Schöningh

Connect...

History for Bilingual Classes

2

Herausgegeben und erarbeitet von:

Iris Faßbender
Colette Granvillano

Sprachliche Betreuung: Ronnie Halligan, Michelle Kloppenburg (Glossar)

© 2015 Bildungshaus Schulbuchverlage
Westermann Schroedel Diesterweg Schöningh Winklers GmbH
Braunschweig, Paderborn, Darmstadt

www.schoeningh-schulbuch.de
Schöningh Verlag, Jühenplatz 1–3, 33098 Paderborn

Das Werk und seine Teile sind urheberrechtlich geschützt.
Jede Nutzung in anderen als den gesetzlich zugelassenen Fällen bedarf der vorherigen schriftlichen Einwilligung des Verlages.
Hinweis zu § 52a UrhG: Weder das Werk noch seine Teile dürfen ohne eine solche Einwilligung gescannt und in ein Netzwerk gestellt werden.
Das gilt auch für Intranets von Schulen und sonstigen Bildungseinrichtungen.

Auf verschiedenen Seiten dieses Buches befinden sich Verweise (Links) auf Internet-Adressen. Haftungshinweis: Trotz sorgfältiger inhaltlicher Kontrolle wird die Haftung für die Inhalte der externen Seiten ausgeschlossen. Für den Inhalt dieser externen Seiten sind ausschließlich deren Betreiber verantwortlich. Sollten Sie dabei auf kostenpflichtige, illegale oder anstößige Inhalte treffen, so bedauern wir dies ausdrücklich und bitten Sie, uns umgehend per E-Mail davon in Kenntnis zu setzen, damit beim Nachdruck der Verweis gelöscht wird.

Druck A 5 4 3 2 / Jahr 2019 18 17 16
Die letzte Zahl bezeichnet das Jahr dieses Druckes.
Alle Drucke der Serie A sind im Unterricht parallel verwendbar.

Umschlaggestaltung: Nora Krull, Bielefeld; Foto © ullstein bild – Hesse
Druck und Bindung: westermann druck GmbH, Braunschweig

ISBN 978-3-14-024721-4

Inhaltsverzeichnis

Zur Arbeit mit dem Buch 6

What is the German's Fatherland? The Difficult Question of German National Identity 8

The Idea and Difficulty of Nation, Nation-state and Nationalism 13
- Political vs. Cultural Nation and Nation-state 13
- Nationalism and Liberalism 14

The Impact of the Napoleonic Wars on Nationalism in Europe: The Examples of Germany and Italy 16
- Prussia's Growth in Strength 16
- Prussia's Revolution "from Above" 16
- The Impact of the Napoleonic Wars on "Germany" 17
- The Unification of Italy 20

The European Peace Framework After the Napoleonic Wars 23
- Reshaping Europe at the Congress of Vienna 23
- The Development of Nationalist and Liberal Movements in the German Confederation between 1815 and 1848 24

"Unity and Liberty" in the German Revolution of 1848/49 28
- The Social and Economic Origins of the Revolution 28
- The Supporters of the Revolution and their Aims 29
- The Development of the Revolution and Reactions to it in Prussia and in Austria 30
- The National Assembly in the Paulskirche in Frankfurt 31
- The Failure of the Revolution 32
- The Legacy of the Revolution 33

German Unification "from Above" 34
- Bismarck Becomes Minister-President of Prussia 34
- The End of Austro-Prussian Dualism 34
- The Unification of Germany 36

Domestic Policy in the Second Empire 38
- The Constitution and Political Parties 38
- "Enemies of the Reich" 39

Foreign Policy in the Second Empire 42
- The Alliance System 42
- Bismarck's Resignation in 1890 43

Sources 44
Paper Practice 155
Vocabulary 156

The First World War – The "Seminal Catastrophe" of the 20th Century?   158

Industrialization and the Coming into Being of the Modern Mass Society   163

(New?) Imperialism   167

Imperialism: Motives and Justifications   168

British, American and German Imperialism   170
- The Example of Britain   170
- The Example of the USA   172
- The Example of Germany   174

Origins and Outbreak of WWI   177

The First "Modern" and "Total" War   181
- The Course of the War until 1917   182
- The "Epochal Year" 1917   183
- War Aims   186
- The End of the War   187

The International Peace Framework After the First World War   188

Sources   189
Paper Practice   335
Vocabulary   336

National Socialism – Germans' Nemesis Up to Today?   338

Political and Ideological Preconditions for National Socialism   343
- Establishing the Republic   343
- 1918–1923: Crises   345
- 1923–1929: Recovery   348

Causes and Consequences of the World Economic Crisis of 1929   350
- 1929–1933: Collapse   350

National Socialist Rule Over Germany and Europe   353
- NS Ideology   353
- Consolidation of Power – Three Phases   355
- Life Under Nazi Control   358
- Foreign Policy: From Triumph to Disaster   360
- The Second World War   362
- The Holocaust/Shoa   365

Sources   368
Paper Practice   487
Vocabulary   488

The Post-war World – On the Verge of the Apocalypse? 490

Conflicts and Peace After the Second World War   494
    The Division of Germany and Europe, 1945 – 1949   494
    Basic Law and Foundation of the FRG and the GDR   499

The Cold War: Cooperation and Conflicts   501
    The Cold War Outside of Europe   501
    Germany as a "Focal Point"   502

The Reunification of Germany After the Peaceful Revolution of 1989   505
    The Collapse of the Soviet Union and the Revolutions in Eastern Europe   505
    The Reunification of Germany 1989/90   507

Sources   510
Paper Practice   565
Vocabulary   567

CONNECT: Revision   568

Peace – Merely the Absence of War?   568

People and Nation – What Is the German's Fatherland?   572

Appendix   574

Key Skills
Task Instructions for Bilingual History Courses   574
Formal Analysis of Sources   576
How to Analyse a Written Primary Source   578
How to Analyse Visual Sources   580
How to Analyse Statistics   584
How to Analyse a Historical Map   586
How to Analyse a Written Secondary Source   587
Making Historical Judgements   588

Language Support
Talking about Visual Sources   589
Talking about Maps   591
Talking about Charts   592
Talking about Democracy   593
Taking Part in a Discussion   593
Giving a Presentation   595
Task Instructions (*Operatoren*)   596

Model solution   598

Glossary   610

Index   624

Bildquellenverzeichnis   629

Zur Arbeit mit dem Buch

Auftaktdoppelseiten führen in die Themen ein, indem sie das Vorwissen aktivieren und Fragehaltungen entwickeln.

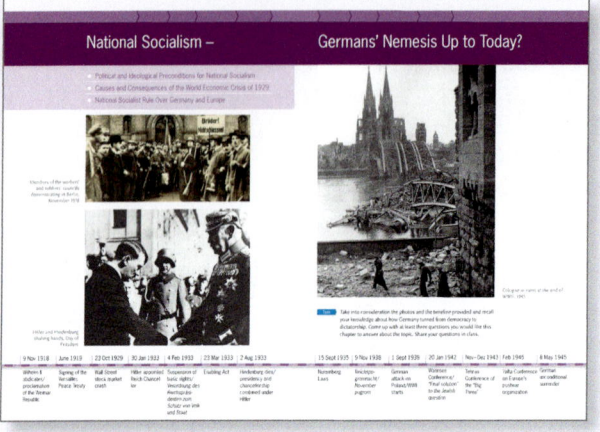

Tabellarische Übersichten beinhalten mit dem Thema verknüpfte Problemfragen wie auch deutsch-englische Schlüsselbegriffe.

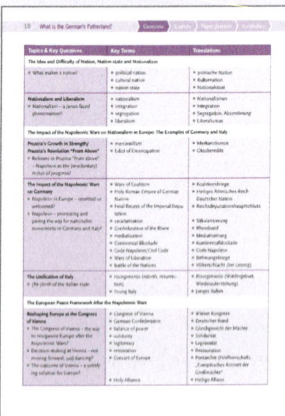

Annotierte Darstellungstexte stellen den relevanten sachlichen Hintergrund und thematisches Vokabular bereit.

Schlüsselbegriffe werden in der Randspalte wiederholt.

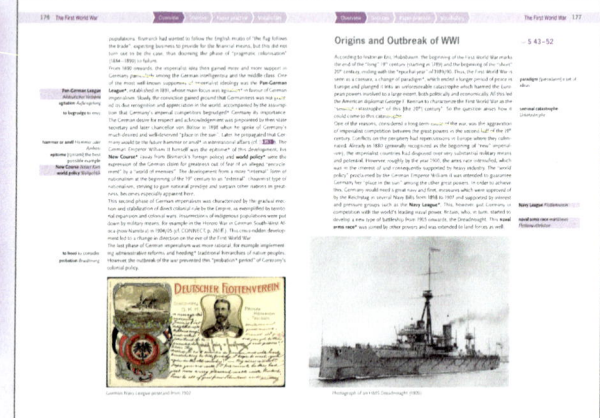

Annotierte Quellen sind mit **vielfältigen Aufgabenapparaten** versehen.

Pre-tasks entlasten die Bearbeitung der Texte vor, indem sie Vorwissen aktivieren, Erwartungshaltungen aufbauen und/oder Wortschatz bereitstellen, der für das Verständnis der Quelle nötig ist. Variierte *tasks* unterstützen das Textverständnis, *post-tasks* regen zu einer vertieften und kreativen Auseinandersetzung an. Dabei werden die drei Anforderungsbereiche des Faches berücksichtigt.

Zur Arbeit mit dem Buch

In jedem Inhaltsfeld bieten spezielle CONNECT-Seiten die Möglichkeit, sich vertieft mit einem bestimmten Aspekt des Themas auseinanderzusetzen.

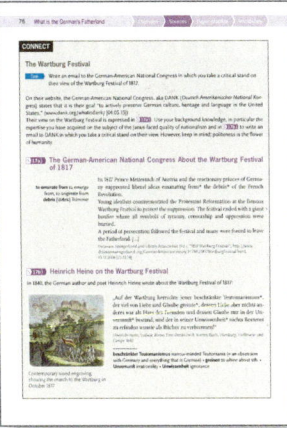

Zu jedem Inhaltsfeld ist eine Auflistung des relevanten thematischen Vokabulars enthalten.

Klausurübungen bieten die Möglichkeit, das Erlernte anzuwenden.

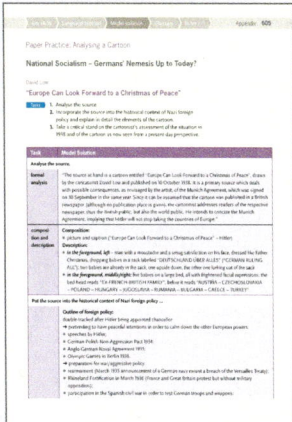

Modelllösungen bieten dabei eine Orientierung.

Ein ausführlicher *skills*-Teil beinhaltet die fachspezifischen Operatoren wie auch zugehörige sprachliche Mittel.

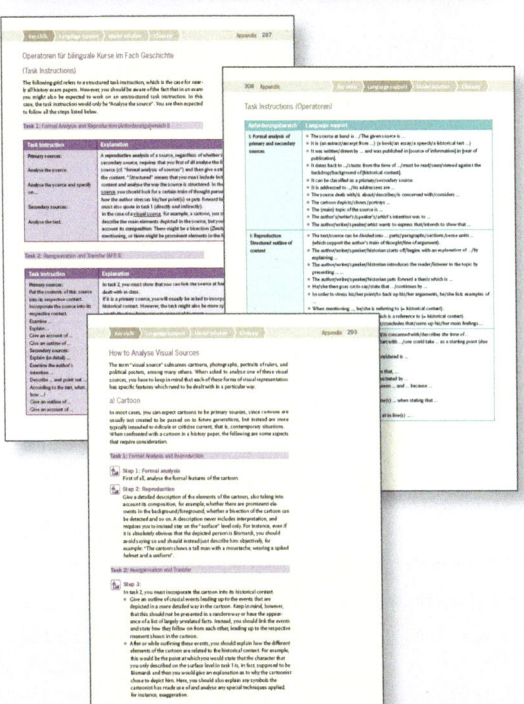

Die **Analyse verschiedener Quellenarten** wird Schritt für Schritt erklärt, weiteres **fachrelevantes Vokabular** wird bereitgestellt.

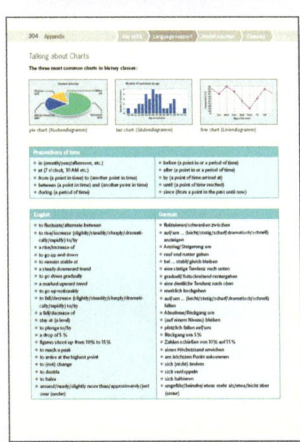

In einem **Glossar** finden sich kurze Erläuterungen zu allen relevanten Schlüsselbegriffen wie auch deutsche Übersetzungen.

What is the German's Fatherland?

- The Idea and Difficulty of Nation, Nation-state and Nationalism
- The Impact of the Napoleonic Wars on Nationalism in Europe: The Examples of Germany and Italy
- The European Peace Framework After the Napoleonic Wars
- "Unity and Liberty" in the German Revolution of 1848/49
- German Unification "from Above"
- Domestic and Foreign Policy in the Second Empire

German cartoon from ca. 1813/14, artist unknown

Embedded text/caption:
Diesen Bock habe ich in Russland geschossen, aber in Deutschland bleibe ich mit ihm im Dreck stecken.

Language support

einen Bock schießen (fig.) to make a boob (coll.) • **Bock** buck • **Wortspiel** pun • **stecken bleiben** to get stuck • **Napoleonshut/Zweispitz** bicorne • **Sporen** spurs

1806	1813	1814/15	1817	1819	1832	1848/49
Confederation of the Rhine	Battle of the Nations	Congress of Vienna	Wartburg Festival	Carlsbad Decrees	Hambach Festival	The 1848/49 Revolutions: "Springtime of the Peoples"

The Difficult Question of German National Identity

"Germania". Painting by Philipp Veit from March 1848, which was hung up in the Paulskirche in Frankfurt, where the National Assembly convened.

The allegorical figure represents Germany and is endowed with various symbols, such as:
- the imperial eagle on her chest,
- the sword, here representing truth and nobility,
- unfettered shackles standing for freedom or independence (from an oppressor),
- oak leaves symbolizing German strength,
- banner and flag in Germany's "national colours" black, red and gold.

Task What would the Germany of 1848 say to the Germany of 1813/14 about the "difficult question of German national identity"? Make use of the information provided on the introductory pages to this chapter and write her speech bubble in your exercise book, making use of your knowledge from previous history classes.

1864	1866	1870/71	1871	1879	1888	1890
German-Danish War	Austro-Prussian War	Franco-Prussian War	Proclamation of the German Empire	Congress of Berlin	Three Emperors' Year	Bismarck resigns

What is the German's Fatherland?

Topics & Key Questions	Key Terms	Translations
The Idea and Difficulty of Nation, Nation-state and Nationalism		
• What makes a nation?	• political nation • cultural nation • nation-state	• politische Nation • Kulturnation • Nationalstaat
Nationalism and Liberalism • Nationalism – a Janus-faced phenomenon?	• nationalism • integration • segregation • liberalism	• Nationalismus • Integration • Segregation, Absonderung • Liberalismus
The Impact of the Napoleonic Wars on Nationalism in Europe: The Examples of Germany and Italy		
Prussia's Growth in Strength/ Prussia's Revolution "From Above" • Reforms in Prussia "from above" – Napoleon as the (involuntary) motor of progress?	• mercantilism • Edict of Emancipation	• Merkantilismus • Oktoberedikt
The Impact of the Napoleonic Wars on Germany • Napoleon in Europe – resented or welcomed? • Napoleon – promoting and paving the way for nationalist movements in Germany and Italy?	• Wars of Coalition • Holy Roman Empire of German Nation • Final Recess of the Imperial Deputation • secularisation • Confederation of the Rhine • mediatisation • Continental Blockade • Code Napoleon/Civil Code • Wars of Liberation • Battle of the Nations	• Koalitionskriege • Heiliges Römisches Reich Deutscher Nation • Reichsdeputationshauptschluss • Säkularisierung • Rheinbund • Mediatisierung • Kontinentalblockade • Code Napoleon • Befreiungskriege • Völkerschlacht (bei Leipzig)
The Unification of Italy • (Re-)birth of the Italian state	• risorgimento (rebirth, resurrection) • Young Italy	• Risorgimento (Wiedergeburt, Wiederauferstehung) • Junges Italien
The European Peace Framework After the Napoleonic Wars		
Reshaping Europe at the Congress of Vienna • The Congress of Vienna – the way to reorganize Europe after the Napoleonic Wars? • Decision-making at Vienna – not moving forward, just dancing? • The outcome of Vienna – a satisfying solution for Europe?	• Congress of Vienna • German Confederation • balance of power • solidarity • legitimacy • restoration • Concert of Europe • Holy Alliance	• Wiener Kongress • Deutscher Bund • Gleichgewicht der Mächte • Solidarität • Legitimität • Restauration • Pentarchie (Fünfherrschaft), „Europäisches Konzert der Großmächte" • Heilige Allianz

The Development of Nationalist and Liberal Movements in the German Confederation between 1815 and 1848 • Pre-March Germany – "restored" to order?	• student unions/fraternities • pre-March • Wartburg Festival • Carlsbad Decrees • Biedermeier • July Revolution • Hambach Festival • Göttingen Seven • Customs Union	• Burschenschaften • Vormärz • Wartburg-Fest • Karlsbader Beschlüsse • Biedermeier • Juli-Revolution • Hambacher Fest • Göttinger Sieben • Zollverein
"Unity and Liberty" in the German Revolution of 1848/49		
The Social and Economic Origins of the Revolution • What makes a revolution?	• pauperism (mass poverty)	• Pauperismus (Massenarmut)
The Supporters of the Revolution and their Aims • 1848 – a "limited" revolution, a revolution nonetheless?	• March Demands	• Märzforderungen
The Development of the Revolution and Revolutions to it in Prussia and Austria • The February Revolution in Paris – the spark that lit the fire?	• Springtime of the Peoples • February Revolution • March Ministries	• Völkerfrühling • Februarrevolution • Märzministerien
The National Assembly in the Paulskirche in Frankfurt • The National Assembly in the Paulskirche – merely a "talking shop" of professors?	• pre(liminary) parliament • Paulskirche Parliament • national assembly • Parliament of Professors • Catalogue of Fundamental Rights • Greater German Solution/Greater Germany • Smaller German Solution/Little Germany	• Vorparlament • Paulskirchen-Parlament • Nationalversammlung • Professorenparlament • Grundrechtekatalog • Großdeutsche Lösung/ Großdeutschland • Kleindeutsche Lösung/ Kleindeutschland
The Failure of the Revolution/The Legacy of the Revolution • 1848/49 – the "Springtime of the Peoples" or doomed to fail right from the start?	• rump parliament • Forty-Eighters • three-class voting system	• Rumpfparlament • 48er • Dreiklassenwahlrecht
German Unification "from Above"		
Bismarck cames Minister President of Prussia/The End of Austro-Prussian Dualism • Austro-Prussian dualism – who was to reign supreme in Germany? • The Customs Union Parliament – a step towards Germany's unification?	• Austro-Prussian dualism • Wars of Unification • German-Danish War • Austro-Prussian War • Battle of Königgrätz • North German Confederation • Customs Union Parliament	• österreichisch-preußischer Dualismus • (Reichs-)Einigungskriege • Deutsch-Dänischer Krieg • Deutscher Krieg • Schlacht bei Königgrätz • Norddeutscher Bund • Zollparlament

What is the German's Fatherland?

The Unification of Germany • A unification "by blood and iron" – Bismarck, the war-monger? • Bismarck – "father" and architect of German unification? • The proclamation of the German Empire – sowing seeds of future conflict in Europe? • The unification "from above" – supported "from below"?	• Ems Telegram/Dispatch • Franco-Prussian War • Battle of Sedan • Treaty of Frankfurt • Second Empire	• Emser Depesche • Deutsch-Französischer Krieg • Schlacht bei Sedan • Frieden zu Frankfurt • Deutsches Kaiserreich

Domestic Policy in the Second Empire

The Constitution and Political Parties • The 1871 Constitution – a fig leaf for absolutism?	• German Conservative Party • National Liberal Party • German Progressive Party • Social Democratic Party • Centre Party	• Deutschkonservative Partei • Nationalliberale Partei • Deutsche Fortschrittspartei • Sozialdemokratische Partei • Zentrum
"Enemies of the Reich" • The "Struggle for Culture" – Catholics as "enemies of the Reich"? • "Carrot-and-stick" – a successful means of combating Socialism? • The Second Empire – the cradle of political anti-Semitism and "Germanization"? • The overall balance of Bismarck's domestic policy – success or failure?	• enemies of the Reich • Papal Infallibility • Struggle for Culture/Culture Struggle • Pulpit Law • Anti-Socialist Laws • social security system • policy of Germanization	• Reichsfeinde • päpstliches Unfehlbarkeitsdogma • Kulturkampf • Kanzelparagraph • Sozialistengesetze • Sozialversicherungssystem • Germanisierungspolitik

Foreign Policy in the Second Empire

The Alliance System • The system of alliances – Bismarck as a "peace politician"? • The overall balance of Bismarck's foreign policy – success or failure?	• "nightmare of coalitions" • Kissingen Dictation • Three Emperors' League • Dual Alliance • Triple Alliance • Three Emperors' Alliance • Reinsurance Treaty • Mediterranean Agreement • Congress of Berlin • "honest broker"	• „Albtraum der Koalitionen" • Kissinger Diktat • Dreikaiser-Abkommen • Zweibund • Dreibund • Dreikaiser-Bund • Rückversicherungsvertrag • Mittelmeerabkommen • Berliner Kongress • „ehrlicher Makler"
Bismarck's Resignation in 1890 • Bismarck's legacy in foreign affairs – consolidating peace in Europe or paving the way for disaster?	• Three Emperors' Year	• Dreikaiserjahr

The Idea and Difficulty of Nation, Nation-state and Nationalism

⇨ S 1–2

When attempting to define the "difficult question of the German fatherland" one must first of all trace back the origins of the term "nation" and define it.
The idea of the nation was developed in the period of the Enlightenment*, realised in the French Revolution and spread throughout Europe by Napoleon and his Grand Army. Whereas, at the beginning of the 19th century, Europe was dominated by princes and founded upon monarchical principles, the term "nation" had come to mean the community of free citizens and was seen as the expression of the people's political will. To the philosophers of the Enlightenment, such as Immanuel Kant (1724–1804) or Jean-Jacques Rousseau (1712–1778), people had natural rights such as freedom and were endowed with reason*. They were expected to unite on the basis of equality and thus form communities, or nations, implying that the nation itself is a historically grown and politically active community of the people. Thus the nation formed an opposing model to the then existing Estate-System* and the monarchical form of rule, which was seen as patronising individuals and keeping them dependent. In contrast to this, the idea of the nation promised emancipation and self-fulfilment.

Enlightenment *Aufklärung*

to be endowed with reason *vernunftbegabt*

Estate-System *Ständegesellschaft*

Political vs. Cultural Nation and Nation-state

One should, however, distinguish between the **political nation*** and the **cultural nation***. Whereas the first relates back to the French Revolution and denotes a state in which power ultimately rests with the people and in which the government is accountable to them, the latter allowed for the people to define themselves as a nation without specific reference to an already existing state. A range of criteria could be applied in order to define the commonalities of a people, for example language, art, culture or history. This is why the concept of the "cultural nation" cannot be grasped easily, as it varies from nation to nation.
The central issue was: who should have the right to found and rule a state – the princes, who employed the principle of the benediction of God* and thus the divine right to rule (princely sovereignty*), to defend their position, or the people (people's sovereignty)? The latter claimed that the community of citizens should form the foundation of a nation instead of a ruler who allegedly ruled by divine will. Only the nation, it was claimed, should be the legitimate sovereign of the state. So it became clear that, right from the beginning, the idea of the nation was closely connected with the idea of a nation-state.
The term **nation-state*** describes states that see themselves as an expression of the politically acting nation. In the 19th century some nation-states came into existence within the boundaries of territorial states dating back to the Early Modern Period. In these cases, a connected national territory was established, as for example in France. So nation-states were formed within an existing state territory.
In other cases, for instance Germany before 1871, so-called "cultural nations" did indeed have a common national consciousness. However, there was no connected national territory. Moreover, there were other states, such as Austria-Hungary, in which different nations lived within the same state (multi-ethnic state*).

political nation *politische Nation*
cultural nation *Kulturnation*

benediction of God *von Gottes Gnaden*
princely sovereignty *Fürstensouveränität*

nation-state *Nationalstaat*

multi-ethnic state *Vielvölkerstaat*

What is the German's Fatherland?

Nationalism and Liberalism

Nationalism*, then, in its broadest sense, centres on the idea that the most important bond in a society is nationality. This leads to the assumption that the nation itself is the highest good and worth preserving, or – in the case of Germany after the Congress of Vienna up to 1871 – fighting for.

However, from the beginning on, the term "nation" was ambiguous* as one can especially see when judging the phenomenon of nationalism with hindsight, aware of its Janus-faced quality.

On the one hand, nationalism is connoted* positively as the identification of a community with a "nation" as well as the foundation of a state based upon the principle of national sovereignty (**integration***). On the other hand, this identification can lead to dissociation* from everything that is considered to be 'different' or to the creation of a common enemy (**segregation***). This other side of the coin became especially apparent in the tensions between the Great Powers prior to the outbreak of the First World War or in National Socialist Germany, where the perception of the nation's alleged superiority led to expulsion* and genocide*. Where the phenomenon of nationalism is concerned, inclusion – that is identification with one's nation – and exclusion – that is disassociation from others – seem to be inevitably intertwined*. Whereas, at the beginning of the 19th century, nationalism can rather be described as an "internal" nationalism, and, in the case of Germany, as a craving for* the creation of a German nation-state founded upon a liberal constitution, the concept was dominated more and more by jingoistic* qualities as the century went by. Its character changed in as far as the Great Powers openly displayed their power and attempted to gain more and more national prestige – as in the case of imperialism.

nationalism *Nationalismus*

ambiguous having more than one meaning

to connote to designate, to suggest an additional idea/emotion not part of the original meaning
integration *Integration*
dissociation considering two people/things to be separate/different/not connected
segregation *Segregation, Absonderung*
expulsion the act of forcing sb. to leave a country
genocide *Völkermord*
to be intertwined to be closely connected
to crave for sth. to desire sth. very much
jingoistic *chauvinistisch, hurrapatriotisch* (cf. chapter 2, imperialism)

"Italia und Germania". Painting by Johann Friedrich Overbeck from 1828, before the unification of Italy (1861) and of Germany (1871). Italia is on the left, Germania on the right.

Liberalism* is sometimes considered as the "twin sister" of nationalism. And, indeed, in some respects, it is hard to distinguish between these two phenomena or to disentangle* their respective meanings.

Like nationalism, liberalism, too, has its roots in the age of Enlightenment. The endorsement* of individual freedom or liberty is central to liberalism, which is against societal or political paternalism* of all kinds. Nationalism and liberalism had in common that both objected to the monarchical order in Europe and that both aimed at the foundation of political power based upon the community of a "nation". However, the extent of political participation was something that was disputed among liberals. The majority of liberals approved of a limited suffrage that would be restricted to property-owning and/or educated classes. Many liberal-nationalists also approved of central executive powers being exercised by the princes. In general, liberalism refers to a body of ideas that centre around five key concepts: constitution, equality, individual freedom, property and reform. A constitution would guarantee individual rights and make the government accountable to the people. As liberals vigorously advocated* equality in the sense of people having natural rights, they were strongly opposed to privileges that were based on birth and not on achievements. They opted rather for a meritocracy*, believing that offices should be granted according to a person's talents and assiduity*. However, material equality was not included in this concept as liberals saw property as bringing with it responsibility and respectability. This partly explains why many of them believed in a limited suffrage that was linked to a person's wealth or to the amount of taxes paid rather than in full, universal manhood suffrage. Liberals generally believed in the peaceful reform of the state rather than in a revolution, hoping to wrest political concessions* that would set constitutional limitations to absolute rule and guarantee certain rights to the people.

Liberalism was by no means a homogeneous* movement though. Despite the fact that the majority of liberals were quite moderate, there were also radical factions who attempted to espouse* revolution for all classes or even opted for the creation of a republic. These divisions were to become particularly apparent in the work of the Frankfurt Parliament in 1848/9, making it very difficult to take quick decisions and contributing to the fact that the parliament tended to be viewed as a "talking shop".

liberalism *Liberalismus*

to disentangle to separate ideas so that they are no longer confused
endorsement support
paternalism a system in which sb. in authority advises and helps people but also controls them by not letting them make their own decisions and choices

to advocate sth. to publicly support a certain way of doing things
meritocracy *Leistungsgesellschaft*
assiduity [ˌæsɪˈdjuːəti] the quality of being hard-working, diligent and thorough

to wrest political concessions *politische Zugeständnisse abringen*

homogenous [ˌhəʊməʊˈdʒiːniəs] of the same type

to espouse sth. to give your support for sth.

Poster created in 1901 on the occasion of the bicentennial of the Kingdom of Prussia

⇨ S 3-10 The Impact of the Napoleonic Wars on Nationalism in Europe: The Examples of Germany and Italy

Prussia's Growth in Strength

As Prussia was to become the state that more and more dominated the German Confederation and, later on, the Second Empire, it is worth tracing back Prussia's growth in strength in the 17th and 18th century that enabled it to assume the leading role in the second half of the 19th century.

elector *Kurfürst*

Frederick William, the Great Elector*, must be considered the founder of the Prussian state. He played an important role in the Westphalian Congress after the Thirty Years War, from which Prussia had made considerable gains, and had managed to defend its scattered possessions. He was succeeded first by Frederick III, who, in turn, was succeeded by Frederick William I. Frederick William I's focus was on the building up of an effective bureaucracy and the creation of a large army disproportionate to the size of his state.

The Prussian tradition itself was, however, mainly established by Frederick II, the Great, who ruled from 1740 to 1786. He turned Prussian bureaucracy into a truly effective instrument of unification. In terms of the economy, he supported **mercantilism***, making sure that state intervention was matched by control of prices and the movement of goods as well as customs prohibitions. He, too, also maintained and expanded the Prussian army, effectively making this endeavour the key aspect of his policy.

mercantilism economic system (Europe, 18th cent.) to increase a nation's wealth by government regulation of all the nation's commercial interests
feudalism ['fjuːd(ə)lɪz(ə)m] *Feudalherrschaft, Lehnswesen*
rigour the quality of being strict/severe
serfdom *Leibeigenschaft*
despot *Gewaltherrscher*

Though feudalism* was in full rigour* in Frederick the Great's times, with the nobility constituting the foundation of his monarchy and peasants still subject to serfdom*, the king came to be seen as an "enlightened despot*", depriving the monarchy of its character as a divine institution. To him, the origin of monarchy lay in the people choosing the wisest and most humane judges and protectors. As he still believed that all republics would end in despotism, his approach came to be known as enlightened absolutism. The prince was considered to be a watchman of the state. According to Frederick the Great: *Der Fürst ist der erste Diener seines Staates* – the prince is the first servant of his state.

Prussia's Revolution "from Above"

epitome [ɪˈpɪtəmi] the best possible example of sth.

During the period of Napoleonic rule, several reforms were carried out in Prussia. As Napoleon was seen as the epitome* of revolution, the Prussian reformers – mainly Karl August Freiherr von Hardenberg (1750–1822), August Graf Neidhardt von Gneisenau (1760–1831), Gerhard Scharnhorst (1755–1813) and Karl Reichsfreiherr vom und zum Stein (1757–1831) – tried to adapt the French reforms to Prussian conditions with the help of a revolution "from above", without the involvement of the people, in order to prevent a revolution "from below", that is by the people. This corresponds to the notion of French nationalism having authoritarian or even totalitarian aspects, and it attracted Prussian reformers who aimed at making careers open to talent and combining liberty with civil order.

Moreover, Prussia had been devastatingly defeated by Napoleon's troops in the battles of Jena and Auerstedt and several severe penalties* had been imposed on

penalty punishment

the state, including a reduction in the size of the Prussian army, territorial losses, and the payment of indemnity* to the French. There existed a growing realisation that there was an urgent need for reform if the country was going to be able to fight France one day.

Broadly speaking, reforms in Prussia can be divided into governmental reforms, intended to prevent a revolution from below, and educational reforms, which were influenced by the ideas of intellectuals such as Fichte. (S 4)

As regards governmental reforms, three main pillars can be distinguished. The **Edict of Emancipation*** of 1807 ended serfdom, feudal privileges and all class distinctions. Jews were also accorded full civil rights with this document, something which constituted a novelty at that time. However, they were still excluded from civil or military offices. Along with this Edict of Emancipation came a land reform in 1811, giving the peasants two-thirds of the land they had worked with, the remaining third going to the land-owning nobles as a compensation for their losses. Finally, military reforms were carried out, aiming at instilling* high morale and efficiency into the Prussian troops by promoting merit*, banning foreign recruits, and introducing compulsory military service.

In respect of education, the Prussian philosopher and minister of education Wilhelm von Humboldt initiated in 1809 a series of reforms which can today still be seen as the foundation of the contemporary German education system. He is accredited with the introduction of the humanistic secondary school and with a reformation of teacher training. In the 18th century already, compulsory primary education, the so-called *Volksschule*, had been introduced in Prussia. Now, more than ever, public schools were seen as appropriate places where a new agenda, instilling nationalist spirit, social obedience* and loyalty to the Crown, could take effect.

The Impact of the Napoleonic Wars on "Germany"

The Napoleonic Wars can be considered as enormously important for the development of a genuine form of German nationalism. Four **Wars of Coalition*** contributed to the fact that the map of Europe changed significantly up to 1812. During these wars, Napoleon and his revolutionary army spread the idea of a nation throughout the whole of Europe. (S 7a–d)

One important reason for Napoleon's stunning victories was that the soldiers of the revolutionary army fully identified with the idea of a French nation. Whereas in former times paid mercenaries* formed the army, the *"Volksarmee"* (the "people's army") can be characterised as soldiers who were proud of French revolutionary ideas.

Another point to be considered when talking about the Napoleonic Wars is that the map of Europe was fundamentally changed as a result of Napoleon's conquests. In 1806, the **Holy Roman Empire of German Nation***, which had previously lasted for almost thousand years, ceased to exist. Territorial reforms carried out by Napoleon that led to the end of the Holy Roman Empire include the **Final Recess of the Imperial Deputation*** in 1803 (Principal Conclusion of the Extraordinary Imperial Delegation) which compensated several German princes for territory annexed by France beforehand in the wake of the French Revolution. Napoleon simply "secularised" (**secularisation***) land belonging to the church and distributed it among German princes. Furthermore, the foundation of the **Confederation of the Rhine*** in 1806 also created a new territorial state*. In addition to these actions, Napoleon "media-

---

indemnity *Entschädigung*

Edict of Emancipation *Oktoberedikt*

to instil to make sb. have a particular feeling or belief
merit *Verdienst* (cf. meritocracy)

obedience [əˈbiːdiəns] doing what you are told to do, obeying orders

Wars of Coalition *Koalitionskriege*

mercenary a soldier who fights for an army that will pay him/her

Holy Roman Empire of German Nation *Heiliges Römisches Reich Deutscher Nation*
Final Recess of the Imperial Deputation *Reichsdeputationshauptschluss*
secularisation *Säkularisation*
Confederation of the Rhine *Rheinbund*
territorial state *Flächenstaat*

mediatisation *Mediatisierung*

Continental Blockade *Kontinentalblockade*
embargo *Embargo, Handelssperre*

tised" (**mediatisation***) the free cities and several regions into smaller states, which meant that the German *Kleinstaaterei* (many mini-states) did not consist of as many small units as had been the case before.

As regards foreign policy and the relationship towards Britain, Napoleon established a **Continental Blockade*** (or Continental System) in 1806 which enabled him to set up an embargo* against British goods. His aim was to weaken Britain economically and financially by forbidding his allies and the areas he had conquered from trading with the British. This embargo was a consequence of the Battle of Trafalgar of 1805. In 1803, the Peace of Amiens, a temporary peace between Britain and France, had broken down, eventually leading to the sea battle of Trafalgar of 1805, in which the combined fleet of Napoleon and his ally Spain was defeated by the British Royal Navy, led by Admiral Lord Nelson, the British national hero, who died in that battle. (cf. S 8)

The Battle of the Nations Memorial, to be found on the site of the battle. Construction was begun after the proclamation of the German Empire in 1871, in commemoration of the first occasion on which German troops from nearly all the independent German states had united in defence against Napoleon (although some Germans did also fight on the French side). On 13 October 1913, the centenary of the battle, the German Emperor William II officially inaugurated the memorial. The figure at the base is Saint Michael portrayed as a Teutonic knight.

Finally domestic reforms were carried out in many European states which, in the long run, supported a sustainable* modernisation. One example of a territory in which reforms were carried out is the area left of the Rhine. Although participation in the process of political decision-making was not possible for the people, they could nonetheless rely on a modern system of administration, the **Code Napoléon/ Civil Code***, that ensured constitutional structures and a tax system based on the financial capability of each single person. Napoleon himself also founded new states, the so-called "satellite states" which were governed by his relatives in accordance with a progressive* legal system, including for example the elimination of feudal and royal privileges in favour of the equality of all citizens before the law, and freedom of speech and worship along with public trial by jury. The states belonging to the Confederation of the Rhine formed another group which, although they were under French influence, were also formally independent. One last group was formed by those states which had not yet been conquered by Napoleon but which felt threatened militarily (Prussia, Austria-Hungary).

All in all, Napoleon's policy of hegemony* triggered numerous reforms in the European territories. However, the final implementation of the idea of a nation came about with the **Wars of Liberation*** against Napoleon. The European states adapted the idea of a nation-state not least because the French Emperor's policy of territorial and military expansion had given rise to feelings of solidarity on their part. The Prussian king Frederick William III actively supported these feelings in order to mobilize his people to fight against France in the Wars of Liberation. These appeals against French rule finally resulted in Napoleon's defeat by a coalition of Russia, Prussia, Austria and Sweden in the **Battle of the Nations*** near Leipzig in 1813. (cf. S9)

sustainable *nachhaltig*

Code Napoléon/Civil Code
Code Napoléon

progressive *fortschrittlich*

hegemony [hɪˈgeməni] political control or influence, especially by one country over other countries
Wars of Liberation
Befreiungskriege

Battle of the Nations
Völkerschlacht (bei Leipzig)

Close to the top of the memorial, there are sculptures of further Teutonic knights, watching over the battle site.

The Unification of Italy

The Unification of Italy

risorgimiento (rebirth, resurrection) *Risorgimento (Wiedergeburt, Wiederauferstehung)*

The term **risorgimento*** (rebirth, resurrection) describes a period of Italian history between 1789 and 1870 and at the same time denotes a heterogeneous political movement aiming at the establishment of Italian unification. Like other European nationalist movements, the Risorgimento was inspired by ideas of the Enlightenment and the French Revolution. After the Congress of Vienna, several uprisings were directed against the predominance of Spain in the "Kingdom of the Two Sicilies" and against the Habsburg monarchy in North and Central Italy. In the long run, Italian unification was implemented "from above" in 1861, under the leadership of Piedmont-Sardinia. With the conquest of Rome in 1870, the erection of an Italian nation-state was finally completed. (cf. S 10)

At the end of the Renaissance and with the downfall of the powerful Italian city-states, Italy had become the playing field of the great European powers. In the course of the Wars of Coalition, which were primarily directed against Austria, Napoleon conquered the Italian peninsula*, leading to the creation of the French vassal states* of the First French Republic. After having crowned himself Emperor, Napoleon founded the kingdoms of Italy and Naples, while the remaining parts of Italy were annexed by France.

peninsula *Halbinsel*
vassal state a state that is subordinate to another state

Similar to the position in the German states, this Napoleonic conquest led to ambivalent feelings among the Italian population. On the one hand, French occupation was resented, but, on the other, the Italian bourgeoisie in particular profited from the introduction of the Code Napoléon and the rule of law* which it established as well as from the abolition of the feudal system. Overall, however, the all-encompassing* French hegemony furthered the idea of Italian unification among the liberal middle class.

In spite of this, the restorative policies applied in accordance with the outcome of the Congress of Vienna shattered these hopes for Italian unification. The liberal middle class but also some enlightened nobles protested against the abandonment of Napoleonic reforms. Uprisings in the Kingdom of the Two Sicilies and in Piedmont in 1820 and in 1830 were put down by Austrian troops. These uprisings had mainly been supported by the so-called *carbonari*, which is Italian for charcoal burners*, and the name of a secret organisation. One of the revolutionaries was Guiseppe Mazzini, who was to become very influential. He founded the secret organisation **Young Italy*** which gained many supporters not only in Italy, but also in other European states. Mazzini has come to be seen as the most important representative of an international nationalism, having had a huge impact on the formation of similar organisations to Young Italy in for example Germany (Young Germany) or Poland (Young Poland), organisations which were later merged into Young Europe. (cf. S 15)

Whereas this form of Italian nationalist movement can be described as radical-democratic, there were also more conservative or moderate forces, such as Pope Pius IX who introduced moderate liberal reforms in the Papal States* and so put pressure on the other Italian states. In addition, the newspaper "Il Risorgimento" – which gave the nationalist movement in Italy its name – espoused the cause of Italian unification under the leadership of King Karl Albert of Piedmont-Sardinia from 1847 on.

In the wake of the 1848/9 Revolutions in Europe, the Italian princes were forced to make more and more concessions. King Karl Albert even turned Piedmont-Sardinia into a constitutional monarchy. In North Italy, the Austrian Danube monarchy remained the main adversary* of Italian nationalists. Already in January 1848 there had been uprisings against Austrian predominance. By March 1848 both Milan and Lombardy declared their independence from Austria and joined the kingdom of Piedmont-Sardinia. Venice declared itself a republic on March 23rd. However, Austrian troops put down the Italian uprisings. Another uprising in Tuscany, in February 1849, which culminated in the foundation of a Tuscan republic, was again successfully put down by Austrian troops who, moreover, managed to re-conquer the revolutionary republic of Venice. So, for the time being, the unification movement in North Italy seemed beaten in military terms.

However, there had also been nationalist uprisings in the south of Italy, for example in Naples and in Rome. After a failed assassination attempt, the Pope had to go into exile in November 1849. Calling for a constituent assembly in the following elections, Mazzini and his supporters gained a decisive victory and the Papal States were declared a republic. Subsequently war broke out between the Roman revolutionary army and French troops. The latter managed to restore papal rule and captured the city of Rome after one month of siege*. In 1850 the Pope returned to Rome and withdrew the moderate reforms he had introduced in 1847.

Though the defeat of the different nationalist uprisings had severely weakened the

rule of law *Rechtsstaatlichkeit*

all-encompassing including everything, present everywhere

charcoal burner *Köhler*

Young Italy *Junges Italien*

Papal States *der Kirchenstaat*

adversary [ˈædvə(r)s(ə)ri] an enemy or opponent

siege [siːdʒ] *Belagerung*

Italian nationalist movement, the kingdom of Piedmont-Sardinia had installed itself at its centre in Turin. The new king, Victor Emanuel II, and his minister-president Cavour pursued a new strategy after the times of revolution. They sought the assistance of other European states in order to achieve Italian unification and so made an alliance with the French Emperor Napoleon III, who, in turn, was interested in weakening Austria. In 1859, the allies defeated the Austrians, who then had to cede* Lombardy to Piedmont-Sardinia. In a series of uprisings, Austrian princes were forced to abdicate in the duchies of Parma, Modena and Tuscany. With Napoleon III's approval, referenda* were carried out in North Italy which resulted in the majority of the people opting for accession* to Piedmont-Sardinia. Despite the successes of this more conservative unification policy, the radical-democratic faction of the nationalist movement was disappointed, having hoped for a unification "from below". When King Victor Emanuel II ceded the territories of Nice and Savoy to Napoleon III to compensate him for his support, they accused him of treason and turned their backs on him. In May 1860, the revolutionary Giuseppe Garibaldi returned from exile and managed to defeat the troops of the king of Naples with the help of 1,000 volunteers. In the course of his triumphal procession via Sicily and into the south of the Italian mainland, many insurrectionists* joined him, especially agricultural workers and peasants, and he had major successes in the south of Italy. On September 7, 1860, Garibaldi, who had in the meantime became a folk hero, even managed to conquer Naples. In order to contain Garibaldi's influence and to prevent him from marching into Rome, troops from Piedmont-Sardinia started to march south. Thus, in summer 1860, two geographically and politically very different nationalist movements confronted each other: the radical-democratic faction, led by Garibaldi, in the south, and the liberal-conservative faction, led by King Victor Emanuel II, in the north. The final decision was the outcome of a referendum held on October 10, 1860, in which the vast majority of the population of the Two Sicilies came out in favour of accession to Piedmont-Sardinia. Accordingly, Garibaldi stepped back and on October 26, 1860, at a meeting in Naples, greeted Emanuel II by addressing him as the "King of Italy". On March 17, 1861, King Emanuel II proclaimed* the Kingdom of Italy in Turin. Thus Italian unification was finally achieved "from above" although the democratic popular movement had decisively contributed to it.

Despite these developments there were still unanswered questions and continued disappointment. The constitution of Piedmont-Sardinia was extended to the whole of Italy but it limited political participation to the upper classes due to a system of suffrage that was closely tied to the amount of taxes paid. It was not until 1912 that universal suffrage was introduced in Italy. The demands of the agricultural workers and peasants for social reforms were not fulfilled and their situation even deteriorated as a result of the introduction of new taxes. Moreover, there were still territorial questions to be settled. In the years to follow there were disputes with the Papal States which could only be solved in 1922 and, in the north, the conflicts with Austria continued. Even though Austria ceded Venetia to Italy after its defeat at the hands of the Prussians in the Battle of Königgrätz in 1866, some regions remained under Austrian influence, despite their being claimed by Italy.

---

to cede to allow sb. to take sth./land from you
referendum plebiscite
accession the occasion when a country formally joins a group of countries (or accepts an agreement)

insurrectionist sb. who attempts to take over control of a country by force

to proclaim *ausrufen*

The European Peace Framework After the Napoleonic Wars

⇨ S 11–21

"Congress of Vienna". Drawing by Jean-Baptiste Isabey, 1815

Reshaping Europe at the Congress of Vienna

From October 1, 1814, until June 9, 1815, the rulers of the major European powers came together at the **Congress of Vienna*** in order to reshape the political map of the continent following the defeat of Napoleonic France. The princes had to agree on various subjects, such as the question of how France should be controlled in future (cf. S 11a–e). One possible solution to that problem was to create buffer states* around France to ensure that France would never become so powerful again. Another question was how the security of Italy and "Germany" could be assured. Italy was now divided into separate states in order to help break the strong French influence imposed by Napoleon. The solution for "Germany" was the foundation of the **German Confederation***. In the first Treaty of Paris in May 1814, France was forced to accept the restoration of the Bourbon monarchy but was treated leniently* in other respects. This was due to considerations that a harsher treaty would cause trouble in the future. In the end, France was allowed to retain its borders of 1792. In the Second Treaty of Paris of November 1815, however, the French borders were reduced to those of 1790, which meant more loss of territory. In the light of Napoleon's "100 Days" rule, the European princes had to rethink their former lenient treatment and now also imposed an indemnity of 700 million francs on France. Moreover, France was to return all looted art treasures and had to bear the costs of an army of occupation which was to remain on French soil until the indemnity was paid off.

As mentioned above, the rulers of the major European powers gathered together. Britain was represented first by the Foreign Secretary, Lord Castlereagh, and later by the Duke of Wellington. Foreign Minister Prince Clemens von Metternich represented Austria, accompanied by Emperor Francis I. The Prussian representative was Prince Karl August von Hardenberg, although King Frederick William III of Prussia joined the Congress as well. Louis XVIII's France was represented by its foreign minister Charles Maurice de Talleyrand-Perigord and Tsar Alexander I spoke for Russia. The main concern of these participants was to exclude France from participating in the negotiations, but the French delegates managed to ensure that France continued to have a say in matters.

Congress of Vienna *Wiener Kongress*

buffer state a country that lies between two other countries that are enemies but is not involved in the argument or war between them

German Confederation *Deutscher Bund*

lenient ['li:niənt] less severe than possible, not harsh

balance of power *Gleichgewicht der Mächte*
solidarity *Solidarität*
legitimacy *Legitimität*
restoration *Restauration*

The main aim of the Congress was to change Europe both politically and territorially in order to create a **balance of power***. The main principles of the congress can be subordinated under the headings of "**solidarity***", "**legitimacy***" and "**restoration***". Restoration implies that the political and social standards of the period before the French Revolution were to be re-established, involving the rehabilitation of the old dynasties as well as the re-establishment of the privileges of the nobility. Legitimacy referred to the justification of the divine right by which the princes governed their territories. The old claims to power of the European dynasties were legitimized by this means. Moreover, the princes agreed to balance their power and to shape a common European policy (**Concert of Europe***). Their aim was to put down revolutionary aspirations but also to secure the new peace. Prussia, Russia and Austria additionally concluded the **Holy Alliance***, intended to preserve Christian values and monarchist rule. The constitutional monarchy Britain did not join this alliance.

Concert of Europe *Pentarchie*

Holy Alliance *Heilige Allianz*

Great Britain was able to expand its overseas Empire and Prussia extended its territory on the left bank of the Rhine and in the old Napoleonic kingdom of Westphalia. Russia gained most of Poland ("Congress Poland") and the Austrian Habsburgs were able to restore the central Italian duchies of Parma, Modena and Tuscany. (cf. S 12–14)

In Germany the German Confederation, consisting of 39 states, was organized in a central assembly chaired by Austria in Frankfurt on Main. The individual states maintained their independence, but Austria assumed a leading role. (cf. S 16)

The Development of Nationalist and Liberal Movements in the German Confederation between 1815 and 1848

The hopes of German nationalists for the creation of a German nation-state were shattered by the final outcome of the Congress of Vienna with the creation of the German Confederation. Despite the restorative policies of the Holy Alliance, the nationalist movement attempted to hold their ground. In particular, the **student unions (or fraternities)***, which had originated from the so-called *Turnvereine*, helped to keep this movement alive. Many of the students had fought against Napoleon in the Wars of Liberation and now demanded the formation of a German nation-state founded upon a liberal constitution.

student unions/fraternities *Burschenschaften*

In general, the period between the Congress of Vienna and the 1848/9 Revolutions is described as **pre-March*** due to the fact that it lasted until revolution broke out in the German Confederation in March 1848. Most commonly pre-March is used as an umbrella term* for the oppositional and revolutionary literature of that time aimed at arousing the political consciousness of the middle class and represented most famously by a group of authors called *Junges Deutschland*.

pre-March *Vormärz*

umbrella term *Sammelbegriff*

In 1817, the student unions organized and gathered for the **Wartburg Festival*** (cf. S 17a–b). The year and the place were deliberately chosen, as 1817, on the one hand, signified the tercentenary* of Martin Luther's nailing of his theses to the door of the castle church in Wittenberg and Wartburg Castle had later been his refuge for a while, and, on the other hand, because 1817 marked the fourth anniversary of the Battle of the Nations near Leipzig where the coalition powers had defeated Napoleon decisively. Both of these historical events – according to the students – were an expression of the German striving for freedom and unity. From 18 to 19 October 1817, around 800 people, predominantly students, but also a few university professors, gathered at the Wartburg. Speeches were made and torchlight processions* organized, which

Wartburg Festival *Wartburg-Fest*

tercentenary [ˌtɜː(r)sənˈtiːnəri] *Dreihundertjahrfeier*

torchlight procession *Fackelzug*

culminated in the burning of so-called "un-German" books, such as the Code Napoleon or "Die Geschichte des Deutschen Reiches" by August von Kotzebue.

The Wartburg Festival gave rise to the nationalist movement. However, when in 1819, August von Kotzebue – who had made fun of the students' nationalist ideas – was murdered by the *Burschenschaftler* Carl Sand, this was taken as a pretext* by the German Confederation, under the leadership of Metternich, to call for the restriction of civil rights and the introduction of censorship in order to contain* liberalism and nationalism, which were seen as endangering the monarchical order established at the Congress of Vienna. These repressive measures, labelled the **Carlsbad Decrees***, were especially directed against students and universities that were seen as "hotspots" of oppositional aspirations*. Student Unions were banned, universities were to be observed by government agents, internal observation committees were introduced and there was strict censorship of any publications comprising under twenty pages. In the event of riots or uprisings, the German Confederation now had the right to interfere in the individual states. (cf. S 18)

This policy of repression and suppression was mainly successful up until the outbreak of the July Revolution in France in 1830 due to the fact that many nationalists, especially those from middle-class backgrounds, retreated into private life. This period has come to be described derisively under the term **Biedermeier***, describing a conservative, restorative and politically resigned form of literature seen as an opposing model to pre-March. (cf. S 19a-b)

In a society based on privilege, the middle class or bourgeoisie at that time were frequently frustrated as they lacked opportunities to climb the social ladder or participate in politics. Students, academics, lawyers and professional men strongly objected to and suffered under the restrictions of their civil rights. Although they firmly believed they were being held back by the established elites, they were also

pretext [ˈpriːˌtekst] *Vorwand*

to contain to prevent from spreading

Carlsbad Decrees *Karlsbader Beschlüsse*
oppositional aspiration *oppositionelle Bestrebung*

Biedermeier *Biedermeier*

"Liberty guiding the people". Painting by Eugène Delacroix in commemoration of the July Revolution of 1830 in France

afraid of the "mob" and attached substantial importance to the possession of property. As a result, they were often unwilling to utter their demands in public or to participate in revolutionary activities.

Despite the existence of so many repressive measures, the cultural nation as such still remained a strong force. German-focused universities as well as German literature and plays kept the national idea alive, especially in educated middle-class circles. When the **July Revolution*** broke out in France in 1830, in the course of which the Bourbon King Charles X was overthrown and replaced by his cousin, Louis-Philippe, social protests and demands for political reform were once again voiced in the German Confederation.

On 27th May 1832 around 25,000 people gathered at the so-called **Hambach Festival*** (cf. S 20). Once again this festival had mainly been organized by the student unions, whose black, red and gold flags had in the meantime become a symbol of German unity, the colours stemming from the uniforms of the Lützov Free Corps which had fought against Napoleon in the Wars of Liberation. The political programme of the Hambach Festival mainly tied in with* that of the Wartburg Festival whereby the anti-French motives that had prevailed* in 1817 had been left behind, reflecting the influence of the French July Revolution and hinting at the fact that the movement had by now gained a European dimension. Not only were demands once again made for German unity, sympathies for nationalist movements in other countries were also uttered, especially in speeches by the radical democratic publishers Johann August Wirth and Jakob Siebenpfeiffer. Nevertheless, the political programme of the Hambach Festival remained inconsistent because liberals and democrats differed on major points.

As a reaction to the Hambach Festival, the 6 (and 10) Articles were implemented in 1832 with the help of which the princes and monarchs, again led by Metternich, attempted to combat the national and liberal oppositional forces. These Articles further aggravated* the restrictions of civil rights that had been embedded in the Carlsbad Decrees.

Ultimately, however, the German nationalist movement could not be halted any longer and its goals were furthered by students who combined both political and social demands which they disseminated* with the help of pamphlets aimed at concerted agitation* against the reactionary state, and in which they in particular attempted to reach the lower classes. Many of them were persecuted and arrested while some managed to escape abroad. The dissemination of their writings was forbidden. When, in 1837, the so-called **Göttingen Seven***, the Brothers Grimm and five other university professors, were dismissed from their university posts, there was an outcry among the oppositional forces. The seven men had protested against the abolition or alteration of the Hanoverian Constitution when the new King Ernest Augustus stated that he was not bound by it and would make any necessary changes he felt fit so that it might reflect his values.

As the German states, especially Prussia and Austria, were unwilling to make any concessions to the liberal and nationalist movement and reacted with means of repression, political tensions increased further, finally leading to the outbreak of the 1848/9 Revolutions in the German Confederation, once again triggered by a revolution in France.

Though political unity still seemed like a utopian dream to some, the economic ties between the individual states had already been strengthened with the introduction of the **Customs Union***. Originally founded by Prussia in 1818, with the intention of

---

July Revolution *Juli-Revolution*

Hambach Festival *Hambacher Fest*

to tie in with sth. *an etw. anknüpfen*
to prevail to be the strongest influence in a situation

to aggravate to make/become worse

to disseminate to spread
concerted agitation *gezielte Agitation/Aufwiegelung*

Göttingen Seven *Göttinger Sieben*

Customs Union *Zollverein*

expanding Prussian trade and industry, it was soon joined by neighbouring states. It was extended in 1834 when Bavaria and Wurttemberg joined and it facilitated* trade thanks to the abolition of internal duties*. This brought the individual states closer to each other at least in economic terms and can thus be seen as making an important contribution to unification, although it did not inevitably lead to such. More importantly, it excluded Austria that pursued an economic policy of protectionism, involving the imposition of high tariff barriers in order to protect its economy against the influx of better or cheaper imports. Thus, a first step was taken to alienate Austria from the German Confederation and at the same time to establish Prussian economic control over the Confederation.

to facilitate to simplify, make easier
duty here: *Abgabe*

The Customs Union and German Unification

⇨ S 22–39

"Unity and Liberty" in the German Revolution of 1848/49

The Social and Economic Origins of the Revolution

When investigating the origins of the revolutionary year 1848, one has to consider both long-term and short-term causes.

One of the long-term causes was the population growth closely connected with increasing industrialisation. Before the year 1848, more than half of the German population was still working in the agricultural sector. The Prussian Reforms (cf. pp. 16 f.) contributed to a considerable amelioration* of the people's living and working conditions, for example, the abolition of serfdom. This paved the way for an immense rearrangement of the economic structures of production. In contrast to former times, when people produced goods mainly for themselves, goods were now manufactured for a broader market. Where the agricultural sector was concerned, this meant that new methods of fertilizing were adapted in order to increase the harvests of crops. The problem was that these new methods did not necessarily generate* new jobs. Many people remained unemployed. This unemployment then led to mass poverty (**pauperism***). Many families were affected by this new phenomenon. One obvious feature was the long working-hours people had to endure*. The weekly work schedule frequently exceeded* 90 hours and child labour as well as female labour was no exception. In order to escape these miserable conditions in the countryside, many people emigrated to the USA or tried to make a better living in the bigger cities. The general misery became very apparent when the Silesian weavers* gave vent to their feelings*. The weavers revolted against the aggravation of their situation, which was due to the increasing import of British textile goods. In 1844, they launched a hunger strike and about 3,000 weavers destroyed machines and demanded higher wages. However, this revolt failed in the end because it was violently put down by Prussian troops and eleven people died.

Another long-term cause was industrialisation itself. Due to the fact that many people were deprived of* their traditional agrarian base, their only alternative was to seek an alternative livelihood* in the new industrial factories. In the big European cities, average life expectancy was very low (for an industrial worker at this time it was only 32), people had to endure poor hygienic conditions which also gave rise to diseases, and most of the new inhabitants were uneducated. Skilled workers*, on the other hand, also became more and more discontent with the fact that machines were taking over their position in the production process. In the middle ages, these craftsmen had been protected by trade guilds*, which were later abolished. Thus, the situation of the skilled workers also contributed to what was an increasingly tense atmosphere in Europe.

One major aspect can be considered to be a short-term cause of the 1848 Revolution, namely the economic crisis that started in 1845. This crisis was triggered by several crop failures* which necessarily led to a severe shortage of food supplies for the population. The crop failures had a major impact on the prices for basic foodstuffs* and people could not afford to pay for their daily bread due to exceedingly high grain* prices. The first riots started in 1845 in the Netherlands and later spread to Stettin and Berlin as well. People protested against having to spend about 70 per cent of their total income to buy food.

---

amelioration improvement

to generate to create
pauperism (mass poverty) Pauperismus (Massenarmut)
to endure to suffer from sth. in a patient way over a long period
to exceed to go above a limit

Silesian weavers schlesische Weber
to give vent to one's feelings seinem Ärger Luft machen

to deprive sb. of sth. to take sth. away from sb.
livelihood ['laɪvlihʊd] sth. (such as a job) that provides the money you need to live
skilled worker Facharbeiter

trade guild Handelsgilde

crop failure Missernte
basic foodstuff Grundnahrungsmittel
grain Getreide

As a result of the increasing food prices, people lost their purchasing power* and consequently the sales* of manufactured goods declined so that employers had to dismiss their workers in order to save money. France was affected very badly by this financial crisis since the French state had subsidized* industries like coal mining and ironmaking with the result that these industries then produced more goods than could be sold under the prevailing conditions at the time. (cf. S 23)

purchasing power *Kaufkraft*
sales *Absatz*

to subsidize to support by giving money (subsidies)

The Supporters of the Revolution and their Aims

The so-called **March Demands*** were first formulated in the southern German states and later taken over by all the other states. Above all, they called for the abolition of the Carlsbad Decrees, the implementation of a constitution, the guarantee of human rights and civil rights, the expansion of political participation and the formation of a united German nation. These demands can be classified as political demands. Social demands included the implementation of social justice, the improvement of the living standard of the lower classes and the right to work. (cf. S 25)

March Demands *Märzforderungen*

Although all German states agreed on the March Demands, there were still inconsistencies among the supporters of the revolution due to the fact that they were by no means a homogenous group. However, not only the middle class was in favour of a revolution, but also the urban lower classes* (such as craftsmen, unemployed people, small traders* and industrial workers). The third group consisted of the rural population*, among them farm workers, peasants and tenants*. The first

urban lower class *städtische Unterschicht*
small trader *Kleingewerbetreibender*
rural population *Landbevölkerung*
tenant *Pächter*

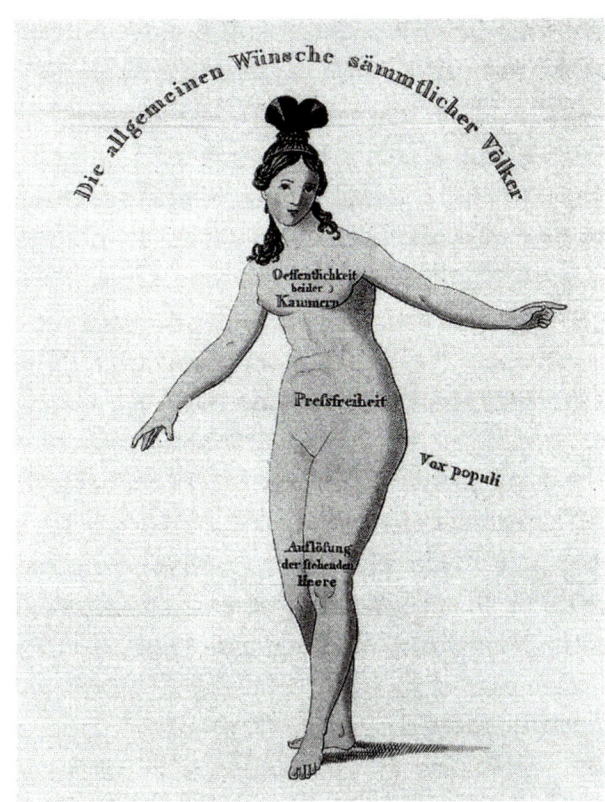

March Demands of the people of Baden

"Die allgemeinen Wünsche sämmtlicher Völker". German copperplate engraving from 1848, ridiculing the March Demands

group wanted to abolish the old class system and monarchic structures, the second fought against the King's troops on the barricades, whereas the third group was mainly driven by material misery, as became obvious though their agitation against symbols of aristocratic domination, such as for example castles.

When it comes to the political dimension, one has to distinguish between the more moderate liberals and the radical democrats. Whereas the former only wanted to enlarge political participation in a limited way and to maintain the monarchy, the latter opted for universal suffrage and a republic. Later in the course of the revolution, the conservatives gained more influence since they were associated with either Prussia or Austria and acted in their interest. However, it is important to keep in mind that there was no such thing as real parties in the modern sense of the term since they only developed in the course of the revolution itself and later had a say in the Frankfurt Parliament.

The Development of the Revolution and Reactions to it in Prussia and in Austria

Springtime of the Peoples *Völkerfrühling*
February Revolution *Februarrevolution*

The **Springtime of the Peoples★** was triggered by the **February Revolution★** in Paris. The Parisians revolted against high prices for bread and an economic slump connected with social injustices. King Louis Philippe was forced to abdicate on 24 February 1848 and the Second French Republic was proclaimed. Soon the unrest spread to Germany and people started to demonstrate in Mannheim, Heidelberg, Karlsruhe, Cologne, Frankfurt on the Main and Munich. As a result, several rulers in the German Confederation installed so-called **March Ministries★**, governments that were supposed to (at least partly) fulfil some of the March Demands. (cf. S 24)

March Ministries *Märzministerien*

concession *Zugeständnis*

King Frederick William IV ruled Prussia in a rather absolutistic manner. In order to avoid meeting the same fate as the French king, he made concessions★ to the large crowd which had gathered in front of his residence in Berlin after having heard of the events in Paris. Up to this point, the assembly of the representatives of the states★ ("United Committees") in Prussia had proved by and large incapable of restricting the king's power. When Frederick William IV dissolved the assembly in March 1848 because they had refused to accept that they were only allowed to convene at the invitation of the king, the assembly turned against him and denied★ him the budget. Faced with the demonstrations that followed, the king then promised to reinstall the assembly and to grant a constitution. The people of Berlin were thankful for the king's concession and gathered in front of the Berlin City Palace when suddenly a shot was fired and the crowd thought they had been betrayed by the king. In the street-fights between revolutionaries and royal troops that followed, 143 people died. In his letter "To my dear Berliners" (cf. S 29), King Frederick William IV attempted to calm down the rather tense situation by promising to remove the troops from the city. The revolution finally seemed to have achieved success in Prussia as well, when a constituent assembly★ was summoned on 22 May 1848.

assembly of the representatives of the states *Ständevertretung*

to deny here: to refuse to grant/give

constituent [kən'stɪtjʊənt] **assembly** *verfassungsgebende Versammlung*
multi-ethnic state *Vielvölkerstaat*
Danube Monarchy *Donaumonarchie (Austria)*

In Austria, Chancellor Metternich became the target of revolutionary groups due to his conservative policies. In general, these groups had the same demands as those in Germany, with one exception: Austria was a multi-ethnic state★ and the Czechs, Hungarians and Italians living in the Danube Monarchy★ had begun calling for their national independence from the German-speaking central power, thus endangering the territorial coherence of the Austrian monarchy.

The demonstrators demanded Metternich's dismissal; he resigned on 13 March

1848 and fled to England. Emperor Ferdinand I promised a constitution and withdrew his troops from Vienna.

The National Assembly in the Paulskirche in Frankfurt

Already in March 1848, Southern German democrats and liberals had summoned a **preliminary parliament*** in Frankfurt, which set up the elections for a German National Assembly. The representatives of the Frankfurt National Assembly were elected in a free, equal and secret election and on 18 May the **Paulskirche Parliament***, the constituent **national assembly***, started its work in Frankfurt. The parliament consisted mainly of educated and respected personalities of the middle class and because of that it was also called the **Parliament of Professors***. Herein lies one of the major points of criticism levelled against this parliament because it neither represented political reality in Germany nor were the revolutionary groups properly represented. (cf. S 30)

One big issue to be dealt with in the National Assembly was whether Germany would become a republic or a monarchy. Due to the long monarchic history of the German states, the vast majority of the representatives opted for the maintenance of a monarchic central power as a regulating force. Another main subject of debate was whether the form of the new state should be federal* or centralised*. Political opinions ranged from those of the radical democrats who preferred a removal of all structures supporting individual states to those of the conservatives who wanted to

preliminary parliament *Vorparlament*
Paulskirche Parliament *Paulskirchen-Parlament*
national assembly *Nationalversammlung*
Parliament of Professors *Professorenparlament*

federal state *Bundesstaat*
centralised state *Einheitsstaat*

Contemporary lithography of the National Assembly in the Paulskirche, after a drawing by Ludwig von Elliott. Over the President's table, one can see the "Germania" painting by Philipp Veit (cf. p. 9).

retain the federal elements to a large extent. Eventually, the liberals gained most support with their model of realizing national unity by setting up a central legislative and a monarchic central power while maintaining the federal elements.

Broad consent was found on the question of the basic rights, as contained in the **Catalogue of Fundamental Rights★**. The aristocracy lost their privileges without exception and without compensation. The people were granted equality before the law, freedom of assembly, opinion and speech. Liberal demands were taken into account in the form of legislation relating to the inviolability of the home and property. The parliament was to be elected according to a system of free and secret voting. (cf. S 31)

The most difficult task was the definition of German territory. Two options were possible: the **Greater German Solution (Greater Germany)★** which favoured unifying all German-speaking peoples under one state within the borders of the German Confederation, and which would also, however, mean including national minorities such as the Poles in East Prussia. In the event that the German-speaking parts of Austria were to be included in the new German state, this would lead to the dissolution of the Danube Monarchy or to the fact that the future German nation-state and some of the non-German parts of Austria would be reigned over by a Habsburg Emperor. Many Austrians were in favour of this model since they expected an increasing degree of Austrian influence. In the end, a decision in favour of the **Smaller German Solution (Little Germany)★** was taken because it was much easier to realize. German territory in Austria was excluded and the future state was to be reigned under Prussian dominance. This development, however, then meant that the German-speaking population in Austria and the Austrian government felt outraged, a fact which became apparent to all when the Austrian representatives left Frankfurt.

The Failure of the Revolution

On 28 March 1849 Prussian King Frederick William IV was offered the crown by the National Assembly. He was supposed to become "Emperor of the Germans". The King refused the "crown from the gutter★" since this would have meant his accepting the sovereignty of the people, something that went against his aristocratic attitudes, according to which he saw himself as king by the grace of God. (cf. S 33, S 34). This was, effectively, the deathblow for the new German state because the whole structure of the constitution was, as a result, rendered invalid and the Parliament could not survive. The representatives of the state governments were ordered to return home and so the Parliament disbanded★. A **rump parliament★** consisting of Southern German delegates retreated to Stuttgart, but it was later dissolved as well. The revolution had failed and many former delegates fled abroad in order to avoid being arrested for high treason★ or lèse-majesty★. They came to be known as the **Forty-Eighters★**.

In May 1849, Prussia introduced the **three-class voting system★** which was to remain in effect until 1918. People were categorized into three classes, depending on what taxes they paid. The system firmly favoured the wealthy voters and thus ensured the continued power of the ruling Prussian conservative politicians. (cf. S 35)

Several reasons have to be considered when attempting to assess why the revolution failed. On the one hand, people were fighting for very different interests, which made it extremely hard to find consensus★. On the other hand, the middle-classes

---

Catalogue of Fundamental Rights *Grundrechtekatalog*

Greater German Solution (Greater Germany) *Großdeutsche Lösung (Großdeutschland)*

Smaller German Solution (Little Germany) *Kleindeutsche Lösung (Kleindeutschland)*

gutter *Gosse*

to disband to break up, to dissolve
rump parliament *Rumpfparlament*
high treason *Hochverrat*
lèse-majesty [ˌliːz ˈmædʒisti] *Majestätsbeleidigung*
Forty-Eighters *48er*
three-class voting system *Dreiklassenwahlrecht*

consensus agreement

were not united in their demands. Although they did want reforms, they were against radical change. Well aware of the effects of the French Revolution, they preferred to seek an agreement with the princes. In addition, the revolution was too widespread, which made it difficult for the revolutionaries to coordinate their activities. Furthermore, the delegates of the National Assembly were rather inexperienced when it came to implementing democracy and this was aggravated by the fact that parliamentary procedures as such were actually non-existent. Finally, the magnitude of the tasks to be solved was considerable and the difficulties involved virtually insurmountable* (creating a constitution, setting up a parliamentary system, solving social problems, establishing national unity). (cf. S 37)

insurmountable impossible to overcome

The Legacy of the Revolution

Altogether, the expectations and hopes of the revolutionaries and liberal citizens were shattered in 1849. However, in the long run, the revolution did influence the development of the German states. Now that the people had stood up and fought against the old restorative structures, their ideas could not be suppressed any more. The majority of the population had now developed a sense of political awareness, and 1848/49 also saw the beginnings of organized political parties.

The constitutional model developed by the Paulskirche Parliament has, in fact, shaped German constitutional history up to today. In the long term, the abolition of feudal rights could not be undone, which meant that the aristocracy never regained the power they formerly possessed. Although the constitution drawn up by the Parliament never came into existence, it continued to exert a major influence on future German constitutions, as can be seen, for example, in the constitution of the German Empire in which universal suffrage was taken over as a progressive element. It also provided a model for the constitution of the Weimar Republic in 1919 (and the basic rights agreed on in 1848/49 are included as the first and inviolable articles of Germany's Basic Law of 1949). The idea of national unity lived on, finding its expression in a large number of newspapers and magazines, and thus creating a vast degree of publicity which at times was still suppressed but which nevertheless survived. (cf. S 38)

German Unification "from Above"

⇨ S 40–48

Bismarck Becomes Minister-President of Prussia

In 1862 there was a constitutional crisis in Prussia. The new Prussian King, William I, wanted to increase the military budget in order to enlarge his army and to prolong* compulsory military service from two to three years, but this was rejected by the Prussian Diet on the grounds that the proposals were too conservative and militaristic. The King and his advisors thus saw one of the most important pillars of royal power, the army, endangered. Since the Prussian Constitution did not provide for a case like this and since neither side wanted to back down, a deadlock* situation came about.

In order to solve this crisis and have his army bill pushed through, William appointed Bismarck minister-president of Prussia. In a speech to the Prussian parliament budget commission, which has become famous as the so-called 'blood-and-iron' speech (S 41) Bismarck outlined his idea of a solution, by claiming that since there was no provision in the Prussian Constitution for a case like this, it was, in the last resort*, upon the King to decide.

Though the army bill was never officially passed, the military budget was nevertheless increased despite the parliament's rejection. For the next four years, Bismarck governed without a budget approved by parliament, as should, in constitutional terms, have been the case. This proceeding* sheds an early light on Bismarck's way of handling politically explosive situations.

The End of Austro-Prussian Dualism

The decision for the Smaller German Solution by the Paulskirche Parliament had laid the foundation for **Austro-Prussian dualism*** (cf. S 40), and raised the question as to which of the two powers would eventually reign supreme in the German Confederation, or in a German nation-state, respectively. The question was to be settled by war.

The so-called **Wars of Unification*** started with the **German-Danish War*** of 1864, which was triggered by the annexation of Schleswig to Denmark due to disputed hereditary claims* in Denmark. Both duchies were autonomous but under Danish sovereignty. However, Schleswig was a member of the German Confederation and many Germans lived there. There was a loud outcry among nationalists in the German Confederation, calling for war with Denmark to re-conquer German Schleswig and also Holstein, where many German-speaking people also lived. Though the Federal Diet in Frankfurt on Main called for armed intervention, Bismarck opted for a solution whereby Prussia and Austria would join forces to combat Denmark. As a result, the Danes promptly forsook* their claims in the Treaty of Vienna. In the Gastein Convention of 1865, Prussia and Austria agreed on a joint administration of Schleswig and Holstein at Austria's insistence. Prussia then occupied Schleswig and Austria administered Holstein.

Soon, however, there were disagreements on how to govern the two regions, which resulted in a military confrontation between Prussia and Austria which can be seen as the decisive battle over who would in future dominate Germany. When Austria broke the Gastein Convention by placing the Schleswig-Holstein question under the control of the Federal Diet, Prussia reacted by occupying Holstein. To add fuel to the flames, Bismarck proposed a new constitution to the Federal Diet which he knew would prove unacceptable to the Austrians. When Austria reacted by calling upon the members of the German Confederation to mobilize their troops against Prussia, Prussia officially declared the end of the German Confederation.

The **Austro-Prussian War*** thus broke out in 1866. Prussia was supported by the smaller northern states and had a well-equipped army under General von Moltke at their disposal; Austria was supported by Hanover and some southern states. In 1866, after only seven weeks of fighting, Austria was decisively defeated in the **Battle of Königgrätz*** in the north of Bohemia. Though the Prussian King William I opted for harsh treaty terms for the Austrians, Bismarck stepped in and convinced William I that it would be better to conclude mild treaty terms since his overall aim was the creation of a German nation-state without Austria, and he was unwilling to anger Austria in such a way that she would then reject the dissolution of the German Confederation or, even worse, form an alliance with France. In the end, Austria not only accepted the end of the German Confederation but also left it up to Prussia to decide on the future reorganization of Germany.

In the final outcome of the Austro-Prussian War, as manifested in the Prague Peace Settlement of 1867, Prussia did not seek any Austrian territory for itself but annexed those northern German states which had allied with Austria, such as for example Hanover, and created the **North German Confederation***, including all the states

Austro-Prussian War *Deutscher Krieg*

Battle of Königgrätz *Schlacht bei Königgrätz*

North German Confederation *Norddeutscher Bund*

"Königgrätz". 1866, lithograph by Christian Sell

north of the river Main. Thus, Germany was at least partly unified north of the Main from 1867 onwards. Since Austria was not a member of the North German Confederation and was thus effectively excluded, this marked the end of the era of Austro-Prussian dualism that had dominated the politics of the German Confederation since its foundation in 1815.

Not only did the establishment of the North German Confederation now effectively exclude Austria from German politics, the creation of the **Customs Union Parliament***, based on the already existing Customs Union, also served to exclude her in economic terms. The southern German states that had allied with Austria in the Austro-Prussian War were first allowed to join the Customs Union and then, in June 1867, forced to accept this Customs Union Parliament. Thus economic unity was accomplished. Though one could argue that this was a step towards a further unification of Germany, one has to bear in mind that in the first elections to this parliament, representatives who were opposed to political unification in fact received most of the votes.

Customs Union Parliament *Zollparlament*

The Unification of Germany

In France this development in Germany was seen critically. Emperor Napoleon III was unwilling to accept German unification, and certainly not without territorial compensations in return. The trigger for war was an incident in Spain.

When in 1868 the Spanish Queen Isabella was deposed*, the Spanish offered the crown to Prince Leopold, a relative of the Prussian King from the Hohenzollern dynasty. Though Bismarck was highly in favour of the Hohenzollern Candidature, the Prussian King was undecided, especially since the French had expressed their concern about a "Prussian puppet on the Spanish throne" in a neighbouring state. To make matters worse, the French themselves also laid claim to the throne.

to depose sb. to force a sovereign out of power

The French sent an ambassador*, Count Benedetti, to King William I, while the latter was spending time in Bad Ems, to entreat* the King to renounce* the offer for all time. This was, however, something William I was unwilling to grant, though he gave in to French demands to reject the immediate offer. Bismarck was informed about the meeting of the two men in a telegram, which has become known as the **Ems Telegram/Dispatch*** (cf. S 43), and it was left to him to decide on its publication. The edited version which Bismarck decided to have published gave the impression that the Prussian King had been rude to the ambassador, which caused an uproar in France. Napoleon III finally had to give in to public demands and declared war on Prussia on July 15, 1870.

ambassador *Botschafter*
to entreat to appeal to, to urge, to plead with
to renounce to state formally that you give up a position, job, etc.
Ems Telegram/Dispatch *Emser Depesche*

Following that, the southern states that were still outside the North German Confederation, namely Baden, Wurttemberg and Bavaria, immediately joined the northern states in fighting the French, which basically meant a unified Germany facing France in the so-called **Franco-Prussian War***. The war was quite short, and the **Battle of Sedan*** on September 2, 1870, dealt a decisive blow to the French and resulted in the surrender* and subsequent war captivity* of Napoleon III.

In January 1871, German troops marched into Paris, and on January 18, 1871, the German Empire was proclaimed in Versailles, with the Prussian King William I now officially bearing the title Emperor William I of Germany.

Franco-Prussian War *Deutsch-Französischer Krieg*
Battle of Sedan *Schlacht bei Sedan*
to surrender to give up
war captivity *Kriegsgefangenschaft*
Treaty of Frankfurt *Frieden zu Frankfurt*

In the **Treaty of Frankfurt***, the peace treaty between France and Germany, France had to cede Alsace-Lorraine to the German Empire, which was a severe blow since both regions were industrial centres rich in coal. Moreover, France was to pay an indemnity of five billion francs to the Germans and a German army was to be stationed in France until the reparations were paid. These terms were very humiliating to the French, but this humiliation had been heightened by the fact that the German Empire had been proclaimed in the Hall of Mirrors* in Versailles, since this was the place where traditionally the French Emperor was crowned. In the years to follow, the French sought revenge for the humiliation endured in 1871, something that Bismarck, however, was eager to prevent.

Not only France, but also other European powers saw the "rise" of Germany's **Second Empire*** in the midst of Europe as a potential threat since they were unsure whether the newly united Empire would wage other wars in order to further enlarge her territory. The creation of the Second Empire was therefore viewed with great concern in many neighbouring states. (cf. S 47 , S 48)

Hall of Mirrors *Spiegelsaal*

Second Empire *Deutsches Kaiserreich*

"The Blood and Bones Meal of Holy Wilhelm". Cartoon by the Dutch artist Altijd op de Loer from 1871

Domestic Policy in the Second Empire

The Constitution and Political Parties

The Constitution of the Second Empire was by and large congruent with* that of the North German Confederation. Since it was left to the federal states to find their own regulations for several matters, the Constitution itself was kept quite short, and did not for example, in contrast to the Paulskirche Constitution of 1849, include a catalogue of fundamental rights.

The German Empire was a federal state consisting of 25 states. The recently annexed Alsace-Lorraine had a special position within the Reich. The Prussian King was at the same time the Emperor of Germany and as such endowed with presidential powers. His title as Emperor was furthermore a hereditary one. He was commander-in-chief of the armed forces* and appointed the Chancellor, in this case, Otto von Bismarck.

The federal states were represented in the federal council*. Prussia, which was the most powerful state, had most of the votes in the federal council and enjoyed the right to veto all decisions. Together with the Reichstag, the federal council made the laws. If the Emperor wanted to declare war, he needed the approval of the federal council, and if he wanted to dissolve the Reichstag, this was officially concluded by the federal council as well.

The German people were represented in the Reichstag, which was elected by universal male suffrage, that is by all males who were 25 years old or older. In contrast to many of the federal states in the Empire, this procedure must be seen as quite progressive. In Prussia itself, for example, the three-class voting system was still in operation and was to remain in force until the collapse of the Empire in 1918.

Like the federal council, the Reichstag could propose laws and – at least in theory – decide on the budget. However, it could be dissolved by royal decree. The Chancellor was only responsible to the Emperor, not to the Reichstag, and could only be dismissed by him.

In the Reichstag itself, a variety of political parties were represented. In general, one can differentiate between five different political directions. From right-wing to left-wing, the very right-wing was represented by the **German Conservative Party*** who were striving for a strengthening of the monarchy and were opposed to the modern tendencies of society. **The National Liberal Party*** was a more moderate conservative party, who, as their name already suggests, put the nation itself at the centre of their political programme. They were loyal to Bismarck, who, in their view, had unified the fatherland. The **German Progressive Party*** was critical of the government. The **Social Democratic Party***, whose ideas were based on the teachings of Karl Marx, represented the interests of the workers and strove to overcome capitalism. However, the ultimate aim of a proletarian revolution took a back seat in favour of more concrete goals that were achievable in the not too distant future and that could be realized by legal means. The **Centre Party***, representing the interests of the Catholic Church, is more difficult to analyse in terms of right-wing or left-wing tendencies.

Bismarck's attitude towards political parties is reflected in the fact that he was not in favour of parliamentary democracy and believed that, in the long run, it would lead to ruin. He did not want to be at the beck and call of* political parties and, accordingly, he sometimes treated the Reichstag in a rather disrespectful manner,

---

⇨ S 49–59

congruent with similar to

commander-in-chief of the armed forces Oberbefehlshaber der Truppen
federal council Bundesrat

German Conservative Party Deutschkonservative Partei
National Liberal Party Nationalliberale Partei

German Progressive Party Deutsche Fortschrittspartei
Social Democratic Party Sozialdemokratische Partei

Centre Party Zentrum

to be at sb.'s beck and call available to do things for sb. else whenever they want

A meeting of the German Reichstag on February 6, 1888. Painting by Ernst Henseler from 1896

threatening the body with dissolution in the event that its members were not in line with his proposals. However, he was also aware of the fact that in order to push his more controversial legislation through, he was in need of support.

"Enemies of the Reich"*

As mentioned above, Bismarck's attitude towards political parties was a rather negative one. The first party to experience this first hand was the Centre Party.
Though disputes between church and state about who was to gain the upper hand had occurred before, this time the struggle intensified when Pope Pius IX proclaimed the dogma of **Papal Infallibility*** in 1870 in order to secure his authority in matters of faith. Six years before, he had already announced in his so-called "Syllabus Errorum" (the list of errors) that he would fight in order to contain secularisation and liberalism. The idea of Papal Infallibility caused uproar among both Protestants as well as Catholics and many of them saw the urgent need of engaging in a "struggle for culture".
When the Pope demanded from Prussia that the state should dismiss all those ecclesiastical* civil servants who had refused to acknowledge* the Pope's stance in this matter, Bismarck refused to comply. The conflict then turned into a fundamental argument concerning the basic question of the influence of the church on the state. And it also provided Bismarck with an opportunity to attack Catholicism and thus also the Centre Party, since, at least in theory, a Catholic's first loyalty was to the Pope and not to the state. Bismarck therefore labelled the members of the Centre Party "enemies of the Reich" and accused them of failing to support Germany reli-

enemies of the Reich Reichsfeinde

Papal Infallibility päpstliches Unfehlbarkeitsdogma

ecclesiastical [ɪˌkliːziˈæstɪk(ə)l] relating to the Christian Church
to acknowledge anerkennen

ably. Accordingly, he stated, members of the Centre Party could not be "good Germans" and members of their party at the same time, and, from then on, they were called "Ultramontanes", from the Latin "ultra montes", meaning "beyond the mountains", whereby the mountains in question here were the Alps, beyond which the Pope resided in Rome. The fact that mainly the southern German states were to a large extent Catholic, least attracted by the idea of German unity and still potential allies of Austria, added to the conflict.

In the course of the *Kulturkampf* **(Struggle for Culture/Culture Struggle)***, Bismarck attempted to strengthen the authority of the state by, for example, dissolving Catholic religious orders*, placing schools under state supervision, forbidding priests to speak about state affairs in their sermons*, according to the terms of the so-called **Pulpit Law*** (cf. S 53a), and by reforming the training of priests. In the entire German Empire, the Jesuit Order was banned and compulsory civil marriage was introduced. Most of this legislation is summed up as the May Laws or Falk Laws, named after Adalbert Falk, who had been appointed Minister of Culture in Prussia in 1872. By and by, attitudes were hardening. Due, however, to the tenacity* of the Catholic Church and the Centre Party's success at the polls in elections in the 1880s, Bismarck finally had to give in and take back some, though not all, of the legislation directed against the Catholic Church. Falk, too, was dismissed from his post in 1879. The growth of the Centre Party had made the "Struggle for Culture" politically unwise. All in all, however, Bismarck's relations with the Centre Party had been severely damaged and he could never fully rely on their support again.

Similar to the "Ultramontanes", the Social Democrats, formed in 1875, were also accused of being disloyal to the Reich since Socialism was a phenomenon with international appeal and the Social Democrats' political programme could be described as anti-bourgeois* and anti-capitalist. This was what made them appear the biggest threat to the existing order, according to Bismarck and other Conservatives. So far the Liberal majority in the Reichstag had rejected the passing of laws that were directed against the alleged "publicly dangerous endeavours of Social Democracy". However, two assassination attempts on the life of Emperor William I were used as a pretext* by Bismarck for blaming the Social Democrats for these actions and thus managing to convince the Reichstag to finally pass the so-called *"Gesetz gegen die gemeingefährlichen Bestrebungen der Sozialdemokratie"*, or **Anti-Socialist Laws*** (cf. S 55). By means of these laws, Socialist associations and trade unions were banned as well as assemblies and the party's press publications. Furthermore, Social Democrats could be banished from the individual federal states. Another means of suppressing the influence of Socialist ideas on the populace was a school reform. The focus clearly lay on teaching loyalty to the Crown and Germany, as well as obedience* to the state order through changing the curricula and instituting state supervision at school to make sure that no "ideas harmful to the existing order", that is Socialist ideas, were instilled in the minds of the young. (cf. S 56, S 57)

Nonetheless, people were still allowed to vote for the Social Democrats in the elections to the Reichstag, which they also did. Despite all the repression that the Social Democrats had to suffer, they gained an increasing number of seats in the Reichstag. In 1890, twelve years after the passing of the Anti-Socialist Laws, there was no longer a majority in the Reichstag in support of their prolongation. In the same year, indeed, the Social Democrats gained the majority of votes in the elections with a total of 1.5 million votes cast in their favour.

The strategy employed by Bismarck to attack Socialism has come to be described as "carrot and stick". Whereas, on the one hand, the Anti-Socialist Laws clearly represent the "stick", that is, the suppression of Socialism by means of repressive measures, the introduction of a **social security system*** can, on the other hand, be considered to be the "carrot". By fulfilling traditional Socialist demands such as health care insurance, old-age pensions or care for the bereaved*, Bismarck hoped to diminish* the attraction of Social Democracy for the working class and thus gain their support for his policies. With the introduction of this social security system, the foundations were laid for today's German social security system, to which, in the period of the Weimar Republic, unemployment insurance was later added.

So far, Bismarck's attempt to eradicate* the "enemies of the state" had been unsuccessful. However, not only Catholics or Socialists were labelled as such, other groups such as Poles or Jews were also targeted by Bismarck. His era saw the rise of political anti-Semitism, as exemplified by the writings of Heinrich von Treitschke and others (cf. S 58 , S 59). Moreover, the Settlement Law of 1886 encouraged German peasants to settle in the eastern provinces of Prussia from which beforehand the Polish inhabitants or Jewish inhabitants of Russian citizenship had been expelled. Those who had nevertheless decided to stay suffered discrimination. Polish, for example, was no longer taught in schools. Similarly, in the annexed territories of Alsace and Lorraine, pupils were also forced to learn German. This policy has become known as the **policy of Germanization***.

social security system *Sozialversicherungssystem*

care for the bereaved *Hinterbliebenenfürsorge*

to diminish to lessen

to eradicate to get rid of completely

policy of Germanization *Germanisierungspolitik*

"The Only Jew-Free Hotel in Frankfurt am Main", colour postcard from 1897, sent from the Kölner Hof

⇨ S 60–66   Foreign Policy in the Second Empire

The Alliance System

Since, following the Franco-Prussian War and the humiliating Treaty of Frankfurt as well as the proclamation of the German Empire in the Hall of Mirrors in Versailles, France was likely to be bent on revenge, Bismarck's first and foremost aim in terms of foreign policy was to prevent any further German engagement in war. He attempted to achieve this objective with the help of a complicated system of alliances that was intended to prevent a war on two fronts against France and Russia by isolating France. He was set on preventing his **"nightmare of coalitions"***, an alliance between France to Germany's west and Russia to Germany's east, or any other alliance of this nature directed against Germany. Additionally, he made a series of defensive alliances to further protect Germany. These cornerstones of Bismarck's diplomacy are outlined in the so-called **Kissingen Dictation*** (cf. S 60) of 1877, which also contains his "three-out-of-five" rule, to the effect that, as long as the world is dominated by an unstable equilibrium of five powers, one should try to be one of three. Already in 1873, Germany, Russia and Austria-Hungary had formed the **Three Emperors' League***, whose function was more mutual consultation in the event of war. However, this alliance had collapsed due to upcoming tension at the Congress of Berlin (see below). In 1879, Germany and Austria-Hungary signed the **Dual Alliance*** in order to strengthen the ties between the two countries. It was agreed that each would assist the other in the event of a Russian attack. When Italy joined the Dual Alliance in 1882, it was extended to the so-called **Triple Alliance***. An alliance with Italy meant secure southern borders for Austria-Hungary and also prevented Italy from forming an alliance with France.

In 1881, the **Three Emperors' Alliance*** was signed by Germany, Austria-Hungary and Russia, stating that in the event of war with a fourth power, they would stay neutral and also that they would attempt to settle Austro-Russian conflicts in the Balkans. However, this Three Emperors' Alliance collapsed in the wake of yet another crisis in the Balkans. Bismarck, however, was aware of the fact that good relations with Russia were needed in order to prevent his "nightmare of coalitions" and so he concluded the **Reinsurance Treaty*** with Russia in 1887 in which both countries (secretly) promised neutrality except for the event that Germany would attack France or Russia Austria. Due to the fact that Russia's rights and interests in the Balkans were confirmed by Germany in this treaty, something which was, of course, contrary to Austria-Hungary's interests, Bismarck had embarked on a bold venture which could turn against him at any minute. With the **Mediterranean Agreement*** between Britain, Austria-Hungary and Italy, concluded in the same year, Bismarck, who had encouraged this agreement, hoped to prevent Russia from further challenging Austria-Hungary in the Balkans. (cf. S 62)

In general, Bismarck's foreign policy was aimed at maintaining the status quo. This is also reflected in his attitude towards the acquisition of overseas colonies. In the first years after the proclamation of the German Empire, Bismarck had always described Germany as "saturated"*, meaning that he did not see a need for the acquisition of overseas colonies and instead he focused more on stabilizing the newly-founded German Empire. He even assumed the role of mediator* at the **Congress of Berlin*** that had been summoned in 1879 as the result of a crisis in the Balkans that particularly affected Austria-Hungary and Russia, in which their interests clashed. With him presiding over the Congress, a settlement was achieved by diplomatic means, thus gaining Bismarck the nickname **"honest broker"**. (cf. S 61)

"honest broker" „ehrlicher Makler"

Bismarck's Resignation in 1890

Emperor William I died in 1888. His son Frederick III succeeded him according to the Prussian dynastic succession*. However, he was severely ill and died after only three months in power. So the next generation had to step in, in this case his son and William I's grandson, William II. Since there were therefore three emperors in power in only one year, we also speak of 1888 as the **"Three Emperors' Year"**. Quite soon it became obvious that there were major differences between the new, young emperor and the old chancellor Bismarck. William was of a new generation, being just 29 at the time of his accession to the throne, Bismarck, however, was already 73 years old. In contrast to his grandfather, William II wanted to rule by himself, striving for a "personal regiment" which would consequently limit Bismarck's scope of action*. Additionally, both differed fundamentally in their views on foreign policy as well as on domestic policy. Due to these private and political differences, Bismarck finally resigned in 1890, not without previously having been urged to do so by the new emperor. (cf. S 63)

succession here: Erbfolge

Three Emperors' Year Dreikaiserjahr

scope of action Handlungsspielraum

Statue of Bismarck in Hamburg, inaugurated in 1906

The Idea and Difficulty of Nation, Nation-state and Nationalism

S1 Andrew Matthews

Revolution and Reaction. Europe 1789–1849

The contemporary historian Andrew Matthews distinguishes between different forms of nationalism in this excerpt.

Pre-task

1. Matthews took the year 1789 as the starting point for his work on nationalism. Revise what you have learned about the "epochal year" 1789 in history class and make the connection to nationalism. What does the French Revolution have to do with the promotion of nationalism?
   TIPS:
   - Abbé Sièyes' "What is the Third Estate"?
   - Tennis Court Oath
   - Declaration of the Rights of Man and the Citizen
   - liberty, equality, fraternity (, or death)
   - Revolutionary Wars

Tasks

2. One very effective and helpful method of attacking a secondary source is to visualize it. Do this with the text by Andrew Matthews: Copy and fill in the boxes and arrows with the help of **S1**.

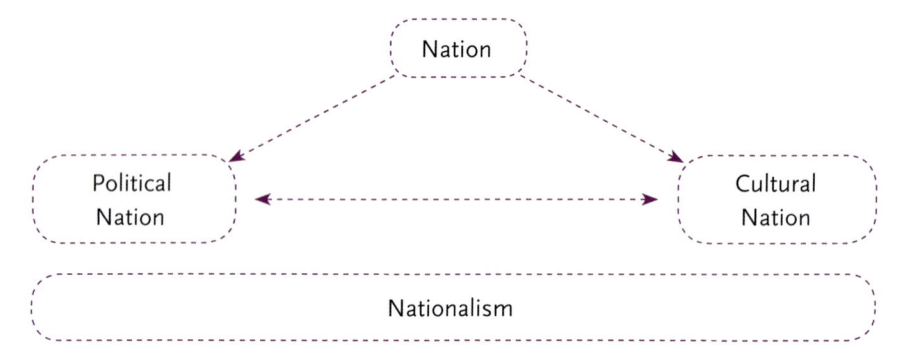

```
                    Nation
                   /      \
                  /        \
          Political  <----  Cultural
           Nation            Nation

              Nationalism
```

3. Explain why, at the turn of the 18th century, France was a political nation and "Germany" a cultural nation.

4. Explain in detail the connection between ideas of the Enlightenment and the phenomenon of nationalism addressed in the text.

Post-task

5. Nationalism can be described as a Janus-faced (two-faced) phenomenon, comprising both inclusion (integration) and exclusion (segregation). Think of situations in which nationalism becomes most apparent (e.g. the Football World Cup or the like) and use these to illustrate the Janus-faced quality of nationalism.

Nationalism

Liberalism is in some respects difficult to disentangle* from nationalism in this period. Both drew their main support from the middle classes and both, in central Europe, were more or less opposed to the established order. And, according to the French model, the sovereignty of the people was the sovereignty of the nation. The term 'nationalism' defies* simple definition. It broadly refers to the notion that the most important bond in society is that of nationality. What then matters is what defines the nation.

Any attempt to define the concept of the nation in more than the most general terms is open to criticism as the criteria we apply are unlikely to fit all nations. [...] Historians have suggested that two concepts of the nation developed at the end of the eighteenth century: on the one hand, a basically political definition of the nation and, on the other hand, an essentially cultural definition.

The political nation

This concept relates to the ideas put forward by Jean-Jacques Rousseau in the eighteenth century and which were applied in 1789 in the French Revolution. In 1789, the people of France claimed to be the French nation (rather than merely the subjects of the king of France) and claimed that political power in the state ultimately rested with them. The French nation wrested* political power from the monarchy and privileged elites. To be French after 1789 was simply to be a citizen of the French state. The idea of the political nation, then, focuses on a people's right to self-determination, its right to choose its own government and the responsibility of that government to respect and protect the people's rights. [...]

The cultural nation

In central and eastern Europe a different concept of the nation developed which did not necessarily have any political overtones*. A nation was defined by reference to a range of criteria such as a common history and culture, a common language and religion, and ties of blood and community derived from long settlement in a particular area. Such a list, of course, will not fit every case, nor is it meant to – to some nations (such as the Germans), history and culture were the defining elements; in others (such as the Poles), it was religion; and for yet others (such as the Italians), it was language. This concept allowed nations to define themselves without specific reference to an existing state. Some ardent* German nationalists, therefore, could see themselves as German and wanted to encourage a sense of Germanness in others without necessarily desiring the creation of a German national state.

Whilst such a distinction is useful, the history of the nineteenth century demonstrates that in the end the two concepts are not mutually exclusive*. As cultural nationalism developed in Europe it was quickly linked to political aspirations* against existing regimes, and the notion of cultural nationhood lent legitimacy to claims for states to be organized on the basis of nations.

Definition of nationalism

At the most basic level, nationalism refers to the belief that the state and the nation should coincide*. Nationalists hold that the nation state is the highest, most desirable and even the only legitimate form of state. Additionally, the state in its constitution and actions should reflect the will of the nation. When nation and state did not coincide (as in a multi-national dynastic empire like that of the Habsburgs*,

---

to disentangle to separate

to defy [dɪˈfaɪ] if sth. defies description, belief, or understanding, it is strange and almost impossible to describe, believe, or understand

to wrest to keep or take away sth. wanted or needed

overtones implications

ardent very enthusiastic

to be mutually exclusive *sich gegenseitig ausschließen*
aspiration goals, hopes

to coincide [ˌkəʊɪnˈsaɪd] to concur, to corrrespond

Habsburgs royal family of the rulers of the Austrian Empire

the multi-state German Confederation or the multi-state Italian peninsula), the nationalists wanted to bring about the nation state or at least seek some political recognition of the nation, especially through some acceptance of national self-government and of the use the national language. [...]

Andrew Matthews: Revolution and Reaction. Europe 1789–1849, Cambridge: Cambridge University Press 2001, pp. 155 f.

S 2 Timothy Baycroft

Nationalism in Europe, 1789–1945

Timothy Baycroft is a contemporary historian who teaches Modern History at the University of Sheffield. In the given text, he elaborates on the impact Napoleonic rule had on Europe.

Pre-task
1. In the given excerpt, Baycroft claims that "[i]n spite of Napoleon's objectives for his greater European empire, it was not his social and administrative organisation that he left behind in Europe, but the seeds of nationalist sentiments which would determine the course of European history for more than one hundred years." (ll. 12 ff.) Make an educated guess as to why Napoleonic rule gave rise to nationalism in Europe.

Tasks
2. Describe the "emotional, nationalist responses" (l. 17) to Napoleonic rule the author refers to.
3. With the help of the overview section, explain the references to the historical context Baycroft makes.
4. Discuss which of the changes brought about by Napoleon would have been either welcomed or resented by the people living in the occupied or annexed territories.

While revolutionary France had only a limited impact on the rest of Europe, France under Napoleon came to dominate the continent. Napoleon had a great plan for Europe, in part motivated by his quest for greater personal power and influence, and in part by a desire to see the social and administrative organisation he had put into place in France extended to the other countries. Through the Civil or Napoleonic Code, he hoped to create a new European civilisation which would be based on the principles of 1789 as he saw them. By this, Napoleon thought mainly of the suppression of feudalism*, and of secularism* and the equality of all before the law. Although he secured a large nationalist, patriotic following in France, by declaring himself emperor he had abandoned the legal principle of the nation as the sovereign basis for the state and the law as it had been conceived by the early leaders of the revolution. In spite of Napoleon's objectives for his greater European empire, it was not his social and administrative organisation that he left behind in Europe, but the seeds* of nationalist sentiments* which would determine the course of European history for more than one hundred years. Based upon resentment of French influence and domination, several other European countries developed emotional, nationalist responses. Great Britain not only lived through 22 years of almost uninterrupted war with France, but after 1807 had to deal with the continental blockade imposed by Napoleon. This blockade led to a crisis of overproduction with significant consequences for the British economy. The resulting hardship and suffering, combined with the threat of invasion and the leading role of the British among the anti-Napoleonic armies after the battle of Trafalgar, contributed to increasing the British national sentiment that had already begun to form among the commercial and political elites who were central to the country's economic greatness. [...] In Italy, where Napoleon had brought greater unity among the different Italian states and revived the use of the term 'Italy', the people began to resent the economic hardships brought about by the blockade, the large numbers of their soldiers killed fighting for Napoleon, and the number of Italian artistic treasures which had been taken away to Paris. Some Italian poets began to call for Italian unity and independence, and they were soon followed by other members of the Italian intellectual and military elite. In the German states, it was the collapse of Prussia at the battle of Jena in 1806 and the harshness of the subsequent French domination that pushed German intellectuals such as Johann Gottlieb Fichte [...] and Karl von Stein to call for unity and support from the greater German nation, which was politically divided rather than culturally uniform. From that time forward, German political unification and liberalisation was a major preoccupation* of the German intellectual elite. These nationalist reactions to Napoleonic domination were by no means felt by the majority of the population in the occupied countries, but the minority who voiced them were persistent* enough not to disappear completely from the scene after Napoleon's fall in 1814–15 and the return of the pre-revolutionary political structure. The years that followed the treaty of Vienna in 1815 would see the steady growth and development of these nationalist sentiments, differing slightly in emphasis and form depending upon the country in question. The active minority who embraced nationalism sought to increase nationalist feeling and win support for the nationalist movements which were already forming around Europe.

Timothy Baycroft: Nationalism in Europe. 1789–1945. Cambridge: Cambridge University Press ⁷2007, pp. 12 f.

feudalism ['fjuːd(ə)lɪz(ə)m] *Feudalismus, Lehnsherrschaft*
secularism lack of religious influence within society

seed (fig.) *Samen, Saatgut*
sentiment feeling

preoccupation the state of being busy thinking about sth.
persistent persevering, relentless, determined

Johann Gottlieb Fichte (1762–1814)

Johann Gottlieb Fichte is considered to be one of the most important representatives of German idealism in philosophy. In the beginning, Fichte was an eager supporter of the French Revolution and its ideas. However, as soon as Napoleon had crowned himself Emperor in 1804 and had revoked the liberal achievements of the Revolution, Fichte rejected him and considered him to be evil. Accordingly, he openly displayed his resistance against the French occupying forces in Berlin, where he delivered his famous "Addresses to the German Nation" speeches (1807–1808), which made him famous among the public, and in which he tackled the issues of creating a German national spirit and instilling it in the people. This is why Fichte is immensely important for the theoretical concept of German nationalism. He placed the blame for recent German humiliations in lost battles on a lack of national spirit and called on the Germans to find or create such a spirit.

When it came to instilling this national spirit in the German people, Fichte saw the public schools as the place where this could and should be done, and so he also had a major influence on the new agenda in public education instituted in Prussia in the wake of the Prussian revolution "from above". Fichte died in Berlin on 19 January 1814.

S 3   Johann Gottlieb Fichte

Reden an die Deutsche Nation

The given source contains excerpts from the fourth and the eighth of Fichte's "Addresses to the German Nation" (cf. biographical account).

Pre-tasks
1. Fichte chose to entitle his lectures "Reden an die Deutsche Nation". What does his choice of words already reveal about the contents and objective of his lectures? Discuss this question in class, taking your results from S 2 into consideration.
2. Fichte aimed at instilling a "national spirit" in the Germans, by for example telling them what sets the Germans apart from other peoples. In class, try to agree on characteristics that all Germans (or Italians, French, Americans, etc.) share. What makes these distinctions difficult, and how can you relate these difficulties to the Janus-faced quality of the phenomenon of nationalism?

Tasks
3. Focus on the excerpt from speech 4: point out what sets the Germans and other peoples of Germanic descent apart.
4. Compare your results from task 3 with your results from task 2: did you think of similar characteristics, such as language?
5. Focus on the excerpt from speech 8: summarize Fichte's views on love of the fatherland.
6. Explain to what extent the Janus-faced quality of nationalism becomes apparent in the given excerpts.
7. In 1938, the National Socialists ordered a renaming of Germany's grammar schools. The schools were supposed to choose a name patron that was in line with National Socialist ideology. On their homepage, a grammar school in Krefeld explains why their school chose Fichte as their name patron, claiming to have picked him in

order to bypass the pressure exerted by the National Socialists [www.fichtekrefeld.de/ueber-uns/tradition/geschichte/fichte/ [04.05.15]. Take a critical stand on their choice.

Post-tasks

8. Revise what you have learned about the notion of "the German" in last year's history class (The Germans from a Roman point of view.). Use this knowledge to refute Fichte's notion of "the German".
9. Do further research on the German philosopher Johann Gottfried von Herder (1744–1803) and his theory of the German *Volksgeist*. Compare his views on "Germanness" and nationalism in a Venn-diagram: what do Fichte and Herder have in common, what sets them apart?

Excerpt from speech 4:

Hauptverschiedenheit zwischen den Deutschen und den übrigen Völkern germanischer Abkunft*

Der zu allererst und unmittelbar der Betrachtung sich darbietende Unterschied zwischen den Schicksalen der Deutschen und der übrigen aus derselben Wurzel
5 erzeugten Stämme ist der, dass die ersten in den ursprünglichen Wohnsitzen* des Stammvolkes* blieben, die letzten in andere Sitze auswanderten, die ersten die ursprüngliche Sprache des Stammvolkes behielten und fortbildeten*, die letzten eine fremde Sprache annahmen, und dieselbe allmählig [sic] nach ihrer Weise umgestalteten*. Aus dieser frühesten Verschiedenheit müssen erst die später erfolg-
10 ten, z.B. dass im ursprünglichen Vaterlande*, angemessen germanischer Ursitte*, ein Staatenbund* unter einem beschränkten Oberhaupte* blieb, in den fremden Ländern mehr auf bisherige römische Weise die Verfassung in Monarchien überging, u. dergl. erklärt werden, keinesweges aber in umgekehrter Ordnung*. Von den angegebenen Veränderungen ist nun die erste, die Veränderung der Hei-
15 math*, ganz unbedeutend. Der Mensch wird leicht unter jedem Himmelsstriche* einheimisch, und die Volkseigenthümlichkeit*, weit entfernt durch den Wohnort sehr verändert zu werden, beherrscht vielmehr diesen und verändert ihn nach sich. Auch ist die Verschiedenheit der Natureinflüsse in dem von Germaniern bewohnten Himmelsstriche nicht sehr gross. Ebensowenig* wolle man auf den
20 Umstand ein Gewicht legen, dass in den eroberten Ländern die germanische Abstammung mit den früheren Bewohnern vermischt worden; denn Sieger, und Herrscher und Bildner des aus der Vermischung entstehenden neuen Volkes waren doch nur die Germanen. Ueberdies erfolgte dieselbe Mischung, die im Auslande mit Galliern, Cantabriern* usw. geschah, im Mutterlande mit Slaven wohl
25 nicht in geringerer Ausdehnung; so dass es keinem der aus Germaniern entstandenen Völker heutzutage leichtfallen* dürfte, eine grössere Reinheit* seiner Abstammung vor den übrigen darzuthun*.
Bedeutender aber, und wie ich dafürhalte, einen vollkommenen Gegensatz* zwischen den Deutschen und den übrigen Völkern germanischer Abkunft begrün-
30 dend, ist die zweite Veränderung, die der Sprache; und kommt es dabei, welches ich gleich zu Anfange bestimmt aussprechen will, weder auf die besondere Beschaffenheit* derjenigen Sprache an, welche von diesem Stamme beibehalten, noch auf die der anderen, welche von jenem anderen Stamme angenommen wird, sondern allein darauf, dass dort eigenes behalten, hier fremdes angenommen
35 wird; noch kommt es an auf die vorige Abstammung derer, die eine ursprüngliche Sprache fortsprechen*, sondern nur darauf, dass diese Sprache ohne Unterbre-

Abkunft origin, descent

Wohnsitz dwelling
Stammvolk ancestral people
fortbilden to develop

umgestalten to form
Vaterland fatherland
Ursitte primary custom
Staatenbund confederation of states
Oberhaupt leader
in umgekehrter Ordnung vice versa
Heimat home
Himmelsstrich geographical area
Eigentümlichkeit peculiarity
ebensowenig here: likewise

Gallier, Cantabrier Gauls, Cantabrians (latter = umbrella term for the peoples living on the northern coast of Spain)
leichtfallen to have no problems with sth.
Reinheit purity
dartun to display
Gegensatz contrast

Beschaffenheit nature

fortsprechen to continue to speak/use the language

Unterbrechung interruption	chung* fortgesprochen werde, indem weit mehr die Menschen von der Sprache gebildet werden, denn die Sprache von den Menschen.

Johann Gottlieb Fichte: „Reden an die deutsche Nation", in: Johann Gottlieb Fichtes sämmtliche Werke. Band 7, Berlin 1845/1846, S. 311–328

Excerpt from speech 8:

<u>Was ein Volk sey, in der höhern Bedeutung des Worts, und was Vaterlandsliebe?</u>

Träger und Unterpfand medium and pledge **irdische Ewigkeit** earthly eternity **hienieden** on earth **gesellschaftliche Ordnung** societal order **Fleiß** diligence **Unterhalt** living **gewähren** to grant **Gerüst** frame **aufblühen** to flourish **göttlich** divine **vollkommen** perfect **Fortgang** development **Behörde** authority **Rücksicht** respect **einförmig** uniform **immerwährend** everlasting **Strenge** strictness **Menschengeschlecht** humankind **keimen** to bud **mühsam** difficult, complicated, tedious ['tiːdiəs]	Volk und Vaterland in dieser Bedeutung, als Träger und Unterpfand* der irdischen Ewigkeit*, und als dasjenige, was hienieden* ewig seyn kann, liegt weit hinaus über den Staat, im gewöhnlichen Sinne des Wortes, – über die gesellschaftliche Ordnung*, wie dieselbe im blossen klaren Begriffe erfasst, und nach Anleitung dieses Begriffes errichtet und erhalten wird. Dieser will gewisses Recht, innerlichen Frieden, und dass jeder durch Fleiss* seinen Unterhalt* und die Fristung seines sinnlichen Daseyns finde, so lange Gott sie ihm gewähren* will. Dieses alles ist nur Mittel, Bedingung und Gerüst* dessen, was die Vaterlandsliebe eigentlich will, des Aufblühens* des Ewigen und Göttlichen* in der Welt, immer reiner, vollkommener* und getroffener im unendlichen Fortgange*. Eben darum muss diese Vaterlandsliebe den Staat selbst regieren, als durchaus oberste, letzte und unabhängige Behörde*, zuvörderst, indem sie ihn beschränkt in der Wahl der Mittel für seinen nächsten Zweck, den innerlichen Frieden. Für diesen Zweck muss freilich die natürliche Freiheit des Einzelnen auf mancherlei Weise beschränkt werden, und wenn man gar keine andere Rücksicht* und Absicht mit ihnen hätte, denn diese, so würde man wohl thun, dieselbe so eng, als immer möglich, zu beschränken, alle ihre Regungen unter eine einförmige* Regel zu bringen, und sie unter immerwährender* Aufsicht zu erhalten. Gesetzt, diese Strenge* wäre nicht nöthig, so könnte sie wenigstens für diesen alleinigen Zweck nicht schaden. Nur die höhere Ansicht des Menschengeschlechts* und der Völker erweitert diese beschränkte Berechnung. Freiheit, auch in den Regungen des äusserlichen Lebens, ist der Boden, in welchem die höhere Bildung keimt*; eine Gesetzgebung, welche diese letztere im Auge behält, wird der ersteren einen möglichst ausgebreiteten Kreis lassen, selber auf die Gefahr hin, dass ein geringerer Grad der einförmigen Ruhe und Stille erfolge, und dass das Regieren ein wenig schwerer und mühsamer* werde.

Johann Gottlieb Fichte: „Reden an die deutsche Nation", in: Johann Gottlieb Fichtes sämmtliche Werke. Band 7, Berlin 1845/1846, S. 377–396

„Fichtes Reden an die deutsche Nation". Painting by Arthur Kampf from 1913/14 which used to be on display in the University of Berlin, but is now destroyed. In the background, one can see the Brandenburg Gate.

| Overview | Sources | Paper practice | Vocabulary | What is the German's Fatherland | 51 |

CONNECT

Prussia's Revolution "from Above"

Task Narrating the historical context of the Prussian reforms in the Napoleonic Era and their impact. The makers of the website www.flowofhistory.com have developed a method of teaching in which they present information in various ways (textual, diagrammatic and auditory modes of input) in order to improve students' understanding of history. They often rely on flow charts to illustrate cause-and-effect relationships, in the given case the cause of the Prussian reforms in the Napoleonic Era and their (short-term and long-term) impact.

The second task of your history paper requires you to do exactly this: to "narrate" the historical context, putting special emphasis on the way that events are linked with each other (check the skills pages for language support, such as sentence connectives). It is of the utmost importance that you do not arbitrarily "list" what happened.

Practise narrating the historical context by turning the given flow chart into a coherent text.

S 4 **Prussian Reforms in the Napoleonic Era and their Impact**

Prussian Reforms in the Napoleonic era and their impact

Napoleon's defeat of Prussia in 1807
↓
Severe penalties imposed on Prussia

- Army cut to 42,000 men
- Indemnities equal to 140% of Prussia's revenues before it lost 1/2 its lands
- Lost nearly half its lands

↓

Prussia realizes need to reform in order to fight France

↙ ↘

Governmental reforms from above to prevent revolution from below
- End serfdom and feudal privileges
- Give peasants 2/3 land they had worked
- Promotions by merit in the army

These, along with Bismarck's later reforms supposedly benefiting factory workers Germans prone to accept w/o questions the rule of a govt. they saw as benevolent

Educational reforms influenced by ideas of Johann Fichte:
- Glorify ancient German tribes to create national traditions
- These traditions should be taught in public schools

Made intellectuals active in school, but also made them subordinate to interests of nation and prone to affirm ideas w/o absolute conviction rather than question them

↓

German people and intellectuals more prone to fall victims to groups who misused these ideas for their own purposes

↙ ↓ ↘

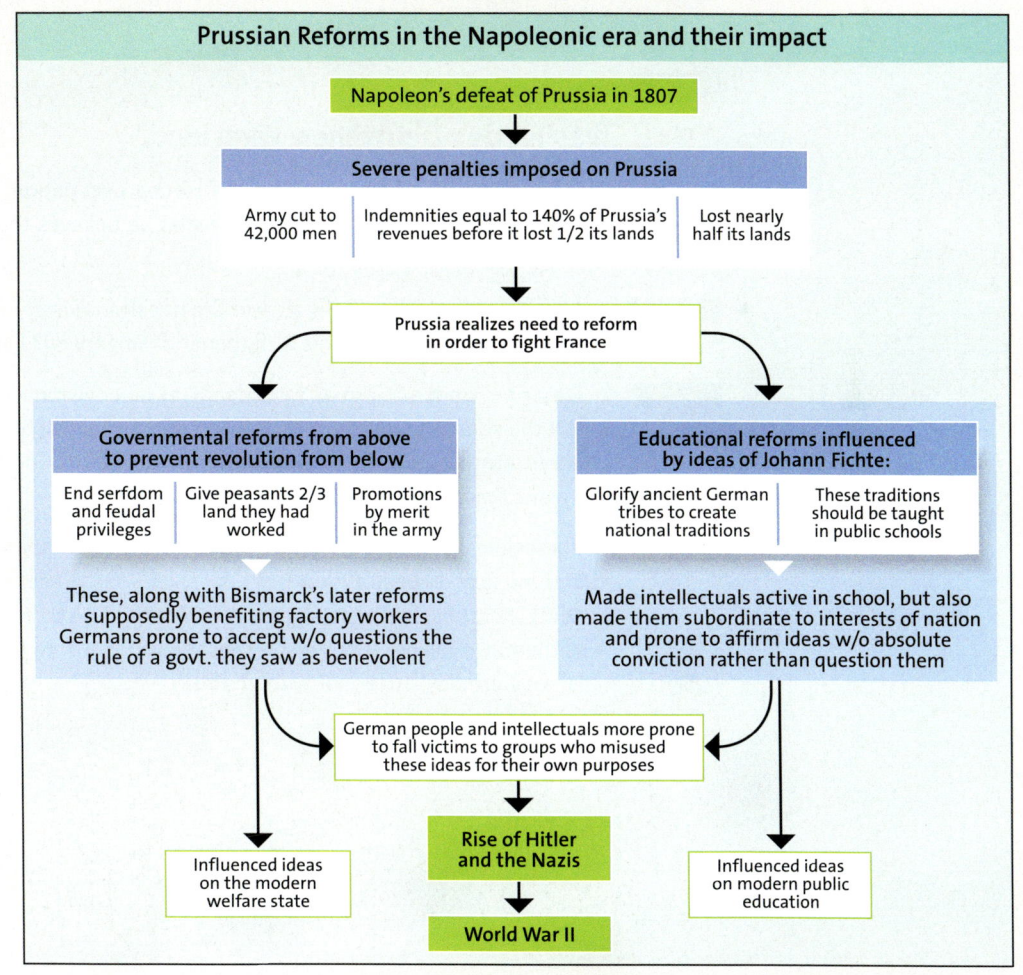

- Influenced ideas on the modern welfare state
- **Rise of Hitler and the Nazis** → **World War II**
- Influenced ideas on modern public education

Chris Butler: "Prussian Reforms in the Napoleonic Era and their Impact", www.flowofhistory.com/category/export/html/121, © Chris Butler 2006 [23.12.14])

Ernst Moritz Arndt (1769–1860)

Ernst Moritz Arndt was a German nationalist author and poet. Today, Ernst Moritz Arndt is seen as a rather ambivalent character in German history due to his anti-Semitic writings.

During the period of the French occupation, Arndt fought against the Napoleonic dominance in 1806 and therefore had to flee to Sweden. Four years later, in 1810, he returned to Germany and started fighting the French again. He wrote several patriotic songs and pamphlets which were sung and read by German nationalists at that time, among them the song "Was ist des Deutschen Vaterland?". When the Carlsbad Decrees came into effect in 1819, Arndt was arrested and his works were confiscated.

In 1841 he became dean of the University of Bonn. When the revolution broke out in the German Confederation in 1848, Arndt became involved and took his seat in the National Assembly at Frankfurt. After the revolution, Arndt retired from public life. He died in Bonn on 29 January 1860.

S 5 — Ernst Moritz Arndt

Was ist des Deutschen Vaterland?

As an opponent of and active fighter against the French occupation, Arndt wrote this song in 1813 in which he gave a definition of what he believes the German fatherland should be like.

Pre-task
1. How would you personally answer the question raised in the title of the song? What constitutes a "fatherland" in general? Discuss.

Tasks
2. Describe Arndt's "German fatherland" as he envisions it in the song.
3. Put the song into its historical context and explain what it reveals about Arndt's attitude towards German unification, and by which means this unification should be achieved.

Post-tasks
4. If possible, listen to a recording of the song and compare message and musical orchestration.
5. Until 1870, this song was regarded as Germany's secret national anthem. Do further research on Ernst Moritz Arndt to find out why it is not Germany's national anthem today.

Original version

Was ist des Deutschen Vaterland?
Ist's Preußenland? Ist's Schwabenland?
Ist's wo am Rhein die Rebe blüht?
Ist's wo am Belt die Möwe zieht?
5 O nein, nein, nein!
Sein Vaterland muss größer sein!

[...]

Was ist des Deutschen Vaterland?
So nenne mir das große Land!
10 Gewiss, es ist das Österreich,
An Ehren und an Siegen reich?
O nein, o nein, o nein, o nein!
Sein Vaterland muss größer sein!

[...]

15 Was ist des Deutschen Vaterland?
So nenne mir das große Land!
Ist's, was der Fürsten Trug zerklaubt?
Vom Kaiser und vom Reich geraubt?
O nein! nein! nein!
20 Das Vaterland muss größer sein.

[...]

Was ist des Deutschen Vaterland?
So nenne endlich mir das Land!
So weit die deutsche Zunge klingt
25 und Gott im Himmel Lieder singt:
Das soll es sein! Das soll es sein!
Das, wackrer Deutscher, nenne dein!
Das ist des Deutschen Vaterland,
wo Eide schwört der Druck der Hand,
30 wo Treue hell vom Auge blitzt
und Liebe warm im Herzen sitzt.
Das soll es sein! Das soll es sein!
Das, wackrer Deutscher, nenne dein!

[...]

35 Das ganze Deutschland soll es sein!
O Gott vom Himmel, sieh darein
und gib uns rechten deutschen Mut,
dass wir es lieben treu und gut!
Das soll es sein! Das soll es sein!
40 Das ganze Deutschland soll es sein!

Ernst Moritz Arndt: „Was ist des Deutschen Vaterland?" in: Des Deutschen Vaterland, Leipzig: Philipp Reclam jun. 1913, pp. 55–56

English translation

Where is the German's fatherland?
The Prussian land? The Swabian land?
Where Rhine the vine-clad mountain laves?
Where skims the gull the Baltic waves?
5 Ah, no, no, no!
His fatherland's not bounded so.

[...]

Where is the German fatherland?
Then name, then name the mighty land!
10 The Austrian land in fight renowned?
The Kaiser's land with honours crowned?
Ah, no, no, no!
His fatherland's not bounded so.

[...]

15 Where is the German fatherland?
Is his the pieced and parcelled land
Where pirate-princes rule? A gem
Torn from the empire's diadem?
Ah, no, no, no!
20 Such is no German fatherland.

[...]

Where is the German fatherland?
Then name, oh, name the mighty land!
Wherever is heard the German tongue,
25 And German hymns to God are sung!
This is the land, thy Hermann's land;
This, German, is thy fatherland.
This is the German fatherland,
Where faith is in the plighted hand,
30 Where truth lives in each eye of blue,
And every heart is staunch and true.
This is the land, the honest land,
The honest German fatherland.

[...]

35 This is the land, the one true land,
O God, to aid be thou at hand!
And fire each heart, and nerve each arm,
To shield our German homes from harm,
To shield the land, the one true land,
40 One Deutschland and one fatherland.

Ernst Moritz Arndt: „The German Fatherland", from: Eve March Tappan (Ed.): The World's Story: A History of the World in Story, Song and Art, 14 Vols., Boston: Houghton Mifflin 1914, Vol. VII: Germany, The Netherlands, and Switzerland, pp. 276–278, the text has been modernized by Jerome S. Arkenberg, © Paul Halsall, www.fordham.edu, November 1998 [07.03.11]

What is the German's Fatherland

S 6   August Heinrich Hoffmann von Fallersleben

Das Lied der Deutschen

Joseph Haydn had composed the melody already in 1797. Back then, however, it was a hymn for Emperor Francis II of the Holy Roman Empire of German Nation and later of Austria (*Gott erhalte Franz den Kaiser* – God save Emperor Francis). In 1841, the German linguist August Heinrich Hoffmann von Fallersleben wrote the lyrics for the "Song of the Germans" which were considered to be revolutionary at that time. The song was a symbol of the March Revolution in 1848, and, in 1922, the whole song became the national anthem of the Weimar Republic.

Pre-task   1. The map below shows how von Fallersleben envisaged Germany. Describe the map and, based on your results, make an educated guess as to why von Fallersleben's lyrics were considered to be revolutionary in 1841.

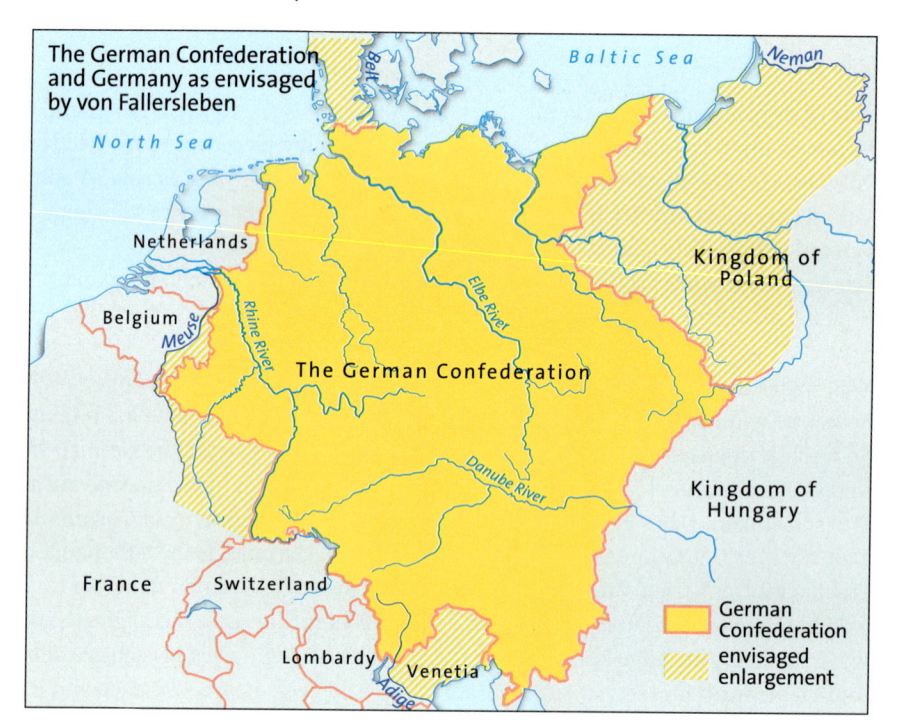

The German Confederation and Germany as envisaged by von Fallersleben

Tasks   2. Give a summary of the "Song of the Germans".
3. Explain the song's title against the backdrop of the lyrics.
4. Today, only the third stanza is sung as Germany's national anthem. Discuss possible reasons for this.

Post-task   5. Today, the *Deutsche Burschenschaft* still sings all three stanzas of the song. Visit their website and find out about their justification for doing so. Take a critical stand on the appropriateness of their view.

Original version

Deutschland, Deutschland über alles,
Über alles in der Welt,
Wenn es stets zu Schutz und Trutze
Brüderlich zusammenhält.
5 Von der Maas bis an die Memel,
Von der Etsch bis an den Belt,
Deutschland, Deutschland über alles,
Über alles in der Welt!

Deutsche Frauen, deutsche Treue,
10 Deutscher Wein und deutscher Sang
Sollen in der Welt behalten
Ihren alten schönen Klang,
Uns zu edler Tat begeistern
Unser ganzes Leben lang.
15 Deutsche Frauen, deutsche Treue,
Deutscher Wein und deutscher Sang!

Einigkeit und Recht und Freiheit
Für das deutsche Vaterland!
Danach lasst uns alle streben
20 Brüderlich mit Herz und Hand!
Einigkeit und Recht und Freiheit
Sind des Glückes Unterpfand;
Blüh' im Glanze dieses Glückes,
Blühe, deutsches Vaterland.

August Heinrich Hoffmann von Fallersleben: "Das Lied der Deutschen", in: Karl Otto Conrady (Hg.): Das große deutsche Gedichtbuch, Frankfurt: Athenäum 1977, S. 485

English translation

Germany, Germany above everything,
Above everything in the world,
When, for protection and defence, it always
takes a brotherly stand together.
5 From the Meuse to the Neman,
From the Adige to the Belt,
Germany, Germany above everything,
Above everything in the world.

German women, German loyalty,
10 German wine and German songs
Shall retain in the world
Their old beautiful chime
And inspire us to noble deeds
During all of our life.
15 German women, German loyalty,
German wine and German song!

Unity and justice and freedom
For the German fatherland!
For these let us all strive
20 Brotherly with heart and hand!
Unity and justice and freedom
Are the pledge of fortune;
Flourish in this fortune's blessing,
Flourish, German fatherland.

August Heinrich Hoffmann von Fallersleben: "Das Lied der Deutschen" (engl. Übersetzung), http://ingeb.org/Lieder/deutsch.html [07.03.15]

Napoleon Bonaparte (1769–1821)

Napoleon Bonaparte was born on the island of Corsica shortly after it had been sold to France by the Republic of Genoa. Born into a noble Corsican family, he was sent to France at the age of nine for the purpose of his education.
When the French Revolution broke out in 1789, Napoleon became an officer in the French army. Supporting the Revolution, he quickly climbed the military career ladder. He was a brilliant military strategist and managed for example to quickly and repeatedly defeat Austrian troops in Italy with an ill-equipped French army.
The French government, fearing Napoleon's rising popularity, sent him to Egypt in 1798 with the task of invading the country and hindering British access to India. However, when, in his absence, royalists in France once again gained in strength due to new coalitions against the country, Napoleon returned to Paris and staged a coup d'état in 1799, therewith making himself ruler (18 *Brumaire*). After having introduced several lasting reforms of the French educational, judicial, financial and administrative systems, he crowned himself Emperor of the French on December 2, 1804.

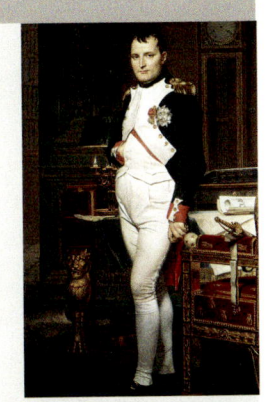

Napoleon in his office, painted by Jacques-Louis David, 1812

He managed to conquer vast parts of Europe with his Grand Army and gained decisive victories, for example in the Battle of Austerlitz (1805) against Austria and Russia or in the Battle of Jena and Auerstedt (1806) against Prussia. However, his Russian campaign failed in 1812, and in 1813 he was defeated in the Battle of the Nations near Leipzig and subsequently forced to abdicate unconditionally and exiled to Elba in 1814.

In 1815 Napoleon managed to escape from this island and returned to the mainland for his so-called "100-Days Rule". His final defeat came in the Battle of Waterloo in present-day Belgium on June 18, 1815, after which he was once again exiled, this time, however, to the faraway British island of St Helena, where he died of stomach cancer on May 5, 1821.

S 7 — How Did Napoleon Attempt to Keep Control over his Empire?

At the height of his power, Napoleon had extended his power over vast areas of Europe, which raises the question of the means he employed in his attempt to maintain control over so huge an empire.

Task Answer the question raised in S 7 by analysing the four maps provided. The skills pages and the following key questions help you:
1. What is the topic of the map (depicted year/period of time etc.)?
2. Which further information does the map's key provide?
3. What is the relevant historical context against which the map must be interpreted?
4. Does the map answer the question properly? If not, do further research.

S 7a+b — "Germany" in 1789 and in 1806

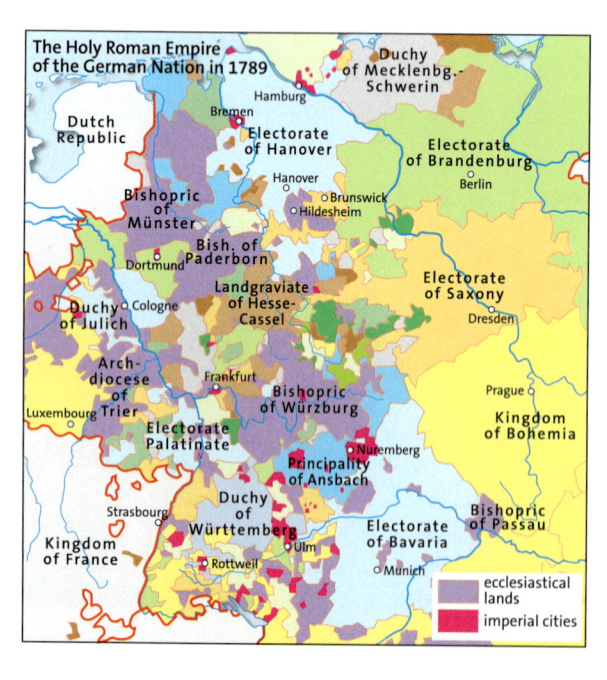

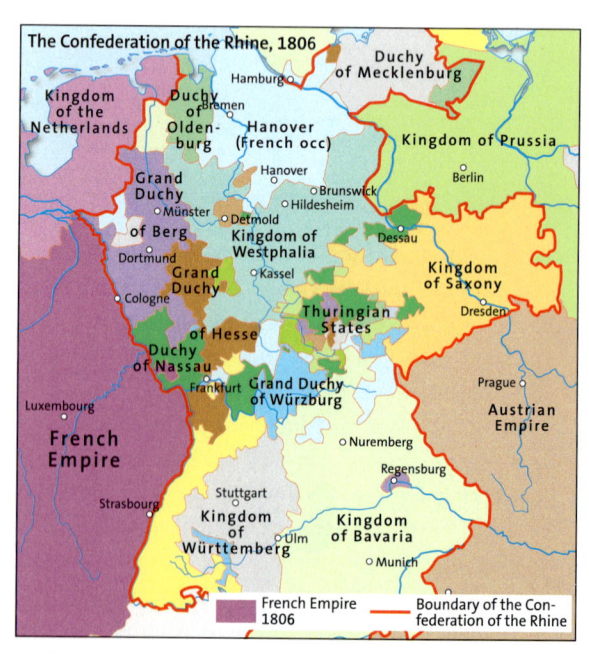

Language support

ecclesiastical property kirchlicher Besitz • **ecclesiastical states** geistliche Gebiete (d. h. Staaten, die z. B. einen Bischof als Landesherrn hatten) • **secular states** weltliche Staaten (d. h. Staaten, die von einem König oder Herzog regiert wurden) • **free imperial city** freie Reichsstadt • **grand duchy** Großherzogtum • **principality** Fürstentum

S 7c Europe under Napoleon

S 7d Europe in 1810: Napoleon's Family System

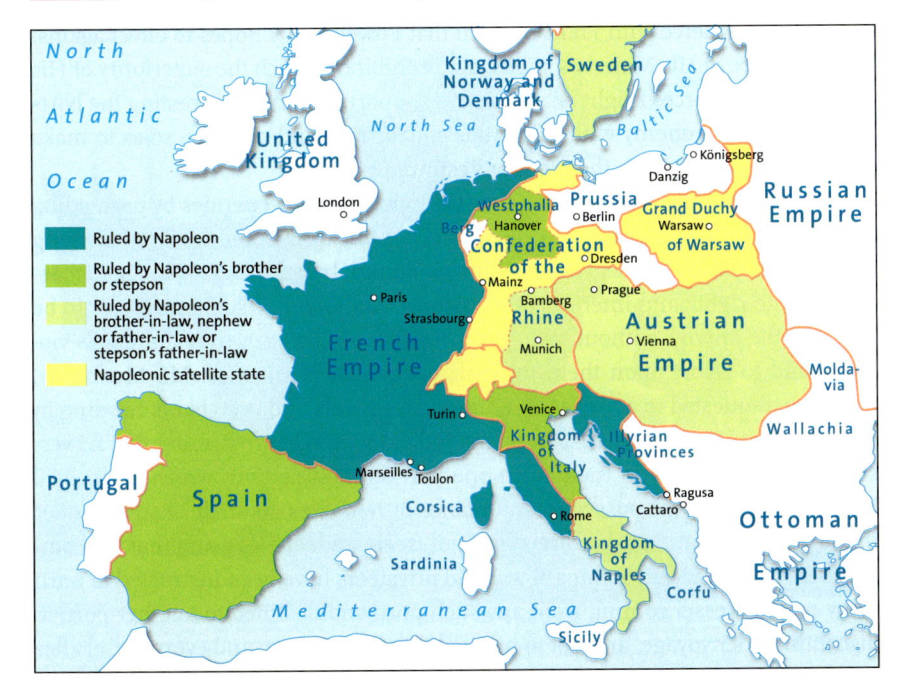

King Frederick William III of Prussia (1770–1840)

Frederick William was born in Potsdam in 1770, the son of Frederick William II of Prussia and Frederika Louisa of Hesse-Darmstadt. He received the usual training of a Prussian prince in the Prussian army and participated in the 1792 to 1794 campaigns against France.

In 1797, he became King of Prussia. His first objective was to restore morality to the court, since he was convinced that his father's court had been dominated by moral debauchery* in both political and sexual respects.

In terms of foreign policy, he at first assumed a neutral stance in the Napoleonic Wars. However, the pro-war parties persuaded him to enter the war in 1806, in which year the Prussian army, led by Frederick William himself, was devastatingly defeated by the French in the battles of Jena and Auerstedt. The Hohenzollern royal family had to flee to East Prussia where they were at the mercy of Tsar Alexander I, who himself had been defeated by the French as well.

After Napoleon's defeat in 1813, Frederick William joined forces with the Coalition powers and travelled with the main army, along with Alexander of Russia and Francis of Austria.

After the Congress of Vienna, Frederick William abandoned the promises for a Prussian constitution which he had made in 1813 and turned towards political reaction. He died in 1840 and was succeeded by his eldest son, Frederick William IV.

debauchery [dɪˈbɔːtʃəri] *Ausschweifungen, Luderleben*

Group 3: Russia

S 11c Representative: Tsar Alexander I (1777–1825), Tsar of Russia (1801–1825)

In 1815, Russia had a population of about 48 million, of which roughly 95% were living in rural areas. Russia's economy was very backward: more than half of the rural population were serfs who were owned by nobles. Most of the rest were state peasants. However, the sheer size of the country and its huge armies accounted for its power. The Tsar ruled autocratically, taking all decisions without reference to government.

autocratic ruling with complete power
liable to likely to

Tsar Alexander had personally led Russia in the war against Napoleon and had then been the first to reach Paris in March 1814. He was a powerful figure at the Congress of Vienna, but the other powers were never quite certain of his intentions. Alexander seemed to be torn between conservatism and liberalism. Although he was an autocratic* ruler, he was attended by a group 5 of liberal advisers. He was also deeply religious and his views were liable to* be influenced by a mystic called Madame Krudener. Finally, it was known that Russia was keen to expand into south-east Asia, at the expense of Turkey. This explains why, in the early stages of the talks, Alexander I had little time for the 'balance of power' idea. Instead, he favoured a Polish state under Russian control, which would, he felt, provide greater security for Poland. Moreover, he wanted a divided Germany, that would pose no threat to Russia, as well as Prussian control of Saxony, which would keep it out of Polish hands.

adapted from: Derrick Murphy (Ed.): Europe 1760–1871, London: Collins Educational 2002, pp. 147 f.

Tsar Alexander I of Russia (1777–1825)

Tsar Alexander I was Emperor of Russia from 1801 to 1825. After the Congress of Vienna, he was the first Russian King of Poland from 1815 to 1825.

He was the grandson of Empress Catherine the Great. After his father, Tsar Paul, had been strangled by a group of officers in a palace revolution in 1801, he succeeded to the throne and was confronted with the difficult task of ruling Russia during the period of the Napoleonic Wars. Whereas, in the first half of his reign, he introduced liberal reforms, the second half of his rule was more arbitrary* in nature, and led to his later revoking* many of his liberal reforms.

Due to his difficult character, some historians have labelled Alexander I the "enigmatic tsar" or the "sphinx". He was brought up according to the principles of the Enlightenment, however, reality in St Petersburg and political intrigues at the Russian court harshly contrasted with the values and ideas he had been taught. After first suffering severe defeats against Napoleon, Alexander I finally managed to drive the French out of Russia in 1812 and even went further, practically chasing them back to France and capturing Paris. This victorious march through Europe had a profound effect on Alexander since he turned to mysticism and religion as guiding principles for restoring peace and order in Russia and Europe. This also helps to explain why he played a key role in the formation of the Holy Alliance, a union of Christian monarchs dedicated to preserving the general peace and the legitimacy of the ruling monarchs against revolutionary uprisings.

Upon his sudden death in 1825, just before his 48th birthday, he was succeeded by his brother Nicholas, since his marriage had produced only one daughter who had died in infancy.

arbitrary *willkürlich* • **to revoke** to take back, to renounce, to say officially that sth. is no longer legal

Group 4: France

S 11d) *Representative:* Charles Talleyrand-Périgord (1754–1838)

In 1815, France had a population of about 29 million, of which roughly 75 % were living in rural areas. Though France was still primarily agricultural, there was some industrial growth, especially in the north. Additionally, it had a powerful army and must be seen as Britain's main rival at sea. From 1815 onwards, France was a constitutional monarchy, although the newly reinstated Bourbon king retained a good deal of power, and the right to vote was very limited in scope. In spite of suffering defeat in 1815, France was still regarded as a powerful nation.

Talleyrand represented the defeated France, on behalf of the newly restored Bourbon monarch Louis XVIII. Crippled as a child, he had entered the Church, becoming a bishop in 1789. However, he had still supported the Revolution and worked for the French Republic in the 1790s, and for Napoleon
5 until 1807. Then he had schemed* for the restoration of the Bourbons and was chief negotiator with the allies in Louis XVIII's cause. His position at the Vienna Congress was not easy, but he was ready to exploit any differences of opinion between the other nations in order to assert French power. He was careful to stress that he spoke for the restored Bourbon monarchy and not for
10 the defeated Napoleon. Talleyrand favoured legitimacy, that is the right of a ruler to hold power by strict hereditary law, as well as restrictions on Prussian expansion, so that Prussia did not pose a direct threat to France. In general he aimed at asserting France's claim to continue to be regarded as a major power.

to scheme [ski:m] to plan

adapted from: Derrick Murphy (Ed.): Europe 1760–1871, London: Collins Educational 2002, pp. 147, 149

Charles-Maurice de Talleyrand-Périgord (1754–1838)

As a diplomat, Charles-Maurice de Talleyrand-Périgord worked as the French chief negotiator at the Congress of Vienna. In that office, he fought for a lenient* treatment of France after Napoleon's defeat.
Since the map of Europe had to be reorganized, Talleyrand demanded a say in the decision-making progress. He managed to secure France's return to the boundaries it had in 1792, without the country having to pay any reparations to the other European powers. In September 1815, Talleyrand resigned from his office and took over the role of a critical statesman.
From 1830 to 1834 he was ambassador to the United Kingdom and here he fought to strengthen the legitimacy of the regime of King Louis-Philippe, who came to power as a result of the July Revolution in 1830.
He died on May 17, 1838.

lenient ['li:niənt] *nachsichtig, mild*

Group 5: Austria

S 11e *Representative*: Prince Klemens von Metternich (1773–1859)

In 1815, Austria had a population of about 25 million, of which roughly 80% were living in rural areas. After Russia, Austria must be considered as the second largest state at that time. Though still largely agricultural, there was very strong industrial growth in the Austrian-owned parts of Italy and in Bohemia. The war years had led to a drain on army finances, which had left the country in severe debt. It is crucial to mention that Austria was a multi-ethnic Empire, meaning it was made up of many different races and ethnicities. It was ruled over by an absolute monarch, the Austrian Emperor.

to preside over to lead

unwieldy [ʌn'wi:ldi] hard to handle

Metternich was the Austrian Foreign Minister who presided over* the Congress, with his master Emperor Francis I. Although he was an extremely able diplomat, his position was not an easy one. Austria itself was a large, unwieldy* central European Empire composed of many different nationalities. It felt threatened by Russia to the east, France to the west and by the ambitions of its peoples from within. It is no wonder, therefore, that much of Metternich's attention at the Congress was taken up in minimizing the spread of liberal and nationalist ideas and working for a balance of power. Metternich thus favoured a strong central Europe – under the influence of Austria – to balance Russia and France, and restrain Russian and Prussian ambitions. In addition, he opted for the continuance of monarchical government and aristocratic leadership.

adapted from: Derrick Murphy (Ed.): Europe 1760–1871, London: Collins Educational 2002, pp. 147–149

Klemens Wenzel Nepomuk Lothar von Metternich-Winneburg (1773–1859)

Metternich was born into an aristocratic family in Coblenz, Germany. At the time of his birth, his father was in the service of the Habsburgs of Austria.
His family had to flee from the French revolutionary armies in 1794 and thus moved to Vienna, the capital of the Austrian Habsburgs, where Metternich served as the Habsburgs' ambassador to Saxony, Prussia and Napoleonic France.
In 1809 Metternich was appointed minister of foreign affairs and as such constantly worked to undermine and erode Napoleon's power. In order not to lose either Russian or French support, Metternich had to employ a very careful form of diplomacy. After the failure of Napoleon's Russian campaign, Austria sided with Russia and Prussia against Napoleon. Two days after the Battle of the Nations, Metternich was invested as a hereditary prince of the Austrian Empire.
In 1814/15 he presided over the Congress of Vienna which owed its final outcome mainly to Metternich's skilful diplomacy, as the former allies present disagreed strongly over the re-organization of Europe after the Napoleonic Wars.
Metternich resented liberalism, nationalism and revolution and was of the opinion that lawful rulers would be better suited to creating functioning and stable societies. In his view, monarchy should share power with the traditionally privileged classes of society and, accordingly, he attempted to stifle* revolutionary movements, by means of the Carlsbad Decrees for instance or the 6 and 10 Articles. This is why, to some, he is seen as the epitome* of reaction and a suppressor of liberty.
The March Revolutions in Vienna in 1848 forced Metternich to resign and to go into exile in England. He returned to mainland Europe 18 months later but only came back to Vienna as late as 1851. He died here in 1859.

---

to stifle to suppress • **epitome** [ɪˈpɪtəmi] the best possible example of sth.

Emperor Francis I of Austria (1768–1835)

Francis I was (as Francis II) the last Holy Roman Emperor of German Nation, ruling as such from 1792 until 1806, when he dissolved the Holy Roman Empire after suffering a defeat against Napoleon in the Battle of Austerlitz. Having founded the Austrian Empire in 1804, he ruled as Francis I of Austria until his death in 1835, being the only double emperor in history between the years 1804 and 1806.
In the Napoleonic Wars, Francis I took over a leading role among Napoleon's opponents. One of several setbacks he suffered was the marriage of state between his daughter Marie Louise and Napoleon in 1810.
At the Congress of Vienna, Austria was a leading member of the newly formed Holy Alliance. Moreover, Francis I was the first President of the newly established German Confederation.
As Francis was a driving factor in the establishment of the Concert of Europe, which aimed at resisting and restricting nationalist and liberal aspirations in Europe in favour of restoring monarchical order and legitimacy, he later in his reign came to be seen as reactionary.
Upon his death in 1835, he was succeeded by his son, Emperor Ferdinand I of Austria, who finally had to abdicate in the wake of the 1848/49 Revolutions in Austria.

What is the German's Fatherland

S 12) The "Dancing Congress" and its Results

After Napoleon's return to power (his so-called 100-Days' Rule) and his subsequent final defeat in the Battle of Waterloo, the statesmen in Vienna eventually agreed on a settlement. However, decision-making processes had been slow, or, as one of the attendees, the Prince of Ligne observed: "The Congress does not move forward, it dances."

Pre-task 1. Read the following remarks about the "Dancing Congress" published in the magazine *Praxis Geschichte* on the occasion of the 200th anniversary of the Congress on Vienna in 2015 and discuss what this suggests about the eventual outcome of Vienna.

> „Sättigungsgefühl"*
>
> Die allgegenwärtige Festdiplomatie stieß allerdings nicht nur auf Anklang: Einzelne Vertreter der gehobenen Kreise konstatierten ein regelrechtes Sättigungsgefühl, und die Wiener Bevölkerung monierte* die hohen Kosten des Fest-Marathons, die vom Steuerzahler getragen werden mussten. Die Äußerung des Fürsten und österreichischen Diplomaten Charles Joseph de Ligne (1735–1814) „Le Congres danse et ne marche pas" („Der Kongress tanzt und arbeitet nicht"), die sich zum geflügelten Wort* entwickelte, täuscht hingegen über die tatsächlich geleistete Arbeit hinweg.
>
> Unstedde, Maren: „Der Kongress tanzt. Der Wiener Kongress als letztes höfisches Fest"; in: Praxis Geschichte 1 (2015), p. 24.
>
> ---
>
> **Sättigungsgefühl:** feeling of satiety • **etw. monieren** to complain about sth. • **sich zum geflügelten Wort entwickeln** to become proverbial

Tasks
2. The given map illustrates major territorial decisions eventually settled on at the Congress of Vienna. Analyse the map with the help of the skills pages. Before doing so, think of a question which you want to answer with the help of the map.
3. Compare the map with the ones depicting Europe under Napoleonic rule (cf. S 7)): who profited most/least in terms of territory gained? Also check the overview section for help.
4. Discuss the impact the territorial settlements might have on future European power constellations.
5. Create an event map for the Congress of Vienna. Label the branches as follows: Where? When? Why? Who? How (principles)? Outcome?
6. The Congress of Europe – a satisfying solution for Europe? Give an evaluation.

INFO: event map

An event map visualizes a historical event like a mind map does. So the event forms the centre of the event map and there are several branches extending from the centre, covering all important aspects relevant here: where it took place, when it took place, who participated and why they gathered there, how it was organized and what its final outcome was. You might also want to include consequences resulting from decisions made at the respective event.

Map of Central Europe, 1815–1866

S13 The Kings' Cake

The contemporary French cartoon "The Kings' Cake" of 1815 satirizes the way that the statesmen at Vienna dealt with reorganizing the map of Europe after Napoleon's final defeat.

Pre-task
1. Focus on the title of the cartoon only. What does it already suggest about the way the cartoonist views the statesmen's behaviour at Vienna, and how can this view probably be explained, bearing in mind the cartoonist's country of origin? Discuss.

Tasks
2. Analyse the formal features of the cartoon (cf. skill pages).
3. Explain the elements of the cartoon against their historical background. In doing so, first identify the people depicted and what or which country they stand for. Next, focus on the symbolism of the map of Europe being torn apart. Consider also who gets which "piece of the cake".
4. Use your results from S11 and S12 to take a critical stand on the cartoonist's assessment of the Congress of Vienna, both from the contemporary point of view at that time and from today's perspective.

People depicted and embedded text from left to right:
(1) The King of Rome[1]: "Daddy takes care of my part."
(2) Napoleon: "Those who reckon without their host reckon twice."
(3) Joachim Murat[1], King of Naples
(4) Metternich: "The price of blood."
(5) Tsar Alexander: "I'm afraid of the ghost."
(6) Frederick William III of Prussia: "Let's take the good pieces."
(7) Emperor Francis: "Those absent have to bear the blame themselves."
(8) Talleyrand (under the table): "From bishop to miller. I'm leading a dangerous life here."
(9) On the map: "Woe betide those who touch this."

---

[1] **The King of Rome:** Napoleon's son Napoleon François-Joseph Charles who, as the heir to the French Empire, was given the title "King of Rome" upon his birth. • [2] **Joachim Murat:** French cavalry leader and King of Naples (*Neapel*) from 1808 to 1815, husband of Napoleon's youngest sister Caroline.

Language Support

to snatch an sich reißen • **to tear apart** zerreißen • **bicorn(e)/two-cornered hat** Zweispitz (Napoleonshut) • **scales** die Waage • **to crouch (down)** kauern • **to reckon without one's host** die Rechnung ohne den Wirt machen • **woe betide sb.** wehe jdm.

S 14 Charles Vane

Memoirs and Correspondence of Viscount Castlereagh

In the text at hand, Castlereagh's brother Charles Vane, who edited and published his brother's memoirs, quotes extracts from a speech the Viscount gave in the British House of Commons on 20 March 1815, following his return from the Vienna settlement, and in response to attacks by the opposition on the procedural methods of the British government and its allies.

Pre-tasks

1. In this source, Vane recalls a speech by his brother delivered in 1815, but the memoirs and correspondence were published in 1848. Does this make the source a primary or a secondary source? Discuss.
2. In his speech to the House of Commons, Castlereagh also presents his views on the Bourbon dynasty in France. What do you believe his views might be, and why? Make an educated guess. (Tip: You might want to consider the way that Britain herself was governed.)

Tasks

3. Outline Castlereagh's line of argument and point out his views on the Bourbon dynasty in France.
4. Explain the British position towards Napoleonic France against the backdrop of the historical context.
5. In the end, Vane speaks about the success of his brother's speech and regrets that the subsequent abandonment of the Concert of Europe has led to "results […] which have afflicted Europe." (ll. 40 f.) Taking into account that the memoirs and correspondence were published in 1848, discuss possible meanings of this conclusion. (Tip: Turn to the respective pages in the overview section.)
6. Castlereagh differed from many other British statesmen who, in the main, preferred Britain's disentanglement from continental affairs. Discuss to what extent Britain's territorial gains after Vienna might have contributed to changing public opinion on this point.

Upon the whole view of the foreign relations of this country, as they have been settled at the Congress, I cannot but help thinking that Parliament will contemplate* with satisfaction those important arrangements. By them, we have obtained many advantages, and not the least, in which we participate with all Europe, is that
5 we are delivered from the danger which might arise from the predominating power of France. The wise measures adopted for this purpose have not degraded France from the high station which she ought to hold among the nations, while they have given to others additional power and security. […] Whatever steps Great Britain may take, upon the issue of the contest which has thus unexpectedly been
10 forced upon us depend all those blessings of peace, and all those advantages of arrangement, of which I have been speaking. Where is the man who can lay his hand upon his heart and say that, of the power of Buonaparte [sic] is re-established in France*, any of those blessings which Europe was about to enjoy can be realized? Who will say, if he again rules the destinies of France, that Europe can be
15 tranquil*, secure, or independent? I consider that in the question now at issue in France is involved the more vital question, whether the world can return to that

to contemplate to consider

the power of Buonaparte is re-established in France reference to the so-called "100-Days Rule"

tranquil calm

moral system by which the happiness and the interests of mankind were to be upheld, or whether we shall remain, as we have been during the last twenty years, under the necessity of maintaining a system of military policy; whether Europe shall in future present the spectacle of an assemblage of pacific* or of armed nations. Shall the nations of the world take up arms to destroy each other, or lay them down to promote each other's happiness? These are the questions to be decided by the result of the present contest in France, – questions of the deepest interest; for if, indeed, the authority of Buonaparte be restored, who can doubt that with him will be restored also that destructive military power? If that military power be reestablished in France, where, let me ask, must we look for peace and prosperity, unless we conquer it with our swords? [...]

Let this country then, let France herself, reflect that upon the result of this new struggle – upon the management of which, or the part which this nation must take, I say nothing at present – must depend all our happiness or all our calamities*. Upon the success of the family of the Bourbon – who in my judgement have done for France the greatest acts of favour that a people could receive, but more especially that act of grace by which peace, so long banished, was restored to her – depends the important question for this country, whether we shall return to that natural and happy state of peace, or whether we shall continue the struggle against the military power of France, [...]. [...]"

This speech, we are told, [...] drew enthusiastic and long continued cheers from all parts of the House; and it is deeply to be deplored* that in after-years the pledge of mutual support has been abandoned; whereas, if Lord Castlereagh's policy had been pursued, it would have probably produced far other results than those which have afflicted Europe.

pacific wanting peace

calamity Katastrophe, Unglück

to deplore to dislike very much

Charles Vane, Marquess of Londonderry (Ed.): Memoirs and Correspondence of Viscount Castlereagh, Second Marquess of Londonderry, Vol. I., London: Henry Colburn 1848, pp. 57–60

S 15 Guiseppe Mazzini
On Nationality (1852)

"The theory of rights enables us to rise and overthrow obstacles, but not to found a strong and lasting accord between all the elements which compose the nation."

Giuseppe Mazzini: The Duties of Man and Other Essays (1860), London: J. M. Dent & Sons 1907

Guiseppe Mazzini (1805–1871) was the founder of the political movement "Young Italy" whose goal was the creation of a united Italian republic. Mazzini believed that a popular uprising would lead to unification and regarded the creation of a democratic Italy as crucial to Italy's development.

Pre-task

1. Mazzini claims that "[t]he question of nationality can only be resolved by destroying the treaties of 1815, and changing the map of Europe and its public law." (ll. 2 f.) In order to explain Mazzini's statement, revise how the Vienna settlements affected Italy.

Tasks

2. Describe Mazzini's concept of "nationality".
3. Incorporate the source into the historical context of the unification of Italy.
4. Explain in how far the Janus-faced quality of nationalism becomes apparent in this abstract.
5. Draw a (rough sketch of a) map of Europe that would correspond with Mazzini's demands for nation-states based on geographical position, traditions and language. Afterwards, discuss the process of making this map: what major issues were you confronted with?

Europe no longer possesses unity of faith, of mission, or of aim. Such unity is a necessity in the world. [...] The question of nationality can only be resolved by destroying the treaties of 1815, and changing the map of Europe and its public law. The question of Nationalities, rightly understood, is the Alliance of the Peoples;
5 the balance of powers based upon new foundations, the organization of the work that Europe has to accomplish. [...]
[The people] still struggle, as do Poland, Germany, and Hungary, for country and liberty; for a word inscribed upon a banner, proclaiming to the world that they also live, think, love, and labour for the benefit of all. They speak the same language,
10 they bear about them the impress of consanguinity*, they kneel beside the same tombs, they glory in the same tradition; and they demand to associate freely, without obstacles, without foreign domination, in order to elaborate and express their idea; to contribute their stone also to the great pyramid of history. It is something moral which they are seeking; and this moral something is in fact, even politically
15 speaking, the most important question in the present state of things. It is the organization of the European task.
It is no longer the savage, hostile, quarrelsome nationality of two hundred years ago which is invoked* by these peoples. The nationality [...] founded upon the following principle: – Whichever people, by its superiority of strength, and by its geo-
20 graphical position, can do us an injury, is our natural enemy; whichever cannot do us an injury, but can by the amount of its force and by its position injure our enemy, is our natural ally, – is the princely nationality of aristocracies or royal races. The nationality of these peoples has not these dangers; it can only be founded by a common effort and a common movement; sympathy and alliance will be its result.
25 In principle, [...] nationality ought only to be [...] the recognized symbol of association; the assertion of the individuality of a human group called by its geographical position, its traditions, and its language, to fulfil a special function in the European work of civilization.
The map of Europe has to be remade. This is the key to the present movement;
30 herein lies the initiative. [...]

Giuseppe Mazzini: "On Nationality (1852)", from: William Clark (Ed.): Essays: Selected from the Writings, Literary, Political and Religious of Joseph Mazzini, London: Walter Scott 1880, pp. 266, 277–278, 291–292

consanguinity blood bond

to invoke to state a law, principle, or idea in order to support an argument

S 16 Alan Farmer and Andrina Stiles

The German Confederation

The hopes of the German nationalists were shattered when the Congress of Vienna did not produce the desired German nation-state, but instead settled on the creation of the German Confederation. In the extract at hand, historians Farmer and Stiles do not only elaborate on the characteristic features of the German Confederation, but also on its strengths and weaknesses.

Pre-task

1. Sort the given aspects paraphrased from the text into possible strengths or weaknesses of the German Confederation. Be prepared to explain your choices.
   - Metternich was the most influential statesman in the Confederation until 1815.
   - The Confederation was a loose association of 39 states.
   - The states were supposed to help each other when in danger.
   - The rulers of the states wanted to retain as much independence as possible.
   - The boundaries were modelled on those of the Holy Roman Empire of German Nation.
   - Representatives to the Federal Diet in Frankfurt were not elected but chosen by the rulers of the states.
   - Decisions in the Diet required unanimity.
   - The single states could neither make foreign alliances that posed a threat to the Confederation nor conclude separate peace treaties in case of war.
   - Military cooperation between Prussia and Austria was necessary for the defence of the Confederation.

Tasks

2. Scan the text for the strengths and weaknesses mentioned above. Seen in their respective context, double-check your categorization from task 1: do you still consider the aspects selected as strengths or weaknesses?
3. Put yourself into the shoes of a German nationalist. Write her/his speech to be given before the Federal Diet in Frankfurt in which you criticize the German Confederation and demand the creation of a German nation-state. Be prepared to back up your claims: what aspects of the German Confederation would you criticize as standing in the way of a future German nation-state, and what have the Germans already sacrificed for the sake of a nation-state?

The most important influence on the future of the German states after 1815 was that of Prince Metternich, Austrian chief minister until 1848. Metternich's aim was the maintenance of Austria's traditional authority over the German states. He was not concerned with German political unity, and his negotiations at Vienna ensured that Germany would become a loose confederation of states under Austrian control.

In June 1815 the German Confederation, comprising 39 states, was established with the aim of 'maintaining the external and internal security and the independence and integrity of the individual states.' Its declared aim was therefore the maintenance of the status quo in individual states through a system of mutual assistance in times of danger, such as internal rebellion or external aggression. It was not concerned with promoting a united Germany. In fact its aim was exactly the opposite, for none of the rulers of the separate states wished to see their independence limited by the establishment of a strong central German government.

Thus, no objection was raised when the boundaries of the Confederation were modelled on those of the Holy Roman Empire rather than on ones that would encourage the development of a nation-state of Germany. So areas peopled by Poles, Czechs, Danes and French were included and provinces with largely German-speaking populations were excluded. States such as Luxemburg, Hanover and Holstein, which were ruled by foreign monarchs (the Dutch King ruled Luxemburg, the British King Hanover and the Danish King Holstein), were within the Confederation while parts of German-speaking Austria and Prussia were not.

The Confederation had only one executive body, the Diet*, which met at Frankfurt. This was a permanent conference of representatives, who were not elected but were sent by their governments with instructions how to act. It was presided over by the Austrian representative. Given that the agreement of every state government was required before any measure could be passed, little was ever achieved. Representatives were more concerned with safeguarding the interests of their own states than working for the Confederation as a whole.

Each state had its own independent ruler, its own government and its own army. The Confederation appointed ambassadors and could make foreign treaties on behalf of its members. Otherwise it had very little control over the 39 individual states, apart from being able to prevent them making foreign alliances which might threaten the security of the Confederation, or concluding separate peace agreements in the event of the Confederation being involved in war. The Constitution of the Confederation, the Federal Act, had empowered the Diet to organise a federal army and to develop commercial and economic co-operation between the states, but local jealousies and fiercely guarded independence meant that nothing of importance was done to unify the Confederation militarily or economically. The defence of the Confederation depended upon the continued co-operation of Austria and Prussia.

The Confederation thus disappointed those Germans who hoped for greater national unity. It has also been criticised by historians who see it as essentially being the Holy Roman Empire mark II – an organisation which had no place in the age of emergent* nation-states. However, the Confederation provided at least a framework within which German states co-existed, albeit* uneasily.

Alan Farmer & Andrina Stiles: "The German Confederation", from: Alan Farmer, Andrina Stiles (Ed.): Access to History – The Unification of Germany 1815–1919, London: Hodder Murray 2007, pp. 3–6

diet national parliament

emergent just beginning to exist
albeit [ɔːlˈbiːɪt] although, even though, even if

CONNECT

The Wartburg Festival

Task Write an email to the German-American National Congress in which you take a critical stand on their view of the Wartburg Festival of 1817.

On their website, the German-American National Congress, aka DANK (*Deutsch Amerikanischer National Kongress*) states that it is their goal "to actively preserve German culture, heritage and language in the United States." (www.dank.org/whatisdank/ [04.05.15])
Their view on the Wartburg Festival is expressed in S 17a. Use your background knowledge, in particular the expertise you have acquired on the subject of the Janus-faced quality of nationalism and in S 17b to write an email to DANK in which you take a critical stand on their view. However, keep in mind: politeness is the flower of humanity.

S 17a The German-American National Congress About the Wartburg Festival of 1817

to emanate from to emerge from, to originate from
debris ['debri:] *Trümmer*

In 1817 Prince Metternich of Austria and the reactionary princes of Germany suppressed liberal ideas emanating from* the debris* of the French Revolution.
Young idealists commemorated the Protestant Reformation at the famous Wartburg Festival to protest the suppression. The festival ended with a giant 5 bonfire where all symbols of tyranny, censorship and oppression were burned.
A period of persecution followed the festival and many were forced to leave the Fatherland. [...]

Delaware Saengerbund and Library Association (Ed.): "1817 Wartburg Festival", http://www.delawaresaengerbund.org/GermanAmericanHistory/HTML/1817WartburgFestival.html, 15.12.2006 [25.12.14]

S 17b Heinrich Heine on the Wartburg Festival

In 1840, the German author and poet Heinrich Heine wrote about the Wartburg Festival of 1817:

„Auf der Wartburg herrschte jener beschränkte Teutomanismus*, der viel von Liebe und Glaube greinte*, dessen Liebe aber nichts anderes war als Hass des Fremden und dessen Glaube nur in der Unvernunft* bestand, und der in seiner Unwissenheit* nichts Besseres zu erfinden wusste als Bücher zu verbrennen!" 5

Heinrich Heine: Ludwig Börne. Eine Denkschrift, Viertes Buch, Hamburg: Hoffmann und Campe 1840

beschränkter Teutomanismus narrow-minded Teutomania (= an obsession with Germany and everything that is German) • **greinen** to whine about sth. • **Unvernunft** irrationality • **Unwissenheit** ignorance

Contemporary wood engraving, showing the march to the Wartburg in October 1817

S18 The Carlsbad Decrees

On 23 March 1819 Carl Ludwig Sand, a theology student at Jena University, killed the journalist and playwright August von Kotzebue at his home in Mannheim. Kotzebue had made fun of the students' liberal and patriotic ideals in his magazine "Literary Weekly". Sand was executed on 20 May 1820. His deed was the subject of controversy: some called him a fanatic, others saw him as a martyr for the cause of German freedom. Using the murder of Kotzebue as a pretext, Metternich summoned a conference of the larger states of the Confederation at Carlsbad (Bohemia) in August, 1819. The Carlsbad Decrees were subsequently laid before the Federal Diet, which, under Austria's influence, reluctantly ratified them.

Pre-tasks

1. Put yourself into the shoes of Metternich after he had heard the news about the murder of Kotzebue. You are determined to put an end to the spreading of nationalist ideas which – you believe – poses a threat to the existing order. You are also aware of the fact that nationalist ideas are mainly disseminated at universities. Which measures would you take to contain the dissemination of these ideas? Prepare a list of suggestions for the next session of the Federal Diet.

2. This German cartoon from 1819, entitled *Der Denker-Club* (The Thinkers' Club), depicts a form of reaction to the restrictions imposed by the Carlsbad Decrees. First, describe the cartoon, also taking the embedded text (see p. 78) into consideration. Second, pinpoint the message conveyed by the artist. Third, compare the message with your list of suggestions as seen from Metternich's perspective (cf. task 1).

3. Use the cartoon to start a word list, containing useful words and phrases for the semantic field of "freedom of speech/expression/the press".

„Der Denker-Club (The Thinkers' Club)." German lithograph, 1819 (artist unknown)

Embedded text:
On the board in the top centre: *Wichtige Frage welche in heutiger Sitzung bedacht wird: Wie lange mochte uns das Denken wohl noch erlaubt bleiben?*
On the board on the top right: *I. Der Präsident eröffnet präcise 8 Uhr die Sitzung./II. Schweigen ist das erste Gesetz dieser gelehrten Gesellschaft./III. Auf das kein Mitglied in Versuchung geraten möge, seiner Zunge freyen Lauf zulassen … so werden beim Eintritt Maulkörbe ausgeteilt./IV. Der Gegenstand, welcher in jedesmalingen Sitzung durch ein reifes Nachdenken gründlich erörtert werden soll, befindet sich auf einer Tafel mit großen Buchstaben deutlich geschrieben. […]"*

Language Support

Sitzung meeting • **Schweigen** silence • **gelehrte Gesellschaft** learned society • **seiner Zunge freien Lauf lassen** to speak openly • **in Versuchung geraten** to be tempted • **Maulkorb** gag, muzzle • **Nachdenken** reflection • **gründlich erörtern** to discuss thoroughly • **mit großen Buchstaben** in capital letters • **Perücke** wig • **jdm./etw. mit der Faust drohen** to shake one's fist at sb./sth. • **den Kopf hängen lassen** to hang one's head

Tasks

4. Find suitable categories under which to subsume the Carlsbad Decrees and continue your word list (cf. task 3) with words and phrases from the text.
5. Identify and explain the ideas which the government had in mind when they spoke of "harmful doctrines hostile to public order or subversive of existing governmental institutions". (ll. 15 f.)
6. With reference to your ideas and results from tasks 1 to 3, explain how Metternich aimed to stifle nationalist movements in the German Confederation.
7. Discuss to what extent it would be justified to call the German Confederation a "police state".

Post-tasks

8. Do further research on the "whistle-blower" Edward Snowden who, in 2013, revealed a number of mass-surveillance programmes undertaken by the American NSA (National Security Agency) and the British GCHQ (Government Communications Headquarters). Present major issues of the scandal in class. Together, discuss if there are any parallels to the Carlsbad Decrees you can draw, and in how far history seems doomed to repeat itself.
9. Up until the present day, Metternich's political achievements have remained controversial. On the one hand, he is seen as symbolizing the oppression of pre-March movements and thus standing in the way of German unification. On the other hand, thanks to a different approach attaching more importance to the securing of peace and stability, Metternich has been labelled the "architect" of this peace through his insistence on the creation of the German Confederation. After all, the period between 1815 and 1914 – notwithstanding the Wars of Unification in 1864, 1866 and 1870/71 – turned out to be one of the longest periods of peace in history. Split up into two factions, one arguing against, the other in favour of Metternich's achievements. Before you start, collect arguments in smaller groups and exchange them amongst each other. Attempt also to anticipate which arguments the other faction might use and how you can refute them.

A special representative of the ruler of each state shall be appointed for each university, with appropriate instructions and extended powers, and shall reside in the place where the university is situated. [...] The function of this agent shall be to see to the strictest enforcement of existing laws and disciplinary regulations; to observe carefully the spirit which is shown by the instructors in the university in their public lectures and regular courses, and, without directly interfering in scientific matters or in the methods of teaching, to give a salutary* direction to the instruction, having in view the future attitude of the students. Lastly, he shall devote unceasing attention to everything that may promote morality, good order, and outward propriety* among the students. [...]

2. The confederated governments mutually pledge themselves to remove from the universities or other public educational institutions all teachers who, by obvious deviation from their duty, or by exceeding the limits of their functions, or by the abuse of their legitimate influence over the youthful minds, or by propagating harmful doctrines hostile to public order or subversive of existing governmental institutions, shall have unmistakably proved their unfitness for the important office entrusted to them. [...]

3. Those laws which have for a long period been directed against secret and unauthorized societies in the universities shall be strictly enforced. These laws apply especially to that association established some years since under the name Universal Students' Union (*Allgemeine Burschenschaft*), since the very conception of the society implies the utterly unallowable plan of permanent fellowship and constant communication between the various universities. The duty of especial watchfulness in this matter should be impressed upon the special agents of the government. The governments mutually agree that such persons as shall hereafter be shown to have remained in secret or unauthorized associations, or shall have entered such associations, shall not be admitted to any public office. [...]

Press Law
I. So long as this decree shall remain in force no publication which appears in the form of daily issues, or as a serial not exceeding twenty sheets of printed matter, shall go to press in any state of the union without the previous knowledge and approval of the state officials. [...]

4. Each state of the union is responsible, not only to the state against which the offense is directly committed, but to the whole Confederation, for every publication appearing under its supervision in which the honour or security of other states is infringed or their constitution or administration attacked. [...]

6. The Diet shall have the right, moreover, to suppress on its own authority, without being petitioned, such writings included in Article I, in whatever German state they may appear, as, in the opinion of a commission appointed by it, are inimical to* the honour of the union, the safety of individual states, or the maintenance of peace and quiet in Germany. [...]

Establishment of an investigating Committee at Mayence
1. Within a fortnight, reckoned from the passage of this decree, there shall convene, under the auspices* of the Confederation, in the city and federal fortress of Mayence, an extraordinary commission of investigation to consist of seven members, including the chairman.

2. The object of the commission shall be a joint investigation, as thorough and extensive as possible, of the facts relating to the origin and manifold ramifica-

---

salutary producing a beneficial effect

propriety [prəˈpraɪəti] behaviour that follows accepted social or moral standards

to be inimical to being adverse often by reason of hostility or malevolence

under the auspices of [ˈɔːspɪsɪz] with the authority, protection, supervision and support of

ramification consequence, development, complication, the often unexpected way in which a decision, process, or event affects other things

tions* of the revolutionary plots and demagogical associations directed against the existing constitution and the internal peace both of the union and of the individual states; of the existence of which plots more or less clear evidence is to be had already, or may be produced in the course of the investigation. [...]

Carlsbad Resolutions", from: J. H. Robinson, (Ed.): Readings in European History, (Boston: Ginn, 1906, 2: 547–550

Karl Ludwig Sand murders August von Kotzebue. Copperplate engraving, 1819

S 19 Vormärz v. Biedermeier

Political attitudes between 1819 and the outbreak of revolution in 1848 can basically be divided into *Vormärz* (pre-March) and Biedermeier and they also find their expression in contemporary paintings.

Work on S 19a and S 19b in pairs and exchange information in order to complete the picture of pre-March Germany. Check the overview section for help and make use of the additional language support provided by the skills pages.

S 19a Carl Spitzweg

Der Sonntagsspaziergang (1841)

Partner A

Tasks (on your own):
1. Describe the painting in detail and point out what the atmosphere is like.
2. Make an educated guess as to the attitude towards politics the people depicted here might have: *Vormärz/Biedermeier*? Give reasons for your choice.

| Tasks | **(with Partner B):**
3. Exchange your findings. Make notes on what your partner tells you.
4. Compare your findings and come to a conclusion as to in how far political attitudes at the time are reflected in the given paintings.

Language Support

Zylinder top hat • **Sonnenschirm** parasol • **Haube** bonnet • **einen Spaziergang machen** to take a walk, to go for a stroll

S 19b Der Zug zum Hambacher Schloss (1832)

Partner B

| Tasks | **(on your own):**
1. Describe the painting in detail and point out what the atmosphere is like.
2. Make an educated guess as to the attitude towards politics the people depicted here might have: *Vormärz/Biedermeier*? Give reasons for your choice.

| Tasks | **(with Partner A):**
3. Exchange your findings. Make notes on what your partner tells you.
4. Compare your findings and come to a conclusion as to in how far political attitudes at the time are reflected in the given paintings.

Language Support

(Um)Zug procession • Menschenmenge crowd • eine Fahne schwenken to wave a flag • Schloss castle • Zinnen battlement • Turm tower • eine Trommel schlagen to beat a drum, to tabour

S 20 Johann August Wirth

Speech at the Hambach Festival

Johann August Wirth was one of the main initiators of the Hambach Festival.

Pre-task
1. Wirth ends his speech by putting an "eternal curse on all those traitors". Who might he be talking about? Discuss.

Tasks
2. Scan the text to find out who Wirth makes out as the "eternal traitors" and point out Wirth's statements.
3. Starting out from Wirth's speech, explain major differences between the Wartburg Festival of 1817 (cf. p. 76) and the Hambach Festival. In your explanation, consider also in how far the Hambach Festival already foreshadowed the so-called "springtime of the peoples", the 1848/49 revolutions.

Post-task
4. After the Hambach Festival, the so-called "6 and 10 Articles" were issued, putting further restrictions on free speech and also banning

the displaying of the "national colours". However, the nationalist movement could not be stopped any longer. Especially those students who were more radical and who put forward not only demands for political but also for social change started to distribute pamphlets with which they wanted to agitate against the reactionary forces. Design such a pamphlet. It should contain the most vital reasons for the creation of a German nation-state and it should pinpoint the current weaknesses. As the ultimate objective was agitation, this should also be mirrored in the language you use for your pamphlet.

5. In 2013, various parties and organizations prepared a Hambach Festival 2.0(13). Do further research on their motivation and their backgrounds in order to explain why they chose Hambach Castle to utter their claims and demands and evaluate the necessity of a Hambach Festival 2.0 (→ http://hambacherfest.de).

Hambacher Fest 2.013
09. Juni 2013
Zum Marsch aufs Hambacher Schloss
Demokratie, Recht und Freiheit

Das Land, das unsere Sprache spricht, das Land, wo unsere Hoffnung wohnt, wo unsere Liebe schwelgt*, wo unsere Freuden blühen, das Land, wo das Geheimniß [sic] aller unserer Sympathien und all' unserer Sehnsucht ruht, dieses schöne Land wird verwüstet und geplündert, zerrissen und entnervt, geknebelt und entehrt*.
5 Reich an allen Hülfsquellen* [sic] der Natur sollte es für alle seine Kinder die Wohnung der Freude und der Zufriedenheit seyn, allein ausgesogen* von 34 Königen, ist es für die Mehrzahl seiner Bewohner der Aufenthalt des Hungers, des Jammers* und des Elendes*. Deutschland, das große, reiche, mächtige Deutschland, sollte die erste Stelle einnehmen in der Gesellschaft der europäischen Staaten,
10 allein beraubt durch verrätherische* [sic] Aristokratenfamilien, ist es aus der Liste der europäischen Reiche gestrichen und der Verspottung* des Auslandes Preiß gegeben. Berufen von der Natur, um in Europa der Wächter des Lichts*, der Freiheit und der völkerrechtlichen Ordnung* zu seyn, wird die deutsche Kraft gerade umgekehrt zur Unterdrückung der Freiheit aller Völker und zur Gründung eines
15 ewigen Reiches der Finsterniß* [sic], der Sclaverei [sic] und der rohen Gewalt* verwendet. So ist denn das Elend unseres Vaterlandes zugleich der Fluch* für ganz Europa. Spanien, Italien, Ungarn und Polen sind Zeuge davon. […] Die Ursache der namenlosen Leiden* der europäischen Völker liegt einzig und allein darin, daß die Herzoge von Oesterreich [sic] und die Kurfürsten* von Branden-
20 burg den größten Theil von Deutschland an sich gerissen* haben, und unter dem Titel der Kaiser von Oesterreich und der Könige von Preußen nicht nur ihre eigenen, durch methodische Plünderung* Deutschlands erworbenen Länder, nach orientalischen Formen beherrschen und deren Kräfte zur Unterdrückung der Freiheit und Volkshoheit der europäischen Nationen verwenden, sondern auch

schwelgen to delight
verwüstet, geplündert, zerrissen, entnervt, geknebelt, entehrt ravaged, plundered, torn, enervated, gagged, disgraced
Hilfsquellen resources
ausgesogen sucked dry
Jammer misery
Elend poverty
verräterisch traitorous
Verspottung mockery
Wächter des Lichts guardian of light
völkerrechtliche Ordnung legal order
ewiges Reich der Finsternis eternal realm of darkness
rohe Gewalt raw force
Fluch curse
namenloses Leiden unspeakable suffering
Kurfürst elector
etw. an sich reißen to seize [siːz]
methodische Plünderung methodical plundering

Übergewicht predominance
fürstliche Alleinherrschaft princely autocracy
dienstbar machen to make serve
Staatsverfassung constitution
Zwecke, Gesinnungen, Interessen aims, convictions, interests

ohnmächtig powerless
in Zerrüttung fallen to disintegrate

öffentliche Angelegenheiten public affairs

Bedürfnisse needs

innigster Völkerbund the most heartfelt league of peoples

ihr Uebergewicht* [sic] über die kleineren Länder Deutschlands benützen, um auch die Kräfte dieser dem Systeme fürstlicher Alleinherrschaft* und despotischer Gewalt dienstbar zu machen*. Bei jeder Bewegung eines Volkes, welche die Erringung der Freiheit und einer vernünftigen Staatsverfassung* zum Ziele hat, sind die Könige von Preußen und Oesterreich durch Gleichheit der Zwecke, Gesinnungen und Interessen* an Rußland geknüpft, und so entsteht jener furchtbare Bund, der die Freiheit der Völker bisher immer noch zu tödten [sic] vermochte. Die Hauptmacht dieses finstern Bundes besteht immer aus deutschen Kräften, da Rußland ohne die Allianz mit Preußen und Oesterreich ohnmächtig* wäre und durch innere Stürme in Zerrüttung fallen* würde. So riesenhaft daher die Macht des absoluten Bundes auch seyn mag, so ist ihr Ende doch in dem Augenblicke gekommen, wo in Deutschland die Vernunft auch in politischer Beziehung den Sieg erlangt, d.h. in dem Augenblicke, wo die öffentlichen Angelegenheiten* nicht mehr nach dem despotischen Willen eines Einzigen, nicht mehr nach den Interessen einer über ganz Europa verzweigten Aristokraten-Familie, sondern nach dem Willen der Gesellschaft selbst und nach den Bedürfnissen* des Volkes geleitet werden. In dem Augenblicke, wo die deutsche Volkshoheit in ihr gutes Recht eingesetzt seyn wird, in dem Augenblicke ist der innigste Völkerbund* geschlossen, denn das Volk liebt, wo die Könige hassen, das Volk vertheidigt, wo die

Painting by Georg Friedrich Kersting, 1815, depicting members of the Lützov Free Corps, whose uniform colours went on to become the colours of Germany's national flag

Könige verfolgen, das Volk gönnt* das, was es selbst mit seinem Herzblut zu erringen trachtet, und, was ihm das Theuerste ist, die Freiheit, Aufklärung, Nationa-
lität und Volkshoheit, auch dem Brudervolke*: das deutsche Volk gönnt daher
diese hohen, unschätzbaren Güter auch seinen Brüdern in Polen, Ungarn, Italien
und Spanien. Wenn also das deutsche Geld und das deutsche Blut nicht mehr den
Befehlen der Herzoge von Oesterreich und der Kurfürsten von Brandenburg, sondern der Verfügung des Volkes unterworfen sind, so wird Polen, Ungarn und Italien frei, weil Rußland dann der Ohnmacht verfallen ist und sonst keine Macht
mehr besteht, welche zu einem Kreuzzuge* gegen die Freiheit der Völker verwendet werden könnte. [...] Wahrlich, ich sage euch, giebt [sic] es irgend Verräther an
den Völkern und an dem gesammten [sic] Menschengeschlechte, giebt es irgend
Hochverräther, so wären es die Könige, welche der Eitelkeit, der Herrschsucht
und der Wollust* willen die Bevölkerung eines ganzen Welttheils elend machen
und dieselbe durch empörende Unterdrückung Jahrhunderte hindurch hindern,
zu dem ihr von Natur bestimmten Zustande von materieller Wohlfart* [sic] und
geistiger Vollendung sich aufzuschwingen. Fluch, ewigen Fluch darum allen solchen Verräthern!

gönnen to grant

Brudervolk fraternal nation

Kreuzzug crusade

Eitelkeit, Herrschsucht, Wollust
vanity, imperiousness, lust
materielle Wohlfahrt material
welfare

Johann Georg August Wirth: Das Nationalfest der Deutschen zu Hambach, Neustadt: Phillip Christmann
1832, Nachdruck, Neustadt: Meininger 1981, S. 41–43

S 21 Deutschlands Vereinigung

The topic of German unification, respectively the formation of a German nation-state, was not only debated at festivals or in pamphlets, but also in newspapers at the time. This is a newspaper article from the *Düsseldorfer Zeitung* (September 3 and 5, 1843).

Pre-task
1. Have a look at the words and phrases taken from this source. Then make an educated guess as to the author's attitude towards "Germany's Union" (cf. headline). Be prepared to explain your answer.

> pieces torn off • connection • heartfelt • no utopian dream • unbearable • savings • special interests • Congress of Vienna • jealousy

Tasks
2. Juxtapose what the author says about a) the weaknesses of the German Confederation and b) the advantages of unification.
3. Explain the references the author makes by incorporating them into the historical context.
4. Evaluate the author's conclusion concerning the question as to why Germany's union had not already come about by 1843. (cf. ll. 42 f.)

Post-task
5. Copy and fill in the time line for the development of German nationalism from 1815 to the late 1830s (the eve of the 1848/49 revolutions) with the help of the materials provided in this sub-chapter. Feel free to add further years/events but distinguish clearly between ACTION (taken by the nationalists) and REACTION (the suppression of further nationalist agitation). Based on your results, discuss to what extent Germany was "restored to order" in the period of time in question.

ACTION(S)

1814/15   1817   1819   1830   1832   1834   1837

REACTION(S)

---

das entschwundene Jahrtausend the millennium gone by
Wiedervereinigung reunification
etw. ersehnen to long for sth.
innige innere Verbindung heartfelt inner bond/sense of union
Wahrzeichen emblem

Wie schmerzlich wir bei dem Rückblick auf das entschwundene Jahrtausend* die von Deutschland abgerissenen Stücke vermissen, und wie sehr wir ihre Wiedervereinigung* ersehnen*, so ist doch für Deutschland, wie es ist, eine innigere innere Verbindung* jedenfalls von viel größerer Wichtigkeit, und in diesem Gefühl liegt es begründet, dass die Stimme der Zeit, wie sie gegen Frankreich nur die Negative des status quo aufgestellt, die Einheit Deutschlands als positives Wahrzeichen* erhoben hat. 5

Und worin könnte diese Einheit anders liegen, als in innigerer politischer Vereinigung? Alles andere, was man zur Vereinigung Deutschlands benutzen will: Gemeinschaftliche Monumente, gleiche Münzen, Maße, Gewichte und Wagenspur*, 10

Wagenspur wagon gauge
Zollverband customs union
Mittel zum Zweck means to an end

selbst ein allgemeiner Zollverband* verhält sich nur als Mittel zum Zweck* oder würde als natürliche Folge der politischen Einheit Deutschlands von selbst ins Leben treten, wenn diese erst erreicht wäre. Die natürliche Schwäche des dermaligen [sic] Zentralpunktes im Konflikte mit dem Nationalwunsche bewirkt diese sonderbaren Zuckungen und Ideenverwechselungen*; dies Hysteron-Proteron* 15

Zuckungen und Ideenverwechslungen twitches and mistaken ideas
Hysteron-Proteron (fig.) putting the cart before the horse
gutmütige Volkspolitik good-natured popular politics
Faseleien drivel
in Misskredit bringen to discredit
unerträglich unbearable

der gutmütigen Volkspolitik* und die Faseleien* über eine von hinten anzufangende deutsche Einheit bringen die Sache selbst am Ende in Misskredit* oder lassen sie als einen utopischen Traum erscheinen, der es doch nicht ist.

Nein, Deutschlands Einheit ist kein utopischer Traum, sie muss so gewiss erreicht werden, als es auf die Dauer unmöglich ist, etwas als notwendig Gefühltes zu 20 unterlassen, und die Idee selbst wird ihrer Verwirklichung umso näher stehen, je unerträglicher* der Vergleich wird des Zustandes, in dem man lebt, mit jenem herrlichen, in dem man leben könnte [...].

Dieses Ziel ist ein kräftiger, politischer Zentralpunkt, dessen Form vorläufig ganz dahingestellt bleiben mag. Aber die natürliche Schwäche des jetzigen Vereinigungspunktes liegt darin, dass wir überall nur einen diplomatischen, keinen politischen Vereinigungspunkt, einen Staatenbund* statt eines Bundesstaates* haben. So haben wir denn statt eines einzigen Deutschlands 38 deutsche Länder, ebenso viele Regierungen, fast ebenso viele Höfe, so und so viele Ständeversammlungen*, 38 verschiedene Gesetze und Administrationen, Gesandtschaften* und 30 25

Staatenbund confederation
Bundesstaat federal state

Ständeversammlung assembly of estates
Gesandtschaft embassy, legation
Konsulat consulate

Konsulate*. Welche enorme Ersparung würde es sein, wenn das alles bei einer Zentralregierung besorgt würde; welche Ersparung an Geld und an Mannschaft würde erwachsen, wenn Deutschland eine einzige Armee erhielte! Aber weit schlimmer als die dermalige Kostenverschwendung ist, dass bei den 38 verschiedenen Staaten ebenso viele Sonderinteressen* obwalten*, die sich bis in das 35 kleinste Detail tagtäglichen Verkehrs* hinein benachteiligen und aufheben. [...]

Sonderinteresse special interest
obwalten to be at work
tagtäglicher Verkehr daily life and commerce

Denkt man nun vollends noch an die Stellung, die das vereinigte Deutschland dem Auslande gegenüber annehmen würde, so scheint es unmöglich, dass sich irgend jemand [sic] gegen die allseitigen Vorteile der Vereinigung verstocken könnte, und man muss sich nur wundern, dass diese Einheit nicht längst zustande gekommen, dass sie jemals aufgehoben worden ist. [...]

Fragen wir aber, warum die deutsche Einheit nicht längst wieder zustande gekommen sei, so kommen wir leider zunächst wieder auf den Wiener Kongress; auf die Eifersucht der auswärtigen Mächte*, die ein einiges Deutschland fürchten, gegenüber den schwachen deutschen Staatsmännern und gegenüber freilich auch einer Masse von Sonderinteressen, die lieber im Kleinen sich wichtig machen, als in der Unterordnung unter ein großes Ganze ihre naturgemäße Stellung* einnehmen wollten. [...]

auswärtige Mächte foreign powers

naturgemäße Stellung natural place

o. V.: „Deutschlands Vereinigung", Düsseldorfer Zeitung 1843 (3. und 5. September), Nr. 244, 246, abgedruckt in: Rheinische Briefe und Akten zur Geschichte der politischen Bewegung 1830–1850, gesammelt und herausgegeben von Joseph Hansen, Bd. I, 1830–1845. Publikationen der Gesellschaft für rheinische Geschichtskunde XXXVI Bd. 1, 1919, S. 589–592

"Unity and Liberty" in the German Revolution of 1848/49

S 22 Allan Todd

Revolutions 1789–1917

Allan Todd is a contemporary historian and lecturer in modern history. In his book "Revolutions 1789–1917", he deals with the French Revolution, the 1848 Revolutions and the Russian Revolution.

Pre-task
1. Come up with your own definition for the term "revolution". It might be helpful to also consider aspects which do not necessarily define a revolution.

Tasks
2. Draw a grid with two columns, one for non-revolutionary forms, the other one for characteristics of a revolution. Fill in the information from the text.
3. Revise what you have learned about the French Revolution in last year's history class. Then discuss to what extent the characteristics of a revolution, as advanced by Todd, can be applied to the French Revolution and if, accordingly, the French Revolution can be called a "model revolution".

Post-task
4. In 1988, the singer and songwriter Tracy Chapman released the song "Talkin' 'Bout a Revolution" which she for example also performed on the occasion of Nelson Mandela's 70th birthday. In 2011, it was also often played in the wake of the so-called "Arab Spring", especially in Tunisia. Do research on the lyrics of the song (e. g. www.azlyrics.com/lyrics/tracychapman/talkinboutarevolution.html) and, against the backdrop of your findings from task 2, assess to what extent the revolution Chapman talks about would indeed qualify as a revolution, or would have the potential to become one.

What a revolution is not
Not all political change and upheaval is a revolution: in fact, the majority of political struggles occurring throughout history have not been revolution. The most common non-revolutionary forms are listed below.
- *Coup d'état/Putsch*. This is essentially the seizure of power by a small group of people, often involving sections of the military. In the main, the aim of such events is to replace one group of rulers with another – the fundamental social and economic features of society are left intact.
- *Civil war*. Similar to a coup, this often starts as a political struggle for power between different groups of people who want to rule. The struggles become so intense that they spill over into the bitter violence of civil war. In the past, such disputes were common amongst royal families and those related to them; nowadays, they are frequently linked to religious or ethnic differences. But, as with coups, the leaders' main aims are usually to change a set of political rulers in order to secure power and privileges for themselves.

- *Revolt/Rebellion*. Though these can be large-scale and violent, they are not normally revolutionary. At the most, they are massive social upheavals which aim to secure a few specific reforms to improve situations which have become unacceptable. Most frequently, however, they are mass protests, organised in opposition to a particular government and some of its laws. Very often, the rebels claim to be attempting to force a return to a time when life was better; this is a feature particularly associated with the numerous peasant revolts which have erupted throughout history.

Though these political phenomena are not revolutions, each one of them can help precipitate* a revolution. Coups and civil wars sometimes generate political weaknesses, and thus create opportunities for revolutionaries, while a large-scale revolt, if prolonged enough, can begin to generate increasingly radical demands and actions. [...]

to precipitate [prɪˈsɪpɪteɪt] to bring on, advance, accelerate, hasten, speed up

Types of revolution

Revolutions have various features in common. [...] *[A]ll* revolutions (as opposed to most coups, for instance) involve mass mobilisations, sometimes led by revolutionary leaders and parties, and sometimes erupting independently of the conscious wishes and intentions of such leaders and parties. While a coup, organised by a few individuals, can seize political control, revolutionaries – no matter how pure and determined – cannot transform a society without the active support and involvement of huge sections of the population.

All revolutions almost always involve a certain amount of violence. This varies according to the relative strength and determination of revolutionaries and dominant groups alike. In fact, most people's image of revolution is no doubt one of crowd violence and organised terror – most likely coloured by stories of the guillotine and Jacobin terror during the 1792–94 upheavals of the French Revolution, or by the operation of the Bolsheviks' Cheka* during the civil war between Reds and Whites from 1918 to 1920. Yet, generally, it is counter-revolution rather than revolution which is more violent.

In part, the amount of mass mobilisation and violence will depend on exactly what kind of revolution is taking place. The two main types are political and social revolutions.

Bolsheviks' Cheka secret police force during the Russian Revolution in 1917 (cf. chapter 2)

Allan Todd: Revolutions 1789–1917, Cambridge University Press: Cambridge 1998, pp. 1–4

S 23 David Blackbourn

The Revolutions of 1848–49

David Blackbourn (*1949) is a British historian who teaches German and European history at Vanderbilt University. In his work "History of Germany 1780–1918. The Long Nineteenth Century", he also focuses on the revolutions of 1848/49 and their impact. In the excerpt at hand, Blackbourn sheds a light on the short-term causes for the outbreak of revolution.

Pre-tasks
1. Revise what you have learned about restoration Europe/the pre-March movements in the German Confederation and identify long-term causes of the 1848/49 revolutions.
2. Discuss possible short-term causes for revolutions in general (cf. S 22, for example).

Tasks

3. Copy the graphic visualization given below and fill it in with the help of the text and your results from task 1. Add two footnotes in which you state the geographical extent of the revolution and who supported it.

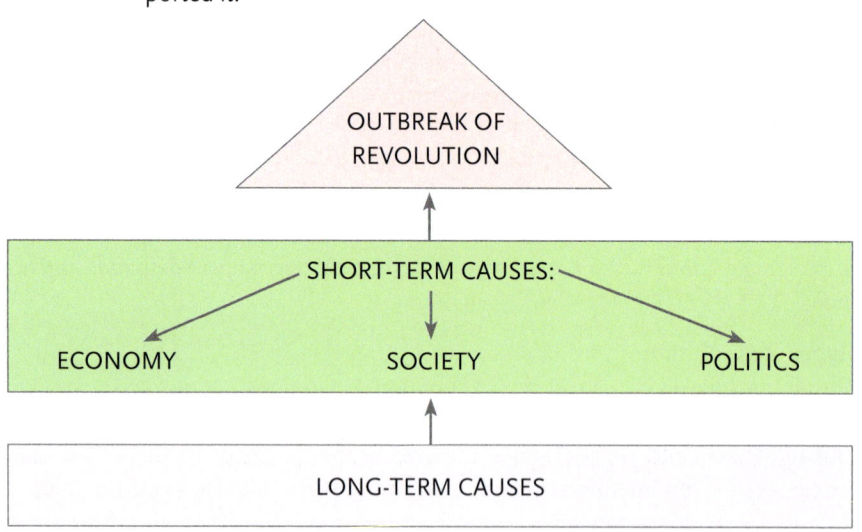

```
        OUTBREAK OF
         REVOLUTION
            ▲
            │
   SHORT-TERM CAUSES:
            │
   ┌────────┼────────┐
   ▼        ▼        ▼
ECONOMY  SOCIETY  POLITICS
            ▲
            │
   LONG-TERM CAUSES
```

4. Use your results from task 3 to give a balanced assessment of the question why revolution broke out in 1848. Include both long-term and short-term causes and rank them according to their importance for the outbreak of revolution.

European revolution was widespread in 1848, but not universal. Revolution did not break out in the backward east, in Russia and the Ottoman Empire, nor in the most advanced western areas of Britain, Belgium and the Netherlands. Its effects were mainly felt in the areas that were, in more than just a geographical sense, in between: by regimes that were neither liberal nor simply regressive, in societies that were no longer predominantly agrarian but in which industry had not yet established itself. In other words, it was the parts of Europe most obviously in transition, politically and socially, which proved the most explosive. [...]

Revolution in Germany was the result of several superimposed* crises. At the economic level, an old-style crisis of harvest failure in 1845–47, more serious than those of 1816–17 or 1830–31, had important and cumulative* effects throughout society. Peasants could not pay their rents, mortgages* and other debts, which led to increased levels of foreclosure* and hurt rural crafts that depended on agricultural prosperity. Crop failure also doubled the price of basic foodstuffs like rye* and potatoes, causing widespread distress among those living on the edge of subsistence*. Even in normal times, food accounted for 80 per cent of spending by poor families. Parts of the rural population were now reduced to eating grass, clover* and potato peelings. The cost of food rose even more steeply in the towns, and this had an important secondary effect. It further reduced the purchasing power available for other produce, driving many businesses into bankruptcy. Textile towns like Krefeld were devastated.

In urban Germany, and in areas where outworking or rural industry was extensive, this last old-style crisis of dearth* coincided with a crisis of a different kind: a downturn of the business cycle in 1847, imported from England, which hit the

---

to superimpose to add

cumulative [ˈkjuːmjʊlətɪv] developing or increasing gradually as a result of more and more additions

mortgage [ˈmɔː(r)ɡɪdʒ] Hypothek

foreclosure Zwangsvollstreckung/-versteigerung

rye Roggen

subsistence the smallest amount of money/food you need to stay alive

clover Klee

dearth [dɜː(r)θ] a situation in which there is not enough of sth.

textile and engineering branches especially hard. Small businesses failed as markets collapsed and creditors* called in their loans. Bankruptcies caused severe pressure on the banks, some of which suspended activities early in 1848, placing hundreds of firms and tens of thousands of workers at risk. Larger concerns, including Borsig and Krupp, laid off men. Yet another problem was therefore added to the crisis of food shortages and rising prices, as the normally high levels of underemployment in German towns now became, in many cases, chronic unemployment. In Pforzheim (Baden) three-quarters of the labour force was idle*. The double aspect of the crisis made it all the more potent. So did the weight of accumulated social grievances – peasants angry at feudal privileges and their exclusion from former common woodlands, craftsmen chafing* over their loss of security, the urban underclass barely subsisting at the best of times. The second half of the 1840s saw growing social unrest. Peasants in Galicia* rose in protest in 1846. The following year there were bread riots and other forms of violent collective action across Germany, from Hamburg, Braunschweig and the eastern provinces of Prussia in the north, to Baden and Württemberg in the South.

Bread riots peaked in the summer of 1847, and it has often been pointed out that the harvest that year was good. But the improved crop could not help peasants who had consumed their seed corn or been foreclosed, just as it meant little to those who remained unemployed or had already fallen victim to bankruptcy. Nor should we expect some automatic relationship between hunger and revolution. Often it was not the most debilitated* who rioted, but the small peasant, journeyman* or struggling master. The psychological impact of the economic double crisis was immense. It further eroded* trust in 'complacent'* governments, placing a question mark against their competence and their very legitimacy, not least among the propertied, the relatively well off and members of the political opposition. [...] Material and nonmaterial grievances reinforced each other to create a crisis mentality. This mood was fostered by events elsewhere, for what happened in Germany belonged to a larger European ferment*. In 1847, unrest in northern Italy prompted Austrian military intervention and raised the political temperature in the German Confederation. The social and political struggles that led to civil war in Switzerland at the end of the year also had an impact on German opinion, especially in the southwest. Revolution broke out in Palermo in January 1848; and when news reached Germany of the February revolution in France that overturned the regime of Louis-Philippe, it seemed to signal that the old order was ripe for collapse everywhere in Metternich's Europe.

David Blackbourn: History of Germany 1780–1918. The Long Nineteenth Century, Malden: Blackwell, 1997 (2007), pp. 104 ff.

creditor Gläubiger/in

idle here: out of work, unemployed

to chafe to feel annoyed and impatient about sth.

Galicia historical and geographical region in Eastern Europe (today: mainly western Ukraine)

debilitated weakened, feeble
journeyman Geselle
to erode to gradually reduce
complacent selbstgefällig

ferment a time of great excitement or seething activity that can for example lead to change or violence

S 24 Carl Schurz

A Look Back at 1848

Carl Schulz (1829–1906) participated in the 1848/49 revolutions in Germany, but became one of the "Forty-Eighters" by emigrating to the USA when the revolution eventually failed to accomplish its goals. Here he became the first German-born American elected to the United States Senate.
In his "Reminiscences", published in 1907, he recalls the beginning of the revolution in Germany.

What is the German's Fatherland?

Pre-task

1. Taking into account that Schurz was one of the Forty-Eighters who left Germany after the failure of the revolution, how do expect him to remember the beginning of the revolution? Choose adjectives from the box which you consider to be appropriate. Give reasons for your choice.

> optimistic • pessimistic • lugubrious (nostalgic) • jaundiced (embittered) • wistful • poignant (melancholic)

Tasks

2. Describe the events, as recalled by Schurz.
3. Examine the atmosphere in the streets, according to Schurz. Afterwards, double-check if you would now still find the adjectives you selected in task 1 appropriate.
4. Incorporate the source into the historical context of the outbreak of revolution. Remember to narrate the context, meaning you must show how events are linked with each other.
5. Based on the text, write a dialogue between two students in the streets in which they express their hopes and possible fears.
6. Hypothesize as to what extent the further course of the revolution is foreshadowed in the given excerpt. Quote from the text to support your hypotheses.

One morning, toward the end of February 1848, I sat quietly in my attic chamber, [...] when suddenly a friend rushed breathlessly into the room, exclaiming: [...] "The French have driven away Louis Philippe and proclaimed the Republic!" [...] We tore down the stairs, into the street, to the market square, the accustomed meeting place for all the student societies after their midday dinner. Although it was still forenoon, the market was already crowded with young men talking excitedly. There was no shouting, no noise, only agitated conversation. What did we want there? This probably no one knew. But since the French had driven away Louis Philippe and proclaimed the republic, something of course must happen here, too. Some of the students had brought their rapiers* along, as if it were necessary to make an attack or to defend themselves. We were dominated by a vague feeling as if a great outbreak of elemental forces had begun, as if an earthquake was impending of which we had felt the first shock, and we instinctively crowded together. [...]

Now had arrived in Germany the day for the establishment of "German Unity", and the founding of a great, powerful, national German empire. First in line the convocation of a national parliament. Then the demands for civil rights and liberties, free speech, free press, the right of free assembly, equality before the law, a freely elected representation of the people with legislative power, responsibility of ministers, self-government of the communes, the right of the people to carry arms, the formation of a civic guard with elective officers and so on – in short, that which is called a "Constitutional form of government on a broad democratic basis."

Republican ideas were at first only sparingly expressed. But the word democracy was soon on all tongues, and many, too, thought it a matter of course that if the princes should try to withhold from the people the rights and liberties demanded, force would take the place of mere petition. Of course the regeneration of the

rapier ['reɪpɪə(r)] a straight two-edged sword with a narrow pointed blade

country must, if possible, be accomplished by peaceable means. [...] Like many of my friends, I was dominated by the feeling that at last a great opportunity had ar-
30 rived for giving to the German people the liberty which was their birthright and to the German fatherland its unity and greatness, and that it was now the first duty of every German to do and to sacrifice everything for this sacred object. We were profoundly, solemnly, in earnest.

Great news came from Vienna! There the students of the university were the first
35 to assail* the Emperor of Austria with the cry for liberty and citizens' rights. Blood flowed in the streets, and the downfall of Prince Metternich was the result. The students organized themselves as the armed guard of liberty. In the great cities of Prussia there was a mighty commotion*. Not only Cologne, Coblenz, and Trier, but also Breslau, Königsberg, and Frankfurt-an-der-Oder, sent deputations to Ber-
40 lin to entreat* the king. In the Prussian capital the masses surged upon the streets, and everybody looked for events of great import. [...]

On the 18th of March we [the students, a few professors and people of all grades in Bonn] too had our mass demonstration. [...] In a moment the city was covered with black, red and gold flags, and not only the Burschenschaft, but almost everybody
45 wore a black-red-gold cockade on his hat.

Carl Schurz: Reminiscences, New York: Doubleday 1908, pp. 112–114, 116–117

to assail to attack violently with blows or words

commotion a condition of civil unrest or insurrection

to entreat to make an earnest request

S 25 March Demands from Dresden

Starting in the southern German states, various groups of people formulated demands to be fulfilled by their respective governments. The so-called March Demands of the citizens of Dresden are listed here.

Pre-task 1. Put yourself into the shoes of the citizens of Dresden: what would you demand from your government? Use the template given below and the language support to formulate your demands.

> *To the High Government of Saxony:*
> *We, the citizens of Dresden, demand from you the following, in order to advance Saxony and the union of Germany as such ...*
>
> *As regards freedom of speech, we ask you to ...*
> *The abolition of censorship of the press is also ...*
> *What is also of the utmost importance to us is that, in future, you refrain from ...*
> *Eligibility to vote and the whole question of suffrage are major issues and so we demand ...*
> *As far as the arming of citizens is concerned, we further want you to ...*
>
> *A cheer for the king! A cheer for the constitution! A cheer for the unity between government and people!*

Tasks 2. Outline the demands of the citizens of Dresden. Did you have similar ideas, or is there anything you would not have expected at all? If so, why?

3. Examine the tone in which the demands are phrased. Focus on how the tone stresses the urgency of the demands on the one hand, but

how it simultaneously contains a conciliatory note to help enable the high government of Saxony to grant the demands put forward.
4. Taking into account the fact that the revolution spread quickly throughout the German Confederation, discuss which of the demands the German princes would probably grant and which they would most certainly reject, and why.
5. Based on your results from task 4 and keeping the historical context in mind, write the proclamation of the high government of Saxony's to the citizens of Dresden in which they respond to the demands.

Kundgebung demonstration
Eintracht unity
erheischen to demand
beseelt inspired

Gewährung granting
Wohlergehen welfare, well-being

unerlässlich indispensable
unabweisbar irrefutable
verheißen to promise

Überweisung referral
ordentliches Gericht court of law
religiöses Bekenntnis religious denomination
willkürliche Verhaftung arbitrary arrest
Haussuchung house search
Untersuchungshaft pre-trial custody
Wählbarkeit eligibility
Schwurgericht jury court
Vereidigung adjuration, swearing-in
Bürgerbewaffnung arming of the people
landesväterlicher Sinn patriotic sense
Huld favour
mit etw. im Einklang stehen to be in line with sth.
Rücktritt resignation
zeitgemäß modern
Achtung respect
Beifall approval

Die drohenden Zeitereignisse machen jedem echten Deutschen die ruhige, aber unverhüllte Kundgebung* dessen, was nach seiner Überzeugung die Eintracht* des Vaterlandes im Innern und nach Außen erheischt*, zur heiligsten Pflicht. [...] Von dieser Überzeugung beseelt* sprechen wir, die unterzeichneten Bürger und Einwohner Dresdens, die Erwartung aus, dass auch von der sächsischen hohen Staatsregierung den Forderungen der Zeit, deren Gewährung* teils für die Ruhe und das Wohlergehen* unseres Sachsenlandes, teils für die einheitliche Entwicklung Deutschlands und „seine Erhebung auf die unter den Nationen Europas ihm gebührende Stufe", unerlässlich* und unabweisbar* ist, dieselbe schleunige Erfüllung werde zu Teil werden, welche ihnen in anderen deutschen Staaten teils verheißen*, teils schon gefolgt ist.
Diese Wünsche sind:
1. Freiheit der Presse, Wegfall des Konzessionszwangs für Zeitschriften und Überweisung* der Pressvergehen an die ordentlichen Gerichte*;
2. Freiheit des religiösen Bekenntnisses* und der kirchlichen Vereinigung.
3. Freiheit des Versammlungs- und Vereinsrechtes.
4. Gesetzliche Sicherstellung der Person gegen willkürliche Verhaftung*, Haussuchung* und Untersuchungshaft*.
5. Verbesserung des Wahlgesetzes namentlich durch Herabsetzung des Zensus und Ausdehnung der Wählbarkeit* auf das ganze Land.
6. Öffentlichkeit und Mündlichkeit der Rechtspflege mit Schwurgericht*.
7. Vereidigung* des Militärs auf die Verfassung.
8. Verminderung des stehenden Heeres, Umbildung des Militärwesens und der Bürgerbewaffnung*. [...]
Wir zweifeln nicht an dem landesväterlichen Sinne* des allverehrten, allgeliebten Königs, wir geben uns seiner Huld* und Weisheit mit Vertrauen hin, wir erwarten aber ebenso zuversichtlich von den Ratgebern der Krone, dass sie klare Einsicht und aufrichtigen Willen genug haben werden, jenen dringenden Forderungen der Neuzeit zu entsprechen, oder dafern dies mit ihren Überzeugungen nicht im Einklang stehen* sollte, dies offen bekennen und durch freiwilligen Rücktritt* von ihrem Amte das gesetzliche Zustandekommen zeitgemäßer* Reformen ermöglichen und sich dadurch der Achtung* und des Beifalls* aller Parteien versichern werden.
Es lebe der König! Es lebe die Verfassung! Es lebe die Eintracht zwischen Regierung und Volk!
Dresden, den 7. März 1848.

"Märzforderungen aus Dresden", in: Karl Obermann (Ed.): Flugblätter der Revolution 1848/49, München: Deutscher Taschenbuch Verlag 1972, p. 49 f.

CONNECT

Die Straße der Demokratie

Task Writing an information brochure for English-speaking tourists planning to visit the "Straße der Demokratie" ("Road to Democracy").

The "Straße der Demokratie" is a joint venture of several cities in the south of Germany, the region in which the German revolution of 1848/49 began and then quickly spread across the rest of the territory. The aim of the project is to keep alive and to revive the revolutionary events, and the places and personalities involved. Search their website for events, places and personalities which you want to include and write an information brochure [→ www.strasse-der-demokratie.eu]. The selected information/persons should be of central importance and representative of the development of the revolution and of democracy in Germany at the time.

S 26 Screenshot „Straße der Demokratie"

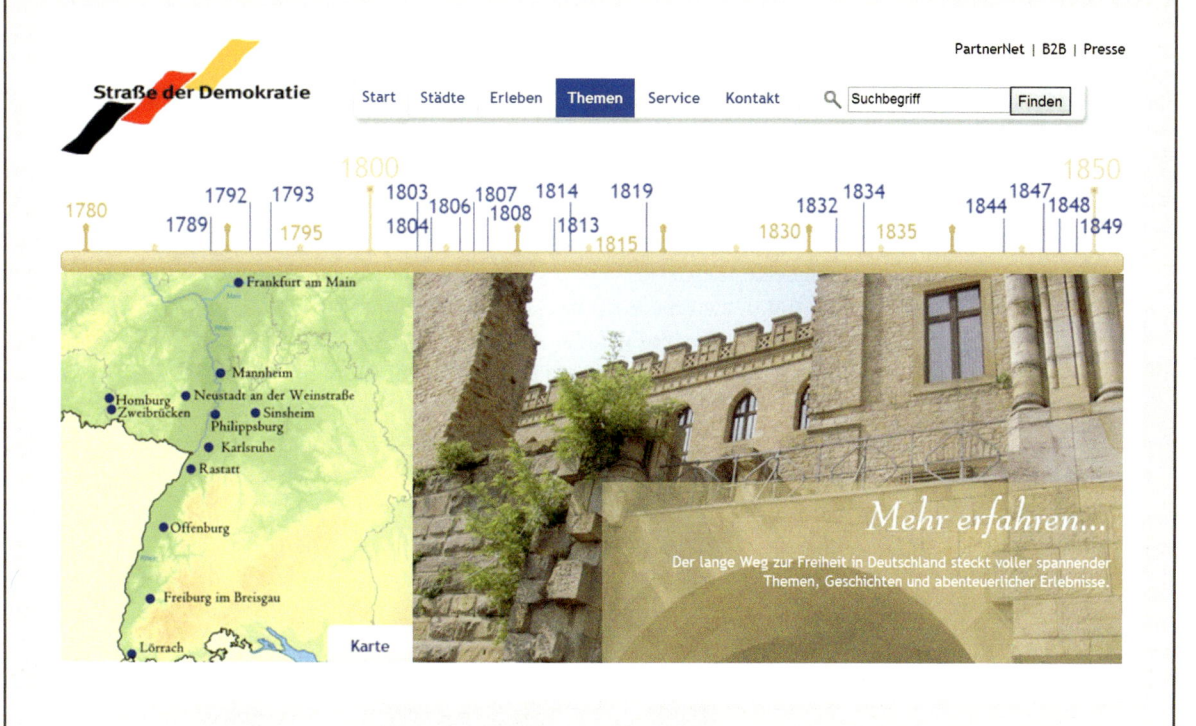

S 27 Frederick William IV

Opening Speech at the *Vereinigter Landtag*

The first Prussian *Vereinigter Landtag* of 1847, summoned by the Prussian King Frederick William IV, did not have rights comparable to "modern" parliaments and was merely intended to give approval to the King's decisions. However, the majority of the representatives was dissatisfied with this role and demanded regular meetings, independent of the monarch. Even though the assembly was dissolved in June 1847, the question of a constitution for Prussia remained unanswered and this situation as such formed an important contribution to the events leading up to the outbreak of revolution in Germany.

Pre-task 1. Have a look at the cartoon and its caption only. Reconstruct the main statement of the King's speech before the *Vereinigter Landtag* based on what you see: how might the king justify the rejection of a constitution?

Tasks 2. Give a summary of the King's rejection of a constitution (in English).
3. Explain the King's view on kingship and monarchy as it becomes apparent in his statement.
4. Compare the statement with the given cartoon: what is the point the cartoonist makes, and how can you relate this to the King's statement?

Post-task 5. How would the King probably react to the revolutionary demands, and why? Predict his actions, based on your results from S 27 .

Erklärung statement
mächtig machend empowering
Vorsehung providence
Treue loyalty
Volksgunst grace/favour of the people

„Es drängt mich zu einer feierlichen Erklärung*: dass es keine Macht der Erde jemals gelingen soll, Mich zu bewegen, das natürliche, gerade bei uns durch seine innere Wahrheit so mächtig machende* Verhältnis zwischen Fürst und Volk in ein conventionelles, constitutionelles zu wandeln, und dass ich es nun und nimmermehr zugeben werde, dass sich zwischen unseren Herr Gott im Himmel und dieses Land eine beschriebenes Blatt gleichsam als zweite Vorsehung* eindränge, um uns mit seinen Paragraphen zu regieren und durch sie die alte, heilige Treue* zu ersetzen. Zwischen uns sei Wahrheit. Von einer Schwäche weiß Ich Mich gänzlich frei. Ich strebe nicht nach eitler Volksgunst*."

Friedrich Wilhelm IV.: "Thronrede zur Eröffnung des ersten Vereinigten Landtags", in: Peter Wende (Ed.): Politische Reden. Kommentierte Ausgabe in zwei Bänden, Band I: 1792–1867, Frankfurt am Main: Deutscher Klassiker Verlag 1990

"Zwischen mir und mein Volk soll sich kein Blatt Papier drängen". German cartoon of 1847 ridiculing the King's speech

| Overview | Sources | Paper practice | Vocabulary | What is the German's Fatherland? | 97 |

King Frederick William IV of Prussia (1795–1861)

King Frederick William IV reigned Prussia from 1840 to 1861.
He served in the Prussian army during the Wars of Liberation against Napoleon in 1814. Even though he rejected both liberalism and the unification of Germany, he, in contrast to his father (Frederick William III of Prussia), eased press censorship and promised to allow democratic elements such as a constitution to play a role in his government. During the course of the revolution, he first insisted on his monarchic power but later changed his mind when the pressure on him increased. On 3 April 1849 he was offered the crown by the Frankfurt Parliament but he refused it since he did not want a "crown from the gutter".
In 1857 a stroke made it impossible for him to reign any longer and so his brother William took over the official functions.
King Frederick William IV died in Bonn on 2 January 1861.

S 28 Barricades in Berlin

This painting composed in 1848 (artist unknown) depicts the barricades and the street fights that took place there as revolution erupted in Berlin on 18 March 1848.

Tasks
1. Describe the painting in detail. Consider in particular the atmosphere captured.
2. Use the overview section to incorporate the painting into the historical context of the outbreak of revolution in Berlin on 18 March 1848.
3. Compare the atmosphere depicted with that illustrated in S 19b and in S 24 . Then discuss to what extent you consider the events in Berlin to constitute an inevitable step in the revolution.

Language Support

Straßenkampf street fight • **jubeln** to cheer, rejoice • **Schutt/Trümmer** debris ['debriː] • **Menschenmenge** crowd

S 29 Frederick William IV

An meine lieben Berliner

After the bloody riots in Berlin, King Frederick William IV issued this proclamation on 21 March 1848.

Pre-task 1. What do you expect the king to say in order to calm down the revolutionaries? Make use of the words and phrases in the box below to reconstruct the proclamation (in German).

> unzählige treue Herzen • aufrührerische und freche Forderungen • tapfere und treue Soldaten • Platz gesäubert werden • Rotte von Bösewichtern • gräuliche Urheber von Blutvergießen • siegreiches Vordringen der Truppen • größerem Unheil vorbeugen • Bewohner meines treuen und schönen Berlins

Tasks 2. Find the words and phrases in the speech and identify their respective contexts. Summarize the speech along the lines of these words and phrases (in English).
3. Characterize the revolutionaries and the soldiers, as presented by the King.
4. Evaluate the appropriateness of the King's reaction to the bloody riots.

Post-task 5. With the help of the overview section and the biographical account of the King, sketch Frederick William IV's further involvement in the revolution.

Einberufungspatent right to summon parliament
Gesinnung attitude

verhallen to die away

wohlgesinnt sympathetic
ungestümes Vordringen tumultuous advancement
arge Absicht bad intention

durch augenscheinliche Lüge verdreht misrepresented through an obvious lie
erhitzte Gemüter high-running feelings

vorbeugen to prevent
unseliger Irrtum disastrous mistake

Durch mein Einberufungspatent* vom heutigen Tage habt Ihr das Pfand der treuen Gesinnung* Eures Königs zu Euch und zum gesamten deutschen Vaterlande empfangen. Noch war der Jubel, mit dem unzählige treue Herzen mich gegrüßt hatten, nicht verhallt*, so mischte ein Haufen Ruhestörer aufrührerische und freche Forderungen ein und vergrößerte sich in dem Maße als die Wohlgesinnten* sich entfernten. Da ihr ungestümes Vordringen* bis in's Portal des Schlosses mit Recht arge Absichten* befürchten ließ und Beleidigungen wider meine tapfern und treuen Soldaten ausgestoßen wurden, musste der Platz durch Kavallerie im Schritt und mit eingesteckter Waffe gesäubert werden und 2 Gewehre der Infanterie entluden sich von selbst, Gottlob! ohne irgend Jemand zu treffen. Eine Rotte von Bösewichtern, meist aus Fremden bestehend, die sich seit einer Woche, obgleich ausgesucht, doch zu verbergen gewusst hatten, haben diesen Umstand im Sinne ihrer argen Pläne, durch augenscheinliche Lüge verdreht* und die erhitzten Gemüter* von Vielen meiner treuen und lieben Berliner mit Rachegedanken um vermeintlich vergossenes Blut! erfüllt und sind so die gräulichen Urheber von Blutvergießen geworden. Meine Truppen, Eure Brüder und Landsleute, haben erst dann von der Waffe Gebrauch gemacht, als sie durch viele Schüsse aus der Königsstraße dazu gezwungen wurden, das siegreiche Vordringen der Truppen war die notwendige Folge davon.

An Euch, Einwohner meiner geliebten Vaterstadt, ist es jetzt, größerem Unheil vorzubeugen*. Erkennt, Euer König und treuster Freund beschwört Euch darum, bei Allem was Euch heilig ist, den unseligen Irrthum*. Kehrt zum Frieden zurück, räumt die Barrikaden die noch stehen hinweg, und entsendet an mich Männer, voll des ächten alten Berliner Geistes mit Worten wie sie sich Eurem König gegenüber geziemen*, und ich gebe Euch mein Königliches Wort, dass alle Straßen und Plätze sogleich von den Truppen geräumt werden sollen und die militärische Besetzung* nur auf die nothwendigen Gebäude, die des Schlosses, des Zeughauses und weniger anderer, und auch da nur auf kurze Zeit beschränkt werden wird. Hört die väterliche Stimme Eures Königs, Bewohner meines treuen und schönen Berlins und vergesset das Geschehene, wie ich es vergessen will und werde in meinem Herzen, um der großen Zukunft Willen, die unter dem Friedens-Segen Gottes für Preußen und durch Preußen für Deutschland anbrechen wird.

Eure liebreiche Königin und wahrhaft treue Mutter und Freundin, die sehr leidend darnieder liegt, vereint ihre innigen, thränenreichen Bitten mit den Meinigen. –

Geschrieben in der Nacht vom 18.–19. März 1848
Friedrich Wilhelm

sich geziemen to be proper

militärische Besetzung military occupation

Johann Georg August Wirth: Die Geschichte der deutschen Staaten, von der Auflösung des Reiches bis auf unsere Tage, 4. Band: Die Deutsche Revolution (Ed. Wilhelm Zimmermann), Karlsruhe: Kunstverlag 1848, pp. 263/264

"Der Champagnerfritze". German cartoon of 1848 (artist unknown), which satirizes the grandiloquent, but basically empty words of the Prussian King

Language Support

sich übergeben to vomit • **Schwall** gush • **Rednerpult** lectern • **sich ergießen** to outpour, to effuse • **Fernrohr** spy-glass • **Missverhältnis** disproportion

CONNECT

A Session in the National Assembly – What Kind of Germany?

Task

1. Staging a session of the Frankfurt Parliament.
   Prepare a discussion in which you simulate a meeting of the National Assembly in session, taking into account the overview section, the biographies and the grid below. Split up into groups. Each group deals with either the democratic right, the liberal centre or the conservative right. Choose one representative of each political group and prepare arguments on his behalf in order to put forward your group demands, taking into account the knowledge you have gained so far. Summarize the arguments in a speech of roughly two minutes to be given in today's session.
   Issues to be addressed in the speeches are:
   - Should there be a Greater or a Little Germany? Why?
   - Should Germany become a federal or a centralized state?
   - Should Germany become a republic or a monarchy?

   Also agree on who is to be the parliament's president for the session, the person in charge of calling people to order and ending speeches in case they get too long.
   When listening to the other speeches, express your approval of statements made by calling out "hear, hear" and show your disapproval by booing.
   After having heard all the speeches, take a vote on the three main issues that were the subject of discussion.

Post-tasks

2. Reflect on the role play by answering the following questions:
   - How did you feel about the atmosphere in parliament?
   - How would you assess the decision-making processes in parliament?
   - Was it hard/easy for you to assume your role? Why?

3. Consider the family background and origin of the Frankfurt MPs provided in the chart below and revise who started the revolution, and why. Then discuss to what extent it would be justified to claim that the revolution was doomed to fail because its parliament was merely a "Parliament of Professors".

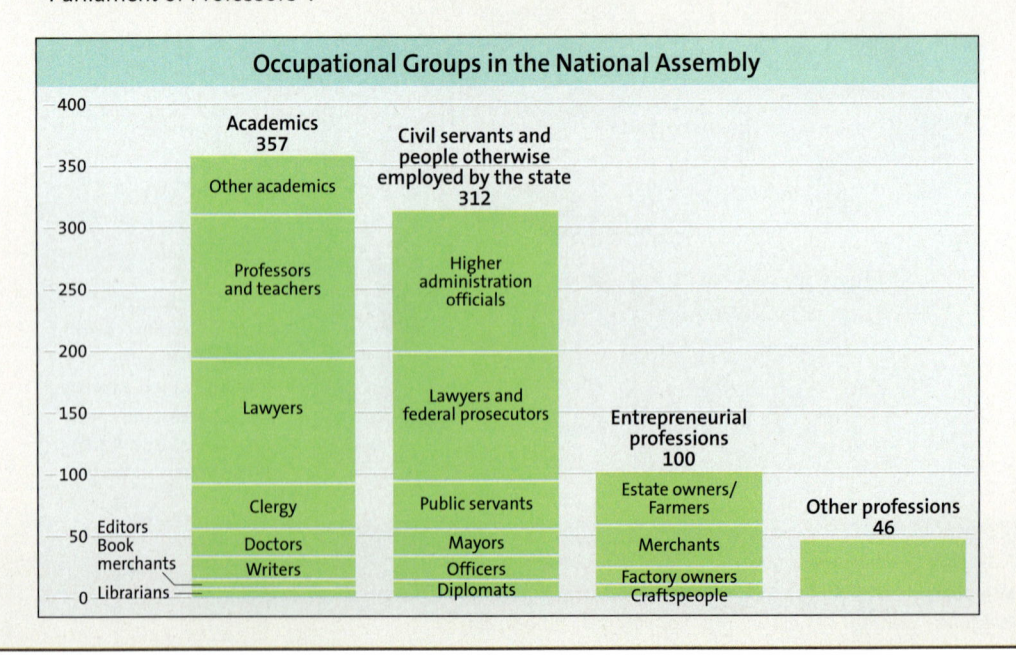

Occupational Groups in the National Assembly

Academics 357	Civil servants and people otherwise employed by the state 312	Entrepreneurial professions 100	Other professions 46
Other academics			
Professors and teachers	Higher administration officials		
Lawyers	Lawyers and federal prosecutors		
Clergy	Public servants	Estate owners/ Farmers	
Editors / Book merchants / Doctors / Writers / Librarians	Mayors / Officers / Diplomats	Merchants / Factory owners / Craftspeople	

S 30 Political Groups in the National Assembly and Some of their Representatives

The French Parliament (in existence since 1814) served as a role model for the German National Assembly. The representatives sat in a specific position in the chamber according to their political attitude. The grid below shows the names of the political groups, their main demands and some of their famous representatives. These political groups were usually named after the place they often met at and can be considered the forerunners of political parties.

Democratic right				Liberal centre					Conservative right
Radical left	Moderate left			Left centre			Right centre		
Donnersberg	Deutscher Hof	Nürnberger Hof	Westendhall	Württemberger Hof	Augsburger Hof	Landsberg	Kasino	Pariser Hof	Café Milani
Greater German republic through rev. action	Republic	Small German hereditary empire with emperor as formal head of state with few rights	Greater German solution	Hereditary empire, Smaller German Solution	Constitutional monarchy with strong Prussia	In favour of Prussian leadership	Greater German solution	Preservation of single monarchies
	Parliamentary-democratic republic			Parliamentary monarchy			Strong monarchic central power; representation of the people limited to legislative		Loose federal framework
	Arnold Ruge (1802 – 1880)	Robert Blum (1807 – 1848) Jakob Venedey (1805 – 1871)	Wilhelm Löwe (1814 – 1886)		Carl Mittermaier (1787 – 1867)	Robert von Mohl (1799 – 1875)	E. M. Arndt (1769 – 1860) Jacob Grimm (1785 – 1863)	Johann Heckscher (1797 – 1865)	Max Gravell (1781 – 1860)

S 31 The Catalogue of Fundamental Rights

The catalogue of fundamental rights (27 December 1848) pre-dates the actual constitution (28 March 1849) by three months.

Pre-task
1. Which rights do you consider to be fundamental rights? Make a list of rights, simultaneously ranking them from the most important to the least important.

Tasks
2. Find categories for the rights granted in the Catalogue of Fundamental Rights.
3. Explain why this document represents a radical break with pre-March "Germany" ("Metternich's Europe").
4. Compare the rights granted here with the March Demands of the citizens of Dresden (cf. S 25). Then assess to what extent this group would have been satisfied with the Catalogue of Fundamental Rights.

Post-task
5. Do further research on fundamental rights as contained in our Basic Law of 1949 and compare these with the rights granted in 1848. Use your findings to refute the thesis that the 1848/49 revolutions in Germany were a complete failure.

§132. Every German has the right of citizenship of the German Reich. He can exercise this right in every German land. [...]

§133. Every German has the right to live in any part of the Reich's territory, to acquire and dispose of property of all kinds, to pursue his livelihood, and to win the right of communal citizenship*. [...]

communal citizenship *Gemeindebürgerrecht*
levy tax

§136. Freedom of emigration shall not be limited by any state; emigration levies* shall not be established. [...]

§137. There are no class differences before the law. The rank of nobility is abolished. [...]

Public office shall be open to all men on the basis of ability.

All citizens are subject equally to military service [...].

§138. The freedom of man shall be inviolable.

capital punishment death penalty
mutiny revolt

§139. Capital punishment*, with the exception of cases prescribed by military law or naval law concerning mutiny*, is abolished, as are sentences to public whipping, branding, and bodily punishment.

§140. The house of every German is inviolable. [...]

§142. The secrecy of letters is inviolable. [...]

§143. Every German shall have the right freely to express his opinion through speech, writing, publication, and illustration.

The freedom of the press shall be suspended under no circumstances through preventive measures, namely, censorship, concessions, security orders, imposts*, limitation of publication or bookselling, postal bans, or other restraints [...]

impost charge, tax

§144. Every German has complete freedom of religion and conscience. [...]

§152. Arts and science, research and teaching, shall be free.

§158. Every person is free to choose his work or profession, and to prepare himself for it wherever and however he wishes.

§161. All Germans have the right to assemble peaceably and without arms; special permission for this is not needed. [...]

§164. Property is inviolable. [...]

§174. All jurisdiction stems from the state. [...]

James Harvey Robinson: Readings in European History, Boston: Ginn and Co. 1904–06, Vol. II, p. 570

S 32 The Paulskirche Constitution

This constitution came into effect on 28 March 1849. However, it was not valid for long since the Prussian King refused to become "Emperor of the Germans" when he was offered the crown.

Pre-task

1. Revise what you have learned about the various political groupings in the Frankfurt Parliament and their views on what Germany should look like in the future. What kind of compromise do you expect in the constitution, as far as a) the question of a republic or a monarchy and b) the question of eligibility and separation of powers are concerned? Discuss.

Tasks

2. Describe the constitution the national assembly eventually agreed on.

3. Explain which political forces were able to enforce their claims.

4. The German crown was offered to the Prussian King Frederick William IV, but he rejected it. Explain why he rejected it, against the backdrop of S 27 and S 29.

Post-task 5. Give a definition of "talking shop" and assess to what extent the Frankfurt Parliament could be labelled as such. Give reasons for your assessment.

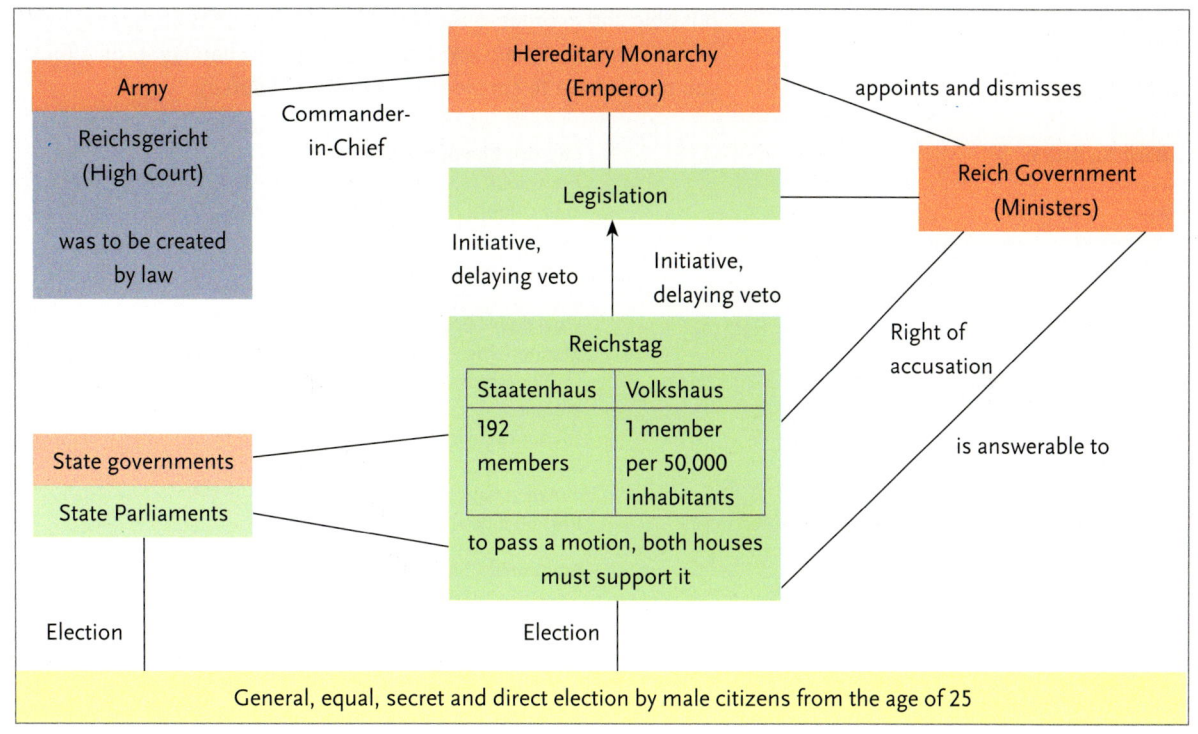

```
                    Hereditary Monarchy
                        (Emperor)              appoints and dismisses
   Army        Commander-
                in-Chief
 Reichsgericht
  (High Court)              Legislation                Reich Government
                                                         (Ministers)
 was to be created    Initiative,    Initiative,
    by law           delaying veto  delaying veto
                                                        Right of
                         Reichstag                      accusation
                    Staatenhaus | Volkshaus
                      192      | 1 member
State governments    members   | per 50,000             is answerable to
State Parliaments              | inhabitants
                    to pass a motion, both houses
                         must support it
  Election                Election
General, equal, secret and direct election by male citizens from the age of 25
```

adapted from: http://en.wikipedia.org/wiki/File:Paulskirchenverfassung_1849_english.svg, 14.01.08 [10.04.15]

S 33 Frederick William IV

Rejection of the Crown

In a private letter written in 1849 to the Prussian delegate to London, Christian von Bunsen, the Prussian King Frederick William IV names his reasons for his rejection of the crown.

Pre-task 1. Once more consider your explanation of why the King rejected the crown (cf. S 32, task 4). Relate your explanation to the following words and phrases taken from the letter:

> von Gottes Gnaden • tausendjähriger Glanz • verunehrt • Ludergeruch der Revolution • imaginärer Reif • legitimer König

Tasks 2. Analyse the source (= analyse the formal features and give a structured outline of content).
3. Discuss to what extent the Frankfurt Parliament could have foreseen the King's rejection of the crown, and why they offered it to him nevertheless.

Post-task 4. Revise what you have learned about King Frederick William IV in this sub-chapter. Consider the overview section, and the sources provided as well as the short biographical account. Imagine you wanted to write a historical novel with Frederick William IV as its protagonist. Use the information to write his character profile. Establishing a character profile is a method often used by writers before writing their novels in order to create a character that is as lifelike as possible and in order to avoid discontinuities in the storyline. The aspects listed can help you when creating the character profile (but you do not have to consider all of them, of course):

Basic Statistics:
Name:
Age:
Nationality:
Hometown:
Occupation:
Talents/Skills:
Birth order:
Siblings (describe relationship):
Spouse (describe relationship):
Children (describe relationship):
Grandparents (describe relationship):
Grandchildren (describe relationship):
Other persons of significance (describe relationship):

Physical Characteristics:
Eye colour:
Hair colour:
Skin colour:
Shape of face:
Distinguishing features:
How does he/she dress?
Mannerisms:
Habits (smoking, drinking etc.):
Hobbies:
Favourite sayings:
Style of dress (elegant, shabby etc.):
Greatest flaw:
Best quality:

Personal Attributes and Attitudes:
Educational background:
Intelligence level:
Any mental illnesses?
Learning experiences:
Character's short-term goals in life:
Character's long-term goals in life:
How does the character see himself/herself?
How does the character believe he/she is perceived by others?
How self-confident is the character?
Does the character seem ruled by emotion or logic or some combination thereof?
What would most embarrass this character?

Emotional Characteristics:
Strengths/Weaknesses:
Introvert or extrovert?
How does the character deal with anger?
With sadness?
With conflict?
With change?
With loss?
What does the character want out of life?
What motivates this character?
What frightens this character?
What makes this character happy?
Is the character judgmental of others?
Is the character generous or stingy?
Is the character generally polite or rude?

abridged from: The Lazy Scholar: "How to Create a Character Profile", The Internet Writing Journal, www.writerswrite.com/journal/jun98/how-to-create-a-character-profile-6986, June 1998 [28.12.14]

nehmen to accept

Ölung anointing

von Gottes Gnaden by grace of God

Glanz resplendence

verunehren to begrime

Ludergeruch hussy stink

Reif circlet

[...] Die Krone, die ein Hohenzoller nehmen* dürfte, wenn die Umstände es möglich machen könnten, ist [...] eine, die den Stempel Gottes trägt, die den, dem sie aufgesetzt wird nach der heiligen Oelung*, „von Gottes Gnaden"* macht, weil und wie sie mehr denn 34 Fürsten zu Königen der Deutschen von Gottes Gnaden gemacht und den Letzten immer der alten Reihe gesellt. Die Krone, die die Ottonen, die Hohenstaufen, die Habsburger getragen, kann natürlich ein Hohenzoller tragen, sie ehrt ihn überschwänglich mit tausendjährigem Glanze*. Die aber, die Sie meinen, verunehrt* überschwänglich mit ihrem Ludergeruch* der Revolution von 1848, der albernsten, dümmsten, schlechtesten, wenn auch, Gottlob, nicht bösesten des Jahrhunderts. Einen solchen imaginären Reif*, aus Dreck und Let-

ten [Lehm*] gebacken, soll ein legitimer König von Gottes Gnaden und nun gar der König von Preußen sich geben lassen, der den Segen hat*, wenn auch nicht die älteste, doch die edelste Krone, die Niemand gestohlen worden ist, zu tragen? Ich sage es Ihnen rund heraus: Soll die tausendjährige Krone deutscher Nation,
15 die 42 Jahr geruht* hat, wieder einmal vergeben werden, so bin ich es, und meines Gleichen, die sie vergeben werden. Und wehe dem*, der sich anmaßt*, was ihm nicht zukommt*!

Leopold von Ranke: Aus dem Briefwechsel Friedrich Wilhelms IV. mit Bunsen, Leipzig: Duncker & Humblot 1873, p. 233 f.

Lehm mud
den Segen hat who is blessed with (verb +-ing)
ruhen to rest
wehe dem woe betide him/her
sich etw. anmaßen to claim sth. without justification, usurp, arrogate
zukommen to be entitled to

S 34 Ferdinand Schröder

Die Ablehnung der Kaiserkrone durch Friedrich Wilhelm IV

This German cartoon by Ferdinand Schröder pokes fun at the King's rejection of the crown. The caption is written in the Berlin dialect, Berlin being the capital of Prussia at that time.

Pre-task
1. The cartoon relies heavily on symbolism. One of the symbols is a house of cards. What does a house of cards usually stand for, and what would it probably represent in the given cartoon? Speculate.

Tasks
2. Describe the cartoon in detail. Do not neglect the composition of the picture.
3. Explain the various elements of the cartoon against the backdrop of their historical context.
4. Discuss if the sun in the background is rising or setting.
5. Take a critical stand on the symbol of the house of cards the cartoonist has made use of.

Embedded text/caption (not given):
„Wat heulst'n, kleener Hampelmann?"
„Ick habe Ihr'n Kleenen 'ne Krone schnitzt, nu will er se nich!"
Persons depicted, from left to right:
Heinrich von Gagern (President of the national assembly) • Germania • Frederick William IV (playing with a bear, representing Russia)

Language Support

Hampelmann Jumping Jack, marionette • **schnitzen** to carve • **Kartenhaus** house of cards • **Schild** shield, buckler • **Pickelhaube** spiked helmet

> S 35   Alan Farmer and Andrina Stiles

The Prussian Constitution

In their work "The Unification of Germany 1815–1919", Farmer and Stiles also focus on the Prussian Constitution of 1849, which they call "a strange mixture of liberalism and absolutism."

Pre-task
1. Which characteristics would you ascribe to liberalism on the one hand, and to absolutism on the other hand? Revise and discuss.

Tasks
2. With the help of the text, visualize the Prussian Constitution of 1848 in form of a diagram.
3. Explain which aspects of the constitution were liberal and which absolutist.
4. Based on your findings, discuss to what extent the Prussian Constitution represented a step towards fulfilling the revolutionaries' demands.

- It guaranteed the Prussians freedom of religion, of assembly and of association, and provided for an independent judiciary.
- There was to be a representative assembly, with two houses. The upper house would be elected by property owners, and the lower one by manhood suffrage.
- Voters were divided into three classes, according to the amount of taxes they paid. This ensured that the rich had far more electoral power than the poor.
- In an emergency, the King could suspend civil rights and collect taxes without reference to Parliament.
- Ministers were to be appointed and dismissed by the King, and were to be responsible only to him and not to Parliament.

to alter to change
- The King could alter* the written constitution at anytime [sic] it suited him to do so.
- The King retained control of the army.

Alan Farmer, Andrina Stiles: The Unification of Germany 1815–1919. London: Hodder Education 2007, p. 42

CONNECT

The 1848/49 Revolutions – "The History of the World Is but the Biography of Great Men"?

The statement quoted above can be traced back to the Scottish writer Thomas Carlyle (1795 – 1881) and expresses the so-called "Great Man theory", saying that history can to a large extent be explained through the impact great men (or heroes) had on it.
However, great women (or heroines) also contributed a lot to the development of the 1848/49 revolutions (and to history in general, needless to say).

Task Write an encyclopaedia entry about the "Great Woman theory" in connection with the 1848/49 revolutions.

Study the biographical account below and the two given sources carefully and analyse what they reveal about women's contributions to the 1848/49 revolutions. Make notes and write your encyclopaedia entry based on these notes.

S 36a Zuruf württembergischer Frauen und Jungfrauen an deutsche Krieger

In 1849, the revolutionary uprisings were put down by the counter-revolutionaries. In this appeal to the soldiers, the women of Württemberg ask them to stop fighting against their own people.

Deutsche Krieger! Ein mächtiger Geist* weht durch alle Gauen* unseres gemeinsamen Vaterlandes! Es ist der Geist der erwachten, wahren Freiheit des deutschen Volkes! Auch an euch, deutsche Jünglinge*, die ihr dem braven deutschen Heere folget, geht der mahnende Zuruf, des Geistes der Frei-
5 heit mitzuwirken*, dass dieses so lang ersehnte Kleinod* endlich unveräußerliches Eigentum* der ganzen Nation werde. Doch nicht mit dem bisher beschrittenen Weg werdet ihr, deutsche Krieger, das köstliche Gut* deutscher Freiheit erringen helfen! [...]
Wohlan denn, deutsche Jünglinge und Männer, hört den Zuruf deutscher
10 Frauen und Jungfrauen: Bedenkt eure Zukunft, bedenkt den friedlichen Bürgerstand*, dem ihr einst wieder angehören wollt, bedenkt das friedliche Glück der Liebe und der Ehe, sowie des häuslichen Herdes*, welches aus der Ferne freundlich euch entgegenlächelt. Hört das Gelübde* deutscher Frauen, welches in heiliger Vaterlandsliebe wir gelobt:
15 „Nie werden wir dem unsre Hand am Altare reichen, dessen Hand von dem Blute seiner deutschen Mitbürger befleckt* wurde!"
„Nie werden wir mit dem unsern häuslichen Herd teilen, der mit Feuer und Schwert dieses, unser Heiligtum, zerstöret hat!!"
„Nie werden wir dem einst in treuer Liebe nah'n, dessen feindliche Waffe
20 Unglück und Verderben* über die deutschen Gauen gebracht hat!!!"
Höret, deutsche Jünglinge, unsern Schwur und des Himmels Vergeltung* treffe uns, wenn wir dieses Gelübde nicht halten! Deutsche Krieger! das Erbe eurer Väter, so lautet ihr Entschluss, welches ihr freventlich* durch eure Waffen zu zerstören trachtet, sei euch entzogen! Es komme denen
25 zugute, die ihr in blindem Wahne* zu Witwen und Waisen* gemacht! Bedenkt diesen Abgrund*, der sich vor euren geblendeten Augen öffnet, und haltet zum Volke, oder der Genius einer glücklichen Zukunft für euch verhüllt trauernd sein Haupt*.
Den 7. Mai 1849
30 Sämtliche Frauen und Jungfrauen* des Königreichs Württemberg.

Gerlinde Hummel-Haasis: Schwestern zerreißt eure Ketten: Zeugnisse zur Geschichte der Frauen in der Revolution von 1848/49. München: Deutscher Taschenbuchverlag, 1982, p. 22 ff.

Geist spirit
Gau district
Jüngling young men
mitwirken to participate
Kleinod treasure
unveräußerliches Eigentum inalienable possession
köstliches Gut delightful gift
Bürgerstand civilian estate
häuslicher Herd domestic hearth
Gelübde oath
beflecken to stain
Unglück und Verderben misery and destruction
des Himmels Vergeltung the wrath of Heaven
freventlich blasphemous(ly)
blinder Wahn blind madness
Waise orphan
Abgrund abyss [əˈbɪs]
verhüllt ... Haupt conceal its face in mourning
Jungfrau maiden

Louise Otto-Peters (1819 – 1895)

Louise Otto-Peters was the youngest of four sisters and was home-schooled until the age of nine. When her parents died shortly after one another, Otto-Peters and two of her sisters lived with her aunt. In 1840, she was engaged to the lawyer Gustav Müller, but he died only one year later.

Otto-Peters published articles in various newspapers, in the beginning under her pen name "Otto Stern". Later, she became part of the democratic movement und founded the first newspaper of the women's movement in 1849, the "Frauen-Zeitung für höhere weibliche Interessen" which, despite censorship, continued to be published until 1852.

In 1851, she was engaged to August Peters who was under arrest for his participation in the March revolution. They married in 1858 and lived in Leipzig from 1860 onwards, where Otto-Peters helped found the first women's education club and the first institute for the higher education for girls. Likewise in the year 1860, the first "Women's Conference" took place in Leipzig at which the foundation of the German Association of Female Citizens (*Allgemeiner Deutscher Frauenverein*) was decided on, whose chairwoman Otto-Peters would become. She also co-edited the Association's magazine "Neue Bahnen" until her death in 1895.

In addition to her numerous publications about women's history and rights, Otto-Peters also published poems, novels and historical writings.

S 36b Louise Otto-Peters

Programm der Frauen-Zeitung

In the first edition of her *Frauen-Zeitung* published in 1849, editor Louise Otto-Peters calls upon women to demand their political rights within the framework of the liberalisation process triggered by the revolution, and to support other women as well.

FRAUEN-ZEITUNG
Ein Organ* für die höheren weiblichen Interessen
Motto: Dem Reich der Freiheit werb'* ich Bürgerinnen. [...]
Nr. 1 Sonnabend, den 21. April 1849
Programm
Die Geschichte aller Zeiten, und die heutige ganz besonders, lehrt: dass diejenigen auch vergessen werden, welche an sich selbst zu denken vergaßen! Das schrieb ich im Mai des Jahres 1848 hinaus in die Welt, als ich zunächst meine Worte an die Männer richtete, die sich in Sachsen mit der Frage der Arbeit beschäftigten – ich mahnte sie damit an* die armen Arbeiterinnen, indem ich für meine Schwestern das Wort ergriff, auf dass sie nicht vergessen wurden! [...] Dieser selbe Erfahrungssatz* ist es, welcher mich zur Herausgabe* einer Frauen-Zeitung veranlasst. Mitten in den großen Umwälzungen*, in denen wir uns alle befinden, werden sich die Frauen vergessen sehen, wenn sie selbst an sich zu denken vergessen!

Organ organ
werben to recruit

anmahnen to admonish

Erfahrungssatz experience
Herausgabe publication
Umwälzungen upheavals

Wohlauf denn, meine Schwestern, vereinigt Euch mit mir, damit wir nicht zurückbleiben, wo alles um alles um uns und neben uns vorwärts drängt und kämpft. Wir wollen auch unser Teil fordern und verdienen an der großen Welt-Erlösung*, welche der ganzen Menschheit, deren eine Hälfte wir
15 sind, endlich werden muss.

Wir wollen unser Teil fordern: das Recht, das Rein-Menschliche* in uns in freier Entwicklung aller unserer Kräfte auszubilden*, und das Recht der Mündigkeit und Selbstständigkeit* im Staat.

Wir wollen unser Teil verdienen: Wir wollen unsere Kräfte aufbieten, das
20 Werk der Welt-Erlösung zu fördern, zunächst dadurch, dass wir den großen Gedanken der Zukunft: Freiheit und Humanität (was im Grunde zwei gleichbedeutende* Worte sind) auszubreiten suchen in allen Kreisen, welche uns zugänglich sind, in den weiteren des größeren Lebens durch die Presse, in den engeren der Familie durch Beispiel, Belehrung und Erzie-
25 hung*.

Wir wollen unser Teil aber auch dadurch verdienen, dass wir nicht vereinzelt streben, nur jede für sich, sondern vielmehr jede für alle, und dass wir vor allem derer zumeist uns annehmen, welche in Armut, Elend und Unwissenheit* vergessen und vernachlässigt* schmachten*.
30 Wohlauf, meine Schwestern, helft mir zu diesem Werke*!

Helft mir für die hier angedeuteten Ideen zunächst durch diese Zeitung [zu] wirken*! [...]

Louise Otto

FRAUEN-ZEITUNG, 1. Jg. 1849, Großenhain/Sachsen, Nr. 1, 21. April 1849, printed in: Margrit Twellmann: Die Deutsche Frauenbewegung im Spiegel repräsentativer Frauenzeitschriften. Ihre Anfänge und erste Entwicklung. Quellen, 1843–1889. Meisenheim am Glan: A. Hain, 1972, p. 34–35

Welt-Erlösung world-redemption
Rein-Menschliche purely personal
ausbilden to cultivate
Mündigkeit und Selbstständigkeit the right to speak for oneself and the right of independence
gleichbedeutend to mean the same

Beispiel, Belehrung und Erziehung example, instruction and bringing up children
Armut, Elend und Unwissenheit poverty, misery and ignorance
vernachlässigt neglected
schmachten to languish
Werk work
wirken to work for

S 37   Alan Farmer and Andrina Stiles

The Failure of the Revolution

On page 48 of their work, Farmer and Stiles present several reasons for the failure of the revolution.

Pre-task
1. In class, collect as many reasons for the failure of the revolution you can think of. Write them down on index cards and put them on the board in arbitrary order.

Tasks
2. Read through the reasons presented by Farmer and Stiles. Identify those you have not thought of yourselves, write them down on index cards and add them to the ones already on the board.
3. Rank the reasons according to their importance for the failure of the revolution.

to omit to leave out

- The Frankfurt Parliament was the product of a middle-class franchise that omitted* the masses. Thus, the Parliament failed to attract mass support.
- The Parliament was divided. Most representatives wanted a constitutional monarchy incorporating liberal ideas of limited democracy. This alienated radicals (who wanted to go much further) and outraged conservatives.
- There was uncertainty about the geographical extent of 'Germany' and no resolution of the *Kleindeutschland-Großdeutschland* debate.
- Discussions in the Parliament were ill-organised. There was plenty of talk but little action.
- Most states were suspicious of a new German authority. Most (especially Prussia and Austria) were determined to preserve their sovereignty.
- The Parliament did not have an administration or an army to carry out its decisions.
- Frederick William of Prussia refused to receive the German crown 'from the gutter'. There was no other obvious German Kaiser.
- The focus should be on Frankfurt's failure, but the defeat of revolution across Germany is relevant.
- Once German princes were back in control, the Parliament stood little chance.

Alan Farmer, Andrina Stiles: The Unification of Germany 1815–1919, London: Hodder Education 2007, p. 48

"Rundgemälde von Europa im August 1849". Cartoon by Ferdinand Schröder, published in the Düsseldorfer Monatshefte, 1849
The man with the spiked helmet (representing the Prussian King Frederick William IV) is "sweeping" the Forty-Eighters out of Europe.

S 38 Roman Herzog

Speech on the Occasion of the 150th Anniversary of the 1848/49 Revolution

On 18 May 1998, the former German Federal President Roman Herzog gave a speech on the occasion of the 150th anniversary of the 1848 revolutions in the Paulskirche in Frankfurt.

| Overview | Sources | Paper practice | Vocabulary | What is the German's Fatherland? | 111 |

Pre-task 1. Keeping in mind the eventual outcome of the revolution, make an educated guess as to what a German Federal President might say on the occasion of the 150th anniversary of the 1848 revolutions. Focus on whether his assessment is more likely to be negative or positive.

Tasks 2. Outline the positive and negative aspects of the revolution mentioned by Herzog. Make use of the language support provided to introduce your sentences, or add further useful words and phrases you can think of.

☺	☹
✓ He praises/lauds/cherishes …	✓ He criticizes/assesses negatively …
✓ Herzog finds it positive/praiseworthy/laudable/important that …	✓ Herzog finds sth. negative/worth criticizing … He is critical of/against …
✓ He appreciates/expresses his appreciation for …	✓ He utters his concern that …
✓ To him, the most important/positive/decisive factor/point is that …	✓ To him, the most important/negative/decisive factor/point is that …
✓ …	✓ …

3. Explain the references Herzog makes by incorporating them into their immediate historical context.
4. Take a critical stand on Herzog's assessment of the 1848/49 revolutions.

Post-task 5. In 2018, the 170th anniversary of the revolutions will be celebrated. Write a letter to Germany's current Federal President in which you make suggestions for celebrations in Germany or discuss whether there should be celebrations at all.

1848 begann in Deutschland eine neue Zeit. Auch wenn es danach schwere Rückschläge* gab: Was hier begann, war auf die Dauer nicht mehr rückgängig zu machen. Das Jahr 1848 war nicht nur der bleibende Anfang der deutschen Demokratiegeschichte – es war auch eine entscheidende Wendemarke* auf dem Weg zum
5 modernen, demokratischen Europa. Denn anders als 1789 war 1848 das Jahr einer wirklich europäischen Bewegung. An vielen Orten und in vielen Sprachen erscholl damals der Ruf nach Partizipation, nach Grundrechten, nach Freiheit. Es wehte der Wind eines Wandels, der die Völker Europas nicht nur veränderte, sondern auch auf neue Weise miteinander verband.
10 Bleiben wir aber zunächst beim deutschen Teil der Geschichte. Ehe hier, an diesem Ort nüchterner* Würde, das Paulskirchen-Parlament zusammentreten konnte, hatte es in Deutschland etwas gegeben, das man seit 1789 zwar kannte, das aber eher mit Furcht und Schrecken genannt wurde: eine Revolution. Es war zwar eine kleine, auch eine weniger blutige und weniger radikale Revolution als
15 1789 – aber dass es sich tatsächlich um eine Revolution handelte, war doch allen Zeitgenossen* klar.
Es kam einiges zusammen, um den revolutionären Funken zu zünden*. Da gab es die Unzufriedenheit der geistigen Elite mit Zensur, Bevormundung* und Un-

Rückschlag setback

Wendemarke turning point

nüchtern level-headed

Zeitgenosse contemporary
zünden to ignite sth.
Bevormundung patronising and dominating behavior

terdrückung, es gab Haft und Kerker für freie Gedanken und ihre öffentliche Artikulation*; da gab es, vor dem Hintergrund des herannahenden* Industriezeitalters, die soziale Frage; es gab das allgemeine Gefühl, dass die alten Strukturen der neuen Zeit nicht gewachsen* waren, und es gab die mächtige Idee, nur ein einiges Deutschland könne Freiheit und Demokratie schaffen und garantieren.

Auf der einen Seite standen die modernen Ideen und aufstrebenden* Kräfte des Bürgertums, auf der anderen Seite herrschten Geburtsadel* und Erbmonarchie, also politische Vorstellungen aus dem tiefsten Gestern. Auf der einen Seite ließen die Anfänge von Eisenbahn, Telegraphie und Schnellpresse die Welt zusammenwachsen, auf der anderen Seite gab es im Deutschen Bund über 30 mehr oder weniger souveräne Staaten. Die Gesellschaft war voller Aufbruch und Veränderung, voller Krisen und wachsender sozialer Not. Die politischen Mächte des Jahres 1848 aber waren rückwärts gewandt* und ideenlos.

Natürlich: Die großen Ambitionen, mit denen man 1848 ans Werk ging, haben sich zunächst nicht erfüllt. Die Revolution ist letztlich gescheitert, die demokratische Gestalt* eines einigen Deutschland hat noch lange auf ihre Verwirklichung* warten müssen. Und doch wies das Jahr 1848 weit in die Zukunft. Die „Paulskirche" ist das eine große Symbol für das Streben der Deutschen nach Einigkeit und Recht und Freiheit, und erst heute können wir hinzufügen: der Fall der Berliner Mauer 1989 ist das andere. Beides sind Sternstunden deutscher Geschichte, mit denen wir sorgfältig umgehen* müssen; sie dürfen nicht in der Routine verordneten Gedenkens* versinken. Das Zusammentreten des ersten, frei gewählten deutschen Parlamentes vor 150 Jahren ist ein Moment in unserer oft so schwierigen Geschichte, auf den wir uns ohne Einschränkung berufen* können, auch wenn wir heute über die Zukunft von Staat und Demokratie nachdenken.

Wenn wir uns – zum Beispiel – daran erinnern, mit welchem Glanz Frankreich das Jubiläum von 1789 gefeiert hat, obwohl an dieser Revolution weiß Gott nicht alles Gold war, dann kann man eigentlich nur begreifen, warum die Geburtsstunde der deutschen Demokratie bei uns nicht zu dem gleichen stolzen Gedanken führt. Müssen wir immer gleich alles perfekt haben? Oder fallen wir gar auf das Bild herein, das sich andere von uns und unserer Geschichte machen?

Noch lange nach Gründung der Bundesrepublik Deutschland geisterte die Parole durch die Welt, die Deutschen können von sich aus kein demokratisches Gemeinwesen schaffen, sie hätten es sich – im Westen – erst von den Siegern nach dem Zweiten Weltkrieg aufdrängen* lassen müssen. Natürlich ist daran manches Wahre, aber zum Teil sind wir an diesem Klischee auch selbst schuld. Ich meine damit nicht nur das Scheitern von Weimar, das in die nationalsozialistische Diktatur führte. Ich meine auch die seltsame Traditionsvergessenheit, durch die die demokratischen und parlamentarischen Tendenzen der deutschen Geschichte immer wieder verschüttet worden sind.

Zugegeben: Die Freiheitsgeschichte unseres Volkes war oft eine Geschichte von Verlierern, von Versuchen, Irrtümern und auch Niederlagen. Und wir können uns unsere Vergangenheit nicht aussuchen. Aber wir können für unser eigenes Selbstbewusstsein, für die Identität unseres Gemeinwesens sehr wohl auswählen, auf welche Traditionen wir uns berufen und an welche wir anknüpfen. 1848 ist dafür der Schlüssel: Damals sind die Prinzipien formuliert worden, die noch heute die Grundlagen unserer staatlichen Existenz ausmachen: Das Bekenntnis* zu Menschenrechten und Demokratie und der gemeinsame Wille, die verschiedenen Regionen und Strömungen in unserem Land zu einem freien Gemeinwesen zu

---

öffentliche Artikulation public mention
herannahen to approach
etw. nicht gewachsen sein to be no match for sth.
aufstreben to emerge
Geburtsadel nobility by birth

rückwärts gewandt old-fashioned

demokratische Gestalt democratic shape
Verwirklichung realization

sorgfältig mit etw. umgehen to handle sth. with care
verordnetes Gedenken decreed remembrance
sich auf etw. berufen to evoke sth., to refer to sth.

jdm. etw. aufdrängen to impose sth. on sb.

Bekenntnis commitment

vereinigen. 1848 gibt uns das Recht, mit Selbstbewusstsein zu sagen: Die demokratische Idee, die Ideen der Freiheit, der Menschen- und Bürgerrechte sind auch ein Teil der deutschen Tradition – auch wenn sie sich erst später wirklich durchgesetzt haben. [...]

_{Roman Herzog: "Rede anlässlich der Veranstaltung '150 Jahre Revolution von 1848/49' in der Paulskirche zu Frankfurt am Main, www.bundespraesident.de/SharedDocs/Reden/DE/Roman-Herzog/Reden/1998/05/19980518_Rede.html, 18.05.1998 [30.03.15]}

S 39 DER SPIEGEL
1848. Die halbe Revolution

On its 150th anniversary in 1998, the German magazine DER SPIEGEL dedicated their front page to the revolution. However, the editors called it a "limited revolution" (*halbe Revolution*) and added the question whether this "limited revolution" was the "beginning of the German disaster".

Pre-task
1. Revise your definition of "revolution" (cf. S 22). What would constitute a "limited revolution"? Collect ideas in class.

Tasks
2. Describe the front page in detail and agree on the most suitable adjective for the atmosphere captured in it.
3. Drawing on your knowledge from previous history classes and the additional information gained in this sub-chapter, explain the connection established between the "limited revolution", Bismarck, William II and Hitler.
4. Discuss to what extent it is justified to call the 1848/49 revolutions "limited", or a revolution at all.

Persons depicted, from left to right: Otto von Bismarck, Adolf Hitler, German Emperor William II

Language Support

halbe Revolution limited revolution
Schlachtfeld battlefield • **Schutt/Trümmer** debris ['debriː] • **Zerstörung anrichten** to wreak havoc • **sich (bedrohlich) abzeichnen** to loom

sung zu regieren (oder die Verfassung zu konsolidieren?); in Frankreich sei das anders, da fehle diese individuelle Selbständigkeit. Eine Verfassungskrise sei keine Schande*, sondern eine Ehre. – Wir sind ferner vielleicht zu „gebildet", um eine Verfassung zu tragen*; wir sind zu kritisch; die Befähigung*, Regierungsmaßregeln*, Akte der Volksvertretung* zu beurteilen, ist zu allgemein; im Lande gibt es eine Menge katilinarischer* Existenzen, die ein großes Interesse an Umwälzungen* haben. Das mag paradox klingen, beweist aber doch alles, wie schwer in Preußen verfassungsmäßiges Leben ist. [...]

Wir haben zu heißes Blut, wir haben die Vorliebe*, eine zu große Rüstung* für unsern schmalen Leib zu tragen; nur sollen wir sie auch utilisieren*. Nicht auf Preußens Liberalismus sieht Deutschland, sondern auf seine Macht; Bayern, Württemberg, Baden mögen dem Liberalismus indulgieren*, darum wird ihnen doch keiner Preußens Rolle anweisen; Preußen muss seine Kraft zusammenfassen und zusammenhalten auf den günstigen Augenblick*, der schon einige Male verpasst ist; Preußens Grenzen nach den Wiener Verträgen sind zu einem gesunden Staatsleben nicht günstig; nicht durch Reden und Majoritätsbeschlüsse* werden die großen Fragen der Zeit entschieden – das ist der große Fehler von 1848 und 1849 gewesen – sondern durch Eisen und Blut.

Wilhelm Schüßler (Ed.): Otto von Bismarck: Reden 1847–1869, Vol. 10: Bismarck: Die gesammelten Werke, ed. Hermann von Petersdorff, Berlin: Otto Stolberg 1924–35, pp. 139 f.

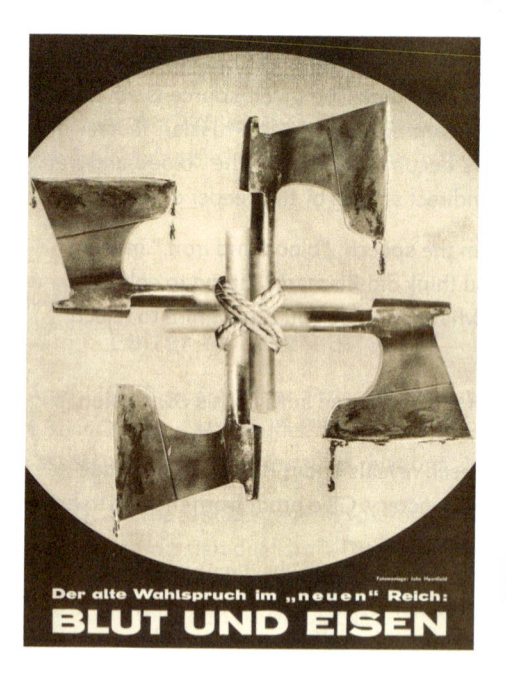

Schande disgrace
tragen here: to put up with
Befähigung ability
Regierungsmaßregeln government measures
Akte der Volksvertretung bills by the national assembly
katilinarisch subversive (after the Roman conspirer Catilina)
Umwälzungen revolutionary change
Vorliebe preference
Rüstung armour
utilisieren to use
indulgieren to indulge in, to react leniently to
günstiger Augenblick favourable moment
Majoritätsbeschlüsse majority decisions

"Blood and Iron". Anti-Hitler artwork by the German artist John Heartfield (born Helmut Herzfeld) of 8 March 1934.

Language Support

Hakenkreuz swastika [ˈswɒstɪkə]

S 42) Lord Augustus Loftus

Letter to Lord Stanley

In the letter below dated 4 August 1866 to Lord Stanley, the British Foreign Minister, the British ambassador in Berlin, Lord Augustus Loftus, reports on Bismarck's diplomacy. The letter was written shortly after a preliminary peace (*Vorfrieden*) had been concluded between Austria and Prussia, effectively ending the Austro-Prussian War.

Pre-task

1. In his letter, Loftus assesses the current situation in Germany. In his conclusion, he attaches importance to the person of Bismarck in relation to the further development in Europe. Have a look at the way he characterizes Bismarck and discuss whether he sees him in a positive or in a negative light, or both. Think of examples to back up your view.

> Bold in conception and energetic in action, unrestrained by scruples and unmoved by principles, governing by fear where he could not win by love, this intrepid*, dexterous*, and powerful Minister has now in his hands the most important part which, perhaps, has ever fallen to the lot of a statesman to fill.
>
> intrepid brave, courageous • dexterous skillful

Tasks

2. Outline Loftus's assessment of the situation.
3. Incorporate the source into the larger historical context of the process of Germany's unification up to 1866 by explaining the references made by Loftus.
4. Against the backdrop of the source, discuss if Loftus sees Bismarck in a positive or in a negative light.

Post-task

5. In 2010, this source was one of the three choices in North-Rhine Westphalia's *Zentralabitur* in Bilingual History. Would it have been your choice, too? Discuss. (Possible criteria: difficulty of the language, tasks, topic, etc.)

The annexation of all the States of Northern Germany to the [River] Main will give to Prussia an increase of about four millions of population. Thus in one month will have been effected, with a rapidity* and success unparalleled in history, changes which even Count Bismarck, in his most elated* moments, never could
5 have anticipated. Indeed, so great, so unexpected has been the success of the Prussian arms, that it is not unlikely to prove an embarrassment, and even a danger, to the political system which Count Bismarck is aiming to establish. His object, and that of the military party, is to create a great and powerful Prussia, extending from the Baltic to the Main, having full command of the maritime ports on the northern
10 coasts, and the important and strategic maritime position of the Elbe Duchies. On the other hand, the desire of the Liberal party in Prussia and in Germany is to create a united Germany under a strong Power – that Power being Prussia – represented by a national parliament, to be established on the basis of the constitution framed by the Frankfort Assembly in 1849. They look to the fulfilment of their
15 long-cherished dream of a German Empire – uniting the whole German nation under one command. But to attain this end (and they judge that the propitious* moment had arrived) Prussia must be fused into Germany, whereas the object of Count Bismarck was to fuse Germany into Prussia.
[T]he sad experience acquired by the Civil War* is a warning to the South German
20 population that the recurrence of a similar misfortune can alone be obviated* by the establishment of a United Germany under one supreme head, with a national representation forming the link of union between the several States.
In my humble opinion a great stride has been made to the attainment of this aim,

rapidity speed
elated extremely happy and excited

propitious [prə'pɪʃəs] favourable

Civil War the Austro-Prussian War
to obviate to avert, to prevent

and the rapid course of events will force Prussia – if not at present, at no distant date – willingly or unwillingly, to rally* the nation round her standard, and to put herself at the head of Germany.

Count Bismarck is wise at this moment to restrict his ambition to the acquirement of Northern Germany. Prussia could not now risk a war with France, and without a collision with her no German unity will be established.

But there is another motive which must weigh powerfully with Count Bismarck – viz.*, a wish not to endanger the advantages already acquired. If at this moment the Imperial crown were offered to the King of Prussia, with the Constitution voted by the National Assembly at Frankfort in 1849, and with the Electoral Law passed by that Assembly, the whole internal system of government in Prussia would be submerged. [...]

For these reasons, therefore, Count Bismarck will resist to the utmost any pressure which may seek to drive him beyond the limits of the preliminaries agreed to at Nikolsburg*, and he will be contented with the creation of a great and powerful Prussia, without aiming to place the Imperial crown on the head of his Sovereign. I may observe that Count Bismarck has passed through with wonderful success one phase of his ambitious undertaking – namely, that of "Demolition." The second phase is about to commence* – namely, the work of Reconstruction. In carrying out this latter phase, Count Bismarck will encounter great difficulties – difficulties, however, which his energy and iron will may succeed in overcoming. The exigencies* of a theoretically constitutional, but a practically absolute, monarchy – the reactionary tendency of a triumphant military party – the strong "particularist" feelings in the dispossessed States, which are not uprooted in a day – the fanaticism of a feudal class, whose political opinions are associated with a past age – and the active pressure of the Progressist* [sic] party, undaunted* by defeat, will severely test the statesmanship, the skill, and the patience of Count Bismarck. [...] Bold in conception and energetic in action, unrestrained by scruples and unmoved by principles, governing by fear where he could not win by love, this intrepid*, dexterous*, and powerful Minister has now in his hands the most important part which, perhaps, has ever fallen to the lot of a statesman to fill. On the success of his policy will not only depend the future greatness and prosperity of his country, but also the maintenance of the security and peace of Europe.

from: Lord Augustus Loftus: The Diplomatic Reminiscences of Lord Augustus Loftus, Second Series, 1862–1879, London: Cassell 1894, Vol. 1, pp. 39, 43–45, 60, 69, 99, 105–108. (original British spelling and syntax)

S 43 The Ems Telegram

When the Spanish Queen Isabella II was deposed in 1868, the Spanish crown was offered to Prince Leopold, a relative of the Prussian King from the Hohenzollern dynasty. Bismarck was clearly in favour of the candidature, but the French found it completely unacceptable, fearing a "Prussian puppet" on the Spanish throne. That is why the French ambassador to Prussia, Count Benedetti, spoke about this matter with King William in Bad Ems. Heinrich Abeken, a close advisor to the king, sent a telegram to Bismarck to inform him about the events, which has come to be known as the "Ems Telegram" or "Ems Dispatch". The version which Bismarck edited before publication triggered the outbreak of the Franco-Prussian War since it provoked the French in such a way that the French King was forced to give in to public demands and to declare war on the North German Confederation.

---

to rally to gather people in order to support a cause

viz. [vɪz] namely

the preliminaries agreed at Nikolsburg the preliminary peace between Austria and Prussia

to commence to begin

exigencies [ˈeksɪdʒ(ə)nsi] difficulties, requirements, urgent needs/demands

Progressist Progressive Party (cf. S 50)
undaunted determined and not afraid to continue doing sth., even though it might be difficult
intrepid brave, courageous
dexterous skillful

S 43a The Original Version

The given source is provided to you in both German as well as English because it is easier to understand by comparing the original and its translation (you will probably find the English translation easier to understand). The following tasks are meant to promote your understanding of this – admittedly – difficult source.

Tasks

1. In a first step, identify who is writing to whom, on whose behalf, and who the people mentioned in the source are. Some help is given in the box below.

   > **Heinrich Abeken:** Prussian representative of the Department of Foreign Affairs
   > - Writes to whom, and on whose behalf (= who told him to write on his behalf)?
   > - Which lines in the source contain Abeken's own words to XX?
   >
   > **Bismarck:** ? (= your Excellency)
   >
   > **H. M. (His Majesty):** ?
   > - In which lines in the source does Abeken quote H. M. directly?
   >
   > **Count Benedetti:** ?
   >
   > **the Prince:** Prince Leopold of Hohenzollern-Sigmaringen (cf. introductory remarks)
   >
   > **Count Eulenburg:** Prussian Minister of the Interior

2. In a second step, reconstruct the events as related by Abeken by answering the given questions:
   - What does Benedetti ask H. M. to promise on the promenade, and in which manner?
   - How does H. M. react to this request, and what reason(s) does he give for his reaction?
   - Why does H. M. refuse to see Benedetti a second time, and what does he ask his aide-de-camp to tell him?

3. Now, explain what one can already conclude from the source as regards the following questions:
   - What has already happened as regards the Hohenzollern Candidature, and how much do the French know about the current state of affairs?
   - How does H. M. see the task of the Prussian government in dealing with the Candidature?
   - Why does H. M. find further talks with the French ambassador superfluous?

4. Compare the German and the English version. Identify problems of or differences in translation and discuss which version you find more accessible, and why.

The Ems Telegram, from Heinrich Abeken to Bismarck (13 July 1870)

His Majesty writes to me: 'Count Benedetti spoke to me on the promenade, in order to demand from me, finally in a very importunate manner, that I should authorise him to telegraph at once that I bound myself for all fu-
5 ture time never again to give my consent if the Hohenzollerns should renew their candidature. I refused at last somewhat sternly, as it is neither right nor possible to undertake engagements of this kind *à tout jamais*. Naturally I told him that I had as yet received no news,
10 and as he was earlier informed about Paris and Madrid than myself, he could clearly see that my government once more had no hand in the matter.' His Majesty has since received a letter from the Prince. His Majesty having told Count Benedetti that he was awaiting news
15 from the Prince, has decided, with reference to the above demand, upon the representation of Count Eulenburg and myself, not to receive Count Benedetti again, but only to let him be informed through an *aide-de-camp*: That His Majesty had now received from the
20 Prince confirmation of the news which Benedetti had already received from Paris, and had nothing further to say to the ambassador. His Majesty leaves it to your Excellency whether Benedetti's fresh demand and its rejection should not be at once communicated both to our
25 ambassadors and in the press.

Wolfgang Windelband, Werner Frauendienst: Bismarck. Die gesammelten Werke, Vol. 6 b (1869–1871), Berlin: Deutsche Verlags-Gesellschaft ²1931, pp. 369, 371

Die Emser Depesche, von Heinrich Abeken an Bismarck (13. Juli 1870)

S. M. der König schreibt mir: 'Graf Benedetti fing mich auf der Promenade ab, um auf zuletzt sehr zudringliche Art zu verlangen, ich sollte ihn autorisieren, sofort zu telegraphieren, dass ich für alle Zukunft mich verpflichte, niemals wieder meine Zustimmung zu geben, 5 wenn die Hohenzollern auf ihre Kandidatur zurückkämen. Ich wies ihn, zuletzt etwas ernst, zurück, da man *à tout jamais* dergleichen Engagements nicht nehmen dürfe noch könne. Natürlich sagte ich ihm, dass ich noch nichts erhalten hätte und, da er über Paris und 10 Madrid früher benachrichtigt sei als ich, er wohl einsähe, dass mein Gouvernement wiederum außer Spiel sei.' S. M. hat seitdem ein Schreiben des Fürsten bekommen. Da S. M. dem Grafen Benedetti gesagt, dass er Nachricht vom Fürsten erwarte, hat Allerhöchstder- 15 selbe, mit Rücksicht auf die obige Zumutung, auf des Grafen Eulenburg und meinen Vortrag beschlossen, den Grafen Benedetti nicht mehr zu empfangen, sondern ihm nur durch seinen Adjutanten sagen zu lassen, dass S. M. jetzt vom Fürsten die Bestätigung der Nach- 20 richt erhalten, die Benedetti aus Paris schon gehabt, und dem Botschafter nichts weiter zu sagen.

S. M. stellt Ew. Exzellenz anheim, ob nicht die neue Forderung Benedettis und ihre Zurückweisung sogleich sowohl unseren Gesandten als in der Presse mitgeteilt 25 werden sollte.

from: L.D. Steefel: Bismarck, the Hohenzollern Candidacy, and the origins of the France-German War of 1879, Harvard 1962, pp. 257 f., reprinted in: Michael Gorman: The Unification of Germany. Cambridge Topics in History, Cambridge: Cambridge University Press 31994, pp. 84 f.

S 43b) The Edited Version

Before Bismarck had the Ems Telegram published, he carefully edited it, and his version eventually caused such anger and resentment among the French that they declared war on the North German Confederation.

Pre-tasks 1. Read Bismarck's description of the amendment given here. Make an educated guess as to the changes made by Bismarck that turned the Ems Telegram into "an answer to a challenge".

> **Bismarck's description of the amendment:**
> "[Several] considerations, conscious and unconscious, strengthened my opinion that war could be avoided only at the cost of the honour of Prussia and of the national confidence of it. [...] I reduced the telegram by striking out words, but without adding or altering [...]. After I had read out the con-

centrated edition to my guests, Moltke* remarked: 'Now it has a different ring; it sounded before like a parley*; now it is like a flourish in answer to a challenge.' [...]"

Michael Gorman: The Unification of Germany. Cambridge Topics in History, Cambridge: Cambridge University Press ³1994, pp. 85 f.

Moltke Chief of the Prussian General Staff • **parley** [pɑː(r)li] a meeting, usually between enemies, to discuss an agreement, negotiation, confab, conversation

2. Based on your ideas from task 1, edit the Ems Telegram in a way that makes it sound like an insult to the French. You are not allowed to write more than 100 words. Use a poster or a transparency to present, compare and discuss your results in class.

Tasks

3. Analyse the edited version by answering the following questions:
   - Does the text still contain the essential facts?
   - What has been omitted?
   - Is the order still the same, or has Bismarck changed something? If there are changes in order, what is the intended/achieved effect?
   - What changes in language contribute to a change in tone?
4. Explain why the edited version of the Ems Telegram caused the Franco-Prussian War.

Nachdem die Nachrichten von der Entsagung* des Erbprinzen* von Hohenzollern der Kaiserlich Französischen Regierung von der Königlich Spanischen amtlich*
5 mitgeteilt worden sind, hat der französische Botschafter in Ems an S.M. den König noch die Forderung gestellt, ihn zu autorisieren, dass er nach Paris telegrafiere, dass S.M. der König sich für alle Zu-
10 kunft verpflichte*, niemals wieder seine Zustimmung* zu geben, wenn die Hohenzollern auf ihre Kandidatur wieder zurückkommen sollten. Seine Majestät der König hat es darauf abgelehnt, den franzö-
15 sischen Botschafter nochmals zu empfangen, und demselben durch den Adjutanten vom Dienst* sagen lassen, dass S.M. dem Botschafter nichts weiter mitzuteilen* habe.

from: Wolfgang Lautermann, Manfred Schlenke (Ed.): Geschichte in Quellen. Das bürgerliche Zeitalter 1815–1914, ed. by Günter Schönbrunn, München: Bayerischer Schulbuch-Verlag 1980, p. 356

Bismarck's edited version of the Ems Telegram, page 1

Entsagung renunciation
Erbprinz hereditary Prince

amtlich official(ly)

sich für alle Zukunft verpflichten to bind oneself for all time
Zustimmung consent

Adjutant vom Dienst aide-de-camp [ˌeɪd də ˈkɑːmp] on duty
mitteilen to communicate

Frederick III
Diary Entry

S 44

The source at hand is an excerpt from a diary entry the Prussian Crown Prince Frederick and later German Emperor (crowned 1888) wrote during the Franco-Prussian War.

Pre-tasks

1. The cartoon at hand, entitled *"Deutschlands Zukunft"*, was published in the Austrian journal *Kikeriki* in 1870. Explain the message the cartoonist conveys, considering the picture, the title and the caption. Do not neglect the fact that it is an Austrian cartoon from 1870 (Wars of Unification).

"Germany's Future"
Embedded text: „Kommt es unter einen Hut? Ich glaube, 's kommt eher unter eine Pickelhaube!"

Language support

Reichsadler imperial eagle • **nach etw. greifen** to catch hold of sth.

2. Considering that it is the Prussian Crown Prince himself who is writing this given source, what do you expect <u>him</u> to write about the Wars of Unification, and, in particular, the Franco-Prussian War? Hypothesize.

Tasks

3. Briefly sum up the Crown Prince's assessment of Germany's current situation and point out his criticism of Bismarck.

4. Take a critical stand on Frederick III's view "dass Deutschland ohne Blut und Eisen, allein mit seinem guten Recht, moralische Eroberungen machen und einig, frei und mächtig werden könne" (ll. 6 ff.), and on the priority he places on the respect that could be gained through the achievements of German culture, science and the German mind.

Post-task 5. Gather evidence from this sub-chapter for and against the thesis that Bismarck was a war-monger. Then give a balanced assessment of this thesis.

Was nützt uns alle Macht, aller kriegerische Ruhm und Glanz*, wenn Hass und Misstrauen* uns überall begegnen, wenn man jeden Schritt uns argwöhnisch* missgönnt*, den wir in unserer Entwicklung vorwärts tun? Bismarck hat uns groß und mächtig gemacht, aber er raubte uns unsere Freunde, die Sympathien der Welt und unser gutes Gewissen. Ich beharre* noch heute fest bei der Einsicht*, dass Deutschland ohne Blut und Eisen, allein mit seinem guten Recht, moralische Eroberungen machen und einig, frei und mächtig werden könne. Dann erlangte es ein ganz anderes Übergewicht als lediglich durch die Gewalt der Waffen, weil deutsche Kultur, deutsche Wissenschaft und deutsches Gemüt* uns Achtung*, Liebe und Ehre eintragen.

Jean Rudolf von Salis: Weltgeschichte der neuesten Zeit, Bd. 1, Basel ²1959, p. 27

Ruhm und Glanz glory and glamour
Misstrauen distrust
argwöhnisch distrustful, mistrustful
missgönnen to begrudge
beharren (auf) to insist (on)
Einsicht insight, awareness, wisdom, understanding

Gemüt mind
Achtung respect

S 45 Thomas Nast
"How is this for High?"

The given cartoon by the American cartoonist Thomas Nast was published in the American political magazine *Harper's Weekly* on 7 January 1871. It shows the crowning of King William I of Prussia as Emperor of Germany, a Germany that, according to the artist, was "tailored" by Bismarck. King Ludwig II of Bavaria, who is depicted holding the mirror for William I, only joined in the Franco-Prussian War in July 1870. In December 1870, in a public letter, he proposed the creation of a unified German Empire, at Bismarck's urgent request to do so.

Pre-tasks 1. Both then and now, Bismarck has often been called the "father" or "architect" of Germany's unification. Can you think of reasons for this? Discuss.
2. The given cartoon is an American one. What can you conclude from this fact as regards the rise of Germany and international politics? Make an educated guess.

Tasks 3. Analyse the source.
4. Explain what the cartoon reveals about the artist's view of Bismarck on the one hand, and of Emperor William I on the other hand. Include the composition of the picture in your considerations here, especially the sizes of the two people in question.
5. Evaluate the cartoonist's decision to present Bismarck as the "tailor" of Germany. Consider the denotation as well as possible connotations of "tailor" in your evaluation (and, of course, the historical context).

Post-task 6. As mentioned in task 1, various metaphors are used when speaking about Bismarck's role in the process of Germany's unification. In class, revise what you have learned about the unification of Germany so far and find a metaphor which you find most appropriate to characterize Bismarck and his role in this process.

Depicted people (from left to right):
Bismarck • William I • King Ludwig II of Bavaria

"HOW IS THIS FOR HIGH?"

Language support

Müllkorb trash basket, wastepaper basket •
schneidern to tailor

S 46 Anton von Werner

The Imperial Proclamation of the German Empire

On 18 January 1871, the Second German Empire was proclaimed in the Hall of Mirrors in Versailles. The Prussian King William I thus became Emperor William I. The artist Anton von Werner was present at the event and not only created one of the most famous paintings in history, but also described the proclamation in his reminiscences.

Pre-task 1. All in all, there are three versions of von Werner's famous painting. The first one dates back to 1877 (the so-called *Schlossfassung*) and was a present of the Grand Duke of Baden and other princes on the occasion of Emperor William I's 80th birthday. It was destroyed during the Second World War. The second version is a woodcut from 1880, and the third version shown here in S 46a was commissioned by the Prussian royal family as a present for Bismarck's 70th birthday in 1885. How do you expect this background to influence the way Bismarck is portrayed in the painting, and why? Discuss.

Tasks 2. Describe the painting and its composition in detail.
3. Connect your results from tasks 1 and 2: how is the fact that this version was a present for Bismarck's birthday reflected in the way he is portrayed in the painting? What can you conclude as regards the way his role in the process of Germany's unification is seen?
4. Compare the artistic presentation of the proclamation of the German Empire with von Werner's eye-witness account of the events. (cf. S 46b)

5. Do further research on the "flaws" in the painting. Focus on: Bismarck's uniform, the decoration he is wearing, the presence of Moltke ... and further "flaws" you can find. Based on your results, including your findings from tasks 1 to 4, discuss what students of history must consider when analysing portraits as "windows to the past". Double-check your ideas with the help of the skills pages (How to analyse portraits, pp. 582 f.).

Post-task 6. Find the other two versions of the painting (cf. task 1) on the Internet and bring them to class. Split up into three groups, each group dealing with one of the paintings. Together, design a freeze frame that shows the relationships and hierarchies between the people depicted. Present and explain your freeze frames in class. Afterwards, evaluate which version you believe to be closest to reality, and why.

S 46a The Friedrichsruh Version

The given version is dubbed the "Friedrichsruh version" since, in view of the fact that it was originally a present for Bismarck's birthday, it could, and can still today, be found at his former estate, Friedrichsruh.

Labels on the painting:
- Emperor William I
- Crown Prince Frederick
- Grand Duke Frederick I of Baden
- Bismarck
- Chief of the General Staff Moltke
- Prussian War Minister von Roon

Language support

Empore gallery • **Stufen** steps • **Läufer** carpet, rug • **jubeln** to cheer

S 46b Erlebnisse und Eindrücke

In his *"Erlebnisse und Eindrücke 1870–1890"*, Anton von Werner describes his impressions of the proclamation of the Second Empire in the Hall of Mirrors in Versailles.

prunklos without pomp
Kürze brevity

hölzern stiff, formal
Vertiefung absorption
Großherzog Grand Duke
siegreich victorious
Er lebe hoch! Long may he live!
Donnergetöse thundering roar
Geklirr clinking, clanging

Und nun ging in prunklosester* Weise und außerordentlicher Kürze* das große historische Ereignis vor sich [...]. Ich wandte ihm meine gespannteste Aufmerksamkeit zu, notierte in aller Eile das Nötigste, sah, dass König Wilhelm etwas sprach, und dass Graf Bismarck mit hölzerner* Stimme etwas Längeres vorlas, hörte aber nicht, was es bedeutete, und erwachte aus meiner Vertiefung* erst, als 5 der Großherzog* von Baden neben König Wilhelm trat und mit lauter Stimme in den Saal hineinrief: 'Seine Majestät, Kaiser Wilhelm der Siegreiche*, Er lebe hoch*!' Ein dreimaliges Donnergetöse* unter dem Geklirr* der Waffen antwortete darauf [...]; von unten her antwortete wie ein Echo sich fortpflanzend das Hurra der dort aufgestellten Truppen. Der historische Akt war vorbei: es gab wieder ein 10 Deutsches Reich und einen Deutschen Kaiser.

Anton von Werner: „Erlebnisse und Eindrücke 1870–1890", from: Rüdiger Hachtmann, Joachim Rohlfes, Volker Ullrich: Deutsche Geschichte. Wie wir wurden, was wir sind. 19. Jahrhundert 1789–1918, Stuttgart: Klett 2002, p. 180

S 47 Benjamin Disraeli

On the "German Revolution"

On 9 February 1871, less than a month after the proclamation of the German Empire on 18 January 1871, the British politician and former (and future) Prime Minister Benjamin Disraeli (cf. also chapter 2: "New" Imperialism) delivered a speech in which he talked about the importance of the rise of Germany for Europe.

Pre-task
1. Disraeli calls the creation of the Second Empire the "German revolution". (l. 5) Anticipate whether he connotes the term positively or negatively. Give reasons for your ideas.

Tasks
2. Sum up Disraeli's view on the "German revolution". Then relate your results to task 1.
3. Explain his statement that "[t]here is no diplomatic tradition which has not been swept away [by Germany]" (ll. 9 f.) against the historical background of the Wars of Unification.
4. Examine why Disraeli, respectively the British, were worried about the rise of Germany in central Europe.
5. The Franco-Prussian War and the subsequent proclamation of the German Empire in the Hall of Mirrors in Versailles (where usually the French kings were crowned) laid the foundation for the alleged Franco-German "hereditary/ancestral enmity" (*Erbfeindschaft*). Explain.
6. Thinking back to the sub-chapter about the 1848/9 revolutions and your definition of the term "revolution", discuss to what extent, if at all, the unification of Germany qualifies as a "revolution", taking into account that it has been dubbed a unification "from above".

Post-task 7. Bismarck was well aware of the worries and fears the rise of Germany created on the continent. Anticipate from previous history classes how he might attempt to lessen these worries and fears by means of foreign policy.

Let me impress upon the attention of the House the character of this war between France and Germany. It is no common war, like the war between Prussia and Austria, or like the Italian war in which France was engaged some years ago; nor is it like the Crimean War*.
5 This war represents the German revolution, a greater political event than the French revolution of last century. I don't say a greater, or as great a social event. What its social consequences may be are in the future. Not a single principle in the management of our foreign affairs, accepted by all statesmen for guidance up to six months ago, any longer exists. There is not a diplomatic tradition which has not
10 been swept away. You have a new world, new influences at work, new and unknown objects and dangers with which to cope, at present involved in that obscurity* incident to novelty in such affairs. We used to have discussions in this House about the balance of power. Lord Palmerston*, eminently a practical man, trimmed the ship of State and shaped its policy with a view to preserve an equilibrium* in
15 Europe. [...] But what has really come to pass? The balance of power has been entirely destroyed, and the country which suffers most, and feels the effects of this great change most, is England.

Hansard Parliamentary Debates, Ser. III, Vol. CCIV, February–March 1871, speech of February 9, 1871, pp. 81–82, original English text reprinted in: William Flavelle Moneypenny, George Earle Buckle: The Life of Benjamin Disraeli, Earl of Beaconsfield, Vol. 2: 1860–1881, London: John Murray 1929, pp. 473–74

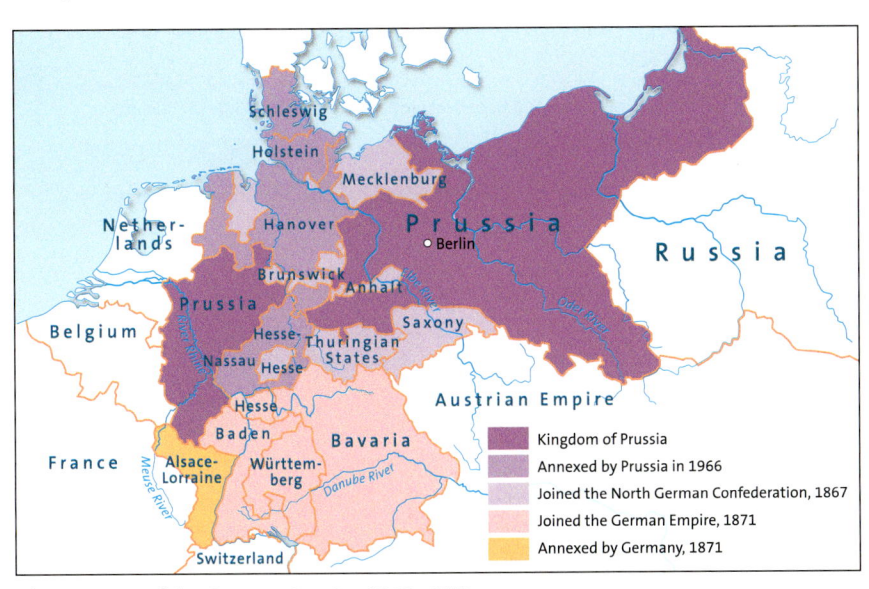

Crimean War (1853–1856) lost by Russia against a coalition of France, Britain, the Ottoman Empire and Sardinia (immediate trigger: rights of Christians in the Holy Land, at that time controlled by the Ottoman Empire)
obscurity a state in which a person or thing is not well known
Lord Palmerston (1784–1865) former British foreign secretary and PM, who stood for the idea of a balance of power in Europe
equilibrium a situation in which there is a balance between different forces or aspects

The creation of the German Empire, 1866–1871

S 48 Lord Odo Russell

Letter to Lord Granville (Excerpts)

On 11 February 1873, the British ambassador in Berlin Lord Odo Russell wrote a confidential letter to Lord Granville, the British Secretary of State for Foreign Affairs, in which he described a meeting with Bismarck.

Pre-task 1. In the box below, you find the beginning and the end of Russell's letter in which he describes the atmosphere of the meeting. Describe the atmosphere and make an educated guess as to Bismarck's intentions in the meeting.

> Prince Bismarck asked me this evening after dinner to come and smoke a Pipe with him in his sitting room. I did so, and found him alone. He said he wished to talk to me on various subjects but as he preferred in his dealings with me to speak with perfect freedom instead of with that diplomatic reserve which the dread of our Blue Books* imposed on Foreign Ministers conversing with English Diplomatists he hoped I would grant him the favour of reporting him privately and not officially. [...]
>
> He then rang his bell, called for a bottle of Beer and another Pipe and went on [...] to repeat his grievance against his Imperial Master for resisting the introduction of a new system of administration under a responsible Premier as in England which he (Prince Bismarck) considered the best method of developing the political education of the Germans and teaching them the art of Self government [sic].
>
> _{Hansard Parliamentary Debates, Ser. III, Vol. CCIV, February–March 1871, speech of February 9, 1871, pp. 81–82, original English text reprinted in: William Flavelle Moneypenny, George Earle Buckle: The Life of Benjamin Disraeli, Earl of Beaconsfield, Vol. 2: 1860–1881, London: John Murray 1929, pp. 473–74}
>
> **Blue Books** handbooks about the correct mode of conduct for British diplomats

Tasks
2. Analyse the source (formal analysis and structured outline of content).
3. Examine Bismarck's intentions, with reference to your results from task 1.
4. Put yourself into the shoes of the addressee of this letter, Lord Granville. You are to report the contents of the letter to the Prime Minister (in 1873: William Ewart Gladstone). Write Granville's report in which you evaluate the sincerity of Bismarck's intentions.

private i. e. confidential

Private.*
Berlin, 11 February 1873.
Dear Lord Granville,
Prince Bismarck asked me this evening after dinner to come and smoke a Pipe with him in his sitting room. I did so, and found him alone. He said he wished to talk to me on various subjects but as he preferred in his dealings with me to speak with perfect freedom instead of with that diplomatic reserve which the dread of our Blue Books imposed on Foreign Ministers conversing with English Diplomatists he

hoped I would grant him the favour of reporting him privately and not officially. –
In the first instance he wished to solicit my cooperation in contradicting calumny*. – It had been reported to him that the Queen of Holland who, for incomprehensible reasons of her own, was a bitter enemy of Prussia and of German Unity, had succeeded during her frequent visits to England in propagating the idea that Prussia sought to annex the Netherlands with a view to acquiring Colonies and a Fleet for Germany [...]. [Bismarck said that] this idea was utterly unfounded. No German Government could ever desire, nor would public opinion ever consent to the annexation of the Netherlands to the German Empire. Germany had long struggled for national unity and now that it was happily established, he thought forty millions of united Germans were sufficient to maintain the national independence they had acquired without having to resort to the conquest of peaceful, industrious and friendly neighbours like the Dutch.
He neither desired Colonies nor Fleets for Germany. [...] Germany was now large enough and strong enough in his opinion, and even the Emperor William's insatiable* desire for more territory had not led him to covet* the possession of the Netherlands.
He had trouble & vexation* enough to combat the Emperor's desire to annex the German Provinces of Austria, the population of which certainly desired to form part of the great German Family, but that desire he would oppose so long as he was in power, because he preferred the Alliance and friendship of Austria to the annexation of Provinces that would add nothing to the strength and security of Germany and the loss of which would lessen the value of Austria as an ally. [...]
After the Danish War the Emperor had not spoken to him for a week so displeased he was His Majesty with him for not having annexed a larger portion of Denmark. – In his opinion Germany had too many Danish speaking subjects and he would willingly pay out of his own pocket to rid Germany of them, but public opinion would not yet allow a German minister to give up any portion of territory so recently acquired. In like manner he held that Germany had too many Polish subjects, but how to deal with them was a question which must depend on the success of measures now under discussion for the neutralization of the antinational Roman Catholic Element in the new Empire. It was now evident that the strength of Germany was in the Protestant North, – her weakness in the Catholic South. [...]
He then rang his bell, called for a bottle of Beer and another Pipe and went on [...] to repeat his grievance against his Imperial Master for resisting the introduction of a new system of administration under a responsible Premier as in England which he (Prince Bismarck) considered the best method of developing the political education of the Germans and teaching them the art of Self government [sic]. [...]
Sincerely yours,
Odo Russell

from: "British Ambassador to Germany, Lord Odo Russell, Berlin, to British Foreign Secretary Lord Granville, London, February 11, 1873", in Paul Knaplund (Ed.): Letters from the Berlin Embassy, 1871–1874, 1880–1885, Washington D. C.: USGPO, 1944, pp. 87–89

calumny a comment about sb. that is not fair or true and is intended to damage the person's reputation

insatiable never satisfied
to covet to very much want sth. that sb. else has
vexation the feeling of being annoyed, confused, or worried

Domestic Policy in the Second Empire

CONNECT

The 1871 Constitution – A Fig Leaf for Absolutism?

Task Evaluating the nature of the 1871 Imperial Constitution.

The Constitution of the Second German Empire resembled that of the North German Confederation from 1867 in vast parts. Both democratic as well as authoritarian elements can be found in it. Despite the fact that officially, the German Empire was a constitutional monarchy, the question arises whether the 1871 Imperial Constitution was not just a "fig leaf" for absolutism, meaning that a few democratic elements were incorporated in order to conceal the fact that the German Empire was basically an absolutist state, with all the power concentrated in the hands of the Emperor. With the help of S 49a – S 49c, evaluate whether this allegation is justified or not. Write down at least fifteen to twenty statements about the Constitution on slips of paper, one slip for each statement, for example "The Chancellor was only responsible to the Emperor." Use the board to sort the slips into either examples of democratic features or of authoritarian features and evaluate whether the claim that the constitution was a "fig leaf" for absolutism is justified or not.

devolution the process of taking power away from a central authority or government and giving it to smaller and more local bodies

electorate all the people who are allowed to vote in an election

S 49a General Features of Constitutional Democracies

Constitutional democracies are usually characterized by the devolution* of some responsibility to local governments or parliaments, such as for example in the Federal Republic of Germany today where the state parliaments for instance decide on education or other matters for themselves.
A parliament, elected by universal manhood suffrage and by a broad electorate* in periodic and frequent elections, is responsible for the central government, foreign policy, the army and matters of defence. State legislation must be a product of parliamentary processes. Both the government and all government ministers are answerable to parliament and cannot make decisions on their own.

authors' text

S 49b General Features of Authoritarian Monarchies

An authoritarian monarchy is characterized by a heavily centralized government in which there is little or no scope for regional initiative. The monarch is in direct control of major state responsibilities, such as foreign policy, the army and the government of the state.
In general, there is no place for universal manhood suffrage and the electorate, if there is any, is restricted. State legislation derives from the monarch and his/her advisers only, no parliament is involved in this process. The monarch is not required to justify or explain his/her actions and thus not accountable to parliament, if there is one at all.

authors' text

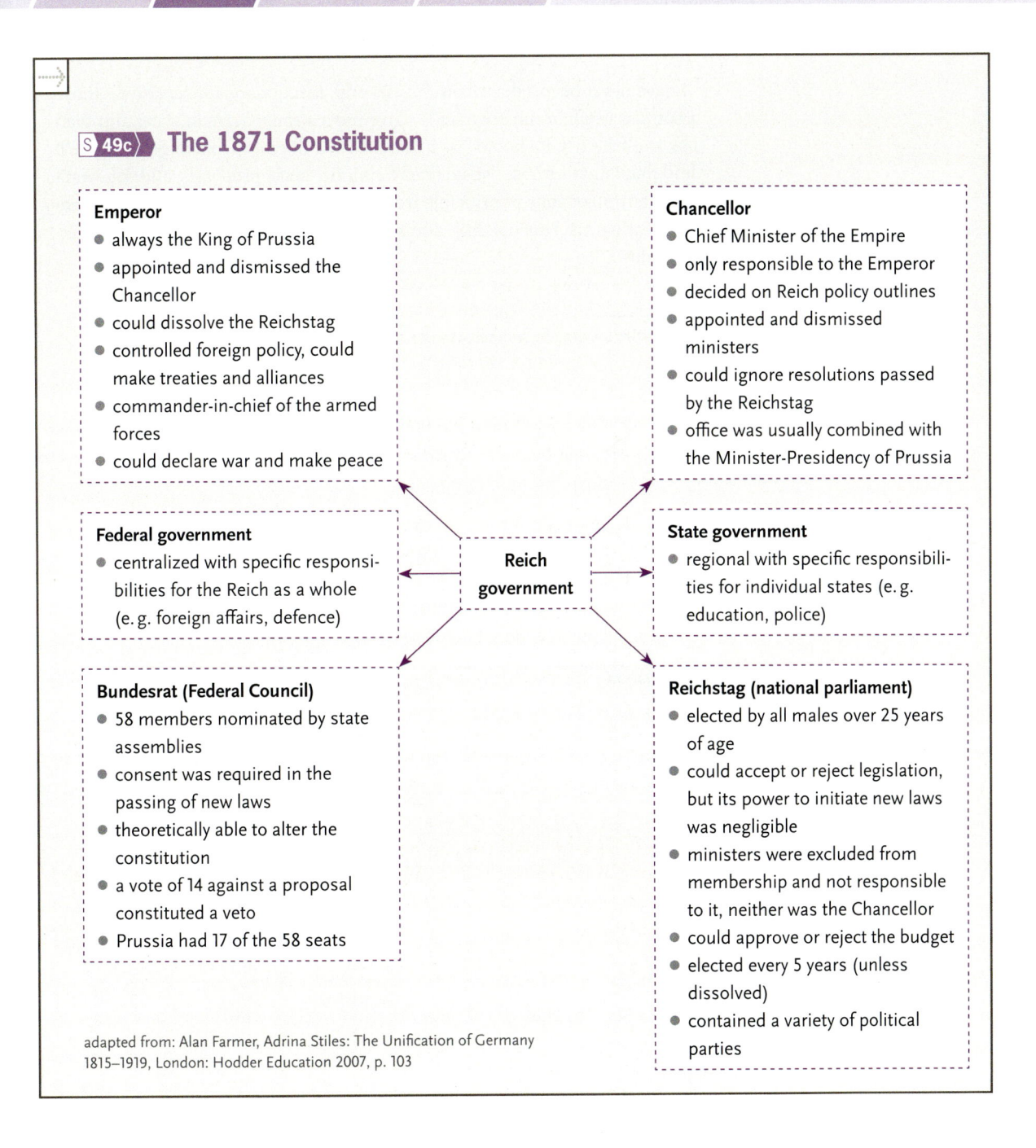

S 49c — The 1871 Constitution

Emperor
- always the King of Prussia
- appointed and dismissed the Chancellor
- could dissolve the Reichstag
- controlled foreign policy, could make treaties and alliances
- commander-in-chief of the armed forces
- could declare war and make peace

Chancellor
- Chief Minister of the Empire
- only responsible to the Emperor
- decided on Reich policy outlines
- appointed and dismissed ministers
- could ignore resolutions passed by the Reichstag
- office was usually combined with the Minister-Presidency of Prussia

Federal government
- centralized with specific responsibilities for the Reich as a whole (e.g. foreign affairs, defence)

Reich government

State government
- regional with specific responsibilities for individual states (e.g. education, police)

Bundesrat (Federal Council)
- 58 members nominated by state assemblies
- consent was required in the passing of new laws
- theoretically able to alter the constitution
- a vote of 14 against a proposal constituted a veto
- Prussia had 17 of the 58 seats

Reichstag (national parliament)
- elected by all males over 25 years of age
- could accept or reject legislation, but its power to initiate new laws was negligible
- ministers were excluded from membership and not responsible to it, neither was the Chancellor
- could approve or reject the budget
- elected every 5 years (unless dissolved)
- contained a variety of political parties

adapted from: Alan Farmer, Adrina Stiles: The Unification of Germany 1815–1919, London: Hodder Education 2007, p. 103

S 50 — The Development of Political Parties

The introduction of universal (male) suffrage across Germany promoted the development of well-organized mass political parties with popular appeal and distinct programmes. However, the origins of political parties are to be found in the Paulskirche Parliament of 1848/49.

Pre-tasks

1. The Bismarck quotation below is taken from a speech he delivered to the Reichstag in 1881. Paraphrase what the quotation reveals about Bismarck's attitude towards political parties.

> "I have never been a doctrinaire* ... Liberal, reactionary, conservative – those I confess seem to me luxuries. ... Give me a strong German state, and then ask me whether it should have more or less liberal furnishings, and you'll find that I answer: Yes, I've no fixed opinions, make proposals, and you won't meet any objections of principle from me. Many roads lead to Rome. Sometimes one must rule liberally, and sometimes dictatorially, there are no eternal rules ..."
>
> D. G. Williamson: Bismarck and Germany 1862–1890, London: Pearson Education ²1998, p. 114

doctrinaire sb. who bases their opinions on very fixed political beliefs, without necessarily considering whether they are practical

Tasks

2. Thinking back to the 1871 Constitution (cf. S 49c), discuss to what extent Bismarck was dependent on the support of political parties to push through his policies.
3. Highlight the key terms which you consider to be crucial in defining the respective party's political programme.
4. Discuss which parties you think Bismarck supported or was opposed to and rank them accordingly from 1 to 6, 6 being most opposed. Be prepared to explain your choices.

		Democrats	Liberals		Conservatives
pre-March era and St. Paul's church					
German Empire	Social Democrats (SPD)	Left Liberals (progressive party)	National Liberals	Centre Party	
Weimar Republic	German Communist Party (KPD)	German Democratic Party (DDP)	German People's Party (DVP)		German National People's Party (DNVP) / National Socialist German Worker's Party (NSDAP)
Federal Republic of Germany	the Left (Party)	The Green Party	Free Democratic Party (FDP)	Christian Democratic Union (CDU)	

The development of political parties

The National Liberals The main support for this party was derived from the educated Protestant middle class and the industrial upper class. The party had two principal aims: (a) the creation of a strong nation-state and (b) the encouragement of a liberal constitutional state; the former in practice being the priority.

The Centre Party A political grouping consisting mainly of Catholics worried by the predominance of Protestants in the new state. Their aim was to defend the interests of the Catholic Church. The party also attracted support from the non-socialist lower classes, particularly in the Rhineland and Southern Germany.

The Social Democratic Party	Composed of socialist groups and having close links with the trade unions, this was predominantly a working-class party. Its socialist programme aimed to promote complete democracy in Germany and to fight for social reforms in the interests of the German working masses.
The German Conservative Party	Mainly composed of landowners. They were sceptical about the unification of Germany, preferring the comfortable familiarity of the old separate states.
The Free Conservatives	Drawn from a wider geographical and social base than the German Conservatives. Contained not just landowners but also industrialists and professional and commercial interests. This group accepted Bismarck's unification and the constitution which followed.
The Progressives	A liberal party but one which, unlike the National Liberals, remained opposed to the pursuit of a powerful nation-state at the expense of liberal constitutional principles. Remained committed to the attainment of parliamentary government.

E. Wilmot: The Great Powers 1814–1914. Challenging History, Walton-on-Thames/Surrey: Thomas Nelson & Sons 1992, p. 268

S 51 „Am Steuer"

This cartoon published in June 1879 in the German satirical journal *Kladderadatsch*, pinpoints the cartoonist's view on Bismarck's way of dealing with political parties.

Pre-task
1. The cartoon presents Bismarck at the helm (*am Steuer*) of a ship, symbolically representing the ship of state. What is the cartoonist suggesting with this metaphor, and under which circumstances does the 1871 Constitution provide for such a position on the part of the Chancellor? Discuss.

Tasks
2. Describe the main elements of the cartoon.
3. Explain the message the cartoonist conveys.
4. Compare Bismarck's view of and attitude towards political parties as presented in the cartoon to his speech in the Reichstag in 1881 (cf. S 50 , task 1).

„Am Steuer" ("At the Helm")
Embedded text:
<u>On the spokes:</u> CONSERVATIV, LIBERAL, ULTRAMONTAN
<u>Caption</u> (not given here):
Die liberale Speiche zu den anderen Beiden: Ueberhebt euch nur nicht! Sobald der Wind sich dreht, bin ich wieder oben.

Language support

Speiche spoke • **am Steuer** at the helm • **ultramontan** – referring to the Catholic Centre Party (pej.), Ultramontanes believed that the Pope had supreme authority in matters of faith • **überhebt euch nicht** don't get cocky • **sich drehen** to shift

S 52 **Lady Emily Russell**

Letter to Queen Victoria

Lady Emily Russell was married to the British ambassador in Berlin, Lord Odo Russell (cf. S 48). In the letter at hand to Queen Victoria dated 27 December 1880, she complains about Bismarck's rule in Germany.

Pre-task
1. Sort the words and phrases taken from the source into references to either Emperor William I or Bismarck.

> completely under the influence • arbitrary and unconstitutional proceedings • absolute power • signs [documents] without question or hesitation • irresponsible power • terror • tacit and cheerful consent • threatening to resign

Tasks
2. Scan the source for the words and phrases, identify and make notes on their respective contexts and give a structured outline of the source on the basis of these notes.
3. Explain by which means and in which manner Bismarck rules at home, according to Lady Russell, and who enables him to do so. Refer to the 1871 Constitution as well in order to examine why this kind of rule was possible at all. (cf. S 49c)
4. With reference to S 48 and S 51 , give an evaluation of Lady Russell's characterization of Bismarck's "chancellor-dictatorship".
5. In the so-called "Three Emperors' Year" of 1888, William I's grandson William II was to ascend the throne. In how far might this have posed a threat to Bismarck? Make an educated guess.

Post-task
6. Do further research on Britain as the "cradle" of parliamentary government. Important aspects to consider: the Magna Carta (1215), the Petition of Right (1628), the Habeas Corpus Act (1679) and the Bill of Rights (1689). Against this background, discuss possible reasons why Lady Russell would be appalled by the way Bismarck (and thus the Emperor) ruled over Germany.

Lady Emily Russell to Queen Victoria.
British Embassy, Berlin, 27th December 1880.
[...] The Crown Prince honoured me with a visit when he first arrived in Berlin, and Odo saw his Imperial Highness out shooting in the Grünewald, when he was graciously invited by the Emperor to join the chasse* prepared for the King of Saxony and Prince George. We were both struck by his Imperial Highness not looking very well, and everyone thinks him rather low and out of sorts, and noticed that at the Jagdfrühstück in the wood, when the Emperor and the King were more than ever cheerful and gracious, the Crown Prince seemed lost in thought, and took no part in the general conversation which was very lively and interesting. Those who know the Crown Prince well think that he is worried and pained to see the Emperor so completely under the influence of Prince Bismarck, whose policy in regard to home questions and Imperial matters he does not approve of; and he fears that the public will hold his Imperial father responsible for the arbitrary* and unconstitutional proceedings which the Chancellor delights in.

chasse [ʃas] hunt

arbitrary *willkürlich*

The initiated* know that the Emperor, since the horrible attempts of 1878*, has allowed Prince Bismarck to have his own way in everything; and the great Chancellor revels* in the absolute power he has acquired and does as he pleases. He lives in the country and governs the German Empire without even taking the trouble to
20 consult the Emperor about his plans, who only learns what is being done from the documents to which his signature is necessary, and which his Majesty signs without questions or hesitation*. Never has a subject been granted so much irresponsible power from his Sovereign, and never has a Minister inspired a nation with more abject* individual, as well as general, terror before. No wonder, then, that the
25 Crown Prince should be worried at a state of things which he has not more personal power or influence to remedy* than anyone else in Prussia, whilst Prince Bismarck lives and terrorises over Germany from Friedrichsruhe [sic] with the Emperor's tacit* and cheerful consent.

Bismarck has gradually appointed a Ministry of Clerks* out of the Government
30 Offices, who do as they are told by him, and he has so terrified the Bundesrath, by threatening to resign whenever they disagreed with him, that they now vote entirely in obedience to his instructions. He now expects that at the next general election he will, by careful management, obtain the absolute majority he requires to carry through his new taxation and commercial policy.
35 If Bismarck should ever die suddenly from indigestion*, which his doctors fear and predict, the difficulty of reforming the general abuses which his personal administration has created will be great, and will impose a hard and ungrateful task on the Sovereign, who will have to find and appoint the Ministers capable of re-establishing constitutionalism in Prussia. [...]

Lady Emily Russell, Berlin, to Queen Victoria, London, December 27, 1880, original English text published in: George Earle Buckle (Ed.): The Letters of Queen Victoria: A Selection from Her Majesty's Correspondence and Journal Between the Years 1862 and 1885, Second Series, Vol. 3, Toronto: Ryerson Press 1928, pp. 168–70.

the initiated die Eingeweihten
1878 in 1878, Emperor William I was twice shot and injured badly (cf. S 55)
to revel to celebrate, to enjoy

hesitation Zögern

abject used for emphasizing how bad, unpleasant, or severe a situation or condition is
to remedy to correct or improve a situation
tacit ['tæsɪt] expressed or understood without being said directly
clerk [klɑː(r)k] sb. whose job is to look after the documents in an office, court, etc.

indigestion Verdauungsstörung

S 53 ▸ The Struggle for Culture

When tensions in the "Struggle for Culture" increased in the early 1870s, Bismarck, backed by the National Liberals, passed a series of laws against papal influence on German politics, aimed at a separation of Church and State.

Pre-task 1. Why would Bismarck possibly consider Catholics "enemies of the Reich"? Make an educated guess. (Tips: To whom do Catholics owe their loyalty? Can the Pope be wrong? Which parts of the Second Empire were predominantly Catholic?)

Tasks 2. Describe the measures implemented in the Pulpit Law (cf. S 53a) and in the School Law. (cf. S 53b)
3. Explain how they were meant to curb the influence of the Church on matters of state.

Post-task 4. Do research on further measures implemented at this time aiming at a final separation of Church and State. Then check whether the changes which took place in this respect are still valid today.

S 53a The "Pulpit ['pʊlpɪt] Law"

The so-called "Pulpit Law" (*Kanzelparagraph*) was included in Germany's penal ['piːn(ə)l] code on 10 December 1871 (StGB §130a).

Geistlicher cleric
Religionsdiener minister of religion
Angelegenheiten des Staates state affairs
in ... Weise in such a way that it endangers the public peace
Verkündung oder Erörterung announcement or discussion
Festungshaft incarceration

Ein Geistlicher* oder anderer Religionsdiener*, welcher in Ausübung oder in Veranlassung der Ausübung seines Berufes öffentlich vor einer Menschenmenge oder welcher in einer Kirche oder an einem anderen zu religiösen Veranstaltungen bestimmten Orte vor mehreren Angelegenheiten des Staates* in einer den öffentlichen Frieden gefährdenden Weise* zum Gegenstande einer Verkündung 5 oder Erörterung* macht, wird mit Gefängnis oder Festungshaft* bis zu zwei Jahren bestraft.

from: Johannes Baptist Kißling: Geschichte des Kulturkampfes im Deutschen Reiche, Bd. 2, Freiburg: 1911, p. 460 ff.

S 53b The School Law

The School Law (*Gesetz betreffend die Beaufsichtigung des Unterrichts- und Erziehungswesens*) was passed on 11 March 1872.

Aufhebung annulment
entgegenstehende Bestimmungen contrary regulations
Aufsicht supervision
Unterrichts- und Erziehungsanstalten school and educational institutions
Lokal- und Kreisschulinspektoren local and district school inspectors

§1. Unter Aufhebung* aller in einzelnen Landesteilen entgegenstehenden Bestimmungen* steht die Aufsicht* über alle öffentlichen und Privat-Unterrichts- und Erziehungsanstalten* dem Staate zu. [...]
§2. Die Ernennung der Lokal- und Kreisschulinspektoren* und die Abgrenzung 5 ihrer Aufsichtsbezirke gebührt dem Staate allein.

from: Johannes Baptist Kißling: Geschichte des Kulturkampfes im Deutschen Reiche, Bd. 2, Freiburg: 1911, p. 460 ff.

S 54 „Zwischen Berlin und Rom"

This cartoon was published in the German satirical magazine *Kladderadatsch* in 1875, the year in which the "Struggle for Culture" had reached its peak.

Pre-task
1. What kinds of skills does playing chess require, and what does the fact that the cartoonist portrays Bismarck and Pope Pius IX playing chess tell you? Hypothesize.

Tasks
2. Analyse the source.
3. Incorporate the source into the historical context of the Struggle for Culture and explain the elements of the cartoon.
4. Taking into consideration the immediate outcome of the Struggle for Culture as well as the long-term impact on Germany (cf. S 53), task 4), take a critical stand on the cartoonist's portrayal of the situation in the game.

Language support

Schachzug move, manoeuvre • **Schachpartie** chess match • **unangenehm** unpleasant • **etwas in petto haben** to have sth. up one's sleeve • **schachmatt** checkmate • **Schachfigur** chess piece

Zwischen Berlin und Rom.
Der letzte Zug war mir allerdings unangenehm; aber die Partie ist deshalb noch nicht verloren. Ich habe noch einen sehr schönen Zug in petto!
Das wird auch der letzte sein, und dann sind Sie in wenigen Zügen matt —— wenigstens für Deutschland.

Depicted people:
Bismarck and Pope Pius IX
Embedded text:
„Der letzte Zug war mir allerdings unangenehm; aber die Partie ist noch nicht verloren. Ich habe noch einen sehr schönen Zug in petto! Das wird auch der letzte sein, und dann sind Sie in wenigen Zügen matt – wenigstens für Deutschland."
on the box: Internirt (arrested) • on the Pope's black chess pieces: Syllabus Errorum (a list of errors) Enzyklika (i. e. "Quod nunquam", directed against the anti-clerical laws) Interdikt (threat of ecclesiastical punishment) • on Bismarck's white chess pieces: Klostergesetz (i. e. dissolution of monasteries in Prussia) Presse

S 55 The Anti-Socialist Laws

Bismarck had made several attempts to curtail the growth of German Social Democracy during the 1870s – for instance through restrictions on the press. But his opponents successfully resisted almost all of these measures, and the number of votes cast for socialist candidates in Reichstag elections continued to increase. Then, in May and June 1878, two attempts were made on the life of Kaiser Wilhelm I, who was badly injured in the second attack. Bismarck blamed the Social Democratic Party and immediately announced new elections to the Reichstag. The newly elected house was more conservative than its predecessor and passed the law reproduced below on October 21.

Pre-tasks

1. Why would Bismarck possibly consider the Social Democrats "enemies of the Reich"? Make an educated guess. (TIPS: What kind of state would Social Democrats prefer? Who should rule? In how far is Socialism international rather than national, and what would Bismarck find dangerous about that?)
2. The official title of the law was "Law against the Publicly Dangerous Endeavours [ɪn'devə(r)] of Social Democracy". What could be meant by "publicly dangerous endeavours" (*gemeingefährliche Bestrebungen*)? Discuss.

Tasks

3. Describe by which means Bismarck attempted to curtail the alleged "publicly dangerous endeavours".
4. Compare the Anti-Socialist Laws to the Carlsbad Decrees of 1819 (cf. S 18). Where can you detect commonalities and/or differences in terms of means and objectives?

Post-task

5. Colloquially speaking, Bismarck's way of treating socialism has been called the "carrot and stick" method (*Zuckerbrot und Peitsche*), with the Anti-Socialist Laws representing the "stick". What could be the "carrot" then? Collect ideas in class.

Gesetz gegen die gemeingefährlichen Bestrebungen* der Sozialdemokratie

§ 1. [1] Vereine, welche durch sozialdemokratische, sozialistische und kommunistische Bestrebungen den Umsturz der bestehenden Staats- oder Gesellschaftsordnung* bezwecken, sind zu verbieten. [...]

§ 9. [1] Versammlungen, in denen sozialdemokratische, sozialistische oder kommunistische auf den Umsturz der bestehenden Staats- und Gesellschaftsordnung gerichtete Bestrebungen zutage treten, sind aufzulösen. [...]

§ 11. [1] Druckschriften*, in welchen sozialdemokratische, sozialistische oder kommunistische auf den Umsturz der bestehenden Staats- und Gesellschaftsordnung gerichtete Bestrebungen in einer den öffentlichen Frieden, insbesondere die Eintracht der Bevölkerungsklassen* gefährdende Weise zutage treten, sind zu verbieten. [...]

§ 17. [1] Wer an einem verbotenen Vereine (§ 6.) als Mitglied sich beteiligt oder eine Tätigkeit im Interesse eines solchen Vereins ausübt, wird mit Geldstrafe* bis zu fünfhundert Mark oder mit Gefängnis bis zu drei Monaten bestraft. Eine gleiche Strafe trifft denjenigen, welcher an einer verbotenen Versammlung (§ 9.) sich beteiligt [...]. [2] Gegen diejenigen, welche sich an dem Vereine oder an der Versammlung als Vorsteher, Leiter, Ordner, Agenten, Redner oder Kassierer* beteiligen oder welche zu der Versammlung auffordern*, ist auf Gefängnis von einem Monat bis zu einem Jahre zu erkennen.

§ 18. Wer für einen verbotenen Verein oder für eine verbotene Versammlung Räumlichkeiten hergibt*, wird mit Gefängnis von [...] bis zu einem Jahr bestraft.

§ 19. Wer eine verbotene Druckschrift (§§ 11, 12) oder wer eine von der vorläufigen Beschlagnahme betroffene Druckschrift (§ 15) verbreitet, fortsetzt oder wieder abdruckt*, wird mit Geldstrafe bis zu eintausend Mark oder mit Gefängnis bis zu sechs Monaten bestraft.

Rüdiger vom Bruch, Björn Hofmeister (Ed.): Deutsche Geschichte in Quellen und Darstellung, Bd. 8: Kaiserreich und Erster Weltkrieg 1871–1918, Stuttgart: Reclam 2002, p. 50 f.

German cartoon ridiculing Bismarck's attempts to push the Anti-Socialist Laws through the Reichstag

Emperor William I of Germany (1797–1888)

William I was born in Berlin on 22 March 1797. He began his military career when his father, King Frederick William III of Prussia, appointed him officer of the Prussian army. His participation in the Wars of Liberation against Napoleon instilled a deep hatred of France in him which was to stamp him for the rest of his life.

Since his older brother Frederick William IV remained childless, William became his official successor after Frederick William's accession to the throne in 1840. In 1849, William took over a leading role in the counter-revolution and helped to strike down the insurrectionists. In 1861, upon Frederick William IV's death, William became Prussian king. One year later, he appointed Bismarck as minister-president of Prussia to solve a constitutional crisis over the army bill. In both the German-Danish War and the Austro-Prussian War, William was commander-in-chief of the Prussian forces and presided over the newly founded North German Confederation. In 1870, he led the German forces in the decisive Battle of Sedan and was then proclaimed Emperor of the German Empire on 18 January 1871. The running of the affairs of state was usually left to his chancellor, Bismarck. William himself concentrated more on representing the new Empire.

William survived two assassination attempts on his life in 1878, which were taken as a pretext by Bismarck to push the Anti-Socialist Laws through the Reichstag.

After a short illness, William died in Berlin on 9 March 1888. He was succeeded by his terminally ill son Frederick III, who was to die only 99 days later and who was in turn succeeded by William I's grandson William II.

S 56 — Emperor William I

Royal Proclamation on Social Policy

A programme of social reforms was announced in this Royal Proclamation (*Kaiserliche Botschaft*) of 17 November 1881 which can be considered Europe's first labour protection acts.

Pre-task
1. Emperor William I claims he is convinced that the remedying of disturbances in the social system cannot solely be achieved by the suppression of "Social Democratic excesses" (l. 5) but must also be sought by the promotion of workers' welfare (here in the form of labour protection acts). In how far is this part of the "carrot-and-stick" policy? Make an educated guess.

Tasks
2. Outline the measures that are to be negotiated in the Reichstag and point out the reasons for the Emperor's decision.
3. Discuss to what extent William I can be considered to be merely Bismarck's mouthpiece when it comes to the fight against Social Democracy.

Wir Wilhelm, von Gottes Gnaden* Deutscher Kaiser, König von Preußen etc., tun kund und fügen hiermit zu wissen*:
[...] Schon im Februar dieses Jahres haben Wir Unsere Überzeugung aussprechen lassen, dass die Heilung der sozialen Schäden* nicht ausschließlich im Wege der
5 Repression sozialdemokratischer Ausschreitungen*, sondern gleichmäßig auf dem der positiven Förderung des Wohles* der Arbeiter zu suchen sein werde. Wir halten es für Unsere Kaiserliche Pflicht, dem Reichstage diese Aufgabe von Neuem ans Herz zu legen*. [...]

von Gottes Gnaden by the grace of God
tun ... wissen announcing and hereby decreeing for all to know
Heilung der sozialen Schäden here in the sense of: the remedying/righting of disturbances in the social system
Ausschreitungen excesses
Förderung des Wohles promotion of welfare
ans Herz legen to recommend warmly

Betriebsunfall industrial accident
Verhandlungen debate
Vorlage bill
gewerbliches Krankenkassenwesen commercial health insurance system
erwerbsunfähig werden to become unfit for gainful employment
begründeter Anspruch legitimate claim
staatliche Fürsorge state welfare

In diesem Sinne wird zunächst der von den verbündeten Regierungen in der vorigen Session vorgelegte Entwurf eines Gesetzes über die Versicherung der Arbeiter gegen Betriebsunfälle* mit Rücksicht auf die im Reichstag stattgehabten Verhandlungen* über denselben einer Umarbeitung unterzogen, um die erneute Beratung desselben vorzubereiten. Ergänzend wird ihm eine Vorlage* zur Seite treten, welche sich eine gleichmäßige Organisation des gewerblichen Krankenkassenwesens* zur Aufgabe stellt. Aber auch diejenigen, welche durch Alter oder Invalidität erwerbsunfähig werden*, haben der Gesamtheit gegenüber einen begründeten Anspruch* auf ein höheres Maß staatlicher Fürsorge*, als ihnen bisher hat zuteil werden können.

Rüdiger vom Bruch, Björn Hofmeister (Ed.): Deutsche Geschichte in Quellen und Darstellung, Bd. 8: Kaiserreich und Erster Weltkrieg 1871–1918, Stuttgart Reclam 2002, p. 54f.

Emperor William II of Germany (1859–1941)

William II was born in Berlin on 27 January 1859 as the son of Prince Frederick William of Prussia, later Emperor Frederick III, and his wife Victoria, Princess Royal of England. The British Queen Victoria was therefore William II's grandmother. The difficult birth caused his left arm to be withered.

When his father died shortly after his accession to the throne in the "Three Emperors' Year" 1888, William II became German Emperor and King of Prussia.

Since William II and Bismarck had different views on how to handle domestic policy, William requested Bismarck to resign on 18 March 1890, which the latter did the following day.

In 1898, the build-up of the German navy began under Alfred von Tirpitz. William, who had uttered the German wish for a "place in the sun", meaning that Germany should also participate in the striving for overseas colonies, supported the naval build-up, which was conceived as an instrument of German colonial or imperial policy. Since Britain had, up to then, been the most important seafaring nation, this naval build-up put a strain on British-German relations, and led later on to a naval arms race between the two countries (cf. chapter 2).

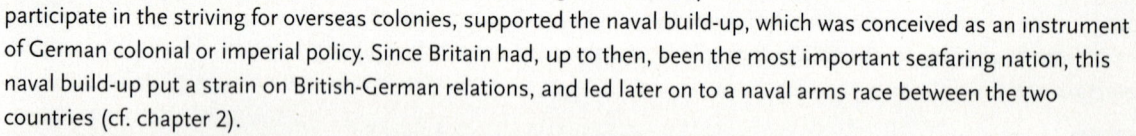

In contrast to Bismarck, William II was not very diplomatic in terms of foreign policy, especially in relation to England. In 1896, for example, he congratulated Boer President Paulus Kruger for having successfully resisted English attacks in the Transvaal region. This so-called Kruger Telegram triggered massive criticism of the Kaiser in England. Moreover, his reign saw a drastic change of the system of alliances carefully constructed by Bismarck. Since William did not renew the Reinsurance Treaty with Russia, Bismarck's 'nightmare of coalitions' finally came about, with two blocs of power opposing each other: the Triple Alliance made up of Germany, Austria and Italy, and the Triple Entente, made up of Great Britain, France and Russia. This can also be traced back to William's bellicose "New Course" in German foreign policy (also cf. chapter 2).

After the outbreak of the First World War, William II called for solidarity and a closing of ranks. However, when Hindenburg and Ludendorff took over the Supreme Command of the army, William more and more lost influence in the field of military matters.

After Chancellor Max von Baden had acted without authority and had proclaimed the abdication of the Emperor on 9 November 1918, William fled to Spa in the Netherlands the next day and here he remained in exile until his death on 4 June 1941.

S 57 Emperor William II

Royal Decree on Reformed School Instruction

This Royal Decree (*kaiserlicher Erlass*) of 1 May 1889 (one year before Bismarck's resignation) postulates the political education of elementary school pupils and the inclusion of contemporary political issues in the curriculum. The rise of Social Democracy in the years before had convinced the Emperor that even the youngest had to be taught to recognize the threats that these alleged "enemies of the Reich" posed. William II wanted the workers to trust in their monarch's beneficence instead.

Pre-task

1. In his Royal Decree, William II states: *"Aber Ich kann Mich der Erkenntnis nicht verschließen, dass in einer Zeit, in welcher die sozialdemokratischen Irrtümer und Entstellungen mit vermehrtem Eifer verbreitet werden, die Schule zur Förderung der Erkenntnis dessen, was wahr, was wirklich und was in der Welt möglich ist, erhöhte Anstrengungen zu machen hat."* (ll. 6 ff.)
Taking into account what you have learned/know about William II, discuss what, to him, might be "true, real and possible".

Tasks

2. With the help of the text, complete the following sentences:
   - The characteristics of Social Democracy are …
   - Schools must … because …
   - The Prussian Kings have always …
   - The best state system is … because …
3. Imagine you were a teacher at Emperor William II School, presented with the Royal Decree. Write a draft for the next teachers' conference at which a new curriculum will be decided on. Copy and fill in the table below.

   Draft curriculum for Emperor William II School

Indispensable topics to be discussed in class:	Objectives:

4. Evaluate the effectiveness of combating Social Democracy with the help of a school reform.
5. Discuss if this Royal Decree is more associated with the category of the "carrot" or the "stick".

Schon längere Zeit hat Mich der Gedanke beschäftigt, die Schule in ihren einzelnen Abstufungen* nutzbar zu machen, um der Ausbreitung sozialistischer und kommunistischer Ideen entgegenzuwirken. In erster Linie wird die Schule durch Pflege der Gottesfurcht* und der Liebe zum Vaterlande die Grundlage für eine
5 gesunde Auffassung* auch der staatlichen und gesellschaftlichen Verhältnisse zu legen haben. Aber Ich kann Mich der Erkenntnis nicht verschließen*, dass in einer Zeit, in welcher die sozialdemokratischen Irrtümer und Entstellungen* mit vermehrtem Eifer* verbreitet werden, die Schule zur Förderung der Erkenntnis dessen, was wahr, was wirklich und was in der Welt möglich ist, erhöhte Anstren-
10 gungen zu machen hat. Sie muss bestrebt sein*, schon der Jugend die Ueberzeugung zu verschaffen, dass die Lehren* der Sozialdemokratie nicht nur den göttli-

Abstufung grade level
Pflege der Gottesfurcht cultivating the fear of God
gesunde Auffassung healthy view
sich verschließen to not deny
Irrtümer und Entstellungen errors and distortions
Eifer zeal

bestrebt sein to strive for
Lehren teachings

Vocabulary:

göttliche Gebote holy commandments
christliche Sittenlehre Christian ethics
unausführbar unfeasible
verderblich detrimental (to) [ˌdetrɪˈment(ə)l]
neue und neueste Zeitgeschichte modern and contemporary history
Staatsgewalt authority of the state
zum Bewusstsein bringen to make aware (of)
heben to improve
Aufhebung der Leibeigenschaft abolition of serfdom
Lohn- und Lebensverhältnisse working-class incomes and living standards
vaterländische Geschichte the history of the fatherland
Gesetzgebung legislation
auf ... Bevölkerung the population that depends on the work of their hands/manual labour
landesväterlicher Schutz fatherly state protection
leibliches und geistliches Wohl physical and spiritual welfare
Fürsorge safeguarding
geordneter Staat well-organized state
Standpunkt der Nützlichkeit utilitarian perspective
unerlässliche Vorbedingung essential prerequisite [prɪːˈrekwəzɪt]
Gedeihen flourishing
Häuslichkeit domestic life

---

chen Geboten* und der christlichen Sittenlehre* widersprechen, sondern in der Wirklichkeit unausführbar* und in ihren Konsequenzen dem Einzelnen und dem Ganzen gleich verderblich* sind. Sie muss die neue und die neueste Zeitgeschichte* mehr als bisher in den Kreis der Unterrichtsgegenstände ziehen und nachweisen, dass die Staatsgewalt* allein dem Einzelnen seine Familie, seine Freiheit, seine Rechte schützen kann, und der Jugend zum Bewusstsein bringen*, wie Preußens Könige bemüht gewesen sind, in fortschreitender Entwickelung [sic] die Lebensbedingungen der Arbeiter zu heben*, von den gesetzlichen Reformen Friedrichs des Großen und von Aufhebung der Leibeigenschaft* an bis heut. Sie muss ferner durch statistische Thatsachen nachweisen, wie wesentlich und wie konstant in diesem Jahrhundert die Lohn- und Lebensverhältnisse* der arbeitenden Klassen unter diesem monarchischen Schutze sich verbessert haben. [...]
Die vaterländische Geschichte* wird insonderheit auch die Geschichte unserer sozialen und wirtschaftlichen Gesetzgebung* und Entwickelung seit dem Beginne dieses Jahrhunderts bis zu der gegenwärtigen sozialpolitischen Gesetzgebung zu behandeln haben, um zu zeigen, wie die Monarchen Preußens es von jeher als ihre besondere Aufgabe betrachtet haben, der auf die Arbeit ihrer Hände angewiesenen* Bevölkerung den landesväterlichen Schutz* angedeihen zu lassen und ihr leibliches und geistliches Wohl* zu heben, und wie auch in Zukunft die Arbeiter Gerechtigkeit und Sicherheit ihres Erwerbes nur unter dem Schutze und der Fürsorge* des Königs an der Spitze eines geordneten Staates* zu erwarten haben. Insbesondere vom Standpunkt der Nützlichkeit*, durch Darlegung einschlagender praktischer Verhältnisse, wird schon der Jugend klar gemacht werden können, dass ein geordnetes Staatswesen mit einer sicheren monarchischen Leitung die unerlässliche Vorbedingung* für den Schutz und das Gedeihen* des Einzelnen in seiner rechtlichen und wirtschaftlichen Existenz ist, dass dagegen die Lehren der Sozialdemokratie praktisch nicht ausführbar sind, und wenn sie es wären, die Freiheit des Einzelnen bis in seine Häuslichkeit* hinein einem unerträglichen Zwange unterworfen würde.

H. Schulthess (Ed.): Kaiserlicher Erlaß vom 1. Mai 1889, Europäischer Geschichtskalender, 1890, p. 166, from: Gerhard A. Ritter, Jürgen Kocka (Ed.): Deutsche Sozialgeschichte 1870–1914. Dokumente und Skizzen, München: Beck ³1982, p. 333–34

S 58 Heinrich von Treitschke

Die Juden sind unser Unglück

Heinrich von Treitschke (1834–1896) was a nineteenth-century historian who was also a National Liberal member of the Reichstag in the 1870s, famous for his multi-volume "History of Germany." In the excerpt below published on 15 November 1879, Treitschke elaborates on the alleged threats the Jews pose for the Germans. Since 1871, Jews in Germany had the same rights as everyone else, but nonetheless they were subject to discrimination and anti-Semitic hostilities.

Pre-task 1. As you know, anti-Semitism is not a new phenomenon in history, but it gained a new and political dimension in the Second Empire. Revise what you have learned about the history of anti-Semitism in class (e.g. the pogroms in the wake of the Crusade of the Poor in the Middle Ages, the Black Death in the 14th century, Nazi Germany): what were Jews often accused of, and why?

Tasks

2. Outline Treitschke's line of argument which leads him to the conclusion that "the Jews are [the Germans'] misfortune." (ll. 33 f.)
3. Explain which common accusations and prejudices against Jews are mirrored in the given source.
4. Against the backdrop of what you have learned about the Janus-faced quality of the phenomenon of nationalism, evaluate to what extent the source at hand exemplifies the negative aspects of nationalism.
5. Make an educated guess: would Treitschke be in favour of or against Bismarck's policies? Give reasons for your ideas.

Post-task

6. Do further research on the so-called *Berliner Antisemitismus-Streit* (1879–1881) and view S 58 in this context.

Was wir von unseren israelitischen Mitbürgern* zu fordern haben, ist einfach: Sie sollen Deutsche werden, sich schlicht und recht* als Deutsche fühlen – unbeschadet* ihres Glaubens und ihrer alten heiligen Erinnerungen, die uns allen ehrwürdig sind*; denn wir wollen nicht, dass auf Jahrtausende germanischer Gesittung*
5 ein Zeitalter deutsch-jüdischer Mischkultur* folge. Es wäre sündlich* zu vergessen, dass sehr viele Juden, getaufte und ungetaufte*, [...] deutsche Männer waren im besten Sinne, Männer, in denen wir die edlen und guten Züge deutschen Geistes verehren. Es bleibt aber ebenso unleugbar*, dass zahlreiche und mächtige Kreise unseres Judentums* den guten Willen, schlechtweg Deutsche zu werden,
10 durchaus nicht hegen. [...] Ich glaube jedoch, mancher meiner jüdischen Freunde wird mir mit tiefem Bedauern Recht geben, wenn ich behaupte, dass in neuester Zeit ein gefährlicher Geist der Überhebung* in jüdischen Kreisen erwacht ist, dass die Einwirkung* des Judentums auf unser nationales Leben, die in früheren Tagen manches Gute schuf, sich neuerdings vielfach schädlich* zeigt. [...]

20 Überblickt man all diese Verhältnisse – und wie vieles ließe sich noch sagen! –, so erscheint die laute Agitation des Augenblicks doch nur als eine brutale und gehässige*, aber natürliche Reaktion des
25 germanischen Volksgefühls* gegen ein fremdes Element, das in unserem Leben einen allzu breiten Raum eingenommen hat. [...] Bis in die Kreise der höchsten Bildung hinaus, unter Männern, die jeden
30 Gedanken kirchlicher Unduldsamkeit* oder nationalen Hochmuts* mit Abscheu von sich weisen würden, ertönt es heute wie aus einem Munde*: Die Juden sind unser Unglück*!

Heinrich von Treitschke: Unsere Aussichten, Preußische Jahrbücher 44, Berlin: Reimer 1879, from: Der „Berliner Antisemitismusstreit" 1879–1881 (Teil 1), ed. by Karsten Krieger, München: K.G. Saur 2003, p. 12–14

Heinrich von Treitschke, 1876

israelitische Mitbürger Israelite fellow citizens
schlicht und recht simply
unbeschadet notwithstanding, regardless of
ehrwürdig sein to hold in reverence
germanische Gesittung Germanic morality
Mischkultur hybrid culture
sündlich sinful
(un)getauft (un)baptized
unleugbar undeniable
Judentum Jewry
Überhebung arrogance
Einwirkung influence
schädlich harmful

gehässig hateful
Volksgefühl racial feeling

kirchliche Unduldsamkeit church intolerance
nationaler Hochmut national arrogance
ertönt ... Munde there rings with one voice
Unglück misfortune

S 59 Theodor Mommsen

Auch ein Wort über unser Judenthum

In this text, the liberal historian Theodor Mommsen (1817–1903) responds to Treitschke and his view that the Jews are Germany's "misfortune".

Pre-task 1. Skim S 58 and your notes on the tasks one more time. Then collect arguments in class to rebut Treitschke.

Tasks 2. Outline the line of argument Mommsen used to disprove Treitschke.
3. Explain Mommsen's remark that Jews have twice committed the original sin. (cf. ll. 10 f.)
4. Discuss to what extent, from a present-day perspective, Mommsen could be called "tolerant".

Post-task 5. Is the overall balance of Bismarck's domestic policy more a success or a failure? Revise what you have learned in this sub-chapter and give an evaluation.

Wahn delusion
erfassen to take hold of
tugendhaft virtuous
jdm. etw. zur Last legen to charge sb. with sth.
streichen to delete
scharf severe
Milderungsgrund extenuating [ɪkˌstenjʊeɪtɪŋ] circumstance
sich hinwegsetzen to ignore
Erbsünde original sin
Okzidentale occidental (Occident = *Abendland*)
Klarheit und Milde clarity and clemency
eine gefährliche Bahn betreten to step on a dangerous path
Stamm tribe
gegenseitig mutual
Alte Liebe rostet nicht. An old flame never dies.
Pommer Pomeranian
Windbeutelei deception
ungeschickt unintelligent
untergraben to undermine

Das ist der eigentliche Sitz des Wahnes*, der jetzt die Massen erfasst* hat, und sein rechter Prophet ist Hr. v. Treitschke. Was heißt das, wenn er von unseren israelitischen Mitbürgern fordert, sie sollen Deutsche werden? Sie sind es ja, so gut wie er und ich. Er mag tugendhafter* sein als sie; aber machen die Tugenden den Deutschen? Wer gibt uns das Recht, unsere Mitbürger dieser oder jener Kategorien wegen der Fehler, welche im Allgemeinen dieser Kategorie, es sei auch mit Recht, zur Last gelegt werden*, aus der Reihe der Deutschen zu streichen*? Wie scharf* man die Fehler dieser Mitbürger empfinden, wie schroff man über alle Milderungsgründe* sich hinwegsetzen* mag, immer wird man logisch wie praktisch höchstens dahin kommen, die Juden für Deutsche zu erklären, welche im Punkte der Erbsünde* doppelt bedacht worden sind. [...]
Es muss in der Auffassung der Ungleichheit, welche zwischen den deutschen Okzidentalen* und dem semitischen Blut allerdings besteht, größere Klarheit und Milde* kommen. Wir, die eben erst geeinte Nation, betreten mit dem Judenkrieg eine gefährliche Bahn*. Unsere Stämme* sind recht sehr ungleich. Es ist keiner darunter, dem nicht spezifische Fehler anhaften, und unsere gegenseitige* Liebe ist nicht so alt, dass sie nicht rosten könnte*. Heute gilt es bei den Juden [...]. Morgen wird vielleicht bewiesen, dass genau genommen jeder Berliner besser sei als ein Semit. Noch etwas weiter hin, und der Pommer* fordert die Erstreckung der Statistik auf die Windbeutelei* und hofft, durch Zahlen zu beweisen, dass dann in den westlichen Provinzen ein doppelter Prozentsatz herausgestellt werde. Es wäre das nicht der ungeschickteste* Weg, um die Einheit unserer Nation zu untergraben*.

Theodor Mommsen: Auch ein Wort über unser Judenthum, Berlin 1880, from: Der "Berliner Antisemitismusstreit" 1879–1881 (Teil 1), ed. by Karsten Krieger, München: K.G. Saur 2003, p. 700 f.

Foreign Policy in the Second Empire

S 60 ▶ The Kissingen Dictation

The so-called "Kissingen Dictation" (*Kissinger Diktat*) sketches the principles of Bismarck's foreign policy. It is a memorandum which Bismarck dictated on 15 June 1877 while spending time in the spa town of Bad Kissingen.

Pre-task
1. In the Kissingen Dictation, Bismarck talks about his "nightmare of coalitions". Have a look at a map of Europe and anticipate what form of alliance would constitute that nightmare for Bismarck, and why.

Tasks
2. Identify Bismarck's "nightmare of coalitions".
3. Based on the text, propose alliances and agreements the Second Empire should make to prevent the "nightmare of coalitions" from coming true.

Ein französisches Blatt* sagte neulich von mir, ich hätte 'le cauchemar des coalitions'*; diese Art Alp wird für einen deutschen Minister noch lange, und vielleicht immer, ein berechtigter bleiben.
Koalitionen gegen uns können auf westmächtlicher Basis mit Zutritt Österreichs
5 sich bilden, gefährlicher vielleicht noch auf russisch-österreichisch-französischer; eine große Intimität zwischen zweien der drei letztgenannten Mächte würde der dritten unter ihnen jederzeit das Mittel* zu einem sehr empfindlichen Drucke* auf uns bieten. In der Sorge vor diesen Eventualitäten*, nicht sofort, aber im Lauf der Jahre, würde ich als wünschenswerte* Ergebnisse der orientalischen Krisis
10 [cf. S 61 ▶] für uns ansehn*:
Gravitierung* der russischen und der österreichischen Interessen und gegenseitigen Rivalitäten nach Osten hin, der Anlass für Russland, eine starke Defensivstellung im Orient und an seinen Küsten zu nehmen, und unseres Bündnisses zu bedürfen*, für England und Russland ein befriedigender status quo, der ihnen
15 dasselbe Interesse an Erhaltung des Bestehenden gibt, welches wir haben, die Loslösung* Englands von dem uns feindlich bleibenden Frankreich wegen Ägyptens und des Mittelmeers, Beziehungen zwischen Russland und Österreich, welche es beiden schwierig machen, die antideutsche Konspiration gegen uns gemeinsam herzustellen, zu welcher zentralistische oder klerikale* Elemente in
20 Österreich etwa geneigt* sein möchten.
Wenn ich arbeitsfähig wäre, könnte ich das Bild vervollständigen und feiner ausarbeiten, welches mir vorschwebt*: nicht das irgend eines Ländererwerbes*, sondern das einer politischen Gesamtsituation*, in welcher alle Mächte außer Frankreich unser bedürfen, und von Koalitionen gegen uns durch ihre Beziehungen
25 zueinander nach Möglichkeit abgehalten* werden.

Institut für Auswärtige Politik in Hamburg (Ed.): Die Auswärtige Politik des Deutschen Reiches 1871–1914, Bd. I, Berlin: Deutsche Verlagsgesellschaft für Politik 1928, p. 58 f.

Blatt newspaper
le cauchemar des coalitions the nightmare of coalitions

Mittel means
empfindlicher Druck severe pressure
Eventualität contingency
wünschenswert desirable
ansehen to consider
Gravitierung here: concentration
bedürfen to need

Loslösung dissociation

klerikal clerical (relating to the Church)
geneigt inclined (towards sth.)
vorschweben to have sth. in mind
Ländererwerb acquisition of territory
Gesamtsituation overall situation
abhalten to keep from (doing sth.)

S 61 The "Honest Broker"

The Berlin Congress of June/July 1878 was held with the purpose of settling a dispute between Austria-Hungary and Russia about the so-called "Oriental Question", meaning the gradual decline of the Ottoman Empire and resulting territorial claims on the part of the European powers. Every conflict in that region had the potential to become a European war, which is why the Berlin Congress was of vital importance. Bismarck mediated between the powers, playing the role of the "honest broker" (*ehrlicher Makler*), a strategy which he had announced would be his intention in a speech about the forthcoming Berlin Congress delivered on 19 February 1878.

Pre-task 1. The given painting by Anton von Werner depicts the final meeting of the Congress in the Reich Chancellery on 13 July 1878. Relate the introductory remarks to the painting: In how far is Bismarck represented as an "honest broker" here?

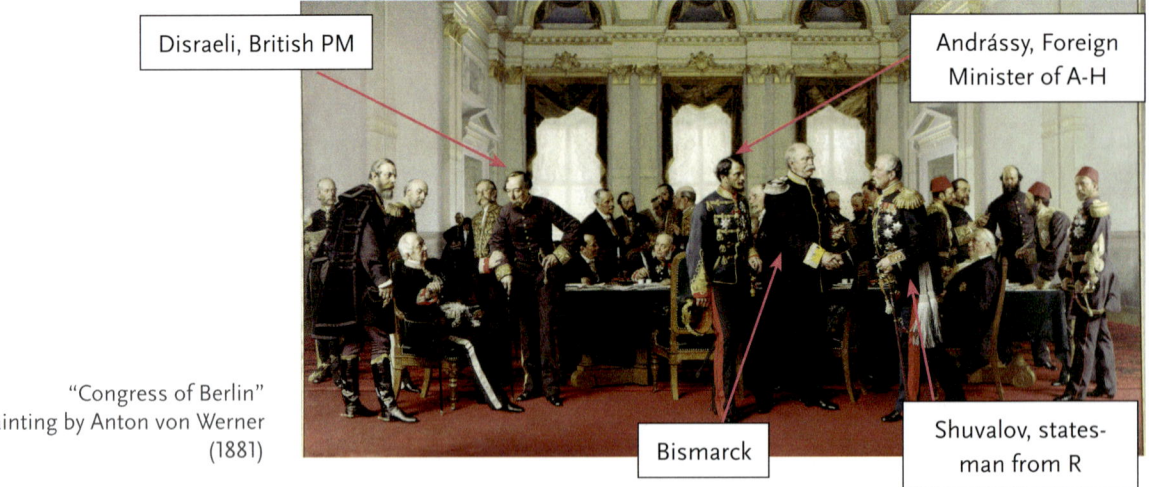

"Congress of Berlin"
Painting by Anton von Werner (1881)

Disraeli, British PM
Andrássy, Foreign Minister of A-H
Bismarck
Shuvalov, statesman from R

Tasks 2. Against the backdrop of the source, use your exercise book and write a thought bubble for Bismarck.
3. Taking into consideration what you have learned about Bismarck so far, take a critical stand on the notion of him as an "honest broker".

Vermittlung mediation
Schiedsrichter here: conciliator, adjudicator, arbitrator
bescheiden modest
ehrlicher Makler honest broker
ein Geschäft zustande bringen to make a deal
langjährig long-standing
fällt der Faden roughly: negotiations get stuck
Scham shame
verstimmt disgruntled

Die Vermittlung* des Friedens denke ich mir nicht so, dass wir nun bei divergierenden Ansichten den Schiedsrichter* spielen und sagen: So soll es sein, und dahinter steht die Macht des Deutschen Reiches, sondern ich denke sie mir bescheidener*, ja – [...] – mehr die eines ehrlichen Maklers*, der das Geschäft wirklich zustande bringen* will. [...]
Ich habe eine langjährige* Erfahrung in diesen Dingen und habe mich oft überzeugt: wenn man zu zweien ist, fällt der Faden öfter*, und aus falscher Scham* nimmt man ihn nicht wieder auf. Der Moment, wo man den Faden wieder aufnehmen könnte, vergeht, und man trennt sich in Schweigen und ist verstimmt*. Ist aber ein Dritter da, so kann dieser ohne weiteres den Faden wieder aufnehmen, ja, wenn getrennt, bringt er sie wieder zusammen. Das ist die Rolle, die ich mir denke.

Otto von Bismarck: Gesammelte Werke (alte Friedrichsruher Ausgabe), 19 Bde., 1924–1933, Bd. 11, p. 526 f.

S 62 William Carr

Bismarck's Foreign Policy, 1871–1890

William Carr (1921–1991) was a British historian of modern Germany. In the given excerpt from his major work "A History of Germany. 1815–1990", he outlines and evaluates Bismarck's foreign policy, especially his system of alliances.

Pre-task 1. Revise what kinds of alliances you envisaged the Second Empire might make in order to prevent the "nightmare of coalitions". (cf. S 60, task 3).

Tasks 2. Copy the country constellation below and, with the help of the overview section as well as the given secondary source, connect the countries with the respective alliances under Bismarck. Use different colours and design a map key as well, outlining the mutual obligations the different alliances would imply as well as Bismarck's motivation in concluding them.

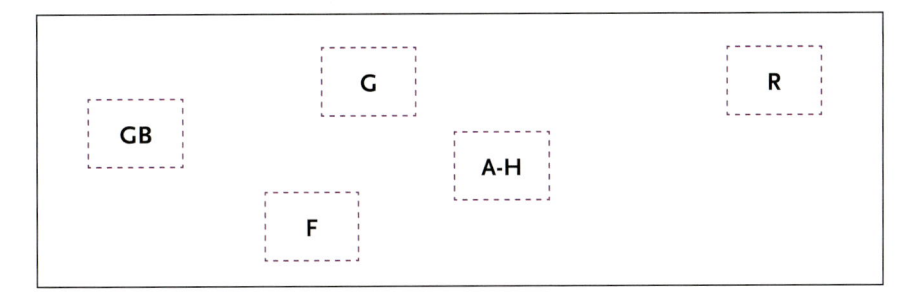

```
                G                           R

   GB
                      A-H

            F
```

3. Compare Bismarck's system of alliances with your ideas and make any necessary changes. Also, explain why you thought similarly or differently.
4. Carr concludes that even though "Bismarck was a past master in diplomatic arts, […] [h]is bullying tactics […] poisoned international relations in this period." (ll. 81 ff.) Take a critical stand on the question whether Bismarck's foreign policy consolidated peace or paved the way for disaster.

How could Bismarck contain the French and avoid a fresh conflagration*? A means lay close at hand. Bismarck had helped to disrupt the old understanding between Austria, Prussia and Russia in order to make Prussia dominant in Germany. Once his purpose was accomplished, the chancellor's instinct as a conserva-
5 tive was to restore the 'entente à trois'. The revival of France confirmed his instinct; a three emperors' league would keep France quiet and preserve the status quo in the east, where all three had Polish subjects to keep in order. Friendship with Russia was essential for geographical reasons as well; Germany faced the real danger of war on two fronts if she was on bad terms with France and Russia simultane-
10 ously. As relations with France were bad, the line to St. Petersburg had to remain open. […] The friendship of Austria was important to Germany not only because it deprived France of a potential ally, but because it gave Bismarck a welcome degree of independence in his dealings with Russia. […]
What happened in the Balkans was of relatively little interest to Bismarck, who

conflagration a very large fire that causes a lot of damage

once remarked that the area was not worth 'the healthy bones of a single Pomeranian musketeer'. Russia could do as she pleased with the Turk as long as she acted in accord with Austria-Hungary. But the effect on Germany's international position of any serious disagreement between Russia and Austria-Hungary mattered a great deal. For if Germany was compelled to choose between them, the rejected suitor* would find a willing ally in France, and an obscure Balkan dispute would quickly develop into a general conflagration. This 'cauchemar des coalitions'*, as Bismarck once called it, was a perpetual* danger because of the resentment France bore Germany. [...]

[W]hen Russo-German relations deteriorated rapidly in the first half of 1879 [because of the crisis in the Balkans], [...][Bismarck met Andrassy, the Austrian foreign minister, in Bad Gastein] and discussed a formal alliance with Austria-Hungary. At first Bismarck proposed an ambitious all-embracing alliance against aggression, to be sanctioned by both parliaments. Andrassy rejected this because he saw no reason why Austria-Hungary should become involved in disputes between Germany and France. Bismarck, anxious that Austria should not succumb to* Russian pressure, or, worse still, look to France for support, gave way. In October 1879 the formal alliance was signed. It was a straightforward defensive alliance committing Germany and Austria-Hungary to resist Russian aggression; but if Germany or Austria-Hungary was at war with a third power, the other partner would remain neutral unless Russia intervened. In effect Germany was bound to aid Austria-Hungary in the event of a Russian attack but Austria-Hungary was not bound to support Germany against France. [...]

By the end of 1879 Russia was thoroughly alarmed by her diplomatic isolation and anxious for an understanding with Germany [...] and in 1881 the Three Emperors' Alliance was signed [by Germany, Austria-Hungary and Russia]. [...] It stated that if one of the three powers was at war with a fourth, the others would remain neutral. [...]

In 1882 Bismarck acquired a new and unexpected ally in Italy [...]. The [Triple] Alliance [between Germany, Austria-Hungary and Italy] was of five years' duration and committed the signatories to uphold the monarchical principle and the existing social and political order. More specifically the three partners agreed to aid each other if one or more was attacked, without provocation on their part, by two or more powers. [...]

Much controversy has surrounded [the Reinsurance] treaty [between Germany and Russia]. [...] The agreement was very limited in scope. During the negotiations Russia wanted each power to remain neutral if the other was at war with a third power; in effect Russia wanted a free hand against Austria, in return for which she offered Germany a free hand against France. But Bismarck refused and told Russia that under the 1879 treaty Germany could remain neutral only if Austria-Hungary attacked Russia; if Russia was the aggressor, Germany was bound to aid Austria-Hungary. On learning this, Russia would only promise neutrality if France attacked Germany; if Germany was the aggressor, Russia would not promise to stay neutral. Thus the element of 'reinsurance' was slight [...]. In a highly secret protocol to the Reinsurance treaty Bismarck had promised moral and diplomatic support for Russia if she took measures to protect her interests at the Straits*; he also promised to support her in Bulgaria [...].

[I]n December 1887 the Second Mediterranean Agreement was signed [by Austria, Italy and Great Britain]; in this secret pact the three powers pledged themselves to

uphold the status quo in the Near East, at the Straits, in Asia Minor and in Bulgaria [...]. Bismarck gave his blessing to the agreement and helped it along actively behind the scenes, for in this way his promise to aid Russia at the Straits – a promise which was, strictly speaking, incompatible with the spirit of the Austro-German treaty and with the text of the Triple Alliance – was neutralised by the readiness of the Mediterranean powers to resist Russia. [...]
Bismarck has long enjoyed a formidable reputation in the field of foreign affairs. His apologists claim that he was largely responsible for preserving peace in Europe for twenty years; he did not want war himself, so it is argued, and he prevented others from going to war by enmeshing the Great Powers in such an intricate* diplomatic web that war became too perilous* an undertaking. This is to exaggerate his influence. A factor of equal importance was the desire of the powers to avoid a major war in Europe. [...] No one would deny that Bismarck was a past master in the diplomatic arts [...]; by cleverly exploiting and fostering* the rivalries among the powers he prevented the formation of any hostile coalition against Germany and obtained for his country an assured place at the top table. These are solid achievements. But, equally, it cannot be denied that his policies ended in failure. His bullying tactics, however successful in the short term, were bitterly resented, especially by the Russians, and poisoned international relations in this period.

intricate complicated
perilous dangerous

to foster to promote

William Carr: A History of Germany, 1815–1990. London: Hodder Education ⁴1991, pp. 146–161

"The Three Emperors; or, the ventriloquist of Varzin*!"
Cartoon by John Tenniel, published in the British satirical magazine *Punch* on 20 September 1884 (on the occasion of the Berlin/Congo Conference, cf. chapter 2).
Persons depicted (from left to right, sitting on the chairs):
Tsar Alexander III • Emperor William I • Emperor Francis Joseph I

Warcine (Varzin) is a village in northern Poland, in the historical region of Pomerania. It was given to Bismarck in 1867 for his services as Prussian minister-president in the Austro-Prussian War and remained in the hands of the Bismarck family until their expulsion in 1945.

| Language support |

ventriloquist [venˈtrɪləkwɪst] Bauchredner • **Fäden** strings • **Bauchrednerpuppe** ventriloquist's dummy

S 63 — John Tenniel

Dropping the Pilot

The cartoon "Dropping the pilot" by Sir John Tenniel was published in the British satirical magazine *Punch* in March 1890. It refers to Bismarck's resignation from his post as German chancellor in 1890.

Pre-task

1. In German textbooks, the title of this cartoon is translated as "Der Lotse geht von Bord" ("The pilot leaves the ship"). Against the backdrop of the historical context of Bismarck's rule way of running the affairs of state and resignation, discuss whether the English original title or the German translation is more appropriate.

Tasks

2. Analyse the source and specify the way the two people are depicted.
3. In both S 51 and S 62, the cartoonists rely on the metaphor of the ship of state. Compare the two representations and focus on the role of the people "at the helm".
4. What might Emperor William II, in the position depicted in the cartoon, perhaps say to Bismarck at this very moment? Use your exercise book and write his speech bubble and Bismarck's reply.

Post-task

5. The overall balance of Bismarck's foreign policy: success or failure? Revise what you have learned in this sub-chapter and give an evaluation.

"Dropping the Pilot"
Persons depicted:
Emperor William II, (Ex-)Chancellor Bismarck

DROPPING THE PILOT.

Language support

Lotse pilot • **Leiter** ladder • **Geländer** handrail • **Bullauge** bull's eye, porthole • **die Arme verschränken** to fold one's arms

S 64 Eugen Richter
Bismarck's System of Government

Eugen Richter was a German politician and publisher. He was one of the leaders of the *Deutsche Freisinnige Partei*, a liberal party that had emerged in 1884. After Bismarck's resignation in 1890, Richter commented on Bismarck's achievements and the impact of his decisions on future German politics.

Pre-task
1. Eugen Richter claims it would have been a blessing for the Reich if Bismarck had been removed earlier. (cf. ll. 3 f.) What might have prompted him to come to this assessment? Gather arguments in class.

Tasks
2. Analyse the source. Specify the criticism of Bismarck that Richter utters.
3. Explain the references made by Richter by incorporating them into their historical context.
4. Take a critical stand on Richter's assessment of Bismarck's system of government.
5. Write Bismarck's reply to Richter in which he justifies his policies as a means to an end in order to consolidate the Second Empire.

Post-tasks
6. Below, you will find sociologist Max Weber's assessment of Bismarck's political heritage, written in 1917 – nineteen years after Bismarck's death during the First World War. Compare his assessment with Richter's and discuss to what extent the respective years of origin of the two texts influence the view on Bismarck.

> **Sociologist Max Weber about Bismarck's political heritage, writing in 1917:**
> "Bismarck left behind him as his political heritage a nation without any political education, […]. Above all, he left behind a nation without any political
> 5 will, accustomed to allow the great statesman at its head to look after its policy for it. Moreover, as a consequence of his misuse of the monarchy as a cover for his own interests in the struggle of political parties, he left a nation accustomed to submit, under the label of constitutional monarchy, to anything which was decided for it […]."
> from: William Carr: A History of Germany, 1815–1990, London: Hodder Education ⁴1991, p. 145

7. Bismarck died in 1898. Choose a perspective from which to write and compose Bismarck's obituary (*Nachruf*) for publication in the newspapers (for example: from the point of view of a Social Democrat, a member of the Centre Party, Emperor William II, …).

Die Entlassung des Reichskanzlers Fürsten Bismarck ist vollendete Tatsache*. Gott sei Dank, dass er fort ist! so sagen wir heute ebenso aufrichtig, wie wir ihm gegenüber stets gewesen sind. Es wäre ein Segen* für das Reich gewesen, wenn er schon viel früher beseitigt* worden wäre. Nicht um der Person willen sagen wir
5 dies, sondern wegen des Regierungssystems, welches Fürst Bismarck befolgte. […]

vollendete Tatsache fait accompli [fɛɪt əˈkɒmpliː]
Segen blessing
beseitigen to remove

Vocabulary

innerste Überzeugung deepest conviction
innere Politik domestic policy
in den Abgrund führen to bring to ruin
sich bekennen to declare support
Frucht product, fruit
geeignet sein to be suited
Zuckerbrot und Peitsche carrot and stick
künstlich großziehen to raise artificially
konfessionelle Gegensätze confessional differences
verschärfen to exacerbate [ɪgˈzæsə(r)beɪt]
Strafbestimmungen criminal regulations
kirchenpolitischer Kampf battle over church policy
Emporwuchern growth
rücksichtslos ruthless(ly)
auf Kosten des allgemeinen Wohles at the expense of the general good
Schutzzollpolitik policy of protective tariffs
anreizen to stimulate
Anschwellen der Steuerlasten rise of the tax burdens
zuungunsten to the disadvantage of
minderwohlhabend less well-off
in rücksichtslosester Weise behandelt treated in the most ruthless manner
in ihrem Ansehen herabgewürdigt belittled in its reputation
Nachwelt posterity
Mitwelt the contemporary world
zur Geltung kommen to show
zu vollem Bewusstsein gelangen to become fully aware of sth.
Nachwirkungen consequences
eine Erbschaft antreten to inherit a legacy
beneiden to envy
Missregierung misgovernment
stumpfe Passivität apathetic passivity
berufen sein to be called upon
Geschick destiny

Es ist unsere innerste Überzeugung*, dass eine Fortsetzung der bisherigen inneren Politik*, wie sie namentlich seit 1877 begonnen, nach einem ebensolchen Zeitraum tatsächlich Deutschland in den Abgrund geführt* haben würde. Dass bei den letzten Wahlen die deutsche Bevölkerung sich zu einem Fünftel zu einer republikanischen Partei bekannt* hat, ist in der Hauptsache die Frucht* des Bismarckschen Regierungssystems, welches nur zu sehr geeignet* war, die Sozialdemokratie bald mittels dargereichten Zuckerbrotes, bald mittels der angewandten Peitsche* künstlich großzuziehen*. Dazu sind die konfessionellen Gegensätze* verschärft* worden, nach der einen Seite durch den mittels Polizei und Strafbestimmungen* geführten kirchenpolitischen Kampf*, nach der anderen Seite durch das Verhalten des Kanzlers zu der Entstehung der antisemitischen Bewegung. Das gewaltige Emporwuchern* der Interessenparteien, welche rücksichtslos* die Ausbeutung der Staatsgewalt auf Kosten des allgemeinen Wohles* erstreben, ist zurückzuführen auf die Schutzzollpolitik* und jene Schutzzollagitationen, zu welchen der Kanzler persönlich in jeder Weise aufgefordert und angereizt* hat. [...]

Nur die falsche Politik des Kanzlers hat das Anschwellen der Steuerlasten* des Reiches in den letzten zehn Jahren um nahezu 400 Millionen, und zwar vorwiegend zuungunsten* der minderwohlhabenden* Klassen verschuldet. [...]

Die Volksvertretung wurde stets in der rücksichtslosesten Weise behandelt* und in ihrem Ansehen herabgewürdigt*, so oft sie dem Kanzler nicht zu Gefallen stimmte. [...]

Erst eine spätere Generation wird ein vollkommen gerechtes Urteil über den Fürsten Bismarck fällen. Wir sind der Meinung, die Nachwelt* wird seine 28 jährige Wirksamkeit in ihrer Gesamtheit weniger in den Himmel heben, als es die Mitwelt* vielfach getan hat. Vor den Augen der letzteren kam voll und ganz zur Geltung*, was er für die Einheit des Vaterlandes getan; aber wie seine falsche innere Politik an dem Volksleben gesündigt, das wird in seinem ganzen Umfang erst späteren Generationen zum vollen Bewusstsein gelangen*, die noch unter den Nachwirkungen* dieser Politik zu leiden haben werden.

Diejenigen Staatsmänner, welche die Erbschaft anzutreten* haben, sind wahrlich nicht zu beneiden*. Es wird noch gar vieles anders werden müssen im deutschen Reich, wenn es gelingen soll, die bösen Folgen einer langjährigen Missregierung* zu überwinden. Aber nachdem der blinde Autoritätskultus, den man mit der Person des Fürsten Bismarck getrieben, gegenstandslos geworden, wird man hoffentlich in allen Kreisen des Volkes die Schäden jener Politik schärfer als bisher erkennen. Vor allem hoffen wir, dass nunmehr in Deutschland überall wieder ein kräftiges, selbstbewusstes, politisches Leben erwacht. Statt in stumpfer Passivität* hinzuhorchen, was von oben kommen wird, muss man sich wieder überall mit dem Gedanken durchdringen, dass das Volk selbst berufen* ist, an seinem Geschicke* mitzuarbeiten. Auf die Dauer wird kein Volk anders regiert, wie es regiert zu werden verdient.

Freisinnige Zeitung, Nr. 68, 20. März 1890. printed in: Gerhard A. Ritter (Ed.): Das Deutsche Kaiserreich 1817–1914. Ein historisches Lesebuch, Göttingen: Vandenhoeck & Ruprecht 51992, pp. 260–62

S 65 Bismarck's Legacy

As you have already seen, the Bismarckian legacy is evaluated differently by his contemporaries, but also by historians. Whereas some see him as a political and diplomatic genius, others maintain that his rule helped to pave the way for the disaster of the First World War.

Pre-task
1. Revise your ideas on S 39 (SPIEGEL cover, limited revolution of 1848/49). Are there any aspects you feel you would like to or now have to add after concerning yourself with this sub-chapter?

Tasks
2. Juxtapose positive and negative aspects of Bismarck's rule, as elaborated on by D. G. Williamson in S 65a.
3. Describe S 65b.
4. Explain the message conveyed in S 65b: which "part" did Bismarck, as purported by the makers of the postcard in 1933, contribute to the rise of Hitler?
5. Take a critical stand on this message, both from D. G. Williamson's (cf. S 65a) and from your own point of view.

Post-tasks
6. Do further research on the so-called "German special path" theory (*Deutscher Sonderweg*) which you will also be confronted with in chapter 3. What does this theory say, and what does it have to do with the Second Empire? Important German historians/representatives in this respect are: Helmuth Plessner, Hans-Ulrich Wehler, Heinrich August Winkler. Discuss possible arguments that might be put forward to refute this theory, too.
7. Have a look at the overview with its key questions and key terms provided at the beginning of this chapter. Take turns with a partner, ask each other the key questions and answer them, using all the necessary key terms.

S 65a D. G. Williamson
Bismarck in Myth and Reality

In this short excerpt from British historian D. G. Wiliamson's work "Bismarck and Germany 1862–1890", he juxtaposes positive and negative aspects of Bismarck's rule.

Bismarck played so important a role in moulding the German state, the creation of which was to have such fateful consequences for Europe that it is unlikely that a definitive and universally accepted assessment of this great statesman will ever be agreed upon by historians. His subtle and impregnable* defence of the powers of
5 the Prussian monarchy and his refusal to revise the constitutional settlement of 1867–71 undoubtedly helped strengthen anti-democratic and liberal sentiments in Germany and preserved the power of the pre-industrial elite. Paradoxically, however, he did create a German state with a very modern infrastructure. Its bureaucracy, industry, educational and state welfare systems were the envy of Edwardian
10 Britain. The weightiest and most serious accusation that can be levelled against him is that he prepared the way for Hitler. Despite the modernity of some aspects of the Reich, in retrospect it is undeniable that Bismarck put a very powerful brake on Germany's constitutional development. He created a semi-constitutional sys-

impregnable difficult to attack, strong

impervious not affected by sth. or not seeming to notice it

tem that seemed impervious* to further evolutionary change. If he had revised the settlement of 1867–71 and laid the foundations for a constitutional monarchy in the eighties, it is just possible that there would have been no war in 1914, or even if this had occurred, that German democracy would have been sufficiently strong to have survived its aftermath without succumbing to Nazism.

D. G. Williamson: Bismarck and Germany 1862–1890, Essex: Longman ²1998, p. 91

S 65b Was der Fürst formte …

The Nazi postcard below from the year 1933 establishes a connection between Frederick the Great, Bismarck, Hindenburg and Hitler.

Was der König – der Fürst – der Feldmarschall – rettete und einigte
eroberte,   formte,   verteidigte,   der Soldat.

Persons depicted (from left to right):
Frederick the Great (Prussian King, 1712–1786) • Otto von Bismarck • Paul von Hindenburg (general, President of the Weimar Republic from 1925 to 1934) • Adolf Hitler

Language support

erobern to conquer • **Fürst** prince • **Feldmarschall** field marshal

Paper Practice: Analysing a Secondary Source

S 66   Michael Gorman

The Unification of Germany: Introduction

In the introduction to his book, the then Head of Humanities at Westfield Community School Michael Gorman gives an overview of the forces that brought about the German unification of 1871.

Model solution
➔ p. 599

Tasks
1. Analyse the text.
2. Give an outline of the larger context of the unification of Germany and explain the references made by the author.
3. Take a critical stand on the historian's assessment of the role played by Bismarck in the process of Germany's unification, as presented in the text.

The declaration of the new German Empire on 18 January 1871 was undoubtedly the most important political event in the history of 19th-century Europe after the Napoleonic wars, thus making it a worthy subject for detailed study. Its impact in the years that follow was enormous. The focus of power in Europe was switched
5 from Paris, where it had been located since the 18th century, to Berlin. Bismarck, as the Chancellor of the new German Empire, had installed himself as the leading statesman in European affairs – historians often call the period 1862–90) the 'Age of Bismarck'. The humiliation of military defeat for Austria (in 1866) and France (in 1870) had important consequences: Austria became Austria-Hungary and
10 turned her attention to the Balkans; France harboured an enduring enmity towards Germany. Both developments portended* ill for the future.
Historians have identified many factors shaping German unification which are of great importance to the more general history of Europe in the 19th century. Foremost among these was the impact of industrialisation, which Germany experi-
15 enced at an increasing pace after 1850. New factory processes led to a greater range and enhanced quality of manufactured goods; transport improved, especially railways; new weapons and techniques could be deployed in warfare; vast amounts of wealth were generated. All of this greatly accelerated* the process of unification.
In addition, the 1850s and 1860s witnessed the growing attraction of *liberalism* and
20 *nationalism*. The chief beneficiaries* of the economic development were the middle classes, especially the entrepreneurs* and financiers. They increasingly demanded that the nation of 'Germany' as an economic unit should be translated into political unification which, they believed, would lead to even greater economic prosperity. They also demanded a greater say in the running of the country; thus
25 the traditional privileges of the aristocracy, accepted without question for so long, were challenged by an alternative ideology.
More than anything, historians have pointed to the political genius of Otto von Bismarck, who played an essential role in manipulating internal and external forces which combined to unify Germany. His influence is crucial in explaining the
30 events leading up to 1871. […]

Michael Gorman: The Unification of Germany, Cambridge: Cambridge University Press ³1994, p. 1

to portend to be a sign or warning of sth. that will happen

to accelerate to speed up

beneficiary [benɪˈfɪʃəri] sb. who profits from sth.
entrepreneur [ˌɒntrəprəˈnɜː(r)] sb. who uses money to start businesses and make business deals

to abolish sth.; abolition/abolishment (n.) *etw. abschaffen; Abschaffung*
to abdicate; abdication (n.) *abdanken; Abdankung*
to be accountable to sb./sth.; accountability (n.) *jdm./etw. rechenschaftspflichtig sein; Rechenschaftspflicht*
adversary ['ædvə(r)səri] enemy, opponent
to aggravate; aggravation (n.) to make sth. bad become worse
to agitate, agitation (n.) to try to cause social or political changes by arguing or protesting, or through other political activity
to ally with sb. [ə'laɪ] [ælaɪ]; **ally (n.)** (to make/conclude/enter into an) **alliance** [ə'laɪəns] *sich mit jdm. verbünden; Verbündete(r); ein Bündnis (eingehen/abschließen)*
to alter ['ɔːltə(r)]; **alteration (n.)** to change; change/modification
ambassador, embassy *Botschafter/in, Botschaft*
to ameliorate; amelioration (n.) to make better/improve; improvement
to annex; annexation (n.) *annektieren; Annexion*
arbitration *Schiedsgerichtsverfahren*
to aspire to sth.; aspiration (n.) to want to achieve sth.; goal, hope
balance of power; equilibrium [ˌiːkwɪ'lɪbriəm] *Gleichgewicht (der Mächte)*
buffer state *Pufferstaat*
to cease [siːs] to stop
ceasefire truce, armistice
to cede to allow sb. to take sth. such as power or land away from you
censorship *Zensur*
to conquer; conquest; conqueror *erobern; Eroberung; der/die Eroberer/in*
constituent [kən'stɪtjʊənt] **assembly** *verfassungsgebende Versammlung*
constitutional/unconstitutional, constitution *verfassungsgemäß/verfassungswidrig, Verfassung*
to convene; convention (n.) to arrange or gather for a formal meeting
to culminate in sth.; culmination (n.) to happen or exist as the final result of a process or situation
to deliberate, deliberations (n., us. pl.) to think about or discuss sth. very carefully, especially before you make an important decision
demonstrator sb. who demonstrates
to disenfranchise sb.; disenfranchisement (n.) to take away sb.'s right to vote

to dismiss sb.; dismissal (n.) (opp.: to appoint sb.; appointment (n.)) *jdn. entlassen; Entlassung (jdn. ernennen/berufen; Ernennung/Berufung)*
to emancipate; emancipation (n.) to give freedoms and rights to sb.
empire; emperor; empress *Reich; Kaiser; Kaiserin*
to endorse sth.; endorsement (n.) support
enemy of the Reich *Reichsfeind*
entente [ɒn'tɒnt] an informal agreement between countries or groups (an "understanding")
equality before the law *Rechtsgleichheit*
to eradicate sth.; eradication (n.) to get rid of sth. completely
to expel sb.; expulsion (n.) *jdn. vertreiben; Vertreibung*
to facilitate, facilitation (n.) to make sth. easier
federal state *Bundesstaat*
franchise the right to vote in elections
freedom of speech/of the press/of assembly *Redefreiheit/Pressefreiheit/Versammlungsfreiheit*
to give in to *nachgeben*
to give rise to sth. to lead to sth.
hegemony [hɪ'geməni] political control or influence, predominance
hereditary monarchy *Erbmonarchie*
to humiliate sb.; humiliation (n.) *jdn. demütigen; Demütigung*
to implement sth.; implementation (n.) to make sth. such as an idea, plan, system, or law, to start to work and be used
indemnity reparations
insurrection uprising, riot
Janus-faced *Janus-köpfig, doppelköpfig*
to liberate; liberation; liberator *befreien; Befreiung; Befreier/in*
to mediate; mediation; mediator *vermitteln; Vermittlungsgespräch/Schlichtung; Vermittler/Schlichter*
meritocracy [ˌmerɪ'tɒkrəsi] *Leistungsgesellschaft, Meritokratie*
middle class, bourgeoisie *Bürgertum, Mittelstand*
multi-ethnic state *Vielvölkerstaat*
national assembly *Nationalversammlung*
national (political) consciousness *Nationalbewusstsein; politisches Bewusstsein*
natural rights *unveräußerliche Rechte*
to negotiate; negotiation (n.) *verhandeln; Verhandlung*
obedience (n.) [ə'biːdiəns]; **obedient (adj.)** *Gehorsam; gehorsam*

to occupy; occupation (n.) *besetzen; Besetzung*
to patronise sb. to behave in a way that shows that you are superior to others, to condescend, to look down on
to persecute sb.; persecution (n.) *jdn. verfolgen; Verfolgung*
predecessor ['priːdɪˌsesə(r)] **(opp.: successor)** *Vorgänger (Nachfolger)*
pretext ['priːˌtekst] *Vorwand*
to proclaim; proclamation (n.) *ausrufen; Ausrufung*
reason *Vernunft*
to repress; repression (n.) *unterdrücken; Unterdrückung*
to resent sth./sb.; resentment (n.) to be/become angry at sth./sb.;
to resign, resignation (n.) to state formally that you are leaving a job/post permanently
to restore; restoration (n.) *etw. wiederherstellen; Restauration*
rule of law *Rechtsstaatlichkeit*
sentiment feeling

to shatter hopes *Hoffnungen zerstören*
sovereignty ['sɒvrɪnti] the right to rule a country
to strive for sth. to try hard to do or get sth.
suffrage the right to vote
to summon (parliament) *(das Parlament) einberufen*
(to) surrender (v.; n.) *sich ergeben, Kapitulation*
surveillance [sə(r)'veɪəns] *Überwachung*
system of alliances *Bündnissystem*
to talk shop, talking shop *fachsimpeln; Quasselbude*
tension *Spannung*
treaty concluded under international law *völkerrechtlicher Vertrag* (between countries)
to unify; unification (n.) to become one
victor the winner of a competition or battle
to voice sth. to express one's opinions or feelings about sth., especially negative feelings
to wage war; to declare war on sb. *Krieg führen; jdm. den Krieg erklären*
to wrest (political) concessions *(politische) Zugeständnisse abringen*

The First World War – The "Seminal

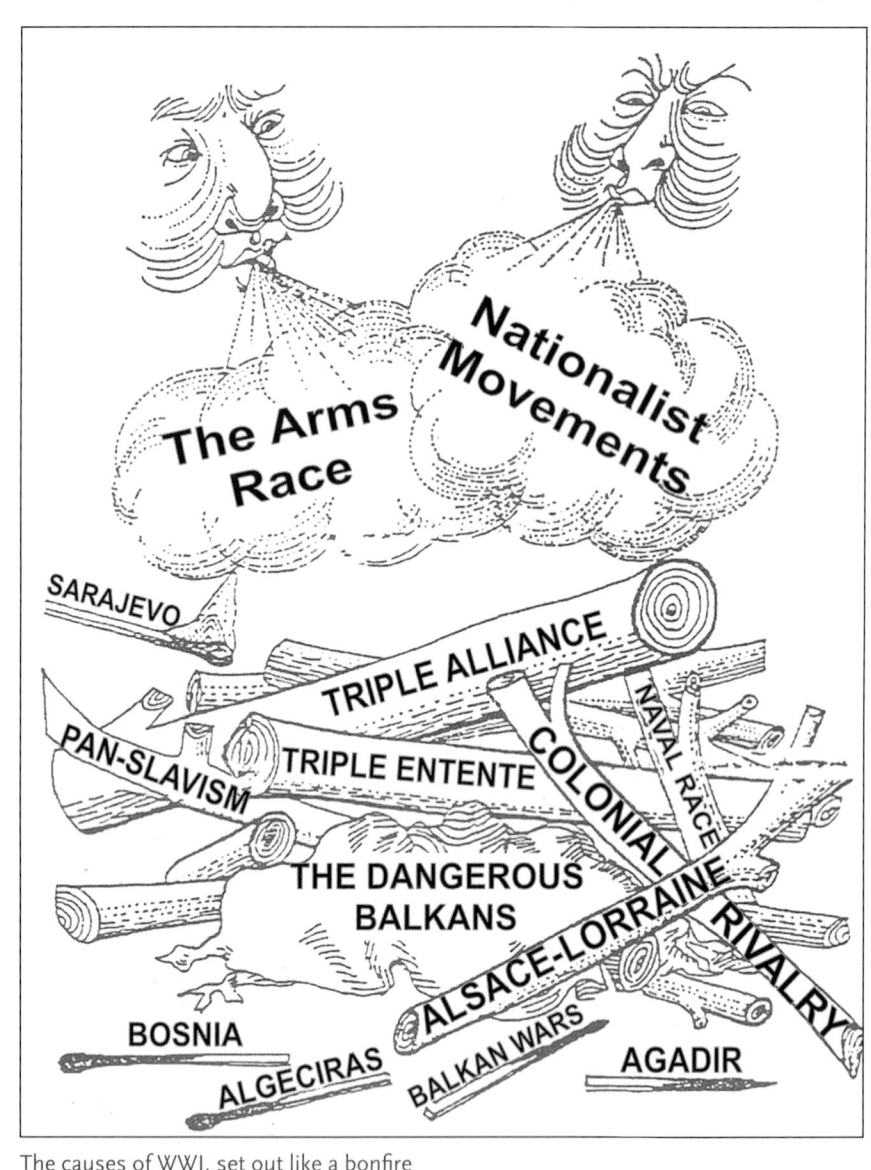

The causes of WWI, set out like a bonfire

1884	1898	1905/06	1908	1911	1912/13	28 June 191
Congo-Conference (Berlin): Scramble for Africa	Fashoda Incident	First Moroccan Crisis	Bosnian Crisis	*Panthersprung* (Second Mor. Crisis)	Balkan Wars	Assassination of Franz Ferdinand in Sarajevo

Catastrophe" of the 20th Century?

- Industrialization and the Coming into Being of the Modern Mass Society
- (New?) Imperialism
- Imperialism: Motives and Justifications
- British, American and German Imperialism
- Origins and Outbreak of WWI
- The First "Modern" and "Total" War
- The International Peace Framework After the First World War

British troops negotiating a trench during the Battle of the Somme, 1916

Task In the introduction to his 1979 book "The Decline of Bismarck's European Order: Franco-Russian Relations 1875–1890", the American diplomat George F. Kennan characterized the First World War as "the seminal catastrophe of this century" (= *die Urkatastrophe*). With the help of the materials and information provided on the introductory pages to this chapter, revise what you remember about World War One, and discuss in how far WWI qualifies as this "seminal catastrophe".

3 Aug 1914	Aug 14	1916	1917	11 Nov 1918	28 June 1919
Germany invades Belgium/ Schlieffen Plan	Battle of Tannenberg	Battle of Verdun/Battle of the Somme	"Epochal year": Russian Rev. and US entry into war	Armistice signed by Germany	Treaty of Versailles signed by Germany

The First World War

Topics & Key Questions	Key Terms	Translations
Industrialization and the Coming into Being of the Modern Mass Society		
• The Industrial Revolution – the "Unbound Prometheus"? • Progress – always "progress"? • A revolution at all? • Industrialization in Germany – from late-bloomer to pioneer? • The "Social Question" – a(n) (un)solvable issue? • The workers and the Industrial Revolution – a change for the better or for the worse? • In how far did industrialization pave the way for the first "modern" war?	• industrialization • urbanization • rural exodus • steam engine • the Social Question • child labour • the Communist Manifesto • workers' movement • trade union • Social Democracy • economic liberalism • free-market economy • division of labour • social security system • welfare • sunrise industries	• Industrialisierung • Urbanisierung/Verstädterung • Landflucht • Dampfmaschine • die Soziale Frage • Kinderarbeit • das Kommunistische Manifest • Arbeiterbewegung • Gewerkschaft • Sozialdemokratie • Wirtschaftsliberalismus • freie Marktwirtschaft • Arbeitsteilung • Sozialversicherungssystem • Sozialhilfe, Fürsorge • Zukunftsindustrien
(New?) Imperialism / Imperialism: Motives and Justifications		
• "New" imperialism? • Imperialism – the "White Man's Burden"?	• New Imperialism • formal v. informal empire • national prestige • jingoism/chauvinism • terra nullius (no-man's land) • to proselytise/missionise • Social Darwinism • outlet markets • social imperialism	• Hochimperialismus • formelle vs. informelle Herrschaft • Nationalprestige • Hurrapatriotismus/Chauvinismus • Terra Nullius (Niemandsland) • bekehren, missionieren • Sozialdarwinismus • Absatzmärkte • Sozialimperialismus
British, American and German Imperialism		
The Example of Britain • Great Britain or Little England? • How did the British attempt to ensure that "the sun never sets on the British Empire"?	• Pax Britannica • raj [rɑːdʒ] • British East India Company • protectorate • "Cape-to-Cairo" • Fashoda Incident/Crisis • Scramble for Africa • Entente Cordiale • Hague Conventions	• Pax Britannica • Raj • Britische Ostindien-Kompanie • Protektorat, Schutzgebiet • „Kap-bis-Kairo" • Faschoda-Krise • Wettlauf um Afrika • Entente Cordiale • Haager Friedenskonferenzen
The Example of the USA • From the Monroe Doctrine to the Roosevelt Corollary: the USA as the "world's constable"?	• manifest destiny • "open-door" policy • dollar imperialism • Monroe Doctrine • Roosevelt Corollary • "big-stick" diplomacy • Good Neighbor policy	• Manifest Destiny • Politik der offenen Tür • Dollar-Imperialismus • Monroe-Doktrin • Roosevelt-Zusatz • Big Stick • Politik der guten Nachbarschaft

The Example of Germany • From "pragmatic colonisation" to Germany's "New Course": In how far did William II's striving for colonies impact international relations? • New Imperialism: The long fuse for WWI? • Imperialism: Enduring legacies for the 21st century?	• "pragmatic colonisation" • Berlin (Congo/West Africa) Conference • "latecomer nation"/"belated nation" • Pan-German League • New Course • world policy	• „pragmatische Kolonialisierung" • Kongo-Konferenz (Westafrika-Konferenz) • „verspätete Nation" • Alldeutscher Verband • Neuer Kurs • Weltpolitik
Origins and Outbreak of WWI		
• In how far did industrialization and imperialism contribute to the outbreak of war? • Was the Schlieffen Plan doomed to fail right from the start? • Europe 1914 – "sleepwalking" into war?	• Navy League • naval arms race • Kruger Telegram • Daily Telegraph Affair • Entente Cordiale • Triple Entente • Triple Alliance • Pan-Slavism • Bosnian Crisis • Balkan Wars • First and Second Moroccan Crises • sabre-rattling • July Crisis • "blank cheque" • Schlieffen Plan • central powers • Spirit of 1914 • ?	• Flottenverein • maritimes Flottenwettrüsten • Krüger-Telegramm • Daily-Telegraph-Affäre • Entente cordiale • Triple Entente • Dreibund • Pan-Slawismus • Bosnien-Krise • Balkan-Kriege • Erste und Zweite Marokko-Krise • Säbelrasseln • Juli-Krise • „Blankovollmacht" • Schlieffen-Plan • Mittelmächte • Augusterlebnis • Burgfrieden
The First "Modern" and "Total" War		
The Course of the War until 1917 • From the "Spirit of 1914" to the war of attrition: In how far was WWI different from any war fought before?	• weapons of mass destriction (WMDs) • stalemate • trench warfare • war of attrition • Battle of Tannenberg • Battle of the Somme • Battle of Verdun • naval blockade	• Massenvernichtungswaffen • Pattsituation • Grabenkrieg • Stellungskrieg • Schlacht bei Tannenberg • Schlacht an der Somme • Schlacht um Verdun • Seeblockade

The First World War

The "Epochal Year" 1917 • "Epochal year" 1917 – the preliminary decision?	• epochal year • unrestricted submarine warfare • Zimmermann Telegram • tsar/czar • autocracy • duma • Bolsheviks • April Theses • Russian Revolution • Soviet Union • council democracy • Treaty of Brest-Litovsk • communism • Marxism-Leninism	• Epochenjahr • uneingeschränkter U-Boot-Krieg • Zimmermann-Telegramm • Zar • Autokratie • Duma • Bolschewiken • Aprilthesen • die Russische Revolution • Sowjetunion • Rätedemokratie • Vertrag von Brest-Litowsk • Kommunismus • Marxismus-Leninismus
War Aims / The End of War • WWI – the "seminal catastrophe" of the 20th century? • Commemorating WWI – time for sorrow or time for pride?	• victory peace • 14 Points • self-determination • League of Nations • stab-in-the-back legend/myth • propaganda	• Siegfrieden • 14 Punkte • Selbstbestimmung • Völkerbund • Dolchstoßlegende • Propaganda

The International Peace Framework After the First World War

• The Treaty of Versailles – an armistice for 20 years? • The League of Nations – making the world safe for democracy?	• Treaty of Versailles • War-Guilt Clause (Article 231) • indemnity/reparations • "Polish Corridor" • Oder-Neisse line • demilitarisation • the "Big Three" • ignominious [ɪgnəʊmɪnɪəs] peace • Anschluss	• Versailler Vertrag • Kriegsschuldartikel (Artikel 231) • Entschädigung/Reparationen • „Polnischer Korridor" • Oder-Neiße-Linie • Entmilitarisierung • die „Big Three" • Schandfrieden • Anschluss

Industrialization and the Coming into Being of the Modern Mass Society

⇨ S 1–17

The term "**industrialization★**" actually describes the construction of industrial plants or enterprises. However, in a broader sense, it comprises all the possible consequences that result from the development of industries, such as the impact on social structures or on the living and working conditions of societies.

In the middle of the 18th century a process of industrialization began that had such a profound impact that even contemporaries used the term "Industrial Revolution" to emphasize the revolutionary and cataclysmic★ importance this wave of industrialization had in terms of changes in the economy and in society. Today, many historians consider the Industrial Revolution to be just as important as the Neolithic Revolution when man became sedentary★ (cf. S2). This process of industrialization began in England in the 18th century, with countries on the continent following by the end of the 18th century.

At the beginning of the 18th century, about 90 % of the population still lived in the country, employed in agriculture and also producing a large amount of their clothing or their tools themselves. This situation had not changed a lot since the Middle Ages. Likewise, too, social hierarchies remained quite stable: birth decided societal status, sons usually took over their fathers' forms of employment. But also in towns, estates and guilds were dominant that had formed in the Middle Ages. Most towns were rather small and still of a more rural character, cities such as London or Paris were an exception to the rule. The production of goods was meant to provide for subsistence★ and these were still manufactured manually.

England was no exception here. However, she led the way in the historical process of industrialization. This is because the agriculturally usable land belonged to a small elite of (usually noble) landowners who rented their land to farmers. These farmers in turn employed wage workers and thus were interested in keeping their business profitable and effective, which is why they tried out new ideas which promised an increase of yields. One example was the three-field crop rotation★ which was replaced by a new system without fallow★ land. Technical novelties such as seed drills★ or metal ploughs★ were introduced, as well as the systematic breeding of animals. On the one hand, all of these changes made agriculture more profitable for the farmers. On the other hand, fewer workers were needed, which led to an increase in the number of people who could not make their living from agriculture anymore. Since they were neither bound by serfdom★ nor by property, many of them moved to the towns and cities looking for a new job, leading to a **rural exodus★** and introducing the phenomenon of **urbanization★**. Another reason for this was the enormous population growth which England experienced from the middle of the 18th century on. Improved hygienic conditions and new medical achievements led to a decline of diseases such as the plague or tuberculosis, which in turn led to a decrease in infant mortality rates and an increase in the birth rate. From 1750 to 1850, the population of England tripled, which also meant an increase in the number of labourers available and rising consumption.

Another reason why England became "the workshop of the world" was that more than half of the entrepreneurs★ and merchants were Puritans who were neither allowed to work in the military nor in the civil service. Puritan belief said that success in this life is the precondition for salvation in the afterworld. This attitude influenced the way the Puritans did business.

---

industrialization *Industrialisierung*

cataclysmic [ˌkætəˈklɪzmɪk] changing a situation in a sudden way

sedentary *sesshaft*

subsistence the smallest amount of food you need to stay alive

three-field crop rotation *Dreifelderwirtschaft*
fallow *brachliegend*
seed drill *Sämaschine*
plough [plaʊ] *Pflug*

serfdom *Leibeigenschaft*
rural exodus *Landflucht*
urbanization *Urbanisierung (Verstädterung)*

entrepreneur [ˌɒntrəprəˈnɜː(r)] sb. who uses money to start businesses and make business deals

trust *Stiftung*
welfare *Sozialhilfe, Fürsorge*

In addition to the efforts of the Church, guilds, trusts* and the private ventures of businesspeople, the state also began to pursue a **welfare*** policy when the growing political consciousness of the workers resulted in waves of strikes from 1871 to 1873, which made the German authorities fear for the security and safety of the authoritarian German Empire (cf. Bismarck's domestic policy, chapter 1).

"Der Segen der Alters- und Invalidenversicherung". German woodcut c. 1890

(New?) Imperialism

⇨ S 18

There are numerous definitions of "imperialism", and even contemporaries called the time before the outbreak of the First World War the "age of imperialism", a period characterized by the striving of the European powers to gain overseas possessions and thus economic and/or political spheres of influence in order to increase their **national prestige*** and power. So imperialism denotes a period of competition between the European powers and later also the USA in connection with seizing what was alleged to be **terra nullius (no-man's land)*** in the final phase of the spreading of the control of the western world into so-called "underdeveloped" regions.

Imperialism as a form of rule is by no means a typical phenomenon of the late 19th and the start of the 20th century since the desire to build empires can already be identified in antiquity, with the Roman Empire being the most momentous* example, historically speaking. Consequently, the term "imperialism" comes from the Latin word *imperium*, meaning "empire" and "rule".

A new dimension of European expansion was reached in the wake of the voyages of discovery from the 15th to the 18th century, with the European naval powers of Spain, Portugal, the Netherlands, England and France securing their spheres of influence in America, India, Australia and Oceania. This trend was gradually slowed down by the American Declaration of Independence from Great Britain (4 July 1776), but imperialism gained new impetus* from the 1870s onwards. Accordingly, this fresh phase of imperialism is called **"new" imperialism***, leading to a renewed race for the partitioning* of the world. In 1872, for example, the British politician Benjamin Disraeli delivered the so-called "Crystal Palace speech" in London, in which he developed the idea of an open, imperialist, colonial and world policy (cf. S 18).

In contrast to previous phases of imperialism, which had been characterized by their predominantly informal and indirect system of control (**informal empire***), new imperialism partly returned to traditional forms of colonial expansion, such as ways of exercising formal rule in the sense of direct military occupation and of taking over political and administrative control (**formal empire***). This meant comprehensive expansion instead of erecting single colonial outposts, which in turn required a more formalized way of exerting authority, subjecting the indigenous peoples to direct control.

However, there were also other, more informal, ways of control, such as exploitation of the resources for trade, or exchange of goods while simultaneously leaving indigenous rule untouched. There was also the development of infrastructure, supported by western financiers and western expertise, as well as cultural influence in its broadest sense. These forms of indirect rule in particular proved to be very effective, since, as a result, the overseas territories became very much dependent on the western world, economically and financially.

On the eve of the First World War, the tensions between the European powers had started to increase on the periphery*, far outside Europe. The antagonisms* developing there, however, led back to Europe where they were hard to contain or resolve. Instead, these tensions were intensified by involvement in arms races and eventually they got out of control. So the question arises as to how far new imperialism can be considered the "long fuse"* leading to the First World War.

---

national prestige *Nationalprestige*

terra nullius (no-man's land) *Terra Nullius (Niemandsland)*

momentous very important because of having an effect on future events

impetus a force that helps sth. to happen or develop more quickly

new imperialism *Hochimperialismus*

to partition to divide into parts

informal empire *informelle Herrschaft*

formal empire *formelle Herrschaft*

periphery [pəˈrɪf(ə)ri] the outer part of an area, far away from the centre

antagonism [ænˈtægəˈnɪz(ə)m] strong opposition

long fuse *lange Zündschnur*

⇨ S 19-24

Imperialism: Motives and Justifications

Generally speaking, imperialism is the attempt to take possession of as much territory as one can by exploiting one's own superiority over others. Such ventures required justification, since imperialism as such is neither naturally given nor necessary. It is by no means the prerogative* of a certain class or societal group, but proponents of colonial expansion were at the time to be found in all milieus and groups of society. These justifications shed light on the way people thought at that time, on the assumptions, motives and prejudices that they considered to be the truth, but they do not necessarily reveal the underlying causes of imperialism. That is why historians investigate the validity* of these assumptions and views, seeking for comparable patterns, while maintaining the necessary critical distance.

The imperialism of the late 19th century is a very complex epoch, defined by very different causes and motivations and supported by very different social groups. However, one can certainly say that decisive motives behind new imperialism can be traced back to economic and social states of development in the respective states. These experienced a period of rapid industrialization and processes of political modernization, leading to the coming into being of new social classes (especially the working class) with new political demands. The industrialised states were thus characterized by technological and power-political superiority over the traditionalist societies on the periphery, leading to a situation in which the latter could not effectively defend themselves against western intrusions*. This meant that the expansion of the imperialist states happened without much resistance. All in all, industrialization was a caesura* that took the European states to a superior level of development, one which was, in itself, a defining characteristic of "new" imperialism.

Consequently, economic motives were of major importance, leading the protagonists involved to search for colonies in order to expand domestic and foreign markets and to establish **outlet markets*** for surplus produce. But colonies were also used for settlements, and when speaking of justifications of imperialism, one should not neglect the factor of religious **missionizing** and **proselytizing*** of the alleged "heathens" in order to spread "civilization". Closely connected to this belief in the "white man's burden" (cf. S 21) was the belief in one's own racial superiority in the general struggle for the "survival of the fittest" (cf. S 20, S 23, S 24).

prerogative Vorrecht

validity Gültigkeit

intrusion becoming involved in sth. in a way that is not welcome

caesura [siːˈʒjʊərə] a complete break

outlet markets Absatzmärkte

to missionize/proselytize [ˈprɒs(ə)lətaɪz] missionieren/bekehren

A grain in the balance will determine which individual shall live and which shall die, – which variety or species shall increase in number, and which shall decrease, or finally become extinct.

Charles Darwin: On the Origin of Species, John Murray, London 1859, p. 467

Charles Darwin

Thus biological theories about the evolution of species were transposed to explain and justify the rule of the western, "civilized" world over the "uncivilized" indigenous peoples. This "might makes right" approach was called **Social Darwinism***, after Charles Darwin's theory of the origin of species and evolution.

A further important motive of new imperialist policy can be seen in the attempt to divert attention away from domestic problems by pointing out the successes of imperialism in order to legitimize political power structures and social hierarchies. This is known as **social imperialism***.

In the decades prior to the outbreak of the First World War in 1914, a further motive became important, namely that of national prestige. A competition of national expansion came into being, underlining strong desires for equal status between the nations. Formal rule over overseas territories became a matter of prestige, since, in the eyes of the public, the respective positions of strength within Europe seemed to be increasingly defined by positions outside of Europe. This competition for power and influence sped up the process of imperial expansion. Yet, since the world was already more or less divided up by the end of the 19th century, these claims could not be realized geographically anymore, as seen by the example of the German Empire. The imperialist "latecomer" Germany thus expressed her wish for equal status in the world ("a place in the sun") and this in turn increased tensions between rivals. So the conflicts on the periphery between the European powers led to tension, which was felt clearly on the continent.

Alongside pluralist approaches to explaining the phenomenon of imperialism, there are also theories that try to explain imperialism by focussing on single aspects, such as the economic theory of John A. Hobson (cf. S 19) or of Lenin (cf. p. 301) both of whom perceived a primacy* of economic motives. National-psychological explanations see nationalist enthusiasm and the hoped-for strengthening of national confidence as the most decisive driving force, in other words an exaggerated degree of nationalism in the form of **jingoism or chauvinism***. There are numerous other theories, and the variety of interpretative patterns* is evidence of the difficulties involved when it comes to interpreting this complex epoch.

Social Darwinism *Sozialdarwinismus*

social imperialsm *Sozialimperialismus*

primacy the fact of being more powerful or important than sth. else

jingoism, chauvinism *Hurrapatriotismus, Chauvinismus*

interpretative pattern *Deutungsansatz*

Renewal of Patriotism. Illustration published in "Le Petit Journal" on March 24, 1912

British, American and German Imperialism

⇨ S 25–42

The Example of Britain

By the 1870s, Great Britain disposed over a huge empire, even despite the secession* of the USA in 1776. After the American Declaration of Independence, the British public was more inclined not to subject colonies to formal rule, but to grant self-administration and to secure direct access to trade without direct control, in the sense of free trade. Great Britain, as the "cradle"* of the Industrial Revolution, had been able to maintain the principle of free trade since her naval superiority and an elaborate system of outposts could secure the supply with foodstuffs and raw materials as well as the exchange of goods all over the world. Naval superiority was also of crucial importance in relation to the fact that the British Empire consisted largely of non-contiguous* territory spread all over the globe, as reflected in the famous saying "The sun never sets on the British Empire".

A certain change of direction was then announced in Benjamin Disraeli's "Crystal Palace speech" (cf. S 18), against the backdrop of the proclamation of the German Empire in 1871. Great Britain in response affirmed* her wish to lead the empire back to its former size and power, and even to expand it. The motives for these intentions can thus be traced back more to reasons of national prestige than to economic justifications. Added to this were nationalist-racist variants such as those advanced by Cecil Rhodes (cf. S 26), but also the vision of a **Pax Britannica***, the idea of peace and prosperity established by British rule.

The demand for a renewed expansion of the empire soon found increasing popularity among the British public, especially since imperialist tendencies were intensified by the fear of the country losing its dominant position on the world market. The target of this "new" British imperialism was Africa, because Africa was more or less unexplored, and because the Suez Canal, opened in 1869, was the most important transport link to India, the "jewel in the crown" of the British Empire.

British rule over India, known as the **raj***, is a good example of the imperial policy "the flag follows the trade", meaning that after having established trade outposts, territorial acquisitions – respectively conquests – would follow. India was originally ruled over by the Muslim Mughal* Empire, from which the **British East India Company***, founded in 1600, won the rights to build several trading posts. When the Mughal Empire began to disintegrate* in the early 1700s, following the setting up of rivalling kingdoms by Mughal princes, both the British and the French competed for power in India, allying with various Indian leaders, but eventually the British managed to drive France out of India by the 1760s. The British East India Company was given the right by the Mughal emperors to collect taxes and subsequently took over jurisdiction in order to protect its interests. However, this jurisdiction also affected some long-established Hindu practices which were ultimately forbidden by the British, such as the practice of Sati (the self-immolation* of widows), which angered the Indians, leading to uprisings such as the Sepoy rebellion of 1857.

After this uprising had been put down by the British, India was taken over as a colony in 1858, and in 1876, the British Queen Victoria assumed the title "Empress of India". Even though the British rule over India brought advantages as well, such as the modernization of infrastructure, improved health care and education, the changes made also rendered India dependent on Britain, not only in economic ways. Studies have also underlined the superiority of British language and culture, leading to the suppression of indigenous cultures. On the other hand, the emergence of an educated Indian middle class also meant an increase in political awareness, resulting in growing resentment against British rule. In 1947, India declared its independence. The British "divide-and-rule" policy of treating Hindus and Muslims in India differently paved the way for the partition of India after it gained its independence. The establishment of India (for the Hindus) and Pakistan (for the Muslims) was to lead to numerous conflicts in the aftermath of 1947, conflicts that have continued up to the present day.

Turning back to the British interest in the Suez Canal, this link to India made Egypt strategically important. This was, however, also recognized by France that wanted to explore Africa from this base. To Russia, Egypt was important for securing her access to the Mediterranean Sea.

After the annexation of Egypt in 1882, the British established **protectorates*** over Kenya (1886) and Uganda (1895) and conquered Sudan (1896–99), also with a view to securing control over the Suez Canal.

protectorate *Schutzgebiet, Protektorat*

The British method of proceeding in Africa combined several approaches. On the one hand, the British government was initially willing to support imperial expansion, despite growing military and economic obligations and diplomatic difficulties. On the other hand, the initiative was more and more left to private colonial companies, such as the British East Africa Company (1888). British acquisitions in the south of Africa were an important contribution to the "**Cape-to-Cairo**"* idea, to the attempt to expand the British sphere of influence with the help of direct military advances from South Africa into northern Africa on the one hand, and similar advances from Egypt into southern Africa on the other. This was bound to lead to clashes with another major colonial power in Africa, namely with France, whose expansion was directed from West Africa to the east. Their geographical point of intersection was in Sudan where expeditionary forces of both countries "met" in Fashoda in 1898, on the upper stretch* of the River Nile. The British general Kitchener threatened with war, which ultimately compelled the French forces under general Marchand to retreat, thus finalizing the French demise. Even though French national pride had suffered, the French still sought to make compromises with England as they could not afford further conflicts due to existing tensions with Germany (cf. chapter 1). The so-called **Fashoda Incident/Crisis*** has gone down in history as a prime example of clashes connected with the **Scramble for Africa***, the partitioning of the "unclaimed" African continent by the European powers (cf. S 40). The aftermath of this crisis is also a good example for illustrating to what extent colonial conflicts on the periphery also had repercussions* on the European centre. In the resulting Sudan Treaty of 1898, both countries settled on their respective spheres of influence. In return for respecting British interests along the River Nile, the French were given a free hand in Morocco. This paved the way for the **Entente Cordiale*** of 1904, a "friendly agreement" between England and France which would later be joined by Russia.

Cape-to-Cairo *Kap-bis-Kairo*

upper stretch *Oberlauf*

Fashoda Incident/Crisis *Faschoda-Krise*
Scramble for Africa *Wettlauf um Afrika*

repercussion a bad effect that sth. has and that lasts for a long time

Entente Cordiale *Entente Cordiale*

An attempt to settle future potential conflicts was also made by the **Hague Conventions*** of 1899 and 1907, by invitation of the Russian tsar and the Dutch queen. At both conferences, delegates from 26, and 44 countries respectively were present in an attempt to develop an international legal order and norms as to how to settle conflicts peacefully. Yet, the delegates could not agree on steps of disarmament*,

Hague Conventions *Haager Friedenskonferenzen*

disarmament *Abrüstung*

arbitration
Schiedsgericht(sbarkeit)
unanimity [juːnəˈnɪməti]
complete agreement
The Hague *Den Haag*

and the idea of compulsory arbitration* failed because Germany, Austria-Hungary, Turkey and several other smaller states voted against it and unanimity* was required. Nevertheless, an international court of arbitration was installed in The Hague* in the Netherlands, and the Hague Conventions were a first step to define laws of war and, consequently, war crimes. A third conference was scheduled for 1914, but did not take place because of the outbreak of the First World War.

The Example of the USA

After declaring their independence from Great Britain in 1776, the USA became a new rival for the European powers. Although the Declaration of Independence was a declaration against rule without the consent of the governed and the USA basically saw themselves as anti-imperialist, they still pursued an imperial policy. The idea of exploring new "frontiers" can be considered to be the leitmotif* of US policy, making the welfare of the country dependent on territorial expansion. The westward expansion, in the course of which Native Americans were expropriated*, can be seen as an imperial process, as well as the acquisition of territories on the continent, such as Florida (1819).

leitmotif a recurring idea or motive

to expropriate to take away property

After the USA had reached the Pacific coast in the course of the westward expansion ("from sea to shining sea"), the expectations of the public were, for several reasons, more and more directed beyond the North-American continent. The USA saw themselves as a dynamic, emergent young nation, the nation of futurity with the God-given mission to take over the lead in the world and to bring the achievements of American civilization and liberty to everyone. This religious sense of mission is called **manifest destiny***.

manifest destiny *Manifest Destiny*

"American Progess". Painting by John Gast, 1872. The woman hovering above the scene is Columbia, the female national personification of the United States. She is depicted bringing "civilization" (for example, trains, telegraph wires) in the course of the westward expansion.

In the 1890s, economic motives were more and more added to this imperialist ideology since the USA had become a major industrial power and simultaneously the biggest exporter of agrarian produce. This led to the view that an expansion of the American market was indispensable*, and the idea gained ground that America should become a naval power in order to secure trade and colonies. From this resulted the demand for colonial settlements: the war against Spain about Cuba, the annexation of Puerto Rico and Guam and the Philippines mark the transition to undisclosed* colonialism.

After the annexation of Texas in 1845 and the conquest of New Mexico and California after a war against Mexico in the years 1846 to 1848, the USA had expressed their sympathy for a Cuban insurrection directed against Spain's colonial rule over Cuba in 1898. In the resulting Spanish-American War of 1898, the Spanish fleet was defeated and Cuba became a republic, according to the terms of the Treaty of Paris. Not only could the USA then secure marine bases, but, as mentioned above, Spain also had to cede* Puerto Rico, the Pacific island of Guam and the Philippines to the USA, each for an indemnity* of 20 million dollars.

All in all, there were three different directions of impact connected with American expansion in the 19th century: (1) the northern continent including Canada and Mexico, (2) the Caribbean and parts of Latin America and (3) the Pacific and East Asia. This way, Spain was driven out of Central America, the Caribbean was turned into an "American" sea, the construction of the Panama Canal (1904–14) secured the canal area, and, as a result of the acquisition of Pacific islands, a bridge to East Asia was established. In general, America's economic expansion corresponded more with the idea of an "informal empire" (with the exception of some major acquisitions such as the Philippines). The main emphasis was on building up an empire of free trade whose main arteries* were to be secured with the help of strongholds.

After the turn of the century, the USA concentrated on preventing any European intrusion into American spheres of interest or into territories that up to that date had remained unaffected (e.g. China). In 1899, they, for instance, protested vehemently against the territorial distribution within the Chinese Empire while at the same time striving for economic influence. The USA was content with an **open-door policy***, not demanding spheres of influence in China, but claiming unhindered access to the Chinese market. This policy of informal imperialism was additionally characterized by its so-called dollar diplomacy, or **dollar imperialism***: American capital was invested in less developed parts of the world in order to boost American foreign trade, but also to assert foreign-political goals (cf. the example of the Panama Canal, see p. 174).

In general, the USA alternated* between officially rejecting formal imperialism while at the same time claiming their own interests by informal means, thus combining formal anti-imperialism with methods of informal imperialism with the goal of realizing their own political and economic interests. This strategy was especially applied to Central and South America where US interests were predominantly concentrated after the collapse of the Spanish and the Portuguese colonial empires. In 1823, the US President James Monroe had declared in the so-called **Monroe Doctrine*** (cf. S 28) that the USA would, in future, no longer be subject to European colonization, therewith also proclaiming American isolationism. Yet, the doctrine also proclaimed that both Central and Latin America belonged to the American sphere of influence and that any European interference there would be considered a "hostile action".

---

indispensable difficult or impossible to live or do without

undisclosed open, not hidden

to cede [si:d] to allow sb. to take sth. such as land away from you
indemnity Entschädigung

main arteries Hauptverkehrsadern

open-door policy Politk der offenen Tür
dollar imperialism Dollar-Imperialismus

to alternate schwanken

Monroe Doctrine Monroe-Doktrin

Roosevelt Corollary *Roosevelt-Zusatz*

In 1904, US President Theodor Roosevelt extended the Monroe Doctrine in his so-called **Roosevelt Corollary**★ (cf. S 30), laying claim to the right of the USA to function as an "international police power" entitled to interfere in the affairs of South American states to guarantee law and order.

By the end of the 19th century, Roosevelt pursued the idea of a link between the Atlantic and the Pacific by means of a canal across Panama which at that time was part of Colombia. When Colombia declined the American offer of $10 million dollars to buy the strip of land required, the Americans encouraged rebels to declare Panama an independent republic, and, in 1903, this newly-created nation then ceded a canal zone of 32 kilometres width to the Americans. The Panama Canal shortened the sea route from the east to the west coast by 15,000 kilometres, from which especially the American economy and the navy profited. Thus whereas the USA was satisfied with an "open-door policy" in Asia, they made use of military means to intervene on their own continent. President Roosevelt described this method of proceeding by using an African saying "Speak softly and carry a big stick", which is why this form of diplomacy has come to be known as **"big-stick diplomacy"**★.

big-stick diplomacy *Big Stick*

Roosevelt's successors also relied on dollar imperialism with regard to Latin America, believing that economic potential could best be realized in a peaceful environment. However, when the Great Depression hit the USA from 1929 onwards and given the increased general resentment against the US line of action from within Latin America, US President Franklin Delano Roosevelt (whose wife Eleanor was the niece of former President Theodor Roosevelt) implemented his so-called **Good-Neighbor Policy**★ in order to improve relations with Central and South America. This policy shifted the focus away from military threats towards economic and political cooperation. In his inaugural address on 4 March 1933, FDR concluded: "In the field of world policy I would dedicate this nation to the policy of the good neighbor – the neighbor who resolutely respects himself and, because he does so, respects the rights of others."[1]

Good-Neighbor Policy *Politik der guten Nachbarschaft*

The Example of Germany

On 27 April 1884, Chancellor Bismarck ordered the German consul in Cape Town to put the possessions of the German merchant Adolf Lüderitz in South-West Africa under imperial protection, and this was followed by the German "protection" of Togo and Cameroon in July of that same year as well as by the acknowledgement of the acquisitions of the German "conqueror" Carl Peters (cf. S 33) in East Africa. Thus, 27 April 1884 can be considered the date of birth of German colonialism. At the beginning, however, the support of the German public authorities was not very strong, which is why Bismarck relied on the initiatives of private investors and companies. His **concessions**★ to Lüderitz, Peters and the like were restricted to military protection and basic administrative tasks, oriented towards the British concept of the "informal empire" (see above), seeking to help Germany stand its ground in the world-wide economic trade competition. That is why Bismarck resorted to mercantile, or trading rule in the colonies concerned and why these were consequently called "protectorates" since the Empire refused to assume formal rule. He himself called this form of colonialism **"pragmatic colonisation"**★ (cf. S 34).

concessions *Zugeständnisse*

pragmatic colonisation *pragmatische Kolonialisierung*

---

[1] Franklin D. Roosevelt, Good Neighbour Policy, 1933, https://history.state.gov/milestones/1921–1936/good-neighbor [06.04.2015]

A photograph from 1885 showing a German traveller in an unnamed colony

Upon assuming office as German chancellor, Bismarck had initially spoken out against Germany joining the "race" for colonies, pursuing a policy of internal and external consolidation of the Empire, especially since the rise of Germany in the midst of Europe had evoked fears of further German territorial aspirations* (cf. chapter 1). However, he changed his mind in 1884, even presiding over the Berlin Conference of the same year.

The **Berlin Conference*** (also known as Congo Conference, or West Africa Conference) was delivered in Berlin from 15 November 1884 to 26 February 1885, with participants from 14 different countries. In the wake of the so-called Scramble for Africa, conflicts had arisen concerning claims to African territory, in particular between Belgium, France and Portugal over the possession of the Congo Basin. At the Berlin Conference, the Scramble for Africa was more or less formalised, by partitioning the continent and thus settling territorial claims, as well as by discussing matters of future trade. The results were contained in the General Act* of 1885.

Up to today, the question remains as to what made Bismarck change his mind in 1884. He was certainly aware of the influence of private investors on German public opinion, and he might have hoped to divert attention away from domestic problems by participating in all the enthusiasm for the colonies (social imperialism). However, foreign policy considerations also seem to have played an important role, his recognizing the opportunity to better relations with the "enemy" France by means of colonial cooperation while simultaneously worsening the relations between Britain and France.

In terms of nation-building and colonialism, the German Empire was, or saw herself, as a "**latecomer nation**", or "**belated nation**"*. In contrast to Britain or France, she could not fall back on older colonial possessions and now laid claim to as yet unappropriated places in the world. Bismarck's strategy of restricting the state's interference to a minimum ultimately proved to be unsuccessful. Private investors were confronted with almost insurmountable* difficulties, for instance underestimating the necessary investments, or insurrections on the part of the indigenous

---

aspiration sth. that you want to achieve

Berlin Conference *Kongo-Konferenz*

General Act *Generalakte*

latecomer/belated nation *verspätete Nation*

insurmountable impossible to deal with successfully

populations. Bismarck had wanted to follow the English motto of "the flag follows the trade", expecting business to provide for the financial means, but this did not turn out to be the case, thus dooming the phase of "pragmatic colonisation" (1884–1890) to failure.

From 1890 onwards, the imperialist idea then gained more and more support in Germany particularly among the German intelligentsia and the middle class. One of the most well-known supporters of imperialist ideology was the **Pan-German League***, established in 1891, whose main focus was agitation* in favour of German imperialism. Slowly, the conviction gained ground that Germanness was not granted its due recognition and appreciation in the world, accompanied by the assumption that Germany's imperial competitors begrudged* Germany its importance. The German desire for respect and acknowledgement was pinpointed by then state secretary and later chancellor von Bülow in 1898 when he spoke of Germany's much-desired and well-deserved "place in the sun". Later, he propagated that Germany would be the future hammer or anvil* in international affairs (cf. S 35). The German Emperor William II himself was the epitome* of this development, his **New Course*** (away from Bismarck's foreign policy) and **world policy*** were the expression of the German claim for greatness out of fear of an alleged "encirclement" by a "world of enemies". The development from a more "internal" form of nationalism at the beginning of the 19th century to an "external", chauvinist type of nationalism, striving to gain national prestige and surpass other nations in greatness, becomes especially apparent here.

This second phase of German imperialism was characterized by the gradual erection and stabilization of direct colonial rule by the Empire, as exemplified by territorial expansion and colonial wars. Insurrections of indigenous populations were put down by military means, for example in the Herero War in German South-West Africa (now Namibia) in 1904/05 (cf. CONNECT, p. 261ff.). This crisis-ridden development led to a change in direction on the eve of the First World War.

The last phase of German imperialism was more rational, for example implementing administrative reforms and heeding* traditional hierarchies of native peoples. However, the outbreak of the war prevented this "probation* period" of Germany's colonial policy.

Pan-German League *Alldeutscher Verband*
agitation *Aufwiegelung*

to begrudge to envy

hammer or anvil *Hammer oder Amboss*
epitome [ɪˈpɪtəmi] the best possible example
New Course *Neuer Kurs*
world policy *Weltpolitik*

to heed to consider
probation *Bewährung*

German Navy League postcard from 1902

Origins and Outbreak of WWI

⇨ **S 43–52**

According to historian Eric Hobsbawm, the beginning of the First World War marks the end of the "long" 19th century (starting in 1789) and the beginning of the "short" 20th century, ending with the "epochal year" of 1989/90. Thus, the First World War is seen as a caesura, a change of paradigm*, which ended a longer period of peace in Europe and plunged it into an unforeseeable catastrophe which harmed the European powers involved to a large extent, both politically and economically. All this led the American diplomat George F. Kennan to characterize the First World War as the "seminal catastrophe* of this [the 20th] century". So the question arises how it could come to this catastrophe.

One of the reasons, considered a long-term cause of the war, was the aggravation of imperialist competition between the great powers in the second half of the 19th century. Conflicts on the periphery had repercussions in Europe where they culminated. Already in 1880 (generally recognized as the beginning of "new" imperialism), the imperialist countries had disposed over very substantial military means and potential. However, roughly by the year 1900, the arms race intensified, which was in the interest of and consequently supported by heavy industry. The "world policy" proclaimed by the German Emperor William II was intended to guarantee Germany her "place in the sun" among the other great powers. In order to achieve this, Germany would need a great navy and fleet, measures which were approved of by the Reichstag in several Navy Bills from 1898 to 1907 and supported by interest and pressure groups such as the **Navy League***. This, however, put Germany in competition with the world's leading naval power, Britain, who, in turn, started to develop a new type of battleship from 1905 onwards, the Dreadnought. This **naval arms race*** was joined by other powers and was extended to land forces as well.

paradigm ['pærədaɪm] a set of ideas

seminal catastrophe *Urkatastrophe*

Navy League *Flottenverein*

naval arms race *maritimes Flottenwettrüsten*

Photograph of an HMS Dreadnought (1906)

The First World War

> Overview › Sources › Paper practice › Vocabulary

Kruger telegram *Krüger-Telegramm*
Boer [bɔː(r)] *Bure*
Daily Telegraph Affair *Daily-Telegraph-Affäre*

On top of this, there were further diplomatic incidents that contributed to a deterioration of British-German relations on the eve of World War One, to some extent caused by a lack of diplomatic skill on the part of the German Emperor. One example here is the so-called **Kruger telegram*** of 1896, sent by William II to the Boer* President of the Transvaal (the South African Republic inhabited by Boers, settlers of Dutch origin), congratulating him on successfully fending off an attack by the British. Another example was the **Daily Telegraph Affair*** of 1908 (cf. S 45).

Entente Cordiale *Entente cordiale*
Triple Entente *Triple Entente*

This provocative German foreign policy prevented on the one hand an Anglo-German understanding, and, on the other hand, ultimately destroyed the system of alliances created by Bismarck. When England and France concluded the **Entente Cordiale*** in 1904, France's diplomatic isolation – as intended by Bismarck – was overcome. This Entente Cordiale was extended to the **Triple Entente*** in 1907 when Russia joined. Thus Bismarck's "nightmare of coalitions" had come true, and two blocs of power faced each other on the eve of the First World War: the Triple Entente and the **Triple Alliance***, consisting of Germany, Austria-Hungary and Italy.

Triple Alliance *Dreibund*

When Russia's expansion into the Pacific area was stopped by her defeat in the Russo-Japanese War of 1905, she more and more turned towards South-Eastern Europe to gain access to the Mediterranean – an area which had shifted into the focus of attention of several powers following the decline of the Ottoman Empire, countries such as for example, Russia, Austria-Hungary and several Balkan peoples striving for independence. These independence movements of the Slav peoples in the Balkans are described by the term **Pan-Slavism***, the desire to create a Greater Slav state, Yugoslavia. This development was especially problematic for Austria-Hungary due to the fact that she was a multi-ethnic empire*. The Austrian emperor was simultaneously the king of Hungary, and ruler over other peoples of Slav descent as well. Thus success on the part of the Pan-Slavist movement would deal a serious blow to Austria-Hungary.

Pan-Slavism *Pan-Slawismus*

multi-ethnic empire *Vielvölkerreich*

Danube ['dænjuːb] *Donau*
Bosnian Crisis *Bosnien-Krise*
powder keg *Pulverfass*
Balkan Wars *Balkan-Kriege*

When the Danube* monarchy (Austria-Hungary) occupied and annexed Bosnia and Herzegovina in 1908 (**Bosnian Crisis***), the conflict in the "powder keg"* of the Balkans intensified (cf. S 46). Even though a Russian intervention could be prevented because of Germany's support for Austria-Hungary, the ensuing **Balkan Wars*** of 1912/13 could not be prevented. The fighting was between Turkey and the united Balkan states of for example Serbia and Bulgaria (and others). Turkey's defeat in the Balkan Wars led to her losing more or less all of her European possessions.

First and Second Moroccan Crises *Erste und Zweite Marokko-Krise*

Another conflict that went on to increase the tensions in Europe came into being in Morocco, where Germany tried to push back the French influence in the **First and Second Moroccan Crises***. After a diplomatic defeat against the Entente powers in the First Moroccan Crisis of 1905/06, a second crisis followed in 1911, which, despite a display of German military presence by sending the gunboat Panther to the port of Agadir, also had an unsuccessful outcome for Germany. Despite this **sabre-rattling*** (in other words, the display or threat of military force), France stayed in Morocco and Germany was refused much-desired territory in the Congo because Britain spoke out against this.

sabre-rattling *Säbelrasseln*

to deviate *to start doing sth. differently than agreed/expected*

These conflicts are evidence of increased bloc-building which more and more deviated* from a policy of keeping peace in Europe according to the principle of a balance of power between the greater powers. Germany had put herself into a difficult situation at the beginning of the century, being more or less isolated and fearing an alleged "encirclement" by hostile nations. Her ally Austria-Hungary was a weak ally

"Solid". Cartoon published in *Punch* magazine on 2 August 1911, during the Agadir Crisis (the Second Moroccan Crisis)

who itself was confronted with many problems which would eventually trigger the war.

The **July Crisis*** of 1914 then ultimately provoked the outbreak of the war which was to become the first "world war" in history (cf. S 47). On 28 June 1914, the Austrian Archduke Franz Ferdinand, heir to the Austro-Hungarian throne, and his wife Sophie were shot by the Serb assassin Gavrilo Princip from the Serb terrorist group "The Black Hand". This assassination had been planned without the knowledge of the moderate Serbian government in Belgrade, but was directed against the policy of Franz Ferdinand to grant the different national groups in Bosnia Herzegovina more autonomy in order to consolidate* Austria-Hungary's rule. The assassination forced Austria-Hungary to react, in an attempt to end the danger disseminating* from an independent Serbia. However, a potential intervention by Russia on behalf of Serbia posed a considerable problem, in view of the fact that Russia was allied with Serbia. This could be prevented, it was hoped, by the German Empire deterring* the Russians by declaring their support for Austria-Hungary, which they did in the form of the so-called **"blank cheque"*** on 6 July 1914 (cf. S 48) issued by the German Emperor William II and the Chancellor Bethmann-Hollweg. This step triggered the following chain of events:

July Crisis *Juli-Krise*

to consolidate *to strengthen*
to disseminate *to spread*

to deter *abschrecken*
"blank cheque" *„Blankovollmacht"*

to extradite [ˌekstrədaɪt] to send sb. accused of a crime back to the country where the crime was committed for trial

- 23 July: Austria-Hungary officially blamed Serbia and presented her with an ultimatum to extradite* the assassin.
- 25 July: When Russia announced her support for Serbia, Serbia rejected the ultimatum.
- 28 July: The Austrians declared war on Serbia and began with the bombardment of the Serbian capital, Belgrade.
- 31 July: Russia began to mobilize her troops to aid the Serbians.
- 1 August: Germany declared war on Russia.
- 3 August: Germany invaded neutral Belgium and declared war on France.

The German invasion of neutral Belgium was part of the German war plan to prevent Germany from being caught up in a two-front war. This plan was called the

Schlieffen Plan *Schlieffen-Plan*

Schlieffen Plan* (cf. S 52), after the Prussian general Count Alfred von Schlieffen (1833–1913), who had devised the plan as a reaction to the Dual Alliance between France and Russia of 1894. The original plan was only slightly altered by his successor Helmuth von Moltke the Younger and had the goal of quickly defeating France before Russia could fully mobilize her troops. The essence of the plan lay in its speed, planning only 42 days for the surrender of France. This meant that German troops would have to march through neutral Belgium, which, however, was actually under the protection of the British, as laid down in a British-Belgian Neutrality Treaty of 1839 (the Treaty of London). Yet the German Chancellor Bethmann-Hollweg is said to have exclaimed that he did not believe Britain would go to war over "this scrap of paper". But on 4 August 1914, Britain declared war on Germany. As a result, the allied powers of the Triple Entente were then at war with the so-called

central powers *Mittelmächte*

central powers*, with Germany and Austria-Hungary, and later the Ottoman Empire (joined the war in 1914) and Bulgaria (joined the war in 1915). The name 'central powers' derives from their location between Russia in the east and Britain and France in the west. Initially, the powers involved expected the war to be over soon, and to end to their advantage. Fuelled by nationalism and general war euphoria, masses of war-enthusiasts marched to war, a war which they believed had been forced upon them and which they deemed necessary for the defence of their own country and interests. This **Spirit of 1914*** was not only a German phenomenon. The

Spirit of 1914 *Augusterlebnis*
? *Burgfrieden*

political parties in Germany also agreed on a so-called policy of **Burgfrieden*** (literally: castle peace), especially the Social Democrats, who also then voted for war credits so as to not endanger the success of the German armies (cf. CONNECT, p. 283).

The First "Modern" and "Total" War

⇨ S 53–66

The war, which had initially been welcomed enthusiastically by many, soon developed to an unforeseeable extent, fuelled by mass mobilization and industrialization. Armies of previously unseen dimensions went to war – in Germany, for instance, more than 13 million soldiers were conscripted*, and more than 6 million of them were finally wounded or killed. The mechanization of the war machinery, made possible by industrialization, developed quickly in the four years of war, from 1914 to 1918.

More complex weaponry and **weapons of mass destruction (WMDs)*** decisively changed the way war was waged, leading to a hitherto* unknown potential for destruction, which in turn led to people dying in masses and to mass destruction. The artillery became more effective with new cannonry (e.g. mortars*) and machine guns and tanks that greatly increased the military strength of the land forces. Due to the naval arms race, the navy could deploy huge battleships as well as submarines. For the first time in the history of warfare, the air force also played an important role, deploying bombs and pursuit planes*. And finally, chemical warfare was first developed in Germany, with poison gases being used from 1915 onwards. (cf. S 53)

However, this first "modern" war not only changed the lives of the soldiers fighting on the front, it also affected the civilian population on the so-called "home front". Men, but also women and forced labourers from abroad, were conscripted for the production of armaments and the population was asked to invest in war bonds*. The increasing lack of supplies led to an economic policy of distributing foodstuffs and punishing black market sales. The daily life of the people was more and more influenced by this war economy. The war was "total" in that it affected everyone, from soldiers to civilians.

to conscript to make sb. join the armed forces

weapons of mass destruction (WMDs) *Massenvernichtungswaffen*
hitherto until the present time
mortar *Minenwerfer*

pursuit plane *Jagdflugzeug*

war bonds *Kriegsanleihen*

"Bravo, Belgium!". Cartoon by Frederick Henry Townsend, *Punch* magazine, 12 August 1914

Language support

thoroughfare Durchfahrt
Gatter gate • **bewachen** to guard • **verteidigen** to defend • **drohen** to threaten [ˈθret(ə)n] • **Knüppel** club

The Course of the War until 1917

The German military leadership, the OHL (*Oberste Heeresleitung* – Supreme Army Command) had planned for a quick victory in the west so as to prevent a war on two fronts against France and Russia. However, the attempt to take the enemy by surprise failed so that the advance of the German army came to a halt at the River Marne in September 1914. There are several factors which account for this failure. One reason was that the Belgian army resisted more forcefully than the Germans had expected them to, thereby delaying the German advance. Nonetheless, the Belgian capital Brussels fell on 20 August. A second reason was that the Germans had miscalculated the time Russia would need to mobilize her troops, and, in fact, Russia mobilized more quickly than expected. That is why the German commander Moltke had to transfer troops from the west to the east to fight against the Russians. However, the French counter-attack directed against the borders of Alsace-Lorraine failed completely. During their march through Belgium, the German forces were briefly held up by the BEF (British Expeditionary Force), but the Germans managed to march further into France. They failed, however, to encircle the city of Paris, as originally planned. In addition, the French armies were reinforced and were able to push the Germans back from the River Marne from 5 to 9 September 1914. The outcome of this battle is often seen as a preliminary indication of the outcome of the war as such since a **stalemate*** came into being, with both sides digging themselves in in trenches which, however, only provided insufficient protection against the new weaponry. Thus this **trench warfare***, which was very typical of the First World War, led to a **war of attrition*** involving very high numbers of casualties,

stalemate *Pattsituation*

trench warfare *(Grabenkrieg*
war of attrition *Stellungskrieg*

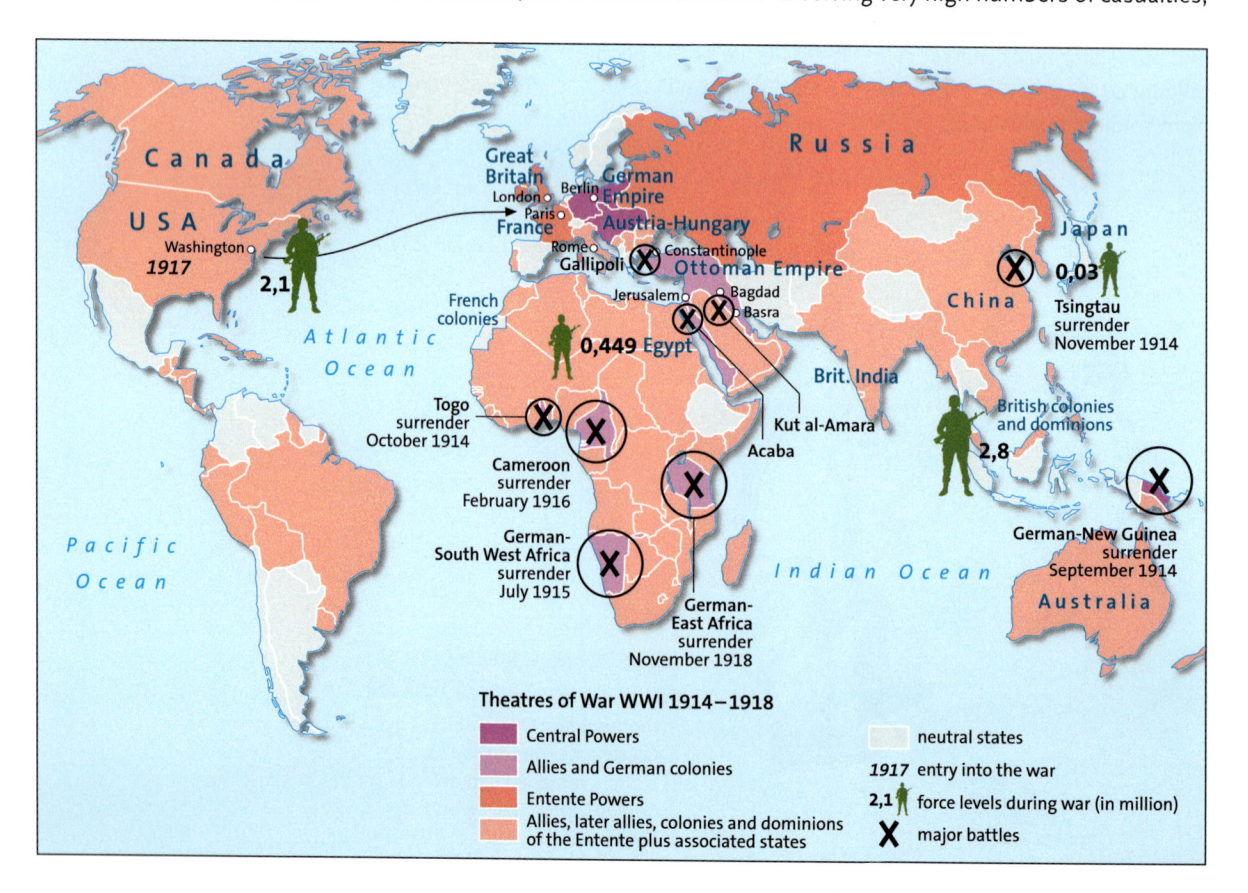

Theatres of War WWI 1914–1918

- Central Powers
- Allies and German colonies
- Entente Powers
- Allies, later allies, colonies and dominions of the Entente plus associated states
- neutral states
- 1917 entry into the war
- 2,1 force levels during war (in million)
- X major battles

due in particular to the use of artillery and poison gas, in which but little ground could be gained. Both sides aimed at "bleeding the enemy white" in these battles of material. Two of the best examples of this war of attrition are the **Battle of Verdun*** in France (February to December 1916) and the **Battle of the Somme*** (cf. S 58). On the eastern front, the advance of the Russian army could be stopped in the **Battle of Tannenberg*** (26–30 August 1914; the victory would later secure Hindenburg and Ludendorff the leadership of the Supreme Army Command from 1916 onwards), but there as well the war turned into a war of attrition in the aftermath. Finally the theatre of war* was expanded when Turkey and Bulgaria entered the war (in 1914 and 1915 respectively) on the side of the central powers, and when Romania entered the war on the side of the allied powers in 1916.

Germany's hopes for naval supremacy were not fulfilled despite the massive build-up of arms that had taken place. Thus the Germans were not able to overcome the **naval blockade*** imposed by the British in order to cut off the central powers from overseas supplies, even though the first operation of submarines led to some German successes.

When the USA entered the war on the side of the allies in April 1917, the balance of power finally shifted in favour of the Entente.

Battle of Verdun/the Somme/ Tannenberg *Schlacht um Verdun/an der Somme/bei Tannenberg*

theatre of war *Kriegsschauplatz*

naval blockade *Seeblockade*

The "Epochal Year" 1917

With hindsight*, it seems justified to call the year 1917 an **epochal year***, a year in which a change of paradigm takes place. With the USA entering the First World War and the Soviet Union coming into existence after two revolutions, the two superpowers whose rivalry would dominate the 20th century entered the world stage.

The USA had several motives for entering the war, namely political, diplomatic and economic ones. However, this intervention marked a clear change in US foreign policy in contrast to, for instance, the Monroe Doctrine or the Roosevelt Corollary (cf. overview US imperialism).

Already in 1914, the German admiralty had declared **unrestricted submarine warfare***, meaning that German submarines would attack any merchant ships or freighters* without warning. On 7 May 1915, the British passenger ship *Lusitania* was sunk off the Irish coast, leaving more than 100 American passengers dead. Even though Germany abandoned unrestricted submarine warfare after this incident, it was resumed in January 1917, which, in turn, led to the USA severing diplomatic relations * with Germany and the US ambassador to Germany leaving Berlin on 3 February 1917. After debates in Congress (cf. S 59), the USA entered the war on the side of the allied powers on 6 April 1917. Another reason for the USA's entry into war was the so-called **Zimmermann Telegram***, a telegram that

with hindsight *im Nachhinein*
epochal year *Epochenjahr*

unrestricted submarine warfare *uneingeschränkter U-Boot-Krieg*
freighter ['freɪtə(r)] a large ship (or plane) that carries goods

to sever ['sevə(r)] **diplomatic relations** *diplomatische Beziehungen abbrechen*

Zimmermann Telegram *Zimmermann-Telegramm*

New York Times headline of 1 March 1917

was sent by Arthur Zimmermann (who was working at the German Foreign Ministry) to his colleague, the German ambassador to Mexico, in January 1917, offering Mexico the return of land seized from it by the USA if it joined the war on the side of the central powers. This telegram was intercepted* by the British, and the decoded version had a huge impact on American public opinion, thus making entry into war more likely.

In Russia, the First World War ended with a revolution (to be precise: two revolutions) which swept away autocratic tsarism, revolutionized the existing societal order, and established a new political system which was to last for more than seven decades: the Soviet Union.

The Russian Empire, reigned over by the **tsars***, was and still is by far the largest state in Europe. Yet, prior to the First World War, it was also the most backward country in economic, social and political respects. The tsar and the nobility still ruled over the people in an **autocracy*** (a system of government in which one person has unlimited and unchecked power), the population had no or but very limited options to participate politically. The serfdom of the peasants had only been abolished in 1861, for example. In 1905, the first revolutionary attempt was put down, after the situation of the people had deteriorated further when Russia was defeated in the Russo-Japanese War. Tsarism was only able to survive this crisis of 1905 because of a clampdown* by the army on the one hand, and because of concessions the tsar made, namely the creation of a constitution and the people's representation in parliament, in the **duma***. But the strains posed by the First World War, which Russia had entered on the side of Serbia against Germany and Austria-Hungary, not only led to the collapse of the Russian army, but also to the collapse of the economy and the supply of the cities. Thus the tsar lost his authority completely.

In February 1917, mass demonstrations and strikes forced the tsar to abdicate (cf. S 60a), and a provisional government took over control with representatives chosen from the duma, in which both the nobility and the bourgeoisie were represented. Simultaneously, workers', peasants' and soldiers' councils* (the Russian word for 'council' is 'soviet') were formed that were intended to check this provisional government. These councils called for an immediate end to the war, for a land reform in favour of the peasants, for the control of the workers over the factories and the immediate summoning of a constituent assembly*. In contrast, the provisional government strove to implement reforms according to the western European model. Soon it became apparent that the provisional government could or would not tackle those problems that were most urgent for the population, such as land reform, because they feared to lay hands on the property of the nobility. Also, they were afraid of losing the sympathies of the western allies by ending the war immediately. In consequence, Lenin and his party, the **Bolsheviks***, gained more and more supporters. In April 1917, Lenin had already foreseen a socialist revolution under the workers' leadership in his **April Theses***, placing the issues of "peace" and "land" at the centre of his demands.

By September 1917, the Bolsheviks (established in 1903) were able to win the majority in the councils. In the night of 24 to 25 October 1917, troops of the Petrograd Soviet (in which the Bolsheviks had the absolute majority) stormed the Winter Palace, the seat of the provisional government. (cf. S 60b) On 25 October 1917, the Second All-Russian Congress of Workers' and Soldiers' Councils decided on:
- the Decree on Peace, offering the warring countries immediate talks about a "just and democratic peace" without territorial losses,

to intercept abfangen

tsar/czar Zar

autocracy Autokratie

clampdown very determined attempt by sb. in authority to prevent sb. from doing sth.
duma Duma

council Rat

constituent [kənˈstɪtjʊənt] *assembly* verfassungsgebende Versammlung

Bolsheviks Bolschewiken

April Theses April-Thesen

- the Decree on Land, which dispossessed the landowners without compensation and which granted the use of the land to everyone who wanted to cultivate it by themselves and
- the establishment of a Council of People's Commissars which was intended to govern the country under Lenin's leadership until the summoning of the constituent assembly.

The two **Russian Revolutions*** of 1917 had turned Russia into the **Soviet Union***, from an autocracy to a **council democracy***.

In the days and weeks after the revolutions of 1917, the Bolsheviks created the legal foundations for the implementation of their demands and promises (e.g. an eight-hour working day), held elections for the constituent assembly, and decreed the nationalization of banks, and the democratization of the army and gender equality. However, the implementation of these decrees proved to be difficult, due to the fact that the revolutionizing of the country posed new problems that had not previously been envisaged.

The new government ended the war with the Central Powers by signing the **Treaty of Brest-Litovsk*** of March 1918 in which the Soviet Union lost one third of its population and more than 80% of its iron and coal deposits as a result of territorial cessions. (cf. S 63)

The Russian Revolutions had not only overthrown one of the most important bulwarks* of absolutism in Europe, they had also brought about a new societal and economic order that claimed to be a better alternative to the capitalist and parliamentarian democracies of the West and a more effective way of overcoming economic and political backwardness. Right from the start, the Soviet Union thus claimed to realize the utopia of **communism***, in which the exploitation of man is overcome by man himself and which enables everyone to develop their full potential.

The driving force behind this revolution was the Russian workers' movement which in turn was a part of the international socialist movement, so that the Russian Revolutions had an impact on the workers' organizations of all the industrialized countries. The evaluation of and way of dealing with these revolutions led to a division of these workers' movements into socialist and communist wings. The Communist International, a union of the parties created in Moscow in March 1919, saw the October Revolution as the beginning and the starting point of a socialist world revolution, with the Soviet Union being the cradle of communism whose policies were to be supported. This coming into being of an alternative societal order threatened the western democracies, all the more so as they saw the communist parties in their respective countries as representatives of the Soviet Union.

The Soviet Union's self-conception was basically rooted in the ideas of Marxism, developed by Karl Marx and Friedrich Engels in the 19th century (cf. S 15) and refined by Lenin to **Marxism-Leninism***. The core of this ideology is what has become known as "historical materialism", according to which the history of mankind is seen as a progression of different societal formations which ultimately ends in the ideal state of communism. The driving force of development is the antagonism between the ruling and the ruled classes (in other words the class struggle). The defining characteristic of the ruling classes is that they possess the means of production (thus also the produce), which is why the ruled classes are forced to sell their manpower for less than it is worth and are thus exploited. The change between the societal formations, up to the next "higher" stage, is always triggered by a revo-

---

Russian Revolutions *Russische Revolutionen*
Soviet Union *Sowjetunion*
council democracy *Rätedemokratie*

Treaty of Brest-Litovsk *Vertrag von Brest-Litowsk*

bulwark *Bollwerk*

communism *Kommunismus*

Marxism-Leninism *Marxismus-Leninismus*

lution in the course of which the ruled classes take over control and become the ruling classes themselves. That is why Marx and Engels considered it to be the historical task of the proletariat (the workers) to overthrow the rule of the bourgeoisie in a socialist revolution and to take over the rule themselves. This, according to Marx and Engels, is the precondition for a classless society and the end of man's exploitation of man.

Lenin amended Marxist theory in three ways: 1) He systematically applied it to the special situation that Russia found herself in, being a country that seemed ill-fitted for a socialist revolution due to its industrial backwardness and the great number of peasants. 2) He developed the concept of a strict party line, the task of the party being the preparation and realization of the socialist revolution. 3) He developed a political theory according to which, in the socialist state, power should be exercised by the councils that were to be directly elected and controlled by the people (council democracy).

In the newly-founded Soviet Union, Marxism-Leninism became the state ideology and this was – in its basic form – to remain in force until the disintegration* of the eastern communist countries in the wake of the "epochal year" 1989.

disintegration falling apart, collapse

War Aims

The warring parties probably had no clear aims in mind at the beginning of the conflict, notwithstanding* previous clearly defined goals such as the re-conquest of Alsace-Lorraine for the French. The actual discussion about war aims only began once the war had started, when different societal groups and institutions announced their respective objectives, for example the September Programme of the Reich government (1914) or the catalogue of war aims issued by the Pan-German League (also 1914). The supporters of the more "ambitious" war aims can, in a simplified way, be divided into the annexionists (mostly from the military) and the supporters of the idea of a Central Europe* (mostly representatives of business) who were rather striving for indirect rule over the continent by means of a customs union, economic interdependence and financial dependence.

notwithstanding despite sth.

Central Europe *Mitteleuropa* (term connoted more historically than geographically here)

In general, it is striking that the German war aims became more and more unrealistic the less likely their realization became. These immoderate* German aims were bound to be an obstacle to the peace talks that followed after the end of the war in 1918. It was not until

immoderate exaggerated

"It's the only way out, Wilhelm!". American cartoon by E.A. Bushnell, October 1918

1917 that a Reichstags majority consisting mainly of Social Democrats, Liberals and members of the Centre Party composed a peace resolution demanding a peace "without annexations and contributions" (indemnity). However, this approach towards a peace based on compromise and understanding remained without consequences since the Reichstag could neither influence foreign policy nor military decisions directly. In the executive branch of the government, the supporters of a **victory peace**★ still had the say.

The allied powers were more reserved as far as the formulation of war aims was concerned. In various documents, one can find, amongst others:
- the political and economic weakening of Germany, both on the continent and as a colonial rival of Britain,
- the re-integration of Alsace-Lorraine into France,
- the restoration of Belgian sovereignty,
- the idea of the River Rhine forming a possible border to France's east.

The **"14 Points"**★ of US President Woodrow Wilson represent the attempt to establish common principles for a post-war order. (cf. S 67) Seeing himself as the opponent of Lenin, Wilson's political strategy was to prevent a sovietisation of the world. Whereas Lenin had initially believed that the First World War would transform the war between peoples into a war between classes (class struggle), Wilson was inspired by the idea of a democratic world revolution under the motto "making the world safe for democracy". (cf. S 59a) Europe was to be reorganized on the basis of **self-determination**★ of the people, the preservation of human rights and a collective peace order. The First World War was thus to serve as a starting point for a new global system of law and order. On Wilson's initiative, the **League of Nations**★ came into being – the forerunner of today's United Nations. (cf. S 75, CONNECT, p. 331)

victory peace *Siegfrieden*

14 Points *14 Punkte*

self-determination *Selbstbestimmung*

League of Nations *Völkerbund*

The End of the War

The USA's entry into the war seemed to spell defeat for Germany and the central powers. However, the Russian Revolutions then appeared to turn the tide in Germany's favour, with the Treaty of Brest-Litovsk effectively ending the war on the eastern front. In the end, US involvement caused the failure of the last German offensive along the River Marne and led to the allied breakthrough on the German western front near Amiens. The anti-war mood at the front was aggravated by desertions and **refusals to obey orders**★.

On 14 August 1918, the OHL declared the war to be unwinnable and sued for an **armistice**★ (cf. S 66a), which was eventually declared on 11 November 1918 in Compiègne. The responsible generals of the OHL, Hindenburg and Ludendorff, resigned from their posts in order to avoid assuming responsibility, and transferred their authority to a parliamentary government, led by Prince Max of Baden (cf. chapter 3). However, about one year later, both would be primarily responsible for the creation of the so-called **stab-in-the-back legend**★ (or myth) that was used by the right-wing as a means of **propaganda**★ against the Weimar Republic. (cf. S 66b)

refusal to obey orders *Befehlsverweigerung*

to sue for an armistice to ask for an armistice (a truce/ceasefire)

stab-in-the-back legend/myth *Dolchstoßlegende*
propaganda *Propaganda*

⇨ S 67–78 The International Peace Framework After the First World War

The Germans had hoped for the conclusion of a peace treaty based on Wilson's "14 Points". In the end, however, the war aims of the Entente powers were more or less realized and fell far behind the "14 Points": In the **Treaty of Versailles**★ (cf. S 68 – S 74, S 78), Germany had to assume the sole guilt for the war in Article 231 of the treaty (the so-called "**War-Guilt Clause**"★) as a legal precondition for the payment of reparations (indemnity). Also, she had to accept territorial losses (for example Alsace-Lorraine, that was returned to France, or the establishment of the "**Polish Corridor**"★ on the basis of the German loss of western Prussia and parts of Upper Silesia★, with the rivers Oder and Neisse forming the new eastern German border along the so-called **Oder-Neisse line**★) and she had to give up her colonies, which were put under the administration of the League of Nations. The German army was reduced to 100,000 soldiers, and **demilitarization**★ (including a ban on tanks and submarines) was extended to the Rhineland, which was to become a demilitarized zone.

The terms had been mainly negotiated by the "**Big Three**"★ (Wilson for the USA, Lloyd George for Britain, and Clemenceau for France), or the "Big Four" including Italy, represented by Orlando. The German delegation was not allowed to take part in the deliberations★ and had no other option than to sign the treaty that was presented to them. This fact, as well as the harsh terms of the treaty (especially Article 231), caused a lot of resentment in Germany where some, due to propaganda, had believed in a victory peace until the very end. The final outcome was regarded by many in Germany as a dictate, an **ignominious peace**★, one which was to provide a breeding ground★ for right-wing propaganda, for example on the part of the National Socialists later.

In the Parisian suburbs, separate peace treaties were concluded with Germany's allies, leading for example to the dissolution of the multi-ethnic empire Austria-Hungary into several smaller states to guarantee the peoples' right to self-determination and to attempt to solve nationality problems. However, this was only partly possible and paved the way for new conflicts to come (e.g. the Sudetenland crisis, cf. p. 361). The German part of Austria had to become an independent state – the **Anschluss**★ with Germany was forbidden.

Treaty of Versailles *Versailler Vertrag*
War-Guilt Clause *Kriegsschuldartikel*
Polish Corridor *Polnischer Korridor*
Upper Silesia *Oberschlesien*
Oder-Neisse line *Oder-Neiße-Linie*
demilitarization *Entmilitarisierung*
Big Three *die Big Three*

deliberations (pl.) discussions in which a subject is considered carefully

ignominious [ˈɪgnəˈmɪniəs] **peace** *Schandfrieden*
breeding ground *Nährboden*

Anschluss *Anschluss*

The First World War   189

Industrialization and the Coming into Being of the Modern Mass Society

S1 The Centennial Mirror, 1776–1876

The lithograph 'Centennial Mirror' was published by the American Geograph Co. on the occasion of the 1876 Centennial Exhibition in Philadelphia, celebrating the 100th anniversary of the American Declaration of Independence (4 July 1776).

Pre-tasks

1. Have a look at the organization and structure of the picture only without focussing too much on detail. Then explain why it is entitled the "Centennial Mirror".
2. Now have a look at the language support on page 190 only. Identify at least two major changes the "Centennial Mirror" depicts. Back up your claims by referring to the relevant vocabulary.

Tasks

3. Describe the "Centennial Mirror" in detail and identify the major changes depicted. Double-check your findings with your ideas from task 2.
4. Put yourself into the shoes of a history teacher who would like to explain the "Centennial Mirror" to their students. Scan the overview section for information you need and select at least two developments and explain them in detail, against the backdrop of the relevant pictures.
5. Discuss in which way the concept of "progress" is depicted here, and to what purpose. You might want to consider who perhaps made this picture, and why.

Post-task

6. Create an "update" to the "Centennial Mirror" that shows current times. Also, write an accompanying commentary that explains your picture.

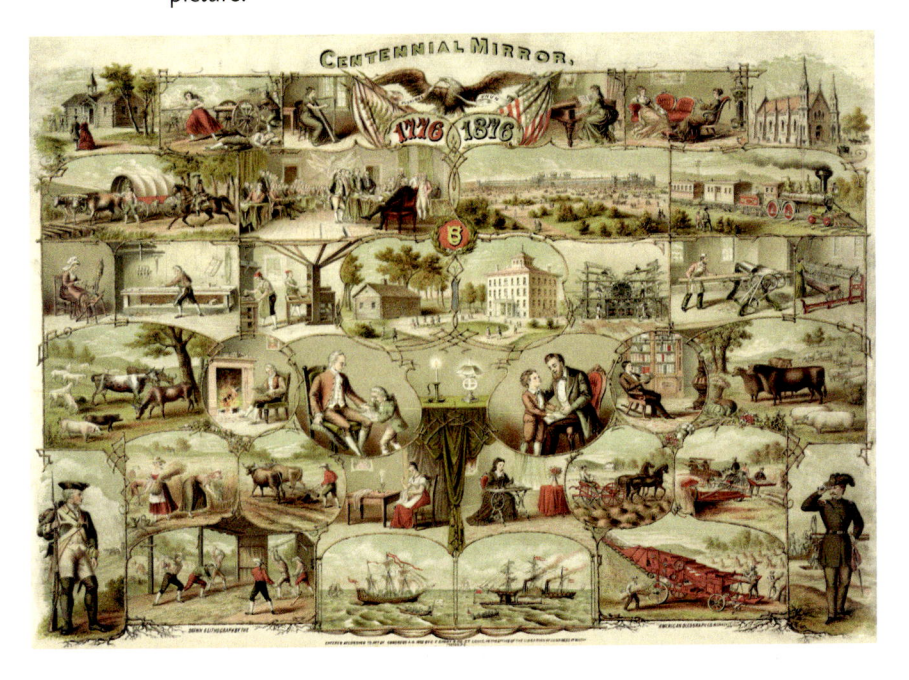

Language support

Weideland grassland • **increase in yield** Ertragssteigerung • **three-field crop rotation** Dreifelderwirtschaft • **fallow** brachliegend • **breeding** die Tierzucht • **Pflug, pflügen** (to) plough [plaʊ] • **Grabenfurche** furrow • **Sähmaschine** seed drill • **Herrenhaus** manor house • **Großgrundbesitzer** (great) landowner • **Webstuhl** loom • **mechanischer Webstuhl** power loom

S2 The Neolithic Revolution

The Neolithic Revolution (sometimes also called the Neolithic Demographic Transition, or Agricultural Revolution) began about 10,000 BCE and describes the shift from nomadism, with its hunting and gathering, to agriculture, with people living in permanent settlements and establishing social classes. The Neolithic Revolution eventually led to the rise of the great civilizations in, for example, Egypt or China.

Pre-task

1. Some historians compare the Industrial Revolution with the Neolithic Revolution, claiming both are of tremendous importance for the development of humankind. Make an educated guess as to what extent both revolutions display similarities, and in how far they differ.

Tasks

2. Copy the table below. With the help of the cartoon provided and the introductory remarks, make notes on major changes occurring in the wake of the Neolithic Revolution. Use the other column to make notes on major changes occurring in the wake of industrialization. Check the overview text and S1 for help.

	Neolithic Revolution	Industrial Revolution
Major changes		

3. Compare both revolutions against the backdrop of your ideas from the pre-task.
4. Justify the use of the term "revolution" in both cases. Think back to the definitions of "revolution" used when talking about the 1848/49 revolutions (cf. chapter 1).

Post-task

5. As you have probably realized, the text embedded in the cartoon is quite ironic, not to say sarcastic, pointing at possible "downsides" of the Neolithic Revolution. Design a similar text for the Industrial Revolution. Aspects to be considered are provided below. Make sure your language fits the language in the given cartoon.

Your KEYS to a BETTER LIFE!	
Move to the cities!	Join the workers' movement!
• ... • ... • ... • ...	• ... • ... • ... • ...

© Science Museum of Minnesota, www.smm.org

> **Language support**
>
> **hunting and gathering** Jagen und Sammeln • **sesshaft** sedentary • **Sesshaftwerdung** sedentism • **domestication** (v.: to domesticate) Domestizierung (Zähmung) von Tieren • **edible** safe or good enough to eat • **to harness** to get control of sth. in order to use it for a particular purpose • **(to) harvest (v./n.)** ernten, die Ernte • **surplus** Überschuss • **submissive** willing to do what others tell you without arguing • **disclaimer** Haftungsablehnung • **deforestation** Abholzung • **desertification** Wüstenbildung • **to diminish** to become less • **cavity** Loch im Zahn

S 3 David Landes

The Unbound Prometheus

In his work "The Unbound Prometheus: Technological Change and Industrial Development in Western Europe from 1750 to the Present", first published in 1969, historian David S. Landes tries to show the interrelatedness of the different factors relevant for the Industrial Revolution.

Pre-task

1. Read the given story about Prometheus [pɹəˈmiːθiəs] in Greek mythology. Then make an educated guess as to why Landes might have called the Industrial Revolution "The Unbound Prometheus".

> From the very first, humans had trouble with the gods. Most gods thought of humans as toys. But some gods found themselves interested in the human race. Some gods even made friends with the humans. One of those gods was named Prometheus.
>
> The first people created by the gods lived happily together. They thought the gods were wonderful. But their children were not as grateful or as content. The children argued among themselves, and sometimes even argued with the gods.
>
> Zeus was very disappointed at mankind. He decided he was not going to give mankind a most important tool – fire! Without fire, humans were not going to last very long.
>
> Prometheus felt sorry for his human friends. Fire was important for many things – like heat and cooking, and hundreds of others. Prometheus stole a lightning bolt from Zeus and gave it to mankind. That's when man discovered fire.
>
> Zeus was furious. He ordered Prometheus chained to a rock as punishment for stealing his lightning bolt, and for going behind his back to help the humans. To make Prometheus even more miserable, Zeus sent storms to beat angry waves against Prometheus, helplessly chained to his rock. Zeus made the sun shine really brightly now and then to burn his skin. Zeus even sent an eagle to nibble at poor Prometheus' body. It was quite a punishment for a god who had only tried to help mankind. But he had defied* Zeus, and that was what made Zeus so angry.
>
> It was Hercules who finally released the helpless god from his chains. By the time Hercules saved him, nearly a thousand years had passed. That's probably not a lot of time if you happen to be immortal*. But humans had changed a great deal over 1000 years. By then, Zeus found humans quite entertaining. Zeus no longer cared if anyone rescued Prometheus or not.
>
> Linn Donn: The Gift of Fire. Zeus and Prometheus, http://greece.mrdonn.org/greekgods/prometheus.html [14.04.2015]
>
> ---
>
> **to defy** [dɪˈfaɪ] to refuse to obey sb. • **immortal** living or existing for ever

Tasks

2. Use the following words and phrases to reconstruct Landes's text. Copy the table and use the empty spaces to add aspects you feel are missing. Make sure to show the interrelatedness of the given facets that Landes also wants to stress.

raw materials	factories	steam engine	textile industry
near and distant markets	demand	mines	metal workings
coal/iron/steel	railroad	steamship	supply
chemical substances			

3. Pick one prime example of interrelatedness and explain it in more detail.

Post-task **4.** Prometheus is inextricably linked with the concept of "hubris", meaning excessive pride and self-confidence, in Prometheus's case defying the Gods, which led to his downfall. Taking this and your knowledge gained about the Industrial Revolution so far into account, write a letter to Mr. Landes in which you take a critical stand on the title he chose to give his book.

The heart of the Industrial Revolution was an interrelated succession of technological changes. The material advances took place in three areas: (1) there was a substitution of mechanical devices for human skills; (2) inanimate* power, in particular steam, took the place of human and animal strength; (3) there was a marked
5 improvement in the getting and working of raw materials, especially in what are now known as the metallurgical and chemical industries.
Concomitant* with these changes in equipment and process went new forms of industrial organization. The size of the productive unit grew: machines and power both required and made possible the concentration of manufacture, and shop and
10 home workroom gave way to mill and factory. [...]
Change begot* change. For one thing, many technical improvements were feasible* only after advances in associated fields. The steam engine is a classic example of this technological interrelatedness: it was impossible to produce an effective condensing engine until better methods of metal working could turn out accurate
15 cylinders. For another, the gains in productivity and output of a given innovation inevitably exerted pressure on related industrial operations. The demand for coal pushed mines deeper until water seepage* became a serious hazard; the answer was the creation of a more efficient pump, the atmospheric steam engine. A cheap supply of coal proved a godsend to the iron industry, which was stifling for lack of
20 fuel. In the meantime, the invention and diffusion of machinery in the textile manufacture and other industries created a new demand for energy, hence for coal and steam engines; and these engines, and the machines themselves, had a voracious* appetite for iron, which called for further coal and power. Steam also made possible the factory city, which used unheard-of quantities of iron (hence coal) in
25 its many storied mills and its water and sewage* systems. At the same time, the processing of the flow of manufactured commodities required great amounts of chemical substances: alkalis, acids, and dyes, most of them consuming mountains of steel in the making. And all of these products – iron, textiles, chemicals – depended on large-scale movements of goods on land and on sea, from the sources
30 of the raw materials into the factories and out again to near and distant markets. The opportunity thus created and the possibilities of the new technology combined to produce the railroad and steamship. Much of course added to the demand for iron and fuel while expanding the market for factory products. And so on, in ever widening circles.
35 In this sense, the Industrial Revolution marked a major turning point in man's history. To that point, the advances of commerce and industry, however gratifying* and impressive, were essentially superficial: more wealth, more goods, prosperous cities, merchant nabobs*. The world had seen other periods of industrial prosperity – in medieval Italy and Flanders, for example – and had seen the line of eco-
40 nomic advance recede* in each case: in the absence of qualitative changes, of im-

inanimate not alive

concomitant simultaneous

to beget to cause
feasible possible

seepage the process of flowing slowly into or out of sth. through small holes

voracious gefräßig, unersättlich

sewage plumbing and drainage systems for waste

gratifying making you feel pleasant and satisfied
nabob magnate
to recede to move back from a high point or level

repercussion after-effect

provements in productivity, there could be no guarantee that mere quantitative gains would be consolidated. It was the Industrial Revolution that initiated a cumulative self-sustaining advance in technology whose repercussions* would be felt in all aspects of economic life. [...] The result has been an enormous increase in the output and variety of goods and services, and that alone has changed man's way of life more than anything else since the discovery of fire [...]. These material advances in turn have provoked and promoted a large complex of economic, social, political, and cultural changes which have reciprocally influenced the rate and course of technological development.

David Landes: The Unbound Prometheus: Technological Change and Industrial Development in Western Europe from 1750 to the Present, Cambridge University Press, Cambridge 1972 [1969], pp. 1–5

"Chained Prometheus". Painting by Peter Paul Rubens (1611–12)

S 4   Paul Kennedy

Industrialization and the Shifting Global Balances 1815–1885

In this text excerpt, Paul Kennedy (*1945), historian at Yale University, examines the impact of the Industrial Revolution(s).

Overview › Sources › Paper practice › Vocabulary   The First World War 195

Pre-task

1. Have a look at the words and phrases provided in the box below. Sort them into positive and negative aspects of the Industrial Revolution, or classify them as neutral. Based on your results, make an educated guess as to Mr Kennedy's stance towards the Industrial Revolution.

> fundamentally important transformation • exploit new sources of energy • stupendous (cf. annotations) • unprecedented increase • self-sustaining • expansion in national wealth and purchasing power • awful costs • proletariat • jerry-built (cf. annotations) cities • widespread benefits • agricultural surpluses of the New World • spectacular • fast-growing population

Tasks

2. Scan the text for the key words in the box and double-check your first ideas with the help of the context. Make any necessary changes.
3. Against the backdrop of the given text, give an outline of the changes the Industrial Revolution brought about.
4. Write and stage a dialogue between Landes (cf. S 3) and Kennedy in which they discuss the importance of the Industrial Revolution and how to assess its impact.

The "Industrial Revolution", most economic historians are at pains to stress, did not happen overnight. It was, compared with the political "revolutions" of 1776, 1789, and 1917*, a gradual, slow-moving process; it affected only certain manufactures and certain means of production; and it occurred region by region, rather
5 than involving an entire country. Yet all these caveats* cannot avoid the fact that a fundamentally important transformation in man's economic circumstances began to occur sometime around 1870 – not less significant, in the view of one authority, than the (admittedly far slower) transformation of savage Paleolithic hunting man to domesticated Neolithic farming man.
10 What industrialization, and in particular the steam engine, did was to substitute inanimate for animate sources of power; by converting heat into work through the use of machines [...] mankind was thus able to exploit vast new sources of energy. The consequences of introducing this novel machinery were simply stupendous*: by the 1820s someone operating several power-driven looms could produce twenty
15 times the output of a hand worker, while a power-driven "mule" (or spinning machine) had two hundred times the capacity of a spinning wheel. A single railway line could transport goods which would have required hundreds of packhorses, and do it far more quickly. To be sure, there were many other important aspects to the Industrial Revolution – the factory system, for example, or the division of la-
20 bour. But the vital point for our purposes was the massive increase in productivity, especially in the textile industries, which in turn stimulated a demand for more machines, more raw materials (above all, cotton), more iron, more shipping, better communications, and so on.
Moreover, as Professor Landes* has observed, this unprecedented increase in
25 man's productivity was self-sustaining. [...]
What the Industrial Revolution in Britain did [...] was to so increase productivity on a sustained basis that the consequent expansion both in national wealth and in the population's purchasing power constantly outweighed the rise in numbers. [...] It

1776 American Revolution
1789 French Revolution
1917 Russian Revolutions
caveat ['kæviˌæt] a warning about the limits of a particular agreement or statement

stupendous very impressive, large, or surprising

Professor Landes cf. S 3

was also true, as social historians remind us, that the Industrial Revolution inflicted awful costs upon the new proletariat which labored in the factories and mines and lived in the unhealthy, crowded, jerry-built* cities. Yet the fundamental point remains that the sustained increases in productivity of the Machine Age brought widespread benefits over time: average real wages in Britain rose between 15 and 25 percent in the years 1815–1850, and by an impressive 80 percent in the next half-century. [...] The new machines not only employed an increasingly large share of the burgeoning* population, but also boosted the nation's overall per capita income; and the rising demand of urban workers for foodstuffs and essential goods was soon to be met by a steam-driven communications revolution, with railways and steamships bringing the agricultural surpluses of the New World to satisfy the requirements of the Old. [...]

The use of inanimate sources of power allowed industrial man to transcend the limitations of biology and to create spectacular increases in production and wealth without succumbing to* the weight of a fast-growing population.

Paul Kennedy: The Rise and Fall of the Great Powers. Knopf Doubleday Publishing Group, 2010, p. 186

jerry-built built very quickly and with as little money as possible, and therefore not of good quality

burgeoning growing or developing quickly

to succumb [səˈkʌm] **to sth./sb.** to lose your ability to fight against sth./sb.

S 5) Adam Smith

The Wealth of Nations

Adam Smith (1723–1790) was a Scottish philosopher and thinker of the Enlightenment and is especially known for being a pioneer in liberal economics. One of his major works is "The Wealth of Nations", published in 1776 (the year in which the American Declaration of Independence was signed), in which Smith outlined – amongst other things – his idea that a nation's prosperity is best achieved by an increased division of labour. In the given extract, two central ideas are elaborated on: the division of labour and the principle of the "invisible hand".

Pre-task 1. Split up into two groups and practise making paper planes. Members of group A follow all ten steps given in the instructions below. Members of group B only practise one step (so split up the steps and decide who is going to practise what). Build two rows of tables facing each other. In two minutes time, try to make as many paper planes as possible. Afterwards, discuss the following questions:
   - Who made more and better paper planes?

Instructions: Paper Planes

Step 1: Take one piece from a stack of paper.
Step 2: Make a centre vertical fold in the piece of paper.
Step 3: Open the paper.
Step 4: Fold the top right corner of the paper in to the fold line.
Step 5: Fold the top left corner in to the fold line.
Step 6: Fold the centre to create the nose.
Step 7: Fold one side down to create one wing.
Step 8: Fold the other side down to create the other wing.
Step 9: Adjust the folds so that the wings are horizontal.
Step 10: Test-fly the airplane.

adapted from: The Power in Our Hands: A Curriculum on the History of Work and Workers in the United States. Teaching Guide. By Bill Bigelow and Norm Diamond, 1988

- What are the reasons for the differences?
- How did the respective group members feel at their workplace? Was it a satisfying job? Why, why not?

Against the backdrop of your findings, try to explain the concept of the "division of labour".

Tasks

2. Sum up Smith's explanations of "the Division of Labour" and explain the metaphor of "the Invisible Hand".
3. Explain why both principles are cornerstones of economic liberalism and a free-market economy.
4. Taking into account the experiences you made with the "paper plane"-activity, examine the impact the "division of labour" probably had on the workers in factories.
5. Skim the short biographical accounts of Karl Marx and Friedrich Engels on pages 210 f. How would the two of them evaluate Smith's economic theory? Discuss.

The Division of Labour

Man has almost constant occasion for the help of his brethren*, and it is in vain for him to expect it from their benevolence* only. He will be more likely to prevail* if he can interest their self-love in his favour, and show them that it is for their own
5 advantage to do for him what he requires of them. Whoever offers to another a bargain of any kind, proposes to do this. Give me what I want, and you shall have this which you want, is the meaning of every such offer; and it is the manner that we obtain from one another that far greater part of those good offices which we stand in need of. It is not from the benevolence of the butcher, the brewer, or the
10 baker that we expect our dinner, but from their regard to their own interest. We address ourselves, not to their humanity but to their self-love. […]

The Invisible Hand

Every individual is continually exerting* himself to find out the most advantageous employment for whatever capital he can command. It is his own advantage,
15 indeed, and not that of the society, which he has in view. But the study of his own advantage naturally, or rather necessarily, leads him to prefer that employment which is most advantageous to the society. […]
As every individual, therefore, endeavours* as much as he can both to employ his capital in the support of domestic industry, and so to direct that industry that its
20 produce may be of the greatest value; every individual necessarily labours to render the annual revenue* of the society as great as he can. […] He intends only his own gain, and he is in this, as in many other cases, led by an invisible hand to promote an end which was no part of his intention. Nor is it always the worse for the society that it was no part of it. By pursuing his own interest he frequently promotes that of
25 the society more effectually than when he really intends to promote it. […]
The division of labour, so far as it can be introduced, occasions*, in every art, a proportionable increase of the productive powers of labour. The separation of different trades and employments from one another seems to have taken place in consequence of this advantage. This separation, too, is generally called furthest in
30 those countries which enjoy the highest degree of industry and improvement; what is the work of one man in a rude* state of society being generally that of several in an improved one. […]

brethren here: people who belong to the same community or group
benevolent [bə'nev(ə)lənt] kind-hearted
to prevail to dominate

to exert oneself to strain oneself, to use a lot of physical or mental effort

to endeavour [ɪn'devə(r)] to try very hard to do sth.

revenue income from business activities or taxes

to occasion to cause

rude here: designed in a simple way

dexterity great skill in using your hands (*Fingerfertigkeit, Geschicklichkeit*)

to facilitate to make easier
to abridge to cut down, reduce

This great increase of the quantity of work which, in consequence of the division of labour, the same number of people are capable of performing, is owing to three different circumstances; first, to the increase of dexterity* in every particular workman; secondly, to the saving of time which is commonly lost in passing from one species of work to another; and lastly, to the invention of a great number of machines which facilitate* and abridge* labour, and enable one man to do the work of many. 35

Adam Smith: An Inquiry in to the Nature and Causes of the Wealth of Nations, Edwin Cannan, ed., Methuen & Co., Ltd., London 1904, www.econlib.org/library/Smith/smWN1.html [14.04.2015]

S 6 Aimé Perret

Die Rast bei der Ernte

In this painting, the French artist Aimé Perret (1847–1927) eternalised his idea of life in the countryside in oil on canvas, showing three young women taking a break from harvesting the crops.

Pre-task 1. Copy the adjectives in the box below which you find most suitable for describing the atmosphere captured in Perret's painting. Think of at least two more and add them to the list.

> rousing (= making you feel emotional, excited, or enthusiastic) • solemn • relaxing • inauspicious (= unheilvoll) • optimistic • pessimistic • calm • celebratory

Tasks 2. Describe the painting in detail, including its composition (cf. skills pages: language support).
3. Use the adjectives you classified as most suitable to describe the atmosphere captured by the artist. Back up your view by referring to specific pictorial elements (e.g. the posture of the people depicted).
4. Write a dialogue between the three women. It should include:
   ✓ how the women are related to each other,
   ✓ where, with whom and how they live,
   ✓ what they do for a living and
   ✓ what they cherish/criticize about their lives.
   Remember: Dialogues are supposed to be <u>acted</u> out, not <u>read</u> out. So make notes only.

Language support

Ernte, ernten (to) harvest • **eine Pause machen** to take a break • **sich ausruhen** to take a rest • **Korb** basket • **Rechen, Harke** rake • **Heuhaufen** haystack

S 7 Adolph von Menzel

Das Eisenwalzwerk

This oil painting by Adolph von Menzel (1815–1905) shows work at a steel mill in the Königshütte (foundry) in Upper Silesia and was created from 1872 to 1875. It is the first large-size German painting that has the immediate work process at its focus and symbolises the process of industrialisation by focussing on the production of steel as the "motor" of industry.

Pre-task
1. Both Perret (cf. S 6) and Menzel lived roughly at the same time, yet their portrayal of the work process is obviously quite different. Think of reasons for this.

Tasks
2. Have a look at the adjectives you chose to describe the atmosphere in Perret's painting (cf. S 6). Using that same list, give evidence from the painting (i.e. pictorial elements) to show that these adjectives do not fittingly describe the atmosphere in S 7 at all.
3. Find adjectives that aptly describe the atmosphere captured. You could look at the box in S 6 again for inspiration.
4. Compare S 6 and S 7 . Focus on the presentation of the work process.
5. With the help of the overview section and S 3 and S 4 , explain in detail why steel was the "motor" of industry (cf. introductory remarks).

Post-task
6. Only after the completion of the painting did von Wenzel give it a title, namely: "Modern Cyclopes". Imagine you were to write an explanation of the title of the painting of not more than 100 words for a museum guide. Do further research on the Cyclopes in ancient Greek mythology and write the explanation, with reference to the pictorial elements.

Language support

Stahl steel • **Eisen** iron ['aɪə(r)n] • **glühen** to glow/heat • **Hochofen** blast furnace • **Zange** pliers ['plaɪə(r)z], pincers • **schmieden** to forge • **schmelzen** to found

S 8) John Leech

A Court for King Cholera

In the wake of industrialization and urbanization, the living conditions in the cities changed dramatically, as illustrated by cartoonist John Leech in a cartoon he entitled "A Court for King Cholera" which was published in the British satirical magazine *Punch* in 1852. Cholera is a serious disease that affects one's stomach and intestines (*Eingeweide, Darm*) and is caused by drinking water or eating food infected with bacteria.

Pre-tasks
1. Write down five words that you associate with the word "king". Then talk to other students: What do you have in common and where do you differ? Do the words you have written down have more negative or more positive connotations?
2. Speculate why the artist chose to give the cartoon the title "A Court for King Cholera". What does this reveal about the status of the illness?

Tasks
3. Analyse the source.
4. Identify and explain "King Cholera's" courtiers (= *Höflinge*): Which conditions in the city made it easy to maintain the "kingship"?

A COURT FOR KING CHOLERA.

Language support

Schmutz dirt • **(un)hygienisch** (un)hygienic [haɪˈdʒiːnɪk] • **Haufen** pile • **Kopfstand** headstand • **überfüllt** over-crowded • **Wäscheleine** washing line

S 9 | Michael Faraday

Observations on the Filth of the Thames

In this letter to the editor to the *Times* of London from 7 July 1855, the English scientist Michael Faraday (1791–1867) warns of the state the river Thames finds itself in and foreshadows dire consequences in case the problem is not taken care of immediately.

Pre-task

1. In his letter, Faraday refers to the colour, the opacity (= *Trübheit*) and the smell of the river Thames. Sort the following phrases from the text into these categories.

   > - the same as that which now comes up from the gully-holes in the streets
   > - pale brown fluid
   > - feculence rolled up in clouds

2. Based on your results, explain why a river in such a state constitutes a severe health risk for the people living in the city.

Tasks

3. Scan the text for the phrases in the box and put them into their respective context: How does Faraday come to the conclusion that the Thames is "a real sewer"? (l. 18)
4. Imagine a meeting was taking place between Michael Faraday and John Leech (cf. S 8) in which the two of them discuss the health issues in London and suggest a list of measures to alleviate the situation. Write their letter of complaint to the mayor of London (in 1855, the Lord Mayor of London was Sir David Salomons). Some ideas and language support are given here.

---

10 July 1855
The City of London

To the Most Honoured Lord Mayor of London, Sir David Salomons,

- We take the pen in our hands because ...
- We have taken the liberty to address you on the issue of ...
- Please pardon the poor paper/the scratchy pen/the ungraceful language ...

- The following observations worry us: ...
- We are truly worried about the conditions in the cities, and about the state of the River Thames.
- To exemplify our worries, let us elaborate on ...

- We suggest/propose/advocate ...
- In order to improve the conditions, we have to ...
- It is imperative that we ...

Respectfully/Faithfully,
(names and professions)

SIR,

I traversed* this day by steam-boat the space between London and Hungerford Bridges between half-past one and two o'clock; it was low water, and I think the tide must have been near the turn. The appearance and the smell of the water forced themselves at once on my attention. The whole of the river was an opaque pale brown fluid. In order to test the degree of opacity, I tore up some white cards into pieces, moistened* them so as to make them sink easily below the surface, and then dropped some of these pieces into the water at every pier the boat came to; before they had sunk an inch below the surface they were indistinguishable, though the sun shone brightly at the time; and when the pieces fell edgeways* the lower part was hidden from sight before the upper part was under water. This happened at St. Paul's Wharf, Blackfriars Bridge, Temple Wharf, Southwark Bridge, and Hungerford; and I have no doubt would have occurred further up and down the river. Near the bridges the feculence* rolled up in clouds so dense* that they were visible at the surface, even in water of this kind.

The smell was very bad, and common to the whole of the water; it was the same as that which now comes up from the gully-holes in the streets; the whole river was for the time a real sewer*. Having just returned from out of the country air, I was, perhaps, more affected by it than others; but I do not think I could have gone on to Lambeth or Chelsea, and I was glad to enter the streets for an atmosphere which, except near the sink-holes, I found much sweeter than that on the river.

I have thought it a duty to record these facts, that they may be brought to the attention of those who exercise power or have responsibility in relation to the condition of our river; there is nothing figurative in the words I have employed, or any approach to exaggeration; they are the simple truth. If there be sufficient authority to remove a putrescent* pond* from the neighbourhood of a few simple dwellings*, surely the river which flows for so many miles through London ought not to be allowed to become a fermenting* sewer. The condition in which I saw the Thames may perhaps be considered as exceptional, but it ought to be an impossible state, instead of which I fear it is rapidly becoming the general condition. If we neglect* this subject, we cannot expect to do so with impunity*; nor ought we to be surprised if, ere many years are over, a hot season give us sad proof of the folly* of our carelessness.

I am, Sir
Your obedient servant,
M. FARADAY.
Royal Institution, July 7

from: Bence Jones (Ed.): The Life and Letters of Faraday, J.B. Lippincott & Co., Philadelphia 1870, pp. 363 f.

to traverse to move over/across an area

to moisten to make sth. slightly wet

edgeways sideways

feculence dirt, waste
dense thick

sewer Abfluss, Abwasser(kanal)

putrescent faulend, verwesend
pond Teich, Becken
dwelling the place where sb. lives
to ferment fermentieren, gären
to neglect vernachlässigen
impunity freedom from any risk of being punished
folly stupidity, madness

S 10) Eric Hobsbawm

The Great Boom

Eric Hobsbawm (1917–2012) was a British Marxist historian, especially famous for having coined the terms "long 19th century" (1789–1914) and "short 20th century" (1914–1989). The given text is an excerpt from one of his major works, "The Age of Capital, 1848–1875", which is part of a trilogy dealing with the 19th century. In the second chapter, entitled "The Great Boom", the historian explores the characteristic features and the impetus generated by the Second Industrial Revolution.

Pre-task

1. The "Second" Industrial Revolution describes a time starting – roughly speaking – in the late second half of the 19th century. Whereas the "First" Industrial Revolution had started in England and had focused on coal and steam as sources of power, the "Second" Industrial Revolution centred on the "sunrise industries" of electricity and chemistry and catapulted Germany to the top of the exporting countries. Revise what you have learned about the German Confederation from 1815 to 1871: Why was Germany a "late-bloomer" in terms of industrial development?

Tasks

2. Scan the text for reasons Hobsbawm gives for Germany's belated industrial development and explain them in more detail, taking into account your ideas from the pre-task.
3. Explain the title of the chapter "The Great Boom" against the backdrop of the given excerpt.
4. According to Hobsbawm, would it be appropriate to speak of a "First" and a "Second" Industrial Revolution? Give an evaluation and back up your view with the help of the text.

[...] The capitalist economy thus received simultaneously (which does not mean accidentally) a number of extremely powerful stimuli. What was the result? Economic expansion is most conveniently measured in statistics and its most characteristic measures in the nineteenth century are steam power (since the steam engine was the typical form of power) and the associated products of coal and iron. The mid-nineteenth century was pre-eminently the age of smoke and steam. Coal output had long been measured in millions of tons, but now came to be measured in tens of millions for individual countries, in hundreds of millions for the world. About half of it – rather more at the beginning of our period* – came from the incomparably largest producer, Great Britain. [...] But by 1870 France, Germany and the United States each produced between one and two million tons, though Britain, still the 'workshop of the world', remained far ahead with almost 6 million or about half the world output. [...]

Such crude* data indicate little more than that industrialization was progressing. The significant fact is that its progress was now geographically much more widespread, though also extremely uneven. The spread of railways and, to a lesser extent, steamships, now introduced mechanical power into all continents and into otherwise unindustrialized countries. The arrival of the railway [...] was in itself a revolutionary symbol and achievement, since the forging* of the globe into a single interacting economy was in many ways the most far-reaching and certainly the most spectacular aspect of industrialization. [...]

The industrialization of Germany was a major historical fact. Quite apart from its economic significance, its political implications were far-reaching. In 1850 the German Federation had about as many inhabitants as France, but incomparably less industrial capacity. By 1871 a united German empire was already somewhat more populous than France, but very much more powerful industrially. And, since political and military power now came to be increasingly based on industrial potential, technological capacity and know-how, the political consequences of industrial development were more serious than ever before. The wars of the 1860s demonstrated this [...]. Henceforth no state could maintain its place in the club of 'great powers' without it. [...]

our period cf. title of Hobsbawm's book

crude not exact or accurate, but often good enough for a particular purpose

forging here: *das Schmieden*

impetus a force that helps sth. to happen or develop more quickly

Still, though it made possible the revolutionary technology of the future, the new 'heavy industry' was not particularly revolutionary except perhaps in scale. Globally speaking, the Industrial Revolution up to the 1870s still ran on the impetus* generated by the technical innovations of 1760–1840. Nevertheless the mid-century decades did develop two kinds of industry based on a far more revolutionary technology: the chemical and (in so far as it was concerned with communications) the electrical. [...]

Eric Hobsbawm: The Age of Capital. 1848–1875, Vintage Books, New York 1996, pp. 39–42

S 11 Grenzverlegenheit

This German cartoon from 1834 must be seen against the backdrop of the creation of the Customs Union (*Zollverein*) in that same year, an extension of the Prussian Customs Union of 1818, under Prussian dominance. Before 1834, the states within the German Confederation (cf. chapter 1) had collected their own taxes and customs. With the creation of the Customs Union, a single market came into being, without internal tariffs (*Binnenzölle*). Austria, following an economic policy of protectionism, was excluded from the Customs Union.

Tasks
1. Describe the cartoon in detail.
2. Make use of your knowledge gained in S 10 and the information provided in the introductory remarks to put the cartoon into its historical context and to explain its elements, including the title.
3. Find an appropriate translation of the cartoon's title into English that expresses the same idea as the one contained in the title *Grenzverlegenheit*.

Embedded text: „Sie sehen, Herr Grenzwächter, dass ich nix zu verzolle hab', denn was hinte auf'm Wagen ist, hat die Lippische Gränz noch nit überschritten, in der Mitt' ist nix, und was vorn drauf is, ist schon wieder über der Lippischen Grenze drüben."

Language support

Grenzwächter border guard • **etw. verzollen** to clear goods/to declare goods • **überschreiten** to cross • **Planwagen** covered wagon • **Ladung** (cart)load

| Overview | Sources | Paper practice | Vocabulary | The First World War 205 |

S 12 Harold Baron

Chemical Industry on the Continent

In the given primary source, the author elaborates on the chemical industry in Germany, the chemical industry being one of the so-called "sunrise industries" (*Zukunftsindustrien*) Germany focused on, which helped her to overtake Britain in terms of economic output.

Pre-task

1. In 1887, Germany's General Electric Company (*Allgemeine Elektrizitäts-Gesellschaft Berlin*, or AEG) evolved from the German Edison Company, founded by Emil Rathenau in 1881. The colour lithograph provided on the right was proposed by Louis Schmidt to feature as the 1888 advertising poster for AEG. Describe the poster and its pictorial elements in detail. Afterwards, discuss the view on "progress" and what constitutes progress. Try to think of specific examples to underline your point of view (e. g. facilitation of everyday life/transport by means of electricity a.s.o.).

Tasks

2. Based on the text, write a job offer for Bayer for the position of a research chemist: What are the benefits of the workplace that you want to emphasize?
3. Discuss to what extent working at Bayer seemed to be a desirable option. Give proof from the text.

Post-task

4. Do further research on Bayer today: To what extent can the company be considered a German "success story"? Present your findings in class.

Language support

Göttin goddess • **Rad** wheel • **Flügel** wing(s) • **Lorbeerkranz** wreath [riːθ] of laurel • **Glühbirne** light bulb • **Blitz** (flash of) lightning

---

One of the most successful firms in Germany engaged in the manufacture of colours and pharmaceutical products, is the Farbenfabriken Friedr. Bayer & Co. of Elberfeld. This chemical works may be regarded as typical of a number of similar concerns engaged in the same branch of industry. [...] It was found in 1891 to be
5 impossible to obtain sufficient land in the immediate vicinity* of the works to permit of the considerable extension which the progress of the company necessitated*. A large site was, therefore, acquired at Leverkusen, which is about five miles north of Cologne on the right bank of the Rhine. The new works at Leverkusen has been planned on a huge scale. Ample provision has been made for the
10 enlargement of the existing plant* for many years to come. [...] The products manufactured by this firm still continue to be chiefly dyestuffs* [...]
A very important branch now being extensively developed is that of pharmaceutical products, such as Phenacetine, the well-known antipyretic, Sulphonal, and Trional, loclothyrine, Salophen, Aspirine, etc. [...]
15 Much research work is carried out in connection with dyeing and printing. Conferences are held daily at which new processes and inventions are brought before the staff and discussed with reference to their value to the firm [...]
The works at Leverkusen cover an estate of about 448 acres, and there is a large

vicinity the area near a particular place

to necessitate to make sth. necessary

plant here: factory
dyestuff *Färbemittel*

open district in the neighbourhood allowing for a further extension and the creation of a garden city for the workmen and employees of the firm. Bayer's works at Leverkusen is certainly one of the best organized chemical establishments in the world. About 3,500 people are employed at Leverkusen alone, and the works are of such a gigantic nature that this number seems to be lost when a visitor is shown through the works [...]

One of the research laboratories was visited [...] The laboratories are arranged very much in the same manner as the University laboratories in this country. Benches and cupboards are provided, and to each bench is led a supply of electricity, compressed air, steam and hot and cold water. The research chemists are paid a salary of about 100 [pounds sterling] for the first year. If a chemist has shown himself to be useful in his first year, a contract is usually made for a term of years in accordance with his capabilities. The research chemist is also remunerated* to some extent by receiving royalties* on the output of products manufactured in accordance with processes invented by himself [...] It is the policy of the large German colour works to keep the chemists strictly to their own department and not to allow them access to other departments. The object of this is to prevent employees becoming conversant* with other than their own work, so that it is less easy for them to carry away secrets to competitors. The contracts under which the employees are engaged are also of a somewhat binding nature. If a chemist desires to leave before the expiration of his contract he cannot as a rule enter the service of a competing firm until the expiration of a prescribed term.

Harold Baron: Chemical Industry on the Continent, Manchester University Press, Manchester 1909, pp. 46–51

to remunerate to pay/reward sb. for their work
royalty Honorar, Tantieme

conversant if one is conversant about sth., one knows about and understands it

S 13 Occupational Breakdown of Germany's Population

Industrialization had a major impact on the way that Germans earned their living. The given figures reveal some of the changes that took place between 1882 and 1907, the phase of the so-called "Second" Industrial Revolution.

Pre-task
1. Brainstorm in class: What have you already learned about changes in occupations in the wake of industrialization? Hint: The figures focus on the following economic sectors: agriculture/industry/trade & commerce/domestic service/administration, military, and independent professions. The unemployed are also considered here.

Tasks
2. Split up into six (expert) groups, each group focussing on one of the economic sectors labelled A to F. In your group, agree on and describe the most decisive changes taking place in your economic sectors. Afterwards, form new (jigsaw) groups in which all six "experts" are assembled. Exchange your findings and make notes.
3. Get back to your "original" expert groups. Double-check your overall findings. Together, explain the impact industrialization had on Germany's occupational breakdown. Select the most important data to back up your analysis.

Post-task
4. Do further research on Germany's occupational breakdown today. Present your findings in class and discuss the reasons for changes that have taken place. The website of Germany's *Statistisches Bundesamt* will be of help here: www.destatis.de.

Gainfully Employed Persons and their Dependents by Economic Sector (in Thousands)

Economic sector	Year	Total number of gainfully employed	Number of women	in %	Family members (d)(7)	Gainfully employed and family members	in % of total population
A. Agriculture	1882	8,236	2,535	30.8	10,564	18,801	41.6
	1895	8,293	2,753	33.2	9,834	18,127	35.0
	1907	9,883	4,599(9)	46.5	7,634	17,517	28.4
B. Industry	1882	6,396	1,127	17.6	9,359	15,756	34.8
	1895	8,281	1,521	18.4	11,652	19,933	38.5
	1907	11,256	2,104	18.7	14,799	26,055	42.2
C. Trade and commerce	1882	1,570	298	19.0	2,665	4,236	9.4
	1895	2,339	580	24.8	3,344	5,683	11.0
	1907	3,478	931	26.8	4,458	7,935	12.9
D. Domestic Service	1882	1,723	1,466	85.1	539	2,261	5.0
	1895	1,772	1,548	87.4	453	2,225	4.3
	1907	1,736	1,570	90.4	320	2,056	3.3
E. Administration, military, and independent professions	1882	1,031	115	11.2	1,027	2,058	4.6
	1895	1,426	177	12.4	1,218	2,644	5.1
	1907	1,739	288	16.6	1,445	3,184	5.2
Total A. through E.	1882	18,957	5,542	29.2	24,154	43,111	95.3
	1895	22,110	6,578	29.8	26,501	48,611	93.9
	1907	28,092	9,493	33.8	28,655	56,747	91.9
F. Those without occupations and those drawing pensions	1882	1,354	702	51.8	756	2,117	4.7
	1895	2,143	1,116	52.1	1,016	3,159	6.1
	1907	3,405	1,792	52.6	1,568	4,973	8.1
Total A. through F.	1882	20,311	6,247	30.7	24,911	45,222	100.0
	1895	24,253	7,694	31.7	27,517	51,770	100.0
	1907	31,497	11,285	35.8	30,223	61,721	100.0

Gerd Hohorst, Jürgen Kocka, and Gerhard A. Ritter, eds., Sozialgeschichtliches Arbeitsbuch: Materialien zur Statistik des Kaiserreichs 1870–1914, Beck, München 1975, vol. 2, p. 66, translated by Thomas Dunlap, *German History in Documents and Images*, German Historical Institute, Washington, DC (http://germanhistorydocs.ghi-dc.org)

Language support

- to fluctuate between/around
- to rise/increase (slightly/steadily/sharply/dramatically/rapidly) to/by
- a rise/increase of
- to go up and down
- to remain stable at
- a steady downward trend
- to go down gradually
- a marked upward trend
- to go up noticeably to fall/decrease (slightly/steadily/sharply/dramatically/rapidly) to/by
- a fall/decrease of
- stay at (a level)
- to plunge to/by
- a drop of xxx %
- figures shoot up from xxx % to xxx %
- to reach a peak
- to arrive at the highest point
- to (not) change
- to double
- to halve
- around/nearly/slightly more than/approximately/just over (under)

S14 A Poor-Relief Doctor Reports from Berlin

The given source is an excerpt from a poor-relief doctor's (*Armenarzt*) report from about 1890, written from a run-down Berlin quarter. The report shows the downside of industrialization and urbanization.

Pre-task

1. As you have learned in the first chapter, the social security system in the Second Empire was quite advanced and served as a model for other countries at that time. The given table from 1913 even claims it to be "an unmatched example for the entire world". Describe the poster and explain why, according to the makers of the poster, Germany's social security system was "an unmatched example for the entire world".

Die deutsche Sozialversicherung steht in der ganzen Welt vorbildlich und unerreicht da.

Die Krankenversicherung
ist seit ihrer Einführung im Jahre 1885 rund 18 Millionen Menschen zugute gekommen. Seit der Reichsversicherungsordnung von 1913 erstreckt sie sich sogar auf etwa die doppelte Anzahl.

1885 1900 1913

Für ärztliche Hilfe und Medikamente wurden 1885 18 Mio. Mark aufgewendet, dagegen im Jahre 1913 171 Mio. Mark.

Invaliden-Fürsorge
16 Millionen Invaliden der Arbeit wurde in den Jahren von 1893 bis 1913 eine Summe von 1805 Millionen Mark ausbezahlt.

Neben der Unterstützung im Invaliditätsfall hat Deutschland durch den Gewerbeschutz auch vorbeugend Grosses geleistet.

Krankenversicherung — Von 1885 5,6 Milliarden M. — bis 1913
Unfallversicherung 2,5 Milliarden M.
Für Invaliden und Hinterbliebene 2,7 Milliarden M.

Tägliche Leistung 1913 mehr als 2¼ Millionen M.

11 Milliarden Mark wurden in der deutschen Arbeiterversicherung-Sozialfürsorge - in der Zeit von 1885 bis 1913 aufgewendet.

Krankenversicherung 1912 in	Deutschland	England	Frankreich
Beiträge in Millionen Mark	464	besitzt ähnliche Einrichtungen erst seit 1912	41
Leistungen in Millionen Mark	426		24
Verhältnis von Leistung zu Beitrag	92%		59%
Leistung pro Fall in Mark	65		40

Altersversicherung
Seit der Errichtung dieses Zweiges der Sozialversicherung hat das Alter auch für den besitzlosen Arbeiter seine Schrecken verloren.

480 1/2 Millionen Mark kamen in der Zeit von 1891 bis 1913 528 000 Altersrentnern zugute. Versichert sind 16 Millionen.

Hinterbliebenen-Fürsorge
ist ein neuer Zweig der Arbeiter- und Angestelltenfürsorge Millionen Mark ausgezahlt.

Alle diese Massnahmen haben zu vermehrter Arbeitsfreudigkeit und Leistungsfähigkeit der deutschen Arbeiterschaft geführt.

L & P / 1013

Language support

Krankenversicherung health insurance • **Invaliden-Fürsorge** care for the disabled • **Altersversicherung** old-age pensions • **Hinterbliebenen-Fürsorge** survivor benefits

2. Now have a look at some observations of the poor-relief doctor in Berlin. Compare his observations with the table praising Germany's social security system: What would you tell the makers of the table if you were in the doctor's shoes?

> a prostitute severely injured by her pimp with a broken plate • every few weeks I had to make out death certificates for suicide couples • cholera • tuberculosis • insufficient diet • artificially induced miscarriages • venereal diseases (cf. annotations)

Tasks
3. Give a definition of the "Social Question", against the backdrop of the text.
4. Imagine an English-speaking friend not in command of the German language had to write a term paper about the "Social Question" and would like to include the most striking of the poor-relief doctor's observations to illustrate the issue. Select the information you think would be most useful to her/him and mediate them into English.

Post-task
5. Revise the different views on the concept of "progress" you have come across so far: Illustrate possible "downsides" of progress with the help of your newly-gained information.

Die Eichendorffstraße, dicht am Nordende der nordsüdlichen Hauptader* Berlins, der Friedrichstraße, und am Stettiner Bahnhof gelegen, gehörte damals zum Quartier latin, das sich, wie mir scheint, seitdem mit der Verbesserung der Transporteinrichtungen immer mehr nach der Gegend des Zoologischen Gartens und dem Savigny-Platze hin verlegt hat. Das heißt, es gab dort viel Kleinbürgertum*, namentlich von alten Leuten, die von der Vermietung der Zimmer an die Studenten lebten, und kolossal viel Prostitution. Es gab außerdem sehr viele Arbeiter, wenn auch nicht gerade von der alleruntersten Schicht der Lumpenproletarier*; mehr Gelernte als Ungelernte*.

Hier sah ich zum ersten Male mit immer wachsendem Verständnis* und immer größerem Grauen* in das Medusenantlitz* der sozialen Frage. Es war eine Kleineleutepraxis, oft sogar eine Armeleutepraxis; es kam immer öfter vor, dass sich ganz arme Familien an mich statt an den offiziellen Armenarzt wendeten; das ganze Elend* der Großstadt entblößte sich vor meinen Augen, und die soziale Bedingtheit so vieler Krankheiten drängte sich mir auf. Als Arzt der Sanitätswache* hatte ich häufig die Folgen von schweren Schlägereien* zu behandeln. Einmal wurde ich in das fürchterlichste Milieu berufen, das ich jemals betreten habe: eine alte Dirne* war von ihrem Zuhälter*, angeblich mit einem zerbrochenen Teller, wahrscheinlich aber mit einem gefährlicheren Instrument, schwer verletzt worden; der Rand des Schulterblattes* lag frei in der klaffenden Rückenwunde*. Alle paar Wochen wurde ich in eines der finsteren kleinen Absteigequartiere* jener Gegend gerufen, um einem Selbstmörderpaare die Totenscheine auszustellen*; und ich hatte eine ganz regelmäßige Einnahme aus der Bescheinigung* von blauen Flecken* und derartigen kleinen Schäden, Attesten, die der erfolgreichen Anstrengung eines Prozesses* dienen sollten. Entsetzliche Roheit* [sic], beschämende* Unbildung*, grässliche Unwissenheit!

Und die übrige Praxis? An der Spitze marschierte die tödliche Seuche*, die damals noch die Säuglinge* der Großstadt mehr als zehntete*: die Kindercholera, die Sommerdiarrhöe, die mir selbst vor langer Zeit meinen geliebten kleinen Bruder Georg geraubt hatte. Wir kannten die Ursache: verdorbene* Milch und schlechte Luft in den überhitzten Mietskasernen*, in die auch die Nacht keine Kühlung bringen konnte, weil die aneinandergedrängten Mauermassen nachts

---

Hauptader artery
Kleinbürgertum petite bourgeoisie
Lumpenproletarier lumpenproletariat
(Un)Gelernte (un)skilled worker
Verständnis sympathy
Grauen horror
Medusenantlitz gorgon's head (in Greek mythology, Medusa was a woman with hair formed from venomous snakes)
Elend misery
Sanitätswache ambulance station
Schlägerei brawl
Dirne prostitute
Zuhälter pimp
Schulterblatt shoulder blade
klaffende Wunde gaping wound
Absteigequartier flophouse
einen Totenschein ausstellen to make out a death certificate
Bescheinigung certification
blauer Fleck bruise
Prozess court action
Roh(h)eit brutality
beschämend shameful
Unbildung lack of education
Seuche disease
Säugling infant
zehnten to kill one tenth of
verdorben spoiled
Mietskaserne tenement house

Hitze ausströmen to radiate heat	die Hitze ausströmten*, die sie am Tage aufgesogen hatten. Vor allem in den engen Höfen mordete die Seuche. Ein berühmter Arzt sagte damals in bitterer Empörung*: „Die armen Kinder werden erst auf dem Totenbette kühl." Wieviel Totenscheine habe ich ausgestellt für solche Würmchen, die ich vorher nie gesehen hatte! Der Tod hatte sie fast mit der Geschwindigkeit eines Blitzes dahingerafft. An zweiter Stelle kam der Zahl nach die Tuberkulose, namentlich in ihrer Gestalt als Lungenschwindsucht*. [...]
Empörung outrage	
Lungenschwindsucht pulmonary tuberculosis	
unzureichende Ernährung insufficient diet	Hier handelte es sich in der Regel um Menschen mit unbelasteter Aszendenz, um ursprünglich gesunde und starke Männer und Frauen, die den Einwirkungen des Fabrikstaubes, der licht- und luftlosen Wohnung und der unzureichenden Ernährung* verfallen waren, oder die sich im Zusammenleben mit anderen Kranken infiziert* hatten. Man musste sie sterben und die Familien zugrunde gehen lassen; gelang es einmal, einen in eine der wenigen damals vorhandenen Anstalten zur Aufnahme zu bringen, so war das fast immer nur eine Atempause; er musste zurück in seine Beschäftigung, und das gefräßige Tier in seiner Lunge wurde seiner Herr. An dritter Stelle stand die Unzahl* der künstlich herbeigeführten Fehlgeburten*, die ich nachzubehandeln hatte, verbrochen in schmutzigen Winkeln von noch schmutzigeren Weibern, die ihren Opfern den letzten Pfennig aus der Tasche zogen und oft genug ihnen dauerndes Siechtum* oder gar den Tod brachten. Und dann das Heer der Geschlechtskrankheiten*, die Prostitution aller Schattierungen, von der eleganten Freundin mehrerer Männer bis herab zur völlig verkommenen unseligen „Tippelschickse"*: „der Menschheit ganzer Jammer" fasst mich noch heute an, wenn ich an all das Elend zurückdenke, das wie ein gespenstischer Film an mir vorüberglitt.
sich infizieren to be/become infected	
Unzahl enormous number	
künstlich herbeigeführte Fehlgeburt artificially induced miscarriage	
dauerndes Siechtum lasting infirmity	
Geschlechtskrankheit venereal [vəˈnɪərɪəl] disease	
Tippelschickse whore	

Franz Oppenheimer: Erlebtes, Erstrebtes, Erreichtes. Lebenserinnerungen, Düsseldorf: Joseph Melzer Verlag, 1964, pp. 100 ff.

Karl Marx (1818–1883)

Karl Marx was born in Trier in 1818 as the third of nine children of the lawyer Heinrich Marx and his wife Henriette. From 1835 to 1841, he studied law and philosophy – first in Bonn, then in Berlin. In 1843, he and his wife Jenny from Westphalia moved to Paris where Marx also became friends with the German poet Heinrich Heine. From 1844 onwards, he, together with Arnold Ruge, was editor of the *Deutsch-Französische Jahrbücher*. In that same year, he also befriended Friedrich Engels (cf. box).

However, the Prussian government pushed for Marx's expulsion from Paris, which made him give up his Prussian citizenship and move to Brussels. In 1847, the League of Communists commissioned him and Engels to come up with a programmatic piece of writing to reorganise the League (cf. S 15).

Together with Engels, Marx also founded the *Deutscher Arbeiterverein* in 1847.

During the 1848/49 revolutions, he returned to Cologne where he edited the left-wing *Neue Rheinische Zeitung*. However, in 1849 he was exiled from Germany and moved to London, where he would remain until his death.

Several publications, often in cooperation with Engels, turned Marx into one of the leaders of the new movement of socialism. In 1864, he was authoritative in the foundation of the International Workers' Association, also called *Erste Internationale*. With his theoretical works, Marx established the scientific and ideological foundation for the socialist movement.

Karl Marx died in London on 14 March 1883.

Karl Marx

Friedrich Engels (1820–1895)

Friedrich Engels was born in Barmen (today a part of the city of Wuppertal) in 1820, the son of a textile factory owner and the eldest of nine children. He left school before his final examinations in order to work in his father's factory. In 1842, Engels first met Karl Marx at the offices of the *Rheinische Zeitung* in Cologne (cf. box on p. 210).

From 1842 to 1844, he continued his commercial apprenticeship in his father's cotton spinning works in Manchester, England. Observing the workers' situation there was to change his political views substantially.

Engels' visit to Paris in 1844 and his writing for the *Deutsch-Französische Jahrbücher* is seen as the beginning of his lifelong friendship with Marx whom he also often supported financially. Together, they wrote the Communist Manifesto for the League of Communists. Engels was actively involved in the 1848/49 revolutions and, after their failure, tried to fuel a second revolution from London. In 1850 he returned to his father's factory in Manchester, where he spent the next twenty years. In 1869, Engels sold his share in the company and settled down only a few blocks from Marx in London. He stayed in England after Marx's death in 1883. He himself died on 5 August 1895, after a short period of illness. He bequeathed* an immense part of his considerable fortune to the German social democratic movement.

Engels in 1877

---

to bequeath to give sb. money/property after you die

S 15 Karl Marx/Friedrich Engels

Das Kommunistische Manifest

The "Communist Manifesto" of 1848 was drafted by Karl Marx and Friedrich Engels and was meant to explain the aims and the policies of the League of Communists (*Bund der Kommunisten*).

Pre-task
1. You have certainly come across some of the catchphrases contained in the Communist Manifesto, such as "A spectre is haunting Europe – the spectre of communism" or "Workers of all countries, unite." Brainstorm in class about what you remember about the ideologies of "capitalism" and "communism" and about the year 1848 in which the Communist Manifesto was published (cf. pp. 28 ff.).

Tasks
2. Outline the cornerstones of the Communist Manifesto. Focus on the class struggle, namely the reasons for the class struggle and how it will eventually be overcome.
3. "Workers of all countries, unite!" (l. 72) Explain a) how this call to action is logically deduced from the line of argument, and b) why it would be especially threatening to capitalism, i.e. "big business".
4. The theory of communism is characterized by a teleological world view (from Greek *telos* = end, and *logos* = reason), directed towards a certain final state and existing for that specific purpose. Visualise the steps towards the final state of communism in a flow chart with the help of the overview section and the given source.

Post-task
5. Write an afterword for the Communist Manifesto in which you take a critical stand on Adam Smith's economic theory (cf. S 5) and its contribution to and legitimation of the exploitation of the proletariat.

Gespenst spectre **Hetzjagd** hunt, chivvy **Guizot** (1787–1874) conservative liberal French politician before 1848	Ein Gespenst* geht um in Europa – das Gespenst des Kommunismus. Alle Mächte des alten Europa haben sich zu einer heiligen Hetzjagd* gegen dies Gespenst verbündet, der Papst und der Zar, Metternich und Guizot*, französische Radikale und deutsche Polizisten. [...]
Klassenkampf class struggle **Freier ... Gesell** free person/slave/patrician/plebeian/baron/serf/guild citizen/journeyman **ununterbrochen** incessant [ɪnˈsesənt]	Die Geschichte aller bisherigen Gesellschaft ist die Geschichte von Klassenkämpfen*. Freier und Sklave, Patrizier und Plebejer, Baron und Leibeigener, Zunftbürger und Gesell*, kurz, Unterdrücker und Unterdrückte standen in stetem Gegensatz zu einander, führten einen ununterbrochenen* [...] Kampf, der jedesmal mit einer revolutionären Umgestaltung der ganzen Gesellschaft endete, oder mit dem gemeinsamen Untergang der kämpfenden Klassen. [...]
Klassengegensatz class antagonism **etw. vereinfachen** to simplify **Lager** camp	Unsere Epoche, die Epoche der Bourgeoisie, zeichnet sich [...] dadurch aus, dass sie die Klassengegensätze* vereinfacht* hat. Die ganze Gesellschaft spaltet sich mehr und mehr in zwei große feindliche Lager*, in zwei große einander direkt gegenüberstehende Klassen – Bourgeoisie und Proletariat. [...]
Widersinn nonsense	In den Krisen bricht eine gesellschaftliche Epidemie aus, welche allen früheren Epochen als ein Widersinn* erschienen wäre – die Epidemie der Überproduktion. [...] Wodurch überwindet die Bourgeoisie die Krisen? Einerseits durch die erzwungene Vernichtung einer Masse von Produktionskräften; andererseits durch die Eroberung neuer Märkte, und die gründlichere Ausbeutung* der alten Märkte.
Ausbeutung exploitation **Mittel** means (pl.)	Wodurch also? Dadurch, dass sie allseitigere und gewaltigere Krisen vorbereitet und die Mittel*, den Krisen vorzubeugen, vermindert. [...]. Aber die Bourgeoisie hat nicht nur die Waffen geschmiedet, die ihr den Tod bringen; sie hat auch die Männer gezeugt, die diese Waffen führen werden – die modernen Arbeiter, die Proletarier.
vermehren to increase **Ware** goods **Schwankung** fluctuation **Mittelstand** middle class **Rentier** rentier [ˈrɒntieɪ] (a person receiving fixed economic income from e.g. bonds, patents) **Handwerker** craftsperson **Konkurrenz** competition **Geschicklichkeit** dexterity	In demselben Maße, worin sich die Bourgeoisie, d. h. das Kapital entwickelt, in demselben Maße entwickelt sich das Proletariat, die Klasse der modernen Arbeiter, die nur so lange leben als sie Arbeit finden, und die nur so lange Arbeit finden, als ihre Arbeit das Kapital vermehrt*. Diese Arbeiter, die sich stückweis verkaufen müssen, sind eine Ware* wie jeder andere Handelsartikel, und daher gleichmäßig allen Wechselfällen der Konkurrenz, allen Schwankungen* des Marktes ausgesetzt. [...] Die bisherigen kleinen Mittelstände*, die kleinen Industriellen, Kaufleute und Rentiers*, die Handwerker* und Bauern, alle diese Klassen fallen ins Proletariat hinab, teils dadurch, dass ihr kleines Kapital für den Betrieb der großen Industrie nicht ausreicht, und der Konkurrenz* mit den größeren Kapitalisten erliegt, teils dadurch, dass ihre Geschicklichkeit* von neuen Produktionsweisen entwertet wird. So rekrutiert sich das Proletariat aus allen Klassen der Bevölkerung. [...]
Lebenslagen living circumstances **ausgleichen** to balance **Lohn** wage **willenlos** will-less **widerstandslos** unresisting	Aber mit der Entwicklung der Industrie vermehrt sich nicht nur das Proletariat; es wird in größeren Massen zusammengedrängt, seine Kraft wächst und es fühlt sie immer mehr. Die Interessen und die Lebenslagen* innerhalb des Proletariats gleichen sich immer mehr aus*, indem die Maschinerie mehr und mehr die Unterschiede der Arbeit verwischt und den Lohn* fast überall auf ein gleich niedriges Niveau herabdrückt. [...] Der Fortschritt der Industrie, dessen willenloser* und widerstandsloser* Träger die Bourgeoisie ist, setzt an die Stelle der Isolierung der Arbeiter durch die Konkurrenz ihre revolutionäre Vereinigung durch die Assoziation. [...]
	Die Kommunisten sind [...] praktisch der entschiedenste immer weiter treibende Teil der Arbeiterparteien aller Länder, sie haben theoretisch vor der übrigen Masse des Proletariats die Einsicht in die Bedingungen, den Gang und die allgemeinen

50 Resultate der Proletarischen Bewegung* voraus. Der nächste Zweck der Kommunisten ist derselbe wie der aller übrigen proletarischen Parteien: Bildung des Proletariats zur Klasse, Sturz* der Bourgeoisieherrschaft, Eroberung der politischen Macht durch das Proletariat. [...] Ihr entsetzt Euch darüber, dass wir das Privateigentum aufheben wollen. Aber in eurer bestehenden Gesellschaft ist das Privat-
55 eigentum für neun Zehntel ihrer Mitglieder aufgehoben; es existiert gerade dadurch, dass es für neun Zehntel nicht existiert. Ihr werft uns also vor, dass wir ein Eigentum aufheben wollen, welches die Eigentumslosigkeit der ungeheuren Mehrzahl der Gesellschaft als notwendige Bedingung voraussetzt*. [...]
Wenn das Proletariat im Kampfe gegen die Bourgeoisie sich notwendig zur Klasse
60 vereint, durch eine Revolution sich zur herrschenden Klasse macht, und als herrschende Klasse gewaltsam die alten Produktionsverhältnisse aufhebt, so hebt es mit diesen Produktionsverhältnissen die Existenzbedingungen des Klassengegensatzes der Klassen überhaupt, und damit seine eigene Herrschaft als Klasse auf. An die Stelle der alten bürgerlichen Gesellschaft mit ihren Klassen und Klassen-
65 gegensätzen tritt eine Assoziation, worin die freie Entwicklung eines jeden die Bedingung für die freie Entwicklung aller ist. [...]
Die Kommunisten [...] erklären es offen, dass ihre Zwecke nur erreicht werden können durch den gewaltsamen Umsturz aller bisherigen Gesellschaftsordnung*. Mögen die herrschenden Klassen vor einer Kommunistischen Revolution
70 zittern*. Die Proletarier haben nichts zu verlieren als ihre Ketten*. Sie haben eine Welt zu gewinnen.
Proletarier aller Länder vereinigt* euch!

from: Jürgen Sandweg, Michael Stürmer: Industrialisierung und Soziale Frage in Deutschland im 19. Jahrhundert, Oldenbourg, München 1979, pp. 71 f.

Bewegung movement

Sturz overthrow

etw. voraussetzen here: to require, to presuppose

Gesellschaftsordnung social order
zittern to tremble
Ketten shackles
sich vereinigen to unite

"Capital and Labour". Cartoon by John Leech, published in the British satirical magazine *Punch* in May 1843.

Language support

Zweiteilung bisection, division into two parts • **Sessel** armchair • **Bediensteter** servant • **Tablett** tray • **Papagei** parrot • **Himmelbett** canopy bed • **Kissen** cushion [ˌkʊʃ(ə)n] • **Aufseher** supervisor • **Minenschacht** shaft • **kriechen** to crawl • **graben** to dig (dug – dug) • **Anker** anchor

CONNECT

The "Social Question" – A(n) (Un)solvable Issue?

There were various attempts to find solutions to the so-called "social question," one of which was embedded in the idea of communism, calling on the proletarians of all countries to unite (cf. S 15). Here are three further views on how to alleviate the lamentable situation vast parts of the working class found themselves in.

Task Presenting and evaluating different attempts to solve the "social question" in a gallery walk.

Split into three groups, each group focussing on one of the attempts presented on the following pages (S 16a – S 16c). Design a poster that contains the gist of your respective approach to tackling the social issues. There are comprehension tasks for each source that are meant to guide you through the most important points.

You should, however, also focus on the motivation of the person/group, and you should assess how realistic and effective an implementation of the approach would be, so look into aspects of practicability.

The presentation of the posters should take place in a gallery walk (see box below) during which "route cards" should be filled out.

Route card template (to be copied into exercise books):

Person/group	Motivation	Suggestions/Ideas	Practicability
Hermann Wagener			
SPD			
Pope Leo XIII			

After the presentations, take a vote in class: Which approach do you consider to be the most realistic and effective? Be prepared to give reasons for your choice.

> **Gallery walk**
> In a museum, the exhibits are usually presented in a gallery and the visitors move from one exhibit to the other, sometimes accompanied by a guide who explains the exhibits.
> In the classroom, the exhibits are the products designed by the various groups, in this case the posters which have been put up in different parts of the classroom. Each group selects a speaker who will stay with the poster and, if necessary, explain it to the other students. The other group members walk around the classroom, from exhibit to exhibit, and make notes on their route cards which will form the basis for the evaluation of the issues under discussion.

S 16a Hermann Wagener

Why the Government Cannot Ignore the Social Question

In this memorandum (*Denkschrift*) to Bismarck dated 29 January 1872, the conservative politician Hermann Wagener (1815–1889) gives reasons for his viewpoint that the "social question" must be tackled by the state, claiming that inaction would have a devastating effect, since enforcing further repressive means (cf. chapter 1: Struggle for Culture, Anti-Socialist Laws) would, in his eyes, pave the way for a domestic "two-front war" against the socialists and the Catholics.

Pre-task

1. With the help of the introductory remarks and the given cartoon, revise what you have learned about Bismarck's domestic policy with regard to socialism and Catholicism. Against this backdrop, make an educated guess why Wagener was afraid of a two-front war in the event that the state would not tackle the "social question".

Tasks

2. State the example of England and America Wagener makes use of.
3. Describe the "practical propositions" (l. 43).
4. Do not forget to explain the author's motivation and to assess the practicability of his approach.

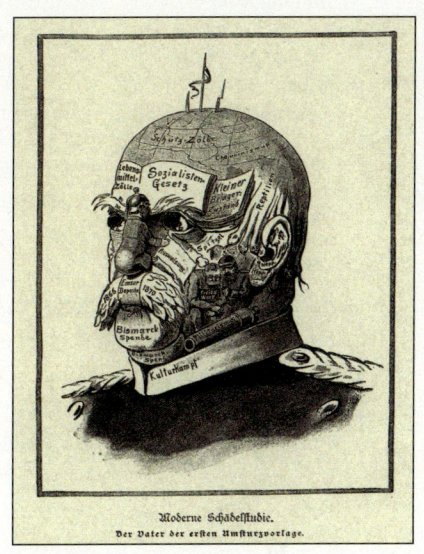

German cartoon published after Bismarck's dismissal in 1890, satirizing his political legacy

Da nach meinem ganz gehorsamsten Dafürhalten* die Art und Weise, in welcher man jetzt auf dem sozialen Gebiete vorgeht, nicht die richtige ist, so erlaube ich mir Euer Durchlaucht* eine kurze Zusammenfassung dessen, was mir dagegen notwendig zu schein scheint, ehrerbietigst* vorzule-
5 gen. [...]
Mir erscheint es [...] als ein überaus gefährliches Unternehmen*, gleichzeitig den Kampf mit der ultramontanen* und der sozialistischen Partei aufnehmen zu wollen und dadurch die Sozialen noch mehr und unwiderruflich* in das klerikale Lager* zu treiben. Mag es immerhin berechtigt und
10 notwendig sein, die bestehenden Gesetze nach allen Seiten energisch zur Anwendung zu bringen* und dadurch insbesondere die auswärtigen* sowie diejenigen Elemente von der sozialen Bewegung fern zu halten, welche antinationale Zwecke verfolgen*, so halte ich es doch für einen entschieden politischen Fehler, die sozialistischen Führer lediglich um ihrer sozialen
15 Bestrebungen willen Ausnahmemaßregeln* zu unterwerfen*, und zwar, ohne gleichzeitig irgendetwas Namhaftes* zur Befriedigung* der berechtigten Bestrebungen* ihrer Anhänger zu tun. [...]
Die neuesten zuverlässigen* Berichte aus England und Amerika ergeben, dass man in England beispielsweise den neunstündigen Normalarbeitstag
20 kaum noch als eine Frage der Gesetzgebung* behandelt, sondern dass die Trade-Unions sich bereits stark genug fühlen, denselben selbstständig durchzusetzen*, und der amerikanische Kongress hat bekanntlich eine Kommission niedergesetzt*, um die Lage des Arbeiterstandes für die Zwecke der Gesetzgebung festzustellen. Dass Letzteres gleichzeitig ein Wahl-

gehorsamstes Dafürhalten in my most humble opinion
Euer Durchlaucht Your Highness
ehrerbietigst respectfully
gefährliches Unternehmen dangerous endeavour [ɪnˈdevə(r)]
ultramontan i.e. the Catholics
unwiderruflich irrevocable
das klerikale Lager the clerical camp
zur Anwendung bringen to apply
auswärtig external
einen Zweck verfolgen to pursue an aim
Ausnahmemaßregel emergency law
jdn. einer Sache unterwerfen to subject sb. to sth.
etwas Namhaftes sth. substantial
Befriedigung satisfaction
Bestrebungen efforts
zuverlässig reliable
Gesetzgebung legislation
durchsetzen to push through
niedersetzen to form

manöver* ist, dürfte die Bedeutung der Maßregel eher steigern* als abschwächen*.

Nach meinem ehrerbietigsten Dafürhalten* sollte die deutsche Reichsregierung diesen Vorgängen folgen und insbesondere auch ihrerseits mit einer gründlichen Enquête* den Anfang machen, wobei ich es als selbstverständlich voraussetze, dass man alles, was auf diesem Gebiet geschieht, mit der größtmöglichsten Publizität behandelt. Außerdem würde es notwendig sein, bei der Auswahl der zu vernehmenden* Personen sich auf eine breitere Basis zu stellen und auch die Leute zu hören, welche mit Recht als gründliche Forscher* auf diesem Gebiete gelten. [...]

Nach allen Erfahrungen der Geschichte ist es aussichtslos*, einen kräftigen Gedanken lediglich mit materiellen Mitteln bekämpfen zu wollen und es gibt dem jetzt sehr mächtigen katholisch-kirchlichen Gedanken gegenüber nur einen Gedanken, der demselben mit Aussicht auf Erfolg politisch ebenbürtig gegenübergestellt werden kann, nämlich den sozialen, und in der Wechselwirkung* dieser beiden Gedanken wird sich nach meinem unvorgreiflichen Dafürhalten die nächste Phase der europäischen Geschichte abspielen.

Die praktischen Vorschläge, welche ich zunächst zu machen haben würde, sind:

1. Niedergang einer Kommission nach dem amerikanischen Vorbilde*, um die Gesetzgebung auf diesem Gebiete vorzubereiten und einzuleiten;
2. Ergänzung der im Handelsministerium* begonnenen Sachverständigenvernehmung* mit möglichster Ausdehnung und Publizität;
3. Praktisches Vorgehen mit dem Institut der Fabrikinspektoren* oder – wenn die andere Bezeichnung besser gefallen sollte – der Arbeitsämter*.

In der Ausbildung namentlich des letzteren Institutes ist die Möglichkeit einer Organisation gegeben, welche auf dem politischen Gebiet selbst der Organisation der katholischen Kirche nicht bloß gewachsen*, sondern sogar überlegen* sein würde. Den materiellen Tendenzen der Gegenwart gegenüber ist der Sozial-Kaiser* stärker als selbst der Sozial-Papst*. [...]

Die Massen der Bevölkerung schwanken gegenwärtig, wohin sie sich wenden sollen. Noch hat die internationale Agitation keine breitere Basis gewonnen, obschon man es hier und da darauf abgesehen zu haben scheint, ihr wohlfeile* Märtyrer zu machen.

Wohin die Massen sich wenden, wird aber nicht allein politisch und parlamentarisch, sondern auch für den Charakter der Armee schließlich von entscheidender Bedeutung sein. Ganz und dauernd zuverlässig wird diese nur dann sein, wenn die Arbeiter, welche das Hauptkontingent* liefern, durch die Leistungen des Reiches für die Reichsidee* gewonnen und an diese gekettet* werden.

Hermann Wagener: Denkschrift an den Reichskanzler Otto von Bismarck, 29. Januar 1872. In: Horst Kohl (Ed.): Bismarck-Jahrbuch, Vol. 6, Verlag von O. Häring: Berlin 1899, pp. 209–214

Wahlmanöver election manoeuver
steigern to add to
abschwächen to detract from
Dafürhalten opinion
Enquête inquiry

vernehmen to listen to

gründliche Forscher thorough researchers
aussichtslos hopeless

Wechselwirkung mutual interaction

Vorbild example

Handelsministerium Ministry of Trade
Sachverständigenvernehmung questioning of experts
Fabrikinspektoren Factory Inspectors
Arbeitsämter employment offices
einer Sache gewachsen sein to match sth.
überlegen superior
Sozial-Kaiser social Kaiser
Sozial-Papst social Pope

wohlfeil opportune

Hauptkontingent main contingent
Reichsidee idea of the Reich
an etw. ketten to be bound to sth.

Photograph taken around 1900, showing the then-leaders of the SPD

S 16b The Social Democratic Party (SPD)

Erfurt Programme

The Erfurt Programme of 1891 was the party programme of the SPD which replaced the Gotha programme of 1875. After the persecution of the socialists under Bismarck (cf. pp. 40 f.), the SPD sought to establish a new position and strategy in order to cope with the impacts of industrialization.

Pre-task
1. Collect words and phrases you use when talking about democracy and political participation, especially those you believe the SPD might include in their party programme (as opposed, for example, to conservative parties).

Task
2. Describe the situation the working class finds itself in, according to the SPD analysis, and state their primary aim.
3. Put the demands into categories and paraphrase them.
4. Where is the difference between socialism and communism (cf. S 15)? Discuss.
5. Do not forget to explain the authors' motivation and to assess the practicability of their approach.

[...] Der Kampf der Arbeiterklasse* gegen die kapitalistische Ausbeutung ist notwendigerweise ein politischer Kampf. Die Arbeiterklasse kann ihre ökonomischen Kämpfe nicht führen und ihre ökonomische Organisation nicht entwickeln ohne politische Rechte. Sie kann den Übergang* der Produktionsmittel* in den Besitz der Gesamtheit nicht bewirken, ohne in den Besitz der politischen Macht gekommen zu sein.

Arbeiterklasse working class

Übergang transfer
Produktionsmittel means of production

Diesen Kampf der Arbeiterklasse zu einem bewussten* und einheitlichen* zu gestalten und ihm sein naturnotwendiges* Ziel zu weisen* – das ist die Aufgabe der Sozialdemokratischen Partei.

Die Interessen der Arbeiterklasse sind in allen Ländern mit kapitalistischer Produktionsweise die gleichen. Mit der Ausdehnung des Weltverkehrs* und der Produktion für den Weltmarkt wird die Lage der Arbeiter eines jeden Landes immer abhängiger von der Lage der Arbeiter in den anderen Ländern. Die Befreiung der Arbeiterklasse ist also ein Werk, an dem die Arbeiter aller Kulturländer* gleichmäßig beteiligt* sind. In dieser Erkenntnis* fühlt und erklärt die Sozialdemokratische Partei Deutschlands sich eins mit den klassenbewussten* Arbeitern aller übrigen Länder.

Die Sozialdemokratische Partei Deutschlands kämpft also nicht für neue Klassenprivilegien und Vorrechte*, sondern für die Abschaffung* der Klassenherrschaft und der Klassen selbst und für gleiche Rechte und gleiche Pflichten aller ohne Unterschied des Geschlechts* und der Abstammung*. Von diesen Anschauungen ausgehend bekämpft sie in der heutigen Gesellschaft nicht bloß die Ausbeutung und Unterdrückung der Lohnarbeiter*, sondern jede Art der Ausbeutung und Unterdrückung, richte sie sich gegen eine Klasse, eine Partei, eine Geschlecht oder eine Rasse.

Ausgehend von diesen Grundsätzen fordert die Sozialdemokratische Partei Deutschlands zunächst:

Allgemeines, gleiches, direktes Wahl- und Stimmrecht* mit geheimer Stimmabgabe* aller über 20 Jahre alten Reichsangehörigen* ohne Unterschied des Geschlechts für alle Wahlen und Abstimmungen. Proportionalwahlsystem*, und bis zu dessen Einführung gesetzliche Neueinteilung* der Wahlkreise* nach jeder Volkszählung*. Zweijährige Gesetzesperioden*. Vornahme der Wahlen und Abstimmungen an einem gesetzlichen Ruhetag. Entschädigung* für die gewählten Vertreter. Aufhebung jeder Beschränkung politischer Rechte außer im Falle der Entmündigung*.

Direkte Gesetzgebung* durch das Volk vermittels des Vorschlags- und Verwerfungsrechts*. Selbstbestimmung* und Selbstverwaltung* des Volks in Reich, Staat, Provinz und Gemeinde*. Wahl der Behörden durch das Volk, Verantwortlichkeit und Haftbarkeit derselben. Jährliche Steuerbewilligung*.

Erziehung zur allgemeinen Wehrhaftigkeit*. Volkswehr* an Stelle der stehenden Heere*. Entscheidung über Krieg und Frieden durch die Volksvertretung. Schlichtung* aller internationalen Streitigkeiten auf schiedsgerichtlichem Wege*.

Abschaffung aller Gesetze, welche die Frau in öffentlich- und privatrechtlicher Beziehung gegenüber dem Manne benachteiligen*.

Erklärung der Religion zur Privatsache. Abschaffung aller Aufwendungen* aus öffentlichen Mitteln zu religiösen und kirchlichen Zwecken. Die kirchlichen und religiösen Gemeinschaften sind als private Vereinigungen zu betrachten, welche ihre Angelegenheiten vollkommen selbstständig ordnen*.

---

bewusst conscious
einheitlich unified
naturnotwendig inherently necessary
weisen to point out
Weltverkehr global commerce
Kulturländer civilized countries
gleichmäßig beteiligt equally involved
in dieser Erkenntnis recognizing this
klassenbewusst class-conscious
Vorrecht prerogative
Abschaffung abolishment
Geschlecht sex
Abstammung here: birth
Lohnarbeiter wage earner
Allgemeines ... Stimmrecht universal, equal and direct suffrage
geheime Stimmabgabe secret ballot
Reichsangehörige citizens of the Reich
Proportionalwahlsystem proportional representation
Neueinteilung redistribution
Wahlkreis constituency [kənstɪtjʊənsi]
Volkszählung census
Gesetzesperiode legislative period
Entschädigung compensation
Entmündigung legal incapacity
direkte Gesetzgebung direct legislation
Vorschlags- und Verwerfungsrat rights of proposal and rejection
Selbstbestimmung self-determination
Selbstverwaltung self-government
Gemeinde municipality
jährliche Steuerbewilligung annual voting of taxes
Wehrhaftigkeit bearing of arms
Volkswehr militia
stehendes Heer standing army
Schlichtung settlement
schiedsgerichtlicher Weg by arbitration
benachteiligen to disadvantage
Aufwendungen expenditures
ordnen to regulate

Weltlichkeit* der Schulen. Obligatorischer Besuch der öffentlichen Volksschulen. Unentgeltlichkeit* des Unterrichts, der Lehrmittel* und der Verpflegung* in den öffentlichen Volksschulen sowie in den höheren Bildungsanstalten* für diejenigen Schüler und Schülerinnen, die kraft ihrer Fähigkeit zur weiteren Ausbildung als geeignet* erachtet werden.

Unentgeltlichkeit der Rechtspflege* und des Rechtsbeistandes*. Rechtsprechung* durch vom Volk gewählte Richter. Berufung* in Strafsachen. Entschädigung unschuldig Angeklagter, Verhafteter und Verurteilter*. Abschaffung der Todesstrafe.

Unentgeltlichkeit der ärztlichen Hilfeleistung einschließlich der Geburtshilfe* und der Heilmittel. Unentgeltlichkeit der Totenbestattung*.

Stufenweise* steigende Einkommens- und Vermögenssteuer* zur Bestreitung aller öffentlichen Ausgaben*, soweit diese durch Steuern zu decken sind. Erbschaftssteuer*, stufenweise steigend nach Umfang des Erbgutes und nach dem Grade der Verwandtschaft*. Abschaffung aller indirekten Steuern, Zölle und sonstigen wirtschaftspolitischen* Maßnahmen, welche die Interessen der Allgemeinheit den Interessen einer bevorzugten Minderheit opfern*.

Zum Schutze der Arbeiterklasse fordert die Sozialdemokratische Partei Deutschlands zunächst:

Eine wirksame* nationale und internationale Arbeiterschutzgesetzgebung* auf folgender Grundlage:

a) Festsetzung eines höchstens acht Stunden betragenden Normalarbeitstages;

b) Verbot der Erwerbsarbeit für Kinder unter vierzehn Jahren;

c) Verbot der Nachtarbeit, außer für solche Industriezweige, die ihrer Natur nach aus technischen Gründen oder aus Gründen der öffentlichen Wohlfahrt Nachtarbeit erheischen*;

d) eine ununterbrochene Ruhepause von mindestens 36 Stunden in jeder Woche für jeden Arbeiter;

e) Verbot des Trucksystems*.

Überwachung aller gewerblichen Betriebe, Erforschung und Regelung der Arbeitsverhältnisse in Stadt und Land durch ein Reichsarbeitsamt, Bezirksarbeitsämter und Arbeitskammern*. Durchgreifende* gewerbliche Hygiene.

Rechtliche Gleichstellung* der landwirtschaftlichen Arbeiter und Dienstboten mit den gewerblichen Arbeitern; Beseitigung der Gesindeordnungen*.

Sicherung des Koalitionsrechts.

Übernahme der gesamten Arbeiterversicherung durch das Reich mit maßgebender Mitwirkung der Arbeiter an der Verwaltung.

„Das Erfurter Programm", (1891), beschlossen auf dem Parteitag der Sozialdemokratischen Partei Deutschland, Erfurt 1891, www.marxists.org/deutsch/geschichte/deutsch/spd/1891/erfurt.htm [09.04.15]

Weltlichkeit secularness
Unentgeltlichkeit free (education, a.s.o.)
Lehrmittel educational materials
Verpflegung meals
höhere Bildungsanstalt higher educational institution
geeignet qualified
Rechtspflege justice
Rechtsbeistand legal assistance
Rechtsprechung jurisdiction
Berufung appeal
Verurteilte(r) convicted person
Geburtshilfe midwifery
Totenbestattung burial
stufenweise graduated
Einkommens- und Vermögenssteuer income and property tax
öffentliche Ausgaben public expenditures
Erbschaftssteuer inheritance tax
Grad der Verwandtschaft degree of kinship
wirtschaftspolitisch economic
opfern to sacrifice
wirksam effective
Arbeiterschutzgesetzgebung work(er) protection
erheischen to require
Trucksystem a truck system is an arrangement in which employees are not paid in standard currency, but in other commodities (such as vouchers)
Reichsarbeitsamt, Bezirksarbeitsamt, Arbeitskammer Reich labour department, district labour bureaus, chambers of labour
durchgreifend rigorous
rechtliche Gleichstellung legal equality
Gesindeordnung the laws regulating the relationship between servant (*Gesinde*) and master (*Herrschaft*) in Prussia

S 16c Pope Leo XIII

Rerum Novarum

Leo XIII (1810–1903) was Pope from 1878 to 1903. His most important social teachings are included in his *Rerum Novarum* (Latin for "of revolutionary change") from 1891 (also known as *Rights and Duties of Capital and Labour*), from which the given source is an excerpt. Pope Leo XIII also strove to end the Struggle for Culture (cf. p. 40) by making compromises with Bismarck.

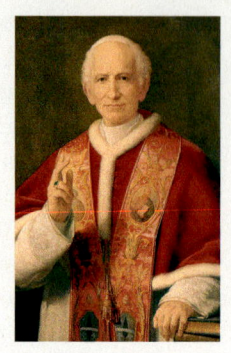

Pope Leo XIII

Pre-task
1. The given source is alternatively entitled "Rights and Duties of Capital and Labour". Make an educated guess as to what Pope Leo XIII might have to say about this subject: would he approve of the communist approach (cf. S 15), or a socialist one? Give reasons for your answer.

Tasks
2. Outline the reasons Pope Leo XIII gives for "the conflict now raging" (l. 8), and how he exemplifies these.
3. Examine the pope's attitude towards socialism, as presented in the given extract.
4. Summarise his proposal on how to alleviate the situation of the working class.
5. Do not forget to explain the author's motivation and to assess the practicability of his approach.

venerable ['ven(ə)rəb(ə)l] very respected
brethren here: the male members of a religious group
the Apostolic See the seat of authority in the Roman Church, i. e. the papacy
cognate related

self-reliance ability to do things for oneself
degeneracy [dɪˈdʒenərəsi] state of immorality
gravity here: the seriousness or importance of sth.
apprehension a feeling of worry or fear
scheme [skiːm] plan

To Our Venerable* Brethren* the Patriarchs, Primates, Archbishops, Bishops, and other ordinaries of places having Peace and Communion with the Apostolic See*.
Rights and Duties of Capital and Labor
That the spirit of revolutionary change, which has long been disturbing the nations of the world, should have passed beyond the sphere of politics and made its influence felt in the cognate* sphere of practical economics is not surprising. The elements of the conflict now raging are unmistakable, in the vast expansion of industrial pursuits and the marvellous discoveries of science; in the changed relations between masters and workmen; in the enormous fortunes of some few individuals, and the utter poverty of the masses; the increased self-reliance* and closer mutual combination of the working classes; as also, finally, in the prevailing moral degeneracy*. The momentous gravity* of the state of things now obtaining fills every mind with painful apprehension*; wise men are discussing it; practical men are proposing schemes*; popular meetings, legislatures, and rulers of nations are all busied with it – actually there is no question which has taken deeper hold on the public mind.

[...] In any case we clearly see, and on this there is general agreement, that
some opportune* remedy* must be found quickly for the misery and
wretchedness* pressing so unjustly on the majority of the working class: for
the ancient workingmen's guilds* were abolished in the last century, and no
other protective organization took their place. [...] Hence, by degrees it has
come to pass that working men have been surrendered*, isolated and helpless, to the hardheartedness of employers and the greed of unchecked competition. The mischief* has been increased by rapacious* usury*, which,
although more than once condemned by the Church, is nevertheless, under
a different guise*, but with like injustice, still practiced by covetous* and
grasping men. To this must be added that the hiring of labor and the conduct of trade are concentrated in the hands of comparatively few; so that a
small number of very rich men have been able to lay upon the teeming*
masses of the laboring poor a yoke* little better than that of slavery itself.
[...] To remedy these wrongs the socialists, working on the poor man's envy
of the rich, are striving to do away with private property, and contend* that
individual possessions should become the common property of all, to be
administered by the State or by municipal* bodies. They hold that by thus
transferring property from private individuals to the community, the present mischievous state of things will be set to rights, inasmuch as each citizen will then get his fair share of whatever there is to enjoy. But their conten-
tions are so clearly powerless to end the controversy that were they carried
into effect the working man himself would be among the first to suffer. They
are, moreover, emphatically* unjust, for they would rob the lawful posses-
sor, distort the functions of the State, and create utter confusion in the community.
[...] What is of far greater moment, however, is the fact that the remedy they
propose is manifestly against justice. For, every man has by nature the right
to possess property as his own. [...] And in addition to injustice, it is only too
evident what an upset and disturbance there would be in all classes, and to
how intolerable and hateful a slavery citizens would be subjected. The door
would be thrown open to envy, to mutual invective*, and to discord*; the
sources of wealth themselves would run dry, for no one would have any interest in exerting his talents or his industry; and that ideal equality about
which they entertain pleasant dreams would be in reality the levelling down
of all to a like condition of misery and degradation. Hence, it is clear that the
main tenet* of socialism, community of goods, must be utterly rejected,
since it only injures those whom it would seem meant to benefit, is directly
contrary to the natural rights of mankind, and would introduce confusion
and disorder into the commonweal*.
[...] The great mistake made in regard to the matter now under consideration is to take up with the notion* that class is naturally hostile to class, and
that the wealthy and the working men are intended by nature to live in mutual conflict. So irrational and so false is this view that the direct contrary is
the truth. [...] So in a State is it ordained* by nature that these two classes

opportune suitable
remedy solution, cure
wretchedness the state of being in a very bad condition
guild Zunft
to surrender sb. to sb. to give sb. to sb. who has defeated you
mischief ['mɪstʃɪf] trouble that sb. has deliberately caused
rapacious extremely greedy
usury Wucher
guise the way that sth./sb. appears to people
covetous envious
teeming containing a large number of people
yoke Joch
to contend to claim that sth. is true
municipal [mjuːˈnɪsɪp(ə)l] kommunal, Gemeinde-

emphatically ausdrücklich

invective (no pl.) Beschimpfungen
discord disagreement

tenet principle, belief

commonweal Allgemeinwohl

notion idea, concept

to ordain to officially order that sth. should be done

to dwell to live
perpetual continuing all the time
strife fighting
efficacy ['efɪkəsi] effectiveness
manifold of many different kinds
intermediary *(Streit-)SchlichterIn*
interpreter here: *der Deuter*

should dwell* in harmony and agreement, […]: capital cannot do without labor, nor labor without capital. Mutual agreement results in the beauty of good order, while perpetual* conflict necessarily produces confusion and savage barbarity. Now, in preventing such strife* as this, and in uprooting it, the efficacy* of Christian institutions is marvellous and manifold*. First of all, there is no intermediary* more powerful than religion (whereof the Church is the interpreter* and guardian) in drawing the rich and the working class together, by reminding each of its duties to the other, and especially of the obligations of justice.

Given at St. Peter's in Rome, the fifteenth day of May, 1891, the fourteenth year of Our pontificate. LEO XIII

adapted from: "Rerum Novarum. Encyclical of Pope Leo XIII on Capital and Labour", www.vatican.va/holy_father/leo_xiii/endyclicals/documents/hf_l-xiii_enc_15051891_rerum-novarum_en.html [02.08.2014]

S 17 Phyllis Deane

The Workers and the Industrial Revolution – an Assessment

In this text, Professor Phyllis Deane (1918–2012), who was a historian of economic history with a focus on Britain during the Industrial Revolution, attempts to give a balanced assessment of the question whether the living standards of the working class improved or deteriorated through industrialization.

Pre-task 1. Scan this sub-chapter for information about the living standards of the working class during industrialization. Make a list of arguments that speak for an improvement or, respectively, a deterioration.

Task 2. In this excerpt, Deane gives a balanced assessment of the question whether the standards of living of the working class improved or deteriorated through industrialization. Copy the graphic representation below and fill in the arrows with arguments Deane puts forward as well as with the conclusion she draws from her argumentation.

Optimistic view:
As a result of falling prices, more regular employment and a wider range of earning opportunities, workers were enabled to enjoy a rising standard of living.
- Mostly right-wing writers (free capitalistic enterprise).

Arguments put forward to support the pessimistic view:

Arguments put forward to support the optimistic view:

Conclusion?

Pessimistic view:
There was a net deterioration in the living conditions of the laboring poor.
- Mostly left-wing writers, feeling sympathy for sufferings of the proletariat.

3. Take a critical stand on Deane's assessment from a contemporary as well as from today's point of view.

Post-task 4. Without the "Second" Industrial Revolution, the First World War as the first "modern" war would not have been possible. Scan this sub-chapter one more time to find evidence for this statement.

One of the most persistent controversies in the history of the industrial revolution is the argument that has raged around workers' standard of living. Two schools have grown up in connection with this topic. The pessimistic view, held by a long line of observers from contemporaries of the process to modern historians, is that
5 the early stage of industrialization in England, though it brought affluence* to some, caused a net deterioration in the standard of living of the labouring poor. The optimistic view, put forward by an equally long list of observers is that although economic change left some workers displaced and distressed, the majority of them were enabled by falling prices, more regular employment and a wider
10 range of earning opportunities to enjoy a rising standard of living.
The controversy had been muddied* by political prejudice and the myopic* views to which prejudice so often gives rise. It is common to find left-wing writers, their sympathies strongly engaged by the sufferings of the proletariat, holding the pessimistic view; and it is equally common to find right-wing writers, more confident of
15 the blessings assured by free capitalistic enterprise, holding the optimistic view. [...]
To some extent it is true that there was a shift in the distribution of incomes in favour of profits and rent and a change in the composition of output in favour of capital goods, exports and goods and services for upper class consumption. But it is manifest* that this is not the whole story. The new factories were not producing
20 entirely for the export or the luxury trade or for producers, and the fact that prices of manufactured consumer-goods fell substantially meant that the working classes gained as consumers where they did not gain as wage-earners. So that while on balance the evidence is strongly in favour of the view that working-class standards of living improved by less than the increase in national income per head would
25 suggest over the first half of the nineteenth century; and while there is no doubt that certain sectors of the labouring poor suffered a serious deterioration in their earning-power because they were made redundant by technical progress, nevertheless it would be difficult to credit an overall decline in real incomes per wage-earning family in a period when aggregate* real incomes for the nation as a whole were
30 growing appreciably* faster than population. In effect, the sustained growth of national product to which industrialization gave rise tended to exert an upward pressure on working-class standards of living in three main ways, none of which implied a rise in the price of labour: (1) by creating more regular employment opportunities for all members of the family – this meant higher earnings per year and
35 per family without a rise in wages per man-hour worked; (2) by creating more opportunities for labour specialization and hence for the higher earnings that semi-skilled or skilled labour can command: here again the average earnings can rise without an increase in the wage rate because the composition of the labour force changes in favour of the higher earning groups; and (3) the upward pressure on the
40 workers' standard of living also operated through the reductions in the price of consumer goods and the widening of the range of commodities which come within the budget of the working classes. Finally, of course, to the extent that it raised real purchasing* power for the masses, industrialization expanded the market for manufactured goods and so justified further increases in investment and output.

Phyllis Deane: The First Industrial Revolution, Cambridge University Press, Cambridge 1965, pp. 238–239, 252–253

affluence ['æf.lu.əns] wealth

to muddy to contaminate
myopic [maɪˈɒpɪk] short-sighted

manifest obvious

aggregate used for describing the total amount of sth. in a country's economy
appreciable significant

to purchase [ˈpɜː(r)tʃəs] to buy

(New?) Imperialism

S 18 Benjamin Disraeli

Crystal Palace Speech

Benjamin Disraeli (1804–1881) was a British conservative politician who served twice as Britain's Minister. The given source contains extracts from his so-called "Crystal Palace speech", given in London in 1872, at which time Disraeli was the leader of the opposition in parliament. In the speech, he outlines the Conservatives' position on the question of Empire.

Pre-tasks
1. Scan the overview section for information on the Crystal Palace speech to put it into the context of British imperialism in the second half of the 19th century.
2. Based on your results, make an educated guess as to the content of Disraeli's speech. You could consider the following two questions:
   - Which arguments might others advance against colonialism that you might want to rebut?
   - What future course should England take, and why?

Tasks
3. Use the two questions provided in task 2 to summarise the gist of Disraeli's speech.
4. Discuss why this speech gave impetus to a new phase of imperialism in England. Use the overview section for help, but also refer back to the given source.
5. Two years after the given speech, Disraeli became Prime Minister after the Conservatives had gained a majority in the elections, however, only at Queen Victoria's intervention (the Queen was on very good terms with Disraeli). He was also the one who officially offered the title "Empress of India" to her in 1876, and who was ennobled by her two years later. Justify Queen Victoria's decision to recognize Disraeli's accomplishments for the British Empire in a short speech to be given at the ennoblement ceremony. Consider the contemporary (British) view, not today's perspective.

Post-task
6. Revise what you have learned about the rise of Germany in the second half of 19th century. Focus on what the other European powers were afraid of after 1871, and why. Against this backdrop, evaluate Disraeli's stance towards Empire.

Tory the conservatives

Gentlemen, there is another and second great object of the Tory* party. If the first is to maintain the institutions of the country, the second is, in my opinion, to uphold the empire of England. [...]
And, gentlemen, of all its efforts, this is the one which has been the nearest to success. Statesmen of the highest character, writers of the most distinguished ability, the most organized and efficient means, have been employed in this endeavour. It has been proved to all of us that we have lost money by our colonies. It has been shown with precise, mathematical demonstration that there never was a jewel in the crown of England that was so truly costly as the possession of India. How often has it been suggested that we should at once emancipate ourselves from this incu-

bus*. Well, that result was nearly accomplished. When those subtle* views were adopted by the country under the plausible plea of granting self-government to the colonies, I confess that I myself thought that the tie was broken. Not that I for one object to self-government. I cannot conceive how our distant colonies can have
15 their affairs administered except by self-government. But self-government, in my opinion, when it was conceded*, ought to have been conceded as a part of a great policy of imperial consolidation*. It ought to have been accompanied by an imperial tariff, by securities for the people of England for the enjoyment of unappropriated* lands which belonged to the sovereign as their trustee*, and by a military
20 code which should have precisely defined the means and the responsibilities by which the colonies should be defended, and by which, if necessary, this country should call for aid from the colonies themselves. It ought, further, to have been accompanied by the institution of some representative council in the metropolis, which would have brought the colonies into constant and continuous relations
25 with the home government. All this, however, was omitted* because those who advised that policy – and I believe their convictions were sincere – looked upon the colonies of England, looked upon our connection with India, as a burden upon this country, viewing everything in a financial aspect, and totally passing by those moral and political considerations which make nations great, and by the influence
30 of which alone men are distinguished from animals.

Well, what has been the result of this attempt during the reign of Liberalism for the disintegration of empire? It has entirely failed. But how has it failed? Through the sympathy of the colonies with the mother country. They have decided that the empire shall not be destroyed, and in my opinion no minister in this country will
35 do his duty who neglects any opportunity of reconstructing as much as possible our colonial empire, and of responding to those distant sympathies which may become the source of incalculable strength and happiness to this land. Therefore, gentlemen, with respect to the second great object of the Tory party also – the maintenance of the Empire – public opinion appears to be in favour of our princi-
40 ples – that public opinion which, I am bound to say, thirty years ago, was not favourable to our principles, and which, during a long interval of controversy, in the interval had been doubtful...

When you return to your homes, when you return to your counties and your cities, you must tell to all those whom you can influence that the time is at hand, that, at
45 least, it cannot be far distant, when England will have to decide between national and cosmopolitan principles. The issue is not a mean one. It is whether you will be content to be a comfortable England, modelled and moulded upon continental principles and meeting in due course an inevitable fate, or whether you will be a great country, – an imperial country – a country where your sons, when they rise,
50 rise to paramount* positions, and obtain not merely the esteem* of their countrymen, but command the respect of the world ...

Benjamin Disraeli: "Crystal Palace Speech", in: T. E. Kebbel (Ed.): Selected Speeches of the Earl of Beaconsfield, Longman, London 1882, Vol. II, pp. 529–534

---

incubus a cause of worry
subtle ['sʌt(ə)l] indirect in a way that prevents people from noticing what you are trying to do

to concede to admit that sth. is true
consolidation Festigung, Stärkung
unappropriated not yet taken possession of
trustee Treuhänder, Bevollmächtigte(r)

to omit to fail to include sth.

paramount more important than all other things
esteem a feeling of admiration and respect

Imperialism: Motives and Justifications

S 19   John Atkinson Hobson

An Early Critique of Imperialism

John Atkinson Hobson (1858–1940) was a British economist, journalist and social reformer whose main interest was the reduction of poverty. He argued that the unequal distribution of wealth was bound to make capitalism unproductive, which is why it could only maintain itself by investing in less-developed countries, thereby pushing colonial expansion.

Hobson's views on imperialism are contained in his 1902 book *Imperialism*.

Pre-task

1. Hobson uses the image of a parasite feeding on the dead body of an animal to describe the relationship between the colonizers and the colonized. Scan the overview section for motives of and justifications of imperialism and explain this image.

Tasks

2. Copy the table below containing a classification of the motives of imperialism. Categorize the motives Hobson refers to accordingly and make notes in the respective column(s).

Exploratory motives	Religious motives	Economic motives	Political motives	Ideological motives

3. Add further aspects you can think of. Check the overview section for help.
4. Explain how Hobson unmasks the hypocrisy of imperialist motives. Focus on his argumentation and his use of language.

Post-task

5. Do further research on Lenin's "Imperialism, the Highest State of Capitalism", written in 1916 and published in 1917. Discuss the probability of Lenin's approach of putting emphasis on economic motives of imperialism.

---

prolific rich, existing in large numbers
seizure ['siːʒə(r)] forceful taking control of
rectification improvement
punitive *Straf-*
incessant [ɪn'ses(ə)nt] continuing for a long time without stopping
Pax Britannica idea of peace through British-dominated prosperity
impudent disrespectful
hypocrisy [hɪ'pɒkrəsi] *Heuchlerei*
to weave *weben*
to buttress to support
to devise to invent
to elevate to improve the status of

The decades of imperialism have been prolific* in wars; most of these wars have been directly motivated by aggression of white races upon "lower races", and have issued in the forcible seizure* of territory. Every one of the steps of expansion in Africa, Asia and the Pacific have been accompanied by bloodshed; each imperialist power keeps an increasing army available for foreign service; rectification* of frontiers, punitive* expeditions and other euphemisms of war are in incessant* progress. The Pax Britannica*, always an impudent* falsehood, has become of recent years a grotesque monster of hypocrisy* [...].

For these business politicians [i. e. those working for the great imperialist powers] biology and sociology weave* thin convenient theories of a race struggle for the subjugation of the inferior peoples, in order that we, the Anglo-Saxons, may take their lands and live upon their labours; while economics buttresses* the argument by representing our work in conquering and ruling them as our share in the division of labour among nations, and history devises* reasons why the lessons of past empires do not apply to ours, while social ethics paints the motive of "Imperialism" as the desire to bear the "burden" of educating and elevating* races of "chil-

dren". Thus are the "cultured" or semi-cultured classes indoctrinated with the intellectual and moral grandeur of Imperialism. For the masses there is a cruder* appeal to hero-worship and sensational glory, adventure and the sporting spirit:
20 current history falsified in coarse* flaring* colours, for the direct stimulation of the combative* instincts. [...]

The normal state of such a country is one in which the fertile lands and the mineral resources are owned by white aliens and worked by natives under their direction, primarily for their gain: they do not identify themselves with the interests of
25 the nation or its people, but remain an alien body of sojourners*, a "parasite" upon the carcass* of its "host", destined to extract wealth from the country and retire to consume it at home. All the hard and manual or other severe routine work is done by natives. [...]

[The] failure to justify by results the forcible rule over alien peoples is attributable
30 to no special defect of the British or other modern European nations. It is inherent* in the nature of such domination.

from: Marvin Perry et. al.: Sources of the Western Tradition II. Houghton Mifflin, Boston 1991, pp. 248–250

crude grob, plump

coarse rude and offensive
flaring shining brightly
combative fighting

sojourner sb. who does not stay permanently
carcass the dead body of an animal

inherent innewohnend

S 20 Joseph Arthur Count de Gobineau
The Inequality of Human Races

Joseph Arthur Count de Gobineau (1816–1882) was a French aristocrat who is considered to be one of the fathers of scientific racism. In his work *An Essay on the Inequality of Human Races*, he established the idea of an Aryan master race which National Socialism would later borrow from. In the given excerpt, Gobineau enlarges on the alleged superiority of the "white" race as opposed to the "black" and the "yellow" races, based on observations of physiological qualities and conclusions he draws from these qualities.

Pre-tasks
1. In the introductory remarks to this source, it says that Gobineau is one of the fathers of "scientific racism". Find a suitable definition for "scientific racism" which you can back up with examples you know from history.
2. One of the pseudo-sciences relied on for scientific racism was the (today discredited) science of phrenology – the measurement of the human skull. In his observations, Gobineau distinguishes between the "negroid variety", the "yellow race" and the "white race", also focussing on the shape of their skulls and drawing conclusions as to mental abilities. Predict his conclusions with the help of the illustration given here.

Tasks
3. Verify (or falsify, and then amend) your predictions with the help of the text: Which mental abilities does Gobineau attribute to the three "varieties"? Which further observations does he make?
4. Explain how and why Gobineau's theory legitimizes imperialism.
5. Discuss the dangers embedded in Gobineau's thesis "that a society is great and brilliant only so far as it preserves the blood of the noble group that created it, [...]." (ll. 45 f.) Give examples from history.

Post-task
6. Do further research on the origins of the scientific discipline of cultural anthropology *(Ethnologie)* and its main representatives, for

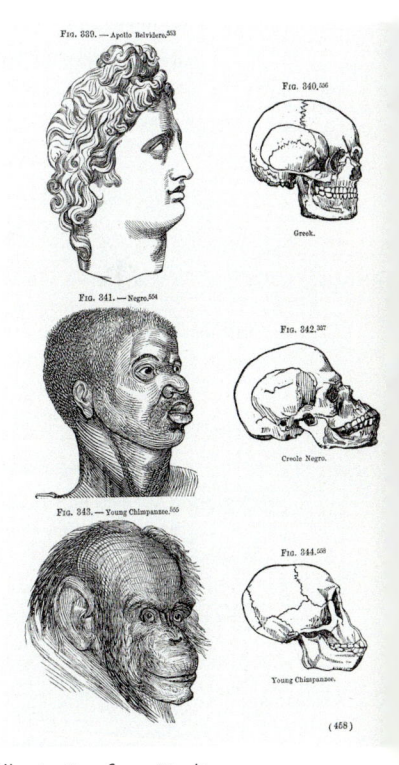

Illustration from "Indigenous Races of the Earth" (1857), in which Josiah Clark Nott and George Robins Gliddon compared the skulls of a "Greek", a "Creole negro" and a "Young chimpanzee".

example Lewis H. Morgan and his 1877 work "Ancient Society". In class, discuss if early cultural anthropology can be considered to be a science in the service of imperialism. Based on your historical judgement, write a critical abstract about the origins of cultural anthropology for young visitors to the Rautenstrauch-Joest Museum in Cologne, the only museum of cultural anthropology in North-Rhine Westphalia.

[I] have been able to distinguish on physiological grounds alone, three great and clearly marked types, the black, the yellow, and the white [...].

The negroid variety is the lowest, and stands at the foot of the ladder. The animal character, that appears in the shape of the pelvis*, is stamped on the negro from birth, and foreshadows his destiny. His intellect will always move within a very narrow circle. He is not however a mere brute, for behind his low receding brow, in the middle of his skull, we can see signs of a powerful energy, however crude its objects. If his mental faculties are dull or even non-existent, he often has an intensity of desire and so of will, which may be called terrible. Many of his senses, especially taste and smell, are developed to an extent unknown to the other two races. The very strength of his sensations is the most striking proof of his inferiority. All food is good in his eyes, nothing disgusts or repels him. What he desires is to eat, to eat furiously, and to excess. [...] It is the same with odours*; his inordinate* desires are satisfied with all, however coarse or even horrible. To these qualities may be added an instability and capriciousness* of feeling that cannot be tied down to any single object, and which, so far as he is concerned, do away with all distinctions of good and evil. We might even say that the violence with which he pursues the object that has aroused his senses and inflamed his desires is a guarantee of the desires being soon satisfied and the object forgotten... [...]

The yellow race is the exact opposite of this type. The skull points forward, not backward. The forehead is wide and bony, often high and projecting. The shape of the face is triangular, the nose and chin showing none of the coarse protuberances* that mark the negro. There is further a general proneness to obesity, which, though not confined to the yellow type, is found there more frequently than in the others. The yellow man has little physical energy, and is inclined to apathy, he commits none of the strange excess so common among negroes. His desires are feeble, his will-power rather obstinate* than violent; his longing for material pleasures, though constant, is kept within bounds. A rare glutton* by nature, he shows more discrimination in his choice of food. He tends to mediocrity* in everything; he understands easily enough anything not too deep or sublime. He has a love of utility* and a respect for order, and knows the value of a certain amount of freedom. He is practical, in the narrowest sense of the word, he does not dream or theorise, he invents little [...].

We come now to the white peoples. These are gifted with reflective energy, or rather with an energetic intelligence. They have a feeling for utility, but in a sense far wider and higher, more courageous and ideal, than the yellow races; a perseverance* that takes account of obstacles and ultimately finds a means of overcoming them; a greater physical power, an extraordinary instinct for order, not merely as a guarantee of peace and tranquillity, but as an indispensable means of self-preservation. At the same time, they have a remarkable, and even extreme, love of liberty, and are openly hostile to the formalism under which the Chinese are glad to vegetate, as well as to the strict despotism* which is the only way of governing the negro.

Such is the lesson of history. It shows us that all civilizations derive from the white
45 race, that none can exist without its help, and that a society is great and brilliant only so far as it preserves the blood of the noble group that created it, provided that this group itself belongs to the most illustrious branch of our species.

Arthur de Gobineau: The Inequality of Human Races. Transl. by A. Collins, London: Heinemann 1915, pp. 205–210

despotism the use of power in a cruel and unreasonable way

An early nineteenth century cartoon of Sarah "Saartjie" Baartman (c. 1790–1815) of the native southwestern African Khoikhoi people, called "Hottentots" by the Dutch settlers in imitation of the sound of the native language (a term considered derogatory today).
Baartman (and other women of the Khoikhoi people) were exhibited at freak shows in Europe as the "Hottentot Venus".
The angel/Cupid sitting on her hip says "Take care of your hearts!"

S 21 Rudyard Kipling
The White Man's Burden

The English novelist and poet Rudyard Kipling (1865–1936) was born in Bombay (today's Mumbai), India, and educated in England, but returned to India in 1882. He is famous for the novel *The Jungle Book*, for example, and was awarded the Nobel Prize for Literature in 1907. Some people regard him as the "chronicler of the British Empire", which is also due to (in)famous poems he wrote.

230 The First World War

Kipling wrote *The White Man's Burden* in 1899, intended to urge the United States to take on the "burden" of imperialism. Shortly before the publication, the Spanish-American War broke out, which is why the full title of the poem is *The White Man's Burden: The United States and The Philippine Islands*.

Pre-task **1.** This advertisement for "Pears' Soap" features Admiral Dewey, an admiral of the United States Navy, who is best known for his victory at the Battle of Manila Bay (1898) during the Spanish-American War by means of which the Americans had taken control of the Philippines. It was published in the American political magazine *Harper's Weekly* around 1900. In a first step, describe the advertisement in detail paying special attention to the use of colours. Do not forget the elements shown in the four corners. In a second step, match the embedded text up with the pictorial elements. In a third step, make an educated guess as to what "the white man's burden" consists of, taking into consideration your findings from the first two steps.

The first step towards lightening
The White Man's Burden
is through teaching the virtues of cleanliness.
Pears' Soap
is a potent factor in brightening the dark corners of the earth as civilization advances, while amongst the cultured of all nations it holds the highest place—it is the ideal toilet soap.

Language support

virtue Tugend

Waschbecken sink • **Bullauge** porthole • **Missionar** missionary • **Fracht** load, cargo

Tasks

2. Read through the poem and state whether the following statements are true or false. Be prepared to give proof by quoting.
   a. It is the "white man's burden" to choose strong men to suppress the native populations.
   b. The native populations give them a warm welcome.
   c. The "white man's burden" is a selfish enterprise.
   d. It is necessary to frequently repeat everything before eventually the benefits offered are understood, if at all.
   e. The white man fights against hunger and diseases.
   f. This work is much appreciated.
   g. The native populations cherish the freedom brought by the white man.
3. Explain the allusion Kipling makes use of in the last two lines given here. Tip: It is a biblical allusion to the Old Testament.
4. Evaluate in how far this poem could be used to justify and legitimize imperialism: Was Kipling a "jingoist"?
5. Put yourself into the shoes of Admiral Dewey (cf. pre-task). Based on the poem, write his piece of advice for those Americans chosen to bring the "blessings of civilization" to the Philippines (cf. introductory remarks): What are their tasks, and what should they expect from the indigenous Philippine population?

Post-task

6. The publishing house responsible for producing this schoolbook is planning to publish a second and shortened edition. Write a letter to the person in charge in which you evaluate whether "The White Man's Burden" by Kipling should still be included.

Take up the White Man's burden –
Send forth the best ye breed –
Go bind★ your sons to exile
To serve your captives' need;
5 To wait in heavy harness,
On fluttered★ folk and wild –
Your new-caught, sullen★ peoples,
Half-devil and half child.

Take up the White Man's burden –
10 In patience to abide★,
To veil the threat of terror
And check★ the show of pride;
By open speech and simple,
A hundred times made plain
15 To seek another's profit,
And work★ another's gain.

Take up the White Man's burden –
The savage wars of peace –
Fill full the mouth of Famine
20 And bid the sickness cease;
And when your goal is nearest
The end for others sought,
Watch sloth★ and heathen Folly
Bring all your hopes to nought. [...]

25 Take up the White Man's burden –
And reap his old reward:
The blame of those ye better,
The hate of those ye guard –
The cry of hosts★ ye humour★
30 (Ah, slowly!) toward the light: –
"Why brought he us from bondage★,
Our loved Egyptian night?" [...]

to bind to commit to

fluttered alarmed
sullen unfriendly, gloomy
sloth laziness

to abide here: to endure

to check here: to control
hosts masses
to humour here: to lure
bondage servitude
to work here: to affect

Rudyard Kipling: The Complete Verse. London: Cathie 1990, pp. 261f.

S 22 John Ruskin

Imperial Duty

John Ruskin (1819–1900) was an English writer and critic. In 1870, he was appointed Professor of Fine Art at Oxford. The given source is an extract from his inaugural lecture on 8 February 1870. The lecture was also published in Ruskin's *Lectures on Art* in 1894.

Pre-task

1. Kipling (cf. S 21) defines the task of bringing "civilization" to the allegedly "uncivilized" peoples as the "white man's burden". Imagine you were to argue it was the "British man's burden": Think of arguments you could advance (from a contemporary perspective) to make this case.

Tasks

2. Point out what, according to Ruskin, makes the English "special".
3. Explain how Ruskin comes to his conclusion that the English must "Reign or Die." (l. 19) In this context, also refer to Ruskin's metaphor of the colonies being "fastened fleets." (l. 28)
4. Compare Ruskin's view to the criticism uttered by Hobson (cf. S 19) and identify motives of imperialism you can detect in Ruskin's lecture.

---

undegenerate pure
dissolute *lasterhaft*
temper *Naturell*

to bequeath to pass down
avarice greed
to covet to want sth. that sb. else has
the most offending souls alive "But if it be a sin to covet honour I am the most offending soul alive." (William Shakespeare: *Henry V*, IV.3)
rapidity speed
empires of Mammon and Belial i.e. of riches and worthlessness/destruction
a sceptred isle "This royal throne of kings, this scepter'd isle." (W. Shakespeare: *Richard II*, II.1)
beneficent [bəˈnefɪs(ə)nt] *wohltätig*
mortal *sterblich*
to perish to die
to seize [siːz] to take
virtue *Tugend*
fidelity loyalty
to disenfranchise here: to take away the rights of a subject
fastened here: fortified

There is a destiny now possible to us – the highest ever set before a nation to be accepted or refused. We are still undegenerate* in race; a race mingled of the best northern blood. We are not yet dissolute* in temper*, but still have the firmness to govern, and the grace to obey. We have been taught a religion of pure mercy, which we must either now betray, or learn to defend by fulfilling. And we are rich in an 5
inheritance of honour, bequeathed* to us through a thousand years of noble history, which it should be our daily thirst to increase with splendid avarice*, so that Englishmen, if it be a sin to covet* honour, should be the most offending souls alive*. Within the last few years we have had the laws of natural science opened to us with a rapidity* which has been blinding by its brightness; and means of transit 10
and communication given to us, which have made but one kingdom of the habitable globe. One kingdom; but who is to be its king? Is there to be no king in it, think you, and every man to do that which is right in his own eyes? Or only kings of terror, and the obscene empires of Mammon and Belial*? Or will you, youths of England, make your country again a royal throne of kings; a sceptred isle*, for all the world 15
a source of light, a centre for peace; mistress of Learning and of the Arts; […].
There is indeed a course of beneficent* glory open to us, such as never was yet offered to any poor group of mortal* souls. But it must be – it is with us, now, "Reign or Die." […]
And this is what she must either do, or perish*: she must found colonies as fast 20
and as far as she is able, formed of her most energetic and worthiest men; – seizing* every piece of fruitful waste ground she can set her foot on, and there teaching these her colonists that their chief virtue* is to be fidelity* to their country, and that their first aim is to be to advance the power of England by land and sea: and that, though they live on a distant plot of ground, they are no more to consider 25
themselves therefore disenfranchised* from their native land, than the sailors of her fleets do, because they float on distant waves. So that literally, these colonies must be fastened* fleets; […].

John Ruskin: Selections and Essays, F.W. Roe (Ed.), New York: Dover Publications 2013, pp. 277 ff.

Linley Sambourne
Man is but a Worm

This cartoon by Linley Sambourne appeared in the British satirical magazine *Punch* in 1881 and satirizes Charles Darwin's recently published work *On the Origin of Species*. Darwin himself is depicted in the centre of the cartoon, left of the man with the top hat. The cartoon was also reprinted in the 1882 *Punch* almanac (a book published every year concerned with the events of the time.).

Pre-task

1. The title of this cartoon alludes to the biblical Psalm 144:4, saying "Man is like a a mere breath; His days are like a passing shadow," expressing the fleeting quality of human life and the wonders of nevertheless being recognized by (an eternal) God. Taking this into account, make an educated guess as to the cartoonist's attitude towards the Church on the one hand and towards Darwin's theories on the other hand.

Tasks

2. Describe the cartoon in detail. Focus on major steps of development, as illustrated by the cartoonist.
3. Recognizing what/whom Sambourne sees as the "final stage" of development, pinpoint the message he wants to convey, taking your results from task 1 into consideration.
4. Discuss how and why Darwin's evolutionary theory could be (mis-)used as a justification for imperialism.

Post-task

5. Creationism (in the USA also called "creation science" to give it an air of (pseudo-)scientific legitimacy) is the belief that the universe originates from some kind of divine being. Creationists therefore reject the theory of evolution. Still today, the debate about whether to teach evolutionary biology or creationism in public schools is going on in many countries, for example in the USA. Do further research on "Resolution 1580", passed by the Parliamentary Assembly of the Council of Europe in 2007 [www.assembly.coe.int]. Present it in class and discuss if it restricts or promotes the freedom of belief in Europe.

Language support

Schwanz tail • **Affe** ape • **aufrechter Gang** upright walk • **Höhlenmensch** cave-dweller • **Zylinder** top hat • **Entwicklung** development • **Spirale** spiral [ˌspaɪrəl] • **Fortschritt** progress • **Evolution** evolution

The First World War

S 24 Herbert Spencer

Principles of Biology

Herbert Spencer (1820–1903) was a British biologist, philosopher, sociologist and writer who some people might consider to be "infamous for his controversial views on society" (cf. task 1).

In his "Principles of Biology (Volume II)", written in 1864, Spencer focuses on the "Laws of Multiplication". The 13th chapter, from which the given extract is taken, is concerned with "Human Population in the Future".

Pre-task 1. In Canada, there is an elementary school which is named after Herbert Spencer. On their school website, they give some information about their name patron. Read the information and speculate what might have made Spencer "infamous for his controversial views on society". Tip: Have a look at his various professions (cf. introductory remarks).

> The school is named after Herbert Spencer, a Victorian era* biologist and philosopher born in England, on April 27th, 1820. Spencer was the editor of The Economist* in 1848 and worked with many of the leading intellectuals of Victorian Britain. One of the most influential figures in sociology and psychology at the time, he is infamous* for his controversial views on society [...]
>
> o.V.: "About Herbert Spencer Elementary School", http://district.sd40.bc.ca/spencer/about 17.02.14]
>
> ---
> **Victorian era** the period of Queen Victoria's reign from 1837 to 1901 • **The Economist** weekly newspaper, first published in 1843 • **infamous** well known for sth. bad

Tasks 2. Copy the graphic visualization provided below and fill it in, with the help of the text. Questions to consider:
- What is the core problem of humankind, and how has Nature found a regulation for this problem, according to Spencer?
- How and why does one go extinct (*aussterben*), how and why does one survive?

Do not forget to add the respective lines and be prepared to give evidence from the text.

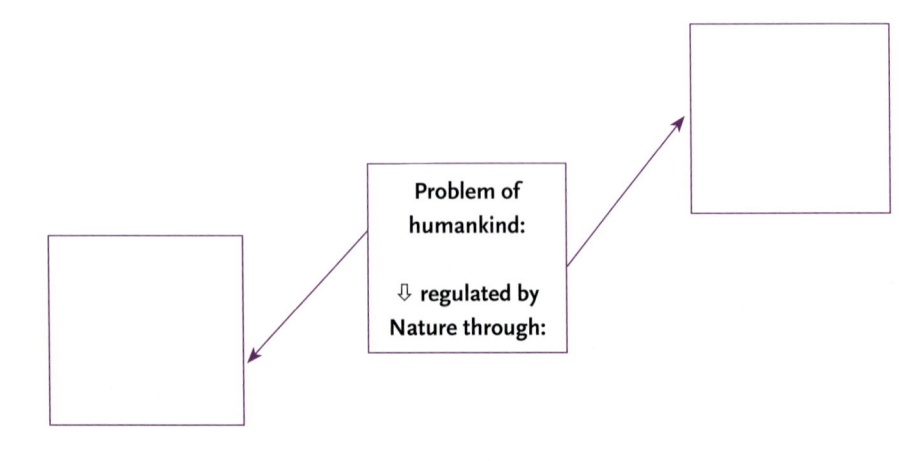

Problem of humankind:

⇩ **regulated by Nature through:**

3. Compare your results with a partner. Together, come up with a catchphrase that best summarizes the gist of Spencer's theory.
4. Present your findings in class. Use appropriate and varied sentence connectives, for example:

> **Talking about causes and effects:**
> - As a consequence of …/Consequently …/Resulting from …/Due to …
> - … is caused by/… leads to …/… results in/… culminates in/… has an impact on …/… can be traced back to …
> - That is why …/Therefore …/So …/Finally …/Ultimately …/In the end …
>
> **Comparing:**
> - Whereas …/On the one hand … on the other hand …
> - Similarly/Likewise/Equally/Not only … but also …
> - In contrast to …/In comparison with …

5. Explain why Spencer's theory served as a justification for imperialism.
6. With the help of your results, evaluate if, and if so, why, Social Darwinism should actually be called "Social Spencerism". Check the overview section and S 23 for help.

Post-task 7. Write a letter to the Canadian Board of Education in which you evaluate if Herbert Spencer is an appropriate name patron for an elementary school.

[…] This constant increase of people beyond the means of subsistence*, causes, then, a never-ceasing* requirement for skill, intelligence, and self-control – involves, therefore, a constant exercise of these and gradual growth of them. […]
In this case, as in many others, Nature secures each step in advance by a succes-
5 sion of trials*; which are perpetually* repeated, and cannot fail to be repeated, until success is achieved. All mankind in turn subject themselves more or less to the discipline described*; they either may or may not advance under it; but, in the nature of things, only those who *do* advance under it eventually survive. For, necessarily, families and races whom this increasing difficulty of getting a living which
10 excess of fertility entails*, does not stimulate to improvements in production – that is, to greater mental activity – are on the high road to extinction*; and most ultimately be supplanted* by those whom the pressure does so stimulate. […]
And here, indeed, without further illustration, it will be seen that premature death, under all its forms and from all its causes, cannot fail to work in the same direction.
15 For as those prematurely carried-off* must, in the average of cases, be those in whom the power of self-preservation* is the least, it unavoidably follows that those left behind to continue the race, must be those in whom the power of self-preservation is the greatest – must be the select* of their generation. So that, whether the dangers to existence be of the kind produced by excess of fertility, or of any other
20 kind, it is clear that by the ceaseless exercise of the faculties* needed to contend* with them, and by the death of all men who fail to contend with them successfully, there is ensured a constant progress towards a higher degree of skill, intelligence, and self-regulation – a better co-ordination of actions – a more complete life.

Herbert Spencer: Principles of Biology. Vol. II. Williams and Norgate, London 1864, pp. 498–500

subsistence the smallest amount of food/drink you need to stay alive
to cease [si:s] to stop

trial here: a painful or difficult experience
perpetual continuing all the time
the discipline described cf. ll. 4 f.

to entail etw. nach sich ziehen
extinction das Aussterben
to supplant to replace

carried-off the dead ones
self-preservation Selbsterhaltung

the select the chosen ones

faculties skills, abilities
to contend to compete against sb., e.g. for a victory/power

British, American and German Imperialism

S 25 ▸ The Devilfish in Egyptian Waters

This American cartoon by an unknown artist from 1882 shows John Bull, the national personification of Great Britain, as the 'octopus of imperialism', grabbing land on every continent.

Pre-task

1. Scan the overview section for information about the peculiarities of British imperialism. Based on your findings, explain why Great Britain is presented as an octopus here.

Tasks

2. Split up into groups and do further research on the land(s) grabbed by the octopus (cf. embedded text). Prepare a one-minute-presentation for each country/territory in which you explain the connection to British imperialism.
3. Against the backdrop of your findings, explain the title of the cartoon.
4. Locate the countries/territories on a map. Use fixing pins, for example. Then explain the famous saying "The sun never set(s) on the British Empire".
5. Also referring back to your results from task 1, discuss the prerequisites for British imperialism to remain/be successful.

Embedded text (clockwise): India, Egypt, Suez Canal, Malta, Helgoland, Australia, Boersland, Gibralter [sic], Cape Colony, Ireland, Cyprus, Jamaica, Canada

Language support

sich etw. schnappen/etw. (er)greifen to grab/seize [si:z] • **Zylinder** top hat • **etw. umspannen** to encompass

Cecil Rhodes (1853–1902)

Cecil Rhodes was born in Bishop's Stortford (England) in 1853. After contracting tuberculosis, he was sent to his brother in South Africa in 1870 to recover. Rhodes stayed and – together with his brother – started to work in the diamond business while simultaneously studying law in Oxford. In 1880, he founded the Beers Mining Company; in 1888, he participated in the foundation of the De Beers Consolidated Diamond Mines that eventually obtained the monopoly in diamond mining in South Africa.

In 1889, the British government entrusted Rhodes with the task of founding the British South Africa Company in order to push forward British rule from the south without defining a specific northern border. The areas administered by this company were then sold to British settlers and named Northern and Southern Rhodesia, after Rhodes (today's Zambia and Zimbabwe).

Being a member of parliament of the Cape Colony, Rhodes was elected Prime Minister in 1890. His vision was to unify the South African republics and the Cape Colony under the British banner. He supported a conspiracy against Boer President Paul Kruger and was accused of having ordered an invasion of the Transvaal, but was eventually acquitted. Nevertheless, Rhodes was forced to resign as Prime Minister. In the time to come, he was preoccupied with the further development of Rhodesia and promoted the construction of railways.

Rhodes died in 1902 and is buried in today's Zimbabwe.

Cecil Rhodes

S 26 Cecil Rhodes

Confessions of Faith

Rhodes originally wrote his "Confessions of Faith" in Oxford in 1877, but made some amendments and changes in Kimberly (South Africa) in that same year. The given extract stems from the amended version and describes Rhodes's views on why the English are destined to rule the world.

Pre-task
1. Think back to Ruskin's views on why the English are destined to rule the world (cf. **S 22**). One of Rhodes's key sentences is that the English are "the finest race in the world and that the more of the world [they] inhabit the better it is for the human race." (ll. 10 f.) Do you expect Rhodes to argue in a similar fashion to Ruskin, (where) do expect differences? Discuss.

Tasks
2. Divide the source into sense units and find headings that summarize these units. Based on your notes, give a structured outline of the contents of Rhodes's "Confessions of Faith".
3. Taking the biographical account of Rhodes into account, explain which motives of imperialism Rhodes represents.
4. Some historians ascribe a mythical component to Rhodes's imperialism. Find examples in the text that support this assessment.
5. Against the background of the text, discuss to what extent Rhodes could be seen as a prime example of a "jingoist".

Post-task
6. In the last part of the extract, Rhodes calls on the British to seize the African continent. Do further research on his plan to link Africa from south to north ("Cape-to-Cairo") by means of telegraph lines and railroads (cf. also the cartoon "The Rhodes Colossus"). Anticipate problems linked to that idea.

If often strikes a man to inquire what is the chief good in life; to one the thought comes that it is a happy marriage, to another great wealth, and as each seizes on his idea, for that he more or less works for the rest of his existence. To myself thinking over the same question the wish came to render myself useful to my country.

I then asked myself how could I and after reviewing the various methods I have felt that at the present day we are actually limiting our children and perhaps bringing into the world half the human beings we might owing to the lack of country for them to inhabit that if we had retained America there would at this moment be millions more of English living. I contend* that we are the finest race in the world and that the more of the world we inhabit the better it is for the human race. Just fancy those parts that are at present inhabited by the most despicable* specimens of human beings, what an alteration there would be if they were brought under Anglo-Saxon influence, look again at the extra employment a new country added to our dominions gives. I contend that every acre added to our territory means in the future birth to some more of the English race who otherwise would not be brought into existence. Added to this absorption of the greater portion of the world under our rule simply means the end of all wars. [...]

The idea gleaming and dancing before one's eyes like a will-of-the-wisp* at last frames itself into a plan. Why should we not form a secret society with but one object the furtherance of the British Empire and the bringing of the whole uncivilized world under British rule for the recovery of the United States for the making of the Anglo-Saxon race but one Empire. What a dream, but yet it is probable, it is possible.

I once heard it argued by my fellow in my own college [...] that it was a good thing for us that we have lost the United States [...] but even from an American's point of view just picture what they have lost, look at their government, are not the frauds* that yearly come before the public view a disgrace to any other country and especially theirs which is the finest in the world. Would they have occurred had they remained under English rule great as they have become how infinitely greater they would have been with the softening and the elevating influences of English rule, think of those countless [...] [thousands] of Englishmen that during the last 100 years would have crossed the Atlantic and settled and populated the United States. Would they

to contend to maintain

despicable extremely unpleasant

will-of-the-wisp sth. that is impossible to achieve (*Irrlicht*)

fraud the crime of obtaining money from sb. by tricking them

"The Rhodes Colossus".
Cartoon satirizing Rhodes's plan to link Cairo and the Cape by means of a telegraph line and a railroad. The title alludes to the Colossus of Rhodes, one of the Seven Wonders of the Ancient World.
Published in the British satirical magazine *Punch*, 10 December 1892

have not made without any prejudice a finer country of it than the low class Irish and German emigrants? All this we have lost and that country loses owing to whom? [...]

We learn from having lost to cling to what we possess. We know the size of the world we know the total extent. Africa is still lying ready for us it is our duty to take it. It is our duty to seize every opportunity of acquiring more and more territory and we should keep this idea steadily before our eyes that more territory simply means more of the Anglo-Saxon race more of the best the most human, most honourable race the world possesses. To forward such a scheme what a splendid help a secret society would be a society not openly acknowledged but who would work in secret for such an object.

Cecil Rhodes: "Confessions of Faith", in: Marvin Perry et. al.: Sources of the Western Tradition II, Houghton Mifflin, Boston 1991, pp. 242–244

S 27 Joseph Chamberlain
Speech to Birmingham Businessmen

Joseph Chamberlain (1836–1914) was an influential British businessman, politician, and statesman who became a Liberal Unionist in alliance with the Conservative Party and was appointed Colonial Secretary. He delivered the given speech to businessmen in Birmingham in 1893, stating his views on British imperialism.

Pre-task
1. In his speech, Chamberlain makes a distinction between the "jingo" and the "Little Englander". With the help of the overview section, give a definition of both terms and hypothesize if Chamberlain considers himself a "jingo", a "Little Englander", or none of the two. Take the introductory remarks to this source into account.

Tasks
2. State the reasons advanced by Chamberlain that speak against the "'Little Englander' hav[ing] their way." (l. 29)
3. Explain at least two rhetorical devices Chamberlain makes use of in this speech to appeal to his audience.
4. Compare Chamberlain's view on the African continent with Rhodes's view (cf. S 26): Where do the two of them argue similarly, where do they differ?

Post-task
5. Since this speech was given to Birmingham businessmen, it is not surprising that Chamberlain frequently referred to the economic benefits of British imperialism as a justification. In specific, he talks about the question of supply and demand (cf. e. g. ll. 1 ff.). Do further research on the economic model of supply and demand in a competitive market: How is an economic equilibrium for price and quantity to be reached, and how can you relate that to the motives of imperialism? Also take into account what you have learned about the "Second" Industrial Revolution and its connection to New Imperialism.

We must look the matter in the face, and must recognize that in order that we may have more employment to give we must create more demand [*hear, hear**]. Give me the demand for more goods and then I will undertake to give plenty of employment in making the goods; and the only thing, in my opinion, that the government

hear, hear used to express agreement with a point made by a speaker can do in order to meet this great difficulty that we are considering is to arrange its policy that every inducement* shall be given to the demand; that new markets shall be created, and that old markets shall be effectually developed [cheers].

You are aware that some of my opponents please themselves occasionally by finding names for me, and among other names lately they have been calling me a Jingo [laughter]. I am no more a Jingo than you are [hear, hear]. But for the reasons and arguments I have put before you tonight I am convinced that it is a necessity as well as a duty for us to uphold the dominion* and empire which we now possess [loud cheers]. For these reasons, among others, I would never lose the hold which we now have over our great Indian dependency [hear, hear], by far the greatest and most valuable of all the customers we have or ever shall have in this country. For the same reasons I approve of the continued occupation of Egypt, and for the same reasons I have urged* upon this government, and upon previous governments, the necessity for using every legitimate opportunity to extend our influence and control in that great African continent which is now being opened up to civilization and commerce; and lastly, it is for the same reasons that I hold that our navy should be strengthened [loud cheers] until its supremacy is so assured that we cannot be shaken in any of the possessions which we hold or may hold hereafter. Believe me, if in any of the places to which I have referred any change took place which deprived* us of the control and influence of which I have been speaking, the first to suffer would be the workingman of this country. Then, indeed, we should see a distress which would not be temporary, but which would be chronic, and we should find that England was entirely unable to support the enormous population which is now maintained by the aid of her foreign trade. […]

If the 'Little Englander'* had their way, not only would they refrain from* taking the legitimate opportunities which offer for extending the empire and for securing us new markets, but I doubt whether they would even take the pains which are necessary to preserve the great heritage which has come down to us from our ancestors [applause].

When you are told that the British pioneers of civilization in Africa are filibusters*, and when you are asked to call them back, and to leave this great continent to the barbarism and superstition in which it has been steeped* for centuries, or to hand over to foreign countries the duty which you are unwilling to undertake, I ask you to consider what would have happened if, one hundred and fifty years ago, your ancestors had taken similar views of their responsibility? Where would be the empire on which now your livelihood depends? We should have been the United Kingdom of Great Britain and Ireland but those vast dependencies, those hundreds of millions with whom we keep up a mutually beneficial relationship and commerce would have been the subjects of other nations, who would not have been slow to profit by our neglect* of opportunities and obligations [applause] …

Joseph Chamberlain: "The Doctrine of Commercial Imperialism", 1893, http://web.viu.ca/davies/H479B.Imperialism.Nationalism/Chamberlain.commercial.imperialism.1883.htm [06.08.2014]

---

inducement sth. that persuades sb. to do sth.

dominion colonies that were granted significant freedom to rule themselves

to urge to advise sb. very strongly about what to do

to deprive sb. of sth. to take sth. away from sb.

Little Englander hist. term for a person opposed to the extension of the British Empire
to refrain from sth. to stop from doing sth.

filibuster sb. who pursues a policy of deliberately delaying sth.
to be steeped in sth. to have a lot of a particular quality/thing

neglect the failure to give sb./sth. the attention they need

| Overview | Sources | Paper practice | Vocabulary | | The First World War | **241** |

S 28 US President James Monroe

The Monroe Doctrine

James Monroe was the fifth President of the USA, serving from 1817 to 1825, and the last one of the so-called "Founding Fathers" to become president. On 2 December 1823, Monroe expressed a doctrine which outlined the cornerstones of the future US foreign policy in his seventh annual message to Congress. This doctrine set the basis for the US policy of "isolationism" and defined the relations between Europe and North as well as Central and South America.

Pre-task 1. The Monroe Doctrine is sometimes summarized in the catchphrase "America for the Americans". Anticipate what exactly the Monroe Doctrine said, with reference to this catchphrase and the given cartoon. Also include the geographical extent of "America", as depicted here.

Language support

Knüppel club • **umspannen** to span

Contemporary American cartoon

Tasks 2. Outline the relations between the USA and Europe, as presented in the Monroe Doctrine.
3. Explain why this doctrine set the basis for the American policy of "isolationism" as regards European affairs: Why would the USA feel the need to declare itself free from future European colonization?

4. As you have seen in the cartoon provided, "America" includes not only North, but also Central and South America, which the US considered as their "sphere of influence". Make an educated guess as to the further development of American "continental" relationships, as already foreshadowed in the Monroe Doctrine. Tip: Have a look at how Uncle Sam in the cartoon would probably use "might to make right".

henceforth from this time on

to comport with to conform with

candour honesty, even when the truth is not pleasant
amicable friendly

[...] The American continents, by the free and independent condition which they have assumed and maintain, are henceforth* not to be considered as subjects for future colonization by any European powers [...]
In the wars of the European powers in matters relating to themselves we have never taken any part, nor does it comport with* our policy to do so. It is only when our rights are invaded or seriously menaced that we resent injuries or make preparation for our defense. With the movements in this hemisphere we are of necessity more immediately connected, and by causes which must be obvious to all enlightened and impartial observers. [...] We owe it, therefore, to candor* and to the amicable* relations existing between the United States and those powers to declare that we should consider any attempt on their part to extend their system to any portion of this hemisphere as dangerous to our peace and safety. [...] Our policy in regard to Europe, which was adopted at an early stage of the wars which have so long agitated that quarter of the globe, nevertheless remains the same, which is, not to interfere in the internal concerns of any of its powers; to consider the governments de facto as the legitimate government for us; to cultivate friendly relations with it, and to preserve those relations by a frank, firm and manly policy, meeting in all instances the just claims of every power, submitting to injuries from none. [...] It is still the true policy of the United States to leave the parties to themselves, in hope that other powers will pursue the same course.

James Monroe: "The Monroe Doctrine", 1900, www.yale.edu/lawweb/avalon/monroe.htm [14.04.15]

S 29 US President William McKinley

Speech on Imperialism

William McKinley was the 25th President of the USA, in office from 1897 until his assassination in 1901. In the given speech, delivered in New York City on 3 March 1900, he elaborates on imperialism and on the USA's tasks as regards other countries.

Pre-tasks 1. Have a look at the words and phrases taken from McKinley's speech that he uses to define the "blessings and [...] burdens" (l. 1) of US imperialism. Make a table and categorize the words and phrases accordingly.

> self-governed people • open door in the Far East • trials and responsibilities • to market products • free people • sales • civilizing agency • purchases • free government • mortgages • life, liberty and the pursuit of happiness

2. Discuss differences between British and US imperialism and any respective reasons for this you can think of.

Tasks

3. Scan the speech for the words and phrases contained in the box on p. 242. Add the respective line numbers to your table and be prepared to elaborate, with the help of the context.
4. Explain the self-perception of the USA with reference to the last line of this speech in which McKinley quotes from the American Declaration of Independence of 1776 ("life, liberty, the pursuit of happiness"). Also consider the concept of "manifest destiny" (cf. overview section).
5. Discuss whether McKinley's speech is in line with the Monroe Doctrine (cf. S 28).

[...] We have our blessings and our burdens, and still have both. We will soon have legislative assurance of the continuance of the gold standard, with which we measure our exchanges, and we have the open door in the Far East through which to market our products. We are neither in alliance nor antagonism for entanglement
5 with any foreign power, but on terms of amity and cordiality* with all. We buy from them all and sell to them all, and our sales exceeded our purchases in the past two years by over one billion dollars. Markets have been increased and mortgages have been reduced. Interest has fallen and wages have advanced. The public debt is decreasing. The country is well-to-do. Its people for the most part are happy and
10 contented. They have good times and are on good terms with the nations of the world. [...]
After 33 years of unbroken peace came an unavoidable war*. Happily, the conclusion was quickly reached without a suspicion of unworthy motive, or practice, or purpose on our part and with fadeless honor on our arms [...].
15 Out of these recent events have come to the United States grave trials and responsibilities. As it was the nation's war, so are its results the nation's problem. Its solution rests upon us all. It is too serious to stifle*. It is too earnest for response. [...] There can be no imperialism. Those who fear it are against it. Those who have faith in the republic are against it. So that there is universal abhorrence for it and
20 unanimous opposition to it. Our only difference is that those who do not agree with us have no confidence in the virtue or capacity or high purpose or good faith of this free people as a civilizing agency: while we believe that the century of free government which the American people has enjoyed has not rendered them irresolute and faithless, but has fitted them for the great task of lifting up and assist-
25 ing to better conditions and larger liberty those distant people who have through the issue of battle become our wards*.
Let us fear not. There is no occasion for faint hearts, no excuse for regrets. Nations do not grow in strength and the cause of liberty and law by the doing of easy things. The harder the task the greater will be the result, the benefit, and the honor.
30 To doubt our power to accomplish it is to lose our faith in the soundness* and strengths of our popular institutions.
The liberators will never become the oppressors. A self-governed people will never permit despotism in any government which they foster and defend.
Gentlemen, we have the new care and can not shift it. And, breaking up the camp
35 of ease and isolation, let us bravely and hopefully and soberly continue the march of faithful service and falter* not until the work is done. It is not possible that 75 million American freemen are unable to establish liberty and justice and good government in our new possessions. The burden is our opportunity. The opportu-

cordial friendly

an unavoidable war McKinley is referring to the Spanish-American War of 1898

to stifle here: to suppress

ward sb. who is officially being looked after (esp. a child)

soundness correctness, solidity, integrity

to falter to stop doing sth. because you have lost your confidence or determination

nity is greater than the burden. May God give us strength to bear the one and wisdom so to embrace the other as to carry to our distant acquisitions the guarantees of "life, liberty, and the pursuit of happiness."

William McKinley: "Speech on Imperialism", in: U.S. Foreign Policy: A Documentary and Reference Guide, A. Kalaitzdis, G. W. Streich (Eds.), ABC-CLIO 2011, pp. 59–60

Theodore "Teddy" Roosevelt (1858–1919)

Theodore "Teddy" Roosevelt Jr. was born in New York City on 27 October 1858, the son of a wealthy and well-established family of Dutch-Jewish descent.

From 1876 to 1881, he studied Law at Harvard University and continued his studies at Columbia University. During that time, he had already become an independent candidate for the Republican Party and was elected into the New York parliament, which made him the youngest deputy ever up to that date. Even though he lost the elections for the office of Mayor of New York in 1886, he became the head of the New York police force in 1895 and, under the presidency of William McKinley (cf. S 29), Assistant Secretary of the Navy. However, he resigned from office in the wake of the Spanish-American War (1898). In 1899, Roosevelt then became governor of the State of New York.

Theodore Roosevelt in 1904

One year later, he became McKinley's Vice-President and succeeded the latter in office in 1901 (McKinley had been assassinated), as the youngest president to date, aged only 42. His mediation efforts in the Russo-Japanese War of 1905, while presiding over an international court of arbitration, gained him a Nobel Peace Prize (the first one for an American so far).

Roosevelt died in Sagamore Hill, New York, on 6 January 1919.

S 30 US President Theodore Roosevelt

The Roosevelt Corollary

On 6 December 1904, President Theodor Roosevelt delivered a speech to Congress which contained his views on US foreign policy. This speech has become known as the Roosevelt Corollary (= *Zusatz, Folgesatz*) to the Monroe Doctrine of 1823 (cf. S 28).

Pre-tasks

1. Roosevelt himself summarized his views on US foreign policy by resorting to an African saying: "Speak softly and carry a big stick, and you will go far." That is why his form of diplomacy has come to be known as "big-stick diplomacy". Discuss what a realization of this proverb in connection with matters of US foreign policy and diplomacy could look like. Tip: a useful word here is "deterrence" (verb: to deter [dɪˈtɜː(r)] sb.), which you should add to your vocabulary notebook.

2. Divide the class into two groups, one focussing on the 1905 cartoon of Roosevelt, the other on the film advertisement of 2004. Individually, make notes on the respective representation of "big stick diplomacy" and of the idea of the US enforcing "world policy". Team up and exchange your results. Then discuss in how far both concepts/ideas seem to be a leitmotif of US foreign policy. Check the overview section for help.

"The World's Constable". American cartoon by Louis Dalrymple from 7 January 1905, depicting Theodore Roosevelt standing between Europe and Latin America.

Advertisement for the 2004 film "Team America: World Police"

Embedded text:
On the club: "The New Diplomacy"
On the scroll tucked under the belt: "Tell your troubles to the policeman"
On the scroll tucked under the left arm: "Arbitration"

Embedded text:
Top: "Putting the "F" back in freedom"
Bottom: "Team America/World Police"

Language support

arbitration mediation • **club** Knüppel • **scroll** Schriftrolle

vermitteln to mediate • **Schiedsrichter** mediator

Language support

etw. schultern to shoulder sth. • **Maschinengewehr** machinegun • **Kampfflugzeug** fighter jet • **Chaos/Verwüstung verursachen** to wreak havoc/cause destruction • **Sehenswürdigkeit** sight

Tasks

3. Outline the cornerstones of the Roosevelt Corollary.
4. Try to find examples of such "flagrant cases of such wrongdoing or impotence" as would entitle the USA to "the exercise of an international police power" (ll. 9 f.), as Roosevelt puts it.
5. Explain the self-perception of the USA, as presented here.
6. Does this doctrine qualify as a "corollary" to the Monroe Doctrine? Give an evaluation, also taking the two contemporary cartoons related to the doctrines into account.
7. As you have read in the biographical account of Roosevelt, he was awarded the Nobel Peace Prize in 1905. Discuss if it is possible to be a "big-stick diplomat" and a peace-maker at the same time.

Post-task

8. Do further research on the so-called "Obama doctrine", the US President's remarks to cadets at the United States Military Academy of West Point, N.Y. on 28 May 2014. Present your findings in class and evaluate if, or to what extent, Obama could also be called a "big-stick diplomat".

It is not true that the United States feels any land hunger or entertains any projects as regards the other nations of the Western Hemisphere save such as are for their welfare. [...] If a nation shows that it knows how to act with reasonable efficiency and decency in social and political matters, [...] it need fear no interference from
5 the United States. Chronic wrongdoing, or an impotence which results in a gen-

flagrant shocking since obvious

detriment ['detrɪmənt] the disadvantage, the state of being harmed or damaged by sth.

eral loosening of ties of the civilized society, may in America, as elsewhere, ultimately require intervention by some civilized nation, and in the Western Hemisphere the adherence of the United States to the Monroe Doctrine may force the United States, however reluctantly, in flagrant* cases of such wrongdoing or impotence, to the exercise of an international police power. [...] We would interfere with them only in the last resort, and then only if it became evident that their inability or unwillingness to do justice at home and abroad had violated the rights of the United States or had invited foreign aggression to the detriment* of the entire body of the American nations. It is a mere truism to say that every nation [...] which desires to maintain its freedom, its independence, must ultimately realize that the right of such independence cannot be separated from the responsibility of making good use of it.

In asserting the Monroe Doctrine, [...] we have acted in our own interest as well as in the interest of humanity at large. [...] Nevertheless there are occasional crimes committed on so vast a scale and of such peculiar horror as to make us doubt whether it is not our manifest duty to endeavour at least to show our disapproval of the deed [...]. In extreme cases action may be justifiable and proper. What form the action shall take must depend upon the circumstances of the case; that is, upon the degree of the atrocity* and upon our power to remedy* it. [...]

atrocity a cruel and violent act
to remedy to deal with a problem or improve a bad situation

Theodore Roosevelt: Annual Message to Congress, December 6, 1904, www.latinamericanstudies.org/us-relations/roosevelt-corollary.htm [7.5.11]

American cartoon, establishing a direct link between the "big-stick diplomacy" of Roosevelt and the foreign policy of US President Obama

CONNECT

The "Banana Wars"

The term "Banana Wars" refers to a series of interventions and occupations by the United States in the Caribbean and in Central America in the time between the Spanish-American War of 1898 and the implementation of the "Good Neighbor Policy" under US President Franklin D. Roosevelt in 1933. The term "Banana Wars" can be traced back to the USA's commercial interests in the respective countries, as exemplified by the policies of the United Fruit Company.

Task Writing an improved *Wikipedia* entry about the "Banana Wars"!

As you might have realized, the term "Banana Wars" sounds quite trivial, seen against the backdrop of (US) imperialism. Still, *Wikipedia* uses the term for their entry without even putting it in quotation marks (cf. S 31).

That is why your task is to write a new and improved article for this Internet platform. In order to do so:

- ✓ Split up into six groups. Each group is going to do research on one of the "Banana Wars" and to give a presentation in class: What triggered the war – what interests were at stake – what was the outcome of the war? Summarise your findings on a poster or choose another method of visualization (transparency, Powerpoint, etc.).
- ✓ After your presentation, briefly explain in how far, or if at all, the war your group did research on fits into the concept of US "dollar imperialism".
- ✓ After having heard all six presentations, write a draft for an improved *Wikipedia* entry. Also, find a name for this series of wars which is more appropriate than "Banana Wars". Be prepared to explain your choice in class.

Selected "Banana Wars", waged by the USA against:

1) Panama	2) Honduras	3) Nicaragua
4) Mexico	5) Haiti	6) the Dominican Republic

S 31 *Wikipedia* Screenshot

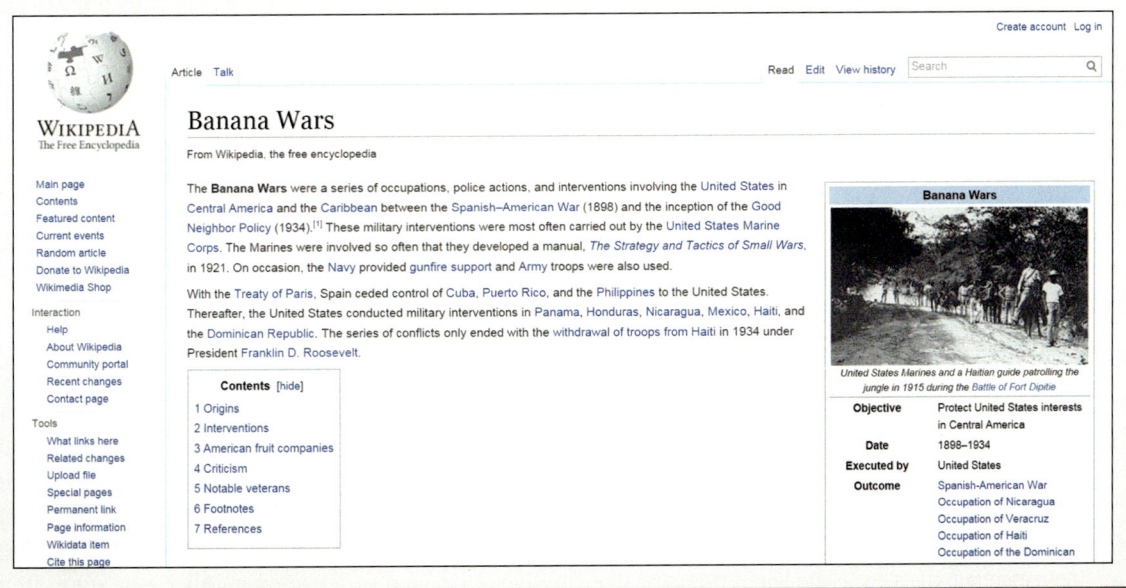

Banana Wars

From Wikipedia, the free encyclopedia

The **Banana Wars** were a series of occupations, police actions, and interventions involving the United States in Central America and the Caribbean between the Spanish–American War (1898) and the inception of the Good Neighbor Policy (1934).[1] These military interventions were most often carried out by the United States Marine Corps. The Marines were involved so often that they developed a manual, *The Strategy and Tactics of Small Wars*, in 1921. On occasion, the Navy provided gunfire support and Army troops were also used.

With the Treaty of Paris, Spain ceded control of Cuba, Puerto Rico, and the Philippines to the United States. Thereafter, the United States conducted military interventions in Panama, Honduras, Nicaragua, Mexico, Haiti, and the Dominican Republic. The series of conflicts only ended with the withdrawal of troops from Haiti in 1934 under President Franklin D. Roosevelt.

Contents [hide]
1 Origins
2 Interventions
3 American fruit companies
4 Criticism
5 Notable veterans
6 Footnotes
7 References

Banana Wars

United States Marines and a Haitian guide patrolling the jungle in 1915 during the Battle of Fort Dipitie

Objective	Protect United States interests in Central America
Date	1898–1934
Executed by	United States
Outcome	Spanish-American War
Occupation of Nicaragua
Occupation of Veracruz
Occupation of Haiti
Occupation of the Dominican

> S 32   Friedrich Kapp

Gegen „kolonialen Chauvinismus"

Friedrich Kapp was a National Liberal Reichstag Deputy. In this address to the annual Congress of German Economists on 22 October 1880, he speaks for those who were not in favour of Germany having overseas colonies.

Pre-task
1. Keeping in mind that the German Empire was a "belated empire" as regards the coming into being of a German nation-state and its participation in the "race for colonies", anticipate which arguments Kapp might advance to convince his audience of the necessity of refraining from colonialism. Also consider who he was actually speaking to.

Tasks
2. Outline the reasons advanced that speak against Germany having overseas colonies. Compare the arguments with your initial thoughts and make any necessary changes/amendments.
3. Explain in how far Kapp recurs to and views patriotism in his speech.

Chauvinist chauvinism here = exaggerated nationalism, jingoism
in den Vordergrund stellen to emphasize, to put in the foreground
Kolonialwesen colonial matters
sich allmählich festsetzen to gradually gain a foothold
ein Einsehen haben to understand
brav well-behaved, worthy
jdn. gewähren lassen to let sb. have their way
paradiesischer Zustand heavenly state of affairs
Misstrauen suspicion
Privatmann private person
günstige Gelegenheit good opportunity
Großmacht great power
Machtmittel instruments of power
behaupten to defend
auf etw. ankommen to risk
missgünstig resentful
jdm. etw. aufdrängen to force sth. upon sb.
etw. totschweigen to keep quiet about sth.
Überzeugung conviction
gerüstet sein to be prepared
Seekrieg naval war
unglücklich sein to fail
in Mitleidenschaft ziehen to have a detrimental [ˌdetrɪˈment(ə)l] effect on

Ich komme jetzt auf einen Punkt, den unsere Kolonial-Chauvinisten* nicht gern in den Vordergrund stellen*. Sie entschuldigen sich gewissermaßen damit, dass sie sagen: wir wollen uns ja nur so sachte in's Kolonialwesen* hineinschieben und uns erst allmählich festsetzen*. Selbst die Engländer werden ein Einsehen haben*, und weil sie wissen, dass wir brave* Leute sind, uns ruhig gewähren lassen*. Nein, meine Herren, das geht nicht so, zu diesem paradiesischen Zustande* gehören zwei: Einer, der es sagt, und ein anderer, der es glaubt; aber glauben tut uns das niemand. Die ganze Welt betrachtet uns mit Misstrauen*, und die Engländer erst recht. Überhaupt kann sich wohl ein Privatmann* da, wo er eine günstige Gelegenheit* erspäht, in eine neue und größere Stellung hineindrücken; ein Staat, eine Großmacht* aber muss mit allen ihren Machtmitteln* eintreten, wenn sie eine neue Position erringen und behaupten* will. Es darf ihr dann selbst auf einen Krieg nicht ankommen*, und wenn sie ihn nicht will, so wird er ihr von ihren missgünstigen* Nachbarn schon aufgedrängt* werden. Aber diese sich ganz von selbst verstehende Perspektive schweigen unsere would-be-Kolonisatoren wohlweislich tot*. Sie denken, erst drücken wir unsere Wünsche durch, und dann mögen die anderen weiter sehen. Ich will diesem Verhalten gegenüber offen meine Überzeugung* dahin aussprechen, dass wir, ohne stets auf Krieg gerüstet* zu sein, und zwar auch auf einen Seekrieg*, den wir möglicherweise Tausende von Meilen von der Heimat zu führen haben, nie eine Kolonie gründen, geschweige denn behaupten können. Und wenn wir in einem solchen Kriege unglücklich sind*, wird dann etwa das Mutterland nicht in Mitleidenschaft gezogen werden*? Ich kenne schon im voraus die Antwort, die mir auf diese bescheidene* Frage zuteil werden wird. Sie überhaupt nur stellen, heißt in den Augen unserer Kolonial-Chauvinisten soviel als schlechter Deutscher, Zweifler* an unserem nationalen Berufe*, Verkleinerer* unseres Volkes, wenn nicht gar Reichsfeind* sein. Derartige persönliche Anklagen mögen füglich unerwidert bleiben, da sie keine sachlichen Widerlegungen* sind. Wir Deutschen aber haben viel wichtigere und dringendere Aufgaben zu erfüllen, als uns unnötigerweise Verlegenheiten* auf den Hals zu laden, als mit fremden Weltteilen anzubinden und Abenteuer zu suchen, die leicht mit ganz überflüssigen* Kriegen enden können. Alles, was wir in fremden Weltteilen brauchen, sind Kohlen- und Flottenstationen* zum Schutze unseres Handels; was darüber ist, ist vom Übel.

Bericht des Referenten Dr. Kapp, 1880 in: Hans Fenske (Hg.): Im Bismarckschen Reich 1871–1890. Darmstadt: Wissenschaftliche Buchgesellschaft, 1978, S. 258–59

bescheiden modest
Zweifler doubter
Beruf mission
Verkleinerer belittler
Reichsfeind enemy of the Reich
sachliche Widerlegung an objective attempt to refute sth.
Verlegenheiten difficulties
überflüssig superfluous [suːəpɜː(r)fluəs]
Kohlen- und Flottenstationen coal and naval stations

S 33 · Carl Peters
Gründungsmanifest der Gesellschaft für Deutsche Kolonisation

This manifesto for the newly founded Society for German Colonization was drafted by the Africa adventurer Carl Peters and published on 28 March 1885. Here Peters portrays colonialism as an economic and patriotic necessity.

Pre-task
1. Have a look at the arguments advanced by Kapp (cf. S 32) and collect arguments Peters could make use of to refute them.

Tasks
2. Outline the reasons advanced that speak for Germany having overseas colonies. Compare the arguments used by Peters with your initial thoughts (cf. task 1) and make any necessary changes/amendments.
3. Explain in how far Peters recurs to and views patriotism in his speech.
4. Stage an argument between Kapp and Peters in which they discuss the advantages and disadvantages of Germany having overseas colonies.

Post-task
5. Do further research on Carl Peters and German East Africa. Centre your research on the question as to what extent the term "protectorate" is appropriate to describe the relationship between colonizers and colonized (consider for example the Maji Maji Rebellion of 1905). Present your findings in class, against the backdrop of your results from task 4.

Deutsche Kolonisation
Die deutsche Nation ist bei der Verteilung* der Erde, wie sie vom Ausgang des 15. Jahrhunderts bis auf unsere Tage hin stattgefunden hat, leer ausgegangen*. Alle übrigen Kulturvölker* Europas besitzen auch außerhalb unseres Erdteils Stätten,
5 wo ihre Sprache und Art feste Wurzel fassen* und sich entfalten* kann. Der deutsche Auswanderer, sobald er die Grenzen des Reiches hinter sich gelassen hat, ist ein Fremdling* auf ausländischem Grund und Boden*. Das Deutsche Reich, groß und stark durch die mit Blut errungene Einheit, steht da als die führende Macht auf dem Kontinent von Europa: seine Söhne in der Fremde müssen sich überall
10 Nationen einfügen*, welche der unsrigen entweder gleichgültig* oder geradezu feindlich* gegenüberstehen. Der große Strom* deutscher Auswanderung taucht seit Jahrhunderten in fremde Rassen ein*, um in ihnen zu verschwinden. Das Deutschtum* außerhalb Europas verfällt fortdauernd nationalem Untergang*.
In dieser, für den Nationalstolz so schmerzlichen Tatsache liegt ein ungeheurer
15 wirtschaftlicher Nachteil für unser Volk! Alljährlich geht die Kraft von etwa 200 000 Deutschen unserem Vaterland verloren! Diese Kraftmasse* strömt meistens unmittelbar in das Lager unserer wirtschaftlichen Konkurrenten* ab und vermehrt

Verteilung partitioning
leer ausgehen to be left empty-handed
Kulturvölker civilized nations
Wurzel fassen to take root
sich entfalten to flourish
Fremdling stranger
ausländischer Grund und Boden foreign territory
sich einfügen to adapt to
gleichgültig indifferent
feindlich hostile
Strom stream
eintauchen submerge
Deutschtum Germandom
Untergang decline
Kraftmasse strength
wirtschaftliche Konkurrenten economic competitors

die Stärke unserer Gegner. Der deutsche Import von Produkten tropischer Zonen geht von ausländischen Niederlassungen* aus, wodurch jährlich viele Millionen deutschen Kapitals an fremde Nationen verlorengehen! Der deutsche Export ist abhängig von der Willkür* fremdländischer Zollpolitik*. Ein unter allen Umständen sicherer Absatzmarkt* fehlt unserer Industrie, weil eigene Kolonien unserem Volke fehlen.

Um diesem nationalen Missstande* abzuhelfen, dazu bedarf es praktischen und tatkräftigen* Handelns. Von diesem Gesichtspunkte ausgehend, ist in Berlin eine Gesellschaft zusammengetreten, welche die praktische Inangriffnahme* solchen Handelns als ihr Ziel sich gestellt hat. Die Gesellschaft für deutsche Kolonisation will in entschlossener und durchgreifender Weise* die Ausführung von sorgfältig erwogenen* Kolonisationsprojekten selbst in die Hand nehmen und somit ergänzend den Bestrebungen* von Vereinigungen ähnlicher Tendenzen zur Seite treten.

Als ihre Aufgabe stellt sie sich in besonderem:
1. Beschaffung eines entsprechenden Kolonisationskapitals.
2. Auffindung und Erwerbung geeigneter Kolonisationsdistrikte.
3. Hinlenkung* der deutschen Auswanderung in diese Gebiete.

Durchdrungen von der Überzeugung, dass mit der energischen Inangriffnahme dieser großen nationalen Aufgabe nicht länger gezögert* werden darf, wagen wir es, mit der Bitte vor das deutsche Volk zu treten, die Bestrebungen unserer Gesellschaft tatkräftig zu fördern! Die deutsche Nation hat wiederholt bewiesen, dass sie bereit ist, für allgemein-patriotische Unternehmungen* Opfer zu bringen*: sie möge auch der Lösung dieser großen geschichtlichen Aufgabe ihre Beteiligung in tatkräftiger Weise zuwenden.

Jeder Deutsche, dem ein Herz für die Größe und die Ehre unserer Nation schlägt, ist aufgefordert, unserer Gesellschaft beizutreten. Es gilt, das Versäumnis* von Jahrhunderten gutzumachen*; der Welt zu beweisen, dass das deutsche Volk mit der alten Reichsherrlichkeit* auch den alten deutsch-nationalen Geist der Väter überkommen* hat!

Carl Peters: „Aufruf der Gesellschaft für Deutsche Kolonisation" (28. März 1885), in: E.A. Jacob: Deutsche Kolonialpolitik in Dokumenten, Gedanken und Gestalten der letzten fünfzig Jahre, Leizip 1938, pp. 85–87

1884 photograph of Carl Peters with a coloured servant

Niederlassung settlement
Willkür arbitrariness
Zollpolitik tariff policies
Absatzmarkt outlet market
Missstand deplorable state of affairs
tatkräftig vigorous
Inangriffnahme initiation
in entschlossener und durchgreifender Weise in a resolute and sweeping manner
sorgfältig erwogen carefully planned
Bestrebung aim
Hinlenkung directing
zögern to postpone
allgemein-patriotische Unternehmungen general patriotic endeavours [ɪn'devə(r)]
Opfer bringen to make sacrifices
Versäumnis omission, oversight
gutmachen to make up for
Reichsherrlichkeit imperial glory
überkommen to inherit

| S 34 | Otto von Bismarck

Zur „pragmatischen" Kolonisierung

Bismarck was not in favour of "formal imperialism", fearing in particular a strain on diplomatic relations with the other powers. However, he later adopted a policy of "pragmatic colonialism" which he explained on 26 June 1884.

Pre-tasks
1. Revise what you have learned about Bismarck's foreign and domestic policy in chapter 1: what were his aims, and how did he try to achieve them? Against this background, explain why Bismarck initially rejected German colonialism.
2. Have a look at the cartoon, entitled "Die Südsee ist das Mittelmeer der Zukunft", published in the German satirical magazine *Kladderadatsch* on 13 July 1884. The tiny flag which one sees in Southwest Africa marks Angra Pequence (*Lüderitzbucht*). Describe the cartoon in detail, also focussing on its composition and the intended effect on the spectator. Afterwards, explain the cartoon's title, taking the pictorial elements and your results from task 1 into consideration.

Embedded text:
"Mir kann es ganz recht sein, wenn die anderen dort unten Beschäftigung finden. Man hat dann endlich Ruhe hier oben."

Language support

etw. ist jdm. recht sth. is all right with sb., sth. suits sb. • **Beschäftigung finden** to be occupied • **seine Ruhe haben** to have some peace and quiet • **Rauchwolke** cloud of smoke

Tasks
3. Point out Bismarck's elaborations on the "French system" (l. 8) and outline how he envisions Germany's "colonial endeavours" (l. 16).

4. With reference to the arguments used, explain why Bismarck calls his approach "pragmatic".

Post-task 5. Do further research on the Berlin Conference of 1884 and the role played by Bismarck. Evaluate if his role and behaviour are in line with his statements on "pragmatic colonialism".

Unternehmung enterprise
hanseatische Kaufleute Hanseatic merchants
Terrainankauf land purchase ['pɜː(r)tʃəs]
Antrag auf Reichsschutz request for imperial protection
etw. einer Prüfung unterziehen to consider
Unterlage foundation
Auswanderer emigrant
herbeiziehen to draw
Garnison garrison
Abneigung aversion
ausführbar practicable
zweckmäßig expedient [ɪkˈspiːdiənt]
Kolonialbestrebung colonial endeavour [ɪnˈdevə(r)]
Gebilde community
überschüssige Säfte superfluous [suːˈpɜː(r)fluəs] strength

kaufmännisch commercial

lehnbar bleiben to remain dependent

Schädigung damage

verfehlt a failure

sich vergreifen to adopt the wrong approach

Privatmann private person
Wurzeln schlagen to put down roots
jdm. etw. versagen to deny sb. sth.

Was die Kolonialfrage im engeren Sinne anlangt, so wiederhole ich die Genesis derselben, wie ich sie damals angegeben habe. Wir sind zuerst durch die Unternehmung* hanseatischer Kaufleute*, verbunden mit Terrainankäufen* und gefolgt von Anträgen auf Reichsschutz*, dazu veranlasst worden, die Frage, ob wir diesen Reichsschutz in dem gewünschten Maße versprechen könnten, einer näheren Prüfung zu unterziehen*. Ich wiederhole, dass ich gegen Kolonien – ich will sagen, nach dem System, wie die meisten im vorigen Jahrhundert waren, was man jetzt das französische System nennen könnte –, gegen Kolonien, die als Unterlage* ein Stück Land schaffen und dann Auswanderer* herbeizuziehen* suchen, Beamte anstellen und Garnisonen* errichten —, dass ich meine frühere Abneigung* gegen diese Art Kolonisation, die für andere Länder nützlich sein mag, für uns aber nicht ausführbar* ist, heute noch nicht aufgegeben habe. [...] Etwas ganz anderes ist die Frage, ob es zweckmäßig*, und zweitens, ob es die Pflicht des Deutschen Reiches ist, denjenigen seiner Untertanen, die solchen Unternehmungen im Vertrauen auf des Reiches Schutz sich hingeben, diesen Reichsschutz zu gewähren und ihnen gewisse Beihilfen in ihren Kolonialbestrebungen* zu leisten, und denjenigen Gebilden*, die aus den überschüssigen Säften* des gesamten deutschen Körpers naturgemäß herauswachsen, in fremden Ländern Pflege und Schutz angedeihen zu lassen. Und das bejahe ich, allerdings mit weniger Sicherheit vom Standpunkte der Zweckmäßigkeit – ich kann nicht voraussehen, was daraus wird –, aber mit unbedingter Sicherheit vom Standpunkte der staatlichen Pflicht. [...]
Unsere Absicht ist, nicht Provinzen zu gründen, sondern kaufmännische* Unternehmungen, aber in der höchsten Entwickelung, auch solche, die sich eine Souveränität, eine schließlich dem Deutschen Reich lehnbar bleibende*, unter seiner Protektion stehende kaufmännische Souveränität erwerben, zu schützen in ihrer freien Entwickelung sowohl gegen die Angriffe aus der unmittelbaren Nachbarschaft als auch gegen Bedrückung und Schädigung* von seiten anderer europäischer Mächte. Im übrigen hoffen wir, dass der Baum durch die Tätigkeit der Gärtner, die ihn pflanzen, auch im ganzen gedeihen wird, und wenn er es nicht tut, so ist die Pflanze eine verfehlte*, und es trifft der Schade weniger das Reich, denn die Kosten sind nicht bedeutend, die wir verlangen, sondern die Unternehmer, die sich in ihren Unternehmungen vergriffen* haben. Das ist der Unterschied: bei dem System, welches ich das französische nannte, will die Staatsregierung jedesmal beurteilen, ob das Unternehmen ein richtiges ist und ein Gedeihen in Aussicht stellt; bei diesem System überlassen wir dem Handel, dem Privatmann* die Wahl, und wenn wir sehen, dass der Baum Wurzel schlägt*, anwächst und gedeiht und den Schutz des Reiches anruft, so stehen wir ihm bei, und ich sehe auch nicht ein, wie wir ihm das rechtmäßig versagen* können.

Otto von Bismarck: Rede vor dem Reichstag, 26. Juni 1884, in: Gustav Adolf Rein et al. (Ed.): Otto von Bismarck: Werke in Auswahl. Jahrhundertausgabe zum 23. September 1862, Vol. 7: Reichsgestaltung und Europäische Friedenswahrung, Part 3: 1883–1890 (ed. by Alfred Milatz), Wissenschaftliche Buchgesellschaft, Darmstadt 2001, pp. 167, 169f.

S 35 Bernhard von Bülow

Hammer oder Amboss

On 11 December 1899, then German Secretary of State for Foreign Affairs Bernhard von Bülow (1849–1929), who was to become one of Bismarck's successors in office as German Chancellor from 1900 to 1909, gave a speech to the Reichstag which has come to be known as the "hammer-or-anvil" speech. The occasion was the announcement of a second proposal for a German fleet.

Pre-task 1. This speech has come to be famous as the so-called "hammer-or-anvil" speech, an image with which von Bülow characterizes the two different directions the German Empire can take in the next (i.e. the 20th) century. Write down what you associate with the two images. Based on your results, make an educated guess as to von Bülow's line of argument.

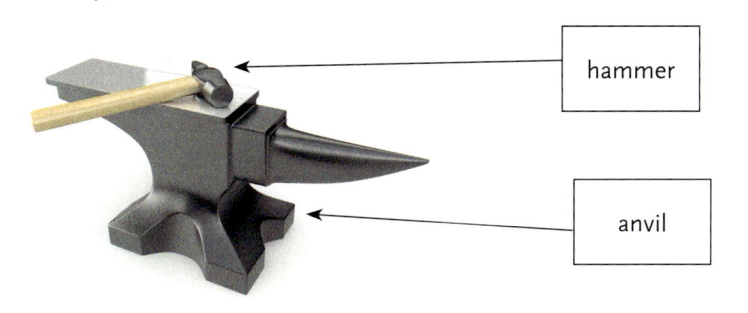

Tasks
2. Outline the demands von Bülow makes, and state his reasons.
3. Explain in how far von Bülow's approach to foreign policy differs from his predecessor in office as Chancellor, Bismarck.
4. Evaluate the seeds of potential conflicts embedded in von Bülow's speech.
5. Discuss what the German Empire would need in order to gain "a place in the sun".

[...] In unserm neunzehnten Jahrhundert hat England sein Kolonialreich, das größte, das die Welt seit den Tagen der Römer gesehen hat, weiter und immer weiter ausgedehnt*, haben die Franzosen in Nordafrika und Ostafrika festen Fuß gefasst* und sich in Hinterindien* ein neues Reich geschaffen, hat Russland in
5 Asien seinen gewaltigen Siegeslauf* begonnen, [...].
Der englische Premierminister hatte schon vor längerer Zeit gesagt, dass die starken Staaten immer stärker und die schwachen immer schwächer werden würden. [...] Wir wollen keiner fremden Macht zu nahe treten*, wir wollen uns aber auch von keiner fremden Macht auf die Füße treten lassen* (Bravo!) und wir wollen
10 uns von keiner fremden Macht beiseite schieben lassen, weder in politischer noch in wirtschaftlicher Beziehung. (Lebhafter Beifall.)
Es ist Zeit, es ist hohe Zeit, dass wir [...] uns klar werden über die Haltung, welche wir einzunehmen haben gegenüber den Vorgängen*, die sich um uns herum abspielen und vorbereiten und welche die Keime in sich tragen für die künftige Ge-
15 staltung der Machtverhältnisse* für vielleicht unabsehbare Zeit*. Untätig beiseite

ausdehnen to increase
festen Fuß fassen to put down roots
Hinterindien the Far East
Siegeslauf course of victory

jdm. zu nahe treten to step on sb.'s toes
auf die Füße treten lassen to have one's feet tramped on

Vorgänge processes
Machtverhältnisse power relationships
unabsehbare Zeit unforeseeable future

untätig beiseite stehen to stand inactively to one side

beispielloser Aufschwung unprecedented blossoming
Tüchtigkeit efficiency, capability, hard work
verflechten to weave (wove – woven) into

Stützpunkt base
Mittel means
Rüstung armaments

wirtschaftliche Fühlhörner ausstrecken to stretch out one's economic antennae

stehen*, wie wir das früher oft getan haben, [...], während andere Leute sich in den Kuchen teilen, das können wir nicht und wollen wir nicht. (Beifall.)
Wir können das nicht aus dem einfachen Grunde, weil wir jetzt Interessen haben, in allen Weltteilen. [...] Die rapide Zunahme unserer Bevölkerung, der beispiellose Aufschwung* unserer Industrie, die Tüchtigkeit* unserer Kaufleute, kurz, die gewaltige Vitalität des deutschen Volkes haben uns in die Weltwirtschaft verflochten* und in die Weltpolitik hineingezogen. Wenn die Engländer von einem Greater Britain reden, wenn die Franzosen sprechen von einer Nouvelle France, wenn die Russen sich Asien erschließen, haben auch wir Anspruch auf ein größeres Deutschland (Bravo! rechts, Heiterkeit links), nicht im Sinne der Eroberung, wohl aber im Sinne der friedlichen Ausdehnung unseres Handels und seiner Stützpunkte*. [...] [...]
Das Mittel*, meine Herren, in dieser Welt den Kampf ums Dasein durchzufechten ohne starke Rüstung* zu Lande und zu Wasser, ist für ein Volk von bald 60 Millionen, das die Mitte von Europa bewohnt und gleichzeitig seine wirtschaftlichen Fühlhörner ausstreckt* nach allen Seiten, noch nicht gefunden worden. (Sehr wahr! rechts.)
In dem kommenden Jahrhundert wird das deutsche Volk Hammer oder Amboss sein. [...]

from: Buchners Kolleg Geschichte, Das Kaiserreich 1871 bis 1918, Bamberg: C.C. Buchners Verlag 1987, S. 137 ff.

S 36 Emperor William II

„Hunnenrede"

The so-called "Hun speech" was given by the German Emperor William II on the occasion of the East-Asia Expedition Corps leaving the port of Bremerhaven on 27 July 1900 in order to assist international forces in putting down the Boxer Rebellion in China. The transcript of the speech provided here is the unofficial version in which William II makes explicit reference to the Huns in the last sentence, whereas this reference is missing in the version published in the newspapers. Nevertheless, this speech gained the Germans the nickname "the Huns", a description spread and mostly used by the British in their anti-German war propaganda.

Pre-tasks 1. Read the (inofficial) ending of the speech given in the box below. Paraphrase the threat uttered by the German Emperor in your own words and discuss why von Bülow (cf. S 35) only gave an edited version to the press.

> Wie vor tausend Jahren die Hunnen unter ihrem König Etzel sich einen Namen gemacht, der sie noch jetzt in Überlieferung und Märchen gewaltig erscheinen lässt, so möge der Name Deutscher in China auf 1000 Jahre durch euch in einer Weise bestätigt werden, dass es niemals wieder ein Chinese wagt, einen Deutschen scheel anzusehen!
>
> from: Manfred Görtemaker: Deutschland im 19. Jahrhundert. Entwicklungslinien, Opladen 1996. (Schriftenreihe der Bundeszentrale für politische Bildung, Vol. 274), p. 357

Tasks

2. Do research on Attila (*Etzel*) and the Hunnic Empire. Based on your results, explain William II's choice of reference.
3. State the tasks of the German Empire, according to the Emperor, and point out the alleged crimes committed by the Chinese that require German retaliation.
4. Analyse the tone of the speech. Focus on the Emperor's diction (choice of words). If possible, listen to the speech (e. g. on YouTube) to see in how far intonation and stress underline the results of your analysis.
5. In his memoirs, von Bülow classified this speech as the worst and probably most harmful ever given by William II. Evaluate this assessment, taking into account a) content and tone of the speech, and b) von Bülow's "hammer-or-anvil" speech (cf. S 35).

Post-task

6. Do further research on the Boxer Rebellion and on the actions taken by the German East Africa Expedition Corps in putting the rebellion down. Present your results in class and, against this backdrop, evaluate to what extent the behaviour of the German troops was in contradiction with Article 23 of the Hague Conventions of 1899 (cf. overview section) given in the box, and in how far the Emperor's speech authorized this form of behaviour.

SECTION II. – ON HOSTILITIES
CHAPTER I. – On means of injuring the Enemy, Sieges, and Bombardments
Article 23
Besides the prohibitions provided by special Conventions, it is especially prohibited: –
To employ poison or poisoned arms;
To kill or wound treacherously* individuals belonging to the hostile nation or army;
To kill or wound an enemy who, having laid down arms, or having no longer means of defence, has surrendered at discretion;
To declare that no quarter will be given;
To employ arms, projectiles, or material of a nature to cause superfluous* injury;
To make improper use of a flag of truce*, the national flag, or military ensigns and the enemy's uniform, as well as the distinctive badges of the Geneva Convention;
To destroy or seize the enemy's property, unless such destruction or seizure be imperatively demanded by the necessities of war.

treacherous ['tretʃərəs] *heimtückisch* • **superfluous** excessive, uncalled for • **truce** ceasefire, armistice

from: Convention with Respect to the Laws and Customs of War and on Land (Hague, II) (29 Juli 1899), http://avalom.law.yale.edu/19th_century/hague02.asp#art 23 [15.11.14]

---

7. As explained in the introduction to this source, this speech earned the Germans the nickname "the Huns", especially in British war propaganda. Have a look at the example given here. Describe it in

detail, explain its respective functions (Tip: Check CONNECT: Propaganda for help, cf. pp. 309 f.) and assess if you consider it to be in line with the way William II presents the Germans in his speech.

US anti-German propaganda poster

Language support
liberty bonds Freiheitsanleihen (a means of financing the war)
überdimensional over-dimensional • **Ungeheuer** monster • **näherkommen** to come closer • **(Blut) tropfen** to drip (blood)

überseeische Aufgaben overseas tasks
Landsleute countrymen
Verpflichtung obligation
jdn. bedrängen to beset sb.

Große überseeische Aufgaben* sind es, die dem neu entstandenen Deutschen Reiche zugefallen sind, Aufgaben weit größer, als viele Meiner Landsleute* es erwartet haben. Das Deutsche Reich hat seinem Charakter nach die Verpflichtung*, seinen Bürgern, sofern diese im Ausland bedrängt* werden, beizustehen. Die Aufgaben, welche das alte Römische Reich deutscher Nation nicht hat lösen können, ist das neue Deutsche Reich in der Lage zu lösen. Das Mittel, das ihm dies ermöglicht, ist unser Heer.

verewigt late, deceased
die Probe ablegen to put to the test
sich bewähren to prove one's worth
eine Probe bestehen to pass a test

In dreißigjähriger treuer Friedensarbeit ist es herangebildet worden nach den Grundsätzen Meines verewigten* Großvaters. Auch ihr habt eure Ausbildung nach diesen Grundsätzen erhalten und sollt nun vor dem Feinde die Probe ablegen*, ob sie sich bei euch bewährt* haben. Eure Kameraden von der Marine haben diese Probe bereits bestanden*, sie haben euch gezeigt, dass die Grundsätze unserer Ausbildung gute sind, und Ich bin stolz auf das Lob auch aus Munde auswärtiger Führer, das eure Kameraden draußen sich erworben haben. An euch ist es, es ihnen gleich zu tun.

harren to await
Unrecht injustice
sühnen to revenge
Völkerrecht international law
umwerfen to overturn
Heiligkeit sacredness

Eine große Aufgabe harrt* eurer: ihr sollt das schwere Unrecht*, das geschehen ist, sühnen*. Die Chinesen haben das Völkerrecht* umgeworfen*, sie haben in einer in der Weltgeschichte nicht erhörten Weise der Heiligkeit* des Gesandten, den Pflichten des Gastrechts* Hohn gesprochen*. Es ist das um so [sic] empörender*, als dies Verbrechen begangen worden ist von einer Nation, die auf ihre uralte Kultur stolz ist. Bewährt die alte preußische Tüchtigkeit*, zeigt euch als Christen im freundlichen Ertragen von Leiden, möge Ehre und Ruhm* euren Fahnen und Waffen folgen, gebt an Manneszucht* und Disziplin aller Welt ein Beispiel. Ihr wisst es wohl, ihr sollt fechten gegen einen verschlagenen*, tapferen, gut bewaffneten, grausamen Feind. Kommt ihr vor den Feind, so wird derselbe geschlagen! Pardon wird nicht gegeben! Gefangene werden nicht gemacht! Wer euch in die Hände fällt, sei euch verfallen*! Wie vor tausend Jahren die Hunnen unter ihrem König Etzel sich einen Namen gemacht, der sie noch jetzt in Überlieferung und Märchen* gewaltig erscheinen lässt, so möge der Name Deutscher in China auf 1000 Jahre durch euch in einer Weise bestätigt werden, dass es niemals wieder ein Chinese wagt, einen Deutschen scheel anzusehen*!

from: Johannes Penzler (Ed.): Die Reden Kaiser Wilhelms II., Bd. 2: 1896–1900. Leipzig o. J., S. 209–212; Manfred Görtemaker: Deutschland im 19. Jahrhundert. Entwicklungslinien. Opladen 1996. Schriftenreihe der Bundeszentrale für politische Bildung, Bd. 274), S. 357

Gastrecht hospitality
Hohn sprechen to mock
empörend outrageous
preußische Tüchtigkeit Prussian virtue
Ehre und Ruhm honour and glory
Manneszucht manliness
verschlagen cunning
verfallen forfeited ['fɔː(r)fɪt]
Überlieferung und Märchen history and legend
jdn. scheel ansehen to look askance at sb.

S 37 Verax

As Others See Us

Verax was the pseudonym used by the English journalist Henry Dunckley (1832–1896). In the given excerpts from one of his articles, entitled "As Others See Us", published in *The Manchester Guardian* on 4 February 1894, Dunckley – as the headline already indicates – takes a closer look at the way Britain is seen by others, but also examines Germany's imperialist ambitions.

Embedded text:
Grandma' Victoria: "Now, Willie dear, you've plenty of soldiers at home; look at these pretty *ships*, – I'm sure you'll be pleased with *them*!"

Pre-tasks

1. In 1889, Emperor William II made a state visit to Britain, then ruled by his grandmother Queen Victoria. During that visit, William II was made Admiral of the Fleet of the Royal Navy, a gesture that, it was hoped, would calm down the enthusiastic and militaristic new Emperor and prevent him from further extending his fleet. This visit is ridiculed in the given cartoon by John Tenniel, published on 3 August 1889 in *Punch* magazine, entitled "Visiting Grandmamma". Based on what you have learned about the imperial ambitions of Emperor William II, write his speech bubble in your exercise book: how do you see yourself, and what, in the final analysis, do you want?

Language support

Schaufel shovel • **Sandburg** sand castle • **Kampfschiff** battleship • **Zaun** fence • **Sonnenschirm** parasol

VISITING GRANDMAMMA.

GRANDMA' VICTORIA. "NOW, WILLIE DEAR, YOU'VE PLENTY OF SOLDIERS AT HOME; LOOK AT THESE PRETTY SHIPS,—I'M SURE YOU'LL BE PLEASED WITH THEM!"

2. With the help of the caption, make an educated guess as to what Queen Victoria might have to say in return.

Tasks

3. Work with a partner. **Partner A** makes notes on the British, as Verax views them, i.e.:
   a. how others see them,
   b. why others see them like that and
   c. how they should see them.

   Partner B makes notes on Verax's view of the Germans, i.e.:
   a. Germany's naval history,
   b. reasons for Germany's naval history and
   c. suggestions for Germany's future.

4. Exchange your findings. Together, write Queen Victoria's speech bubble in your exercise books (key words only, expressing how she is seen by others and how she sees herself (representing the British), as well as what she thinks about her grandson's (= Germany's) naval ambitions. Before writing: decide on the tone you want to use when speaking to William II. The tone should match up with the cartoon's composition and Verax's statements. Check the box below for ideas.

Tone can for example be …

accusatory (*anklagend*) • amused • bitter • cheerful • condescending (*herablassend*) • contemptuous (*verächtlich*) • defiant (*trotzig*) • diplomatic • earnest • encouraging • forthright (*geradeheraus*) • gentle • impersonal • judgemental (*wertend*) • mocking (*verspottend*) • neutral • objective • patronising (*gönnerhaft*) • quizzical (*spöttisch*) • rude • sarcastic • snobbish • threatening • vindictive (*rachsüchtig*) … etc.

---

ample enough, often more than needed
unmitigated unrestricted

innocency innocence
guile the use of clever but dishonest behaviour to trick people
rectitude a very moral and correct way of behaving
testimony *Aussage*
impartial *unparteiisch*

to appropriate to take possession of
Hanseatic League *die Hanse* (an economic alliance of trading cities during the late Middle Ages and Early Modern Period)
submissiveness willingness to do what you are told
to attain to to succeed in getting sth.
to aspire to want to achieve sth.

Any of us who are concerned to know in what light we are regarded by other nations have lately had ample* means of satisfying their curiosity. […] We learn to our surprise that our foreign policy is one of unmitigated* selfishness. […]
It is well to find out what the rest of the world thinks of us. Acting always in the innocency* of our hearts, unconscious of any guile*, and persuaded of our perfect rectitude*, we may not quite know ourselves. Possibly, perhaps probably, the accusations levelled at us may not be quite just, but yet it may be worth while to pay some attention to the testimony* of outside observers, even though they may not be absolutely impartial*. […]
What is the impression which the spectacle of this world-wide empire is likely to make, and does make, upon other nations? Does it not, at any rate, offer some reasonable explanation of the protests and rather jealous remarks we hear them utter from time to time? Does it not happen to be true that we have so far appropriated* the wide spaces of the world as to leave but small room for such colonising capacities as they have, or think they have? They are not at all in the same position. Germany, though one of the oldest group of States in Europe, is new as a single political power, and has entered the sphere of naval enterprise rather late. Since the days of the Hanseatic League*, Germany has had but few ships, and till lately but little foreign commerce. The problems she has had to solve have been of a domestic order. Long reduced to comparative helplessness of her princes and the submissiveness* of her people, she had to attain to* unity within herself before she could aspire* to influence abroad. Now, when she gathers up her energies and

surveys the globe, she finds most of it already occupied and complains no room has been left for her. We could hardly be expected to repress the energies of our
25 people and wait till she could join us, so that we might both "start fair" [...]. Germany has done great things for herself, and that may well be accepted as something like a compensation. The greatest military Power on the continent, only yesterday celebrating exploits* which echoed throughout the world, may well recognise without grudging* our superiority at sea, and permit us quietly to enjoy the
30 empire we have won [...].

from: The Manchester Guardian, 4. February 1897

exploit: here: a brave or exciting act
grudging envy

S 38 Eyre Crowe

Memorandum

Eyre Crowe (1864–1925) was working at the British Foreign Office, when, on 1 January 1907, he wrote a memorandum in which he also assessed Germany's imperial ambitions and motivations.

Pre-task 1. Revise Verax's assessment of Germany's imperial ambitions and motivations (cf. S 37). Make an educated guess as to changes that took place in the British assessment of this issue up to 1907, the year in which the given memorandum was written. Be prepared to justify your views.

Tasks 2. Point out the characteristics of Britain's foreign policy, according to Crowe, and outline his view on the "purposes of [Germany's] foreign policy", as well as her motives (l. 6).
3. Explain in detail Crowe's attitude towards Germany's foreign policy. In doing so, also put his references to the development of Germany into the historical context.
4. Put the source into the historical context of the development of British-German relations on the eve of the First World War by comparing S 37 and S 38 and by elaborating on the time in between.

[...] The general character of England's foreign policy is determined by the immutable* conditions of her geographical situation on the ocean flank of Europe as an island State [sic] with vast oversea colonies and dependencies, whose existence and survival as an independent community are inseparably bound up with the posses-
5 sion of preponderant* sea power. [...]
For purposes of foreign policy the modern German Empire may be regarded as the heir, or descendant of Prussia. [...] With the events of 1871 the spirit of Prussia passed into the new Germany. In no other country is there a conviction so deeply rooted in the very body and soul of all classes of the population that the preserva-
10 tion of national rights and the realization of national ideas rest absolutely on the readiness of every citizen in the last resort to stake himself and his State on their assertion and vindication*. With "blood and iron" Prussia had forged* her position in the councils of the Great Powers of Europe. [...]
Germany had won her place as one of the leading, if not, in fact, the foremost
15 Power [sic] on the European continent. But over and beyond the European Great

immutable impossible to change

preponderant more powerful than others

vindication defence
to forge schmieden

Powers there seemed to stand the "World Powers". It was at once clear that Germany must become a "World Power". The evolution of this idea and its translation into practical politics followed with a singular consistency the line of thought that had inspired the Prussian Kings in their efforts to make Prussia great. [...] "I want more territory," said Prussia. "Germany must have Colonies [sic]," says the new world-policy. And Colonies were accordingly established, in such spots as were found to be still unappropriated, or out of which others could be pushed by the vigorous assertion of a German demand for "a place in the sun" [...].

No modern German would plead guilty to a mere lust of conquest for the sake of conquest. But the vague and undefined schemes of Teutonic expansion ("die Ausbreitung des deutschen Volkstums") are but the expression of the deeply rooted feeling that Germany has by the strength and purity of her national purpose, the fervour* of her patriotism, the depth of her religious feeling, the high standard of competency, and the perspicuous* honesty of her administration, the successful pursuit of every branch of public and scientific activity, and the elevated character of her philosophy, art, and ethics, established for herself the right to assert the primacy of German national ideals. And it is an axiom* of her political faith that right, in order that it may prevail*, must be backed by force, the transition is easy to the belief that the "good German sword," which plays so large a part in patriotic speech, is there to solve any difficulties that may be in the way of establishing the reign of those ideals in a Germanized world.

Eyre Crowe: "Memorandum on the Present State of British Relations with France and Germany", January 1, 1907, in: G.P. Gooch, H. Temperly (Ed.): British Documents on the Origins of the War, 1898–1914. Vol. III, Her Majesty's Stationery Office (HMSO), London 1926–38, pp. 402–406

fervour enthusiasm
perspicuous *deutlich*

axiom a statement that is generally believed to be true
to prevail to triumph, to come out top, to be the strongest element in a situation

L'INGORDO TROP DUR

Italian cartoon ridiculing William II's "New Course"

CONNECT

The Herero-Nama Uprising of 1904/05

One of the few German colonies in Africa was German Southwest Africa, today's Namibia. In 1883, the German merchant Franz Adolf Lüderitz had established a trading post in Angra Pequence, naming it Lüderitzbucht and the neighbouring area he had acquired Lüderitzland. Subsequently, the German Empire took over the "protection" of the colony. However, exploitation and mistreatment of the native tribes led to an uprising of the Herero and Nama tribes in 1904. Under the command of Lothar von Trotha, the revolt was put down violently, ending in a German victory at Waterberg River.

In 2004, on the occasion of the centenary of the Herero Uprising, then German Minister for Economic Co-operation and Development apologised for the German deeds, yet refused to pay indemnity for the wrong suffered by the tribes at the hands of the Germans.

Task — Write a letter to the German Minister for Economic Co-operation and Development Gerd Müller in which you evaluate if the FRG (Federal Republic of Germany) should pay indemnity to the Herero and Nama. Your evaluation should first of all define in how far the actions of the German Empire back then can be characterized as genocide, and, on this basis, propose the paying of indemnity, or not. (The FRG argues that the UN Convention on genocide was agreed on after the 1904/5 uprising, which is why it does not apply in this instance.)

Sources **S 39a–d** give you further insight into the matter, but also do research on your own on the events that eventually led to the Herero Uprising of 1904

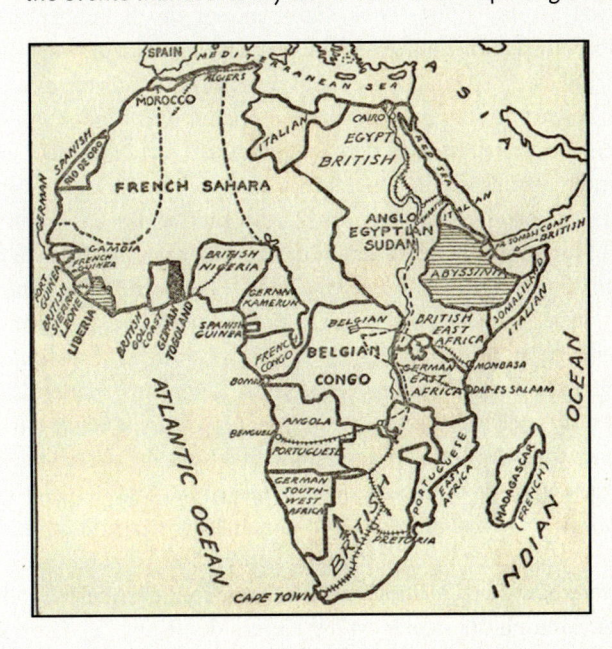

Map taken from the *Deutscher Kolonial-Atlas* of 1918, illustrating German possessions in Africa prior to 1914

S 39a — United Nations

Convention on the Prevention and Punishment of the Crime of Genocide

On 9 December 1948, the United Nations General Assembly ratified Resolution 260 (III), or the "Convention on the Prevention and Punishment of the Crime of Genocide". The article at hand presents criteria for defining genocide and making the crime of committing genocide punishable. This had been deemed necessary in the light of the recent impression of the Holocaust.

In the present Convention, genocide means any of the following acts committed with intent to destroy, in whole or in part, a national, ethnical, racial or religious group, as such:
(a) Killing members of the group;
(b) Causing serious bodily or mental harm to members of the group;
(c) Deliberately inflicting on* the group conditions of life calculated to bring about its physical destruction in whole or in part;
(d) Imposing measures intended to prevent births within the group;
(e) Forcibly transferring children of the group to another group.

"Convention on the Prevention and Punishment of the Crime of Genodice," adopted by Resolution 260 (III) A of the United Nations General Assembly on 9 December 1948; www.hrweb.org/legal/genocide.html [16.10.14]

to inflict sth. on sb. to cause sth. unpleasant to happen

S 39b Winfried Speitkamp
The Herero-Nama Genocide of 1904/05

Winfried Speitkamp is Professor of Modern History at the University of Kassel. In the given text, he elaborates on the suppression of the Herero Uprising and on its impact and aftermath.

[Nach der Schlacht am Waterberg im August 1904] änderte [Generalleutnant Lothar von] Trotha [1904–1905 Kommandeur der Schutztruppe*] seine Strategie. Nunmehr begann er einen Vernichtungsfeldzug*, der die Herero in die Halbwüste* Omaheke trieb und sie aus dem Land verjagen* sollte. In brutaler Weise wurden auch flüchtende Frauen und Kinder von den Wasserstellen* vertrieben und in den Tod geschickt. Am 2. Oktober erging der so genannte Schießbefehl: 'Die Herero sind nicht mehr deutsche Untertanen [...]. Das Volk der Herero muss [...] das Land verlassen. Wenn das Volk dies nicht tut, so werde ich es mit dem Groot Rohr [Kanone] dazu zwingen. Innerhalb der deutschen Grenze wird jeder Herero mit oder ohne Gewehr, mit oder ohne Vieh, erschossen, ich nehme keine Weiber oder Kinder mehr auf*, treibe sie zu ihrem Volke zurück oder lasse auch auf sie schießen.' [...] Die Folgen der Kämpfe waren verheerend. Über die genauen Zahlen der Opfer besteht nach wie vor wenig Klarheit. In Deutsch-Südwestafrika sollen vor dem Krieg etwa 80 000 Herero und 20 000 Nama gelebt haben. Am Ende des Krieges nahmen die deutschen Truppen 1906 8 889 Herero gefangen, davon kamen wohl noch einmal 7700 in den Militärlagern um. In den Sammellagern* der Rheinischen Missionsgesellschaft befanden sich bis 1907 12 500 Herero, weitere 2 000 flohen. Nach anderer, ebenfalls als offiziell deklarierter Zählung überlebten 14 769 Herero den Krieg [...]. Grob geschätzt wird häufig, dass 80 Prozent der Herero und 50 Prozent der Nama dem Krieg zum Opfer gefallen seien.* [...]
Mit den jeweiligen* Tausenden Toten und der Zerstörung der natürlichen Existenzgrundlage* Vieh [...] brach die soziale Struktur innerhalb der betroffenen sozialen Gruppen und Ethnien zusammen. Die kolonialpolitische Reaktion, die Enteignung*, Umsiedelung*, Reservate und Arbeitszwang umfasste, tat ihr Übriges. [...]

Schutztruppe protecting force
Vernichtungsfeldzug campaign of annihilation
Halbwüste semi-desert
verjagen to drive/chase away
Wasserstelle watering holes, sources of water

aufnehmen to take in

Sammellager internment camp

zum Opfer fallen to fall prey/victim to
jeweilig respective
Existenzgrundlage means of existence
Enteignung dispossession
Umsiedelung relocation

Deutsch-Südwestafrika wurde fortan [...] ganz zur Kolonie der Siedler ausgebaut. Der Aufstand hatte den Weg dazu frei gemacht.* Nach dem Krieg
30 setzte eine starke Zuwanderung von Weißen ein, ihre Zahl stieg von 4640 im Jahr 1903 auf 14830 im Jahr 1913. Eisenbahnbau und Diamantfunde einerseits, Eindämmung* und Disziplinierung der Herero und Nama andererseits steigerten die Attraktivität der Kolonie. Die Überlebenden der Aufstände stellten keine Gefahr mehr dar. [...] Alle über sieben Jahre alten
35 Afrikaner hatten nun immer eine Passmarke* mit sich zu führen. Für jeden Afrikaner wurde ein Dienstbuch* angelegt, dass die Polizeibehörde an den Dienstherren aushändigte.*

Winfried Speitkamp: Deutsche Kolonialgeschichte. Stuttgart 2005, pp. 125 f., 133 ff.

den Weg frei machen to clear the way

Eindämmung containment

Passmarke registration badge
Dienstbuch employment service book
aushändigen to hand over to, to deliver

S 39c) Surviving Herero

This photograph of about 1905 shows surviving members of the Herero tribe after their escape through the desert of Omaheke.

Language support

ausgemergelt emaciated [ɪˈmeɪsieɪtɪd], haggard • **verhungern** to starve to death • **nichts als Haut und Knochen** nothing but skin and bone

S 39d Heidemarie Wieczorek-Zeul

Speech on the Occasion of the Commemoration of the Centenary of the Herero-Name Uprising of 1904

Here are extracts from a speech given by then Minister for Economic Co-operation and Development Heidemarie Wieczorek-Zeul in Okakarara on 14 August 2004.

Gewalttat atrocity
Vorfahren ancestors

verblendet von blinded by
Wahn delusion
Sendbote messenger
Vernichtung extermination

Vergebung forgiveness
Trauer grief
Versöhnung reconciliation

weltoffen cosmopolitan
Wiedervereinigung reunification

Achtung respect

NEPAD New Partnership for Africa's Development: plan by the African Union for social and economic development
bekennen to acknowledge

[...] Es gilt für mich an diesem Tage, die Gewalttaten* der deutschen Kolonialmacht in Erinnerung zu rufen, die sie an Ihren Vorfahren* beging, insbesondere gegenüber den Herero und den Nama. [...]

Vor hundert Jahren wurden die Unterdrücker – verblendet von* kolonialem Wahn* – in deutschem Namen zu Sendboten* von Gewalt, Diskriminierung, Rassismus und Vernichtung*.

Die damaligen Gräueltaten waren das, was heute als Völkermord bezeichnet würde – für den ein General von Trotha heutzutage vor Gericht gebracht und verurteilt würde.

Wir Deutschen bekennen uns zu unserer historisch-politischen, moralisch-ethischen Verantwortung und zu der Schuld, die Deutsche damals auf sich geladen haben. Ich bitte Sie im Sinne des gemeinsamen „Vater unser" um Vergebung* unserer Schuld.

Ohne bewusste Erinnerung, ohne tiefe Trauer* kann es keine Versöhnung* geben.

Versöhnung braucht Erinnerung.

Des Gedenkjahr 2004 sollte auch ein Jahr der Versöhnung werden.

Wir ehren heute die Toten. Wer sich nicht erinnert, wird blind für die Gegenwart. Mit dem Erinnern sollten wir Kraft für Gegenwart und Zukunft gewinnen. [...]

Deutschland hat die bittere Lektionen der Geschichte gelernt: Wir sind ein weltoffenes* Land, das inzwischen in vielerlei Hinsicht multikulturell ist. Wir haben die deutsche Wiedervereinigung* auf friedlichem Wege erreicht und freuen uns, einer erweiterten Europäischen Union anzugehören. Wir sind engagiertes Mitglied der Vereinten Nationen und setzen uns weltweit für Frieden, die Achtung* der Menschenrechte, Entwicklung und Armutsbekämpfung ein. Wir leisten der Bevölkerung Afrikas kontinuierliche Hilfe und unterstützen die NEPAD*-Initiative intensiv.

Wir bekennen* uns zu unserer besonderen historischen Verantwortung gegenüber Namibia und wollen die enge Partnerschaft auf allen Ebenen fortsetzen. Nach vorne schauend will und wird Deutschland Namibia weiter dabei unterstützen, die Entwicklungsherausforderungen anzugehen, das gilt vor allem für die Unterstützung bei der notwendigen Landreform. [...]

Rede von Bundesministerium Heidemarie Wieczorek-Zeul bei den Gedenkfeierlichkeiten der Herero-Aufstände am 14. August 2004 in Okakarara, www.windhuk.diplo.de/Vertretung/windhuk/de/03/Gedenkjahre_2004_2005/Seite_Rede_BMZ_2004-08-14.html [16.02.15]

| Overview | Sources | Paper practice | Vocabulary | The First World War 265 |

S 40 Thomas Pakenham

The Scramble for Africa

Thomas Pakenham is an Anglo-Irish historian (*1933). The source below is an excerpt from his book "The Scramble for Africa", published in 1990.

Pre-task
1. In German, the "Scramble for Africa" is translated as "Wettlauf um Afrika". Depict the "results" of the scramble: make out the "winners" and the "losers" in the race for African colonies with the help of the map.

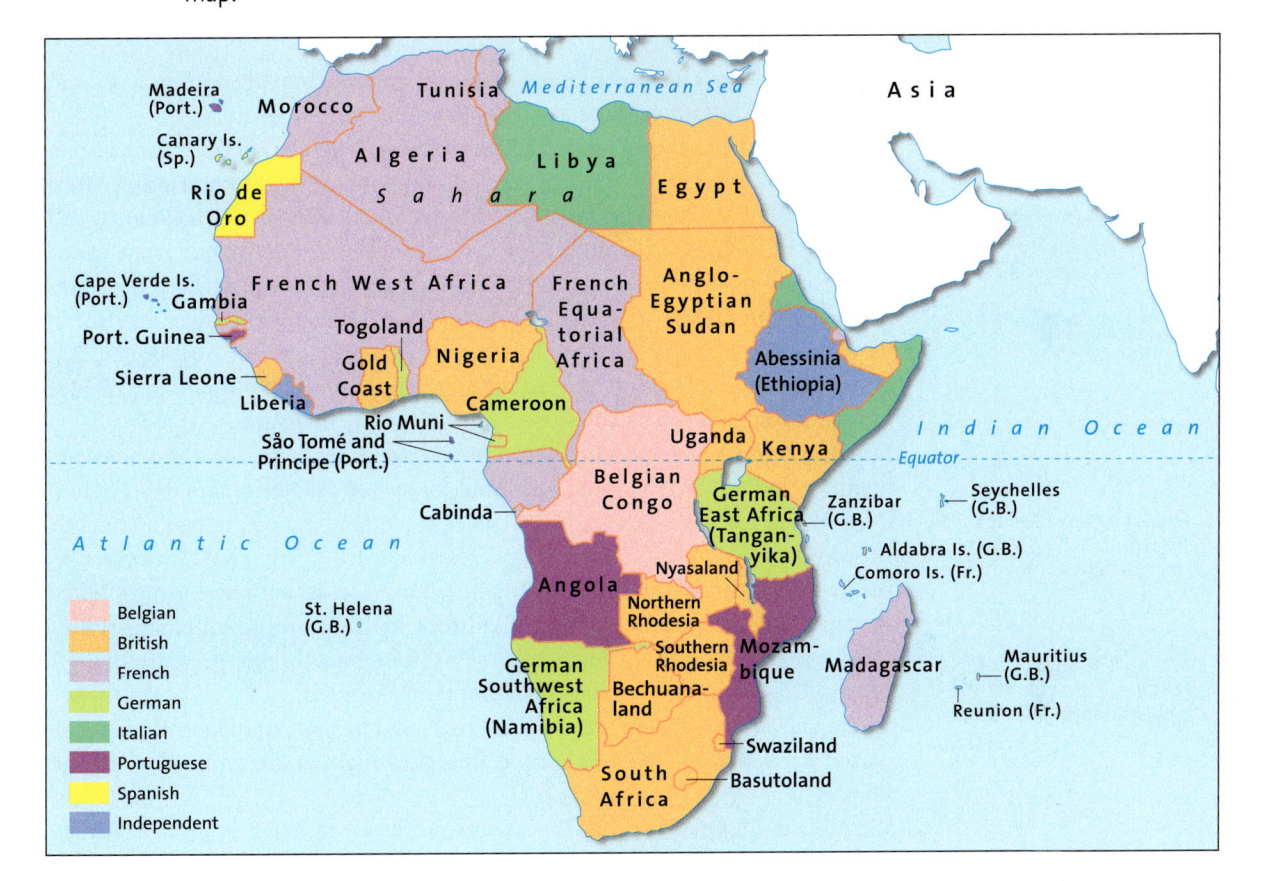

Map of Africa showing colonial possessions:
- Belgian
- British
- French
- German
- Italian
- Portuguese
- Spanish
- Independent

Tasks
2. Give a structured outline of the text. In order to do so, determine the sense units and give each a heading. Write your outline along the lines of these headings, and do not forget to quote from the text (direct and indirect quotations).
3. Explain in detail the reasons for the "scramble" that Pakenham mentions.
4. Rank the reasons in order of their importance. Explain your ranking in class.
5. Evaluate to what extent the "scramble" contributed to "poison[ing] the political climate in Europe" (l. 21) and thus, in the long run, to the outbreak of World War One.

Post-task
6. Pakenham concludes that "Europe had imposed its will on Africa at the point of a gun. It was a lesson that would be remembered, fifty

years later, when Africa came to win its independence." (ll. 47 f.) Illustrate this conclusion by doing further research on the rule of Leopold II (cf. ll. 17 ff.) over the Congo, and the impact this has up to today (in the Congo and in the way it is perceived today in Belgium). If you like, split up into groups and include further African countries in your research, for example South Africa, as an example of a former British colony, or Namibia, as a former German colony, or any other country you want to learn more about. Present your results in class (for example in a gallery walk) and take a critical stand on Pakenham's conclusion.

The Scramble for Africa bewildered everyone, from the humblest African peasant to the master statesmen of the age, Lord Salisbury* and Bismarck.
Ever since Roman times, Europe had been nibbling at the mysterious continent to the south. By the mid-1870s, much was still mysterious. It was known that Africa straddled* the equator with uncanny* precision. But no explorer had penetrated far along the dangerous latitude of zero towards the interior. No one knew which was Africa's greatest river or where it led. Europeans pictured most of the continent as 'vacant': legally res nullius, a no-man's land. If there were states and rulers, they were African. If there were treasures they were buried in African soil. But beyond the trading posts on the coastal fringe, and strategically important colonies in Algeria and South Africa, Europe saw no reason to intervene.
Suddenly, in half a generation, the Scramble gave Europe virtually the whole continent: including thirty colonies and protectorates, 10 million square miles of new territory and 110 million dazed* new subjects, acquired by one method or another. Africa was sliced up like a cake, the pieces swallowed by five rival nations – Germany, Italy, Portugal, France and Britain (with Spain taking some scraps) – and Britain and France were at each other's throats. At the centre, exploiting the rivalry, stood one enigmatic* individual arid* self-styled philanthropist*, controlling the heart of the continent: Leopold II, King of the Belgians.
By the end of the century, the passions generated by the Scramble had helped to poison the political climate in Europe, brought Britain to the brink of a war with France [...].
Why this undignified rush by the leaders of Europe to build empires in Africa? Anglo-French rivalries explains a great deal – but not enough. Historians are as puzzled now as the politicians were then. [...]
To these events historiography has added a pack of jostling* theories. We have Eurocentric explanations [...] that surplus capital in Europe was the driving force behind expansion into Africa; Afrocentric explanations where the emphasis is placed on sub-imperialism in Africa itself; and combinations of the two [...]. But there is no general explanation acceptable to historians – nor even agreement whether they should be expected to find one. [...]
At first European governments were reluctant to intervene. But to most people in their electorates, there seemed a real chance of missing something. Africa was a lottery and a winning ticket might earn glittering prizes. [...] Perhaps Africa was the answer to the merchants' prayers. There might be new markets out there in this African garden of Eden, and tropical groves* where the golden fruit could be plucked by willing brown hands.
Or perhaps the lottery would pay best in terms of prestige. Overseas empires

---

Lord Salisbury British PM (1885, 1886–92, 1885–1902)

to straddle to be on both sides of sth.
uncanny strange and mysterious

dazed so surprised that you cannot react

enigmatic mysterious
arid dull
philanthropist [fɪˈlænθrəpɪst] benefactor

to jostle to compete

grove a group of trees

would soothe the amour-propre* of the French army, humiliated by its collapse in
40 the Franco-Prussian war. And it would no less bolster the pride of the political
parvenus* of Europe, Germany's Second Reich and a newly united Italy. Then
there were the diplomatic advantages. Cards drawn in the jungle could be played
out in the chancelleries in Europe. No harm for Bismarck to consolidate his position by making mischief* between France and Britain. And what about a place in
45 the sun for emigrants – and a way to retain as citizens all those young sons of the
Reich now taking the boat and vanishing without trace in Africa? [...]
Europe had imposed its will on Africa at the point of a gun. It was a lesson that
would be remembered, fifty years later, when Africa came to win its independence.
[...]

Thomas Pakenham: The Scramble for Africa. 1876–1912, Weidenfeld and Nicolson, London: 1991, pp. 15 ff.

amour-propre ['æmʊə(r) 'prɒprə] self-respect
parvenu ['pɑː(r)və͵njuː] sb. from a low social class that has become rich or important but is not accepted as an equal by other rich or important people
mischief ['mɪstʃɪf] troublemaking

S 41 Bonnie G. Smith

Epilogue

Bonnie G. Smith is Professor of History at Rudgers University in New Jersey, USA. In her collection of sources on imperialism from 2000, she wrote an epilogue in which she evaluates the enduring legacy of the phenomenon of imperialism.

Pre-task 1. Keeping in mind what you have learned about (new) imperialism in this sub-chapter, collect possible enduring legacies of this phenomenon that shape the world up to today. Also consider whether these legacies are positive or negative.

Tasks 2. Outline the legacies of imperialism advanced by Smith. Were your ideas (cf. task 1) similar or very different? Why (not)? Discuss.
3. Against the backdrop of the text and taking into consideration what else you have learned about (new) imperialism, prepare a balance sheet for this phenomenon: what would you put on the debit, what on the credit side? Be prepared to elaborate.

All the imperialist nations claimed to be benefiting those they conquered and oppressed. [...] Despite its disintegration after World War II, imperialism as a system of direct political rule of conquered areas left an enduring legacy. It had truly internationalized commerce and politics because of the systems of rapid transportation
5 and communication embodied in the railroad, steamship, telegraph, and telephone involved in imperialism's triumph. In these circumstances Western culture lost the distinctiveness* that it might have retained from Europe's relative isolation. Instead, Western civilization became a culture profoundly dependent on taking and incorporating ideas, customs, and resources from the rest of the world.
10 Although there was a great deal of borrowing in the other direction as well, some have argued that imperialism had far less effect outside the West in cultural terms. Instead, the real effect of imperialism elsewhere was in its plunder and rapacious* devastation of resources, whether that plundering was committed by the English, Belgians, Russians, Americans, or Japanese. [...]
15 Another legacy of imperialism is the incredible and increasing global violence that has since the 19th century killed hundreds of millions in colonial conquest and forced labor, world wars, wars of liberation, and civil wars – all of them connected

distinct easy to recognize because of being different from other people or things of the same type

rapacious never satisfied until you have taken everything that you can

to pit against to make sb. compete or fight against sb. or sth. else

acquisitive greedy

in one way or another to imperialism and its aftermath. It is one of imperialism's many paradoxes that while it made people more aware than ever before of the world's multiple races, accomplishments, and cultures, it set a trend of pitting* humans against one another in an orgy of conquest, competition, and hatred. Yet at the same time, around the globe population soared, health improved, technology became more modern, and concerns for human rights advanced.

A final legacy and paradox of imperialism is that its end saw the world increasingly divided between the prosperous peoples of the former imperial powers and poorer peoples who had once been colonized. Differences in wealth became greater, and a new or neo-imperialism had replaced the old. This neo-imperialism was based – as it had been before political conquest in the 19th century – on trading superiority and on a culture of curiosity, acquisitiveness*, and conquest. Although the age of high imperialism ended long ago, it continues to shape our present world.

Bonnie G. Smith: Imperialism. A History in Documents, Oxford University Press, New York 2000, pp. 164f.

S 42 William Carr

The Germany of William II, 1890–1914

William Carr (1921–1991) was a historian of modern German history. In his work "History of Germany, 1815–1945", first published in 1969, he also focuses on changes from Bismarck's Germany to William II's Germany, explaining why Germany embarked on world policy.

Pre-task
1. Carr determines three major reasons why Germany turned towards world policy, namely 1) economic pressures (changes brought about in the wake of industrialization), 2) psychological pressures (changes in the phenomenon of nationalism, Social Darwinism), and 3) political pressures (radicalization, radical interest groups). Revise the sub-chapters on industrialization and (new) imperialism and elaborate.

Tasks
2. Skim the text: how does Carr elaborate on the pressures operating in Germany? Make any necessary additions to your ideas from task 1.
3. Carr explains why Germany turned from Bismarck's "saturated Empire" (cf. chapter 1) to William II's "New Course". To what extent could one also use Carr's elucidations to explain why the First World War broke out? Give an evaluation.

Post-task
4. Revise the two sub-chapters on industrialization and (new) imperialism. Find aspects that speak for industrialization and (new) imperialism as the "long fuse" (*lange Zündschnur*) of the First World War. Copy the illustration below into your exercise books and label the fuse accordingly.

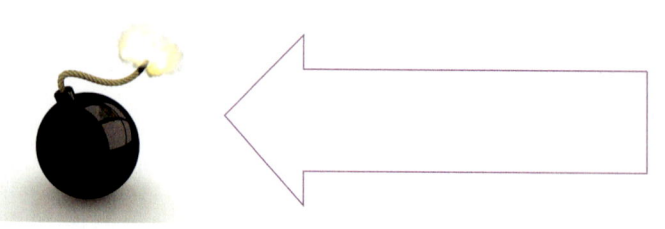

The close of the nineteenth century was a real turning-point in German history. The Reich broke with Bismarck's foreign policy and embarked on Weltpolitik, with all that this implied for the future. Germany suddenly evinced* a new interest in colonial expansion and acquired some possessions in the Pacific; she initiated the scramble for China; she laid the basis of a powerful navy and she became more deeply involved in the affairs of Asia Minor than ever before. Like any broad trend in foreign policy, Germany's transition to Weltpolitik was a response to internal pressure, part economic, part psychological and part political.

Industrialisation impelled* all advanced countries to look beyond their frontiers for raw materials to feed the new factories, for markets for manufactured goods and for outlets for accumulated capital, all of which could only be found outside of Europe. [...]

Secondly, psychological pressures operated in the same direction. When France was defeated in 1870, the victory was hailed in Germany as a vindication* of the superior moral and cultural power of the German way of life. By the turn of the century a profound change had come over nationalism in all lands. The biological ideas of Lamarck* and Darwin robbed nationalism of its idealism; nationality was now equated with a community of blood rather than a community of ideas; Natural Selection applied to relations between states as much as to the animal kingdom; the struggle for markets and raw materials and the urge to expand overseas were interpreted as outward signs of a deep unceasing struggle between nations in a world 'red in tooth and claw'* where the right of the strongest was law. In this age of 'national missions' Germany was well to the fore, determined to play a role overseas commensurate* with her economic and military might. As Bernhard von Bülow observed in a speech in 1897: 'we do not wish to put anyone in the shade but we demand our place in the sun'.

Thirdly, there were political pressures. By the end of the century demographic change and accelerated economic development were altering the structure of German politics. [...] Left as well as Right derived benefit from [a] radicalisation process. [...] [The] right-wing activists were active supporters of Weltpolitik. They supplied the membership for numerous pressure groups originating mainly in the 1890s including the Pan-German League [or] the Navy League [...].

William Carr: A History of Germany, 1815–1990. Hodder Arnold, London ⁴1991, pp. 173 ff.

to evince to show clearly

to impel to compel, induce, motivate

vindication justification

Lamarck Jean-Baptiste Lamarck (1744–1829), a French early proponent of the idea that evolution occurred and proceeded in accordance with natural laws
red in tooth and claw reference to the sometimes violent natural world, in which predatory animals sometimes cover their teeth and claw with the blood of their prey
commensurate proportional

"Germany at sea" – German postcard, ca. 1900

Origins and Outbreak of WWI

S 43 Steven E. Ozment

A Mighty Fortress. A New History of the German People

Steven E. Ozment is Professor of Ancient and Modern History at Harvard University. In his work on the "new" history of the German people, he also (cf. **S 42**) reflects on changes in Germany's foreign policy from Bismarck to William II but seeks to take away the sole guilt for the deterioration of European relations from the Emperor.

Pre-tasks

1. The given cartoon, entitled "L'enfant terrible", was drawn by John Tenniel and published in *Punch* magazine on 6 May 1890. Describe the elements of the cartoon and, after that, pinpoint the message Tenniel is conveying.
2. Explain the immediate historical context the cartoon is referring to.
3. The term "enfant terrible" can have different meanings: a) a child whose inopportune remarks cause embarrassment/a person known for shocking remarks or outrageous behaviour, or b) a usually young and successful person who is strikingly unorthodox, innovative, or avant-garde[1]. Against the backdrop of the cartoon, discuss which meaning the cartoonist would have chosen.
4. Think of arguments to rebut or at least mitigate Tenniel's view.

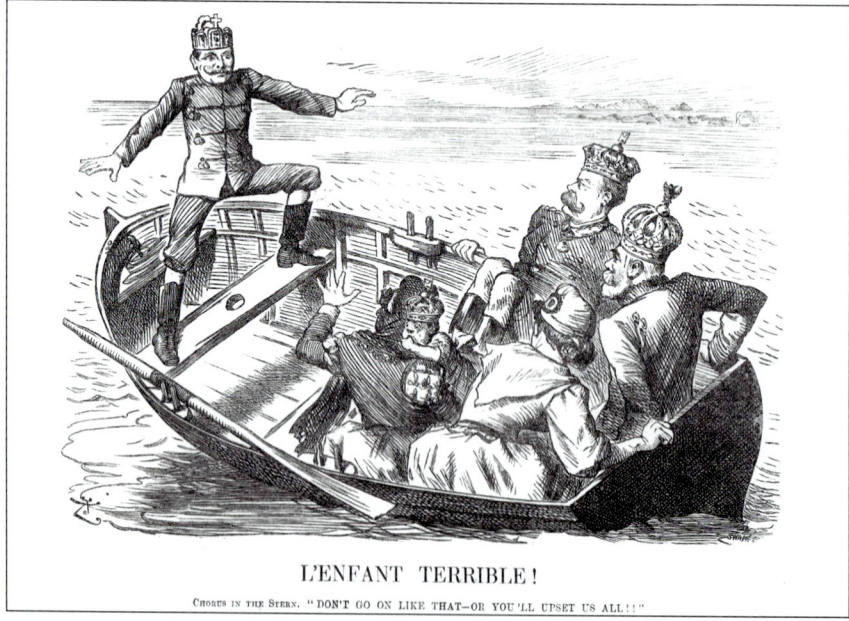

L'ENFANT TERRIBLE!

Chorus in the Stern. "DON'T GO ON LIKE THAT—OR YOU'LL UPSET US ALL!!"

Language support

Gleichgewicht balance • **Ungleichgewicht** imbalance • **schaukeln** to rock, to swing • **kentern** to capsize

---

[1] www.merriam-webster.com/dictionary/enfant%20terrible [19.04.15]

5. Scan the text for arguments you could use to support the cartoonist's view on the one hand, and to refute/mitigate this view on the other hand.
6. Revise the graphic visualization of Bismarck's system of alliances (cf. chapter 1, p. 147, task 2). Put a transparency over your visualization and, with the help of the text, add the changes that take place under William II.
7. Discuss in which way(s) changes in the system of alliances brought Europe closer to war.

Bismarck made Germany strong by centering it around Prussia and keeping its foreign policy focused. In doing so he defeated efforts by the Austrians and Bavarians to perpetuate the old sprawling empire* with its ancient divisions and rival states. His compact empire gave the chancellor a freer hand in dealing with parliament and the European great powers. Instead of casting a hated imperial shadow across Europe, Germany became its honest broker, turning its geographical position in Middle Europe to international advantage in keeping the peace.

By contrast Emperor William provoked international conflict by projecting an expansive Germany. Determined to see Germany become a world power, he plunged the empire into Europe and the developing colonial world. Although no one knew what the future held, the imperial government's every commanding step in that direction was one toward war.

However, if Bismarck's balanced Europe began to look like a house of cards, Emperor William was not solely to blame. In the end the miscalculations of the Foreign Ministry, on which the emperor's new chancellor, Leo von Caprivi, had relied, had more to do with Germany's foreign policy slide than the emperor's interference and bravado*. Caprivi, a former chief of the Admiralty, had been a poor choice for the rapidly changing 1890s. He fell quickly under the spell of Bismarck appointee* and hater Frederick von Holstein, who now controlled the ministry. On Holstein's recommendation, Caprivi did not renew the Reinsurance Treaty with Russia, which since 1887 had guaranteed Russian neutrality in the event of a western, or southern, invasion of Germany. [...]

Within five years of the treaty's lapse*, France and Russia had become trading partners, and before two more had passed, they were defensive allies, each promising each other to strike Germany should Germany mobilise against either. Suddenly Germany was in the great power pincers* it so feared, a peril* the Reinsurance Treaty might have averted. When the time came for the British to choose sides, the Germans had unfortunately become their economic and military rivals. [...]

Competing smartly with France and Russia in the colonial world, Britain opened diplomatic doors for a Germany desperate to establish its presence there. Without British neutrality Germany's forward leaps during the 1890s, both colonial and European, would have been impossible. But after the turn of the century, Britain progressively ceased to be Germany's friend. [...]

As early as 1907, British diplomats described Germany as "out to dominate Europe", while Russia, more fearful of Germany than ever, began closing ranks with Britain. Agreeing on their respective possessions in colonial Asia, the two great powers joined with France to create an informal, but scary, association of Germany's most feared rivals, something Bismarck's diplomacy had spared the Germans. If and

sprawling empire reference to the Holy Roman Empire which had ceased to exist in 1806 (cf. chapter 1)

bravado a confident way of behaving to impress people, often to hide insecurities
appointee sb. who has been chosen to do a particular job

the treaty's lapse Ozment speaks of the Reinsurance Treaty here

pincers tool made of two crossed pieces of metal, here: reference to the fact that Germany now had to face the threat of a war on two fronts
peril danger

when war broke out, Germany now faced attack on both its eastern and western fronts, with only a self-preoccupied* Austria-Hungary and an ever-retreating Italy for allies (the aged and weary Triple Alliance). Largely by its own saber rattling, and to its peril, Germany had made itself the center of great-power attention.

Steven E. Ozment: A Mighty Fortress – A New History of the German People, Granta, London (2005), pp. 233–235

to be self-occupied to think and worry exclusively about one's own problems

S 44 L'empereur d'Allemagne en voyage (The German Emperor on a Voyage)

The given cartoon by Henri Meyer was published on the front cover of the Parisian newspaper *Le Petit Journal* on 6 November 1898. It shows the German Emperor William II during a voyage to Palestine.

Pre-tasks
1. Have a look at the language support only. What does it tell you about the cartoonist's view on the German Emperor? Discuss.

Tasks
2. With the help of the language support, describe the cartoon in detail. Pay special attention to the composition of the picture.
3. Explain the artist's interpretation of the Emperor's self-portrayal when abroad.
4. Put yourself into the shoes of the photographer shown in the cartoon. The editor of the newspaper you are working for is not happy with the picture you brought him, criticizing its bias and influence on the readership's perception of the Emperor. Write a short explanation of your picture in which you justify why it was nearly impossible to take a more "neutral" picture, given the circumstances.

Language support

Heiligenschein halo • **Brustpanzer** cuirass [kwɪˈræs] • **Pickelhaube** spiked helmet • **Epauletten** epaulettes (= the decorative elements on the shoulders) • **Eisernes Kreuz** Iron Cross (a military decoration in Prussia, later on also in the Second Reich and Nazi Germany) • **Sporen** spurs (pl.) • **gerade** straight • **Körperhaltung** posture • **Menschenmenge** crowd • **Pinsel und Staffelei** brush and easel

S 45 The *Daily Telegraph* Affair

On 28 October 1908, William II gave an interview to the British *Daily Telegraph*, which was to cause not only tension with Britain, but also led to criticism of the Emperor's behaviour in Germany itself.

Pre-task
1. Revise what you have learned about British-German relations at the time the given interview was published. Based on your results, discuss how you would advise William II to treat the British in an official public interview.

Tasks
2. In the interview, William repeats that he considers himself to be a friend of England, but that the English make it hard for him to maintain this friendly attitude. Summarize what he accuses the English of.
3. Write a speech bubble for S 44 in your exercise book in which you point out how the Emperor sees himself, according to the interview.
4. As said in the introductory remarks, William II also faced criticism in Germany for his behaviour, which was seen as increasingly erratic. Give proof from the text to explain this criticism.
5. Write a letter to the editor of *The Daily Telegraph* from a contemporary British perspective in which you comment on the interview and evaluate its possible impact on British-German relations.

Post-task
6. At the end of the interview, William II says that "[t]here has been nothing in Germany's recent action with regard to Morocco which runs contrary to the explicit declaration of [his] love and peace." (ll. 35 ff.) This quotation is a reference to the First Moroccan Crisis. Do further research on the Second Moroccan Crisis and the *Panthersprung* to put this quotation into perspective.

We have received the following communication from a source of such unimpeachable* authority that we can without hesitation comment on the obvious message which it conveys to the attention of the public.
[...]
As I have said, his Majesty honoured me with a long conversation, and spoke with impulsive and unusual frankness. "You English," he said, "are mad, mad, mad as March hares*. What has come over you that you are so completely given over to suspicions quite unworthy of a great nation? What more can I do than I have done? I declared with all the emphasis at my command, in my speech at Guildhall*, that my heart is set upon peace, and that it is one of my dearest wishes to live on the best of terms with England. Have I ever been false to my word? Falsehood and prevarication* are alien to my nature. My actions ought to speak for themselves, but you listen not to them but to those who misinterpret and distort* them. That is a personal insult which I feel and resent*. To be forever misjudged, to have my repeated offers of friendship weighed and scrutinized* with jealous, mistrustful eyes, taxes my patience severely. I have said time after time that I am a friend of England, and your press – or, at least, a considerable section of it – bids the people of England refuse my proffered* hand and insinuates* that the other holds a dagger. How can I convince a nation against its will?

unimpeachable impossible to doubt or criticize
mad as March hares in the breeding season (in March), hares tend to behave in an erratic way (also cf. the mad March hare in Lewis Carroll's *Alice's Adventures in Wonderland*)
Guildhall former town hall and still the administrative centre in the City of London
prevarication *Tatsachenverdrehung*
to distort *verzerren*
to resent to be angry about sth.
to scrutinize to examine sth. very carefully
proffered offered
to insinuate [ɪnˈsɪnjueɪt] to say sth. unpleasant in an indirect way

an die Waffen appellieren to resort to arms
hetzen to agitate
Feuer schüren to add fuel to sth.
Seiner k. und k. (königlichen und kaiserlichen) Apostolischen Majestät Emperor Francis Joseph I
Notwendigkeit necessity
kriegerische Aktion warlike operation
bedauern to regret
günstig opportune

gen, an die Waffen zu appellieren*. Doch werde es bei den anderen Mächten der Tripleentente gegen uns hetzen* und am Balkan das Feuer schüren*. Er begreife sehr gut, dass es Seiner k. und k. Apostolischen Majestät* bei seiner bekannten Friedensliebe schwer fallen würde, in Serbien einzumarschieren; wenn wir aber wirklich die Notwendigkeit* einer kriegerischen Aktion* gegen Serbien erkannt hätten, so würde er (Kaiser Wilhelm) es bedauern*, wenn wir den jetzigen, für uns so günstigen* Moment unbenützt liessen. [...]

Ladislaus Graf von Szögyény-Marich (Berlin) an Leopold Graf von Berchtold (5. Juli 1914), in: Ludwig Bittner et al. (Ed.): Österreich-Ungarns Aussenpolitik von der Bosnischen Krise 1908 bis zum Kriegsausbruch 1914, Österreichischer Bundesverlag für Unterricht, Wissenschaft und Kunst, Wien 1930, Vol. 8, No. 10.058

Cartoon illustrating the July Crisis, 1914

CONNECT

The Fischer Controversy

Fritz Fischer (1908–1999)

Fritz Fischer was the first German historian to set in motion a major debate between historians in post-war (i.e. after 1945) Germany.
Born in Ludwigstadt in 1908, he first studied in Erlangen, then in Berlin. Already in the early years of the Weimar Republik, Fischer was active in völkisch youth groups where he was a member of an ultra-right-wing free corps. In 1933, he joined the SA (Nazi *Sturmabteilung*, stormtroopers) and in 1937 he became a member of the NSDAP (National Socialist German Workers' Party, Nazi Party). In 1939, he was given a scholarship to study under NS historian Walter Frank who also recommended him for a professorship at Hamburg university.

Yet after the war, Fischer repeatedly claimed not to have been a supporter of National Socialism. His 1961 book *Griff nach der Weltmacht* then generated the aforementioned debate among historians, which – after Fischer – is called the Fischer Controversy. Fischer was mainly accused of "reading history backwards". Fischer died aged 91 in Hamburg in 1999.

S 49 Frank McDonough
The Fischer Thesis

In his book *The Origins of the First and Second World Wars*, historian Frank McDonough reserves a special section for the Fischer Thesis, or Fischer Controversy.

Task
- Put a supporter of Fritz Fischer on the Hot Seat.
  In order to do so, proceed as follows:
  - Read carefully through McDonough's explanation of the Fischer Thesis and make notes on the cornerstones of the thesis. Do additional research to elaborate on Fischer's approach. Then think of a) further arguments you could advance in favour of Fischer's cause and b) arguments you could use to disprove him (think of the main accusation levelled against Fischer of "reading history backwards", for example).
  - Find a volunteer for the Hot Seat.

Putting somebody on the **Hot Seat** means asking him/her all kinds of questions, especially uncomfortable and tough ones in order to really find out about his/her attitude/opinion about a certain topic.

Preparation for the person on the Hot Seat
- Tune into your character! Take some notes about aspects you really would like to stress in your opening sentence. Remember that your statement has to match the person's attitude.

Preparation for the questioners
- Try to cover aspects that are not clear to you after having read the text.
- Prepare at least three (if possible) provocative questions you would like to ask the person on the Hot Seat. Be careful not to be offensive or insulting!
- Make sure that you ask questions which cannot be answered with 'yes' or 'no'.

Procedure
- Arrange a circle of chairs around one chair in the middle (the Hot Seat).
- The person on the Hot Seat opens the question period with a short statement.
- Every student participating is allowed to ask his/her question (watch out that each question is asked only once).
- The person on the Hot Seat answers each question as best as he/she can. He/she is allowed to say "no comment" only once.

Evaluation
- After having been put on the Hot Seat, the student who took the role of the character should state how/she felt during the interrogation.
- Discuss whether this method gave you a deeper insight into the question/topic.
- What worked out well, what could be improved next time?

Fischer's approach was very conventional, concentrating on the archives of the German leadership and focusing on the aims and policies of four key German figures: the Kaiser; Bethmann Hollweg, the chancellor; Gottlieb von Jagow, the foreign secretary; and Helmuth von Moltke, the chief of the army's general staff. [...] Only one chapter in the book deals with the origins of the war. Even so, Fischer is associated with the idea of German responsibility for the outbreak of war. On this issue, Fischer makes the following claims:

1 Germany was prepared to launch the First World War in order to become a great power.

2 Germany encouraged Austria-Hungary to start a war with Serbia, and continued to do so, even when it seemed clear that such a war could not be localised.

3 Once the war began, Germany developed a clear set of aims, already discussed before the war, to gain large territorial gains in central and eastern Europe, very similar to Hitler's later craving for* *Lebensraum* ('living space') in eastern Europe. [...]

The two most unorthodox aspects of Fischer's thesis were the prominence given to domestic factors in shaping Germany's foreign policy (*Primat der Innenpolitik*), as opposed to the established German view that external factors shaped foreign policy (*Primat der Außenpolitik*), and the new evidence that he assembled concerning the actions of Bethmann Hollweg, the German chancellor. [...] Fischer suggested that German foreign policy was viewed by the Kaiser and his government as a key means of diverting attention from domestic discontentment.

However, Fischer's most remarkable claims are reserved for Bethmann Hollweg. [...] In Fischer's view, Bethmann Hollweg was no puppet of the militarists, but the prime mover of German policy during the July Crisis of 1914, and a key figure in the development of Germany's expansionist aims once war began. Bethmann Hollweg was deeply gloomy about the Balkan situation, realised that Austria-Hungary required Germany's full support, and believed that Germany had to break free from its diplomatic 'encirclement'. To this end, the German chancellor attempted to improve Anglo-German relations, and hoped that the British government might remain neutral in any future war. The 'blank cheque' given to Austria-Hungary during the July Crisis, and Bethmann Hollweg's last-minute pleas for British neutrality, were therefore essential parts of a pre-existing German policy. Thus, Fischer believes that the First World War was no preventative war, born of fear and desperation; it was planned and launched by Germany with the aggressive aim of dominating Europe. [...]

Frank McDonough: The Origins of the First and Second World Wars. Cambridge University Press, Cambridge 1997, pp. 25–27

to crave for sth. to want sth. very much and in a way that is hard to control

| S 50 | Christopher Clark

The Sleepwalkers. How Europe Went to War in 1914

Christopher Clark is an Australian historian (*1960) and Professor of Modern History at the University of Cambridge. His book "The Sleepwalkers. How Europe went to war in 1914", published in 2012, has aroused a lot of controversy again about the war-guilt question and has turned the book into a major bestseller, not only in Germany.

Pre-tasks

1. Clark uses the metaphor of "sleepwaking" to characterize the way Europe went to war in 1914. Read the very last sentence of his book given in the box below and paraphrase it in your own words. Then explain the "sleepwalking" metaphor.

> "In this sense, the protagonists of 1914 were sleepwalkers, watchful but unseeing, haunted by dreams, yet blind to the reality of the horror they were about to bring into the world."
>
> Christophes Clark: The Sleepwalkness. How Europe went to war in 1914. Penguim Books, Londone 2012, p. 562

2. Make a list of connotations you connect with "sleepwalking". Then discuss what Clark implies by employing this image.

Tasks

3. Outline the arguments Clark makes use of that lead him to conclude that "the outbreak of war was a tragedy, not a crime." (ll. 36 f.)
4. Against the backdrop of the text, explain the book's title.
5. Write a letter to Clark's publishing house in which you take a critical stand on his view of the outbreak of war. Also, suggest (other/further) appropriate metaphors instead of/in support of the "sleepwalking" metaphor.

Post-task

6. Have a look at two very contrary positions on why the war broke out in 1914. Imagine one side of your classroom represented the one position, the other side the other position. Find your own place in between these two views, or decide to support one completely. Find your place in the classroom and be prepared to give reasons for your position.

David Lloyd George
(cf. CONNECT, pp. 317 ff.):

"The nations slithered over the brink into the boiling cauldron of war."

Fritz Fischer
(cf. CONNECT, pp. 278 ff.)

Germany is responsible for starting the war.

We need to distinguish between the objective factors acting on the decision-makers and the stories they told themselves and each other about what they thought they were doing and why they were doing it. All the key actors in our story filtered the world through narratives that were built from pieces of experience glued to-
5 gether with fears, projections and interests masquerading as maxims*. In Austria,

maxim a phrase or saying that includes a rule or moral principle about how you should behave

Hilfsmittel device	
um … durchbrechen to break through the enemy lines	
beispiellos unprecedented [ʌnˈpresɪˌdentɪd]	
Schub surge	
drahtlose Funktelefone wireless phones	
Geschütz cannon	
Jagdflugzeug pursuit plane	
Kampfzone combat zone	
jdn. befördern to promote sb.	
Tränen vergießen to shed tears	

zur Neige. Militärs suchten nach neuen Waffen und Hilfsmitteln* jeder Art, um die gegnerischen Linien zu durchbrechen* – und nahmen dafür Milliardenbeträge in die Hand.

Das Ergebnis: ein beispielloser* Technisierungsschub*. Wissenschaftler entwickelten drahtlose Funktelefone*; Ingenieure konstruierten Geschütze*, deren Granaten sogar 120 Kilometer weit flogen; Jagdflugzeuge* verwandelten den Himmel erstmals in eine Kampfzone*. […]

Fritz Haber, der Vater des Gaskriegs, wurde nach dem erfolgreichen deutschen Angriff bei Ypern 1915 sogar zum Hauptmann befördert*. Angeblich vergoss er darüber Tränen* des Glücks.

DER SPIEGEL, Ausgabe 4/20 (2014), S. 5

S 54 John McRae

In Flanders Fields

The poem "In Flanders Fields" was written by Major John McRae of the First Brigade Canadian Field Artillery. He is believed to have composed it in May 1915, during the second battle of Ypres, after having witnessed the death of his friend Alexis Helmer the day before.

The poem's reference to the poppy flower (*Mohnblume*, cf. picture provided) has inspired the wearing of the traditional Remembrance Poppy in order to commemorate the victims of World War One since 1920, and is still worn on Remembrance Day (November 11, the day of the armistice in 1918). Poppies were the first flowers to grow again on the churned-up Flanders battlefields.

Pre-task 1. Against the backdrop of **S 53**, make a list of the possible disasters of the First World War that one should not forget. Start your list with the words "Lest we forget …" and continue in the same style of writing.

Poppy flowers in remembrance of the war. The phrase "Lest we forget" as a reminder not to forget the disaster of war is taken from Rudyard Kipling's poem "Recessional".

Tasks
2. Describe the scene presented in the first stanza and state the call to action contained in the third stanza.
3. Analyse the atmosphere of the poem. Consider who is speaking and the antithetical use of life and death.
4. A publishing house is planning a special anthology containing works of fiction and non-fiction concerned with the First World War. Write a letter to the person in charge in which you evaluate to what extent the poem at hand would be a valuable contribution to that anthology.

In Flanders fields the poppies blow
Between the crosses, row on row,
That mark our place; and in the sky
The larks*, still bravely singing, fly
5 Scarce heard amid the guns below.

lark *Lerche*

We are the Dead. Short days ago
We lived, felt dawn*, saw sunset glow,
Loved and were loved, and now we lie
In Flanders fields.

dawn *Morgendämmerung*

10 Take up our quarrel with the foe*:
To you from failing hands we throw
The torch*; be yours to hold it high.
If ye* break faith with us who die
We shall not sleep, though poppies grow
15 In Flanders fields.

foe enemy

torch *Fackel*
ye you

John McRae: "In Flanders Fields", in: Winston Groom: A Storm in Flanders: The Ypres Salient, 1914–1918: Tragedy and Triumph on the Western Front, Grove Press, 2007, p. 117

S 55 Andreas Probst

A Letter from the Trenches (*Feldpostbrief*)

Letters sent home from the trenches offer us invaluable insights into the conditions the soldiers had to suffer. Here you can read about the experiences of the German sergeant Andreas Probst, which he wrote about in a letter to his parents and siblings on 5 June 1915, from the battlefield in France. Probst was reported missing only three days later. Soon after, his parents were officially informed about their son's death when his grave was discovered in a French cemetery.

Pre-task
1. World War One was a war of attrition in which millions of soldiers died in and between the trenches, with only little ground being gained (stalemate). What do you expect Probst to write to his parents about life in the trenches? Make an educated guess, considering the physical condition of the soliders, the noise, and the smell they had to endure.

Tasks
2. Describe the situation on the battlefield. Distinguish between the physical condition of the soldiers, the noise and the smell.
3. Based on your findings, design and create an anti-war propaganda postcard.

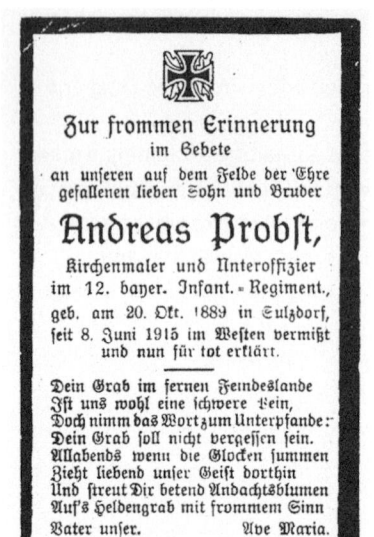

In-memoriam notice for Andreas Probst after the official declaration of death.
The poem reads as follows:

„Dein Grab im fernen Feindeslande
Ist uns wohl eine schwere Pein*,
Doch nimm das Wort zum Unterpfande*:
Dein Grab soll nicht vergessen sein.
Allabends wenn die Glocken summen
Zieht liebend unser Geist* dorthin
Und streut Dir betend Andachtsblumen*
Auf's Heldengrab mit frommem Sinn.
Vater unser*. Ave Maria."

Lebenszeichen – Feldpostbriefe erzählen: pädagogische Handreichung/von Christof Beitz. Volksbund Deutsche Kriegsgräberfürsorge e.V., Landesverband Bayern. – München: Volksbund Dt. Kriegsgräberfürsorge, 2003

Pein anguish • **Unterpfand** pledge • **Geist** spirit • **Andachtsblumen** flowers of devotion • **Vaterunser** Lord's Prayer

---

Lebenszeichen sign of life
Pfingsten Whitsuntide ['wɪts(ə)n‚taɪd]
Fronleichnam Corpus Christi
Massenmord mass murder

Graben trench

erschöpft exhausted [ɪɡˈzɔːstɪd]
verschüttet entombed [ɪnˈtuːm],

Opfer sacrifice
unbeschreiblich beyond words
Leiche corpse, dead body

Überzahl superior numbers

Vaterland fatherland
Verwüstung devastation
trostlos grim, desolate

fortgehen to continue

Marketender sutler (hist.: a civilian merchant who sells provisions to an army in the field of war)

Am 5. Juni 1915,
Liebe Eltern und Geschwister!
Ein Lebenszeichen* sollt Ihr haben, kaum zu glauben, dass da noch ein Mensch leben kann, denn es sind furchtbare Kämpfe. Pfingsten*, Fronleichnam* und andere Tage waren grausam. Die Franzosen stürmten in Massen an. Das ist kein Krieg mehr, sondern Massenmord*, viele unserer Kameraden mussten wieder dran glauben. In drei Tagen habe ich keine Minute geschlafen, denn es war keine Zeit da, wir hielten aus, alles war in einem Graben*, Franzosen und Deutsche, jedoch haben wir uns aufs äußerste gewehrt. Zerfetzt und voll Dreck, ganz erschöpft* kamen wir in Ruhe. Es war furchtbar, dieses Krachen und Zittern, Tösen, einfach alles ging drunter und drüber, förmlich verschüttet* waren wir, viele sind noch verschüttet, dies ist hart; da darf bald eine bessere Zeit kommen, denn was dieses Opfer* kostet ist unbeschreiblich*.
Massen von Leichen* liegen umher und dieser Geruch bei der Hitze, wenig zu trinken gibt es, viel Durst, viele Steine und wenig Brot. Aber sie sollen nicht durchkommen mit ihrer Überzahl*.
Doch hatte ich wieder großes Glück und danke unserm Herrgott. Ihr dürft Gott danken, dass der Feind nicht in unserem schönen Vaterland* ist, denn diese Verwüstungen*, trostlos*.
Ihr habt tatsächlich den Himmel, in einer Hölle kann es nicht ärger zugehen wie dieser Tage bei uns. Geht nur in die Kirche, betet, dass baldiger Frieden kehrt. So kann es nicht fortgehen*.
Hoffen das Beste und vertrauen auf Gott.
Für heute herzliche Grüße
euer Andreas
Schicken braucht ihr mir vorläufig kein Paket mehr, wir können hier alles beim Marketender* einkaufen.

Lebenszeichen – Feldpostbriefe erzählen: pädagogische Handreichung/von Christof Beitz. Volksbund Deutsche Kriegsgräberfürsorge e.V., Landesverband Bayern. – München: Volksbund Dt. Kriegsgräberfürsorge, 2003

S 56 Erich Maria Remarque

Im Westen Nichts Neues

The novel 'All Quiet on the Western Front' (*Im Westen Nichts Neues*) by Erich Maria Remarque was published in 1929. It tells the story of six young German soldiers who volunteer to fight in the First World War, and it chronicles their intellectual, spiritual and physical demise. The first-person narrator is called Paul Bäumer, a very young soldier, who exposes details of life on the Western front and is eventually shot in the head when leaving the protection of his trench upon seeing a butterfly flying by. Remarque had fought on the Western front himself at the age of eighteen, suffering several injuries, taking with him the horrors he experienced there.

Since, upon its publication, many readers believed that the novel called into question the values set forth by Germany's 'fatherland propaganda', it was banned and later on publicly burned by the Nazis. Remarque lost his German citizenship in 1938 and was forced to move to Switzerland and, later, to the United States.

The (American) film version dates back to 1930 and was the first film to win both the Academy Awards ('Oscars') for Outstanding Production and Best Director.

Pre-task 1. With the help of the introductory remarks, discuss what the title of the novel reveals about Remarque's views on the First World War.

Tasks 2. Use the poster as well as the two quotations from the novel to double-check your ideas from task 1.
3. Examine Remarque's attitude towards the war.
4. Discuss in how far "All Quiet on the Western Front" qualifies as a reliable source for history classes, also taking the author's background into account.

Post-task 5. If possible, watch an excerpt from the film in class in which actual trench warfare is shown. Discuss the cinematic realization, keeping in mind that the film is from 1930. Pay special attention to the sound.

French film poster, 1930

Anklage accusation
Bekenntnis confession

entkommen to escape

Dieses Buch soll weder eine Anklage*
noch ein Bekenntnis* sein.
Es soll nur den Versuch machen,
über eine Generation zu berichten,
die vom Kriege zerstört wurde –
auch wenn sie seinen Granaten entkam*.

Erich Maria Remarque: Im Westen nichts Neues. Köln: Kiepenheuer & Wietsch 1993, S. 5

sich quälen to agonize
gefasst composed

Er fiel im Oktober 1918, an einem Tage, der so ruhig und still war an der ganzen Front, dass der Heeresbericht sich nur auf den Satz beschränkte, im Westen sei nichts Neues zu melden.
Er war vornübergesunken und lag wie schlafend an der Erde. Als man ihn umdrehte, sah man, dass er sich nicht lange gequält* haben konnte; – sein Gesicht hatte einen so gefassten* Ausdruck, als wäre er beinahe zufrieden damit, dass es so gekommen war.

Erich Maria Remarque: Im Westen nichts Neues. Köln: Kiepenheuer & Wietsch 1993, S. 197

S 57   Wilfred Owen

Dulce Et Decorum Est

The Latin words *Dulce Et Decorum Est* (*Pro Patria Mori*) are taken from an ode by the Roman poet Horace (65 BCE – 8 BCE) and can be translated as "it is sweet and right (to die for your country)". The given poem was written by the English poet and soldier Wilfred Owen (1893–1918) and published after his death, in 1920. Owen was killed in action on 4 November 1918, his mother received the telegram informing her about her son's death on 11 November 1918 (Armistice Day).

Pre-task

1. Read the words and phrases in the box below, taken from Owen's poem (check the annotations for help in case there are words you do not know). Use them to extend the title of the poem with "buts". Write at least three sentences.
   - It is sweet and right to die for your country, but …

> coughing • sludge • haunting flares • blood-shod • lame • blind • fatigue • gas • yelling • stumbling • floundering • choking • froth-corrupted lungs

Tasks

2. Describe the scenario the poet creates.
3. Examine the poet's attitude towards the war, as illustrated by the choice of words and stylistic devices.
4. Discuss possible addressees of the given poem (cf. last stanza: "If you …").
5. In 1915, Owen suffered a number of traumatic experiences (for example: he suffered from concussion after having fallen into a shell hole and lay on the bank of the river for several days among the bodily remains of a fellow officer). Eventually he was diagnosed as "shell shocked" and treated in a hospital in Edinburgh. Yet, he returned to the front in 1918 where he was killed a week before the

Wilfred Owen

armistice was signed. Against this background, evaluate his reliability as an eye-witness to the war.

Post-task 6. Do research on the poem "Pro Patria" by Sir Owen Seaman (the title is also taken from Horace), written in August 1914. Examine what both poems have in common, and where they differ. Based on your findings, discuss which one you would prefer to read in a history schoolbook, and why.

Bent double, like old beggars under sacks,
Knock-kneed, coughing like hags*, we cursed through sludge*,
Till on the haunting flares* we turned our backs
And towards our distant rest* began to trudge*.
5 Men marched asleep. Many had lost their boots
But limped on, blood-shod. All went lame; all blind;
Drunk with fatigue*; deaf even to the hoots*
Of disappointed shells that dropped behind.

GAS! Gas! Quick, boys – An ecstasy of fumbling,
10 Fitting the clumsy helmets* just in time;
But someone still was yelling out and stumbling
And floundering* like a man in fire or lime* –
Dim, through the misty panes* and thick green light
As under a green sea, I saw him drowning.

15 In all my dreams, before my helpless sight,
He plunges at me, guttering, choking, drowning.

If in some smothering dreams you too could pace*
Behind the wagon that we flung him in,
And watch the white eyes writhing* in his face,
20 His hanging face, like a devil's sick of sin;
If you could hear, at every jolt*, the blood
Come gargling from the froth*-corrupted lungs,
Obscene as cancer, bitter as the cud*
Of vile*, incurable sores on innocent tongues –
25 My friend, you would not tell with such high zest*
To children ardent* for some desperate glory,
The old Lie: Dulce et decorum est
Pro patria mori.

Wilfried Owen: "Dulce Et Decorum Est", in: Horst Meller, Klaus Reichert (Eds.): Englische Dichtung. Von R. Browning bis Heaney, München: C. H. Beck 2000, p. 126

hag an old woman who is ugly and unpleasant
sludge thick soft mud
flare rocket burning with a bright glare to light up the targets
distant rest a camp away from the front line
to trudge to walk somewhere with heavy, slow steps
fatigue [fəˈtiːg] extreme tiredness
hoot the noise made by shells in the air
helmet here: gas mask
to flounder to move with great difficulty and in an uncontrolled way
lime white substance that burns living tissue
panes glass in the eyepieces of the gas masks
to pace to walk
to writhe sich winden

jolt Ruck, Erschütterung
froth Schaum
cud wiedergekäutes Futter
vile extremely unpleasant
high zest idealistic enthusiasm
ardent keen

CONNECT

General Haig and the Battle of the Somme – Butcher or Hero?

Sir Douglas Haig (1861–1928)

Sir Douglas Haig was born in Edinburgh in 1861 and studied first in Oxford, then at the Royal Military Academy in Sandhurst, afterwards serving as an officer in the cavalry, mostly stationed in India, where he was made Chief of Staff of the Indian army in 1909.

In the first two years of WWI, Haig commanded the first corps of the BEF – the British Expeditionary Force, which he had helped to build up from 1906 onwards, to prepare for the event of a possible war with Germany. On 10 December 1915, Haig was appointed Commander-in-chief of the whole BEF. As such, he was the person in charge and responsible for the Battle of the Somme which began on 1 July 1916. Two years later, he would oversee the British advances on the western front that would eventually contribute to the Allied victory over Germany.

Until his retirement in 1921, Haig commanded the British Home Forces. He died on 28 January 1928.

Sir Douglas Haig

Task

On the occasion of the centenary (*Hundertjahrfeier*) of the First World War in 2014, British historian Gary Sheffield gave a lecture which he called "Douglas Haig reassessed". His main point was that Haig was neither a hero nor a butcher, but still was mainly responsible for the victory of the Allies.

Put yourself into the shoes of a fellow historian of Sheffield's who opposes his view, clearly seeing Haig as a "butcher" rather than a "hero" and the Battle of the Somme as a prime example of trench warfare and the futility of the fighting. Prepare a lecture you want to give in response to Sheffield's.

- Think of a catchy title for the university calendar which reveals your point of view, but which is also worded in a catchy way so as to attract a greater number of students.
- Do further research on the Battle of the Somme (purpose – course – outcome/gains or losses) including the war plan in theory and in action (cf. S 58).
- Make yourselves familiar with arguments advanced by Sheffield to plan your rebuttal.
- Write your lecture and rehearse it before giving it! Use the checklist below!

A good lecturer …	✓
… conveys the main information to their audience.	
… makes the immediate point clear.	
… frames the information, i.e. puts it into a broader context.	
… proceeds from sub-topic to sub-topic in an organized way.	
… uses appropriate visual tools.	
… uses visuals in a way that makes following the lecture and/or note-taking easier (e.g. appropriate font sizes, readability, etc.).	
… answers questions well.	
… uses technical terms appropriately as well as a formal register with correct pronunciation and effective intonation.	
… keeps the audience's interest up.	
… lectures at an appropriate level (neither too difficult nor too easy).	

adapted from: Deborah Moskowitz: "Things a Good Lecturer Usually Does", The How-to collection, www.columbia.edu/cu/biology/faculty/mowshowitz/howto_guide/lecturer.html [14.04.2015]

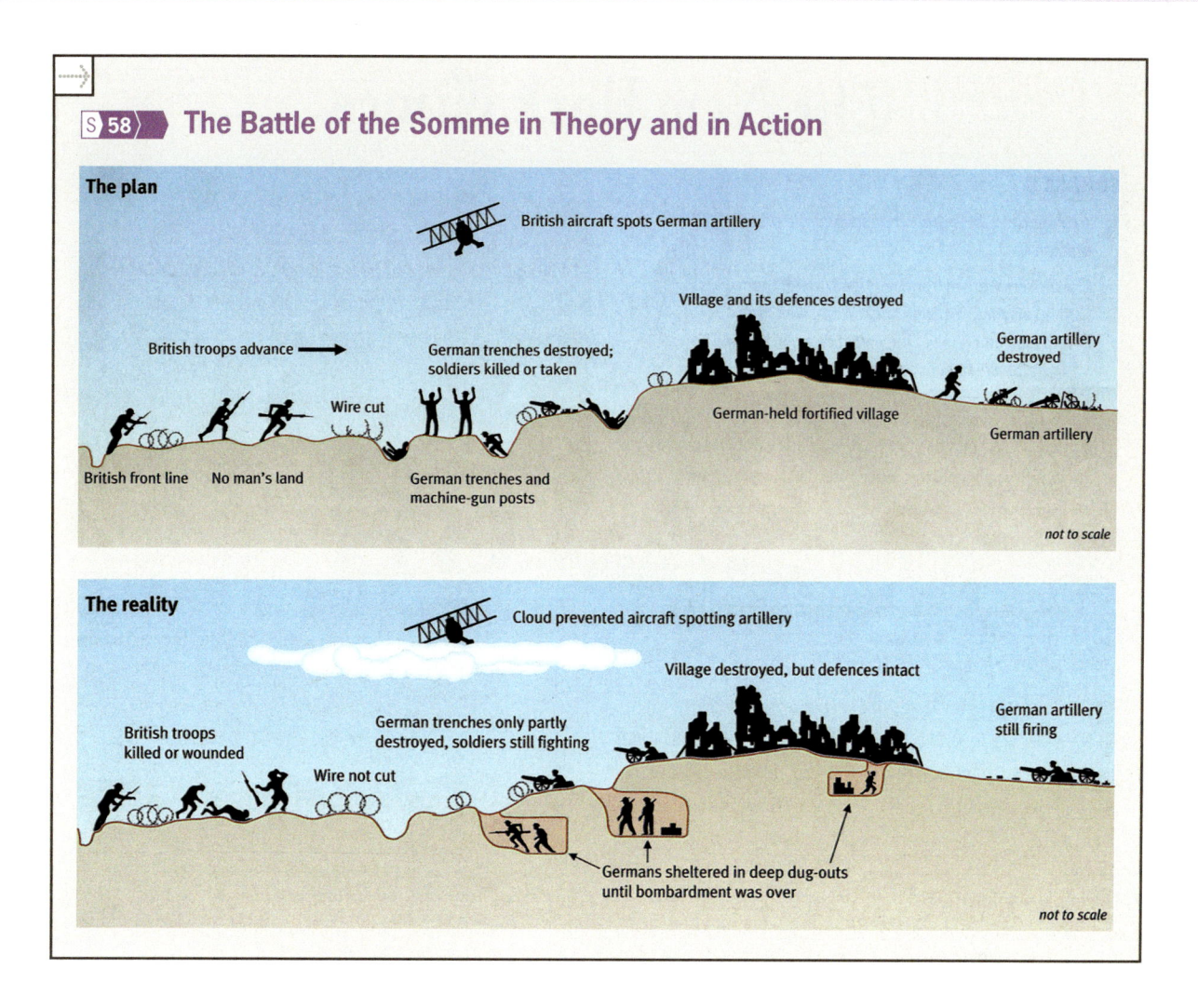

S 58 The Battle of the Somme in Theory and in Action

The plan

- British aircraft spots German artillery
- British troops advance
- German trenches destroyed; soldiers killed or taken
- Wire cut
- Village and its defences destroyed
- German-held fortified village
- German artillery destroyed
- German artillery
- British front line
- No man's land
- German trenches and machine-gun posts

not to scale

The reality

- Cloud prevented aircraft spotting artillery
- British troops killed or wounded
- German trenches only partly destroyed, soldiers still fighting
- Wire not cut
- Village destroyed, but defences intact
- German artillery still firing
- Germans sheltered in deep dug-outs until bombardment was over

not to scale

New York Times front page of 1915, reporting about the sinking of the Lusitania (cf. overview section).

S 59 The USA and WWI: Intervention or Neutrality?

On 4 February 1915, the Germans had declared unrestricted submarine warfare. On 7 May 1915, a German submarine had sunk the British passenger ship *Lusitania* off the Irish coast on its way to New York. Of the almost 2,000 passengers only 761 survived. This had already turned American public opinion against Germany. In the ensuing period, Germany renounced unrestricted submarine warfare, but then announced its resumption in January 1917. In addition, the Zimmermann Telegram added to increasing tensions between Germany and the USA. That is why the United States severed diplomatic relations with Germany on 3 February 1917, and the American ambassador left Berlin.

On 6 April 1917, the American Congress voted on whether the USA should enter World War One or not. In order to convince Congress to vote in favour of entry into war, President Woodrow gave a speech on 2 February 1917. The opposing view was represented by Robert M. La Follette, a member of Congress who answered Wilson on 4 February 1917.

Pre-tasks 1. With a partner, take turns to describe the propaganda poster. Make use of the language support provided. Afterwards, pinpoint the reasons the poster gives for the necessity of joining (or rather: continuing) the war.

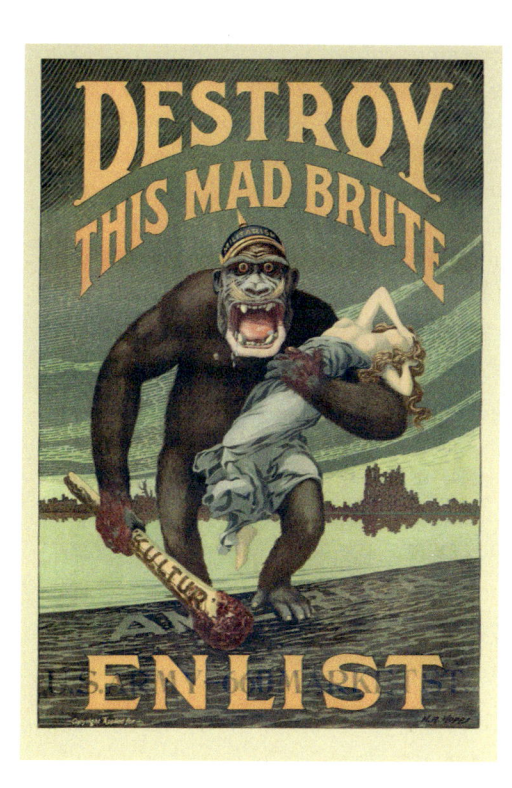

American WWI propaganda poster, 1917

Language support

brute *Unmensch, Grobian* • **to enlist** *sich freiwillig melden* • **Affe** ape • **Pickelhaube** spiked helmet • **Schlagstock** club

2. With another partner, now take turns to describe the cover illustration for a popular American anti-war song of 1915. Make use of the language support provided. Pinpoint the reasons the illustration provides against entering the war. If possible, listen to the song and try to understand the gist [dʒɪst] (= the main/most important points) of the lyrics.

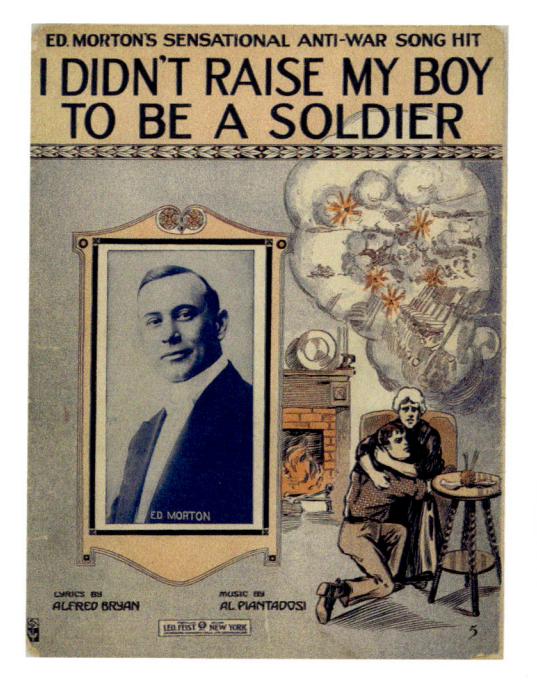

Cover illustration, 1915

Language support

Schlachtfeld battlefield • **marschieren** to march • **Kamin** fireplace, hearth • **umarmen** to hug

Tasks

3. Split into two groups, one group dealing with S 59a, the other with S 59b. Match up the source with the picture (cf. pre-tasks) and add arguments advanced that speak for/against the USA joining the war.

4. Put yourself into the shoes of two members of Congress who are still undecided as regards the impending vote on the USA's entry into war. Write a dialogue in which you have the two of them discuss the issue in question, against the backdrop of the given speeches and the historical context. Make sure that the arguments are related to each other, and that there is a logical ending to the dialogue (which could also be to agree to disagree, however).

Post-task

5. The USA's decision to enter the war has often been called the "preliminary decision", meaning that the balance of power thus shifted in favour of the allies. However, it would still take about 1.5 years for Germany and the central powers to surrender. What might have played into the hands of the Germans? Make an educated guess.

S 59a Woodrow Wilson

War Message to Congress

President Wilson delivered this "war message" on 2 February 1917, four days before Congress would vote on entering the war.

[...] It is a war against all nations. American ships have been sunk, American lives taken, in ways which it has stirred* us very deeply to learn of, but the ships and people of other neutral and friendly nations have been sunk and overwhelmed in the waters in the same way. There has been no discrimination*. The challenge is to all mankind. Each nation must decide for itself how it will meet it. The choice we make for ourselves must be made with a moderation* of counsel* and a temperateness* of judgment befitting our character and our motives as a nation. We must put excited feeling away. Our motive will not be revenge or the victorious assertion* of the physical might of the nation, but only the vindication* of right, of human right, of which we are only a single champion. [...]
We are accepting this challenge of hostile purpose because we know that in such a government, following such methods, we can never have a friend; and that in the presence of its organized power, always lying in wait to accomplish* we know not what purpose, there can be no assured security for the democratic governments of the world. We are now about to accept gage* of battle with this natural foe* to liberty and shall, if necessary, spend the whole force of the nation to check and nullify* its pretensions* and its power. We are glad, now that we see the facts with no veil* of false pretense* about them, to fight thus for the ultimate peace of the world and for the liberation of its peoples, the German peoples included: for the rights of nations great and small and the privilege of men everywhere to choose their way of life and of obedience. The world must be made safe for democracy. Its peace must be planted upon the tested foundations of political liberty. We have no selfish ends to serve. We desire no conquest, no dominion. We seek no indemnities for ourselves, no material compensation for the sacrifices we shall freely make. We are but one of the champions of the rights of mankind. We shall be satisfied when those rights have been made as secure as the faith and the freedom of nations can make them. [...]

President Wilson's Declaration of War Message to Congress, April 2, 1917; Records of the United States Senate; Record Group 46; National Archives, www.archives.gov [14.04.15]

---

to stir to make sb. feel very strongly about sth.

discrimination here: a difference that is recognized

moderation the quality of being reasonable/not extreme

counsel advice

temperateness behaving in a calm and controlled way

assertion a strong claim

vindication justification

to accomplish to achieve

gage (AmE; BrE: gauge) [geɪdʒ] Fehdehandschuh

foe enemy

to nullify to make sth. lose its effect/power

pretension Anspruch

veil [veɪl] Schleier

pretense Vortäuschung

Woodrow Wilson (1856–1924)

Woodrow Wilson was the 28th President of the USA (1912–1921).
Born in Virginia in December 1856, he attended Davidson College in 1873/74 and studied at Princeton University from 1876 to 1879, after which he studied law at the University of Virginia until 1883. He earned his PhD* at John-Hopkins-University in Baltimore in 1885 and then taught at college and university up to 1890, when he became professor of law and national economy at Princeton. Wilson also served as Princeton's president from 1902 to 1910.
In 1910, he was elected as Democratic governor of New Jersey, and two years later, he won the presidential elections against acting President William Howard Taft.
At the beginning of WWI in 1914, Wilson was a strong proponent of US neutrality but changed his mind in 1917, the year in which the USA entered the war, influenced by Germany's resumption of unrestricted submarine warfare. Wilson justified this change of mind by claiming that the American intervention was a "crusade for democracy".
In a speech to Congress on 8 January 1918, Wilson outlined his plan for a post-war world order in the so-called "14 Points" (cf. S 67). In November 1918, he travelled to France to participate in the peace talks, advocating a League of Nations as an indispensable* part of the peace treaty. However, the Treaty of Versailles was rejected by the American Senate in March 1920, which meant the USA would also not join the League of Nations. Nonetheless, Wilson was awarded the Nobel Peace Prize for the year 1919.
In 1919, a stroke had left him hemiplegic*, which is why he did not run for another term in office in 1921 and was succeeded by the Republican Warren G. Harding. Woodrow Wilson died in Washington, D. C. on 3 February 1924.

*PhD Doctor of Philosophy (= the highest university degree) • **indispensable** essential, crucial, difficult or impossible to exist without • **hemiplegic** [ˈhɛmɪˈpliːdʒɪk] *halbseitig gelähmt*

S 59b Robert M. La Follette

Reply to Wilson's War Message

Robert M(arion) La Follette Senior (1855–1925) was an American Republican (and later Progressive) politician and a member of Congress.
In the given source below, you can read excerpts from his reply to President Wilson's War Message, delivered on 4 April 1917.

If we are to enter upon this war in the manner the President demands, let us throw pretense to the winds, let us be honest, let us admit that this is a ruthless war against not only Germany's Army and her Navy but against her civilian population as well, and frankly state that the purpose of Germany's hereditary European en-
5 emies* has become our purpose. [...]
Countless millions are suffering from want* and privation*; countless other millions are dead and rotting on foreign battlefields; countless other millions are crippled and maimed*, blinded, and dismembered*; upon all and upon their children's children for generations to come has been laid a burden of debt* which
10 must be worked out in poverty and suffering, but the "whole force" of no one of the warring nations has yet been expended*; but our "whole force" shall be expended,

hereditary enemy *Erbfeind*
want a lack of sth.
privation hardship
to maim *verstümmeln*
to dismember sb. *jdn. zerstückeln*
burden of debt [det] *Schuldenlast*
to expend to use up or spend a lot of time, money, energy, etc.

shambles (pl.) mess

so says the President. We are pledged by the President, so far as he can pledge us, to make this fair, free, and happy land of ours the same shambles* and bottomless pit of horror that we see in Europe today.

Just a word of comment more upon one of the points in the President's address. He says that this is a war "for the things which we have always carried nearest to our hearts – for democracy, for the right of those who submit to authority to have a voice in their own government." In many places throughout the address is this exalted sentiment* given expression.

exalted [ɪgˈzɔːltɪd] **sentiment** a feeling of great importance
peculiarly especially

It is a sentiment peculiarly* calculated to appeal to American hearts and, when accompanied by acts consistent with it, is certain to receive our support; but in this same connection, and strangely enough, the President says that we have become convinced that the German government as it now exists [...] can never again maintain friendly relations with us, [...] and repeatedly throughout the address the suggestion is made that if the German people would overturn their government, it would probably be the way to peace. So true is this that the dispatches* from London all hailed* the message of the President as sounding the death knell* of Germany's government. [...]

dispatch telegram
to hail to describe sth. as very good
death knell [nel] (fig.) an event/a situation that is a sign of the end of sth.

from: Jeremi Suri: American Foreign Relations Since 1898: A Documentary Reader. John Wiley & Sons, 2010, pp. 34 f.

Tsar Nicholas II (1868–1918)

Nicholas II was the eldest son of Tsar Alexander III of the Romanov dynasty and the last tsar of Russia.

Born in Pushkin in 1868, he was schooled privately and studied law at the university of St. Petersburg from 1885 to 1890 while simultaneously receiving a military education.

He became tsar of Russia upon his father's death in November 1894 and, in that same month, married the German princess Alexandra of Hesse-Darmstadt, one of the granddaughters of the British Queen Victoria. Their marriage produced five children: four daughters and one son, crown prince Alexis (*1904). However, Alexis was born a haemophiliac*, meaning that even tiny cuts could potentially kill him. A simple peasant pretending to be a monk and a prophet came to court and was indeed able to help the crown prince (even though he could not heal the disease). This man called himself Rasputin and gained more and more influence over the tsarist family.

Tsar Nicholas II, c. 1909

After Russia's defeat in the Russo-Japanese War of 1905, there were waves of protests and strikes against the tsar's way of ruling the country, which eventually forced Nicholas II to make concessions and to introduce basic rights and a legislative body, the duma (the Russian parliament), on the basis of universal suffrage. Yet, the tsar then dissolved parliament whenever he felt like doing so and restricted the right to vote to the wealthy classes. This, as well as the Romanovs' attachment to Rasputin, further harmed the Romanovs' reputation.

In 1914, Russia entered WWI. After major defeats, the tsar took over as commander-in-chief of the armed forces, but all over the country there were workers' mutinies because of a lack of supplies and dissatisfaction among the population. In February 1917, the duma formed a committee from which a provisional government would evolve. When Nicholas II ordered the dissolution of the duma and commanded the soldiers to shoot at the insurrectionists* on 11 March, the soldiers refused to obey and Nicholas had to abdicate (cf. S 60a).

On 21 March 1917, Nicholas II and his family were put under arrest and later banned to Siberia. On 16 July 1918, the whole family was murdered by Bolshevik (cf. biographical information about Lenin, S 60b) troops in Yekaterinburg.

haemophilia [hiːməˈfɪliə] *Bluterkrankheit* • **mutiny** a refusal by a group to accept sb.'s authority, esp. a group of soldiers or sailors • **insurrectionist** sb. who participates in an uprising (= an insurrection)

S 60 Revolutions in Russia

In 1917, Russia witnessed two revolutions which eventually turned Russia from an autocracy into a council democracy.

Pre-tasks
1. In their World War One commemorative edition, *The Sun* used the pun "Tsar Wars" for their cover story of the Russian Revolution, playing on the similar sound of the words "Star" as in George Lucas's *Star Wars*, and "Tsar", the title of the autocratic ruler of pre-revolutionary Russia. Make an educated guess: what were people in autocratic Russia dissatisfied with, and in how far would communist ideas be tempting to them? Revise what you have learned about communist ideas so far (cf. S 15 , The Communist Manifesto).
2. Before working on S 60a and S 60b , do research on how (un)successful Russia was in World War One (e.g. the Battle of the Masurian Lakes). Use the information to elaborate on your ideas from task 1.

Tasks
3. Work in pairs, focussing on either the revolution of March or that of November. Copy the table below and fill in the information given in your text. Then exchange with your partner.

	March Revolution, 1917	November Revolution, 1917
cause/trigger (long-/short-term)		
course		
outcome/aftermath (long-/short-term)		

4. Together, find additional categories (e.g. loss of lives ... impact ...) and compare both revolutions: how was Russia eventually turned from an autocracy into a council democracy?

Post-task
5. Revise your ideas on the question as to in how far the USA's entry into war might have meant a preliminary decision influencing the outcome of the war (to the detriment of Germany). In how far could the Russian Revolution have played into the hands of the Germans? Discuss.

S 60a The March Revolution

The year 1917 began with icy temperatures and the war was still going very badly for Russia. During the month of March, conditions in Russia grew even worse and tensions increased, especially in the Russian capital of Petrograd (originally Saint Petersburg, named Petrograd in 1914, then Leningrad in 1924 and Saint Petersburg again in 1991).

Wednesday 7 March
The managers of the giant Putilov steel works locked out their 20,000 workers after pay talks broke down. This meant that 20,000 tough, angry steel workers were now out on the streets in a mood for trouble. Workers in other factories went on strike in support of the steel workers.

Thursday 8 March
Fifty factories closed down and 90,000 workers went out on strike. As this was International Women's Day there were also thousands of socialist women on the streets, demonstrating. [...]

Friday 9 March
200,000 workers were on strike. [...]

Saturday 10 March
250,000 workers were on strike. There was no public transport and no newspapers. Food shortages continued. [...]
Later in the day, Cossacks* refused to attack a procession of strikers when they were ordered to do so.

Cossacks semi-military groups

Sunday 11 March
The President of the Duma*, Michael Rodzianko, sent this telegram to the Tsar:
"The situation is serious. The capital is in a state of anarchy. The government is paralysed; the transport system has broken down; the food and fuel supplies are completely disorganised. Discontent is general and on the increase. There is wild shooting on the streets; troops are firing at each other. It is urgent that someone enjoying the confidence of the country be entrusted with the formation of a new government."
The Tsar's response to this telegram was to order the Duma to stop meeting.

Duma name of the Russian parliament (up to today)

Monday 12 March
At six o'clock in the morning a mutiny* began in the Volinsky regiment of the army: a sergeant shot his commanding officer dead. The soldiers then left their barracks* and marched into the centre of Petrograd. [...]
Later in the day the Duma held a meeting, despite the Tsar's order not to do so. It set up a twelve-man committee called the Provisional Government to take over the government.
That evening, revolutionaries set up a Soviet, or council, of workers and soldiers in Petrograd. The Petrograd Soviet also intended to take over the government and immediately began to organise food supplies for the city.

mutiny Meuterei, Aufruhr

barracks a group of buildings in which members of the armed forces live and work

Tuesday 13 March
Tsar Nicholas sent a telegram to the Duma, saying that he would share power with the Duma. Michael Rodzianko, the Duma leader, replied:
"The measures you propose are too late. The time for them has gone. There is no return."

Wednesday 14 March
Leading army generals sent telegrams to Nicholas*, informing him that none of the army supported him. Nicholas, 500 km away in army headquarters, now tried to return to Petrograd to take control of the situation.

Nicholas Tsar Nicholas II

Thursday 15 March

Nicholas, now 250 km away from Petrograd where revolutionaries had halted his train, agreed to abdicate and [...] gave the crown to his brother, Grand Duke Michael [...].

Grand Duke Michael, however, feared that he would be just as unpopular as Nicholas, and within twenty-four hours he, too, had abdicated. Russia was now a republic – a country governed not by a monarch but by an elected leader. [...]

Josh Brooman: Russia in War and Revolution. Russia 1900–24 (Longman 20th Century History Series). Longman: New York [20]2007, pp. 18 f.

Russian soldiers demonstrating in February 1917 (the Russians still used the Julian calendar, so in Russia it was March, whereas in Germany it was February because of the Gregorian calendar used).

Lenin (1870–1924)

Vladimir Iljitsch Uljanov Lenin was born in Simbirsk (today's Uljanovsk) in 1870 and already started studying Marxist writings when attending secondary school. When his brother Alexander was hanged in 1887 because of a planned attack on the Tsar, Lenin joined the revolutionary movement.

He studied Law in Samara and worked there as a lawyer from 1891 to 1893 when he moved to St. Petersburg, continuing to participate in the revolutionary movement and establishing contacts with leading socialists.

With Julij Martov, Lenin founded the League of Struggle for the Emancipation of the Working Class *(Kampfbund zur Befreiung der Arbeiterklasse)*, a forerunner of the Russian Social Democratic Labour Party *(Sozialdemokratische Arbeiterpartei Russlands)*, which was to split into the Mensheviks (led by Martov) and the Bolsheviks (led by Lenin) in London in 1903.

From 1895 to 1900, Lenin spent two years in prison and three years in banishment in Siberia because of political agitation. In exile in Europe, he participated in the foundation of the magazine "Iskra", describing his vision of a revolutionary political party and from then on he used only the alias Lenin.

In 1912, he finally separated the Bolsheviks from Social Democracy, led the newly-established party magazine "Pravda" and appointed Joseph Stalin into the party's central committee.

Lenin

In exile in Switzerland from 1914 to 1917, Lenin – supported and organized by the German government in order to weaken the Russian enemy from within – returned to Russia after the March Revolution of 1917 (cf. S 60a) and propagated the fight against the Provisional Government. In his "April Theses", Lenin outlined his radically revolutionary programme, demanding immediate peace, a land reform and a council democracy. When an uprising failed in July, Lenin fled to Finland, but he returned after the successful November Revolution (cf. S 60b) which brought the Bolsheviks to power. Hereafter, Lenin proclaimed a council democracy.

From 1918 onwards, the Bolsheviks built up a quasi-dictatorial system of government, radically suppressing oppositional forces. In the resulting Russian civil war from 1918 to 1920, Lenin consequently employed the newly-established secret service tcheka as well as military force. However, because of growing states of emergency and protests, he announced his New Economic Policy in 1921 in order to improve the feeding of the population and to raise the standard of living.

Lenin suffered three strokes within a short space of time in 1922 and 1923 and could thus not prevent the take-over of his position by Stalin, of whom he had warned in advance. He died in Gorki near Moscow on 21 January 1924.

S 60b The November Revolution

After the March Revolution, a provisional government had been set up. However, this government competed with the Petrograd Soviet for power. Also, the commander-in-chief of the armies, General Kornilov, was planning to take over control. That is why the Prime Minister of the Provisional Government, Kerensky, allowed the Bolsheviks (= the Communists) to set up a defence force called the Red Guards to defend the Russian capital of Petrograd (originally Saint Petersburg, named Petrograd in 1914, then Leningrad in 1924 and Saint Petersburg again in 1991), which they did. This put them in a very powerful position by October 1917.

The state of Russia in September 1917
During the summer of 1917 peasants began to take control of the land on which they grew their food. They had been waiting since March for the Provisional Government to give them land, but it had failed to do so. On more than 2,000 farms peasants killed their landlords and divided the land up among themselves. In other areas they seized the lands of the Church and the Tsar.
Kerensky tried to stop the peasants from grabbing land by sending soldiers on 'punishment expeditions' into the countryside. Several expeditions went out, whipping peasants and burning their homes. But Kerensky could not find enough loyal troops to do this dirty work for him, so in most areas the violence between landlords and peasants continued.
The violence in the countryside delayed the harvest on many farms, and this led to food shortages. [...] [S]o now people faced the winter with the threat of famine.
In the armies discipline was breaking down. The Petrograd Soviet's Order No. 1 in March had already led many soldiers to disobey the orders given by their officers. Now, thousands of soldiers were deserting from the army every week, most of them with the intention of going back to their villages to make sure they got their fair share of land.
On the front lines Bolsheviks encouraged soldiers to lay down their weapons and to give up fighting. Everywhere in the army there was drunkenness, chaos and violence. [...]

The November Revolution

In October 1917 Lenin returned to Petrograd from his hiding place in Finland. [...] The Bolshevik leaders agreed to stage an armed uprising against the Provisional
25 Government. Leon Trotzky, the Bolshevik chairman* of the Petrograd Soviet, drew up the plans and set up headquarters in the Smolny Institute, a disused school. [...] By the night of 6 November the Red Guards were well armed with rifles from the Peter and Paul Fortress, and they were ready for action. During the night they began to take control of all the most important locations in Petrograd. [...]
30 The Provisional Government had its headquarters in the Winter Palace and was guarded only by army cadets and the Women's Battalion of the army. On the evening of 7 November a cruiser, the Aurora, which Bolshevik sailors had captured, sailed up the river Neva and fired blank shells at the Winter Palace. Later the guns in the Peter and Paul fortress also opened fire on the Palace. Then the Red Guards
35 stormed the Winter Palace. The Cadets and the Women's Battalion gave up without a fight. The ministers of the Provisional Government surrendered* and were taken away under arrest.
The Bolsheviks now controlled Petrograd, the capital of Russia. The next day Lenin announced that he was setting up a new government. The Bolsheviks had come to
40 power after a single day of rebellion in which eighteen people had been arrested and two people had been killed.

chairman the person in charge

to surrender sich ergeben

Josh Brooman: Russia in War and Revolution. Russia 1900–24 (Longman 20th Century History Series). Longman: New York ²⁰2007, pp. 22 f.

S 61 — Russia's Provisional Government

Note to the US Government

This note was dispatched by Russia's Provisional Government to the US government on 23 June 1917.

Pre-task
1. In their note to the US government, the provisional government refers to and quotes from Wilson's "war message" (cf. S 59a). Make an educated guess: what would they quote, and why?

Tasks
2. Identify the quotation from Wilson's "war message" and outline the situation the new Russia finds herself in, according to the Provisional Government.
3. With the help of the overview section as well as S 60a and S 60b, put the source into its historical context and explain the Provisional Government's motivation in sending this note.
4. Not even half a year after this note was dispatched, the November Revolution turned Russia into the Soviet Union. In what way would a diplomatic note from the new Soviet government to the US government differ from the one at hand, and why? Discuss.

On behalf of the Russian Provisional Government and on behalf of all the people of new Russia, I have been first of all sent here to express their gratitude to the Government of the United States for the prompt recognition of the new political order in Russia. This noble action of the world's greatest democracy has afforded
5 us strong moral support and has created among our people a general feeling of profound appreciation.

Close and active relationship between the two nations based upon complete and sincere understanding encountered inevitable obstacles during the old regime because of its very nature. The situation is now radically changed with free Russia starting a new era in her national life.

The Provisional Government is actively mobilizing all its resources and is making great efforts to organize the country and the army for the purpose of conducting the war. We hope to establish a very close and active cooperation with the United States, in order to secure the most successful and intensive accomplishment of all work necessary for our common end. [...]

New Russia, in full accord with the motives which impelled* the United States to enter the war, is striving to destroy tyranny, to establish peace on a secure and permanent foundation and to make the world safe for democracy. [...]

Guided by democratic precepts*, the Provisional Government is meanwhile reorganizing the country on the basis of freedom, equality, and self-government, rebuilding its economic and financial structure.

The people are realizing more and more that for the very sake of further freedom law must be maintained and manifestation of anarchy suppressed. In this respect local life has exemplified a wonderful exertion of spontaneous public spirit. [...]

With all emphasis may I state that Russia rejects any idea of separate peace. I am aware that rumours were circulated in this country that a separate peace seemed probable. I am happy to affirm that such rumours are wholly without foundation in fact.

Russian Note of Thanks to the U.S. Government, 23 June 1917, in: Source Records of the Great War, Vol. V, ed. Charles F. Horne, National Alumni 1923

to impel to force

precept ['priːsept] a rule, instruction, or principle that teaches correct behaviour

S 62 Gottfried Niedhart

Visionen von der "Einen Welt"

In the given extract, the German historian Gottfried Niedhart, who specializes in international relations in the 20th century, examines the reasons that make 1917 an "epochal year".

Pre-task
1. The given article was published in the magazine *Praxis Geschichte* in 2007. Have a look at the front cover of the issue dealing with the "epochal year 1917". Describe it in detail, also taking the composition into account. Then explain what/whom the editors consider to be decisive in making 1917 an "epochal year".

Tasks
2. Outline the reasons the author gives for making the year 1917 stand out.
3. Against the backdrop of the text, evaluate to what extent the bipolar post-1945 world, characterized by the antagonism between the USA and the Soviet Union, was the culmination of a development that started in 1917.

Post-task
4. Do further research on the "epochal year" 1789: what makes it an "epochal year", and why could it be seen as the beginning of the "long" 19th century (ending with the First World War)? Present and discuss your findings in class.

[...] Das Jahr 1917 gilt als Epochenjahr, weil es zwei Tendenzen der Moderne verdichtete*. Das 19. Jahrhundert war das Jahrhundert der Nationalstaaten und, wie sich in der Vorgeschichte* des Ersten Weltkriegs zeigte, des übersteigerten* Nationalismus. Es war aber auch ein Jahrhundert des Internationalismus mit einer Vielzahl von Kooperationen und Organisationen. Industrie, Handel und Banken drängten energisch über die nationalen Grenzen und regionalen Einzugsgebiete* hinaus und entwickelten Formen der Zusammenarbeit und der Absprachen*, so dass ein arbeitsteilig* organisierter Weltmarkt entstand. Das Netz der globalen Interdependenz, wie es an der Wende zum 20. Jahrhundert bestand und dann durch den Ersten Weltkrieg zerrissen wurde, sollte erst lange nach dem Zweiten Weltkrieg wieder erreicht werden. Diese frühe Form der Globalisierung brachte das transnationale Phänomen der bürgerlichen* Internationale hervor, die marktwirtschaftlich orientiert* war. [...]

Betrachtet man die Eckdaten*, die das Epochenjahr 1917 geprägt* haben, so wird deutlich, dass Nationalismus und Internationalismus in der Gestaltung ihrer Kriegsführung sowie in der Formulierung ihrer Kriegsziele und Friedensvorstellungen nebeneinander herliefen und sich zugleich wechselseitig ausschlossen*. Wie es im Krieg gar nicht anders sein konnte, waren Haltung und Politik in allen Staaten durchgehend vom Nationalismus geprägt. Eine Steigerung* wurde allerdings erreicht, als das Deutsche Reich am 1. Februar 1917 den uneingeschränkten U-Boot-Krieg verkündete. Die Antwort darauf erfolgte am 6. April 1917 mit dem Eintritt der USA in den Krieg [...]. Dies hatte mit konkreten amerikanischen Interessen zu tun, war aber von der Grundidee der „bürgerlichen Internationale" begleitet, die sich von der weltweiten Verbreitung der Marktwirtschaft und der Demokratie eine stabile Weltordnung ohne Krieg erhoffte.

Das Demokratie-Argument erhielt einen deutlichen Impuls* durch die am 8. März ausgebrochene Revolution in Russland, die infolge des dort noch geltenden julianischen Kalenders als Februarrevolution geführt wird und am 15. März 1917 zur Abdankung* des Zaren führte. Damit schien sich in Russland der Weg zur parlamentarischen Demokratie zu eröffnen, der allerdings schon nach kurzer Zeit mit der Oktoberrevolution der Bolschewiki (7. November nach gregorianischem Kalender) beendet war. Mit dieser welthistorisch einschneidenden* Weichenstellung* wurde die revolutionäre Variante des internationalen Sozialismus zu einem Akteur*, der seit 1917 die kommunistische Revolutionierung weltweit anstrebte* [...].

Für die Entwicklung der internationalen Beziehungen war die Tatsache bedeutsam, dass sich seit 1917 auch die Sozialistische Internationale mit der Führung eines Staates verband. Moskau stand hinfort Washington gegenüber, der Ost-West-Konflikt, der nach dem Zweiten Weltkrieg zum Kalten Krieg werden sollte, war entstanden. [...]

Gottfried Niedhart: „Visionen von der „Einen Welt". Machtpolitik und Ideologie im Epochenjahr 1917"; in: Praxis Geschichte: Epochenjahr 1917. Visionen für den Weltfrieden. 1 (2007), Westermann, Braunschweig 2007, pp. 4–11

verdichten to condense
Vorgeschichte preliminary events
übersteigert exaggerated
Einzugsgebiet trading area
Absprache agreement, consultation, accord
arbeitsteilig based on the division of labour

bürgerlich civic
marktwirtschaftlich orientiert market-oriented
Eckdaten key data
prägen to form, to stamp

sich wechselseitig ausschließen to be mutually exclusive
Steigerung escalation

Impuls stimulus

Abdankung abdication

einschneidend radical, incisive
Weichenstellung (new) setting of the course
Akteur player
etw. anstreben to strive for sth.

S 63 The Treaty of Brest-Litovsk

The Treaty of Brest-Litovsk was signed by the Soviet Union and the Central Powers on 3 March 1918, effectively ending the war on the eastern front for Germany. However, the issue of making peace with the Central Powers had been heavily disputed in the Soviet Union, and the terms of the treaty led many Russians to call it a "robber peace".

S 65b Propaganda Posters

American poster

Austrian poster

French poster ("Germany is the war")

German postcard

Paul von Hindenburg (1847–1934)

Paul von Hindenburg was born in Posen (today's Poznan, PL) in 1847, son to a Prussian officer and landowner.

After attending a cadet school in Wahlstatt and in Berlin, Hindenburg participated in the Battle of Königgrätz in 1866 and in the Battle of Sedan during the Franco-Prussian War of 1870/71. (cf. chapter 1)

Despite his retirement from military service, he was once again recruited to serve in WWI, taking over the joint command of the 8th Army, together with Erich Ludendorff on 21 August 1914. After the German successes against the Russians in the Battle at the Masurian Lakes (1915), Hindenburg was given the supreme command over all German troops on the eastern front, and after the dismissal of Erich von Falkenhayn, he and Ludendorff took over the Supreme Army Command *(OHL – Oberste Heeresleitung)* in August 1916.

Paul von Hindenburg

On 29 September 1918, after the failure of the spring offensive, the *OHL* demanded immediate armistice talks and a parliamentary government, and on 9 November 1918 Hindenburg advised Emperor William II to flee to the Netherlands. One day later, he pushed for the signing of the armistice (which was eventually signed on 11 November 1918).

In 1919, Hindenburg retired and moved to Hannover. However, in 1925, the right-wing parties convinced him (he had no allegiance to any party himself) to run for the office of President in the second round of the elections, which he then won. He consequently swore an oath on the Weimar constitution, despite his openly displayed favour of a monarchy.

Hindenburg was also elected for a second term in office in 1932, winning against Adolf Hitler. However, after appointing Brüning Chancellor in 1930 without asking the parliament for approval, he, in effect, introduced a period of presidential cabinets. After von Papen's and Kurt von Schleicher's chancellorships, Hindenburg eventually appointed Hitler Chancellor on 30 January 1933, with von Papen as Vice-Chancellor. By signing the so-called Reichstag Fire Decree *(Reichstagsbrandverordnung;* cf. chapter 3), he paved the way for the National Socialist dictatorship, and he also enhanced the public image of the Nazis by participating in the Nazi-orchestrated "Day of Potsdam" (cf. chapter 3).

Hindenburg died on 2 August 1934. After his death, Hitler merged the offices of President and Chancellor into that of the *Führer* of Germany.

S 66 Hindenburg about the End of WWI

As the main figure in the OHL, Hindenburg advised the German government to sue for an armistice in October 1918 (cf. S 66a). One year later, he had to make a testimony about the end of the war before a parliamentary board of enquiry *(parlamentarischer Untersuchungsausschuss)* (cf. S 66b).

Pre-task 1. Revise what you have learned about the reasons for Germany's defeat. Against this backdrop and taking into account the autobiographical account of Hindenburg provided here, decide what/whom Hindenburg would probably make responsible. Give reasons for your views.

Tasks

2. Copy the table below and fill it in with the help of S 66a and S 66b.

Hindenburg in 1918	Hindenburg in 1919
Germany could not win the war because …	Germany could have won the war if …
• …	• …
• …	• …
• …	• …
Responsible for Germany's defeat: ?	Responsible for Germany's defeat: ?

3. Turn to the overview section of chapter 3 and read the information about the end of World War One in Germany. Against this backdrop, explain in detail Hindenburg's references to the "revolutionary influence" the troops were allegedly exposed to.

4. As you have seen, Hindenburg totally contradicts himself in 1919, see also the change in first and in final sentence here which reveals the 1919 statement as a lie. Discuss Hindenburg's possible motivations for taking a very different stance in 1919.

5. Both Hindenburg and Ludendorff propagated the so-called "stab-in-the-back"-myth. In German, it is called "Dolchstoßlegende". Explain the differences in meaning and evaluate if the German or the English term is more accurate and/or appropriate.

S 66a Paul von Hindenburg

Dispatch to Prince Max von Baden

On 3 October 1918, Hindenburg sent a note to Chancellor Max von Baden, explaining why Germany should sue for an armistice.

Oberste Heeresleitung Supreme Army Command
auf etw. bestehen to insist on sth.

nach menschlichem Ermessen in all probablity, as far as it is humanly possible to tell
Aussicht prospect
fest gefügt stehen to stand strong
schwer wiegend momentous
etw. ist geboten it is imperative
ersparen to spare

Die Oberste Heeresleitung* bleibt auf ihrer am Sonntag, dem 29. September d. J., gestellten Forderung der sofortigen Herausgabe des Friedensangebotes an unsere Feinde bestehen*.
Infolge des Zusammenbruchs der mazedonischen Front, der dadurch notwendig gewordenen Schwächung unserer Westreserven und infolge der Unmöglichkeit, die in den Schlachten der letzten Tage eingetretenen sehr erheblichen Verluste zu ergänzen, besteht nach menschlichem Ermessen* keine Aussicht* mehr, dem Feind den Frieden aufzuzwingen.
Der Gegner seinerseits führt ständig neue, frische Reserven in die Schlacht. Noch steht das deutsche Heer fest gefügt* und wehrt siegreich alle Angriffe ab. Die Lage verschärft sich aber täglich und kann die O.H.L. zu schwer wiegenden* Entschlüssen zwingen.
Unter diesen Umständen ist es geboten*, den Kampf abzubrechen, um dem deutschen Volke und seinen Verbündeten nutzlose Opfer zu ersparen*. Jeder versäumte Tag kostet Tausenden von tapferen Soldaten das Leben.

from: Matthias Herrmann: Die Dolchstoßlegende. Hintergrund und politische Wirkung, in: Geschichte lernen, Heft 52 (1996), p. 48–53, p. 53

S 66b Paul von Hindenburg

Testimony before the Parliamentary Board of Enquiry

In a testimony before the Parliamentary Board of Enquiry of 18 November 1919, Hindenburg explains why Germany lost the First World War.

Wir wussten, was wir vom Heer, der oberen und niederen Führung, nicht zuletzt von dem Mann im feldgrauen Rock* zu fordern hatten und was sie geleistet* haben. Aber trotz der ungeheuren Ansprüche an Truppen und Führung, trotz der zahlenmäßigen Überlegenheit* des Feindes konnten wir den Kampf zu einem
5 glücklichen Ende führen, wenn die geschlossene* und einheitliche* Zusammenwirkung von Heer und Heimat eingetreten wäre. Darin hatten wir das Mittel zum Sieg gesehen, den zu erreichen wir den festen Willen hatten.
Aber was geschah nun? Während sich beim Feinde trotz seiner Überlegenheit ein Zusammenarbeiten aller Parteien und Schichten zeigte, sodass sie sich in dem
10 Willen zum Siege immer fester zusammenschlossen, und zwar umso mehr, je schwieriger ihre Lage wurde, da machten sich bei uns die Parteiinteressen geltend*. [...] Ich wollte kraftvolle und freudige Mitarbeit* gewinnen, bekam aber Versagen* und Schwäche. [...] Die Heimat hat uns von diesem Augenblick an nicht mehr gestützt. Wir erhoben oft unsere warnende Stimme. Seit dieser Zeit
15 setzte auch die heimliche Zersetzung* von Heer und Flotte ein. Die Wirkung dieser Bestrebungen* war der Obersten Heeresleitung während des letzten Kriegsjahres nicht verborgen geblieben. Die braven Truppen, die sich von der revolutionären Einwirkung* frei hielten, hatten unter der Einwirkung der revolutionären Kameraden schwer zu leiden. Unsere Forderung, strenge Zucht* und
20 strenge Handhabung* der Gesetze durchzuführen, wurde nicht erfüllt. So mussten unsere Operationen misslingen, so musste der Zusammenbruch kommen, die Revolution bildete nur den Schlussstein*. Ein englischer General sagt mit Recht: Die deutsche Armee ist von hinten erdolcht* worden. Wo die Schuld liegt, bedarf keines Beweises.

from: Matthias Herrmann: Die Dolchstoßlegende. Hintergrund und politische Wirkung, in: Geschichte lernen, Heft 52 (1996), p. 48–53, p. 52 f.

feldgrauer Rock field-grey uniform
etw. leisten to accomplish sth.
jdm. zahlenmäßig überlegen sein to outnumber sb.
geschlossen as one man
einheitlich uniform (adj.)

geltend machen to bring sth. to bear
Mitarbeit cooperation
Versagen failure
heimliche Zersetzung clandestine ['klænde‚staɪn] corruption
Bestrebungen endeavours
Einwirkung influence
Zucht discipline
Handhabung handling

Schlussstein apex ['eɪpeks]
von hinten erdolcht stabbed in the back

314 The First World War

> Overview | **Sources** | Paper practice | Vocabulary

Language support

jdn. **erstechen** to stab sb. • **Verbrecher** criminal

DNVP (*Deutschnationale Volkspartei*) election poster of 1924

Embedded text:
Wer hat im Weltkrieg dem deutschen Volk den Dolchstoß versetzt? Wer ist schuld daran, dass unser Volk und Vaterland so tief ins Unglück stürzen musste? Der Parteisekretär der Sozialdemokraten Vater sagt es nach der Revolution 1918 in Magdeburg:
„Wir haben unsere Leute, die an die Front gingen, zur Fahnenflucht* veranlasst. Die Fahnenflüchtigen* haben wir organisiert, mit falschen Papieren ausgestattet, mit Geld und unterschriftslosen Flugblättern* versehen. Wir haben diese Leute nach allen Himmelsrichtungen*, hauptsächlich wieder an die Front geschickt, damit sie die Frontsoldaten bearbeiten und die Front zermürben* sollten. Diese haben die Soldaten bestimmt, überzulaufen*, und so hat sich der Zerfall allmählich*, aber sicher vollzogen."
Wer hat die Sozialdemokratie hierbei unterstützt? Die Demokraten und die Leute um Erzberger.
Jetzt, am 7. Dezember, soll das Deutsche Volk den zweiten Dolchstoß erhalten. Sozialdemokraten in Gemeinschaft mit den Demokraten wollen uns zu Sklaven der Entente machen, wollen uns für immer zugrunde richten*.
Wollt ihr das nicht, dann wählt deutschnational!

―――――――
*****Fahnenflucht** desertion • **Fahnenflüchtige** deserters • **Flugblatt** leaflet • **Himmelsrichtung** cardinal direction • **zermürben** to demoralize • **überlaufen** to change sides • **allmählich** gradual(ly) • **zugrunde richten** to destroy

The International Peace Framework After the First World War

On 11 November 1918, Germany signed an armistice – the war was over. Now the Allies had to decide on a peace treaty with the defeated nations, a treaty that would, on the one hand, punish those responsible for the war but that would also prevent future wars.

S 67 Woodrow Wilson

14 Points

In his so-called "14 Points" of 8 January 1918, US President Woodrow Wilson outlined his vision for a peaceful post-war world order.

Pre-task
1. Revise Wilson's "war message" to Congress (cf. S 59a). From his speech, deduce how he might imagine a post-war order.

Tasks
2. Find categories under which to put the "14 Points".
3. Use an atlas to explain the impact of the territorial changes envisioned by Wilson.
4. Against the backdrop of the source, explain why Germany hoped for a peace settlement based on the "14 Points".
5. In 1919, Wilson was awarded the Nobel Peace Prize. Put yourself into the shoes of a member of the committee deciding on the awardees. Write a recommendation for your fellow members of committee in which you justify why Wilson deserves the Nobel Peace Prize for his post-war visions on peace.

[...] I. Open covenants* of peace, openly arrived at, after which there shall be no private international understandings of any kind but diplomacy shall proceed always frankly and in the public view.
II. Absolute freedom of navigation upon the seas, outside territorial waters, alike
5 in peace and in war, except as the seas may be closed in whole or in part by international action for the enforcement of international covenants.
III. The removal, so far as possible, of all economic barriers and the establishment of an equality of trade conditions among all the nations consenting to* the peace and associating themselves for its maintenance.
10 IV. Adequate guarantees given and taken that national armaments will be reduced to the lowest point consistent with domestic safety.
V. A free, open-minded, and absolutely impartial* adjustment of all colonial claims, based upon a strict observance of the principle that in determining all such questions of sovereignty the interests of the populations concerned must have
15 equal weight with the equitable* claims of the government whose title is to be determined.
VI. The evacuation of all Russian territory and such a settlement of all questions affecting Russia as will secure the best and freest cooperation of the other nations of the world in obtaining for her an unhampered* and unembarrassed opportu-
20 nity for the independent determination of her own political development and national policy and assure her of a sincere welcome into the society of free nations

covenant Abkommen

to consent to to agree to

impartial unparteiisch

equitable fair and reasonable

unhampered free from difficulties

under institutions of her own choosing; and, more than a welcome, assistance also of every kind that she may need and may herself desire. [...]

VII. Belgium, the whole world will agree, must be evacuated and restored, without any attempt to limit the sovereignty which she enjoys in common with all other free nations. [...]

VIII. All French territory should be freed and the invaded portions restored, and the wrong done to France by Prussia in 1871 in the matter of Alsace-Lorraine, which has unsettled the peace of the world for nearly fifty years, should be righted, in order that peace may once more be made secure in the interest of all.

IX. A readjustment of the frontiers of Italy should be effected along clearly recognizable lines of nationality.

X. The peoples of Austria-Hungary, whose place among the nations we wish to see safeguarded and assured, should be accorded the freest opportunity to autonomous development.

XI. Rumania, Serbia, and Montenegro should be evacuated; occupied territories restored; Serbia accorded free and secure access to the sea; and the relations of the several Balkan states to one another determined by friendly counsel* along historically established lines of allegiance and nationality; [...].

XII. The Turkish portion of the present Ottoman Empire should be assured a secure sovereignty, but the other nationalities which are now under Turkish rule should be assured an undoubted security of life and an absolutely unmolested* opportunity of autonomous development, and the Dardanelles should be permanently opened as a free passage to the ships and commerce of all nations under international guarantees.

XIII. An independent Polish state should be erected which should include the territories inhabited by indisputably Polish populations, which should be assured a free and secure access to the sea, and whose political and economic independence and territorial integrity should be guaranteed by international covenant.

XIV. A general association of nations must be formed under specific covenants for the purpose of affording mutual guarantees of political independence and territorial integrity to great and small states alike. [...]

We have no jealousy of German greatness, and there is nothing in this programme that impairs* it. We grudge her no achievement or distinction of learning or of pacific* enterprise such as have made her record very bright and very enviable. We do not wish to injure her or to block in any way her legitimate influence or power. We do not wish to fight her either with arms or with hostile arrangements of trade if she is willing to associate herself with us and the other peace-loving nations of the world in covenants of justice and law and fair dealing. We wish her only to accept a place of equality among the peoples of the world, – the new world in which we now live, – instead of a place of mastery.

President Woodrow Wilsons's Fourteen Points, 8 January, 1918, in: The Avalon Project. Documents in Law, History and Diplomacy, http://avalon.law.yale.edu [17.04.2015]

counsel advice and help

unmolested unbehelligt

to impair to damage
pacific wanting peace

CONNECT

The "Big Three" at Versailles

The negotiations of the terms of the peace treaty of Versailles were mainly conducted by the so-called "Big Three": George Clemenceau for France, David Lloyd George for Britain and Woodrow Wilson for the USA (actually it would be more appropriate to speak of the "Big Four", including Vittorio Orlando for Italy). The German delegation was excluded from participating in the talks. The task of the "Big Three" was not an easy one, since all three of them had their very own ideas and aims and had somehow to find a consensus.

Task
You are to stage a conversation, representing that between the "Big Three" during the negotiations. Get into three groups, each group representing one of the three participants/countries. With the help of your role card and the additional information provided, prepare the demands you want to put forward, as well as an opening statement that contains the gist of your most important point. Your conversation should centre on answers to the questions given in the box below, because these were the issues the "Big Three" also had to resolve at Versailles. Remember that agreement is needed, so that you might have to compromise in some points. Choose one group member to represent your country's viewpoint up front and one substitute to help out.
One student should take over the role of the moderator (cf. role card). In the event that you do not represent your group up front, be prepared to take minutes on the other two viewpoints you have not worked on and to read out your minutes after the discussion.

The "Big Three" at Versailles. From left to right: Clemenceau, Wilson, Lloyd George

Questions to be discussed:
- Who should be made guilty for the war, and for which reasons?
- Should Germany be forced to demilitarise? If so, to what extent?
- Should Germany pay indemnity? If so: why and how much?
- Should Germany cede territory? If so, which territory, why, and to whom?
- Should Austria and Germany be allowed to join?

S 68 Role Cards "The Big Three at Versailles"

ROLE CARD: Moderator 	Preparatory tasks:
	• Puzzle out a strategy → think about what the participants might say and which questions you want to ask them in case the discussion gets stuck.
	What you have to tell the others:
	1. Welcome the participants.
	2. Give an explanation of the procedure and the rules.
	• The participants should first introduce themselves and give their opening statement.
	• In the second round, each of the participants has to react to a point made by one of their 'opponents'.
	• They are not allowed to interrupt each other or to be rude, otherwise you will call them to order.
	What you are in charge of doing:
	Opening the talk and moderating it:
	• Make sure that each participant has a fair share in the discussion.
	• Make sure they discuss matters in a decent, reasonable way.
	• Try to calm them down if they get too worked up about their subject.
	• Try to move the conversation along when it gets stuck or loses substance by
	  – asking provocative questions
	  – providing thought-provoking impulses.
	Finishing the talk:
	When time is up, finish the discussion by giving a rough summary of the results and thank the participants for the (lively) discussion.

ROLE CARD: FRANCE  Represented by CLEMENCEAU 	France had to cope with most losses in WWI, with about 1,250,000 French casualties and with the fact that about 90% of the French coal and iron industry had been taken away by the Germans. By the end of the war, huge parts of France and French roads had been destroyed in the fighting or deliberately destroyed by the retreating Germans. WWI meant a second German invasion for France (cf. Franco-Prussian War of 1870/71, chapter 1). France was represented by her Prime Minister George Clemenceau, nicknamed "the Tiger" because of his unrelenting attitude towards Germany. He wanted to make Germany pay for the damage caused and ensure that Germany would never again be able to rise to power. His three major demands were: 1. Alsace-Lorraine should be returned to France, 2. France should take possession of the Rhineland to act as a bulwark against a future German attack, 3. Germany should pay reparations ($200 billion).

| ROLE CARD: BRITAIN

Represented by LLOYD GEORGE | Britain had spent about 8 billion pounds on the war and was indebted to the USA. In addition, there were about 750,000 British casualties.
Britain was represented by her Prime Minister David Lloyd George. Lloyd George, in contrast to many of his countrymen, realized that too harsh a punishment would stand in the way of a lasting peace.
His three major demands were:
1. Germany should not be treated too harshly, to avoid her starting another war in the future for this reason.
2. France should not be given the Rhineland. Instead, the Rhineland should become a demilitarized zone.
3. Germany should pay reparations ($120 billion). |
|---|---|
| ROLE CARD: USA

Represented by WILSON | After their entry into war on 6 April 1917, the USA suffered 113,000 casualties. Even though no actual fighting had taken place on American soil, the USA had lent the allies, especially Britain, a lot of money. As many Americans had been against entering the war at all, the public now preferred returning to their state of non-interference in European affairs, even though they wanted to have their expenses paid back, of course.
The USA was represented by their President Woodrow Wilson. As opposed to many of his fellow countrymen, Wilson's vision of the future was contained in his "14 Points", which were meant to create a lasting peace (cf. S 67). His major demands are embedded in these "14 Points". |

320 The First World War

Aus Versailles.
Die deutschen Unterhändler. Von links nach rechts: Leinert, Melchior, Giesberts, Brockdorf-Rantzau, Landsberg, Schücking.

Photograph of the German delegation to Versailles

S 69 Count von Brockdorff-Rantzau

Speech on the Occasion of the Presentation of the Treaty Draft to the Germany Delegation

The German delegation in Versailles was not allowed to take part in the negotiations but was only presented the draft of the treaty to be signed. On this occasion, the German foreign minister gave a speech on 7 May 1919 in which he expressed German willingness to accept punishment in return for fair treatment.

Pre-task
1. Before reading, anticipate what Brockdorff-Rantzau might have to say about the following questions:
   - Why did the war break out in 1914?
   - How much indemnity should Germany pay?
   - How can a lasting peace be ensured?

Tasks
2. Summarize how Brockdorff-Rantzau in fact answers the questions raised in task 1.
3. Take a critical stand on Brockdorff-Rantzau's view on the outbreak of war.

Post-tasks
4. Write one sentence for each of the "Big Three" in response to this speech: utter either sympathy for or criticism of Germany's stance, as befitting your position (cf. CONNECT: The "Big Three" at Versailles, pp. 317 ff.).

erhaben grand
dauerhaft lasting
Wir ... über we are aware of
Ohnmacht powerlessness

Meine Herren! Wir sind tief durchdrungen von der erhabenen* Aufgabe, die uns mit Ihnen zusammengeführt hat: Der Welt rasch einen dauerhaften* Frieden zu geben. Wir täuschen uns nicht über* den Umfang unserer Niederlage, den Grad unserer Ohnmacht*. Wir wissen, dass die Gewalt der deutschen Waffen gebrochen ist; wir kennen die Wucht* des Hasses, die uns hier entgegentritt*, und wir haben die leidenschaftliche Forderung gehört, dass die Sieger uns zugleich als Überwundene* zahlen lassen und als Schuldige bestrafen sollen.

Es wird von uns verlangt, dass wir uns als die allein Schuldigen bekennen*; ein solches Bekenntnis* wäre in meinem Munde eine Lüge. Wir sind fern davon, jede Verwantwortung dafür, dass es zu diesem Weltkrieg kam, und dass er so geführt wurde, von Deutschland abzuwälzen*. [...]

Keiner von uns wird behaupten wollen, dass das Unheil* seinen Lauf erst in dem verhängnisvollen* Augenblick begann, als der Thronfolger* Österreich-Ungarns den Mörderhänden zum Opfer fiel. In den letzten 50 Jahren hat der Imperialismus aller europäischen Staaten die internationale Lage chronisch vergiftet. Die Politik der Vergeltung* wie die Politik der Expansion und die Nichtachtung* des Selbstbestimmungsrechtes* der Völker hat zu der Krankheit Europas beigetragen, die im Weltkrieg ihre Krise erlebte. Die russische Mobilmachung* nahm den Staatsmännern die Möglichkeit der Heilung und gab die Entscheidung in die Hände der militärischen Gewalten. [...]

Unsere beiderseitigen Sachverständigen* werden zu prüfen haben, wie das deutsche Volk seiner finanziellen Entschädigungspflicht* Genüge leisten* kann, ohne unter der schweren Last* zusammenzubrechen*. Ein Zusammenbruch würde die Ersatzberechtigten* um die Vorteile bringen, auf die sie Anspruch haben*, und eine unheilbare Verwirrung* des ganzen europäischen Wirtschaftslebens nach sich ziehen. Gegen diese drohende Gefahr mit ihren unabsehbaren Folgen* müssen Sieger wie Besiegte auf der Hut sein. Es gibt nur ein Mittel, um sie zu bannen: das rückhaltlose Bekenntnis* zu der wirtschaftlichen und sozialen Solidarität der Völker zu einem freien und umfassenden Völkerbund.

Meine Herren! Der erhabene Gedanke, aus dem furchtbarsten Unheil der Weltgeschichte durch den Völkerbund den größten Fortschritt der Menschheitsentwicklung herzuleiten, ist ausgesprochen und wird sich durchsetzen*; nur wenn sich die Tore zum Völkerbund aller Nationen öffnen, die guten Willens sind, wird das Ziel erreicht werden, nur dann sind die Toten dieses Krieges nicht umsonst gestorben*. Das deutsche Volk ist innerlich bereit, sich mit seinem schweren Los abzufinden*, wenn an den vereinbarten Grundlagen des Friedens nicht gerüttelt wird. Ein Frieden, der nicht im Namen des Rechts von der Welt verteidigt werden kann, würde immer neue Widerstände gegen sich aufrufen. Niemand wäre in der Lage, ihn mit gutem Gewissen zu unterzeichnen, denn er wäre unerfüllbar*. Niemand könnte für seine Ausführung die Gewähr*, die in der Unterschrift liegen soll, übernehmen.

Wir werden das uns übergebene Dokument mit gutem Willen und in der Hoffnung prüfen, dass das Endergebnis unserer Zusammenkunft von uns allen gezeichnet werden kann.

from: W. Lautemann/M. Schlenke (Hrsg.): Geschichte in Quellen, Bd. V.: Weltkriege und Revolutionen 1914–1945, München 21970, S. 126 ff.

Wucht vehemence
die ... entgegentritt that we are confronted with
Überwundene the defeated
dass ... bekennen that we admit our sole guilt
Bekenntnis confession
(die Verantwortung) abwälzen to shift (the responsibility)
Unheil disaster
verhängnisvoll fatal ['feɪt(ə)l]
Thronfolger heir [eə(r)] to the throne
Vergeltung retaliation
Nichtachtung disrespect, contempt
Selbstbstimmungsrecht right to self-determination
Mobilmachung mobilisation
Sachverständige experts
Entschädigungspflicht duty to pay indemnity
Genüge leisten to satisfy
Last burden
zusammenbrechen/Zusammenbruch to collapse
Ersatzberechtigter party entitled to compensation
auf etwas Anspruch haben to have claim to sth.
unheilbare Verwirrung inextricable ['ɪnɪk'strɪkəb(ə)l] confusion
unabsehbare Folgen unforeseeable consequences
rückhaltloses Bekenntnis (zu) wholehearted commitment (to)
sich durchsetzen to prevail
umsonst sterben to die in vain
sich abfinden to accept

unerfüllbar unaccomplishable
Gewähr guarantee

S 70 ▶ The Treaty of Versailles (Excerpts)

On 28 June 1919, the Treaty of Versailles was signed by the German delegation. The Allied Powers concluded separate peace treaties with Germany's allies, for example the Treaty of St. Germaine with Austria-Hungary in which the *Anschluss* of the German-speaking part of Austria with Germany was forbidden.

Pre-task

1. In Germany, the treaty caused outrage and demonstrations, with people calling it a dictate and an "ignominious peace" (*Schandfrieden*). What do you expect the treaty to contain if it caused this reaction? Make an educated guess.

Tasks

2. Categorize the articles into impact on 1) territory, 2) economy, 3) military, or 4) others.
3. Compare the Treaty of Versailles with Wilson's "14 Points" (cf. S 67). Use your results and the historical context of the World War in general to evaluate the Germans' reaction to the treaty.
4. Which one of the "Big Three" got most of what he wanted? Give an evaluation.
5. Put yourself into the shoes of Brockdorff-Rantzau (cf. S 69). Write a telegram to the German government in which you comment on the terms of the treaty you are confronted with, also referring back to what you had initially hoped for.

fortification *Befestigungsanlage*

ARTICLE 42:
Germany is forbidden to maintain or construct any fortifications* either on the left bank of the Rhine or on the right bank to the west of a line drawn 50 kilometres to the East of the Rhine.
ARTICLE 45:
As compensation for the destruction of the coal mines in the north of France and as part payment towards the total reparation due from Germany for the damage resulting from the war, Germany cedes* to France in full and absolute possession [...] the coal mines in the Saar Basin.
ARTICLE 49:
Germany renounces in favour of the League of Nations [...] the government of the territory defined above. At the end of fifteen years from the coming into force of the present Treaty the inhabitants of the said territory shall be called to indicate the sovereignty under which they desire to be placed.
Alsace-Lorraine. The High Contracting Parties, recognizing the moral obligation to redress* the wrong done by Germany in 1871 both to the rights of France and to the wishes of the population of Alsace and Lorraine [...] agree upon the following...
ARTICLE 51:
The territories which were ceded to Germany [...] on February 26, 1871, and [...] May 10, 1871, are restored to French sovereignty as from the date of the Armistice of November 11, 1918. [...]
ARTICLE 119:
Germany renounces* [...] all her rights and titles over her overseas possessions.
ARTICLE 159:
The German military forces shall be demobilised and reduced [...].
ARTICLE 160:
By a date which must not be later than March 31, 1920, the German Army must not comprise more than seven divisions of infantry and three divisions of cavalry. After that date the total number of effectives in the Army of the States constituting Germany must not exceed 100,000 men [...]. The Army shall be devoted exclusively to the maintenance of order within the territory and to the control of the frontiers. [...]

to cede [si:d] *to allow sb. to take sth. from you*

to redress *wiedergutmachen*

to renounce *to state formally that you give up sth.*

ARTICLE 231:
The Allied and Associated Governments affirm and Germany accepts the responsibility of Germany and her allies for causing all the loss and damage to which the Allied and Associated Governments and their nationals have been subjected as a consequence of the war imposed upon them by the aggression of Germany and her allies.

ARTICLE 232:
The Allied and Associated Governments recognize that the resources of Germany are not adequate [...] to make complete reparation for all such loss and damage. The Allied and Associated Governments, however, require, and Germany undertakes, that she will make compensation for all damage done to the civilian population of the Allied and Associated Powers and to their property during the period of belligerence* of each as an allied or associated power against Germany.

from: Dave Powers [Ed.]: Important Documents in American History: A Collection of the important Documents Throughout America's History, Lulu.com, 2010, pp. 121 ff.

belligerence [bəˈlɪdʒərəns]
warfare

Demonstration in Berlin against the Treaty of Versailles, 1919

S 71 Deutschlands Verstümmelung

The given map, entitled "Germany's Disfigurement", is taken from a geo-political history atlas from 1929 and is part of a series of four maps in all. The titles of the other three maps are: *Deutschlands Versklavung* (showing the financial losses as compared to pre-war standards), *Deutschlands Entwaffnung* (showing demilitarised and occupied territory) and *Deutschlands Einriegelung* (showing Germany's alleged "encirclement" by hostile troops). Since the map shown here also includes Austria, the editors seem to view Austria as a part of Germany's "disfigured" territory.

The editors of the maps, Franz Braun and Arnold Hillen Ziegfeld, intended to show the existential threat Germany had to suffer due to the Treaty of Versailles and as such supported revisionist claims made especially by conservative and right-wing forces in the republic.

Pre-task 1. Look up a map of Europe and identify the territory Germany in fact lost because of the Treaty of Versailles. Based on your findings, discuss the potential the Treaty of Versailles offered for right-wing, nationalist propaganda in Germany, also taking the title of the given (propaganda) map into account.

Tasks

2. State the topic of the map and describe it.
3. Explain the means the editors of the map employ to make this map not only different from "normal" maps, but which also turn this map into an instrument of cartographic agitation depicting Germany as the "victim" of the Allied powers (e.g. the colouring, the inclusion of "statistics", etc.).

Post-task

4. Split up into three groups and do research on the other three maps of this series. For each, identify the respective articles of the Treaty of Versailles that are being criticized, and analyse the means by which the medium of maps is here exploited for propaganda purposes (cf. task 3 and CONNECT: Propaganda, pp. 309 ff.).

Embedded text:
Verstümmelung disfigurement • **unbesetzt** unoccupied • **jdm. etw. vorenthalten** to deny sb. sth. • **jdm. etw. entreißen** to wrest sth. away from sb.

Language support

Übertreibung exaggeration • **jdn. aufhetzen** to incite sb. to do sth., to instigate

S 72 US Senator William E. Borah

The League of Nations

William Edgar Borah was a Republican senator from the state of Idaho who was known for his isolationist views. This is the reason he was opposed to the USA joining the League of Nations, but he was also against signing the Treaty of Versailles. In this speech delivered in the Senate on 19 November 1919, Borah presents reasons to convince the Senate of his point of view and make the other senators vote against the ratification of the Versailles Treaty.

Pre-task

1. In his speech, Borah explicitly expresses his concern about possible violations of the Monroe Doctrine (cf. **S 28**). Explain why this concern makes clear his stance immediately.

Tasks

2. Outline Borah's concerns about the League of Nations and state his main points of criticism in respect of the Treaty of Versailles.
3. Incorporate the source into the context of the Treaty of Versailles and explain in detail Borah's views.
4. Even though the League of Nations originated from Wilson's "14 Points" (cf. **S 67**), the USA did not join it, and they also did not sign the Treaty of Versailles, but instead a separate peace treaty with Germany in 1921. Taking the "traditional" American policy up to 1917 into consideration, give an evaluation of these American decisions.

Mr. President, I am not misled by the debate across the aisle* into the view that this treaty will not be ratified. I entertain little doubt that sooner or later – and entirely too soon – the treaty will be ratified with the league of nations in it, and I am of the opinion with the reservations* in it as they are now written. […]
5 You have put in here a reservation upon the Monroe Doctrine. I think that, in so far as language could protect the Monroe Doctrine, it has been protected. But as a practical proposition, as a working proposition, tell me candidly*, as men familiar with the history of your country and of other countries, do you think that you can intermeddle in European affairs and keep Europe from intermeddling in your af-
10 fairs? […]
When this league, this combination, is formed, four great powers representing the dominant people will rule one-half of the inhabitants of the globe as subject peoples – rule by force, and we shall be a party to the rule of force. There is no other way by which you can keep people in subjection. You must either give them inde-
15 pendence, recognize their rights as nations to live their own life and to set up their new form of government, or you must deny them these things by force. That is the scheme*, the method proposed by the league. It proposes no other. […]
[Y]our treaty does not mean peace – far, very far, from it. If we are to judge the future by the past it means war. Is there any guaranty of peace other than the guar-
20 anty which comes of the control of the war-making power by the people? Yet what great rule of democracy does the treaty leave unassailed*? The people in whose keeping alone you can safely lodge the power of peace or war nowhere, at no time and in no place, have any voice in this scheme for world peace. Autocracy which has bathed the world in blood for centuries reigns supreme. Democracy is every-
25 where excluded. This, you say, means peace.
Can you hope for peace when love of country is disregarded in your scheme, when

aisle [aɪl] *(Mittel-)Gang*; here: political term → chairs in the US Senate are arranged in a semi-circle, divided by a large central aisle; Democrats sit on the right, Republicans on the left (viewed from the presiding officer's desk)
reservation here: a feeling of doubt
candid honest and direct, even when the truth is not pleasant

scheme [skiːm] plan

unassailed → **unassailable** impossible to criticize or argue with

the spirit of nationality is rejected, even scoffed at? Yet what law of that moving and mysterious force does your treaty not deny? With a ruthlessness unparalleled your treaty in a dozen instances runs counter to the divine law of nationality. Peoples who speak the same language, kneel at the same ancestral tombs, moved by the same traditions, animated by a common hope, are torn asunder*, broken in pieces, divided, and parcelled out to antagonistic nations. And this you call justice. This, you cry, means peace. [...]

No; your treaty means injustice. It means slavery. It means war. And to all this you ask this Republic to become a party. You ask it to abandon the creed* under which it has grown to power and accept the creed of autocracy, the creed of repression and force. [...]

from: Robert Byrd: The Senate, 1789–1989: Classic Speeches, 1830–1993, ed. by W. Wolff, U.S. Government Printing Office, Washington, pp. 569 f.

asunder apart

creed a set of (religious) beliefs

S 73 Will Dyson

Peace and Future Cannon Fodder

The cartoon below by the Australian cartoonist Will Dyson was published in the British *Daily Herald* on 13 May 1919, about one month before the Treaty of Versailles was signed.

Pre-task
1. What does the title of the cartoon reveal about the cartoonist's stance? Discuss.

Tasks
2. Describe the cartoon and its composition.
3. Explain in detail the elements of the cartoon, including its title.
4. Evaluate the cartoonist's view on the Treaty of Versailles from a <u>contemporary</u> perspective: was it a "peace" or rather an "armistice for twenty years"?

Embedded text:
The Tiger: "Curious! I seem to hear a child weeping!"
1940 CLASS (above the child's head)
PEACE TREATY (on the scroll of paper at the bottom of the pillar)

Language support

cannon fodder Kanonenfutter •
to weep weinen

Säule pillar • **Zylinder** top hat •
Gehstock cane

S 74 John Maynard Keynes
The Economic Consequences of the Peace

In 1920, the English economist John Maynard Keynes analysed how the Treaty of Versailles would affect not only Germany economically, but other countries as well.

Pre-task
1. The given chapter begins with the sentence "This chapter must be one of pessimism." What might an economist most likely criticize about the effect of Versailles on Germany and other countries? Hypothesize.

Tasks
2. Divide the source into sense units and find headings for each. With the help of your headings, double-check your ideas from task 1.
3. Explain the references to the "Council of Four" (l. 8) by incorporating Keynes's remarks into the historical context.
4. Give an evaluation of Keynes's view, against the backdrop of the question as to what extent the Treaty of Versailles was just an "armistice for twenty years".
5. Discuss in how far Keynes's 1920 assessment of the Treaty of Versailles played into the hands of right-wing propaganda against the Weimar Republic, including, for example, National Socialist propaganda.

This chapter must be one of pessimism. The Treaty includes no provisions for the economic rehabilitation of Europe, – nothing to make the defeated Central Empires into good neighbors, nothing to stabilize the new States of Europe, nothing to reclaim Russia; nor does it promote in any way a compact of economic solidar-
5 ity amongst the Allies themselves; no arrangement was reached at Paris for restoring the disordered finances of France and Italy, or to adjust the systems of the Old World and the New.
The Council of Four paid no attention to these issues, being preoccupied* with others, – Clemenceau to crush the economic life of his enemy, Lloyd George to do
10 a deal and bring home something which would pass muster* for a week, the President to do nothing that was not just and right. It is an extraordinary fact that the fundamental economic problems of a Europe starving and disintegrating before their eyes, was the one question in which it was impossible to arouse the interest of the Four. Reparation was their main excursion into the economic field, and
15 they settled it as a problem of theology, of politics, of electoral chicane*, from every point of view except that of the economic future of the States whose destiny they were handling…
The essential facts of the situation, as I see them, are expressed simply. Europe consists of the densest aggregation* of population in the history of the world. This
20 population is accustomed to* a relatively high standard of life, in which, even now, some sections of it anticipate improvement rather than deterioration*. In relation to other continents Europe is not self-sufficient; in particular it cannot feed itself. Internally the population is not evenly distributed, but much of it is crowded into a relatively small number of dense industrial centers. This population secured for
25 itself a livelihood before the war, without much margin of surplus, by means of a delicate and immensely complicated organization, of which the foundations were supported by coal, iron, transport, and an unbroken supply of imported food and

to be preoccupied to be busy with
to pass muster to reach the expected or necessary standard

chicane [ʃɪˈkeɪn] deception, trickery, chicanery, a part of a road, especially a track for racing cars, with a bend shaped like the letter 'S' (*Hindernis im Motorsport*)
aggregation *Verdichtung*
accustomed to used to
deterioration [dɪˌtɪərɪəˈreɪʃ(ə)n] worsening

to deprive sb. of sth. to take sth. away from sb.
redundant unnecessary

rapid quick

remnant a small, remaining part of sth.

raw materials from other continents. By the destruction of this organization and the interruption of the stream of supplies, a part of this population is deprived of* its means of livelihood. Emigration is not open to the redundant* surplus. For it would take years to transport them overseas, even, which is not the case, if countries could be found which were ready to receive them. The danger confronting us, therefore, is the rapid* depression of the standard of life of the European populations to a point which will mean actual starvation for some (a point already reached in Russia and approximately reached in Austria). Men will not always die quietly. For starvation, which brings to some lethargy and a helpless despair, drives other temperaments to the nervous instability of hysteria and to a mad despair. And these in their distress may overturn the remnants* of organization, and submerge civilization itself in their attempts to satisfy desperately the overwhelming needs of the individual. This is the danger against which all our resources and courage and idealism must now co-operate.

Excerpt from THE ECONOMIC CONSEQUENCES OF THE PEACE by John Maynard Keynes. Copyright © 1920 by Houghton Mifflin Harcourt. Publishing renewed 1948 by Lydia Lopokova Keynes. Reprinted by permission of Houghton Mifflin Harcourt Publishing Company. All rights reserved.

The League of Nations (Völkerbund)

The League of Nations as an instrument for keeping peace and to "make the world safe for democracy" was proposed by US President Wilson in his "14 Points" (cf. S 67). However, the USA did not join the League (cf. e.g. S 72). Headquartered in Geneva, Switzerland, the League was organized around its Secretariat, led by a Secretary-General.
Decisions were to be made in the Assembly which met once a year and was attended by three delegates per country. However, decisions required unanimity, which was never achieved, and so motions were passed on to the Council.
The great powers at that time (GB, F, I, Japan) had a permanent seat there and met up to four times a year as well as in times of crisis. By unanimous decision, they could impose (moral/economic/military) sanctions on nations that had violated the peace.
Legal disputes between nations were dealt with by the Court at The Hague (NL) and special world problems (e.g. the spread of diseases) were dealt with in the Commissions. Finally, there was the ILO (International Labour Organization), concerned with the surveillance of working conditions world-wide and with establishing a code of good practice.
By 1933, the League had 33 members, but immediately after the war, the defeated nations had not been allowed to join, and neither was Russia (because of the communist government) – at least until 1934.
As far as the League's power and effectiveness were concerned, they could condemn countries by expressing their disapproval (but usually to little avail). Another possibility was the imposition of economic sanctions and also military force. Since the League did not have its own army, it had to rely on the militarily strong members (e.g. GB, F) to assert its demands.

The semi-official emblem of the League of Nations, used from 1939 to 1941

"The Gap in the Bridge". Cartoon by Leonard Raven-Hill, making fun of the "gap" caused by the USA not joining the League of Nations. British *Punch* magazine, 10 December 1920

S 75 The League of Nations

Covenant (Excerpts)

The Covenant of the League of Nations was adopted in Paris on 29 April 1919. The USA, however, did not join the League.

Pre-task 1. Make a connection between the foreword to the League's Covenant and the given cartoon: what would the cartoonist say to the goals agreed on by the member states, and why?

A cartoon entitled 'Overweighted', depicting Woodrow Wilson handing a heavy olive branch, representing the League of Nations, to a dove of peace, 1919

Foreword to the Articles of the Covenant of the League of Nations:

THE HIGH CONTRACTING PARTIES,
In order to promote international co-operation and to achieve international peace and security
by the acceptance of obligations not to resort to war,
5 by the prescription of open, just and honourable relations between nations,
by the firm establishment of the understandings of international law as the actual rule of conduct among Governments, and
by the maintenance of justice and a scrupulous* respect for all
10 treaty obligations in the dealings of organised peoples with one another,
Agree to this Covenant of the League of Nations.

Preamble to the Covenant of the League of Nations, Versailler Treaty, June 28, 1919, in: C. H. Ellis: The Origin, Structure & Working of the League of Nations, The Lawbook Exchange, Ltd., 2003, p. 487

---

scrupulous [ˈskruːpjʊləs] very careful to be honest and to do what is morally correct

Tasks

2. Outline the agreements and mutual obligations contained in the Covenant.
3. Explain the message of the cartoon "Overweighted" against the backdrop of the text.
4. Discuss strengths and potential weaknesses of the League of Nations.
5. Evaluate to what extent Wilson's "14 Points" (cf. S 67) were put into practice in the Covenant.

[...] ARTICLE 2
The action of the League under this Covenant shall be effected through the instrumentality of an Assembly and of a Council, with a permanent Secretariat. [...]
ARTICLE 5
[...] Except where otherwise expressly provided in this Covenant or by the terms of the present Treaty, decisions at any meeting of the Assembly or of the Council shall require the agreement of all the Members of the League represented at the meeting. [...]
ARTICLE 8
The Members of the League recognise that the maintenance of peace requires the reduction of national armaments to the lowest point consistent with national safety and the enforcement by common action of international obligations*. [...]
ARTICLE 11
Any war or threat of war, whether immediately affecting any of the Members of the League or not, is hereby declared a matter of concern to the whole League, and the League shall take any action that may be deemed* wise and effectual to safeguard the peace of nations. In case any such emergency should arise the Secretary General shall on the request of any Member of the League forthwith* summon a meeting of the Council. [...]
ARTICLE 16
Should any Member of the League resort to war [...], it shall ipso facto* be deemed to have committed an act of war against all other Members of the League, which hereby undertake immediately to subject it to the severance* of all trade or financial relations, the prohibition of all intercourse between their nationals and the nationals of the covenant-breaking State, and the prevention of all financial, commercial or personal intercourse between the nationals of the covenant-breaking State and the nationals of any other State, whether a Member of the League or not. It shall be the duty of the Council in such case to recommend to the several Governments concerned what effective military, naval or air force the Members of the League shall severally contribute to the armed forces to be used to protect the covenants of the League. [...]

Preamble to the Covenant of the League of Nations, Versailles Treaty, June 28, 1919, in: C. H. Ellis: The Origin, Structure & Working of the League of Nations, The Lawbook Exchange, Ltd., 2003, p. 487 ff.

obligation sth. one must do, for legal or moral reasons

to deem halten für

forthwith immediately

ipso facto (Lat.: "by the fact itself") used for showing that sth. is true or obvious because of a fact that has just been mentioned

severance ['sev(ə)rəns] the process of ending sth.

American cartoon by Daniel Fitzpatrick, satirizing the doubters of the League of Nations in the USA. Published in the St. Louis Post (date unknown)

CONNECT

The League of Nations

S 76 — **Making the World Safe for Democracy?**

Task Learning from history? In 1943, at the Tehran Conference, the Allies decided to replace the League of Nations with a new body, the United Nations. The last official meeting of the League of Nations took place in Geneva in 1946.

Split the class into two halves. One half is going to do further research on one of the "successes" of the League of Nations, namely the case of the Åland Islands in the Baltic Sea (1920–21). The other half is going to do further research on one of its "failures", in this case the so-called "Far Eastern Crisis" or "Mukden/Manchurian Incident" (1931).

Back in class, find a partner who has worked on the other research task. Team up and inform each other, focussing on:
- what the conflict was about,
- how the League of Nations reacted and
- the outcome of the conflict.

Together, discuss which strengths and which weaknesses of the League of Nations become apparent. Then write a piece of advice for the participants of the Tehran Conference who are about to decide on the organisation of the new body, the United Nations: what aspects should they keep, which changes do you consider necessary? For further food of thought on this question, you could also check http://nigelgraves.co.uk/history/league.htm.

Do follow-up research on exactly this question: what was kept and which changes were made when the League of Nations was turned into the United Nations? In your comparison, do not only focus on structural or organizational aspects, but also on the praise or the criticism both organisations were and still are confronted with. The website of the UN also offers important information on its history. (www.un.org)

The Palace of Nations (Palais des Nations) in Geneva, Switzerland.
Built between 1929 and 1939, it was the headquarters of the League of Nations and, since 1946, it has functioned as the headquarters of the United Nations.

S 77 Michael Gove

Why Does the Left Insist on Belittling True British Heroes?

On 2 January 2014, then British Secretary for Education Michael Gove wrote an article for the *Daily Mail* in which he presents his view on how the First World War should be commemorated.

Pre-tasks

1. In order to commemorate the centenary of the outbreak of war, there was an art installation at the Tower of London, created by artist Paul Cummins and realized by theatre designer Tom Piper. The art installation was entitled "Blood-swept Lands and Seas of Red", inspired by the words of a soldier fighting in Flanders who described the scenery as the "blood-swept lands and seas of red where angels fear to tread". The art installation consisted of 884,246 ceramic poppy flowers, each representing one British/Commonwealth soldier who died during the First World War. Have a look at the two pictures of the artwork. What kind of commemoration do they suggest: a time for sorrow or a time for pride? Give reasons for your answer.

The Tower of London clad in red ceramic poppies

2. Read the headline of Gove's article. Anticipate what kind of commemoration Gove would probably suggest: a time for sorrow or a time for pride?

Tasks

3. Point out Gove's view on how the First World War should be commemorated and describe the "misunderstandings and misrepresentations" (ll. 18 f.) he attempts to clarify.
4. Revise the historical context of the First World War and collect arguments with which to disprove Gove's position of commemorating the war not only with sorrow, but also with pride. Put special emphasis on the war as the first "modern" and "total" war.
5. Put Mr. Gove on the Hot Seat! (cf. p. 279 for an explanation of the method).

Post-tasks

6. The "Poppy Appeal" on Remembrance Day, as celebrated in the Commonwealth countries, has often been criticized, too. Do further research on what in particular is criticized in this connection (look for "white poppies" or "purple poppies", for instance).
7. In Britain (as well as in France), the First World War is called the "Great War". Discuss why this is not the case in Germany.
8. Germany does not celebrate Remembrance Day in a way that attracts substantial media attention. Discuss if Germany should celebrate Remembrance Day, and if so, how. Make a list of suggestions.

The past has never had a better future. Because history is enjoying a renaissance in Britain. After years in which the study of history was declining in our schools, the numbers of young people showing an appetite for learning about the past, and a curiosity about our nation's story, is growing once more. [...]

5 [C]hallenges we face today – great power rivalry, migrant populations on the move, rapid social upheaval, growing global economic interdependence, massive technological change and fragile confidence in political elites – are all challenges our forebears faced. Indeed, these particular forces were especially powerful one hundred years ago – on the eve of the First World War. Which is why it is so important
10 that we commemorate, and learn from, that conflict in the right way in the next four years. The Government wants to give young people from every community the chance to learn about the heroism, and sacrifice, of our great-grandparents, which is why we are organising visits to the battlefields of the Western Front.

The war was, of course, an unspeakable tragedy, which robbed this nation of our
15 bravest and best. But even as we recall that loss and commemorate the bravery of those who fought, it's important that we don't succumb to some of the myths which have grown up about the conflict.

Our understanding of the war has been overlaid by misunderstandings, and misrepresentations which reflect an, at best, ambiguous attitude to this country and,
20 at worst, an unhappy compulsion* on the part of some to denigrate* virtues such as patriotism, honour and courage.

The conflict has, for many, been seen through the fictional prism of dramas such as Oh! What a Lovely War, The Monocled Mutineer and Blackadder,* as a misbegotten shambles* – a series of catastrophic mistakes perpetrated by an out-of-
25 touch elite. [...]

Professor Sir Richard Evans, the Cambridge historian and Guardian writer, has criticised those who fought, arguing, 'the men who enlisted in 1914 may have thought they were fighting for civilisation, for a better world, a war to end all wars, a war to defend freedom: they were wrong'.
30 And he has attacked the very idea of honouring their sacrifice as an exercise in 'narrow tub-thumping* jingoism'. [...]

The First World War may have been a uniquely horrific war, but it was also plainly a just war. [...] The ruthless social Darwinism of the German elites, the pitiless approach they took to occupation, their aggressively expansionist war aims and their
35 scorn* for the international order all made resistance more than justified. And the war was also seen by participants as a noble cause. Historians have skilfully demonstrated how those who fought were not dupes* but conscious believers in king and country, committed to defending the western liberal order.

compulsion a very strong feeling of wanting to do sth.
to denigrate ['denɪˌgreɪt] to defame, to slander, to blacken, to put down, to find fault with
Oh! What a Lovely War musical that ironically ciriticises WWI
The Monocled Mutineer British TV series dramatizing the life of an army deserter
Blackadder comedy series featuring Rowan Atkinson
shambles sth. that is very badly organised
tub-thumping loud and determined in the way you express you opinion

scorn contempt, disrespect

dupe Tölpel

to acquire sth.; acquisition (n.) to gain or obtain sth.
advantageous [ˌædvənˈteɪdʒəs] **(adj.); advantage (n.) (opp.: disadvantageous; disadvantage)** *vorteilhaft; Vorteil (unvorteilhaft, nachteilig; Nachteil)*
affluent [ˈæfluːənt] **(adj.); affluence (n.)** wealthy; wealth/prosperity
antagonism [ænˈtæɡəˌnɪz(ə)m] feelings of hatred and opposition
armistice truce, ceasefire
to assassinate sb.; assassination (n.); assassin (n.) *ein Attentat auf jdn. verüben; Attentat; Attentäter*
barbed wire *Stacheldraht*
to begrudge to envy
breadline the level of income of very poor people
casualty [ˈkæʒuəlti] sb. who is injured or killed in an accident or military action
cataclysmic [ˌkætəˈklɪzmɪk] **(adj.); cataclysm (n.)** catastrophic, disastrous, destructive; disaster, catastrophe
child labour *Kinderarbeit*
to civilize *zivilisieren*
to compete for sth.; competition (n.); competitor (n.) *um etw. in Wettstreit treten; Wettstreit; Konkurrent*
to conscript sb.; conscription (n.) *jdn. einziehen; Wehrpflicht*
customs (pl.); tariff; toll *Zoll; Zollgebühr; Zoll/Maut*
decline (v.; n.) a continual decrease in the number, quality or value of sth.
to deteriorate [dɪˈtɪəriəreɪt]; **deterioration (n.) (opp.: to improve; improvement)** to become worse (to become better)
to disintegrate; disintegration (n.) to fall apart
to dispossess sb.; dispossession (n.) (syn.: to expropriate; expropriation) to take away sb.'s possessions/property
division of labour *Arbeitsteilung*
to encircle; encirclement (n.) *einkreisen/umzingeln; Einkreisung/Umzingelung*
to enslave sb. to make sb. a slave
entrepreneur [ˌɒntrəprəˈnɜː(r)]; **entrepreneurial (adj.)** *Unternehmer; unternehmerisch*
to expand, expansion (n.) to grow, to extend, to augment, to spread
to exploit, exploitation (n.) *ausbeuten, Ausbeutung*
to extradite sb.; extradition (n.) to send to another place by force, to officially send sb. who has been accused or found guilty of a crime back to the country where the crime was committed
famine [ˈfæmɪn] *Hungersnot*

free-market economy *freie Marktwirtschaft*
to fuel sth. to feed, to give nourishment, to strengthen
heathen [ˈhiːð(ə)n] **(adj.; n.) (syn.: pagan)** *heidnisch; Heide*
heir [eə(r)], **heiress** [ˈeəres] *Erbe, Erbin*
indemnity reparations
indigenous [ɪnˈdɪdʒənəs] native
inferior (ad.); inferiority (n.) (opp.: superior, superiority) (+ to sb./sth.) *unterlegen; Unterlegenheit (überlegen, Überlegenheit)*
to intensify; intensification (n.) to increase in degree or strength
iron [ˈaɪə(r)n] **ore; pig iron** *Eisenerz; Roheisen*
jingoism (chauvinism) *Hurrapatriotismus*
to justify; justification (n.) *rechtfertigen; Rechtfertigung*
to meet demands (supply and demand) *der Nachfrage nachkommen (Angebot und Nachfrage)*
outbreak (of war) *(Kriegs-)Ausbruch*
outlet market *Absatzmarkt*
outpost here: a small place far away from other towns, usually where trading takes place
to partition to divide into parts
periphery [pəˈrɪf(ə)ri] the outer part of an area, far from the centre
(coal) pit *(Kohlen-)Grube*
plant here: factory
poison gas *Giftgas*
to proselytize [ˈprɒs(ə)lətaɪz] **(syn.: to missionize)** to try to persuade people to share your religious or political beliefs
protectorate *Protektorat; Schutzgebiet*
raw materials *Rohstoffe*
sense of mission *Sendungsbewusstsein*
serf, serfdom *Leibeigener, Leibeigenschaft*
to settle; settlement (n.); settler (n.) *sich niederlassen/besiedeln; Niederlassung/Siedlung; Siedler/in*
to sever [ˈsevə(r)] **diplomatic relations** *diplomatische Beziehungen abbrechen*
skilled worker *Facharbeiter/in*
social security system *Sozialversicherungssystem*
to specialize in sth.; specialization (n.) *sich auf etw. spezialisieren; Spezialisierung*
sphere of influence *Einflussbereich*
steam engine *Dampfmaschine*
stalemate *Pattsituation*
to starve; starvation (n.) to suffer or die because there is not enough food
steam engine *Dampfmaschine*
stronghold *Bollwerk, Festung, Hochburg*

subsistence the smallest amount of food one needs to stay alive
surplus more of sth. than is necessary
to take possession of sth. *etw. in Besitz nehmen*
tank *Panzer*
trade union *Gewerkschaft*
trench; trench warfare *Schützengraben; Grabenkrieg*

tycoon a rich and powerful person who is involved in business or industry
wage worker; day labourer *Lohnarbeiter; Tagelöhner*
war of attrition *Abnutzungskrieg, Zermürbungskrieg*
weapons of mass destruction (WMDs) *Massenvernichtungswaffen*
welfare *Sozialhilfe, Fürsorge*

National Socialism –

- Political and Ideological Preconditions for National Socialism
- Causes and Consequences of the World Economic Crisis of 1929
- National Socialist Rule Over Germany and Europe

Members of the workers' and soldiers' councils demonstrating in Berlin, November 1918

Hitler and Hindenburg shaking hands, Day of Potsdam

9 Nov 1918	June 1919	23 Oct 1929	30 Jan 1933	4 Feb 1933	23 Mar 1933	2 Aug 1933
Wilhelm II abdicates/ proclamation of the Weimar Republic	Signing of the Versailles Peace Treaty	Wall Street stock market crash	Hitler appointed Reich Chancellor	Suspension of basic rights/ *Verordnung des Reichspräsidenten zum Schutz von Volk und Staat*	Enabling Act	Hindenburg dies/ presidency and chancellorship combined under Hitler

Germans' Nemesis Up to Today?

Cologne in ruins at the end of WWII, 1945

Task Take into consideration the photos and the timeline provided and recall your knowledge about how Germany turned from democracy to dictatorship. Come up with at least three questions you would like this chapter to answer about the topic. Share your questions in class.

15 Sept 1935	9 Nov 1938	1 Sept 1939	20 Jan 1942	Nov–Dez 1943	Feb 1945	8 May 1945
Nuremberg Laws	*Reichspogromnacht*/ November pogrom	German attack on Poland/WWII starts	Wannsee Conference/ "Final solution" to the Jewish question	Tehran Conference of the "Big Three"	Yalta Conference on Europe's postwar organization	German unconditional surrender

Topics & Key Questions	Key Terms	Translations
Political and Ideological Preconditions for National Socialism		
Establishing the Republic • The "revolution from above": Why was a democratic regime born out of Germany's defeat? • What were the strengths and weaknesses of the Weimar Constitution?	• November Revolution • sailors' mutiny • workers' and soldiers' councils • Council of the People's Deputies • Spartacists • Imperial Council Convention • parliamentary vs. council democracy • Weimar Coalition (Centre Party/SPD/DDP) • Weimar Constitution • emergency decree (article 48) • Basic Rights	• Novemberrevolution • Matrosenaufstand • Arbeiter- und Soldatenräte • Rat der Volksbeauftragten • Spartakus-Gruppe • Reichsrätekongress • parlamentarische vs. Rätedemokratie • Weimarer Koalition (Zentrum/SPD/DDP) • Weimarer Verfassung • Notverordnung (Artikel 48) • Grundrechte
1918–1923: Crises • Which impact did the challenge from the political Left have and how strong was the challenge from the political Right? • Why did the Weimar Republic survive the years of crises?	• Ebert-Groener pact • free corps • Spartacist Uprising • Kapp Putsch • fulfilment policy • Ruhr occupation (passive resistance) • political assassinations • hyperinflation • Munich Beer Hall Putsch	• Ebert-Groener-Pakt • Freikorps • Spartakusaufstand • Kapp-Putsch • Erfüllungspolitik • Ruhrbesetzung (passiver Widerstand) • politische Morde • Hyperinflation • Hitlerputsch
1923–1929: Recovery • Was Stresemann a good European or a good German? • In how far is the term "recovery" (in)appropriate to describe the years 1923–1929?	• "Golden Twenties" • Dawes Plan • policy of détente • Treaty of Locarno • League of Nations • Young Plan • Treaty of Rapallo	• „Goldene Zwanziger" • Dawes Plan • Entspannungspolitik • Vertrag von Locarno • Völkerbund • Young Plan • Vertrag von Rapallo
Causes and Consequences of the World Economic Crisis of 1929		
1929–1933: Collapse • What were the causes and the consequences of the world economic crisis of 1929? • Why was the NSDAP so successful from 1930 to 1932?	• Great Depression/slump • Wall Street Crash/Black Friday • Grand Coalition • Presidential Cabinets • deflationary policy • "Cabinet of Barons"	• Große Depression/Abschwung • Börsencrash/Schwarzer Freitag • Große Koalition • Präsidialkabinette • Deflationspolitik • „Kabinett der Barone"

• January 30, 1933: "seizure of power", "takeover of power", "handing-over of power" or "sneaking into power"? • Was the Weimar Republic doomed to fail? Why (not)?		

National Socialist Rule Over Germany and Europe

NS Ideology • How did anti-Semitism change through history? • Where can the origins of Nazi ideology be found and why was it so appealing to some parts of Weimar society? • How did the Nazis ensure that their ideas were spread among the people?	• 25-Points Programme • anti-Semitism • Social Darwinism • leader principle • People's Community • "Aryan master race" • living space • Ministry of Public Enlightenment and Propaganda • "euthanasia"	• 25-Punkte-Programm • Antisemitismus • Sozialdarwinismus • Führerprinzip • Volksgemeinschaft • „arische Herrenrasse" • Lebensraum • Reichsministerium für Volksaufklärung und Propaganda • „Euthanasie"
Consolidation of Power – Three Phases • Control at the centre: Why do the Reichstag Fire Decree and the Enabling Act play a prominent role in the Nazi consolidation of power? • Control beyond the centre: Where is the difference between "control at the centre" and "control beyond the centre" and how was the "final stage" prepared? • The final stage: How did Hitler win the support of the army? • Which preconditions for the establishment of a dictatorship were implemented by the completion of the third phase?	• Reichstag Fire • Decree for the Protection of People and State ("Reichstag Fire Decree") • Enabling Act • SA (storm troopers) • Day of Potsdam • Gleichschaltung/Bringing into Line • German Labour Front • "Law against the establishment of political parties" • Concordat • Night of the Long Knives • SS/SD/Gestapo	• Reichstagsbrand • Verordnung des Reichspräsidenten zum Schutz von Volk und Staat („Reichstagsbrandverordnung") • Ermächtigungsgesetz • SA (Sturmabteilung) • Tag von Potsdam • Gleichschaltung • Deutsche Arbeitsfront (DAF) • „Gesetz gegen die Neubildung von Parteien" • Konkordat • Röhm-Putsch • SS (Schutzstaffel)/SD (Sicherheitsdienst)/Gestapo (Geheime Staatspolizei)
Life Under Nazi Control • How successful was Nazi economic policy? • What role did Nazi ideology envisage for women? • How were the minds of the German youth won by the Nazis? • Was there any kind of opposition to the regime and what was it like?	• Four-year plan • League of German Girls/National Socialist Women's League • Reich Labour Service • Hitler Youth • resistance • Confessing Church • 20 July plot • Kreisau Circle	• Vierjahresplan • Bund Deutscher Mädel/Nationalsozialistische Frauenschaft • Reichsarbeitsdienst • Hitlerjugend • Widerstand • Bekennende Kirche • Attentat vom 20. Juli 1944 • Kreisauer Kreis

Foreign Policy: From Triumph to Disaster • Which factors made Hitler's foreign policy so successful until 1939? • To what extent did appeasement policy make the Nazis stronger?	• appeasement policy • Hossbach Memorandum • Munich Agreement • Rome-Berlin Axis	• Beschwichtigungspolitik • Hoßbach-Niederschrift • Münchner Abkommen • Achse Berlin-Rom
The Second World War • How did the ideological features of the Third Reich contribute to enhancing Hitler's means of waging war? • How did Hitler ensure that his war plans could be realized? • To what extent can the Second World War be considered as totally different from all other previous wars?	• Blitzkrieg • Hitler-Stalin Pact/Additional Secret Protocol • Battle of Britain • Operation Barbarossa • Battle of Stalingrad • Pearl Harbor • Atlantic Charter • D-Day/Operation Overlord • total war • unconditional surrender • war of annihilation	• Blitzkrieg • Hitler-Stalin-Pakt/Geheimes Zusatzprotokoll • Luftschlacht um England • Operation Barbarossa • Schlacht um Stalingrad • Pearl Harbor • Atlantik-Charta • D-Day/Operation Overlord • totaler Krieg • bedingungslose Kapitulation • Vernichtungskrieg
The Holocaust/Shoa • By which steps was the disenfranchisement of the Jews accomplished? • Why was the "final solution to the Jewish question" not implemented before the outbreak of WWII?	• Holocaust/Shoa • deportation • concentration/extermination camps • Aryanization • Nuremberg Laws of Citizenship and Race • "Night of Broken Glass"/November Pogrom • "final solution to the Jewish question"/Wannsee minutes • genocide	• Holocaust/Shoa • Deportation • Konzentrationslager/Vernichtungslager • Arisierung • Nürnberger Rassegesetze • „Reichskristallnacht"/Novemberprogrom • „Endlösung der Judenfrage"/Wannseeprotokoll • Genozid, Völkermord

Political and Ideological Preconditions for National Socialism

Establishing the Republic

⇨ S 1–5

The First World War did not only bring about drastic changes for the European societies, it also profoundly influenced the international system of politics. Returning to the old order was no longer an option for the countries involved in the "great seminal catastrophe of the (twentieth) century", as US historian and former diplomat George F. Kennan put it. One driving factor amongst others for the establishment of a democratic political system in what was then the German Empire was the American notion of self-determination of the people. This had been one reason why the USA entered WWI, and therefore the USA demanded a democratisation of its war enemies. Added to that, the mobilisation of the masses since August 1914 and the participation of left-wing parties in political decision-making contributed to widespread expectations in terms of increased political rights. Hence, a boost of democracy seemed inevitable. Furthermore, WWI had crushed the liberal economic system of the 19th century and had destroyed the prosperity of a large number of people. On the other hand, it had definitely boosted the arms industry. A new economic order was, however, not about to come about on its own.

Surprisingly enough, the first impulses for a reform of the political system in Germany came from the German Military High Command* itself, according to which every continuation of the war would have meant a threat of German territories being occupied and an aggravation* of peace conditions after the fall of Bulgaria in September 1918. Hence, the High Command not only demanded an immediate request* for an armistice but also the setting up of a civil government including the existing political parties. The new chancellor of the Reich, Prince Max of Baden, agreed to an armistice and addressed US President Woodrow Wilson on 3 October 1918. Shortly afterwards, a mass movement started when orders were given that the German fleet should leave the port of Wilhelmshaven on 29 October 1918 for the North Sea. The sailors feared that this, in military terms, senseless manoeuvre* would endanger the efforts for peace and so they started to demonstrate – the **November Revolution*** began. Navy officials arrested about 1,000 sailors, which then triggered a broad display of solidarity among sailors, soldiers and workers. This was the beginning of the **sailors' mutinies*** in Kiel and other large ports of the North Sea during which the first **workers' and soldiers' councils*** were founded. Soon, these councils spontaneously formed all over Germany as organs of an emerging desire for self-administration or **grassroots democracy***. The established political parties had to somehow react to this new mass movement and to its demands (e.g. abdication of the German emperor Wilhelm II, political reforms) and thus, also in order not to lose influence over the development, the party leadership of the SPD decided to take over control. The Social Democrat Philipp Scheidemann proclaimed* the republic on 9 November 1918, after Prince Max of Baden had declared that Emperor Wilhelm II would abdicate and, on the same day, Baden transferred his office of Reich Chancellor to Friedrich Ebert, leading member of the SPD. In the prevailing revolutionary situation, however, this process was not sufficient to legitimize the new government since the population wanted a clear cut with the old system. The SPD then offered to the USPD (Independent Socialist Party) negotiations about the

Military High Command Oberste Heeresleitung (OHL)

aggravation worsening of a situation

request question or petition

manoeuvre [məˈnuvər] military practice, operation

November Revolution Novemberrevolution

sailors' mutiny Matrosenaufstand

workers' and soldiers' councils Arbeiter- und Soldatenräte

grassroots democracy Basisdemokratie

to proclaim to announce, to declare

joint common, shared

Council of the People's Deputies Rat der Volksbeauftragten

Spartacists Spartakus-Gruppe

amnesty pardon, often by government

proportional representation Verhältniswahlrecht

constituent assembly verfassungsgebende Versammlung

inconsistent contradictory, conflicting

parliamentary democracy parlamentarische Demokratie

council democracy Rätedemokratie

Imperial Council Convention Reichsrätekongress

to be in session tagen

to dispossess sb. of sth. to deprive sb. of sth.

majority vote Mehrheitswahlrecht

creation of a joint* revolutionary government. The USPD rejected any participation of middle-class politicians in such a government, but agreed to the formation of a **Council of the People's Deputies*** under the joint leadership of Friedrich Ebert (SPD) and Hugo Haase (USPD), consisting of three SPD and three USPD politicians respectively.

A majority of the workers euphorically welcomed this agreement between both socialist parties as the long-expected victory of the working class but there were critical voices nonetheless, such as from the left wing of the USPD, and especially from the **Spartacists*** led by Rosa Luxemburg and Karl Liebknecht. Both socialist parties had in common that they wanted to abolish censorship and introduce an amnesty* for political crimes and a new system of suffrage (women's suffrage, lowering the voting age to 20, introduction of proportional representation*). However, the parties differed in their idea of a constituent assembly* due to their inconsistent* ideas about how to turn Germany into a democratic state, i.e. what form of democracy and what kind of national assembly should be installed. The SPD opted for a **parliamentary democracy*** whereas the USPD favoured a **council democracy***. Eventually, the SPD succeeded in preparing a constitutional convention. From 16 to 18 December 1918, the so-called **Imperial Council Convention*** was in session* in Berlin and after long and hard discussions they agreed on elections for a national assembly at the earliest possible date, namely 19 January 1919. Until that date, the convention had complete executive and legislative power in order to dispossess* competing institutions of any legitimacy to govern Germany (cf. S1, S2). The elections for the national assembly were then held on 19 January 1919 as planned according to the new system of proportional representation (in contrast to the former majority vote* of the former empire). Furthermore, the voting age was reduced to 20 and women were given the right to vote. As to the election result, Germany experienced a jolt to the left: the Centre Party (together with the Bavarian People's Party) gained 19.7 per cent of the votes, the DDP (German Democratic Party) 18.5 per cent and the SPD 37.9 per cent of the votes. Voter participation figures were high

From left to right: Wilhelm Dittmann, Otto Landsberg, Hugo Haase, Friedrich Ebert, Emil Barth, Philipp Scheidemann

at 83 per cent and 36.8 million people were eligible to vote*. On 11 February 1919, the national assembly elected Friedrich Ebert as Reichspräsident (President of the Reich) and head of state and Ebert then established a coalition of SPD, Centre Party and DDP, the so-called **Weimar Coalition***.

Apart from achieving peace, the most important task of the national assembly was to create a constitution (quite similar to the position of the national assembly in 1848) and after six months of consultation, the **Weimar Constitution*** (cf. S5) came into effect* on 14 August 1919. With this constitution, the new republic clearly distanced itself from the idea of a council democracy as wished for by the USPD. The position of the Reichstag (parliament) was strengthened in comparison to the constitution of 1871, and the Reichsrat (chamber of the federal states) was limited to an advisory role in terms of legislation. This meant that the Reichstag had far more power and influence. The same was true for the Reichspräsident, whose power became obvious in connection with the instrument of the so-called **emergency decree (article 48)***. A new aspect was the introduction of plebiscitary elements*, which formed a counterweight to the Reichstag. Plebiscites* were possible if the Reichspräsident submitted a law, which had already been passed by the Reichstag, to the people before it came into effect or if a bill* was entertained* in a plebiscite by at least ten per cent of the voters. Originally, the **Basic Rights*** section was supposed to be kept rather short, however, it grew larger during long discussions. The problem, however, was that due to the fact that it was the parliament's task to fill those rights with life, they turned out in effect to be of minor value*. Another interesting aspect is that the Basic Rights were put at the very end of the constitution, which shows how unimportant the politicians considered them to be (in contrast to the Paulskirche constitution of 1848/49 and the Basic Law of the Federal Republic of Germany of 1949). Moreover, it was possible to change every Basic Right, like every article of the constitution, with a two-thirds-majority.

1918–1923: Crises

Whereas the USPD could strongly rely on well-organized, fiercely determined workers in the big industrial centres such as Berlin and Central Germany, the moderate SPD was willing to cooperate with the middle-class and representatives of the old order. Under these circumstances, cooperation with the OHL became especially significant and was initiated after a secret telephone call by general Wilhelm Groener (successor of Ludendorff) to Ebert on 10 November 1918. Thus, the **Ebert-Groener pact*** was sealed (cf. S6). For the time being, such a collaboration between the leaders of the OHL and the People's Deputies seemed unavoidable in the light of the impending armistice and the return of the army. However, Groener was also thinking in terms of domestic policy, fearing that the republic might turn out to become even more left-wing oriented. The leaders of the SPD shared this fear. For Ebert, Groener's offer to cooperate with the new government meant that the OHL now officially approved of it. Technically speaking, the OHL was still in charge of governing because Wilhelm II had transferred command to the OHL before he fled. At that time, it was not clear whether the People's Deputies would be able to politically control the OHL and whether a new (republican) army could be established.
A threat to security was the **Spartacist uprising*** of January 1919 (cf. S7). The trigger was the dismissal of the Berlin police superintendent* Emil Eichhorn (USPD). The USPD and the KPD had called for a demonstration against his dismissal.

---

to be eligible to vote *wahlberechtigt sein*
Weimar Coalition *Weimarer Koalition*

Weimar Constitution *Weimarer Verfassung*
to come into effect *in Kraft treten*

emergency decree (article 48) *Notverordnung (Artikel 48)*
plebiscitary [pləˈbɪsɪtəri] **element** *plebiszitäres Element*
plebiscite [ˈplɛbəsaɪt] vote by which the people of a country or region express their opinion for or against an important proposal
bill *Gesetzesentwurf*
to entertain here: to support
Basic Rights *Grundrechte*
to be of minor value to be of less importance, value

⇨ S 6–15

Ebert-Groener pact *Ebert-Groener-Pakt*

Spartacist uprising *Spartakusaufstand*
superintendent *Polizeipräsident*

In the course of these demonstrations, armed Spartacists occupied the publishing house* of the SPD magazine *Vorwärts* and Karl Liebknecht even declared the government dismissed. However, the movement lacked a strong leadership and that is why it eventually failed. The government resorted to* the support of the OHL. Two right-wing **free corps*** groups played a decisive role in suppressing agitation. Former officers had formed them after the regular troops had disbanded over Christmas (cf. S 8). The free corps later continued to play an important role in the future of the Weimar Republic, since they tried to prolong their existence as soldiers in times of peace. Fighting was often their only focus in life and the enemy was no longer identified in terms of the foreign enemies of Germany but in terms of the left-wing movement. Rosa Luxemburg and Karl Liebknecht were arrested by a group of officers and soldiers and then brutally abused and killed on 15 January 1919. The perpetrators* had to face a military court but were only given mild sentences*. One effect of this Spartacist uprising was that the national assembly could not meet in the now rather turbulent Berlin. Instead they met in Weimar, which gave the first German republic its name.

Apart from the burden of the Versailles Treaty and the stab-in-the-back myth (cf. chapter 2), the young republic had to face threats from both the political left and right. Between 1920 and 1923, the republic had to resist two attempted coups from the right. The first happened on 13 March 1920, when Wolfgang Kapp, a senior official* and right-wing politician, was proclaimed new Reich Chancellor after General Walther von Lüttwitz had ordered the occupation of governmental buildings in Berlin. Kapp and Lüttwitz had the support of several free corps, which should, according to the provision of the Treaty of Versailles to reduce Germany's army to 100,000 men, actually have been dissolved. However, the **Kapp Putsch*** failed due to a national strike on the part of the workers and the refusal of civil servants to follow Kapp's orders. As a consequence, workers started to march against the free corps, especially in the Ruhr area, Thuringia* and Saxony, but this fight was settled bloodily by troops of the Reichswehr.

The year 1923 in particular was one of perpetual crisis. Fulfilling the reparation payments was an enormous burden and obstacle for the German government. Germany's aim was to keep the payments relatively low whereas the victorious powers wanted to be compensated for their losses at all costs, regardless of what damage this would do to Germany's productive and financial capacities. France even had the long-term weakening of Germany's economy and military in mind since it was not totally convinced that this could be achieved through the provisions of the Versailles Treaty alone. After several government crises, the advocates of the so-called **fulfilment policy*** prevailed*. They were eager to strictly adhere* to the reparation provisions. The plan was to show to the victorious powers that the compensation demands were unrealisable, would cause a financial crisis, and would thus have to be revised. France in particular did not believe in such a scenario and when Germany fell behind* with its payments, France occupied the Ruhr area in January 1923 (**Ruhr occupation***, cf. S 12). Consequently, German trade unions and the German government called upon the population to start a campaign of **passive resistance*** and to go on strike. Both measures, in turn, had a devastating effect on the German currency*. The rapid loss in value of the Reichsmark developed into soaring* inflation by the autumn of 1923. Not surprisingly, industrial production decreased and the number of people unemployed increased. Wages and salaries could no longer keep up with the prevailing **hyperinflation*** (cf. S 13). To make

---

publishing house *Verlagshaus*

to resort to to make use of, to employ
free corps *Freikorps*

perpetrator criminal
sentence sentence is immiment *(?)*

senior official high-ranking civil servant

Kapp Putsch *Kapp-Putsch*

Thuringia *Thüringen*

fulfilment policy *Erfüllungspolitik*
to prevail to dominate
to adhere [æd'hɪər] **to sth.** to conform to or follow rules exactly
to fall behind with sth. to lag
Ruhr occupation *Ruhrbesetzung*

passive resistance *passiver Widerstand*
currency paper and coin money of a country
soaring high, fast-rising
hyperinflation *Hyperinflation*

matters worse, farmers and retailers* refused to trade in their goods for valueless money, which is why by autumn 1923 a total breakdown of the local supply system was imminent. The population started looting* groceries and blamed the government, which thus lost more and more authority. Hyperinflation did not, however, pose a problem for everybody. One group which even profited from it were clever entrepreneurs (and the owners of material assets* in general) since hyperinflation allowed for the repayment of credit with less valuable money. The second winner of hyperinflation was the state itself whose debt problem had, in effect, nearly vanished as money lost its value. Creditors* (i.e. moneylenders), in contrast, almost totally lost their economic position and banks their equity capital base*.

This fulfilment policy had also been the reason for several **political assassinations*** in 1920/21. The entire period was characterised by a climate of right-wing hate campaigns and assassination attempts on leading democratic politicians. The republic's first minister president Philipp Scheidemann survived an assassination attempt, whereas USPD-politician and former member of the Council of People's Deputies Hugo Haase, Matthias Erzberger (Centre Party) and DDP-politician Walther Rathenau fell victim* to assassinations. With Erzberger and Rathenau, the political terror unfortunately hit two very talented politicians who had also been engaged in a policy of understanding with the victorious powers. After the murder of Rathenau, the Reichstag passed a law to protect the republic, which penalized* conspiracies to political murder and allowed the banning of extremist organizations. The legislation, however, did not have any great influence.

The second putsch attempt from the political right took place on 8 and 9 November 1923 in a beer hall in Munich, and has thus been called the **Munich Beer Hall Putsch*** (cf. S 15). It started when Gustav Ritter von Kahr, an extreme right-wing politician who was in charge of the executive power in Bavaria, made the troops stationed in Bavaria subject* to the command of Munich, thus effectively disempowering* the government in Berlin. General Hans von Seeckt, commander in chief of the German Army, however, refused to interfere militarily. The National Socialist German Workers' Party (NSDAP) and its leader Adolf Hitler played a decisive role

retailer merchant, seller

to loot to steal goods

material asset *Sachwert*

creditor *Gläubiger*
equity capital base *Eigenkapitalbasis*
political assassinations *politische Morde*

to fall victim to sb./sth. *jdm./etw. zum Opfer fallen*

to penalize to punish

Munich Beer Hall Putsch *Hitlerputsch*
to subject sb. to so. *jdn. jdm. unterstellen*
to disempower to deprive of power, to make weak or unimportant

Participants in the putsch in front of the court house

in developments. Already back then, Hitler's rhetorical talent had become apparent and the old right-wing extremists took advantage of that by letting Hitler campaign for their cause. Hitler accused Kahr of having been too cautious and at the end of 1923 he saw the time come to crush "Marxist Berlin". On 8 November Hitler used the occasion of a meeting summoned by Kahr in a Munich beer hall to proclaim the "national rising*". He had armed party members enter the beer hall and declared the Bavarian and Berlin government deposed*. Furthermore, he forced Kahr and von Lossow, the troop commander, to agree to a provisional government. Hitler's plans failed when later both Kahr and Lossow decided otherwise and on 9 November ordered the violent dispersion* of groups of National Socialists who had demonstrated in front of the Feldherrnhalle in Munich. Hitler was arrested and tried for treason* in February 1924 and von Seeckt banned the NSDAP. However, Hitler used the trial against him to attack the Weimar regime and further expound* his views. The judges acquitted* Ludendorff, also a participant in the putsch, and sentenced Hitler to the minimum possible sentence of five years in prison which Hitler did not have to completely serve*. He was released after only nine months.

1923–1929: Recovery

The years of recovery are inextricably* connected with the politician Gustav Stresemann (cf. biography). In 1926, he was even awarded the Nobel Peace Prize together with Aristide Briand, the French foreign minister, for his policy of understanding with France. In terms of foreign trade, Germany was reintegrated into the world market with the help of the USA and thus experienced an economic rebound*.

As chancellor, Stresemann made an important decision, namely to end the passive resistance in the Ruhr area, which had been a reaction to the Ruhr occupation, by stabilising the currency through the introduction of a new currency, the Rentenmark, on 15 November 1923. In fact, the problem of market stabilization could not be solved only by the mere introduction of a new currency as such, what really counted was the stabilization of its value. In order to achieve that, state expenditure* was cut and no new money was printed. Furthermore, Germany's central bank, the Reichsbank, had to embark on* a rather restrictive monetary policy, which unfortunately made credit more expensive. The result was a rising unemployment rate and business failures*.

This financial policy resulted in a division of society not only in terms of working relations but also on a cultural level. On the one hand, a new attitude to life developed especially in Berlin in the so-called **Golden Twenties*** which found its expression in literature, theatre, film, music, painting, design and architecture. These years were shaped by a new direction in arts, the so-called *Neue Sachlichkeit* (New Objectiveness). However, this new development did not find acceptance among the population as a whole. Some harshly criticised it as being decadent and even degenerated*, in the main people who clung to* traditional values and forms of expression. This division also made it difficult for political parties to succeed in forming stable coalitions. The middle-class cabinets between 1924 and 1927, partly with and partly without the DNVP, could rely on the SPD when it came to foreign policy, but in domestic matters the SPD usually played an oppositional role.

Under Stresemann, Germany was soon able to overcome its international isolation, also due, of course, to the fact that the victorious powers had an interest in stable agreements with Germany. The **Dawes Plan*** in 1924 provided for a new settlement of the reparation payments. It refrained* from formulating the complete immediate demand of reparations and instead it defined increasing annual rates between one and 2.5 bn Reichsmark for the years 1924/25 to 1928/29. Furthermore, a reparation agent controlled not only German financial policy but also the transfer of payments to foreign countries, whereby the stability of the German currency had to be taken into account at all times. Thus, one-sided reparation demands were not allowed any more. It was a success for Stresemann that Germany participated equally in the relevant negotiations, in contrast to the situation in 1919. Most important was that Germany again was an internationally accepted credit receiver and US loans in particular contributed to Germany's financial recovery.

In fact, the Dawes Plan was an attempt to stabilize the Versailles system with German acceptance. However, the success of this undertaking remained in doubt as long as there was no understanding between Germany and France. As foreign minister, Stresemann pursued a **policy of détente***. In the **Treaty of Locarno*** (cf. S19) of October 1925, Germany on the one side and France and Belgium on the other side, abstained from* any violent alteration of the existing borders, which then again were guaranteed by England and Italy. The consequence was that Germany entered the **League of Nations*** in 1926. A final solution for the reparation question was eventually found with the help of the **Young Plan*** according to which Germany was to make repayments until 1987/88 (cf. S18). The controls of the Dawes Plan did not apply anymore and French troops had to withdraw from the Rhineland by 30 June 1930.

Stresemann's western-oriented policy can be considered a deliberate decision against a one-sided strategy aiming at a rapprochement* with Russia with regard to foreign affairs. This had been demanded by right-wing conservative politicians after the **Treaty of Rapallo*** (1922). This treaty settled the resumption* of diplomatic relations between Germany and Russia after they had been interrupted by WWI and the Russian Revolution. However, in the Treaty of Berlin (1926), Stresemann promised Germany's neutrality in case Russia went to war with a third power and apart from that, the military cooperation between both states, which allowed for Germany to secretly avoid provisions settled in the Versailles Treaty concerning arms limitation, was continued.

to refrain from to not do

policy of détente *Entspannungspolitik*
Treaty of Locarno *Vertrag von Locarno*
to abstain from sth. cf. to refrain
League of Nations *Völkerbund*
Young Plan *Young-Plan*

rapprochement *Annäherung*

Treaty of Rapallo *Vertrag von Rapallo*
resumption *Wiederaufnahme*

Stresemann, Chamberlain, Briand and von Schubert during negotiations on the Treaty of Locarno, 1925

Causes and Consequences of the World Economic Crisis of 1929

⇨ S 21–26

1929–1933: Collapse

Great Depression/slump *Große Depression/Abschwung*
Wall Street Crash *Börsencrash*
Black Friday *Schwarzer Freitag*

The **Great Depression*** started with a rapid **slump*** followed by the **Wall Street Crash*** on 24 October 1929 and its effects reached Europe the next day, which was a Friday, and thus called **Black Friday***. The events in the USA triggered a worldwide decline in industry and trade. However, the Wall Street Crash was more a symptom than a cause of a crisis which had its roots in the USA. In the 1920s, the USA had, like no other country before, embarked on mass production of consumer goods and had promoted consumer credit. Thus, a slowdown* of demand, high risks of speculation in shares* and the worldwide decline of agricultural prices were enough to start the cataclysm*.

slowdown *Abschwächung*
speculation in shares *Aktienspekulation*
cataclysm *catastrophe*

One reason why the crisis in the USA affected the other industrial countries so fast lies in the fact that the USA had at this time an enormous influence on the world economy. Between 1926 and 1929 the USA was responsible for 42 per cent of the world's industrial production and bought about 40 per cent of the world's most important raw materials while at the same time reducing capital exports, i. e. credit. This led to a massive destabilisation of the already weak European banking system and thus the scope of action* of European governments was limited. The crisis worsened because the USA did not take over responsibility for stabilizing the whole system. As the biggest creditor, it would have been their obligation to open their borders for visible exports* and services for the rest of the world in order to keep the international flow of payments* balanced. Against this background, the European states saw no other alternative but to search for other solutions to the crisis.

scope of action *Handlungsspielraum*

visible export *Warenexport*
flow of payments *Zahlungsströme*

For the young Weimar Republic, the slump had the effect that its moderate economic recovery suddenly came to a stop since foreign loans were now no longer being paid. The unemployment rate increased so sharply that the unemployment insurance bodies could no longer pay their contributions*. The Weimar Coalition (Centre Party/SPD/DDP) broke up over the question of how to reconstruct the unemployment insurance system. On 27 March 1930 the government under chancellor Müller resigned and a new **Grand Coalition*** was formed which effectively meant the end of the parliamentary phase of the Weimar Republic and the beginning of the era of the so-called **Presidential Cabinets***.

contribution *Beitrag*

Grand Coalition *Große Koalition*

Presidential Cabinet *Präsidialkabinett*

to quintuple [kwɪnˈtupəl] *verfünffachen*

New elections were held on 14 September 1930 in which the NSDAP managed to quintuple* their votes in comparison to 1928, making them the second-largest party in the Reichstag. It was not unemployed people who voted for the NSDAP in the first place, they rather voted for the KPD. However, there was a connection between people's confession and their electoral behaviour and it turned out that the NSDAP gained far more support in Protestant communities than in those with a predominantly Catholic population. During the election campaign of 1930, the NSDAP presented itself as young and fresh, but also as determined, disciplined and forceful. The positive election result was also a consequence of the fact that the party had laid the foundation for a new organization since its new foundation in February 1925. By 1928 already, the party had more than 100,000 registered members whose average age* lay below thirty. After the unsuccessful putsch of 1923, Hitler promised to take over power legally, although the party's real aims were quite obvious.

average age *Durchschnittsalter*

Since 1929/30, the government possessed a sufficient amount of material which explicitly proved the NSDAP's unconstitutional* aims and methods, however, this information was withheld*. This cautious treatment of the NSDAP by the government and the judiciary in turn made the party more acceptable to the middle-class. Heinrich Brüning (Centre Party) became the new chancellor. Before the elections, General Kurt von Schleicher, chief minister of the Ministry of the Reichswehr, had campaigned for the appointment of Brüning as chancellor by Hindenburg. The new government was supposed to launch a conservative change of policy. After the SPD had dropped out of the government, Brüning had no parliamentary majority anymore. Nevertheless, the Reichspräsident promised Brüning extraordinary powers according to Article 48 of the Weimar constitution, which Brüning, in turn, considered useful for his further actions. Brüning's cabinet failed to pass a programme for reconstructing* Germany's finances, which would also have included increased unemployment insurance contributions*. However, Reichspräsident Hindenburg made use of Article 48 and passed the programme via emergency decree.

Brüning's first and foremost aim was the reconstruction of Germany's national finances primarily by means of a long-term cut in expenditure especially in the field of social policy. This, of course, meant great sacrifices for the workers. Brüning's **deflationary policy*** (cf. S 21), in combination with the effects of the Great Depression, led to a continuous increase in unemployment rates. By 1932, over six million people were jobless, and many companies collapsed since the people's purchasing power* sank drastically as a result. However, this dramatic situation led to a total cancellation* of reparation payments being agreed on at the Lausanne Conference in 1932. Unfortunately, this foreign policy success could not compensate the population for the harsh consequences of unemployment and by 1931/32 Brüning had lost all credit with the electorate. In the end, the higher-income earners around Hindenburg talked the Reichspräsident into dismissing Brüning as chancellor.

Brüning resigned on 30 May 1932, whereas five weeks before Hindenburg had been re-elected as Reichspräsident. Kurt von Schleicher presented Hindenburg the then rather unknown Franz von Papen, whose **Cabinet of Barons*** would be able to rely on the DNVP in order to govern. However, Hindenburg, Schleicher and his advisers also fatefully thought of stabilizing the presidential cabinet by including the NSDAP. Hitler's demand for early elections was fulfilled and the elections of 31 July 1932 brought about the expected increase in support for the NSDAP. Apart from the KPD and the Centre Party, all other parties lost votes. Hitler, however, strengthened by the election result, refused to merely support the government but boldly claimed the chancellorship for himself. At that point, Hindenburg sharply refused Hitler's claim, issuing a public explanation to this effect on 13 August 1932. The plan to involve the NSDAP had failed and the only exit now was to announce new elections. The results of 6 November 1932 confirmed the crisis of the NSDAP and their votes dropped from 37 per cent to now 33 per cent. Further negotiations proved unsuccessful because of Hitler's renewed stubborn claims to the post of chancellor.

After Papen's resignation, von Schleicher himself took over the office of chancellor on 3 December 1932. Shortly after that, Hindenburg was confronted with the wish of influential people from industry and agriculture to appoint Hitler chancellor (cf. S 24). On 4 January 1933, Hitler and von Papen met in Cologne and agreed on a future government under Hitler's leadership. Apart from Hitler, the cabinet was to consist of only two other National Socialists. Papen was to become vice chancellor and since Alfred Hugenberg, party leader of the DNVP, was to become a member

unconstitutional against the constitution
to withhold to keep back

to reconstruct here: *sanieren*
increased contributions *Beitragserhöhungen*

deflationary policy *Deflationspolitik*

purchasing power *Kaufkraft*

cancellation calling off, erasure

Cabinet of Barons „*Kabinett der Barone*"

of the cabinet as well, it seemed as if Hitler would somehow be framed and hopefully influenced and held in check by conservatives. Eventually, Hindenburg agreed to this solution and to another dissolution of the Reichstag, which the Nazis had demanded. On 30 January 1933 Hitler was appointed chancellor. He was not elected chancellor and he also did not "seize" power in a revolutionary act. The chancellorship was instead handed over to him through the Reichspräsident following the tradition of the Presidential Cabinets (cf. S 26).

Cabinet von Papen, also called the "Cabinet of Barons"

National Socialist Rule Over Germany and Europe

NS Ideology

⇨ S 27–28

Anti-Semitism as a hostile, highly prejudiced and aggressive attitude towards the Jewish minority was not invented by Hitler and the Nazis. Influenced by religion in the first place, this attitude underwent a process of transformation as the ideas of the Enlightenment spread in Europe in the 18th century among parts of the bourgeoisie* and later among the working classes. In the late 19th century, however, a more devious modern form of anti-Semitism, supposedly connected with biological characteristics, became important for German history in particular. Its pseudo-scientific* principles were less important for its effectiveness than its political usefulness was for conservatives. Jews were literally "made" enemies of the state by nationalist politicians, professors and clergymen in the German Empire after 1871. This new enemy was intended to focus the fears caused by the Industrial Revolution and thus serve as a scapegoating integrating factor in the new empire. The objective* of this form of anti-Semitism remained for a long time unclear but finally culminated* in the demand for a "solution to the Jewish question". Although this idea had at first but little influence on politics, it intensified anti-Semitic prejudice in large parts of the population and some smaller radical nationalist groups were even inspired by it to call for an expulsion* and extermination* of the Jews. During the social crisis in the aftermath of the First World War, this kind of anti-Semitism gained supporters among the bourgeoisie and petite bourgeoisie*. The NSDAP was only one of many national and racial parties propagating anti-Semitism, however, they did this more aggressively than the others. This development was strengthened in the final phase of the Weimar Republic when von Gayl (DNVP), the home secretary* in 1932, called for a limitation of the naturalisation* of people belonging to a "minor culture", effectively meaning Jews, who had been immigrating to Germany since 1918.

Since the 19th century, German Jews had, on the other hand, connected more and more to German culture. Despite this process of assimilation, the Jews were, however, never totally integrated into German society and their contributions to science and culture and their participation in fighting in the First World War for Germany did not save them from being discriminated against. Since 1910, the proportion of Jews in the German population had decreased and about two thirds of the German Jews lived in big cities (approximately one third in Berlin alone). They were represented in above-average* terms in some respected professions, such as those of doctors, lawyers, and merchants. However, they remained a minority in the financial sector and the same is true in the fields of science and art. In Berlin alone in 1932, about 50,000 businesses were owned by Jews, which only made up 6 per cent of all businesses, but these shops accounted for 26 per cent of the total revenue*. Especially in the retail* industry there were a large number of small and very small shops the continued existence of which was not only threatened by the Great Depression but also by larger businesses. The owners of such small shops were the target group of NSDAP politics since they could be easily mobilised with the help of the familiar anti-Semitic prejudice.

In its time and also beyond, the NSDAP was considered to be a party with an ideol-

bourgeoisie middle class

pseudo-scientific ['sudoʊ] not real

objective goal
to culminate to end up

expulsion [ɪkˈspʌlʃən] banishment
extermination complete destruction
petite bourgeoisie Kleinbürgertum

home secretary Innenminister
naturalisation Einbürgerung

above-average überdurchschnittlich

revenue Umsatz
retail Einzelhandel

ogy whose programme was not aimed at realities and possible compromises but rather geared towards an ideology. In fact, the party did not develop its own programme, which would have been important for its policy, instead it followed a racial* and national policy which already became clear in the party's **25-Points Programme*** (cf. S 27). The core of NS ideology was an extreme form of nationalism combined with aggression against all non-Germanic peoples, especially against Jews (**anti-Semitism***) (cf. S 14). Expansive and imperialist aims were justified by pseudo-scientific theories of a racial biology (**Social Darwinism***). Violence as a political means was legitimized by the law of nature, i.e. the law of the jungle* and thus also war became a necessary part of the racial conflict*.

Faced with the complicated realities of a modern industrial society, the party only had anti-Enlightenment and anti-democratic answers and an authoritarian **"leader principle"*** was supposed to overcome antagonisms* in society by establishing a harmonious **People's Community*** in which class differences were eliminated. According to Nazi ideology, this People's Community, consisting only of members of the **"Aryan master race"***, needed **living space*** in which they could dwell*. This was one of the reasons why Hitler started the Second World War. Belonging to this "master race" gave the Germans the feeling of being special, precious and a "chosen people".

National Socialist racism can be traced back to an already existing tradition of racist ideas in the 18th century. In fact, Hitler did not invent European anti-Semitism and it is not a particular German problem. Pogroms against Jews, especially in Eastern Europe, have a long history. The special feature of National Socialist anti-Semitism is its biological aspect, as already mentioned above.

The ideological blurring* of its programme allowed the party to integrate large groups of voters who felt attracted by the simple basic concept of the enemy* and the fanatic radicalness of party propaganda. The humiliating effect on German national consciousness of the events of 1918 played a big role when it came to attempting to explain the fact that lots of National Socialist followers felt attracted by Germanic racial fanaticism.

However, this rather unrealistic ideology was believed by a large section of the German population as a kind of substitute* for religion. The **Ministry of Public Enlightenment and Propaganda*** played an important role in spreading those ideas (cf. S 28). Both main enemies of National Socialism, liberal capitalism and communism, could be merged* into one large concept of the enemy. In propagandistic terms, Jews led both the communist Soviet government and US banks in Wall Street. With this in mind, it was easy to address those parts of the population who feared a communist overthrow (cf. Spartacist uprising) as well as those suffering from the effects of the Great Depression or from high interest* payments. Declaring the victorious powers of WWI, especially the USA, as being undercut* by Jews, made it easy to

Propaganda postcard from 1939

Vocabulary (margin):

- **racial** *völkisch*
- **25-Points Programme** *25-Punkte Programm*
- **anti-Semitism** *Antisemitismus*
- **Social Darwinism** *Sozialdarwinismus*
- **law of the jungle** *Recht des Stärkeren*
- **racial conflict** *Rassenkampf*
- **leader principle** *Führerprinzip*
- **antagonism** contrast
- **People's Community** *Volksgemeinschaft*
- **"Aryan master race"** *„arische Herrenrasse"*
- **living space** *Lebensraum*
- **to dwell** to live
- **blurring** *Verwischung*
- **concept of the enemy** *Feindbild*
- **substitute** sb. or sth. that takes the place of another
- **Ministry of Public Enlightenment and Propaganda** *Ministerium für Volksaufklärung und Propaganda*
- **to merge** to bring or come together
- **interest** here: *Zinsen*
- **to undercut** *untergraben, unterwandern*

blame them as a whole for having lost WWI and for the harsh provisions of the Versailles Treaty. Hence, every form of aggression in German politics could be explained as a contribution to Germany's rescue and defence.

Especially in the first years of National Socialist rule, the Germans were willing to ignore the other side of the coin, namely the persecution and exclusion of minorities, among them homosexuals, Jews, political opponents and the mentally ill*. A particularly dark chapter of German history is the **"euthanasia"*** programme, the destruction of so-called "life unworthy of life"*.

Consolidation of Power – Three Phases

Hitler's appointment as chancellor was strongly welcomed by the old political right. An authoritarian government under Hitler, dependent on the Reichspräsident and former field marshal Hindenburg, seemed to be a guarantee for the political power of the old elites of the military, the nobility and the landowners as well as for big industry and the upper classes, since they all opted for a strong state pursuing national power politics*. Furthermore, this move should, they felt, help erase the consequences of the First World War in respect of domestic and foreign policy, for which, ironically, those "old elites" were to blame in the first place.

When it came to the matter of the consolidation of power, chancellor Hitler, home secretary Frick, minister (without portfolio) Göring, and propaganda minister Goebbels pursued a policy of contrasting measures, such as propaganda ceremonies to help gain and confirm supporters, apparent cooperation with possible opponents, formal legality to calm down the cautious, and open terror and pressure to intimidate and stop opponents.

Nazi consolidation of power can be divided into three phases: control at the centre, control beyond the centre and the final stage. When the Reichstag building went up in flames on 27 February 1933, Hitler used the opportunity to abolish the Basic

mentally ill *Geisteskranke/r*
"euthanasia" [ˌjuθəˈneɪʒə] *Euthanasie*
"life unworthy of life" „*lebensunwertes Leben*"

⇨ **S 29–32**

power politics *Machtpolitik*

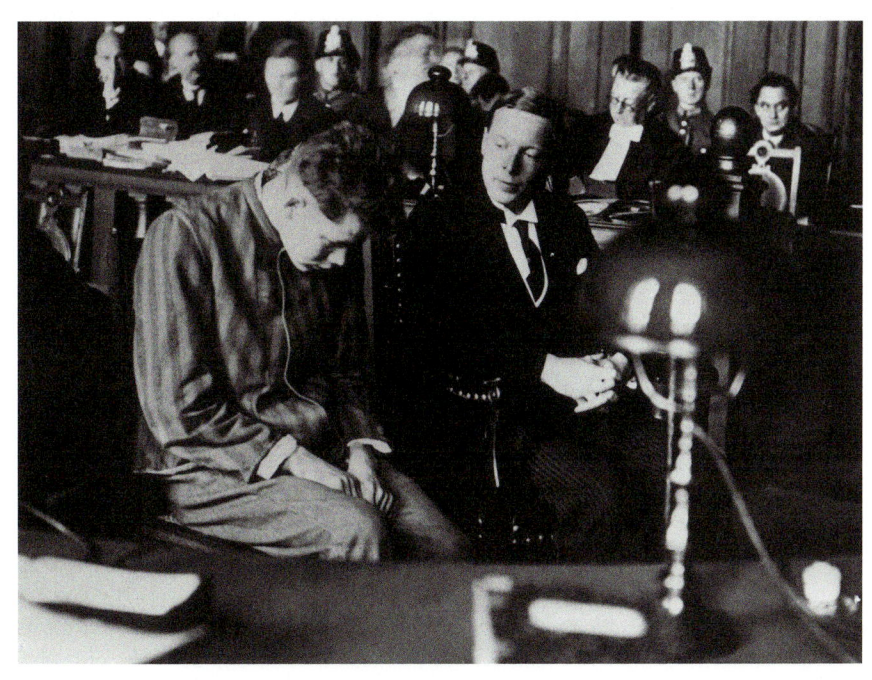

Marinus van der Lubbe with his interpreter, 24 September 1933

Rights. The former Dutch communist Marinus van der Lubbe was made responsible for the **Reichstag Fire***. The Nazis turned the fire into a signal for an uprising of the KPD and thus propaganda against the threatening communist danger kicked into action. In the very night of the 27 February, Göring, without any legal basis for his measures, ordered the closure of KPD party bureaus. Party leaders and high-ranking officials were arrested and the party press was abolished. Furthermore, home secretary Frick presented the **Reichstag Fire Decree (Decree for the Protection of People and State*)** which suspended* the most important basic rights in the constitution. In fact, this effectively marked the end of the rule of law* (cf. S 30). The conservatives in the government agreed to this since they thought that the decree was only directed against the leftists and that, according to the constitution, it could only be in effect for a limited time. The last word would still lie with the Reichspräsident. However, the Reichstag Fire Decree remained valid until 1945 and served as a kind of Basic Law of the Third Reich, thus making it even more important than the **Enabling Act*** (cf. S 31). By March, 10,000 people (mostly communists but also Social Democrats and members of other parties and groups) in Prussia alone, had been taken into "protective custody"* and by the end of October, 500 to 600 people had been killed and about 100,000 arrested. Despite all the national enthusiasm and propaganda, and in spite of intimidation and terror, the NSDAP was not able to achieve an absolute majority in the elections on 5 March 1933. Hence, Hitler still had to cooperate with the (albeit weakened) DNVP to form a government.

The newly elected Reichstag was supposed to meet on 21 March for its constituent session. In order to commemorate the opening of the first German Reichstag in 1871 under Bismarck, a ceremony in the Potsdam Garrison Church* was prepared. This ceremony was intended to show that the National Socialist movement stood in the tradition of Prussia. The day was introduced by Protestant and Catholic festival services* attended by uniformed members of the **SA*** and leading representatives of the NSDAP such as Göring and Himmler. Communist and Social Democratic representatives were not invited or their attendance prevented by "important work to be done in the concentration camps", as Frick explained. This was also the reason why the parliamentary group* of the KPD could not attend the opening session of the Reichstag that very afternoon in the Kroll Opera House. The elimination of the KPD was a manoeuvre in order to pass the Enabling Act which basically meant an end of the separation of powers by combining the legislative and the executive branch in the hands of the government. In order to pass this constitutional amendment*, a two-thirds majority was needed. However, this would have been endangered if 85 per cent of the representatives had participated in the voting since the NSDAP had 288 votes and the conservatives and liberals together 85. Thus, "protective custody" for 81 KPD members and 15 SPD members turned out to be a ruthless method of securing the majority. In the end, 444 deputies (among them the Liberals and the Centre Party) voted in favour of the Enabling Act and thus for their own disempowerment. Only the SPD unanimously* voted against it.

Now that control at the centre had been achieved, control beyond the centre was the next step, which meant the **Bringing into Line*** of the German federal states. The corresponding law came into effect on 31 March and on 7 April the federal governments were replaced by Reich Governors (*Reichsstatthalter*). The same day another law was passed which restored the civil service (*Gesetz zur Wiederherstellung des Berufsbeamtentums*). The idea behind this was that all civil servants of Jewish origin and/or with a democratic attitude were dismissed. On 10 May the **German**

Labour Front* replaced all trade unions*. The SPD was banned on 22 June and by the end of July all the other political parties had dissolved themselves. The **"Law against the establishment of political parties"*** of 14 July left the NSDAP as the only legal party in Germany.

Already on 20 July 1933, Hitler could present a foreign policy success, namely the signing of a **Concordat*** with the Catholic Church, i.e. Pope Pius XI. The German government guaranteed the existence and freedom of action of religious, cultural and charitable* Catholic organizations and, in turn, the Vatican prohibited priests and members of monastic orders from participating in political actions, something which had previously been quite common in the Centre Party. Given the pope's authority, this agreement was a rather reassuring signal for German Catholics to cooperate with the National Socialist German state and can be seen as the last step taken to gain control beyond the centre.

All these repressive measures became possible due to a massive use of terror, mostly carried out by the SA. This party army had grown to over three million members by 1933 and the problem was that most of them were now no longer needed due to a lack of political opposition. Thus, SA leader Ernst Röhm planned to turn the organization into a militia*. This plan conflicted with Hitler's promise to the Reichswehr that it would remain the only group with the right to bear arms. Röhm, however, did not give in and so he and other leading members of the SA were arrested on 30 June 1934 under the pretext* of planning a putsch. The very next day, 83 SA members were executed in the **Night of the Long Knives***, among them also the former chancellor Kurt von Schleicher. The Nazi propaganda term for this event was the "Röhm Putsch". Surprisingly enough, Hitler's reputation grew considerably among the public despite the obvious crimes and violations of the constitution. Nazi propaganda had accused Röhm and other high-ranking SA members of being homosexual which made Hitler appear as a man with a clear political agenda who stood for relentless moral cleanliness. Another military organization took advantage of the crushing of the SA, namely the **SS***. The SS was, under the leadership of Heinrich Himmler, now responsible for controlling and watching over the concentration camps. Later Himmler developed the **SD*** of the SS into a secret police which operated Germany-wide. Another group was the **Gestapo*** which had also been led by Himmler since 1934, and, in 1939, the Gestapo, the criminal investigation department* and the Ordnungspolizei (Order Police) were joined together with the SD to form the Reichssicherheitshauptamt (Reich Main Security Office). The concentration camps with their SS-run plants had been under the control of the SS-Wirtschafts- und Verwaltungshauptamt (SS Main Economic and Administrative Department) since 1942. These and other departments formed kinds of ministries in the SS state which became more and more powerful and can be regarded as the centre of terror.

Another important role was played by the courts. The normal courts stuck to the unjust rulings of the Unrechtsstaat in which the exercise of power was not properly constrained by the law and the notorious Sondergerichte (special courts) pronounced even more radical sentences. After the Reichstag Fire, the Volksgerichtshof (People's Court) was founded and this had gained regular status by 1936. It was not possible to appeal* against the verdict of this court. Its President Roland Freisler, who also sentenced the members of the 20 July plot to death, was known for his furious trials.

Hitler completed the final stage of his consolidation of power when he combined

---

German Labour Front *Deutsche Arbeitsfront*

"Law against the establishment of political parties" *„Gesetz gegen die Neubildung von Parteien"*
Concordat *Konkordat*

charitable humanitarian

militia [mə-'li-shə] a group of people who are not part of the armed forces of a country but are trained like soldiers
pretext a reason that you give to hide your real reason for doing something
Night of the Long Knives *Röhm-Putsch*

SS *SS (Schutzstaffel)*
SD *SD (Sicherheitsdienst)*
Gestapo *Gestapo (Geheime Staatspolizei)*

criminal investigation department *Kriminalpolizei*

to appeal *Rechtsmittel einlegen*

the offices of Reichspräsident and chancellor in one person and proclaimed himself "Führer und Reichskanzler" after Hindenburg's death on 2 August 1934.

One and a half year after having been appointed chancellor, the NSDAP under Hitler had assumed absolute political power in Germany. Possible domestic competitors had been crushed. However, there was still a certain and sometimes openly hostile attitude visible among some parts of the population. For the regime this meant the necessity for increased effort to achieve unconditional support and consent from the whole German population in order to consolidate its power. On the one hand, successes in foreign policy and in the economic field were intended to strengthen the inner willingness for an agreement between rulers and ruled. On the other hand, the development of the surveillance* apparatus and an enforced ideological coverage* were to secure consensus through exterior pressure and terror.

surveillance [sərˈveɪləns] close observation, control
coverage inclusion

⇨ S 33–37

Life Under Nazi Control

One crucial reason why National Socialist ideas gained widespread support among the German population was the high unemployment rate resulting from the Great Depression and the miserable living conditions it brought about. Thus, fighting unemployment was the fundamental political issue for vast sections of the population. The myth that Hitler fought joblessness successfully can be proven wrong by examining which measures were taken. First of all, boosting the arms industry was intended to prepare for war and the same was true for the expansion of the motorways (work on which had already started during the Weimar Republic). The poor financial system inevitably must have led to inflation, respectively bankruptcy. Cutting wages meant a low level of consumption for lots of people. Finally, not including women's work, calling people up for the Reichsarbeitsdienst (RAD) and the introduction of conscription* in 1935 made it possible to sugar-coat* the unemployment statistics. In general, the economy was organized by the state. The state planned, gave orders and controlled whereas private property was not abolished. However, social classes were no longer relevant since the People's Community provided the concept of a society without conflict. By 1936 already, it became clear that Hitler's economic policy was leading to enormous debts. Nonetheless, Hitler did not listen to advice from experts in this field and in June 1936 he declared the **Four-year plan*** (cf. S 33). This plan accounted for a radical reduction of imports in order to save foreign exchanges*. The required raw material was to be won in Germany. Despite great efforts, however, Germany did not succeed in managing without imports. Furthermore, the planned control over the private economy was not achieved since several companies undermined the state's measures. In 1939, it became apparent that the aims of the Four-year plan could not be achieved and that the German industry was not properly prepared for a long war.

conscription allgemeine Wehrpflicht
to sugar-coat here: to cover up the truth

Four-year plan Vierjahresplan

foreign exchanges Devisen

inconsistent contradictory

The role of women in National Socialist society was rather inconsistent*. On the one hand, they were seen as having the "honourable" task of reproducing and maintaining the German "race", while, on the other hand, it was also the Nazi party's aim to view women and girls as "Volksgenossinnen" (national comrades) and organize them in women's organizations, such as the **League of German Girls*** and later the **National Socialist Women's League*** (cf. S 34). Women who wanted to study had to join the **Reich Labour Service*** and by 1938 already, a so-called "Pflichtjahr" (compulsory year, which can be seen as the equivalent of military service for men) was introduced for all women and girls between the ages of 14 and 25

League of German Girls Bund Deutscher Mädel
National Socialist Women's League Nationalsozialistische Frauenschaft
Reich Labour Service Reichsarbeitsdienst

which was usually fulfilled in the domestic economy or in farming. When it came to professional life, the Nazis made it clear at a very early stage, with the "Law for the Reduction of Unemployment" (*Gesetz zur Verminderung der Arbeitslosigkeit*, 1 June 1933) that women should not start a career at all. However, when the war started in September 1939, conditions for women changed again. One has to keep in mind that women were seen as makeshifts* who were to return to their original roles as mothers when Germany had achieved the "final victory".

The **Hitler Youth*** had its origins in the period before Hitler took over government, but when Hitler became chancellor it became a mass movement. In the course of Bringing into Line, the Hitler Youth remained the only youth organization and a special law made membership compulsory (25 March 1939) (cf. S 35). However, the influence of the organization on the young people was sometimes not as strong as intended by the Nazis. Many young people were able to defy* control and of course families were able to work against the pressure to participate and identify with Nazi goals as well. Additionally, there was also sporadic* **resistance*** against the total control of the regime. Still, oppositional youth groups were the exception and there was no such thing as open rebellion (cf. S 37). Small oppositional groups can, however, be seen as proof that the NS regime did not succeed in totally controlling and indoctrinating* youth as a whole.

When assessing resistance against National Socialist dictatorship, one has to make a distinction between deliberately fighting the regime, refusing to actively take part in everyday life in the manner desired by the Nazis and finally an inner mental dissociation* from Nazi ideology and its control. Open resistance definitely came from the political left, from the workers' movement, and among them, the communists played the most prominent role. The first wave of terror hit the communists and also members of the SPD and trade unions. Many people were arrested and taken to concentration camps where they could be abused and tortured by the SA and SS. After this phase of terror, deliberate, state-run persecution through the Gestapo and the SS followed, so that all attempts of the KPD, the SPD, and socialist and Christian trade unions to build up illegal organizations failed. By 1935, there were hardly any communists or socialists left. Although large parts of the Protestant and Catholic Church had collaborated with the regime, the most crucial form of resistance came from these quarters. Their main concern, however, was not about being politically active against National Socialism, instead they were more worried about the independence of their own institutions. Even the most brutal measures against political opponents or Jewish fellow citizens did not cause the churches to decry* such behaviour or oppose it despite the fact that it definitely

A family drawn by Wolfgang Willrich, undated

makeshift substitute

Hitler Youth *Hitlerjugend*

to defy to resist or fight

sporadic happening often but not regularly
resistance *Widerstand*

to indoctrinate to teach sb. to fully accept the ideas, opinions, and beliefs of a particular group and to not consider other ideas, opinions, and beliefs
dissociation separation

to decry to express strong disapproval of sth.

went against Christian ideals of humanity. However, some priests showed more courage, such as Graf von Galen who openly condemned euthanasia. The **Confessing Church*** (of which Dietrich Bonhoeffer was a key founding member) opposed Nazi policy and the integration of Protestant Christians into the NS state.

Confessing Church *Bekennende Kirche*

The military and the administration also included pockets of resistance. Attempts were made to keep out very active NSDAP members, to help the persecuted, or to try to counter aggressive foreign policy measures by diplomatic means. Many people who supported the Weimar Republic before 1933 resigned from official posts and from the civil service, even when they were not formally dismissed. Many scientists and artists preferred to preserve their mental and inner integrity rather than to collaborate with the regime.

Critical thinking directed against the regime became more frequent, especially among the military, once the war began to turn in 1942/43 and with the ever stronger strain* on the population. Nonetheless, a majority still refused the violent removal of the NS government even when the participants of the **20 July plot*** to kill Hitler were arrested and executed. Without the support of the population, every serious form of resistance had to remain futile*, however, the fact that there were individuals and groups engaged in active resistance became enormously important for German morale and self-respect in the period after Germany's defeat.

strain emotional pressure
20 July plot *Attentat vom 20. Juli 1944*
futile pointless, useless

At the beginning of 1942, the **Kreisau Circle*** had formed around the jurist Helmuth James von Moltke, consisting of young members of the military, the diplomatic and civil services, as well as trade unions and the SPD. For them it was obvious that an overthrow would only be possible with the help of leading military staff. Since 1943, Claus Schenk Graf von Stauffenberg, a German army officer, had been planning Hitler's assassination. He wanted to kill Hitler on 20 July 1944 in his headquarters. Stauffenberg, however, was not successful and Hitler survived the assassination attempt virtually unscathed. One day later in a radio address, he announced that the perpetrators would receive their just punishment. None of the main plotters* and hardly any of their confidants* survived. Often, just being related to the plotters was enough cause for subsequent persecution. About 7,000 people were arrested and hundreds were executed. However, the majority of the population remained silent and followed Hitler without resistance until the very end, their main concern being to save themselves.

Kreisau Circle *Kreisauer Kreis*

plotter person who secretly plans to do sth. illegal or harmful
confidant trusted friend

⇨ S 38–43

Foreign Policy: From Triumph to Disaster

Although it is absolutely clear that the consequence of NS policy had to be war, it is debatable whether this policy was determined by the person of Hitler or inevitably had to emerge from the political and economic structures of National Socialism. In practical terms, NS foreign policy was at first aimed at hiding its true objective, namely a war to expand German territory, from foreign countries (cf. S 38). Thus, the hopes of other European people, and especially of the Western powers, for peace had to be kept alive. The wish for peace was widespread in the light of many countries' own domestic economic and social problems as well as colonial issues. The Soviet Union was weakened internationally by interior struggles connected with the industrial policies introduced by Stalin. Hitler's foreign policy success can thus be traced back to different factors: Nazi peace propaganda, the hope for peace in other countries, loyal civil servants in the Department of Foreign Affairs, and the growing readiness on the part of the Western powers to make concessions*.

concession *Zugeständnis*

One argument frequently brought forward is that the **appeasement policy*** of the Western nations had paved the way for Hitler's triumph because the powers responsible should not have tolerated the first violations of the Versailles Treaty (cf. S 40–43). However, the Western powers had also suffered from the consequences of the Great Depression, some even worse than Germany and over a longer period of time. The Western powers had not embarked on large-scale manufacturing of armaments and Britain in particular had to deal with the burdens caused by growing opposition in its colonial empire. The politicians in charge believed that making concessions would prevent war. Thus, Germany's demands for complete international equality was seen as basically justified and the politicians hoped that Germany could be incorporated into the international community of states if they made concessions concerning the revision of the provisions of the Versailles Treaty.

Shortly after the Concordat with the Vatican, Germany left the League of Nations in autumn 1933, which was an open challenge* to the Versailles Treaty. On 26 January 1934, Germany signed a non-aggression pact with Poland, which the world public saw as proof of Germany's will for agreement.

The overwhelming results of the plebiscite in Saarland in January 1935 in favour of re-joining Germany were a cause of great joy in the whole of Germany. Two months later, Hitler announced the introduction of conscription to build up an army of 750,000 soldiers. The Naval Agreement with Britain in the same year, however, ended a conflict which had lasted since the turn of the century. By granting Germany permission to construct a fleet 35 per cent of the size of the British fleet, Britain itself abandoned the terms of the Treaty of Versailles. In March 1936, German soldiers marched into the demilitarised Rhineland and since France showed no reaction, Hitler felt emboldened* in his plans and at a meeting on 5 November 1937 he told his top ministers and commanders of the need to increase rearmament efforts in order to prepare for war in the 1940s. This was the subject of the so-called **Hossbach Memorandum***, named after the colonel who took the minutes.

The question is whether the Western powers should have interfered at this point, when Germany's armaments industry was still in its infancy. In March 1938, Hitler annexed Austria (Anschluss), wiping out the provision not to permit the unification of Germany with Austria, which the Germans had perceived as humiliating. In May 1938, the Sudeten Germans in Czechoslovakia were encouraged to start turmoil, causing the Czech government to prepare for war. This triggered a meeting between British prime minister Neville Chamberlain and Hitler in September at which the transfer of the Sudetenland to Germany was arranged. The **Munich Agreement*** of 30 September confirmed that the Sudetenland should be handed over to Germany by 10 October. These negotiations demonstrated that the Western powers, and Britain in particular, wanted to preserve peace at all costs.

Despite all these massive steps, Hitler had been able to calm down the Western powers many times. He assured them that Germany only wanted to regain its equality and its national self-determination. He claimed that the final problem of German foreign policy had been solved with the take-over of the Sudetenland and declared that Germany had no further claims. By the end of 1938, Germany had 79 million inhabitants, almost as many as France and Britain together (88 million). The fact that Germany had now had great success with its aggressive policy meant more domestically than the repeatedly uttered demands for a revision of the Versailles Treaty. In effect, there had been a shift in political power in Europe.

The behaviour of foreign countries was characterised by worries and fear, but also

---

appeasement policy *Beschwichtigungspolitik*

challenge objection

to embolden to make sb. more confident

Hossbach Memorandum *Hoßbach-Niederschrift*

Munich Agreement *Münchner Abkommen*

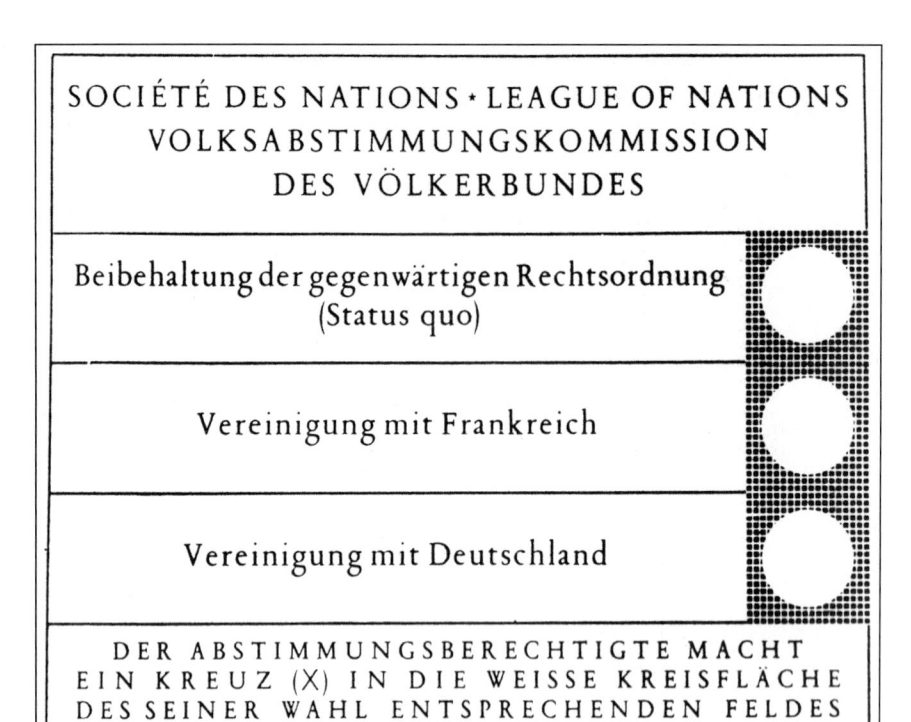

> SOCIÉTÉ DES NATIONS · LEAGUE OF NATIONS
> VOLKSABSTIMMUNGSKOMMISSION
> DES VÖLKERBUNDES
>
> Beibehaltung der gegenwärtigen Rechtsordnung (Status quo) ○
>
> Vereinigung mit Frankreich ○
>
> Vereinigung mit Deutschland ○
>
> DER ABSTIMMUNGSBERECHTIGTE MACHT EIN KREUZ (X) IN DIE WEISSE KREISFLÄCHE DES SEINER WAHL ENTSPRECHENDEN FELDES

Ballot paper for the Saarland referendum, 13 January 1935

fascist ['fæʃɪst] *faschistisch*

by respect. The modern German air force had already demonstrated its military power in the Spanish Civil War (1936–39) when it had supported the fascist* General Franco in his fight against the Republicans. The destructive aggressiveness of the National Socialists had become apparent when the German air force completely ruined the city of Guernica because it was still loyal to the legal government. Since fascist Italy also participated in the war and supported Franco, it came to an approximation* between Germany and Italy, resulting in the establishment of the **Rome-Berlin Axis***. This coalition eventually became a formal alliance between both states when Italy joined the Anti-Comintern Pact between Germany and Japan against the Soviet Union in 1937.

approximation closeness

Rome-Berlin Axis *Achse Berlin-Rom*

stronghold *Bollwerk*

to lurk *lauern*

Britain attempted to use Nazi Germany as a stronghold* against the Soviet Union despite the fact that the danger of an anti-democratically governed Europe seemed to be lurking*. It was only in 1938, after the Munich Agreement had been violated by Germany, that British policy changed and communism was no longer considered the main threat for peace in Europe but National Socialism. In the meantime, however, the German population had found increasing favour with the courses of action taken by Hitler due to his successful track record* in terms of domestic and foreign policy.

track record achievement

⇨ S 44–50

The Second World War

None of the big industrial states had overcome the Great Depression of 1929–1933 better than Germany. However, Germany had achieved this by armament only. The threat of a new war had been obvious since 1936 for all the potential enemies of Germany and this meant that it was necessary to attempt to postpone the outbreak of war for as long as possible. For Germany, a very early start to a war was more fa-

Europe in April 1944

Europe in April 1944
- Front line, 5 April 1944
- German Reich with allied countries and occupied territories
- Allied territories
- Neutral countries

vourable, as had already become visible during the crisis over the Sudetenland where concessions on the part of the Western powers and the mediation of the Italian dictator Benito Mussolini had prevented a war limited to Europe. The British and French armies had to cope with the problems of the obsolescence* of their military equipment and a limitation of armaments. Thus, the policy of appeasement was their only option when it came to dealing with Hitler's aspiration* to expand. Britain had voluntarily reduced its army to 100,000 soldiers while the Soviet Union was not ready for war due to its preoccupation with internal conflicts. It was only in 1939 that the French government believed itself to be in a position to appropriately respond to a German attack. However, the French air force was still so weak that only the deployment of the complete British Royal Air Force could have compensated for its inferiority. To add to the difficulties, it was not possible for Britain and France to take effective offensive action against Germany after it had attacked Poland on 1 September 1939.

By way of contrast, the German army was the most modern in the whole of Europe despite the fact that it still lacked the substantial reserves necessary for waging war. Hence, high losses in specialist combat units, such as the parachutists*, could not

obsolescence [ɒbsəˈlɛsəns] *Überalterung*

aspiration goal

parachutist *Fallschirmspringer*

be compensated for easily. In order to nevertheless gain control over Europe and the world, the alternative was quick wars of **aggression*** lasting only a few months, the so-called **Blitzkrieg***. The internal conflicts in Europe until 1939 played **to*** these plans and Hitler feared nothing more than another two-front war like in the First World War. In order to prevent that, Poland, which had an authoritarian and anti-Communist government, was intended to secure the east, thus giving Germany a free hand against France and Great Britain. However, the Polish refused to join the Anti-Comintern Pact at the beginning of 1939.

It was also by no means easy to establish a system of alliances against Germany after 1933. Although the Soviet Union, Britain and France felt equally threatened by Germany, their distrust of each other was too great. In fact, negotiations between these three powers failed in summer 1939 because the Soviet Union demanded the right to march through Poland. Germany saw its chance and signed a non-aggression pact with the Soviet Union on 23 August 1939 (**Hitler-Stalin Pact*** (cf. S 44)). An **Additional Secret Protocol*** settled the **partition*** of eastern Europe between these two powers. On 1 September 1939 Germany then attacked Poland and with that the Second World War had begun. To Hitler's surprise, Britain and France declared war on Germany according to their **contractual obligations*** with Poland. By mid-September, the German army had surrounded Warsaw and at this point Soviet troops crossed the Polish border and occupied the eastern part of Poland along the line agreed on in the Hitler-Stalin Pact. Half of this new territory was incorporated into Germany, the other half was then administered by Germany as a so-called **General Government***. German troops went on to conquer and occupy Denmark, Norway and France between April and June 1940. Since British prime minister Winston Churchill repeatedly refused to accept any German offers for an alliance, Germany launched the **Battle of Britain*** (July – October 1939) in which the United Kingdom was severely bombed by the German air force (cf. S 45). Although an invasion of Great Britain was prepared, this enterprise failed and the large-scale air attacks were finally stopped. On 22 June 1941, Germany started to pursue the core idea of its ideology, namely to conquer living space in the east, by attacking the Soviet Union in the **Operation Barbarossa***. Despite initial successes, the tide for the German army turned in the late autumn of 1941 when temperatures sank rapidly. As a result, a large number of weapons did not work anymore and many soldiers froze to death due to inappropriate clothing. The German **advance*** stopped near Moscow but the city of Stalingrad was encircled by the end of 1942 by the 6th Army (**Battle of Stalingrad***). However, the 6th Army was then forced to surrender in February 1943 and this marked a turn in the course of the war. The USA entered the war on 8 December 1941 with a declaration of war against Japan after Japan had attacked the headquarters of the United States Pacific Fleet in **Pearl Harbor***, on the Hawaiian island of Oahu the day before. As a reaction to the German attack on the Soviet Union, the USA and Britain drafted their goals for a post-war world in the **Atlantic Charter*** on 14 August 1941 and in July 1943 the British and US air forces launched a bomb war on German cities such as Cologne, Hamburg, Dresden and Würzburg, which were almost completely destroyed. Finally, the plans for **Operation Overlord*** were put into practice. This military operation was the name for the allied invasion in Normandy on 4 June 1944, commonly known as **D-Day*** (cf. S 50).

The war in the Pacific ended with the two atomic bombs dropped on the Japanese cities of Hiroshima (6 August 1945) and Nagasaki (9 August 1945). When signs that the war would be lost became clear with defeat in the Battle of Stalingrad in 1942,

---

war of aggression Angriffskrieg
Blitzkrieg Blitzkrieg
to play to sth. here: entgegenkommen

Hitler-Stalin Pact/Additional Secret Protocol Hitler-Stalin-Pakt/geheimes Zusatzprotokoll
partition division

contractual obligation vertragliche Verpflichtung

General Government Generalgouvernement

Battle of Britain Luftschlacht um England

Operation Barbarossa Operation Barbarossa

advance Vormarsch

Battle of Stalingrad Schlacht um Stalingrad

Pearl Harbor Pearl Harbor

Atlantic Charter Atlantik-Charta

Operation Overlord/D-Day Operation Overlord/D-Day

the National Socialist leadership proclaimed a **total war*** in order to mobilise the last forces. However, by the winter of 1944/45 German resistance had for the most part collapsed and chaos reigned (cf. S 48). When Berlin was encircled by the Red Army, Hitler committed suicide in his Führerbunker on 8 May. The same day the German Wehrmacht agreed on an **unconditional surrender*** and thus the Second World War ended.

In total, about 55 million people lost their lives in this war, which is considered the greatest catastrophe in the history of humankind. Its special character as a **war of annihilation*** is not only due to its worldwide expansion from Europe to Africa, Asia and the Pacific or to the use of progressive weaponry but, above all, to the racist and inhumane* policy of annihilation practised in territories occupied by Germany.

total war *totaler Krieg*

unconditional surrender *bedingungslose Kapitulation*

war of annihilation *Vernichtungskrieg*

inhumane brutal, heartless

The Holocaust/Shoa*

Due to the military success of the years 1939–1941, Germany had been able to reign over most of the European continent and detailed plans had been worked out as to how the continent should be governed and exploited. In relation to the western countries at least, the Nazis stuck to the conventions regulating behaviour towards enemy forces, abiding by* the conventions of international law and treaties. In matters of resistance, however, executions and **deportations*** into **concentration camps*** were directly ordered.

⇨ S 51–56

Holocaust/Shoa *Holocaust/Shoa*

to abide by sth. to stick to sth.

deportation *Deportation*

concentration camp *Konzentrationslager*

Concentration and extermination camps and major "euthanasia" centres

German policy was much more brutal in eastern Europe than in the west since the objective was to gain living space. Millions of native inhabitants were to make way for German "settlers". Thus plans for mass executions soon complemented* plans for gigantic expulsion campaigns (for example 20 million Poles). The intention was to reduce the number of Slavic peoples such as Poles, Ukrainians and Russians, replace them by Germans, and then enslave the rest of the population. Jews were to be completely exterminated.

Increasing anti-Semitism in the Weimar Republic and a growing Jewish self-consciousness influenced by Zionism (a nationalist movement, which emerged in the late 19th century, supporting the creation of a Jewish homeland) had already given rise to prejudice against Jews and misgivings about Germany on the part of Jews themselves. The actual persecution of German Jews happened in four phases. It began with a fierce terrorisation of Jewish business people whereby Jewish socialists and communists were persecuted in a particularly hateful way by the SA. The first centrally directed anti-Jewish action occurred on 1 April 1933 with the boycott of Jewish shops, ordered by propaganda minister Goebbels and Julius Streicher, editor of the Nazi propaganda magazine *Stürmer*. Already in 1933/34, the **Aryanization*** of Jewish shops took place by forcing owners to sell their shops. The legal exclusion of Jewish citizens was introduced in autumn 1935 with the **Nuremberg Laws of Citizenship and Race***. However, these measures did not yet allow the Nazis to take over Jewish private property, which would have eased the strained* financial situation of the Reich (cf. S 52).

In this situation, a 17-year-old Polish Jew assassinated a German diplomat in Paris on 7 November 1938 in order to attract the attention of the international public to the fate of about 18,000 Jews who were expelled from Germany. Rather than viewing this assassination as the action of one single person, Nazi propaganda exploited* the act as part of an international Jewish conspiracy. Soon, isolated riots occurred but when the German diplomat died on 9 November, the Nazis ordered the police in a secret telex* not to interfere in the actions against the Jews and to prepare the arrest of 20,000–30,000 (wealthy) Jews. In the night of 9 to 10 November synagogues were burned down and many Jewish shops were looted and destroyed. Due to the many broken shop windows, the Nazis created the term "Reichskristallnacht" or **"Night of Broken Glass"*** as it has become known in English. The more neutral term is the **November Pogrom*** (cf. S 53). Thousands of people were abused, at least 90 (but probably many more) were murdered and 30,000 were put into concentration camps. A lot of German people looked away, although some also felt shocked, not so much because of the aim of the pogrom but rather because of the extreme violence involved. There were many cases where people actively helped and some also expressed their compassion* and shame. For the Nazis, the November Pogrom was neither a success in terms of domestic nor of foreign policy but it did not trigger any resistance in Germany. After being deprived of the right to exercise their profession, the majority of German Jews had lost their livelihood*. Those who wanted to leave Germany often failed due to the costs of the journey and also because of reservations on the part of the countries they wanted to emigrate to which envisaged problems because of a possible wave of immigrants. Further laws and decrees were passed under Goebbels, Göring and SD chief Heydrich which all aimed at further deprivation* of the German Jews. Already in 1938, Jewish citizens had to declare property valued at over 5,000 Reichsmark and they were cynically fined* 1.12 billion Reichsmark as compensation for the damage caused in the No-

---

to complement to accompany

Aryanization *Arisierung*

Nuremberg Laws of Citizenship and Race *Nürnberger Rassegesetze*
strained tense

to exploit here: *instrumentalisieren*

telex *Fernschreiben*

"Night of Broken Glass"/ November Pogrom *„Reichskristallnacht"/Novemberpogrom*

compassion sympathy

livelihood income

deprivation *Beraubung, Entrechtung*
to fine to financially penalise

vember Pogrom. Furthermore, they had to give their complete jewellery to the state and from 1939 onwards, those who wanted to emigrate had to pay a charge*. Up until October 1941, it was still in some cases possible for Jews to leave Germany but from 1940 onwards the German government planned mass deportations to the east only, whereby the destination* and the fate of the deportees was intentionally left open. Soon, however, these plans, too, were outdated. With the attack on the Soviet Union, first the German army and then the troops of the SD and the Sicherheitspolizei (Security Police) started planned mass executions of Polish-Jewish citizens. By 1942, over one million people of Slavic or Jewish origin had fallen victim to this "racial reorganization".

The **"Final Solution to the Jewish Question"***, effectively the extermination of all European Jews, was agreed upon at the Wannsee Conference, held on 20 January 1942 near Berlin. Hitler approved of the **Wannsee minutes*** (cf. S 54), although he did not issue any written order. The consequence was the establishment of a huge apparatus, organized with military precision, whose only aim was to arrest, transport and finally kill millions of people and to record their deaths. Many of those people had to undergo unbelievable suffering in conditions we nowadays cannot even imagine. The extent of the crimes committed in this systematic **genocide***, the criminal energy of those who gave orders and those who obeyed them, but also the ability of the bureaucrats, managers, civil servants, judges, doctors, engineers, soldiers etc. to push aside those crimes, cannot be understood today. The fact that Heinrich Himmler himself, facing the loss of the war, ordered a stop to the gassing* in Auschwitz on 1 November 1944, is proof of Nazi awareness of this being the most inhumane crime ever committed by humans.

charge fine

destination journey's end

"Final Solution to the Jewish Question"/Wannsee minutes „Endlösung der Judenfrage"/ Wannsee-Protokoll

genocide Genozid, Völkermord

gassing Vergasung

Political and Ideological Preconditions for National Socialism

S 1 Max Cohen-Reuss

Speech at the first Imperial Council Convention

In this speech, delivered on 19 December 1918, the journalist and Social Democrat Max Cohen-Reuss elaborates on the question of Germany's future political system: national assembly (i. e. parliamentary democracy) or council democracy.

Pre-task
1. Make an educated guess as to which arguments Cohen-Reuss might bring forward in favour of a national assembly. Take the historical context into consideration by having a look at the overview section.

Tasks
2. Outline and explain the reasons why Cohen-Reuss favours elections for a National Assembly. Compare with your results from task 1.
3. State which concessions Cohen-Reuss is willing to make with the old authorities and explain why he thinks that these concessions are necessary.

günstig positive

Wie man auch über die Arbeiter- und Soldatenräte denken mag – ich denke ziemlich günstig* über sie und werde darauf noch zurückkommen –, in jedem Falle drücken die Arbeiter- und Soldatenräte nur einen Teilwillen, niemals aber den Willen des ganzen deutschen Volkes aus. Diesen festzustellen, darauf kommt es an.

Die Gefahr, in der wir schweben, ist, glaube ich, sehr viel größer, als die meisten es sich vorstellen.

Wirtschaftsleben economic life
Voraussetzung precondition
Wiederaufbau reconstruction

Wenn es so weitergeht wie bisher, dann wird unser gesamtes Wirtschaftsleben*, das doch die Voraussetzung* für den Wiederaufbau* Deutschlands ist, lahm gelegt, ohne dass wir in der Lage sind, etwas Neues an seine Stelle zu setzen. [...]

Parteigenosse party comrade

Kameraden und Parteigenossen*! Nun glaube ich, dass im Augenblick die Dinge sich so entwickelt haben, dass für die Wiederaufrichtung unseres wirtschaftlichen Lebens eine vorhergehende Neuregelung unserer politischen Verhältnisse notwendig ist. Es ist in dieser kritischen Zeit und im Augenblick umgekehrt, wie wir Sozialisten es meist angenommen haben. Für den Augenblick ist die Politik die Voraussetzung der Ökonomie geworden, und ich glaube, dass wir eine geregelte Verwaltung in Deutschland nur durch die Nationalversammlung herstellen können, die uns die demokratische Verfassung gibt und das Deutsche Reich wieder aufbaut und seine auseinander strebenden Teile zusammenhält. [...]

selbstverständlich sein to go without saying
zur Geltung kommen to show to advantage, to come into its own

Parteigenossen! Es sollte eigentlich für jeden Sozialisten selbstverständlich* sein, und das war es auch bisher, dass der Volkswille so schnell wie möglich zur Geltung* kommt. Ich will darauf hinweisen, dass es bis zur Mitte des Jahres 1917 die freieste Feststellung des Volkswillens auf Grund eines gleichen Wahlrechts für alle Männer und Frauen das selbstverständliche Programm aller sozialistischen Parteien der ganzen Welt war. [...]

verfassungsgebende Konstituante constituent assembly
Bolschewist Bolshevik (i.e. Russian communists)

Parteigenossen! In der glorreichen Revolution Russlands vom Frühjahr 1917 wurde als erste Forderung aufgestellt: die allgemeine verfassungsgebende Konstituante* für das Russische Reich! Erst den Bolschewisten* war es vorbehalten, hierin eine Änderung eintreten zu lassen. Man kann es aber gar nicht scharf genug betonen*, dass auch die Bolschewisten nicht von Anfang an gegen die Nationalversammlung waren. [...]

Nun frage ich Sie, Parteigenossen – wir wollen uns einmal ganz ruhig darüber unterhalten: was hat der Bolschewismus, die Diktatur des Proletariats in Russland erreicht? Nach meiner Überzeugung nichts, was zur Förderung* des Sozialismus, sondern nur, was dazu dienen kann, den Sozialismus auf Jahrzehnte hinaus zu diskreditieren. [...]

Parteigenossen, man kann eben Sozialismus durch Gewalt und Dekrete* nicht einführen; das hat uns das russische Beispiel gezeigt. Sozialisierung ist ein organischer* Entwicklungs- und Umbildungsprozess*, bei dem neue Wirtschaftsformen neben werdenden und auch alten Formen zusammen existieren werden. Wenn man aber diesen Entwicklungsprozess nicht in sorgsamster* Weise fördert, kommt die Katastrophe. [...]

Die Genossen sagen: wenn eine baldige Nationalversammlung zusammentritt, bekommen wir keine sozialistische Mehrheit, wir müssen deshalb die Sozialisierung vorher so schnell wie möglich beschließen. Parteigenossen, ich bin direkt der gegenteiligen Auffassung. Wenn wir eine sozialistische Mehrheit bekommen wollen, müssen wir die Nationalversammlung so schnell wie möglich einberufen. [...] Wenn die Genossen der U.S.P.*, die an eine solche Mehrheit nicht glauben, sich mit der alten Partei für die Wahlen zusammentun, was mein sehnlichster Wunsch* wäre, dann wird hier eine feste Reihe entstehen, die alle bürgerlichen Parteien schlagen wird und schlagen muss. [...]

Es ist selbstverständlich, dass wir alle so viel Sozialismus wollen, wie durchführbar* ist. Aber persönlich habe ich die Überzeugung, es wird nicht mehr Sozialismus durchführbar sein, als die Mehrheit des Volkes will. Denn ein Sozialismus, der vorher durchgeführt wäre, hätte sehr geringen Bestand, wenn die Mehrheit des Volkes anderer Meinung wäre. [...]

betonen to emphasize, to stress

Förderung support

Dekret decree

organisch organic, natural
Entwicklungs- und Umbildungsprozess process of development and transformation
sorgsam careful

U.S.P. Independent Socialist Party (USPD)

sehnlichster Wunsch burning desire

durchführbar feasible

The Imperial Council Convention met in the House of Representatives in Berlin.

nüchtern sober
gering einschätzen to underestimate

Parteigenossen, schätzen Sie wirklich bei ganz ruhiger, nüchterner* Überlegung den Widerstand der bürgerlichen Kreise und der Intelligenz so gering* ein, dass wir, wenn wir sie politisch entrechten, gegen ihren Willen die Wirtschaft führen können? [...]

Gesamtkomplex complete complex

Nun aber müssen wir vor allen Dingen und zuerst – und das hängt natürlich mit dem Gesamtkomplex* der Fragen, die ich hier zu entwickeln mir erlaubt habe, zusammen – Frieden haben, einen Vorfrieden und dann einen schnellen, endgültigen Frieden. Glaubt jemand, der die Interessen der Entente kennt, dass diese Frieden schließen wird mit einem Deutschland, das nicht zu geordneten Zuständen und nicht zur Aufnahme seiner Produktion gekommen ist? Die Entente denkt gar nicht daran.

from: Peter Longerich (Hg.): Die Erste Republik. Dokumente zur Geschichte des Weimarer Staates, München (Piper) 1992, pp. 67–72

S 2 Ernst Däumig

Speech at the first Imperial Council Convention

Ernst Däumig, socialist and journalist, delivered a speech at the first Imperial Council Convention on 19 December 1919 as well. His topic, too, was whether Germany should become a parliamentary democracy or a council democracy.

Pre-task
1. Make an educated guess as to which arguments Däumig might bring forward in favour of a council democracy.

Tasks
2. Outline and explain the reasons why Däumig favours a council democracy for Germany. Compare these with your results from task 1.
3. When contrasting council democracy and parliamentary democracy, Däumig mostly uses negatively connoted words and expressions. Find them in the text and explain their implications.
4. Take a critical stand on Däumig's assumption that a parliamentary democracy stands in the way of the German people governing itself (cf. ll. 41 ff.).

sich einen Strick um den Hals legen to put a rope around one's neck
einleuchten to be clear
gleichbedeutend equivalent (to)
für etw. plädieren to advocate sth.
Konzession concession
nichts als Schall und Rauch sein to be nothing but hollow words, to be nothing but smoke and mirrors
breitspurig pompous
einnisten to nest
im Gefolge in its wake
Staffage decoration
Marionette puppet

Wenn die Geschichte dieser Revolutionswochen in Deutschland geschrieben wird, dann wird man sich lächelnd fragen: Waren denn die Leute so blind, dass sie nicht sahen, dass sie sich selbst den Strick um dem Hals legten*? Denn das muss doch jedem Denkenden einleuchten*, dass die jubelnde Zustimmung zur Nationalversammlung gleichbedeutend* ist mit einem Todesurteil für das System, dem Sie jetzt angehören, für das Rätesystem. [...]

Genossen und Kameraden, Sie haben vorhin, als Genosse Cohen so warm für die Nationalversammlung plädierte* und sogar für einen frühen Termin eintrat, zum Teil lebhaft applaudiert; Sie haben aber zweifellos damit Ihr eigenes Todesurteil gesprochen. Denn die Konzessionen*, die vom Genossen Cohen und anderen Leuten gemacht werden, dass ja, wenn die Nationalversammlung komme, das Rätesystem noch weiterbestehen könne, sind ja doch nur Schall und Rauch*. Was soll denn dieses Rätesystem neben einem sich breitspurig* einnistenden* parlamentarisch-demokratisch-bürgerlichen System, wie es die Nationalversammlung einmal im Gefolge* hat! Eine leere Staffage*, eine Marionette*! Im Wirtschaftsleben werden mit Hilfe der Nationalversammlung und des Bürgertums die Gewerkschaften alten Stils* natürlich die Arbeiterräte aus den Betrieben ganz schnell herausgedrängt* haben. Das machen sie heute schon und haben es schon gemacht. Ach nein, dieses beides lässt sich eben nicht miteinander vereinigen, man muss das eine oder das andere wollen. Aber das sage ich Ihnen: all Ihre Illusionen auf ein neues, freies, auch kulturell und geistig freies Deutschland, auf ein deutsches Volk, das diesen alten Untertanengeist* von sich geworfen hat, der ja heute noch knüppeltief drinsitzt im deutschen Volk, auf ein Deutschland, in dem das Volk auch wirklich aktiven Anteil an seinen Geschicken* nimmt und nicht alle zwei, drei Jahre mit einem Stimmzettel* in der Hand zur Wahlurne* läuft, erreichen Sie nicht mit diesem alten System. [...]

Die Diktatur ist zweifellos mit dem Rätesystem verbunden. Aber was sich in Russland durch die historischen Gesetze aufzwang, braucht noch lange nicht in Deutschland der Fall zu sein*. Ich gehöre nicht zu denen, die mechanisch und sklavisch* das russische Beispiel nachzuahmen* versuchen. Ich bin Deutscher, und ich bin stolz darauf, Deutscher zu sein. Die 20 Jahre, die ich jetzt in der Partei bin, habe ich dazu verwandt, die deutsche Kultur, die deutsche Dichtung*, die deutsche Literatur den Massen da unten zugänglich* zu machen, weil die bürgerliche Gesellschaft nach dieser Richtung hin Millionen jahraus, jahrein* geistig beraubt hat. Aber das, was sich aus der großen Geschichte der russischen Revolution ergibt*, haben wir uns nutzbar* zu machen, und ich habe stets zu denen gehört, die den Verzweiflungskampf der Bolschewisten gestützt haben. [...]

Wir müssen ja doch aufräumen* mit dieser ganzen alten Verwaltungsmaschine, die wir haben in Reich und Bundesstaaten und Kommunen*. Die Selbstverwaltung* muss doch mehr und mehr die Aufgabe sein, die dem deutschen Volke erwachsen* muss, anstatt des Regiertwerdens. Wie wollen Sie aber ein Volk in weitest gehendem Maße zur Selbstverwaltung erziehen, wenn Sie es politisch einfach so dahintrotten* lassen und wenn Sie Erwählte in irgendein Parlament schicken, die dann wieder die üblichen Redebächlein* fließen lassen und den Parteihader* erscheinen lassen, aber sonst an den Dingen draußen beim Volk nichts ändern!

from: Peter Longerich (Hg.): Die Erste Republik. Dokumente zur Geschichte des Weimarer Staates, München (Piper) 1992, pp. 72–75

alten Stils old-fashioned
herausdrängen to crowd sth./sb. out

Untertanengeist culture/spirit of subservience
Geschick fate
Stimmzettel ballot paper
Wahlurne ballot box

der Fall sein to be the case
sklavisch slavish
nachahmen to imitate
Dichtung poetry
zugänglich machen to make accessible
jahraus, jahrein year in, year out
sich aus etw. ergeben to result from sth.
nutzbar machen to make useful, to harness
aufräumen to do away with sth., to get rid of sth.
Kommune local authority
Selbstverwaltung self-administration
aus etw. erwachsen to accrue from sth.
trotten to jog
Redebächlein stream of speech
Hader quarrel

Rosa Luxemburg (1871–1919)

Rosa Luxemburg was born in Zamosc, Poland, on 5 March 1871, as the daughter of a businessman. She became politically interested and engaged at the age of 16 and joined the first Marxist party in Poland. From 1889 to 1897, Luxemburg studied political sciences and national economy at the University of Zürich. During that time, she published articles in workers' newspapers and magazines and was connected with leading personalities of both the Polish and the Swiss Socialist movements. A fictitious marriage in 1897 made it possible for her to immigrate to Germany. From then on, she became an active member of the SPD and spoke at many party congresses and at international Socialist congresses. Due to repeated anti-war political statements on her part, she was arrested and sent to prison. On 15 January 1919, Rosa Luxemburg and her comrade Karl Liebknecht were assassinated by counter-revolutionary soldiers during the Spartacist Uprising.

S 3 Rosa Luxemburg
„An die Proletarier aller Länder"

Rosa Luxemburg's appeal was published on 25 November 1918 in the Spartacist newspaper *Die Rote Fahne*. She elaborates on the current situation after the overthrow of the German Empire and calls for action.

Pre-task

1. In her appeal, Luxemburg sharply contrasts the proletarians with the capitalists. Have a look at the words and phrases below and sort them into those two categories.

> rücksichtslos • Not und Elend • friedlich gesinnt • brüderliche Solidarität • unmenschlich • herrschende Klassen • blühende Gärten • ausgesogen, ausgepresst • zerbrochenes Werkzeug • die Massen, weitere Kreise • brutal • zur Schlachtbank getrieben

Tasks

2. Read the appeal, and check your results from the pre-task. Then, search for more contrasts and complete the table below.

proletarians	capitalists
friedlich gesinnt	brutal
…	…

3. Summarize the arguments Luxemburg puts forward against the national assembly.
4. Explain the expression „Deutschland ist schwanger mit der sozialen Revolution" (l. 47).
5. Evaluate which statements are owed to the immediate revolutionary situation and which can be considered part of the communist ideology.

Post-task

6. Discuss in how far Luxemburg's, Däumig's and Cohen-Reuss's views are in accordance with democratic principles.

Genosse comrade
Schlachtbank slaughterhouse
aussaugen to suck sth. dry
aushungern to starve out
Geißel scourge [skɜrdʒ]

Internationale Communist International (i.e. international communist organization)

An die Proletarier aller Länder.
Proletarier! Männer und Frauen der Arbeit! Genossen*!
In Deutschland hat die Revolution ihren Einzug gehalten. Die Massen der Soldaten, die vier Jahre lang zur Schlachtbank* getrieben wurden um kapitalistischer Profite willen, die Masse der Arbeiter, die vier Jahre lang ausgesogen*, ausge‑ 5
presst, ausgehungert* wurden, sie haben sich erhoben. Das furchtbare Werkzeug der Unterdrückung: der preußische Militarismus, die Geißel* der Menschheit, liegt gebrochen am Boden; seine sichtbarsten Vertreter und damit die sichtbarsten Schuldigen an diesem Kriege, der Kaiser und der Kronprinz, sind außer Landes geflüchtet. Überall haben sich Arbeiter- und Soldatenräte gebildet. 10
Proletarier aller Länder, wir sagen nicht, dass in Deutschland alle Macht wirklich in die Hände des arbeitenden Volkes gelangt, dass der volle Sieg der proletarischen Revolution bereits errungen sei. Noch sitzen in der Regierung alle jene Sozialisten, die im August 1914 unser kostbarstes Gut, die Internationale*, preisgegeben haben, die vier Jahre lang die deutsche Arbeiterklasse und die 15
Internationale zugleich verraten haben.
Aber, Proletarier aller Länder, jetzt spricht der deutsche Proletarier selbst zu euch.

Wir glauben, das Recht zu haben, in seinem Namen vor euer Forum zu treten. Wir haben vom ersten Tage dieses Krieges uns bemüht, unsere internationalen Pflichten zu erfüllen, indem wir jene verbrecherische Regierung mit allen Kräften bekämpften und sie als wahre Schuldige des Krieges brandmarken*.

Genossen der Krieg führenden Länder, wir kennen eure Lage. Wohl wissen wir, dass eure Regierungen nun, da sie den Sieg errungen haben, manche Volksschichten* durch den äußeren Glanz des Sieges blenden*. [...] Wir wissen, dass euch in euren Ländern das Proletariat die furchtbarsten Opfer an Fleisch und Gut gebracht hat, dass es des grauenhaften Gemetzels* müde ist, dass der Proletarier jetzt nach Hause zurückkehrt und zu Hause Not und Elend findet, während in der Hand weniger Kapitalisten Milliardenvermögen angehäuft* sind. Er hat erkannt und wird weiter erkennen, dass der Krieg auch von euren Regierenden geführt worden ist um der großen Geldsäcke willen. [...] Der Imperialismus aller Länder kennt keine „Verständigung", er kennt nur ein Recht: den Kapitalprofit, nur eine Sprache: das Schwert, nur ein Mittel: die Gewalt. [...]

Proletarier aller Länder! Dieser Krieg muss der letzte sein! Das sind wir den 12 Millionen hingemordeter Opfer, das sind wir unseren Kindern, das sind wir der Menschheit schuldig. [...]

Die Bestie Kapital, die die Hölle des Weltkrieges heraufbeschworen* hat, ist nicht imstande, sie wieder zu bannen, wirkliche Ordnung herzustellen, der gequälten Menschheit Brot und Arbeit, Frieden und Kultur, Recht und Freiheit zu sichern. [...] Der Sozialismus allein ist nicht imstande, das große Werk des dauernden Friedens zu vollbringen, die tausend blutenden Wunden der Menschheit zu heilen, die vom Zuge der apokalyptischen Reiter des Krieges niedergestampften Fluren* Europas in blühende Gärten zu verwandeln, an Stelle der vernichtenden Produktivkräfte* verzehnfachte* neue hervorzuzaubern, alle physischen und sittlichen* Energien der Menschheit zu wecken und an Stelle des Hasses und der Zwietracht brüderliche Solidarität zu setzen, Eintracht* und Achtung* für alles, was Menschenantlitz* trägt. [....] Darum blickt das Proletariat Deutschlands in dieser Stunde auf euch. Deutschland ist schwanger mit der sozialen Revolution, aber den Sozialismus kann nur das Weltproletariat verwirklichen. [...]

Proletarier aller Länder! Wir rufen euch auf, das Werk der sozialistischen Befreiung zu vollbringen, der geschändeten Welt wieder Menschenantlitz zu verleihen und jenes Wort wahr zu machen, mit dem wir uns in alten Tagen oft begrüßten und mit dem wir auseinander gingen:

Die Internationale wird die Menschheit sein!

Es lebe die Weltrevolution des Proletariats!

Proletarier aller Länder vereinigt euch! [...]

„Die Rote Fahne", 25. November 1918, qtd. in: Rosa Luxemburg. Ausgewählte Reden und Schriften, II. Band, pp. 612–616

---

brandmarken to brand, to denounce

Volksschicht part of the population
blenden to blind
Gemetzel massacre

anhäufen to accumulate

heraufbeschwören to provoke sth.

Flur field

Produktivkräfte productive forces
verzehnfachen to increase tenfold
sittlich moral
Eintracht concord
Achtung respect
Menschenantlitz human countenance

Friedrich Ebert (1871–1925)

Friedrich Ebert was born in Heidelberg on 4 February 1871. His original profession was that of a saddler. He joined the Socialist German Workers' Party and the saddlers' trade union in 1889 and thus started his political career. In May 1891, Ebert moved to Bremen and, in 1893, he became the editor of the *Bremer Bürger-Zeitung*, an SPD party organ. After presiding over the SPD party convention in 1904 in Bremen, Ebert became better known nationwide. On 20 September 1913, he was elected joint party chairman of the SPD (together with Hugo Haase) at the party convention in Jena. In general, Ebert supported war loans for World War I, whereas his co-chairman Haase rejected them. On 6 January, both Haase and Ebert returned to Berlin and after Haase resigned as party chairman in 1916, Ebert, together with Philip Scheidemann, became chairman of the SPD group in the Reichstag. In April 1917, discussions about war loans led to a split-off of the Independent Socialist Party (USPD) and the left-wing extremist Spartacus League. When strikes broke out in Berlin in January 1918, Ebert opted for a fast end to them, which resulted in him being called "traitor of the workers" by the political left and "traitor of the fatherland" by the right. Nevertheless, on 11 February 1919, he was elected Germany's first Reichspräsident. Ebert died on 28 February 1925 of appendicitis.

Friedrich Ebert

S 4 Friedrich Ebert

„Rückkehr auf den Weg der Gesetzmäßigkeit"

Friedrich Ebert gave this speech at the opening of the national assembly in Weimar on 6 February 1919.

Pre-task
1. The title of Ebert's speech suggests that Germany had left the path of legality in the past and is now on its way towards following it again. Use your knowledge about Germany's role and responsibility in the First World War and explain in how far the German Empire had acted "illegally".

Tasks
2. Scan the text for references to the "nasty legacy" (l. 36) the new provisional government has to face and explain them.
3. Point out Ebert's attitude towards the revolution.
4. Explain how he characterizes the policy of the provisional government.

Meine Damen und Herren, die Reichsregierung begrüßt durch mich die Verfassunggebende Versammlung der deutschen Nation. Besonders herzlich begrüße ich die Frauen, die zum ersten Mal gleichberechtigt im Reichsparlament erscheinen.
Die provisorische Regierung verdankt ihr Mandat der Revolution; sie wird es in die Hände der Nationalversammlung zurücklegen.
In der Revolution erhob sich das deutsche Volk gegen eine veraltete, zusammenbrechende Gewaltherrschaft. Sobald das Selbstbestimmungsrecht des deutschen Volkes gesichert ist, kehrt es zurück auf den Weg der Gesetzmäßigkeit*. Nur auf der breiten Heerstraße der parlamentarischen Beratung und Beschlussfassung* lassen sich die unaufschiebbaren* Veränderungen auch auf wirtschaftlichem und sozialem Gebiete vorwärts bringen, ohne das Reich und sein Wirtschaftsleben zugrunde zu richten*.

Weg der Gesetzmäßigkeit path of legality
Beschlussfassung resolution
unaufschiebbar not to be delayed
zugrunde richten to destroy

Deshalb begrüßt die Reichsregierung in dieser Nationalversammlung den höchs-
15 ten und einzigen Souverän in Deutschland. Mit den alten Königen und Fürsten
von Gottes Gnaden* ist es für immer vorbei.

Wir verwehren niemandem eine sentimentale Erinnerungsfeier. Aber so gewiss
diese Nationalversammlung eine große republikanische Mehrheit hat, so gewiss
sind die alten gottgegebenen Abhängigkeiten für immer beseitigt. Das deutsche
20 Volk ist frei, bleibt frei und regiert in aller Zukunft sich selbst.

Diese Freiheit ist der einzige Trost, der dem deutschen Volke geblieben ist, der
einzige Halt, an dem es aus dem Blutsumpf des Krieges und der Niederlage sich
wieder herausarbeiten kann. [...]

Wir haben den Krieg verloren. Diese Tatsache ist keine Folge der Revolution [...],
25 es war die Kaiserliche Regierung des Prinzen Max von Baden, die den Waffenstill-
stand einleitete, der uns wehrlos* machte. Nach dem Zusammenbruch unserer
Verbündeten und angesichts der militärischen und wirtschaftlichen Lage konnte
sie nicht anders handeln. Die Revolution lehnt die Verantwortung ab für das
Elend, in das die verfehlte* Politik der alten Gewalten und der leichtfertige* Über-
30 mut* der Militaristen das deutsche Volk gestürzt haben. [...]

Deutschland darf nicht wieder dem alten Elend der Zersplitterung* und der Verengung* anheimfallen*. Geschichte und Anlage hemmen zwar, einen straff zen-
tralisierten Einheitsstaat zu bilden. Viele Stämme und Dialekte sind in Deutschland vereinigt, aber sie müssen in einer Nation und einer Sprache zusammenklin-
35 gen. [...]

Die provisorische Regierung hat eine sehr üble Erbschaft* angetreten. Wir waren
im so eigentlichen Wortsinne die Konkursverwalter* des alten Regimes; alle
Scheuern*, alle Lager waren leer, alle Vorräte gingen zur Neige*, der Kredit war
erschüttert, die Moral tief gesunken. Wir haben [...] gestützt und gefördert vom
40 Zentralrat der Arbeiter und Soldatenräte unsere beste Kraft eingesetzt, die Gefahren und das Elend der Übergangszeit zu bekämpfen.

Wir haben der Nationalversammlung nicht vorgegriffen*. Aber wo Zeit und Not
drängten, haben wir die dringlichsten Forderungen der Arbeiter zu erfüllen uns
bemüht. Wir haben alles getan, um das wirtschaftliche Leben wieder in Gang zu
45 bringen. Wenn der Erfolg nicht unseren Wünschen entsprach, so müssen die
Umstände, die das verhinderten, gerecht gewürdigt werden.

Sorgenvoll blickt uns die Zukunft an. Wir vertrauen aber trotz alledem auf die
unverwüstliche* Schaffenskraft* der deutschen Nation. Die alten Grundlagen der
deutschen Machtstellung sind für immer zerbrochen. [...]
50 Wie der 9. November 1918 angeknüpft hat an den 18. März 1848, so müssen wir
hier in Weimar die Wandlung vollziehen vom Imperialismus, von der Weltmacht
zur geistigen Größe. [...] So wollen wir an die Arbeit gehen, unser großes Ziel fest
vor Augen, das Recht des deutschen Volkes zu wahren, in Deutschland eine starke
Demokratie zu verankern und sie mit wahrem sozialen Geist und sozialistischer
55 Tat zu erfüllen.

So wollen wir wahr machen, was Fichte der deutschen Nation als ihre Bestimmung* gegeben hat: „Wir wollen errichten ein Reich des Rechtes und der Wahr-
haftigkeit, gegründet auf Gleichheit all dessen, was Menschenantlitz trägt."

from: Herbert Michaelis, Ernst Schraepler (Eds.): Ursachen und Folgen. Vom deutschen Zusammenbruch
1918 und 1945 bis zur staatlichen Neuordnung Deutschlands in der Gegenwart, Bd. 3, Berlin (n.d.),
pp. 247 ff.

---

von Gottes Gnaden by grace of God

wehrlos defenceless

verfehlt failed
leichtfertig thoughtless, careless
Übermut arrogance
Zersplitterung fragmentation
Verengung restriction
anheimfallen to fall victim to sth.

üble Erbschaft nasty legacy
Konkursverwalter liquidator
Scheuer barn
zur Neige gehen to run short

jdm. bei etw. vorgreifen to anticipate sth.

unverwüstlich indestructible
Schaffenskraft creative power

Bestimmung destiny, purpose

National Socialism

CONNECT

The Weimar Constitution: the basis for "the Most Radical Democracy in Europe" or a recipe for chaos?

Task — Assessing the strengths and weaknesses of the constitution and the Germans' attitude towards democracy:

The German theologian and member of the German Democratic Party (DDP) Ernst Troeltsch (1865–1923) called German democracy the "most radical" one in Europe in his essay "Die deutsche Demokratie".

- First, take a critical stand on his statement by comparing the Weimar Constitution and the corresponding articles (S 5a) with the 1871 Constitution (cf. chapter 1, S 49c). Focus on
  - the head of state,
  - the Reichstag (parliament) and
  - the federal states.
- Second, study the profiles of the political parties (S 5b) and their election posters. Order each party from the most left-wing to the most right-wing and explain the party's attitude towards the Weimar democracy. In doing so, refer to symbolic elements of the election posters as well.
- Third, study the election results for the National Assembly and the Reichstag from 1919 until 1933 (S 5c). Transfer the information into a line graph for better visualization. Taking your results from the two previous tasks into consideration, explain why governing the Weimar Republic became ever more difficult.
- Fourth, explain the meaning of the front page (S 5d) and, incorporating your present knowledge, the meaning of the question "a republic without republicans?".

S 5a The Weimar Constitution

Basic Rights Arts. 109–164 — Possibility of restriction according to Art. 48

- **President of the Reich** — appointment (on proposal of the Reichsrat); supreme command
- **Reichsgericht** (Imperial Court of Justice)
- **Reichsregierung (government)** — appointment/dismissal
  - Reich Chancellor — proposal → Reich Ministers
- emergency act (Art. 48) → emergency decree
- **Reichswehr** (armed forces)
- **Reichstag** — 1919: 421 to 1933: 647 deputies; dissolve / confidence; vote on
  - KPD | SPD | Z | DVP | DNV | NSDAP
  - President
- **Reichsrat** — 66 votes (1925); veto; chairman (member of the government)
- **18 Länder (federal states)** — Ministerpräsident, Ministerpräsident

Legend: legislation, executive, judiciary, legislative initiative (§)

- direct election for 7 years
- proportional representation for 4 years
- **voters** (over 20) universal, equal, direct and secret right to vote
- **plebiscite** (upon request of the Reichspräsident)
- **petition for a referendum** (by 1/10 of the voters)

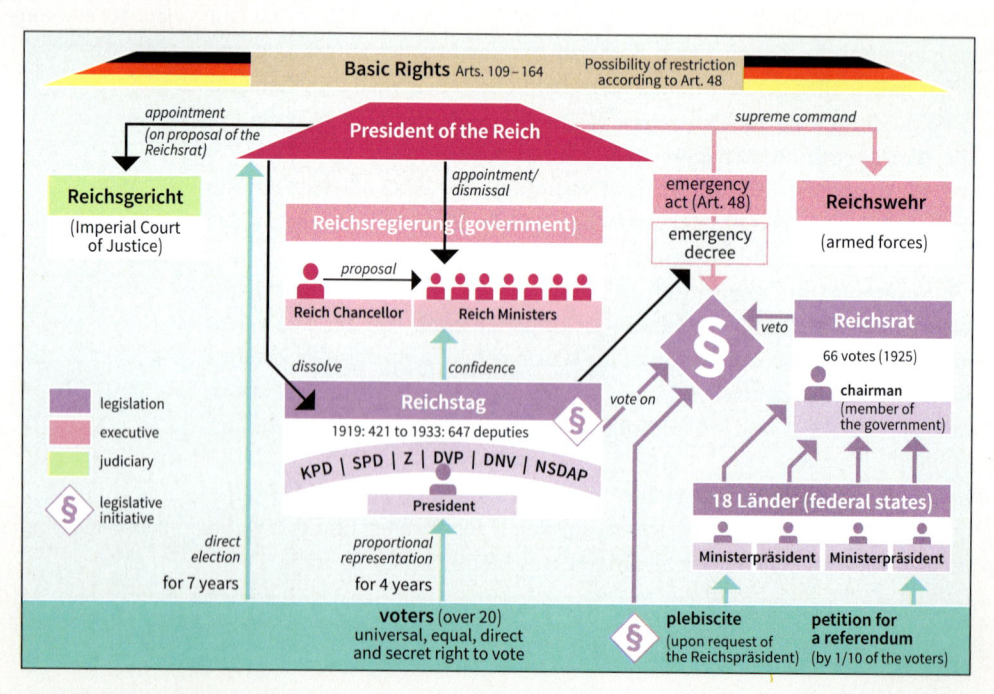

Präambel
Das deutsche Volk, [...] von dem Willen beseelt*, sein Reich in Freiheit und Gerechtigkeit zu erneuern und zu festigen, dem inneren und dem äußeren Frieden zu dienen und den gesellschaftlichen Fortschritt zu fördern, hat sich diese Verfassung gegeben. [...]

Artikel 1
Das Deutsche Reich ist eine Republik. Die Staatsgewalt geht vom Volke aus.
Artikel 2
Das Reichsgebiet besteht aus den Gebieten der deutschen Länder. [...]
Artikel 20
Der Reichstag besteht aus den Abgeordneten des deutschen Volkes.
Artikel 21
Die Abgeordneten sind Vertreter des ganzen Volkes. Sie sind nur ihrem Gewissen* unterworfen und an Aufträge nicht gebunden*.
Artikel 22
Die Abgeordneten werden in allgemeiner, gleicher, unmittelbarer* und geheimer Wahl von den über zwanzig Jahre alten Männern und Frauen nach den Grundsätzen der Verhältniswahl gewählt. [...]
Artikel 23
Der Reichstag wird auf vier Jahre gewählt. Spätestens am sechzigsten Tage nach ihrem Ablauf muss die Neuwahl stattfinden. [...]
Artikel 41
Der Reichspräsident wird vom ganzen deutschen Volke gewählt.
Wählbar* ist jeder Deutsche, der das fünfunddreißigste Lebensjahr vollendet hat. [...]
Artikel 43
Das Amt des Reichspräsidenten dauert sieben Jahre. Wiederwahl ist zulässig.
Vor Ablauf der Frist* kann der Reichspräsident auf Antrag des Reichstags durch Volksabstimmung abgesetzt* werden. [...]
Artikel 48
Wenn ein Land die ihm nach der Reichsverfassung oder den Reichsgesetzen obliegenden* Pflichten nicht erfüllt, kann der Reichspräsident es dazu mit Hilfe der bewaffneten Macht anhalten*.
Der Reichspräsident kann, wenn im Deutschen Reiche die öffentliche Sicherheit und Ordnung erheblich gestört oder gefährdet wird, die zur Wiederherstellung der öffentlichen Sicherheit und Ordnung nötigen Maßnahmen treffen, erforderlichenfalls mit Hilfe der bewaffneten Macht einschreiten. Zu diesem Zwecke darf er vorübergehend die in den Artikeln 114, 115, 117, 118, 123, 124 und 153 festgesetzten Grundrechte ganz oder zum Teil außer Kraft setzen. [...]
Artikel 76
Die Verfassung kann im Wege der Gesetzgebung geändert werden. Jedoch kommen Beschlüsse des Reichstags auf Abänderung der Verfassung nur zustande, wenn zwei Drittel der gesetzlichen Mitgliederzahl anwesend sind und wenigstens zwei Drittel der Anwesenden zustimmen. [...]

---

von etw. beseelt sein to be inspired by sth.

Gewissen conscience ['kɒnʃəns]
an etw. gebunden sein to be bound to sth.
unmittelbar direct

wählbar eligible

Frist deadline
jdn. absetzen to remove sb. from office

jdm. obliegen to fall to sb.
jdn. dazu anhalten, etw. zu tun to admonish sb. to do sth.

unverletzlich inviolable
Beeinträchtigung infringement
Entziehung suspension

Brief-, Post- und Fernsprechgeheimnis privacy of correspondence, posts and telecommunications

gewährleisten to guarantee

Enteignung expropriation

Artikel 114
Die Freiheit der Person ist unverletzlich*. Eine Beeinträchtigung* oder Entziehung* der persönlichen Freiheit durch die öffentliche Gewalt ist nur auf Grund von Gesetzen zulässig. [...]

Artikel 115
Die Wohnung jedes Deutschen ist [...] unverletzlich. Ausnahmen sind nur auf Grund von Gesetzen zulässig. [...]

Artikel 117
Das Briefgeheimnis sowie das Post-, [...] und Fernsprechgeheimnis* sind unverletzlich. Ausnahmen können nur durch Reichsgesetz zugelassen werden.

Artikel 118
Jeder Deutsche hat das Recht, innerhalb der Schranken der allgemeinen Gesetze seine Meinung durch Wort, Schrift, Druck, Bild oder in sonstiger Weise frei zu äußern. [...]
Eine Zensur findet nicht statt. [...]

Artikel 153
Das Eigentum wird von der Verfassung gewährleistet*. Sein Inhalt und seine Schranken ergeben sich aus den Gesetzen.
Eine Enteignung* kann nur [...] auf gesetzlicher Grundlage vorgenommen werden. [...]

Artikel 181
[...] Das deutsche Volk hat durch seine Nationalversammlung diese Verfassung beschlossen und verabschiedet. Sie tritt mit dem Tage ihrer Verkündung in Kraft.

Schwarzburg 11. August 1919.

Der Reichspräsident
Ebert.
Das Reichsministerium
Bauer, Erzberger, Hermann Müller, Dr. David, Noske, Schmidt, Schlicke, Giesberts, Dr. Mayer, Dr. Bell.

Reichsgesetzblatt 1919, Nr. 152, S. 1383 ff., in: Ernst Rudolf Huber (Ed.): Dokumente zur Deutschen Verfassungsgeschichte, Band 4. Stuttgart: W. Kohlhammer, 1978–1992, pp. 151 ff.

S 5b) Political Parties

Catholic Centre Party (Zentrum, or, Z)
In terms of ideology and class, the Catholic Centre Party (Zentrum, or, Z) was more diverse than any of its Weimar rivals. Its one area of uniformity was its commitment to protect the interests of Germany's Catholics; about 34% of the population. Thus, it is not surprising that the largest number of Centre Party supporters were Catholic, although Protestants also supported the party and were included in its legislative delegation. Even some of Ger-

many's Jews (1% of the population) voted for the Catholic Centre party. Catholic women voted for the party in very high numbers. While it had a left-liberal trade union wing, and a right-conservative nationalist wing, the weight of its support placed the party at the centre of the political spectrum. The Centre Party was vital to the stability of the Republic, and it was a part of every Weimar government. Its leaders served as chancellors for nine administrations and were included in each of the twenty-one cabinets that ruled during the fourteen years of the Republic. With the change in leadership of the party in 1928, it drifted towards its more conservative wing which had evolved into the Bavarian People's Party (BVP). Independent of the national Catholic Centre party, the BVP often positioned itself in opposition to the Weimar government.

"Weimarer Political Parties", by Paul Bookbinder, www.facinghistory.org [17.04.2015]

Embedded text:
„Wer schützt Familie – Heimat – Arbeit? Das Zentrum"

Language support

Schild buckler • **Pflug** plough/plow

Election poster of the Centre Party, 1930

Communist Party (KPD)

The German Communist Party (KPD) was founded at the end of December 1918 in the midst of revolutionary chaos. Its earliest members came from the ranks of the radical Spartacist group that had been crushed by the army under orders from a transitional government dominated by Social Democrats. Drawing on a membership of more radical workers and a small group of radical intellectuals, the party was fundamentally opposed to the existence of the Weimar Republic and, although a leftist party, was particularly antagonistic to the democratic leftist Social Democratic Party. The Communists were in favour of a Russian style dictatorship and during the Weimar period fell more and more under the control of the Communist International based in Moscow. While the party had a strong feminist agenda, as well as the only prominent woman party leaders and the most women candidates for office across the political spectrum, this position did not translate into substantial female voting support. Although the party opposed anti-Semitism and had Jews among its leaders, very few German Jews voted Communist. During the crisis of the last Weimar years the parties voting strength grew substantially as it attracted support from the growing ranks of the unemployed.

"Weimarer Political Parties", by Paul Bookbinder, www.facinghistory.org [17.04.2015]

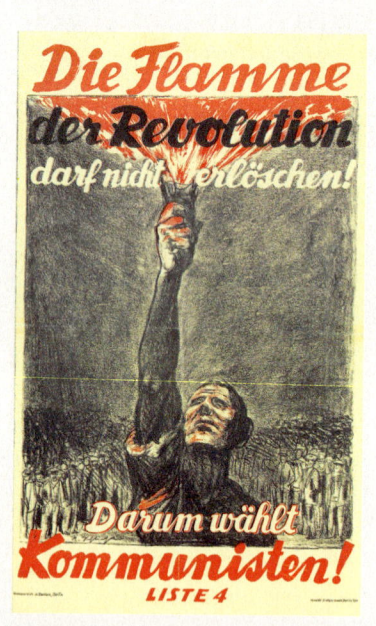

Embedded text:
„Die Flamme der Revolution darf nicht erlöschen! Darum wählt Kommunisten! Liste 4"

Language support

erlöschen to go out

Election poster of the Communist Party, 1924 (© Hessisches Landesmuseum Darmstadt/Foto: Wolfgang Fuhrmannek)

German Democratic Party (DDP)
The German Democratic Party's (DDP) largely Protestant membership was drawn from the middle class, often from professional groups of lawyers, doctors and liberal academics. Some of its leaders were converts to democracy and republicanism, but the party was firmly* supportive of the Weimar Republic and resistant to militarism and anti-Semitism. It attracted more Protestant than Catholic voters and many of Germany's Jews voted for the party. While the party fits on the left side of the political spectrum, it stressed its moderation. Unfortunately for the Weimar Republic, this party received its greatest vote totals in 1919 and saw its support erode* for most of the Weimar period. Contributing to the decline of the Democratic Party were the untimely deaths of Max Weber and Friedrich Naumann, its most prominent leaders. Yet, in spite of its declining support, the party played a significant role during the Weimar years, and was an eager participant in coalition governments. In an effort to revive its fortunes in the final days of the Republic, the Democratic Party reconstituted itself as the "State Party."

"Weimarer Political Parties", by Paul Bookbinder, www.facinghistory.org [17.04.2015]

firm strong

to erode to deteriorate

Embedded text:
„Säubert das Reich! wählt Deutsche Demokraten! LISTE 6"

Language support

säubern to cleanse [klenz]

Election poster of the German Democratic Party, 1919

German Nationalist People's Party (DNVP)

The supporters of the German Nationalist People's Party (DNVP) were generally Protestant and represented a mix of landowners and industrialists with crafts people and civil servants and farmers who followed the lead of the wealthy landowners. The party also attracted the more conservative elements among the white collar clerical and retail sales workers. It was militaristic, resistant to republican government, opposed to attempts to fulfil the terms of the Versailles treaty, and anti-Semitic.

"Weimarer Political Parties", by Paul Bookbinder, www.facinghistory.org [17.04.2015]

Embedded text:
„Wählt Schwarz-Weiß-Rot! Das ist Deutschnational!"

Language support

Ast branch

Election poster of the German Nationalist People's Party, around 1924. This poster shows the party's anti-republican attitude by ridiculing the newly designed "Reichsadler" by contrasting it with the eagle of the German Empire.

German People's Party (DVP)

The German People's Party (DVP) represented owners of small and middle-sized businesses and white-collar workers, and its support was much stronger among Protestants than Catholics. It lacked the rural base of the nationalists and was more moderate in its nationalism and less extreme in its anti-Semitism. The party had a core group which was willing to support and participate in Weimar coalition government, and these reform conservatives kept Gustav Stresemann as party leader. At the same time, other People's Party members were never reconciled to the new Republic.

"Weimarer Political Parties", by Paul Bookbinder, www.facinghistory.org [17.04.2015]

Embedded text:
„Wählt meine Partei
Die Deutsche Volkspartei"

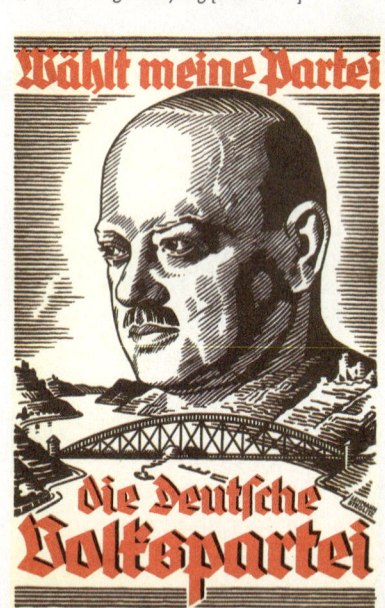

Election poster of the German People's Party, 1930. This poster uses former German foreign minister Gustav Stresemann for identification purposes. The river depicted here is the Rhine and Stresemann is looking westwards.

National Socialist German Workers Party (NSDAP or Nazi-Party)

The National Socialist German Workers Party (NSDAP or Nazi-Party), founded in 1919 as the German Workers party, began its move toward prominence when Adolf Hitler emerged as its principal speaker and leader. The National Socialists initially attracted young men who had been in the military and had not been able to reintegrate themselves into the civilian society and economy. The party also drew support from members of the lower middle class, shopkeepers, artisans* and white-collar workers. The party was unequivocally* opposed to the Weimar Republic and in 1923 its members, led by Hitler, tried unsuccessfully to seize government by force. After this failed attempt, the party reverted* to a strategy of gaining power through the electoral process without ever changing its fundamental opposition to democracy and the republican government. Anti-Semitism and the threat that the Jews represented to Germany were at the core of the Nazi ideology. During the later twenties, the base of National Socialist support expanded considerably. Although most of the top leaders of the party including Hitler,

artisan a person who is skilled at making things by hand
unequivocally clearly, strongly, unambiguously
to revert to to return to

were Catholic, and the party had begun in Catholic Munich, fewer Catholics proportionally voted for the party than did Protestants. This voting pattern came about because the Catholic Church urged its members to avoid supporting the Nazis. This opposition on the part of the Catholic Church to the Nazis was later dropped once Hitler achieved power. While the Nazis were slow to attract women supporters (the programme for women was summarized by the slogan "Children, the Kitchen and the Church"), women became the fastest growing group of supporters by the early 1930s. By 1932, the Nazis had become the most popular political party and they had the largest legislative delegation.

"Weimarer Political Parties", by Paul Bookbinder, www.facinghistory.org [17.04.2015]

Embedded text:
„Nimmer wird das Reich zerstöret –
wenn ihr einig seid und treu"
„Nationalsozialisten"

Election poster of the National Socialist German Workers Party, 1933. The person on the left is Hindenburg.

Social Democratic Party (SPD)

The Social Democratic Party (SPD) drew its support from blue-collar trade union skilled workers, and at times from more progressive white-collar workers and intellectuals. While the party had proportionally more Protestant than Catholic supporters, it did attract Catholic workers. In some parts of Germany landless farm workers voted for the party. German women from working class families voted for the Social Democratic Party in large numbers. Some of Germany's Jews also voted for the Social Democratic Party. From 1919 to 1932, the Social Democratic Party was the party that received the most votes in national elections and had the largest legislative delegation. The SPD was committed to further reform of Weimar society and hoped to eventually make the institutions and economy of Weimar more egalitarian*. This party was a bulwark* of the Republic and was the most active opponent of anti-Semitism during the Weimar years.

"Weimarer Political Parties", by Paul Bookbinder, www.facinghistory.org [17.04.2015]

egalitarian equal
bulwark support

Election poster of the Social Democratic Party, 1920

S 5c Elections for the National Assembly (1919) and the Reichstag

	19 Jan. 1919		6 June 1920		4 May 1924		7 Dec 1924		20 May 1928		14 Sept 1930		31 July 1932		6 Nov 1932		5 Mar 1933	
NSDAP	votes in thousands				1918		907		810		6409		13745		11737		17277	
	mandate	percent			32	6.5	14	3.0	12	2.6	101	18.3	230	37.3	196	33.1	288	43.9
DNVP	3721		4249		5696		6206		4381		2458		2177		2959		3136	
	44	10.3	71	15.1	95	19.5	103	20.5	73	14.2	41	7.0	37	5.9	52	8.3	52	8.0
DVP	1345		3919		2694		3049		2679		1578		436		662		432	
	19	4.4	65	13.9	45	9.2	51	10.1	45	8.7	30	4.5	7	1.2	11	1.9	2	1.1
Zentrum and BVP	5980		5083		4860		5253		4657		5132		5781		5325		5499	
	91	19.7	85	18.0	81	16.6	88	17.3	78	15.2	87	14.8	97	15.7	90	15.0	92	13.9
DDP since 1930 DStP	5641		2333		1655		1920		1505		1322		371		336		334	
	75	18.5	39	8.3	28	5.7	32	6.3	25	4.9	20	3.8	4	1.0	2	1.0	5	0.9
(M)SPD	11509		6104		6009		7881		9153		8577		7959		7248		7182	
	165	37.9	102	21.7	100	20.5	131	26.0	153	29.8	143	24.5	133	21.6	121	20.4	120	18.3
USPD	2317		5046		235		99		21		–		–		–		–	
	22	7.6	84	17.9	–	0.8	–	0.3	–	0.1	–	–	–	–	–	–	–	–
KPD	–		589		3693		2709		3264		4592		5283		5980		4848	
	–	–	4	2.1	62	12.6	45	9.0	54	10.6	77	13.1	89	14.3	100	16.9	81	12.3
others	483		869		2518		2365		4298		4821		1126		1176		634	
	7	1.6	9	3.0	29	8.6	29	7.8	51	24.7	72	13.9	11	3.1	12	3.3	7	1.6
voter turnout	83.0		79.2		77.4		78.8		75.6		82.0		84.1		80.6		88.8	
deputies	423		459		472		493		491		577		608		584		647	

Parties: NSDAP = National Socialist Geman Workers Party; DNVP = German Nationalist People's Party; DVP = German People's Party; Zentrum = Centre Party; BVP = Bavarian People's Party; DDP = German Democratic Party; DStP = German State Party; (M)SPD = (Majority) Social Democratic Party; USPD = Independent Social Democratic Party of Germany; KPD = Communist Party

from: Reinhard Sturm: "Zerstörung der Demokratie 1930–1932", in: Informationen zur Politischen Bildung, 23.12.2011, www.bpb.de/geschichte/nationalsozialismus/dossier-nationalsozialismus/39537/zerstoerung-der-demokratie?p=3 [17.04.15]

S 5d Simplicissimus

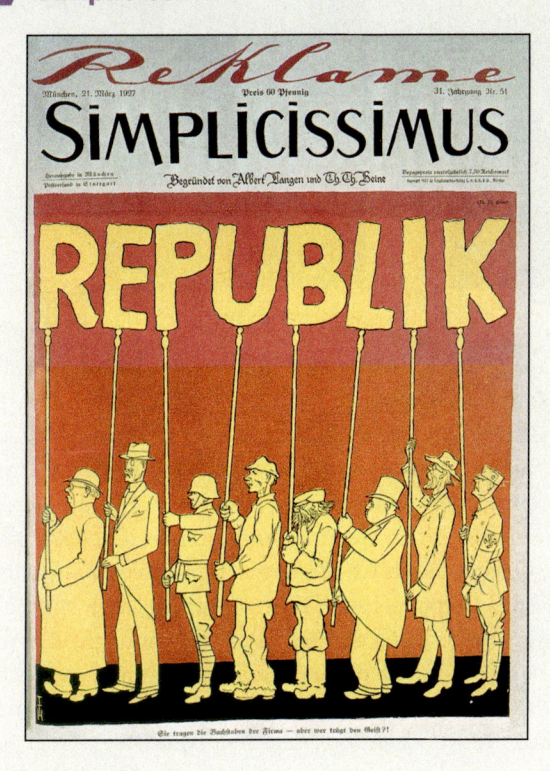

Front page of the German satirical magazine *Simplicissimus*, 21 March 1927. The persons depicted from left to right represent:
the clergy • academics • members of the *Wehrmacht* • the working class • people on welfare • "big business" • middle-class citizens • members of the SA (*Sturmabteilung*, storm troopers)

S 6 Wilhelm Groener

On the Ebert-Groener Pact

In the year 1957, Wilhelm Groener published a retrospective on the Ebert-Groener pact.

Pre-task
1. Have a look at the overview section and make sure that you know what the Ebert-Groener pact was about.

Tasks
2. Analyse the source.
3. Both Groener and Ebert wanted to end the war, however, they had different underlying ideas as to what Germany's future should look like. On 10 November 1918, they had a telephone conversation in which they talked about further procedures. Write the speech bubble and thought bubble for both of them in your exercise book (speech bubble: open conversation; thought bubble: underlying thoughts/ assumptions).
4. Assess whether the Ebert-Groener pact was justified in the face of the revolutionary situation Germany found itself in. Also consider Ebert's alternatives.

Friedrich Ebert   Wilhelm Gröner

[...] In den ersten Tagen nach Eintreffen in Wilhelmshöhe hatte ich eine nächtliche Unterredung im Hause des Oberpräsidenten v. Windheim mit dem Reichstagspräsidenten Fehrenbach, den ich zu einer Rücksprache mit der Heeresleitung gebeten hatte. Ich fragte ihn, ob er in der Lage sei, den Reichstag einzuberufen, damit wenigstens eine legale Institution vorhanden war, die die bürgerlichen Stimmen gegen die radikalen zur Geltung brachte*. Wir dachten natürlich nicht an Berlin als Ort des Zusammentritts, sondern hätten Kassel am liebsten gesehen, wohin man im Falle des Gelingens auch Ebert kommen lassen konnte. Aber Fehrenbach erklärte jede Einschaltung des Reichstags für unmöglich; es gäbe höchstens ein Rumpfparlament, und er fürchte, dass nicht einmal die Rechtsparteien erscheinen würden. Der Reichstag sei eben ein verbrauchtes* Instrument.

So hatte unsere ganze Aufmerksamkeit dem heimkehrenden Heer und der Art seiner Verwendung gegen die Revolution – d.h. gegen die von Unabhängigen* und Spartakus drohenden Gefahren – zu gelten.

In den allerersten Tagen nach dem 9./10. November hatten wir uns in der O.H.L. in dem Traum gewiegt*, dass wir genügend zuverlässige Truppen haben würden, um einen Grenzschutz am Rhein aufzubauen. Diese Hoffnung erwies sich als trügerisch*. Die in vollster Ordnung zurückmarschierenden Truppen blieben in der Hand ihrer Führer bis zu dem Augenblick, da sie am Rhein in die revolutionäre Atmosphäre eintraten; von da ab war kein Halten* mehr. Die von der Heeresleitung an die Marschstraßen ausgesandten „Serumspritzer", tüchtige*, geschickte Offiziere, die die Truppen gegen den Geist der Revolution immun machen sollten, hatten keinen wesentlichen Erfolg. Es gab Regimenter, die während des Rückmarsches sich vornahmen, sobald sie in ihren Garnisonen wären, den Revolutionären, besonders den Matrosen, den Garaus zu machen*; wenn sie aber in den Kasernen waren, wurden alle diese guten Vorsätze* vergessen und der Einfluss der Offiziere war dahin. So schnell wie möglich entlassen zu werden, war der Wunsch jedes einzelnen. Die Sorge um Haus und Hof, um die Familie überwog den vaterländischen* Gedanken. [...]

So blieb nur die Aufstellung einer Freiwilligen-Armee, die allein den Kampf gegen die städtischen Arbeitermassen aufnehmen konnte. [...] In Wilhelmshöhe wurde nun der Plan wieder aufgegriffen und im Einverständnis mit Ebert unter der Decke* weiterentwickelt.

Ehe diese Freiwilligentruppen in Erscheinung traten, hatten wir erst eine schwere Schlappe einzustecken, die die Untauglichkeit* der noch bestehenden Feldheerteile erwies*.

Vocabulary:
- **zur Geltung bringen** to emphasize, to bring to bear
- **verbraucht** used up
- **Unabhängige** Independent Socialist Party
- **im Traum wiegen** to feel optimistic about sth.
- **trügerisch** deceptive, delusory
- **kein Halten** no holding back
- **tüchtig** capable
- **jdm. den Garaus machen** to do sb. in, to murder sb., to kill sb.
- **gute Vorsätze** good intentions
- **vaterländisch** patriotic
- **unter der Decke** secretly
- **Untauglichkeit** incapability
- **erweisen** to show, to reveal

Es war von entscheidender Bedeutung, wer von den sich befehdenden* sozialistischen Gruppen Herr von Berlin war. Zusammen mit Ebert bereiteten wir den „Einzug" von zehn Divisionen nach Berlin vor, um seine Regierung fest in den
40 Sattel zu setzen. Einer meiner besten Mitarbeiter, Major v. Harbou, traf die Vorbereitungen, zum Führer der Truppen wurde General Lequis bestimmt. Aber der Berliner „Vollzugsausschuß" [Vollzugsausschuß der Berliner A. u. S. Räte unter Führung der Radikalen, der sich als eine Art Nebenregierung aufgemacht hatte] war voll Misstrauen* und verlangte, dass die Truppen ohne Munition einzögen.
45 Die O.H.L. musste erst Ebert energisch den Rücken steifen*, damit er sich diesem Ansinnen widersetzte. In diesem Zusammenhang wandte sich Hindenburg zum ersten Mal persönlich mit einem von mir entworfenen Brief an Ebert, in dem er ihm nochmals darlegte, unter welchen Voraussetzungen und Bedingungen er und das Offizierskorps sich zur Verfügung gestellt hatten, und in dem er ihn auf
50 die von ihm (Ebert) übernommene nationale Verantwortung hinwies. In diesem Brief heißt es: „Wenn ich mich mit nachstehenden Zeilen an Sie wende, so tue ich dies, weil mir berichtet wird, dass auch Sie als treuer deutscher Mann Ihr Vaterland über alles lieben unter Hintanstellung* persönlicher Meinungen und Wünsche, wie auch ich es habe tun müssen, um der Not des Vaterlandes gerecht zu
55 werden. In diesem Sinne habe ich mich mit Ihnen verbündet zur Rettung unseres Volkes vor dem drohenden Zusammenbruch." Das Offizierskorps habe sich der Regierung zur Verfügung gestellt, es könne und müsse dafür verlangen, dass ihm die Unterstützung zuteilwerde gegen die unerhörten Übergriffe der heimischen A. u. S.-Räte. „Es liegt auf der Hand, dass wir aus diesen Zuständen nur heraus-
60 kommen können, wenn die Regierung über ein Organ verfügt, das ihren Anordnungen und den bestehenden Gesetzen rücksichtslos Geltung zu verschaffen* vermag. So wie die Verhältnisse liegen, kann dies Organ nur die Armee sein, und zwar eine Armee, in der schärfste Disziplin herrscht. Die Disziplin steht und fällt aber mit der Autorität der Führer und der Fernhaltung der Politik aus dem Heere.
65 ... Soll die Armee ein brauchbares Machtmittel in der Hand der Regierung bleiben, so muss die Autorität des Offiziers sofort mit allen Mitteln wiederhergestellt und die Politik aus dem Heere entfernt werden." [...]
Vom 10. Dezember ab zogen die Truppen in Berlin ein, aber die angestrebte Wirkung, die Stärkung der Regierung, blieb aus, weil sich das Durcheinander der
70 Berliner Gewalten und Personen einschließlich Ebert nicht zu einer ganzen Tat aufraffen* konnten. Diese musste rasch erfolgen, denn auch die ausgesiebten* Truppen des Feldheeres erlagen auf die Dauer der revolutionären Luft der Hauptstadt. Weihnachten zu Hause feiern wurde zur Parole, die Leute waren nicht mehr zu halten. Eberts für das soldatische Empfinden völlig unverständliche Verhalten
75 am 23. Dezember, der, als er von der Volksmarine-Division des Matrosen Dorrenbach in der Reichskanzlei gefangengesetzt war, den zu seiner Befreiung anrückenden Soldaten das Schießen verbot, hat den Kampfgeist noch weiter herabgedrückt.
In der Nacht vom 23. zum 24. Dezember traf das Generalkommando Lequis die
80 letzten Vorbereitungen zur Aushebung der Volksmarine-Division in Schloß und Marstall. Der Verlauf des 24. ist bekannt: nach anfänglichen Erfolgen wurde nachmittags durch das Anrücken* großer Arbeitermassen mit Frauen und Kindern aus Richtung Alexanderplatz die Absperrung der Schlossinsel durchbrochen und der letzte Rest der Einzugsdivisionen zur Auflösung gebracht. Der Drang, an
85 Weihnachten zu Hause zu sein, hatte sich stärker erwiesen als die militärische

---

befehden to feud, to quarrel bitterly

Misstrauen distrust

jdm. den Rücken steifen to back sb. up

Hintanstellung disregard

etw. Geltung verschaffen to enforce sth.

sich dazu aufraffen etw. zu tun to bestir oneself to do sth., to get up the energy to do sth.
aussieben to sieve, to sift

Anrücken advancement

Disziplin. Der Einzug der Truppen war damit in seiner Wirkung endgültig missglückt.

In die Ereignisse der Berliner Tage habe ich wenig persönlich eingegriffen; nur zweimal sah ich mich gezwungen, Ebert scharf auf die Bedingungen unseres Bündnisses hinzuweisen.

Den ersten Anlass gab die auf dem Kongress der A. u. S.-Räte in Berlin am 18. Dezember gegen die Offiziere verfasste Resolution, die durchgeführt die Räteherrschaft und die völlige Auflösung der Disziplin bedeutet hätte. Die Mehrheitssozialisten ließen sich einschüchtern. Darauf antwortete die O.H.L. mit einem Telegramm, in dem Hindenburg für seine Person und mich mit sofortigem Rücktritt drohte, wenn sich die Regierung auf den Boden dieser Resolution stellte. Abends am Telefon machte ich Ebert in der schärfsten Form klar, dass die Heeresleitung mit dieser Frage stehe und falle. Ebert bat mich, nach Berlin zu kommen; ich sagte zu, um auch die letzte Möglichkeit, die Regierung Ebert zu stützen, nicht unversucht zu lassen. [...]

Wilhelm Groener, Lebenserinnerungen, Jugend, Generalstab, Weltkrieg, Friedrich Frhr. Hiller von Gaertringen (Ed.). Göttingen: Vandenhoeck & Ruprecht, 1957, pp. 472–75

S7 Aufruf des Spartakusbundes zur Fortführung der Revolution

This leaflet was published on 10 November 1918 in the course of the elections for the Imperial Council Convention. The Spartacists demanded a continuation of the revolution and called on the workers and soldiers not to be satisfied with the abolition of the monarchy alone.

Language support

Junkertum Junker •
Hydra hydra [ˈhaɪdrə] •
Militarismus militarism
• **den Kopf abschlagen**
to cut sb.'s head off

Pre-tasks

1. Describe the pictorial elements of the front page of the leaflet and make an educated guess about how the Spartacists might want to achieve their aims.
2. The second sentence of this leaflet says "Suspicion is the first democratic virtue!" Why should the German people be suspicious and of whom? Discuss.

Tasks

3. After having read the source, answer the question of the pre-task again and compare with your initial thoughts.
4. Identify the Spartacists' first and foremost aim and explain what they accuse the current government of.
5. Give an account of the measures the Spartacists want the "proletariat" to take in order to transform German society.

Sichert die von euch errungene Macht!
Misstrauen ist die erste demokratische Tugend!

Die rote Fahne weht über Berlin! Würdig* habt ihr euch an die Seite der Städte gestellt, in denen schon das Proletariat und die Soldaten die Macht übernommen haben. Wie aber die Welt auf euch geschaut hat, ob ihr eure Aufgabe lösen werdet, so sieht die Welt jetzt auf euch, wie ihr sie lösen werdet. Ihr müsst in der Durchführung
5 eines sozialistisch-revolutionären Programms ganze Arbeit machen. Mit der Abdankung von ein paar Hohenzollern ist es nicht getan. Noch viel weniger ist es getan damit, dass ein paar Regierungssozialisten mehr an die Spitze treten. Sie haben vier Jahre lang die Bourgeoisie unterstützt, sie können nicht anders, als dies weiter tun. Misstraut denen, die von Reichskanzler- und Ministerstellen herunter glauben, eu-
10 re Geschicke* lenken zu dürfen. Nicht Neubesetzung der Posten von oben herunter, sondern Neuorganisierung der Gewalt von unten herauf. Sorget, dass die Macht, die ihr jetzt errung[e]n habt, nicht euren Händen entgleite* und dass ihr sie gebraucht für euer Ziel. Denn euer Ziel ist die sofortige Herbeiführung* eines proletarisch-sozialistischen Friedens, der sich gegen den Imperialismus aller Länder wendet, und
15 die Umwandlung der Gesellschaft in eine sozialistische.
Zur Erlangung dieses Zieles ist es vor allem notwendig, dass das Berliner Proletariat [...] erklärt, folgende Forderungen mit aller Entschlossenheit und unbezähmbarem* Kampfwillen zu verfolgen:
1. Entwaffnung der gesamten Polizei, sämtlicher Offiziere sowie der Soldaten,
20   die nicht auf dem Boden der neuen Ordnung stehen; Bewaffnung des Volkes; alle Soldaten und Proletarier, die bewaffnet sind, behalten ihre Waffen.
2. Übernahme sämtlicher militärischer und ziviler Behörden und Kommandostellen durch Vertrauensmänner des Arbeiter- und Soldatenrates.
3. Übergabe aller Waffen- und Munitionsbestände* sowie aller Rüstungsbetriebe
25   an den Arbeiter- und Soldatenrat.
4. Kontrolle über alle Verkehrsmittel durch den Arbeiter- und Soldatenrat.
5. Abschaffung der Militärgerichtsbarkeit*; Ersetzung des militärischen Kadavergehorsams* durch freiwillige Disziplin der Soldaten unter Kontrolle des Arbeiter- und Soldatenrates.
30 6. Beseitigung des Reichstages und aller Parlamente sowie der bestehenden Reichsregierung; Übernahme der Regierung durch den Berliner Arbeiter- und Soldatenrat bis zur Errichtung eines Reichs- Arbeiter- und Soldatenrates.
7. Wahl von Arbeiter- und Soldatenräten in ganz Deutschland, in deren Hand ausschließlich Gesetzgebung und Verwaltung liegen. Zur Wahl der Arbeiter-

würdig worthy

Geschick fate

etw. entgleitet jds. Händen sth. slips from sb.'s hands
Herbeiführung the bringing about of sth.

unbezähmbar dauntless

Bestand stock

Militärgerichtsbarkeit military jurisdiction
Kadavergehorsam slavish obedience

und Soldatenräte schreitet das gesamte erwachsene werktätige Volk in Stadt und Land und ohne Unterschied der Geschlechter.
8. Abschaffung aller Dynastien und Einzelstaaten; unsere Parole lautet: einheitliche sozialistische Republik Deutschland.
9. Sofortige Aufnahme der Verbindung mit allen in Deutschland bestehenden Arbeiter- und Soldatenräten und den sozialistischen Bruderparteien des Auslandes. [...]

Arbeiter und Soldaten! Eine jahrtausendealte Knechtschaft* geht zu Ende; aus den unsäglichen* Leiden eines Krieges steigt nun die neue Freiheit empor*. Vier lange Jahre haben die Scheidemänner, die Regierungssozialisten, euch durch die Schrecken eines Krieges gejagt, haben euch gesagt, man müsse „das Vaterland" verteidigen, wo es sich nur um die nackten Raubinteressen des Imperialismus handelte: jetzt, da der deutsche Imperialismus zusammenbricht, suchen sie für die Bourgeoisie zu retten, was noch zu retten ist, und suchen die revolutionäre Energie der Massen zu ersticken.

Es darf kein „Scheidemann" mehr in der Regierung sitzen; es darf kein Sozialist in die Regierung eintreten, solange ein Regierungssozialist noch in ihr sitzt. Es gibt keine Gemeinschaft mit denen, die euch vier Jahre lang verraten haben.
Nieder mit dem Kapitalismus und seinen Agenten!
Es lebe die Revolution!
Es lebe die Internationale!

from: Gerhard A. Ritter, Susanne Miller (Eds.): "Die deutsche Revolution 1918–1919. Dokumente". Frankfurt ²1968

Knechtschaft servitude
unsäglich unspeakable
emporsteigen aus to emerge from

Language support

Garde-Kavallerie Guard Cavalry Division • **verwegen** bold, swashbuckling

Free Corps recruiting poster, 1919

S 8 Gesetz zur Bildung einer Freiwilligen Volkswehr

This law was passed on 12 December 1918. It allowed the formation of an army of volunteers which can be regarded as the basis for the formation of the free corps.

> **Pre-task** 1. The Macmillan Dictionary defines "militia" as "a group of ordinary people who are trained as soldiers to fight in an emergency" (www.macmillandictionary.com/dictionary/british/militia [16.06.15]). Recall your historical knowledge: why was Germany in a state of emergency in December 1918?

> **Task** 2. Choose at least three aspects you find worth discussing in terms of how far the militia might pose a threat to a future democratic Germany. Then talk to a partner and agree on one aspect.

1. Zur Aufrechterhaltung* der öffentlichen Ordnung und Sicherheit ist eine freiwillige Volkswehr zu bilden.
2. Die Vollmachten* zur Aufstellung* der Abteilungen dieser Volkswehr erteilt ausschließlich der Rat der Volksbeauftragten, der auch Zahl und Stärke der Abteilungen festsetzt.
3. Die Volkswehr untersteht ausschließlich dem Rate der Volksbeauftragten. Sie verpflichtet sich der sozialistisch-demokratischen Republik durch Handschlag*.
4. In die Volkswehr werden nur Freiwillige aufgenommen. Sie wird außerhalb des Rahmens des Heeres stehen. Gerichtliche und Disziplinarverhältnisse werden noch geregelt.
5. Die Freiwilligen wählen ihre Führer selbst, und zwar etwa hundert Freiwillige (Hundertschaft) einen Führer und drei Zugführer*; mehrere Hundertschaften* bilden eine Abteilung und wählen den Abteilungsführer und einen Stab*. Ihm steht ein Vertrauensrat von fünf Freiwilligen beratend* zur Seite.
6. Jeder Freiwillige ist im Dienste zum Gehorsam gegenüber seinen selbstgewählten Führern verpflichtet.
7. Für die Annahme der Freiwilligen ist Vorbedingung
   a) in der Regel Zurücklegung des vierundzwanzigsten Lebensjahres,
   b) körperliche Rüstigkeit*,
   c) längerer einwandfreier* Frontdienst.

from: Dokumente und Materialien zur Geschichte der deutschen Arbeiterbewegung, Series 2, Vol. 2: November 1917 – Dezember 1918, Institut für Marxismus-Leninismus beim ZK der SED (Ed.), Berlin, Dietz, 1957, pp. 597–98

Aufrechterhaltung maintenance

Vollmacht authorization
Aufstellung establishment

durch Handschlag by handshake

Zugführer platoon leader
Hundertschaft group of one hundred
Stab staff
jdn. beraten to advise sb.

körperliche Rüstigkeit physical well-being, sound physical constitution
einwandfrei unobjectionable, correct

Kapp soldiers with the imperial war flag in Berlin

S 9 Morgan Philips Price

On the Enemies of the Republic

Morgan Philips Price (1885–1973) was a British politician. From 1919 to 1923, he was a correspondent for the British newspaper *Daily Herald* in Germany. On 5 April 1923, he reports about anti-republican sentiments in Bavaria.

Pre-task
1. Who are the enemies of the republic? Have a look at **S 5b** again for help.

Tasks
2. Explain who the enemies of the republic are, according to Philips Price.
3. Scan the source for information about the mood in Bavaria. What kind of language does Philips Price use in order to convey this mood? Give an explanation.
4. Explain what the author hints at when he says that "Bavaria is dominated by men who have learnt nothing and forgotten nothing since 1914" (l. 18).

goose-step Gänsemarsch
gait way a person moves or walks

White Guards military arm of the White movement, anti-Communist forces who fought against the Bolsheviks in the Russian Civil War (1917–1922/23)
lavish grand

foolhardy rash, reckless

topsy-turvy chaotic nature
martial military

to seethe to boil
anathema sth. hated
all will get short shrift alle können einen kurzen Prozess erwarten
hour of reckoning Stunde der Abrechnung
locksmith Schlosser
to whip up to arouse, to inflame

worthy prominent person
to resort to to make use of
harangue [hə-'raŋ] forceful or angry speech

Iron crosses. Armed Reichswehr troops wearing steel helmets and with a hint of the goose-step* in their marching gait*. A cluster of young *Hakenkreuzler* (Swastika-wearers) roaring 'To Hell with the French beasts!', 'Down with the Jews!', 'Deutschland über Alles!' Flaming placards on every street corner announcing another Fascist meeting at which Hitler, Mussolini's mimic, will speak on Germany's Hour of Revenge. Police, troops, civilian White Guards* and more police. These are a few of the random sights that greet the visitor in Munich. I was walking across one of this city's magnificent parks and paused before a lavish* brown mansion. 'Is this the ex-king's palace?' I asked a passer-by. 'That', he corrected me, 'is the next king's residence.'

There is little in Munich to indicate that Bavaria belongs to the republic. Flags of the old monarchy are more frequent than the republican colours. To be a republican in Munich is to be indiscreet if not foolhardy*. There is, indeed, nothing to suggest that anyone except the Bavarian worker has paid the price of stubborn militarism. The war has left plentiful traces in the topsy-turvy* of Bavaria's economic life. But the fanatical chauvinism, the hatred of democracy and the martial* tunes to which Munich's tired feet are shuffling along – all imply that Bavaria is dominated by men who have learnt nothing and forgotten nothing since 1914.

Bavaria is seething* with hatred – hatred of Protestant North Germany, of the French, Jews, Republicans, Liberals and, above all, Socialists. All are anathema*. All will get short shrift* when the hour of reckoning* strikes. At least, so they say. Adolf Hitler, a native Austrian and a locksmith* by trade [sic] has pushed his way to the leadership of the Bavarian counter-revolutionary movement. A skillful demagogue, who wins converts to Fascism by drinking beer with the common people, he has mastered the routine of whipping up* popular passions.

'How can we help the Fatherland?' I heard Hitler ask his audience. 'I'll tell you how. By hanging the criminals of November 1918!' (These criminals are, of course, the republican workers of Germany.) 'By punishing the worthies* of the Republic we shall gain the respect of foreign nations', cried Hitler. 'If we had resorted to* arms two years ago, we would never have lost Silesia and there would have been no Ruhr problem.' At this point in his harangue* a company of Hitler's 'shock troops' paraded across the platform beneath the banner of monarchist Germany. Such scenes are daily occurrences in Munich.

The reaction in Bavaria is intricate*. It consists of numerous groups, all united in their determination to overthrow the republic and trample* upon Labour, and yet divergent in the means which they propose to employ. One speaker will shout loudest when denouncing the French, another when excoriating* the Jews and a third when damning the German constitution. But all are openly agreed that their common purpose is to fight organised Labour.

Three groups dominate the rising Bavarian reaction. First, there is the separatist movement led by ex-Crown Prince Rupprecht, the former Bavarian Premier von Kahr and the clerical-farmer deputy, Dr. Heim. Briefly summarized, their policy demands greater autonomy for Bavaria within the Reich, restoration of the Wittelsbach dynasty in Munich, union with Austria (except Vienna) and a reinforcement of clerical (Roman Catholic) influence in the Government. Second, there are the Fascists, guided by Hitler, for whom the Roman church and the monarchy are minor details, and who are mainly concerned with the forcible subjugation* of Labour, suppression or expulsion* of Jews, and a Fascist dictatorship with its roots in Bavaria but extending throughout Germany. Third, there is the Ludendorff element, anti-clerical and anti-separatist, relying upon the ex-officers and the Prussian Junkers for a revival of Pan-German militarism. All three factions are busily preparing civil war, storing up arms and munitions and building illicit* White Guards armies. A steady stream of funds pours into their treasury from German industrial magnates*. Well-informed citizens forecast a counter-revolutionary uprising in Bavaria within a few weeks. They say this will be the signal for a 'White' offensive in all Germany.

Morgan Philips Price: Dispatches from the Weimar Republic, Versailles and German Fascism. London and Sterling, Virginia: Pluto Press, 1999, pp. 155–56

intricate complicated

to trample upon sth. *etw. mit Füßen treten*

to excoriate [ek-'skȯr-ē-ˌāt] to criticize sb. or sth. very harshly

subjugation the act of defeating and gaining control over sb. or sth. by the use of force

expulsion banishment, driving out

illicit illegal

industrial magnate *Großindustrielle/r*

S 10 William Carr

The German Revolution 1918–1920

Historian William Carr elaborates on the German Revolution as a whole.

Pre-task
1. In his assessment of the outcome of the German Revolution, William Carr focuses on the Majority Socialists, the Independent Socialists and the Communists. Check the overview section again and find out which aims those three groups pursued for Germany.

Tasks
2. Analyse the text.
3. Copy and complete the grid below. Explain what responsibility Carr ascribes to the Majority Socialists, the Independent Socialists and the Communists for the, from their point of view, disappointing outcome of the revolution.

	Role during the revolution
MSPD	
USPD	
Communists	

4. Take a critical stand on Carr's assessment.

All the same, the achievements of the Revolution were undoubtedly limited. The empire had gone and the dynasties too – but they were harmless anachronisms* by this time. Universal suffrage and the secret ballot were introduced in all states and the reign of parliamentary democracy began – but all this had been achieved before the November Revolution which merely confirmed* a new political order brought into being – but only in part – by the fiat* of the Supreme Command. By 1920 very few Germans took pride in the part they had played in the Revolution. The Republic was accepted by many Germans not as a superior form of government but as a convenient* means of filling a void* left by the collapse of monarchy. It was widely – but quite erroneously* – believed that the alternative to a conservative parliamentary regime was a Red dictatorship which only a tiny minority wanted. The structure of German society was hardly affected by the revolution. The spirit of Imperial Germany lived on in the unreformed civil service, the judiciary and the officer corps. Nor did the powerful industrial barons have much to fear from the revolution. If one believes, as many socialists did in 1918, that democracy is fatally weakened unless the citadels of power and privilege are subjected to the general will, then the outcome of the German Revolution was certainly a disappointment for which the three Socialist parties bear much of the responsibility.

Firstly, the Majority Socialists. The sincerity* of their belief in the principles and practice of parliamentary democracy cannot be doubted. What can be called in question is their imperfect understanding of the socio-political complex post-imperial Germany. Their obsession with correct constitutional procedures blinded them to other equally important considerations. [...] The Majority Socialist leaders were harassed* men, deeply concerned about the German fatherland but morbidly* suspicious of left-wing critics and far too immersed in* the day-to-day problems of government to perceive the general direction in which they were drifting. The Communist uprising made matters worse in this respect. For, as they had conspicuously* failed to arm their own supporters, the Socialists were forced to turn to the Supreme Command for support; almost without noticing it, they became deeply dependent on the sworn enemies of democracy and socialism. They received little thanks for their strenuous* efforts to preserve democracy. The Communists never forgave them for 'betraying the revolution'; while the right wing soon forgot what it owed to Ebert and his associates and denounced all socialists indiscriminately* as 'November traitors' who had 'stabbed the fatherland in the back', a legacy which weighed heavily on the party throughout the Weimar period. [...]

The Independent Socialists, on the other hand, were much more perceptive* in their social analysis. From the start they insisted that a considerable degree of political and economic change was essential if democracy was to flourish in the uncongenial* climate of post-imperial Germany. [...] The high hopes were not realised. Throughout the whole of its short life this party was gravely weakened by internecine* strife between the parliamentary right and the revolutionary left. When the Independents were in the government, the left wing continually sniped* at them and reduced still further what limited influence the ministers had on their Majority Socialist colleagues. By the time they decided to withdraw from the government the Independents had lost many supporters to the Communists, who now became the focal point of resistance to Ebert in Berlin. Indeed the very act of withdrawal was a blunder* which dangerously accentuated* the tension between right and left and made conflict unavoidable. During Spartacus week the Independents were hopelessly divided. In March 1919 they abandoned their belief in parliamentary methods and declared in favour of government by workers' councils, although they were careful to point out that the dictatorship of the proletariat could only be established with the full support of the working class. The fortunes of the party revived in 1920. But when the Independents decided to seek affiliation* with the Third International*, the party was finally split asunder*; a third of the members joined the Communists, and the remainder* eventually found their way back to the Majority Socialists by 1922. [...] It is tempting* to suppose that the Independents represented a viable* alternative to Ebert and Liebknecht. The sad truth is that the party lacked basic cohesion* and simply could not rely on the support of all members at times of crisis. Had the Independents remained inside the Social Democratic party, they might conceivably have arrested its progress to the right and compelled* Ebert to modify his views on socialism. Alternatively, had they joined the Communists *en bloc* they might well have diverted* the new revolutionary party from a disastrous course of action. As it was, the Independents fell tragically between two stools and so exerted little positive influence on the course of events.

Finally, the Communists must bear some share of responsibility for the failure to give the Revolution a positive social content. Radical utopians who got upper hand in the party in December 1918 were hypnotised by the spectacle of the Russian Revolution and easily persuaded themselves that Germany, too, was ripe for proletarian revolution. This was a monumental miscalculation. Rightly or wrongly the German working class was solidly committed to parliamentary democracy. The ill-advised *coup d'état* merely* drove Ebert further to the right into the arms of the forces of action. It finally extinguished what admittedly slim chance still remained of achieving a measure of socialism before the constituent assembly met. The long-term consequences were even more serious. Communist support of insurrectionary* tactics cut the party off from the main stream of the working-class movement, and kept it divided at a time when proletarian solidarity might have helped to stabilize democracy in Germany. When the left Independents joined them in 1920 it looked as if the Communists might at last become a mass party and adopt more realistic tactics. [...]

William Carr: A History of Germany 1818–1990, London 1991, p. 248–251

affiliation association with an organization
Third International Communist International
asunder into parts
remainder rest
tempting attractive
viable possible
cohesion [koʊˈhiʒən] union
to compel to force so. to do sth.
to divert to change the direction or use of (sth.)

merely only

insurrectionary rebellious

S 11 "A Transparent Dodge*"

dodge Trick

The British satirical magazine *Punch* published this cartoon in December 1921.

Pre-task
1. Have a look at the "Big Three at Versailles" (S 73, chapter 2) and at the Treaty of Versailles again (S 75). What was Britain's attitude towards Germany like?

Tasks
2. Describe the cartoon and its composition.
3. Explain in detail the elements of the cartoon.
4. Take a critical stand on the cartoonist's message. In doing so, assess whether Germany could afford the reparation payments.

Embedded text:
A TRANSPARENT DODGE
Germany: "Help! Help! I drown! Throw me the life-belt!"
Mr. Lloyd George & M. Briand: "Try standing up on your feet."

Language support

life-belt Rettungsring • **to drown** ertrinken

S 12 Theo Matejko

„Hände weg vom Ruhrgebiet"

This propaganda poster of the *Kultur-Liga* against the occupation of the Ruhr area was published in Berlin in 1923.

Pre-task

1. Have a look at the "Big Three at Versailles" (S 73, chapter 2) and at the Treaty of Versailles again (S 75). What was France's attitude towards Germany like?

Tasks

2. Describe the poster and its composition.
3. Explain in detail the elements of the poster, including its title. Focus on the representation of France here.
4. Take a critical stand on the representation of France and the poster as a whole.

Language support

Gewehr rifle • **wahnsinnig** lunatic • **nach etw. greifen** to grab for sth.

S 13 Rudolf Pörtner

Memories about Inflation

The German author Rudolf Pörtner recalls his memories about inflation.

Pre-task 1. Describe the pictures below. What information about inflation do they convey?

Tasks 2. Analyse the source.
3. Explain the advantages and disadvantages of inflation the author mentions.

People queuing in front of a Berlin grocery, 1923

Wallpapering [tapezieren] with worthless banknotes

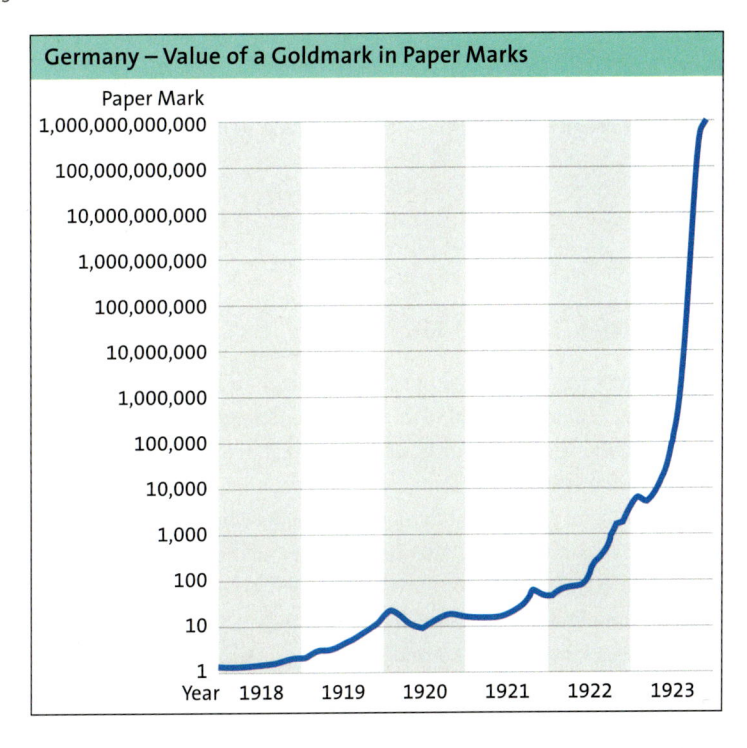

Germany – Value of a Goldmark in Paper Marks

Nutznießer beneficiary	Ich will nicht verschweigen, dass wir zunächst Nutznießer* der fürchterlichen Geldvernichtung waren. Das Ehepaar Pörtner hatte sich 1922 kurzfristig entschlossen, ein im Entstehen begriffenes Haus in der Melberger Kronprinzenstraße, auf der Westseite von Bad Oeynhausen, zu kaufen. Kostenpunkt: 800 000 Mark. Als wir am 1. April 1923 einzogen, war das ein Betrag, der selbst sensible Gemüter nicht mehr zu beunruhigen vermochte. Ein Griff in die Westentasche genügte, alle Verbindlichkeiten* einschließlich der hypothekarischen Eintragungen aus der Welt zu schaffen*.

Ich will nicht verschweigen, dass wir zunächst Nutznießer* der fürchterlichen Geldvernichtung waren. Das Ehepaar Pörtner hatte sich 1922 kurzfristig entschlossen, ein im Entstehen begriffenes Haus in der Melberger Kronprinzenstraße, auf der Westseite von Bad Oeynhausen, zu kaufen. Kostenpunkt: 800 000 Mark. Als wir am 1. April 1923 einzogen, war das ein Betrag, der selbst sensible Gemüter nicht mehr zu beunruhigen vermochte. Ein Griff in die Westentasche genügte, alle Verbindlichkeiten* einschließlich der hypothekarischen Eintragungen aus der Welt zu schaffen*.

Leider war das Haus erst halb fertig, als wir es übernahmen: halb fertig, miserabel gebaut, aus Altmaterialien zusammengeschustert*. Inzwischen arbeiteten die Handwerker nur noch gegen Naturalien. Damit konnten wir natürlich nicht dienen, und das Geld, das Vater ausbezahlt bekam, zuletzt zweimal täglich, reichte gerade für das nackte Leben. Noch im hohen Alter hat er häufig von dem defekten Ofenrohr* in der Küche (also unserem Lebensraum) erzählt, aus dessen Löchern und Ritzen ein bronchien- und schleimhautfeindlicher* Rauch quoll*, ohne dass wir die Möglichkeit gehabt hätten, dem Übelstand abzuhelfen*. Es gab ja keine Ofenknie* und wenn, dann nicht für die lächerlichen Milliardenscheine, die acht Tage nach Erscheinen nicht einmal mehr das Papier wert waren, aus dem sie bestanden.

Was die Ablösung der homöopathisch ausgedünnten* Währung durch die Rentenmark im November 1923 bedeutete, lässt sich heute nicht mehr ermessen. Es war, als wenn ein Ertrinkender, in einer Springflut von Papiergeld fast schon versunken, plötzlich Boden unter den Füßen verspürt hätte. Als mein Vater mit dem ersten wertbeständigen Zahlungsmittel heimkehrte, traten wir wie zur Besichtigung einer säkularen Kostbarkeit* an, und es verschlug* uns fast den Atem, als wir die erste Rentenmark zunächst beäugen, dann sogar wie eine wundertätige Reliquie in die Hand nehmen durften. Die Stöße* übrig gebliebenen Inflationsgeldes haben wir dann genutzt, die getünchten* Wände unserer wenig einladenden Toilettenanlage zu tapezieren, unseren Lokus, mit Verlaub zu sagen, in ein Billionenkabinett zu verwandeln. Die Hauptattraktion war eine aus Millionenscheinen montierte Zahl mit sechsunddreißig Nullen, die in Worten auszudrücken uns nie gelungen ist. Wir hätten schon einen Astronomen zurate ziehen* müssen.

from: Rudolf Pörtner (Ed.): Alltag in der Weimarer Republik. Erinnerungen an eine unruhige Zeit, Econ, Düsseldorf 1990, pp. 360f.

Vocabulary:
- **Nutznießer** beneficiary
- **Verbindlichkeiten** liability
- **aus der Welt schaffen** to dispose of
- **etw. zusammenschustern** to cobble sth. together
- **Ofenrohr** stovepipe
- **bronchien- und schleimhautfeindlich** to be hostile to the bronchia and the mucosa
- **quellen** to gush
- **etw. abhelfen** to remedy sth.
- **Ofenknie** curved part of a stovepipe
- **ausdünnen** to thin out, to dilute
- **Kostbarkeit** treasure
- **jdm. den Atem verschlagen** to take one's breath away
- **Stoß** pile
- **getüncht** whitewashed
- **jdn. zurate ziehen** to consult sb.

Adolf Hitler (1889–1945)

Adolf Hitler was born on 20 April 1889 in Braunau am Inn (in what was then Austria-Hungary) as the son of the customs officer Alois Hitler and his wife Clara. In 1905 he quit school at the age of 16 and showed no interest in further secondary education. It was at that time that he started to become interested in pan-Germanism and became acquainted with anti-Semitism. In 1905, Hitler moved to Vienna where he tried in vain to enrol as a student at the Academy of Fine Arts. After he had spent all the money he had inherited, Hitler was forced to live in shelters for the homeless. His experiences in Vienna, the capital of the multi-ethnic state of Austria-Hungary, and the reading of anti-Semitic newspapers and books clearly determined Hitler's world-view and planted the seed for his racially-based anti-Judaism as well as his radical hostility towards Marxism and liberalism. On 24 May 1913, Hitler moved to Munich in order to avoid military service in the Austrian-Hungarian army. However, on 16 August 1914, he voluntarily joined the Bavarian Army as an Austrian citizen and in December he was awarded the Iron Cross Second Class for bravery. He was wounded in October 1916, but, nevertheless, he joined his regiment again in March 1917. In August 1918 he received the Iron Cross First Class. One month later, Hitler was temporarily blinded during a mustard gas attack and, while in hospital, he heard about Germany's defeat in WWI.

After the war, Hitler returned to Munich and in September 1919 he visited an assembly of the *Deutsche Arbeiterpartei* (DAP) which he joined a few days later. The DAP soon renamed itself *Nationalsozialistische Deutsche Arbeiterpartei Deutschlands* (NSDAP). An attempted putsch in Munich on 9 November 1923 failed and Hitler was sentenced to five years in prison. However, he was released after only nine months during which he wrote his book *Mein Kampf*. On 30 April 1925, Hitler had renounced his Austrian citizenship with the consequence that he was stateless and could not run for public office. However, on 25 February 1932 he was appointed administrator for the state of Brunswick which made him a citizen of Germany one day later. On 30 January 1933, Reichspräsident Hindenburg appointed him chancellor. In the following year and up until 1945, Hitler was successful in eliminating his enemies and any kind of political opposition, turning Germany into a dictatorship and surviving several assassination attempts.

Hitler gave his last speech to the German people on the radio on 30 January 1945 in which he still talked about the "Endsieg" (ultimate victory) despite the fact that the allied forces were advancing into Germany. On 29 April, Hitler married his girlfriend Eva Braun in his "Führerbunker" in Berlin and one day later both committed suicide.

S 14 25-Punkte-Programm der Nationalsozialistischen Deutschen Arbeiterpartei

This party programme already stems from 24 February 1920.

Pre-task
1. Anticipate what the Nazi Programme might state about the categories below on the basis of the overview section. Compare your ideas with a partner.
   - Social welfare
   - Jews
   - Civil liberties
   - Economics
   - Foreign policy
   - Land
   - Government

Tasks
2. After having read the programme, compare with your ideas from the pre-task.
3. Turn each paragraph into a catchy slogan.
4. Explain the underlying motives behind each paragraph. For help, read the part about the international peace framework in chapter 2 (p. 188) again.
5. Who do you think the Nazis were trying to appeal to here? Rank the groups of society from top to bottom (top = supporters; bottom = opponents). Then, assign your slogans to the groups of society.
   - Civil servant
   - Army general
   - Unemployed artist
   - Small farmer
   - Catholic priest
   - Protestant student
   - Unemployed ex-soldier
   - Catholic unemployed worker
   - Shop keeper
   - Junker
   - Industrial worker

[...]

1. Wir fordern den Zusammenschluss aller Deutschen auf Grund des Selbstbestimmungsrechtes der Völker zu einem Groß-Deutschland*.

2. Wir fordern die Gleichberechtigung des deutschen Volkes gegenüber den anderen Nationen, Aufhebung der Friedensverträge von Versailles und St. Germain.

3. Wir fordern Land und Boden (Kolonien) zur Ernährung unseres Volkes und Ansiedlung unseres Bevölkerungsüberschusses.

4. Staatsbürger kann nur sein, wer Volksgenosse ist. Volksgenosse kann nur sein, wer deutschen Blutes ist, ohne Rücksichtnahme auf Konfession. Kein Jude kann daher Volksgenosse sein. [...]

6. Das Recht, über Führung und Gesetze des Staates zu bestimmen, darf nur dem Staatsbürger zustehen. Daher fordern wir, dass jedes öffentliche Amt, gleichgültig welcher Art, gleich ob im Reich, Land oder Gemeinde nur durch Staatsbürger bekleidet* werden darf.

Wir bekämpfen die korrumpierende Parlamentswirtschaft einer Stellenbesetzung nur nach Parteigesichtspunkten* ohne Rücksichtnahme* auf Charakter und Fähigkeiten. [...]

8. Jede weitere Einwanderung Nicht-Deutscher ist zu verhindern. Wir fordern, dass alle Nicht-Deutschen, die seit 2. August 1914 in Deutschland eingewandert sind, sofort zum Verlassen des Reiches gezwungen werden. [...]

13. Wir fordern die **Verstaatlichung** aller (bisher) bereits vergesellschafteten (**Trust**) Betriebe.

14. Wir fordern die Gewinnbeteiligung* an Großbetrieben.

15. Wir fordern einen großzügigen Ausbau der Alters-Versorgung.

16. Wir fordern die Schaffung eines gesunden Mittelstandes und seiner Erhaltung, sofortige **Kommunalisierung der Groß-Warenhäuser** und ihre Vermietung zu billigen Preisen an kleine Gewerbetreibende, schärfste Berücksichtigung aller kleinen Gewerbetreibenden bei Lieferung an den Staat, die Länder oder Gemeinden.

17. Wir fordern eine unseren nationalen Bedürfnissen angepasste **Bodenreform**, Schaffung eines Gesetzes zur unentgeltlichen* Enteignung* von Boden für gemeinnützige* Zwecke. Abschaffung des Bodenzinses und Verhinderung jeder Bodenspekulation.

18. Wir fordern den rücksichtslosen Kampf gegen diejenigen, die durch ihre Tätigkeit das Gemein-Interesse schädigen. Gemeine Volksverbrecher, **Wucherer***, **Schieber*** usw. sind **mit dem Tode zu bestrafen**, ohne Rücksichtnahme auf Konfession und Rasse. [...]

23. Wir fordern den gesetzlichen Kampf gegen die bewusste politische Lüge und ihre Verbreitung durch die Presse. Um die Schaffung einer deutschen Presse zu ermöglichen, fordern wir, dass sämtliche Schriftleiter* und Mitarbeiter von Zeitungen, die in deutscher Sprache erscheinen, **Volksgenossen** sein müssen [...].

Zeitungen, die gegen das Gemeinwohl verstoßen, sind zu verbieten. Wir fordern den gesetzlichen Kampf gegen eine Kunst- und Literaturrichtung, die einen zersetzenden* Einfluss auf unser Volksleben ausübt [...].

25. Zur Durchführung alles dessen fordern wir die Schaffung einer starken Zentralgewalt des Reiches. Unbedingte Autorität des politischen Zentralparlaments über das gesamte Reich und seine Organisationen im Allgemeinen. [...]

25-Punkte-Programm der Nationalsozialistischen Deutschen Arbeiterpartei (24.02.1920), in: documentArchiv.de [Hrsg.], www.documentarchiv.de/wr/1920/nsdap-programm.html [17.04.15]

S 15 Adolf Hitler

Speech at the Putsch Trial in Munich

After the failed putsch of 8/9 November 1923, Hitler, Ludendorff and eight co-defendants were put on trial at the People's Court in Munich from 26 February until 1 April 1924. Despite the fact that the rebels [*Putschisten*] were accused of high treason, they only received a very lenient punishment.
The source below is an excerpt from Hitler's address at the conclusion of the trial from 1 April 1924.

Pre-task 1. Try to anticipate Hitler's line of argument with the help of the extracts provided below.

> Zerbrecher des Marxismus • Die Saat ist reif, die Stunde ist gekommen! • dass ich die Führung des politischen Kampfes in meine Faust bekomme • Deutschlands Schicksal liegt nicht in der Republik oder der Monarchie • dass die eiserne Faust unserer Feinde von uns genommen wird • vor allem sollte wieder eingeführt werden die höchste Ehrenpflicht, die wir als Deutsche kannten, [...] die Wehrpflicht • Denn nicht Sie, meine Herren, sprechen das Urteil über uns, das Urteil spricht das ewige Gericht der Geschichte • die Göttin des ewigen Gerichtes der Geschichte [...] spricht uns frei

Tasks 2. Analyse the source. In the structured outline of content, focus on Hitler's line of argument.
3. Explain Hitler's attitude towards the court.

Post-task 4. As a British journalist, you have decided to write an article about the future of the Weimar Republic, after having attended the trial. First, you have to assess the strengths and weaknesses of the Weimar Republic. Second, recall how the republic coped with its enemies both from left and right. Finally, state your personal opinion about whether you think that the Weimar Republic was doomed to fail from the beginning.

[...] Lossow sagte hier, er habe im Frühjahr mit mir gesprochen und damals nicht beobachtet, dass ich etwas für mich erstrebe, sondern dass ich nur Propagandist und Weckrufer* sein wollte.
Wie klein denken doch kleine Menschen! Nehmen Sie die Überzeugung hin*,
5 dass ich die Erringung eines Ministerpostens nicht als erstrebenswert ansehe. [...] Was mir vor Augen stand, das war vom ersten Tage an mehr, als Minister zu werden. Ich wollte der Zerbrecher* des Marxismus werden. Ich werde diese Aufgabe lösen, und wenn ich sie löse, dann wäre der Titel eines Ministers für mich eine Lächerlichkeit. Als ich zum ersten Mal vor Wagners* Grab stand, da quoll mir das
10 Herz über vor Stolz*, dass hier ein Mann ruht, der es sich verbeten* hat, hinauf zu schreiben: Hier ruht Geheimrat Musikdirektor Exzellenz Baron Richard von Wagner. Ich war stolz darauf, dass dieser Mann und so viele Männer der deutschen Geschichte sich damit begnügen, ihren Namen der Nachwelt* zu überliefern*, nicht ihren Titel. Nicht aus Bescheidenheit* wollte ich damals „Trommler"
15 sein; das ist das Höchste, das andere ist eine Kleinigkeit. [...]

Weckrufer wake-up caller

etw. hinnehmen to accept sth.

Zerbrecher here: destroyer
Richard Wagner (1813–1883) German composer
vor Stolz überquellen to be filled with pride
sich etw. verbitten to refuse to tolerate sth.
Nachwelt ensuing ages
überliefern to pass on
Bescheidenheit modesty

| **Anklageschrift** indictment [ɪnˈdaɪtmənt] |
| **die Zähne zusammenbeißen** to grit one's teeth |
| **sich zur Verfügung stellen** to place oneself at sb.'s disposal |
| **zu etw. berufen sein** to be called to sth. |
| **höhnisch** scornful |
| **Direktorium** directory |
| **jdm. treu ergeben sein** to be loyal to sb. |
| **schmählich** ignominious |
| **Staatshaushalt** budget |
| **Drohne** drone |
| **Zwangslage** plight, tight spot, dilemma |
| **Schar** band |
| **Bataillon** battalion |
| **Regiment** regiment |
| **Division** division |
| **Kokarde** cockade (a decoration that is worn on a hat especially as part of a uniform to show a person's status, rank, etc.) |
| **letztes Gottesgericht** Day of Judgement |

Herr Staatsanwalt, so wie Sie in der Anklageschrift* betonen, dass wir mit zusammengebissenen Zähnen* warten müssten, bis die Saat reif geworden wäre, so haben auch wir gewartet, und als der Mann kam, haben wir gerufen: Die Saat ist reif, die Stunde ist gekommen! Dann erst habe ich mich nach langem Zögern zur Verfügung gestellt*. Ich verlangte, dass ich die Führung des politischen Kampfes in meine Faust bekomme, und zweitens habe ich verlangt, dass die Führung der Organisation, die wir alle ersehnten und die auch Sie innerlich genau so ersehnen, der Held bekommt, der in den Augen des ganzen jungen Deutschlands nun einmal berufen* ist hierzu. Höhnisch* erklärte der Zeuge, man musste Ludendorff nehmen, weil dann die Reichswehr nicht schießen würde. Ist das ein Verbrechen von mir? Lag darin etwa ein Hochverrat, dass ich zu Lossow sagte: „Wie Sie den Kampf beginnen, muss es zum Kampf kommen; wie ich es mir vorstelle, kommt es nicht zum Kampf." [...]

Was wollten wir am 8. November, abends? Im Reiche wollten die Herren alle ein Direktorium*. Was man im Reiche angestrebt hat, kann man in Bayern nicht verdammen. Das Direktorium war in Bayern schon da, es bestand aus den Herren Kahr, Lossow und Seisser. Von einer legalen Regierung haben wir nichts mehr gewusst, wir haben nur gefürchtet, dass bei der letzten Entscheidung vielleicht noch Hemmungen kommen könnten.

Ich bin kein Monarchist, sondern letzten Endes auch Republikaner. Pöhner ist Monarchist, Ludendorff treu ergeben* dem Hohenzollernhaus. Wir alle, die wir so verschieden eingestellt sind, standen zusammen. Deutschlands Schicksal liegt nicht in der Republik oder der Monarchie, sondern dem Inhalt der Republik oder Monarchie. Was ich bekämpfe, ist nicht die Staatsform als solche, sondern der schmähliche* Inhalt. Wir wollten in Deutschland die Voraussetzungen dafür schaffen, die allein es möglich machen, dass die eiserne Faust unserer Feinde von uns genommen wird. Wir wollten Ordnung schaffen im Staatshaushalt*, die Drohnen* ausweisen, den Kampf gegen die internationale Börsenversklavung aufnehmen, gegen die Vertrustung unsrer ganzen Wirtschaft, den Kampf gegen die Politisierung der Gewerkschaften, und vor allem sollte wieder eingeführt werden die höchste Ehrenpflicht, die wir als Deutsche kannten, die Pflicht zur Waffe, die Wehrpflicht. Und da frage ich Sie: Ist das, was wir gewollt haben, Hochverrat? [...]

Nun wird gesagt: Aber Exzellenz v. Kahr, v. Lossow und v. Seisser wollten den Vorgang am 8. November abends nicht. Die Anklageschrift sagt, dass wir die Herren in eine Zwangslage* hineingestoßen haben. In die Zwangslage waren wir durch die Herren selber geraten, sie haben uns in die Zwangslage hineingestoßen. Herr v. Kahr hätte ehrenhaft sagen müssen: Herr Hitler, wir meinen unter Staatsstreich etwas anderes, wir meinen unter Marsch auf Berlin etwas anderes. Er hätte die Pflicht gehabt, uns zu sagen: Wir meinen mit dem, was wir hier machen, etwas anderes als das, was Sie glauben. Er hat das nicht getan, die Folgen kommen ausschließlich auf die drei Herren. [...]

Die Armee, die wir herangebildet haben, die wächst von Tag zu Tag, von Stunde zu Stunde schneller. Gerade in diesen Tagen habe ich die stolze Hoffnung, dass einmal die Stunde kommt, dass diese wilden Scharen* zu Bataillonen*, die Bataillone zu Regimentern*, die Regimenter zu Divisionen* werden, dass die alte Kokarde* aus dem Schmutz herausgeholt wird, dass die alten Fahnen wieder voranflattern, dass dann die Versöhnung kommt beim ewigen letzten Gottesgericht*, zu dem anzutreten wir willens sind. Dann wird aus unseren Knochen und aus unseren Gräbern die Stimme des Gerichtshofes sprechen, der allein berufen ist, über uns zu Gericht zu sitzen*. Denn nicht Sie, meine Herren, sprechen das Urteil über uns, das Urteil spricht das ewige Gericht der Geschichte, das sich aussprechen wird über die Anklage, die gegen uns erhoben ist. Ihr Urteil, das Sie fällen werden, kenne ich. Aber jenes Gericht wird uns nicht fragen: Habt Ihr Hochverrat getrieben oder nicht? Jenes Gericht wird über uns richten, über den Generalquartiermeister* der alten Armee, über seine Offiziere und Soldaten, die als Deutsche das Beste gewollt haben für ihr Volk und Vaterland, die kämpfen und sterben wollten. Mögen Sie uns tausendmal schuldig sprechen, die Göttin des ewigen Gerichtes der Geschichte wird lächelnd den Antrag des Staatsanwaltes und das Urteil des Gerichtes zerreißen; denn sie spricht uns frei.

über jdn. zu Gericht sitzen to sit in judgement on sb.

Generalquartiermeister quartermaster general

„Die Rede Hitlers während des Prozesses zum Hitler-Putsch (Februar 1924)" from: Albrecht Tyrell (Ed.) Führer befiehl ... Selbstzeugnisse aus der „Kampfzeit" der NSDAP. Dokumentation und Analyse. Düsseldorf: Droste Verlag, 1969, pp. 64–67

S 16 Retter Stresemann

Provided below is the front page of the German satirical magazine *Simplicissimus* from 14 May 1923, about six months before the introduction of the Rentenmark.

Pre-task
1. Read Stresemann's biography (p. 404) and the overview section and explain why (or if) he "saved" Germany.

Tasks
2. Analyse the cartoon and explain its elements in detail.
3. Explain the message of the cartoon.

Embedded text:
„Er schaut nach rechts, er schaut nach links – er wird mich retten!"

Language support
jdn. retten to save sb. •
Zipfelmütze jelly bag cap •
schweben to float •
Gleichgewicht balance •
Seiltänzer tightrope walker

Gustav Stresemann (1878–1929)

Gustav Stresemann was born on 10 May 1878 as son of a beer bottler and distributor in Berlin. From 1987 until 1900, he studied political economy at the University of Berlin. In 1903, Stresemann married Käte Kleefeld, the daughter of a Jewish industrialist. The couple had two sons. In the same year, he joined the National Liberal Party and served as a member of the Dresden town council from 1906 – 1912. In 1907, Stresemann became the youngest deputy in the Reichstag and stayed in that office until 1912. During this time, he often struggled with the right-wing faction of his party about the expansion of social legislation. In 1914, Stresemann was elected member of the Reichstag and, as a member of the "Deutscher Kolonialverein", he supported a policy of annexation for the German Empire. In 1917, he became party leader of the National Liberal Party. However, on 22 November 1918 he co-founded the Deutsche Volkspartei (DVP). On 13 August 1923, Stresemann was appointed chancellor of a Weimar Grand Coalition consisting of the DVP, the Centre Party, the DDP and the SPD. As chancellor, he ordered the ending of the policy of passive resistance in the Ruhr area and brought an end to inflation by introducing the *Rentenmark*. On 2 November, however, the Reichstag was dissolved again and, from that year on, Stresemann was Germany's foreign minister until his death in 1929. In 1926, he was awarded the Nobel Peace Prize together with Aristide Briand, the French foreign minister, for his Locarno policy.

S 17 Gustav Stresemann
Brief an den ehemaligen deutschen Kronprinzen

Stresemann wrote this confidential letter to the former German crown prince on 7 September 1925. His topic is German foreign policy.

Pre-task 1. Have a look at the expressions taken from the letter below. Come up with an explanation why this letter was confidential and not official.

> Reparationsfrage • Sicherung des Friedens • Wiedererstarkung Deutschlands • Korrektur der Ostgrenzen • Anschluss von Deutsch-Österreich • Rückgewinnung Elsaß-Lothringens

Tasks 2. Explain the aims of German foreign policy, according to Stresemann.
3. Point out where Stresemann sees differences in terms of east and west.
4. What relevance does Germany's entry to the League of Nations have, according to Stresemann? Explain.

Post-task 5. Write the German crown prince's reply to this letter.

absehbar foreseeable
erträglich tolerable
Wiedererstarkung regaining of strength
Stammesgenossen fellow Germans
Joch yoke
Wiedergewinnung regaining
polnischer Korridor Polish Corridor
Oberschlesien Upper Silesia

Die deutsche Außenpolitik hat nach meiner Auffassung für die nächste absehbare* Zeit drei große Aufgaben: Einmal die Lösung der Reparationsfrage in einem für Deutschland erträglichen* Sinne und die Sicherung des Friedens, die die Voraussetzung für eine Wiedererstarkung* Deutschlands ist.
Zweitens rechne ich dazu den Schutz der Auslandsdeutschen, jener 10 bis 12 Millionen Stammesgenossen*, die jetzt unter fremdem Joch* in fremden Ländern leben.
Die dritte große Aufgabe ist die Korrektur der Ostgrenzen: die Wiedergewinnung* von Danzig, vom polnischen Korridor* und eine Korrektur der Grenze in Oberschlesien*.

Im Hintergrunde steht der Anschluss von Deutsch-Österreich, obwohl ich mir klar darüber bin, dass dieser Anschluss nicht nur Vorteile für Deutschland bringt, sondern das Problem des Deutschen Reiches sehr kompliziert. [...]

Wollen wir diese Ziele erreichen, so müssen wir uns aber auch auf diese Aufgaben konzentrieren. Daher der Sicherheitspakt, der uns einmal den Frieden garantieren und England sowie, wenn Mussolini mitmacht, Italien als Garanten* der deutschen Westgrenze festlegen soll. Der Sicherheitspakt birgt andererseits in sich den Verzicht auf eine kriegerische Auseinandersetzung mit Frankreich wegen der Rückgewinnung* Elsaß-Lothringens, ein deutscher Verzicht, der aber insoweit nur theoretischen Charakter hat, als keine Möglichkeit eines Krieges gegen Frankreich besteht. [...]

Die Frage des Optierens* zwischen Osten und Westen erfolgt durch unseren Eintritt in den Völkerbund nicht. Optieren kann man [...] nur, wenn man eine militärische Macht hinter sich hat. Das fehlt uns leider. Wir können weder zum Kontinentaldegen* für England werden, wie einige glauben, noch können wir uns auf ein deutsch-russisches Bündnis einlassen. Ich warne vor einer Utopie, mit dem Bolschewismus zu kokettieren*. Wenn die Russen in Berlin sind, weht die rote Fahne vom Schloss, und man wird in Russland, wo man die Weltrevolution wünscht, sehr zufrieden sein, Europa bis zur Elbe bolschewisiert zu haben, und wird das übrige Deutschland den Franzosen zum Fraß geben.

Dass wir [...] bereit sind, mit dem russischen Staat, an dessen evolutionäre Entwicklung ich glaube, uns auf anderer Basis zu verständigen* und uns durch unseren Eintritt in den Völkerbund durchaus nicht nach Westen zu verkaufen, ist eine Tatsache, über die ich E.K.H.* gern [...] Näheres sagen würde. [...]

Das Wichtigste ist für die unter 1. berührte Frage der deutschen Politik das Freiwerden deutschen Landes von fremder Besatzung. Wir müssen den Würger* erst vom Hals haben*. Deshalb wird die deutsche Politik, wie Metternich von Österreich wohl nach 1809 sagte, in dieser Beziehung zunächst darin bestehen müssen, zu finassieren* und den großen Entscheidungen auszuweichen*.

Gustav Stresemann: Vermächtnis, Vol. II, Henry Bernhard (Ed.), Ullstein, Berlin 1932, pp. 553 ff.

Garant guarantor

Rückgewinnung cf. *Wiedergewinnung*

optieren to opt for sth.

Degen dagger

mit etw./jdm. kokettieren to flirt with sth./sb.

sich verständigen to agree

E.K.H. (Eure königliche Hoheit) Your Royal Highness

Würger strangler

vom Hals haben to get rid of

finassieren to manage or bring about with finesse

etw. ausweichen to evade sth.

S 18 Gustav Stresemann

Rede zum deutschen Beitritt zum Völkerbund

Gustav Stresemann addressed the League of Nations on 10 September 1926, about one year after his letter to the former German crown prince.

Pre-task 1. Since this is a public speech and an official document, what do you expect Stresemann to say about Germany joining the League of Nations? What might be the difference compared to his confidential letter to Germany's former crown prince? Hypothesize.

Tasks 2. Explain which tasks Stresemann sees for Germany in relation to its foreign policy. Then, compare these with what Stresemann said in S 17. Where are there similarities, where differences?

3. Judging from S 17 and S 18, would you characterize Stresemann as a "good European" or a "good German"? Explain your position.

Genugtuung satisfaction	Der Herr Vorsitzende dieser hohen Versammlung hat ebenso wie der Herr Vorsitzende des Völkerbundsrates die Güte gehabt, mit Worten der Freude und Genugtuung* den Eintritt Deutschlands in den Völkerbund zu begrüßen. Beiden Herren den Dank Deutschlands zum Ausdruck zu bringen und diesen Dank auszudehnen auf die hohe Versammlung, ist meine erste Pflicht, wenn ich von dieser Stelle aus vor Ihnen das Wort nehme. Ich verbinde damit den Dank an die Regierung der Schweizerischen Eidgenossenschaft*, die in traditioneller Weise die großzügige Gastfreundschaft ihres schönen Landes nun auch Deutschland als Mitglied des Völkerbundes erweist.
Schweizerische Eidgenossenschaft Switzerland	

Seit der Begründung des Völkerbundes ist ein Zeitraum von mehr als sechs Jahren verstrichen. Es hat somit einer längeren Entwicklung bedurft, bis die politische Gesamtlage so gestaltet war, dass die deutsche Mitgliedschaft im Völkerbund möglich wurde. Noch in diesem Jahre sind große Schwierigkeiten zu überwinden gewesen, ehe dem Entschluss Deutschlands der einmütige* Beschluss des Völkerbunds folgte. Fern liegt es mir, über diese Dinge der Vergangenheit zu sprechen. Die Aufgabe der lebenden Generation ist es, den Blick auf die Gegenwart und auf die Zukunft zu richten. Nur eines lassen Sie mich sagen: Wenn ein Geschehnis wie der Eintritt Deutschlands in den Völkerbund erst in einer so langen Entwicklung herangereift ist, so trägt vielleicht dieses Geschehnis gerade deshalb eine besondere Gewähr in sich für seine innere Beständigkeit* und seine fruchtbare Auswirkung.

einmütig unanimous

Beständigkeit stability

ungetrübt untarnished

Deutschland tritt mit dem heutigen Tage in die Mitte von Staaten, mit denen es zum Teil seit langen Jahrzehnten in ungetrübter* Freundschaft verbunden ist, die zum anderen Teil im letzten Weltkrieg gegen Deutschland verbündet waren. Es ist von geschichtlicher Bedeutung, dass Deutschland und diese letzteren Staaten sich jetzt im Völkerbund zu dauernder, friedlicher Zusammenarbeit zusammenfinden. Diese Tatsache zeigt deutlicher, als Worte und Programme es können, dass der Völkerbund berufen sein kann, dem politischen Entwicklungsgang der Menschheit eine neue Richtung zu geben. Gerade in der gegenwärtigen Epoche würde die Kultur der Menschheit auf das schwerste bedroht sein, wenn es nicht gelänge, den einzelnen Völkern die Gewähr zu verschaffen, in ungestörtem, friedlichem Wettbewerb die ihnen vom Schicksal zugewiesenen Aufgaben zu erfüllen. Die grundstürzenden Ereignisse eines furchtbaren Krieges haben die Menschheit zur *Besinnung** über die den Völkern zugewiesenen Aufgaben gebracht. Wir sehen in vielen Staaten den Niederbruch wertvollster, für den Staat unentbehrlicher geistiger und wirtschaftlicher Schichten. Wir erleben die Bildung von neuen und das Hinsinken von alten Formen der Wirtschaft. Wir sehen, wie die Wirtschaft die alten Grenzen der Länder sprengt und neue Formen internationaler Zusammenarbeit erstrebt. Die alte Weltwirtschaft hatte für ihre Zusammenarbeit keine Satzungen* und Programme, aber sie beruhte auf dem ungeschriebenen Gesetz des traditionellen Güteraustausches zwischen den Erdteilen. Ihn wiederherzustellen, ist unsere Aufgabe. Wollen wir eine ungestörte weltwirtschaftliche Entwicklung, dann wird das nicht geschehen durch Abschließung der Gebiete voneinander, sondern durch Überbrückung* dessen, was bisher die Wirtschaft der Völker trennte.

zur Besinnung bringen to bring sb. to sb.'s senses

Satzung statute

Überbrückung bridging

Wichtiger aber als alles materielle Geschehen ist das seelische Leben der Nationen. [...]

Die politische Auswirkung dieser Gedanken liegt in einer inneren Verpflichtung der Staaten zu gemeinsamem, friedlichem Zusammenwirken. Diese innere Verpflichtung zu friedlichem Zusammenwirken besteht auch für die großen moralischen Menschheitsfragen. Kein anderes Gesetz darf für sie gelten als das Gesetz der Gerechtigkeit. Das Zusammenarbeiten der Nationen im Völkerbunde muss und wird dazu führen, auch auf diese moralischen Fragen im Völkerleben die gleiche Antwort zu geben. Denn das sicherste Fundament für den Frieden ist eine Politik, die getragen wird von gegenseitigem Verstehen und gegenseitiger Achtung der Völker. Deutschland hat sich schon vor seinem Eintritt in den Völkerbund bemüht, im Sinne friedlichen Zusammenwirkens zu arbeiten. Davon zeugt* die deutsche Initiative, die zu dem Pakt von Locarno führte. Davon zeugen die jetzt nahezu mit allen Nachbarstaaten abgeschlossenen deutschen *Schiedsverträge**. Die deutsche Regierung ist entschlossen, diese Politik mit aller Entschiedenheit weiterzuverfolgen*. Sie kann mit Genugtuung feststellen, dass diese Gedanken – anfangs in Deutschland heftig umkämpft – sich allmählich immer mehr das deutsche Volksbewusstsein erobert haben, so dass die deutsche Regierung auch für die große Mehrheit des deutschen Volkes spricht, wenn sie erklärt, dass sie sich an den Aufgaben des Völkerbundes mit voller Hingebung* beteiligen wird.

Von diesen Aufgaben hat der Völkerbund in sechsjähriger Tätigkeit bereits einen wesentlichen Teil in Angriff genommen und in ernster Arbeit gefördert. Die deutsche Delegation verfügt nicht über die Erfahrungen, die den übrigen hier versammelten Mitgliedern zur Seite stehen. Gleichwohl glaubt sie die Ansicht zum Ausdruck bringen zu können, dass bei den weiteren Arbeiten zunächst jene Gebiete besondere Beachtung verdienen, bei denen die einzelnen Völker durch Einordnung in gemeinsame Einrichtungen die eigene Leistungsfähigkeit* zu steigern vermögen. Neben mancher anderen Schöpfung des Völkerbundes kommt hier vor allem das Streben nach einer internationalen Rechtsordnung in Betracht, das in der Gründung des *Weltgerichtshofs* sichtbaren Ausdruck gewonnen hat.

Von besonderer Bedeutung für die Festigung einer Friedensordnung zwischen den Völkern sind ferner die Bestrebungen, die sich auf die *Abrüstung* beziehen. Die völlige Abrüstung Deutschlands ist durch den Vertrag von Versailles als Beginn der allgemeinen Abrüstung festgesetzt worden. Möge es gelingen, einer allgemeinen Abrüstung in praktischer Arbeit näherzukommen und damit den Beweis zu erbringen, dass eine starke positive Kraft den großen Idealen des Völkerbundes schon jetzt innewohnt*.

Deutschlands Beziehungen zum Völkerbund werden freilich nicht ausschließlich durch die jetzt gegebene Möglichkeit der Mitarbeit an den großen allgemeinen Zielen bestimmt. Der Völkerbund ist vielmehr in mancher Beziehung auch Erbe und Vollstrecker der Verträge von 1919. Daraus haben sich, wie ich offen ausspreche, in der Vergangenheit vielfach Gegensätze zwischen dem Völkerbund und Deutschland ergeben. Ich hoffe, dass sich die Behandlung der hierbei in Betracht kommenden Fragen infolge unserer künftigen Mitarbeit im Völkerbunde leichter gestalten wird. [...] Deutschland wünscht mit allen Nationen, die im Völkerbunde und im Rate des Völkerbundes vertreten sind, auf der Grundlage gegenseitigen Vertrauens zusammenzuarbeiten.

Noch hat der Völkerbund sein Ziel nicht erreicht, alle Weltmächte in sich zu umfassen. [...]

Erst durch die *Universalität* wird der Bund vor jeder Gefahr geschützt, seine politische Kraft zu anderen Diensten als zu reinen Friedensdiensten einzusetzen. Nur auf der Grundlage einer Gemeinschaft, die alle Staaten ohne Unterschied in voller

zeugen von to be evidence of

Schiedsvertrag arbitration agreement
weiterverfolgen to pursue

mit voller Hingebung with total devotion

Leistungsfähigkeit productivity

innewohnen to be inherent to

umspannen to encompass

um etw. ringen to struggle for sth.

erhaben sublime

Gleichberechtigung umspannt*, können Hilfsbereitschaft und Gerechtigkeit die wahren Leitsterne des Menschenschicksals werden.

Nur auf dieser Grundlage lässt sich der Grundsatz der Freiheit aufbauen, um den jedes Volk ringt* wie jedes Menschenwesen. Deutschland ist entschlossen, sich in seiner Politik auf den Boden dieser erhabenen* Ziele zu stellen. Für alle hier versammelten Völker gilt das Wort eines großen Denkers, dass wir Menschen uns zu dem Geschlecht bekennen, das aus dem Dunkel ins Helle strebt. Möge die Arbeit des Völkerbundes sich auf der Grundlage der großen Begriffe *Freiheit, Friede und Einigkeit* vollziehen, dann werden wir dem von uns allen erstrebten Ziele näherkommen. Daran freudig mitzuarbeiten, ist Deutschlands fester Wille.

Gustav Stresemann, Vermächtnis. Der Nachlass in drei Bänden, Henry Bernhard (Ed.), Vol. 2, Berlin 1932, pp. 591–595

CONNECT

Critical voices on the Treaty of Locarno

Although the Treaty of Locarno contributed decisively to Germany's international acceptance, there were also critical voices opposing the treaty.

Election poster of the DNVP, 1928

National Socialism

Task Presenting and evaluating different opinions on the Treaty of Locarno.

- Copy the grid and form five groups. Each group deals with a different source and works on the tasks assigned by completing the grid. In your group, agree on the information you want to convey to the course as a whole.

	Arguments in favour of/against the treaty	Overall attitude towards the treaty	Notes
Fehrenbach			
Wels			
Bartels			
Hugenberg			
Strasser			

- In a second step, mix the groups so that each group consists of someone who has worked on a different source. Present your information to the other students and take notes on what the others tell you. Complete the grid with the given information.

S 19a) Constantin Fehrenbach

„Sind die Verträge ein Instrument des Friedens?"

On 24 November 1925, one month after the ratification of the treaty, former Reich Chancellor Constantin Fehrenbach (1852–1926) comments on the treaty. Fehrenbach was a member of the Centre Party and chancellor from 25 June 1919 until 4 May 1921.

Tasks
1. Analyse the source.
2. Explain how Fehrenbach answers the question raised in the headline and how he justifies his opinion.

Wir fragen uns: sind diese Verträge in Wirklichkeit ein Instrument des Friedens, eines Friedens, dem Deutschland in Ehren zustimmen kann?
Dazu ist unseres Erachtens zunächst erforderlich, dass sowohl in der Form wie in der Sache die volle Gleichberechtigung Deutschlands gewahrt ist
5 und dass dem deutschen Volke nichts zugemutet* wird, was seiner nationalen Würde und unveräußerlichen, durch die natürliche Ordnung der Dinge garantierten Rechten eines jeden Staatsvolkes zuwiderliefe*. Diese Bedingung ist erfüllt. Nach der formalen Seite ist das unbestritten. Aber auch der Inhalt der Verträge entspricht der gestellten Anforderung.
10 Wir leisten keine neue – diesmal freiwillige – Unterschrift unter das Versailler Diktat. [...]
Wir sprechen in dem Vertrag von Locarno auch keinen Rechtsverzicht* auf deutsches Land und Volk aus. [...]
Die gleiche Folgerung ergibt sich aus dem Charakter der Schiedsverträge,
15 die sowohl mit den westlichen wie mit den östlichen Nachbarstaaten Deutschlands vorgesehen sind. [...] Sie enthalten keine uneingeschränkte

jdm. etw. zumuten to expect sth. from sb.

etw. zuwiderlaufen to run contrary to sth.

Rechtsverzicht waiving of rights, giving up of rights

Unterwerfung unter irgendwelche Schiedssprüche, es sei denn, dass es sich lediglich um eine Auslegung von Rechtsbestimmungen handelt.
Wir ziehen daraus den Schluss: die Gleichberechtigung Deutschlands mit den übrigen Vertragsstaaten ist in Locarno gewahrt worden, und unveräußerliche Rechte der Nation sind keineswegs preisgegeben.

from: H. Michaelis, E. Schraepler (Eds.): Ursachen und Folgen. Vol. VI: Die Weimarer Republik: Vertragserfüllung u. innere Bedrohung 1919/1922, Berlin 1960 ff., p. 421

S 19b Otto Wels

„Wir stehen jetzt am Scheidepunkt"

On 24 November 1925, Otto Wels, deputy of the SPD, utters his concerns in the Reichstag.

Tasks
1. Analyse the source.
2. Explain how, according to Wels, a peaceful world can be achieved.
3. How does Wels assess the relationship between Germany and Soviet Russia and how does he see the Treaty of Rapallo? Explain.

[...] Wie man auch zu den Verträgen von Locarno und zu dem Eintritt Deutschlands in den Völkerbund stehen mag, das fühlt ein jeder: wir stehen jetzt am Scheidepunkte der europäischen Politik. Es fragt sich jetzt, ob eine neue Welt, in der der Gedanke des Friedens lebendige Kraft haben soll, das Leben der Völker Europas in Zukunft beherrschen wird, oder ob die Mächte, die, auf Gewalt und kriegerischen Auseinandersetzungen fußend, dem Fortschritt, dem moralischen und materiellen Wiederaufbau den Weg dauernd versperren sollen.

Die ungeheure Wirtschaftskrise, die sich über die ganze Welt erstreckt, zwingt allen Staaten, zwingt allen Bevölkerungsschichten die Erkenntnis auf, dass der Periode des Wiederaufbaus nach den Jahren der kriegerischen Zerstörung die Wege geebnet werden müssen durch ein neues Verhältnis der Staaten Europas zueinander. [...] Was seit Jahrzehnten in Europa fehlte, das Bedürfnis nach europäischer Solidarität, das ist heute ein sichtbares Bedürfnis* aller europäischen Völker geworden. [...] Es zeigt sich jetzt allerdings mehr denn je die Notwendigkeit, die Allgemeininteressen Europas, die mit den Interessen jedes einzelnen Landes identisch sind, den selbstsüchtigen Interessen von Gruppen, Cliquen und Parteien voranzustellen. [...]

Es handelt sich gerade darum, das Bündnissystem der Vorkriegszeit und damit den Gegensatz, der zwischen Alliierten und Deutschland bestand, aus der Welt zu schaffen. Deutschland soll in Zukunft gleichberechtigt neben jenen Mächten stehen, nicht um mit ihnen gegen Russland zu marschieren, sondern um den Völkerbund aufzubauen, der schließlich auch Russland umfassen wird.

Die Fragestellung Völkerbund oder Bündnis mit Sowjetrussland dient nicht der Herbeiführung des Friedens, sondern diese Fragestellung schließt den

Bedürfnis need

Gedanken an eine kommende Auseinandersetzung mit Gewalt in sich. Das Ziel der Politik aber, die nach Locarno geführt hat, ist die Ausschließung
30 des Krieges und die Vorbereitung des Friedens. Deutschland braucht kein Bündnis mehr mit Sowjetrussland. Deutschland und Russland haben den Vertrag von Rapallo. Vor dem Tage von Locarno gelangte der deutsch-russische Handels- und Wirtschaftsvertrag zum Abschluss. Hinter diesem Vertrage steht auf deutscher Seite der Wille, mit Russland in Frieden und
35 Freundschaft zu leben, wirtschaftliche Vorteile aus dieser Verbindung zu ziehen und auch Russland bei seinem wirtschaftlichen Aufbau zu helfen. Unsere Überzeugung ist es, dass Russland nicht dauernd aus der europäischen Wirtschaft und aus seinen Völkerleben ausgeschaltet werden kann ohne schwere Schädigung der übrigen Welt. Darum denkt in ganz Deutsch-
40 land kein Mensch daran, sich nach dem Westen deshalb zu orientieren, weil er zwischen Deutschland und Russland einen Kordon* errichten will. [...]

Kordon line of people, military posts, or ships surrounding an area to close or guard it

from: H. Michaelis, E. Schraepler (Hrsg.): Ursachen und Folgen. Vol. VI: Die Weimarer Republik: Vertragserfüllung u. innere Bedrohung 1919/1922, Berlin 1960 ff., p. 414

Otto Wels (1873–1939)

Otto Wels was born on 15 September 1873 as the son of an innkeeper in Berlin. Wels started working as a paper hanger *[Tapezierer]* in 1891 and in that same year he also joined the SPD. From 1895–1897 he served in the military. While working as a trade union official, Wels was also a member of the *Vorwärts* press committee. In 1907, he became party secretary of the province of Brandenburg and on 12 January 1912 he, for the first time, achieved a mandate for the Reichstag. One year later, Wels, supported by August Bebel, became a member of the SPD executive committee. Despite his political engagement, he did not make an appearance during WWI. It was only on 9 November 1918 that Wels joined the workers' and soldiers' council in Berlin and became military commander of the city. In 1919 and 1920 he was a member of the national assembly and party leader of the SPD. Wels also played a role in the Kapp Putsch since he led the national strike against it.

Otto Wels served as a member of the Reichstag from 1920 until 1933. After Heinrich Brüning (Centre Party) had become chancellor in 1930, Wels openly supported the toleration of Brüning's cabinet which had lost the support of the DNVP. With the rise of the NSDAP, Wels worked more and more against this right-wing influence by for example organizing the Eiserne Front ("Iron Front"), an anti-Nazi group. Wels, however, became famous and respected mainly because of his last speech given in the Reichstag on 23 March 1933 in which he spoke out frankly against the Enabling Act proposed by Hitler. Wels left Germany shortly afterwards and went into exile in Prague and later in Paris where he nevertheless continued to work for an exile organization of the SPD. Otto Wels died in the French capital on 16 September 1939.

S 19c Wolfgang Bartels
„Was ist Locarno?"

On 30 October 1925, Wolfgang Bartels from the KPD commented on the Treaty of Locarno in the Prussian Landtag.

Tasks
1. Analyse the source.
2. How does Bartels answer the question raised in the headline and what are his arguments? Explain.

Büttel negative expression for sb. who obligingly carries out what she/he is told
ausliefern to hand over
verschenken to give sth. away

Aufrechterhaltung maintenance

verschärfte Ausbeutung increased exploitation
Entrechtung deprivation of rights

[...] Was ist Locarno? Wenn man die einzelnen Verträge und ihre Paragraphen durchgeht. So sehen wir, dass Deutschland hinreichend Garantie gibt, aber dafür lediglich die Garantie erhält, dass es Kriegsbütteldienste* leisten darf und andererseits Deutschland als Kriegsschauplatz ausliefern* muss. Locarno bedeutet in Wirklichkeit [...] die Auslieferung der Rheinlande, es bedeutet direkt ein Verschenken* preußisch-deutschen Gebietes, es bedeutet Garantie des Einmarsch- und Durchmarschrechtes durch Deutschland, es bedeutet die Kriegsdienstverpflichtung der deutschen Bevölkerung für die Entente gegen Russland, es bedeutet vor allem die Anerkennung der Aufrechterhaltung* des Besatzungsregimes und es bedeutet erneut das Bekenntnis zu dem Versailler Vertrag. Es bedeutet darüber hinaus verschärfte Ausbeutung*, verschärfte Entrechtung*, Unterdrückung, Elend, Übel, Not und alles, was im Gefolge des neuen Krieges eben zu erwarten ist. [...]

from: H. Michaelis, E. Schraepler (Hrsg.): Ursachen und Folgen. Vol. VI: Die Weimarer Republik: Vertragserfüllung u. innere Bedrohung 1919/1922, Berlin 1960 ff., p. 396

S 19d Alfred Hugenberg
„Ich bin kein Pazifist"

On 15 November 1925, Alfred Hugenberg from the DNVP makes his remarks on the Treaty of Locarno. Apart from being a member and representative of the DNVP, Hugenberg was also a businessmen who later served as Minister of Economy and Minister of Agriculture in Hitler's first cabinet.

Tasks
1. Analyse the source.
2. Explain the dangers Hugenberg sees for Germany's future arising from the terms of the treaty.

etw. Rechnung tragen to allow for sth.

[...] Sachlich betrachtet ist vor allem die Auffassung falsch, dass Locarno einen zehn- bis zwanzigjährigen Frieden bedeute. Gerade das Gegenteil ist richtig. Ich bin kein Pazifist, aber ich muss der Tatsache Rechnung tragen, dass Deutschland waffenlos ist, und muss deshalb verlangen, dass die deutsche auswärtige Politik mit einer dieser Tatsache Rechnung tragenden* Vorsicht geführt wird! Seit unserem Zusammenbruch hat mir immer als größte Sorge vorgeschwebt, dass Deutschland der Kriegsschauplatz zwischen Russland und dem Westen werden, dass Deutschland den Fehler einer Verfeindung mit Russland wiederholen könnte. [...]

Manche Leute sind sich des Unterschiedes in der Struktur des Westens und des Ostens Deutschlands nicht bewusst. Das dichtbevölkerte industrielle Rheinland zu französieren, würde den Franzosen auch dann nicht gelingen, wenn sie es – was Gott verhüte – eine Zeitlang beherrschten. Ganz anders im weiten Osten mit seinem ausgedehnten Großgrundbesitz* und seiner dünnen Bevölkerung. Was wir in Polen heute sehen, kann sich für den ganzen deutschen Osten wiederholen! Man muss auch als Gegner anerkennen, dass alle Regierungen seit der Revolution diesen gefahrvollen, sich jedermann aufdrängenden Tatbestand* berücksichtigt haben. Es ist Herrn Stresemann vorbehalten geblieben, mit diesem Feuer zu spielen. Denn Locarno, wie es geworden ist, bedeutet tatsächlich und trotz aller Vorbehalte, dass Deutschland in dem Gegensatz Westmächte – Russland optiert und damit – waffenlos wie es ist – sich leichtsinnig mitten in Gegensätze hineinspielt, bei deren Austragung es nur die Rolle des furchtbar Leidenden spielen kann. […]

Großgrundbesitz large estate

Tatbestand facts

H. Michaelis/E. Schraepler (Eds.): Ursachen und Folgen. Berlin: Dokumenten-Verlag Wendler & Co. 1958 ff., Vol. VI, p. 398

S 19e) Gregor Strasser

On 24 November 1925, the National Socialist deputy Gregor Strasser talks about the Treaty of Locarno in the Reichstag.

Tasks
1. Analyse the source.
2. Explain what Strasser explicitly criticizes about the treaty.

Wir Nationalsozialisten, wir Frontsoldaten und wir Frontoffiziere […] verzichten nun und nimmer auf Elsass-Lothringen. Wir verzichten nie auf Eupen und Malmedy*, auf die Saar und auf unsere Kolonien. Wir verzichten auf Nordschleswig so wenig wie auf Memel und Danzig, wie auf Westpreußen und Oberschlesien. Wir jungen Deutschen kennen unsere großdeutsche Aufgabe, und wir speisen* die Brüder in Österreich und in Sudeten-Deutschland nicht mit leeren Worten ab. […] Unser Staat, der […] ein in sich geschlossener geworden ist, wird einst die Verträge von Versailles, London* und Locarno wie Papierfetzen* zerreißen können, weil er sich stützt auf das, was Sie bewusst im deutschen Volke zerschlagen, wofür kein Opfer gebracht werden darf, nämlich auf die Bildung eines in sich geschlossenen Volkes.

Eupen und Malmedy geographical area in eastern Belgium

jdn. mit etw. abspeisen to fob sb. off with sth.

Verträge von London Dawes Plan

Papierfetzen scrap of paper

Detlef Junker u. a. (Eds.): Deutsche Parlamentsdebatten II, 1919–1939, Frankfurt/Main 1917, pp. 180 f.

Stresemann delivering his last speech in front of the general assembly of the League of Nations, 9 September 1929

S 20 Gustav Stresemann
Rede vor dem Völkerbund

On 9 September 1929, Stresemann delivered his last speech to the League of Nations before he died on 3 October. He not only elaborates on what the League of Nations has achieved so far but also voices demands for the future.

Pre-task 1. Anticipate what Stresemann might have said about the achievements of the League of Nations and what he might envision for the future. Talk to a partner.

Task 2. After having read the source, compare your results with your ideas from the pre-task: what has been achieved, what has to be done in the future?

Post-task 3. After having dealt with S 18 , you were asked to characterize Stresemann as either a "good European" or a "good German". Do some research on the European Union today (http://europa.eu/index_en.htm) and find out which of the measures that Stresemann demanded back then have been realized today. Then, think again about your initial judgement.

erörtern to debate

Errungenschaft achievement

Ich komme zu der Frage, die in der Debatte dieser Tage erörtert* worden ist. Das war die Neugestaltung der Staatenverhältnisse in Europa. [...] Es gibt sehr viele, die jede Erörterung eines solchen Gedankens von vornherein abgelehnt haben. [...] Was erscheint denn an Europa, an seiner Konstruktion vom wirtschaftlichen Gesichtspunkte aus so außerordentlich grotesk? Es erscheint mit grotesk, dass die ⁵ Entwicklung Europas nicht vorwärts, sondern rückwärts gegangen zu sein scheint. [...] Ist es nicht grotesk, dass Sie auf Grund neuer praktischer Errungenschaften* die Entfernung von Süddeutschland nach Tokio um 20 Tage verkürzt haben, sich aber in Europa selbst stundenlang mit der Lokomotive irgendwo aufhalten lassen müssen, weil eine neue Grenze kommt, eine neue Zollrevision* stattfindet, als wenn das Ganze ein Kleinkrämergeschäft* wäre, das wir in Europa innerhalb der gesamten Weltwirtschaft noch führen dürfen? [...]

Durch den Versailler Vertrag ist eine große Anzahl neuer Staaten geschaffen worden. Ich diskutiere hier nicht über das Politische des Versailler Vertrages, denn ich darf annehmen, dass meine Anschauungen darüber bekannt sind. Aber das Wirtschaftliche möchte ich doch betonen und sagen, dass es unmöglich ist, dass Sie zwar eine große Anzahl neuer Staaten geschaffen, aber ihre Einbeziehung in das europäische Wirtschaftssystem vollkommen beiseite gelassen haben. Was ist denn die Folge dieser Unterlassungssünde* gewesen? Sie sehen neue Grenzen, neue Maße*, neue Gewichte, neue Usancen*, neue Münzen, ein fortwährendes Stocken* des Verkehrs. [...]

Wo bleibt in Europa die europäische Münze, die europäische Briefmarke? Sind diese aus nationalem Prestige heraus geborenen Einzelheiten nicht sämtlich Dinge, die durch die Entwicklung der Zeit längst überholt* wurden und diesem Erdteil einen außerordentlichen Nachteil zufügen*, nicht nur im Verhältnis der Länder zueinander, nicht auch nur in dem Verhältnis zu den Weltteilen, sondern auch im Verhältnis anderer Weltteile, die sich oft viel schwerer in diese Dinge hineinversetzen* können als ein Europäer, der es allmählich auch nicht mehr versteht? Wir in unserem Kreise, wir haben die nüchterne* Aufgabe, die Völker einander näherzubringen, ihre Gegensätze zu überbrücken. Zweifeln wir nicht daran: sie sind einander nicht so nahe, wie es zu wünschen wäre; zweifeln wir nicht daran: es gibt Gegensätze. Es handelt sich um eine harte Arbeit: vorwärtszukommen, diese Gegensätze zu vermindern und uns jenem Zustand zu nähern, den wir alle erhoffen.

Henry Bernhard (Eds.): Gustav Stresemann. Vermächtnis. Bd. 3. Berlin 1932, pp. 577f.

Zollrevision customs inspection
Kleinkrämergeschäft corner shop

Unterlassungssünde sin of not having done sth. against sth.
Maß measure
Usance custom
Stocken stagnation

jdn. überholen to pass by
zufügen to inflict

sich in jdn. hineinversetzen to put oneself in the position of sb.
nüchtern matter-of-fact

Causes and Consequences of the World Economic Crisis of 1929

S 21 John Hite and Chris Hinton

How Did German Governments React to the Slump?

The following text is an excerpt taken from a British schoolbook dealing exclusively with the Weimar Republic and Nazi Germany.

Pre-tasks
1. Describe the vicious circle presented below.
2. When confronted with an economic slump, governments have different options how to tackle it. They could either embark on a policy of non-intervention, meaning the government just waits until the economy recovers on its own, or they could start to intervene in economic affairs by for instance printing money.
   In small groups, discuss which strategies would lead to which consequences. Take into account the visualization as well.

Tasks
3. Rank the "particular factors operating in Germany" according to their importance for the strategy adopted by the German governments.
4. Evaluate the German government's reaction to the slump against the backdrop of the strategy you would have adopted.
5. Discuss what effect this had on the perception of the democratic system of the Weimar Republic in the eyes of the German population.

The depression in Germany after 1929 is often blamed on external events, chiefly the Wall Street Crash. However, as this chart shows, the internal situation in Germany played a major part in the crisis.

Offstage: the Government
No government was prepared to intervene in a major way to reflate the economy. Müller's coalition government 1928–30 could not agree on cuts. Brüning's government 1930–32 tried to use the slump for its own political and foreign policy purposes.

The component parts of the economic crisis
a) Agriculture: many farmers, hit by high interest rates, were going bankrupt by 1927; they were then hit by falling prices.
b) Industry suffered a trade recession from 1929 on.
c) Finance was hit by a banking collapse in the summer of 1931 when five banks went bankrupt.

Germany: Weakness in economy → Loss of confidence → Workers have less money → Wages reduced

USA: Wall Street Crash October 1929 → America loans and investments withdrawn → Fall in demand as people buy less → Businesses lower prices to try to attract customers

World: General lack of confidence → Growth of protectionism → Decline in world trade → Businesses cut back production → Workers laid off

causes / Vicious circle

Like the governments of most other countries hit by the slump, for a long time [they] did very little. This was partly due to the widespread international belief that governments were fairly powerless to help. There were also particular factors operating in Germany:

- Germany had recovered from a minor slump in 1926 without the government taking action.
- It was hard for a coalition government to agree on action, particularly if this called for sacrifices. In March 1930 the Müller SPD-led government collapsed when it failed to agree on what cuts in unemployment relief to make.
- Most crucially, the government was terrified by the thought of a recurrence of the hyperinflation crisis of 1923. It believed that spending its way out of the crisis (for example, by maintaining welfare levels and increasing expenditure on public works) without raising taxes could provoke another inflationary crisis.
- Legal restrictions on the Reichsbank (as part of the Dawes and Young Plans) meant it could not greatly increase the amount of money printed nor devalue the mark.
- The government found it difficult to borrow money. Many potential German investors had lost their savings in 1923 and were unable or reluctant to lend money. Foreigners shared this lack of confidence in German finances. Foreign governments who might have made loans insisted on terms that were unacceptable to the government.

The main approach of governments after 1929 was to reduce expenditure to cope with the fall in tax revenue as economic activity declined. For example, between 1928 and 1933 the budget for war victims' pensions was cut by one-third [...]. Eventually, but too late, the government became more interventionist. Once reparations were suspended in 1931, Chancellor Brüning set up some public work schemes and his successor Papen began to allocate* unused land to dispossessed peasants and workers. But these measures were a classic example of 'too little too late'. The economy did start to improve late in 1932, but this was too imperceptible* to influence the voters. [...]

John Hite/Chris Hinton (Eds.): Weimar & Nazi Germany. London (Hodder) 2000, p. 105

to allocate to officially give sth. to sb., or to decide that sth. can be used for a specific purpose
imperceptible difficult to notice

People reading election posters for the Reichstag elections, 24 September 1930

S 22 Hellmut von Gerlach

On the Electoral Success of the NSDAP

On 6 October 1930, roughly one month after the elections on 14 September 1930, Hellmut von Gerlach, co-founder of the DDP, published this comment about the voters of the NSDAP. Gerlach went into exile in Austria after the Nazis took over complete power.

Pre-task
1. Go back to S 14 again and refresh your knowledge about the aims of the NSDAP.

Tasks
2. According to Gerlach, which parts of the German population voted for the NSDAP? Give a summary.
3. Describe what motives, according to Gerlach, people had for voting for the Nazi party.
4. Assess Gerlach's attitude towards those who voted for the NSDAP by taking his choice of words into account.

Hakenkreuz swastika
auf etw. eingeschworen sein to be committed to sth.
Mitläufer follower, nominal member
labil unstable
Stammkunde regular customer
Laufkunde casual customer
Gunst der Umstände favourable circumstances
Ungunst disfavour, unfavourable circumstances
sich etw. wähnen to consider oneself to be sth.
ostelbische Granden grandees from east of the River Elbe
hospitieren to sit in on, to spend a while with, to observe
sich gebärden to behave
sich etw. dünken to believe oneself to be
berüchtigt notorious
Stehkragenproletarier negative for workers who do not feel that they actually belong to the working class
Standesgefühl feeling of belonging to a certain class
Hetzphrase phrase, catch-cry, slogan of agitation
Konkurrent competitor
bedauerlich unfortunate
Gewerbetreibende/r craftspeople, contractor, tradespeople, manufacturer, small industrialist
Kleinkaufleute small merchants
Einsicht understanding, insight

Die Hitlerwähler setzen sich aus zwei Kategorien zusammen: einer kleinen Minderheit von Nationalsozialisten, die auf das Hakenkreuz* eingeschworen* sind, und einer riesigen Mehrheit von Mitläufern*. Keine andere deutsche Partei ist so labil* wie die nationalsozialistische, das heißt bei keiner anderen ist das Missverhältnis zwischen Stammkunden* und Laufkunden* ebenso groß. [...] 5
Idealisten mit verwirrtem Kopf, insgesamt ein paar hunderttausend Mann, das ist Hitlers Kerntruppe. Die Millionen der Wähler, die er diesmal mustern konnte, dank der Gunst der Umstände*, das heißt dank der Ungunst* der Wirtschaftslage, rekrutieren sich aus den verschiedensten Schichten.
Da sind Arbeiter, relativ genommen nicht sehr viele, aber eine Million wird es 10 doch wohl immer gewesen sein. Es sind Landarbeiter, die sich immer noch vom „gnädigen Herrn" abhängig wähnen* und von ostelbischen Granden* für Hitler kommandiert wurden. Es sind jene labilen Elemente, die erst bei den Kommunisten hospitiert* haben und sich nun den Nationalsozialisten zuwenden, weil diese sich noch radikaler gebärden*. Es sind junge Leute, Friseurgehilfen, Chauffeure 15 usw., die sich etwas Besseres dünken* als die Masse der gewerkschaftlich organisierten Fabrikarbeiter. [...]
Da sind Massen von Angestellten, [...] die berühmten oder berüchtigten* Stehkragenproletarier*. Ihr Interesse müsste sie in eine Einheitsfront mit den Arbeitern führen. Aber ihr „Standesgefühl"* ist stärker als ihre soziale Einsicht. 20
Da ist das Gros der Studenten und sonstigen jungen Akademiker. Bei ihnen fällt die antisemitische Hetzphrase* auf besonders dankbaren Boden. Der Jude wird eben als unbequemer Konkurrent* empfunden. Sie sind fanatisch nationalistisch. Den Krieg kennen sie nicht. [...]
Da sind bedauerlich* viele Beamte. Ihre politische Freiheit verdanken sie aus- 25 schließlich der Republik. Aber leider hat ihnen die Republik mit der politischen Freiheit nicht auch zugleich das politische Denken geben können. [...]
Da ist vor allem der große Block des sogenannten selbständigen Mittelstandes. Diese Millionen von Handwerkern, Gewerbetreibenden* und Kleinkaufleuten* führen seit der nach 1871 einsetzenden großindustriellen Entwicklung einen ver- 30 zweifelten Kampf um ihre Existenz. Es fehlt ihnen an wirtschaftlicher Einsicht*.

Darum fallen sie auf jeden Schwätzer* herein, der ihnen die Wiederherstellung des „goldenen Bodens" durch Kampf gegen Juden und Warenhäuser*, gegen Börse und Gewerbefreiheit* verspricht. [...]

from: Heinrich Bennecke: Wirtschaftliche Depression und politischer Radikalismus: 1918–1938. München: Olzog 1970, pp. 346 ff.

Schwätzer babbler
Warenhaus general store
Gewerbefreiheit freedom of trade, economic freedom

S 23 Franz von Papen
Pläne für die Verfassung

Chancellor Franz von Papen presents his plans for a reform of the constitution to Bavarian industrialists on 12 October 1932.

Pre-task
1. Have a look at the Weimar Constitution again (cf. S 5a). Where exactly does the power lie in this constitution? Explain.

Tasks
2. After having read the source, state where the power lies in von Papen's reformed constitution.
3. Point out how von Papen justifies his plans.
4. Explain which of these proposals violate the Basic Law.

Franz von Papen

Wir wollen eine machtvolle und überparteiliche* Staatsgewalt schaffen, die nicht als Spielball von den politischen und gesellschaftlichen Kräften hin- und hergetrieben* wird, sondern über ihnen unerschütterlich* steht [...]. Die Reform der Verfassung muss dafür sorgen, dass eine solche machtvolle und autoritäre Regie-
5 rung in die richtige Verbindung mit dem Volke gebracht wird.
An den großen Grundgesetzen [...] soll man nicht rütteln, aber die Formen des politischen Lebens gilt es zu erneuern. Die Reichsregierung muss unabhängig von den Parteien gestellt werden. Ihr Bestand* darf nicht Zufallsmehrheiten ausgesetzt sein. Das Verhältnis zwischen Regierung und Volksvertretung muss so
10 geregelt werden, dass die Regierung und nicht das Parlament die Staatsgewalt handhabt*. Als Gegengewicht* gegen einseitige*, von Parteiinteressen herbeigeführte Beschlüsse des Reichstags bedarf Deutschland einer besonderen Ersten Kammer mit fest abgegrenzten Rechten und starker Beteiligung an der Gesetzgebung. Heute ist das einzige Korrektiv* gegen das überspitzte* parlamentarische
15 System und gegen das Versagen des Reichstags die Verordnungsgewalt des Reichspräsidenten auf Grund des Artikels 48 der Reichsverfassung. Sobald aber wieder stetige und normale Verhältnisse herrschen, wird auch kein Anlass mehr sein, Artikel 48 in der bisherigen Weise anzuwenden. [...]
Die Reichsregierung hat bei ihrem Antritt als oberstes Ziel ihrer Innenpolitik die
20 Vereinigung aller wahrhaft nationalen Kräfte proklamiert. Das Ziel bleibt unverrückbar bestehen – es muss bestehen bleiben – um Deutschlands willen – auch wenn die Wege heute auseinander führen. Nichts kann das Vertrauen in den Aufstieg der Nation mehr hindern als die Unstabilität der politischen Verhältnisse, als Regierungen, die nur Treibholz* sind auf den Wellen der Partei und abhängig von
25 jeder Strömung*. Diese Art der Staatsführung der Parteiarithmetik ist im Urteil des Volkes erledigt.

Heinz Hürten (Eds.): Weimarer Republik und Drittes Reich 1918–1945 (Deutsche Geschichte in Quellen und Darstellung, Vol. 9), Stuttgart 1995, pp. 132 ff.

überparteilich above party lines

als Spielball hin- und hergetrieben werden to be at the mercy of
unerschütterlich steadfast

Bestand existence

handhaben to manage
Gegengewicht counterbalance
einseitig one-sided

Korrektiv corrective
überspitzt exaggerated

Treibholz driftwood
Strömung current

S 24 Appeal to Hindenburg to Appoint Hitler Chancellor

In the middle of November 1932, leading personalities in industry and the economy appealed to Hindenburg to appoint Hitler chancellor.

Pre-task
1. Anticipate why Hitler could have been an appropriate candidate for leading personalities in industry and business.

Tasks
2. Point out the arguments brought forward in order to convince Hindenburg.
3. Assess these arguments in terms of how convincing they are.

Der Ausgang der Reichstagswahl vom 6. November [...] hat gezeigt, dass das derzeitige Kabinett [...] für den von ihm eingeschlagenen Weg keine ausreichende Stütze im deutschen Volk gefunden hat, dass aber das von Eurer Exzellenz* gezeigte Ziel eine volle Mehrheit im deutschen Volke besitzt, wenn man – wie es geschehen muss – von der staatsverneinenden* kommunistischen Partei absieht*. Gegen das bisherige parlamentarische Parteiregime sind nicht nur die Deutschnationale Volkspartei und die ihr nahe stehenden kleineren Gruppen, sondern auch die Nationalsozialistische Deutsche Arbeiterpartei grundsätzlich eingestellt und haben damit das Ziel Eurer Exzellenz bejaht*. [...]

Es ist klar, dass eine des Öfteren wiederholte Reichstagsauflösung mit sich häufenden*, den Parteikampf immer weiter zuspitzenden* Neuwahlen nicht nur einer politischen, sondern auch jeder wirtschaftlichen Beruhigung und Festigung entgegenwirken* muss. Es ist aber auch klar, dass jede Verfassungsänderung, die nicht von breitester Volksströmung getragen ist, noch schlimmere wirtschaftliche, politische und seelische Wirkungen auslösen wird. [...]

Wir bekennen uns frei von jeder engen parteipolitischen Einstellung. Wir erkennen in der nationalen Bewegung, die durch unser Volk geht, den verheißungsvollen* Beginn einer Zeit, die durch Überwindung des Klassengegensatzes die unerlässliche* Grundlage für einen Wiederaufstieg der deutschen Wirtschaft erst schafft. Wir wissen, dass dieser Aufstieg noch viele Opfer erfordert. Wir glauben, dass diese Opfer nur dann willig* gebracht werden können, wenn die größte Gruppe dieser nationalen Bewegung führend an der Regierung beteiligt wird.

Die Übertragung der verantwortlichen Leitung eines mit den besten sachlichen und persönlichen Kräften ausgestatteten Präsidialkabinetts an den Führer der größten nationalen Gruppe wird die Schlacken* und Fehler, die jeder Massenbewegung notgedrungen* anhaften*, ausmerzen und Millionen Menschen, die heute abseits stehen*, zu bejahender Kraft mitreißen.

Wolfgang Michalka/Gottfried Niedhart (Eds.): Deutsche Geschichte 1918–1933, Frankfurt/Main 1992, pp. 224f.

Eure Exzellenz Your Excellency
staatsverneinend negating the state
von etw. absehen here: to leave sth. aside
bejahen to support sth.
sich häufen to happen very frequently
zuspitzen to get worse
entgegenwirken to work against sth.
verheißungsvoll promising
unerlässlich vital
willig willingly
Schlacke slag, dross
notgedrungen unavoidably, inevitably
anhaften to adhere to
abseits stehen to be out in the cold, to stand in the shadows

S 25 Ian Kershaw

How Hitler Won Over the German People

Ian Kershaw (*1943) is a British historian who became known for his two-volume biography of Hitler. Here, Kershaw tries to explain why people were easily won over by the Nazis.

> **Pre-task**
> 1. Kershaw quotes a German newspaper from 4 August 1934, one day after Hitler had merged the offices of chancellor and president, declaring himself "Führer", with the headline "Today Hitler Is All of Germany". Explain the meaning of this headline. In a first step, make notes on everything you think Hitler stands for, then, in a second step, do the same for Germany. Compare with a partner.
>
> **Tasks**
> 2. Compare your results from the pre-task with Kershaw's interpretation of the quotation.
> 3. Kershaw names various aspects that he believes contributed to Hitler's success. Focus on the following aspects and explain them in detail:
>   - "fertile terrain"
>   - the Versailles Treaty
>   - foreign policy
>   - Nazi ideology

There were still many Germans who were sceptical of Hitler when he became chancellor in 1933. But Führer propaganda and military success soon turned him into an idol. The adulation* helped make the Third Reich catastrophe possible.

"Today Hitler Is All of Germany." The newspaper headline on Aug. 4, 1934 reflected the vital shift in power that had just taken place. Two days earlier, on the death of Reich President Paul von Hindenburg, Hitler had lost no time in abolishing the Reich Presidency and having the army swear a personal oath of unconditional obedience to him as "the Führer of the German Reich and People." He was now head of state and supreme commander of the armed forces, as well as head of government and of the monopoly party, the NSDAP. Hitler had total power in Germany, unrestricted by any constitutional constraints. The headline implied even more, however, than the major change in the constellation of power. It suggested an identity of Hitler and the country he ruled, signifying a complete bond between the German people and Hitler. [...]

Fertile Terrain Prepared the Way
It was a manufactured consensus, a propaganda construct, with repression of political opponents, "racial enemies" and other outsiders to the proclaimed "national community" as the other side of the coin. The "superman" image of Hitler amounted to the central component of the fabrication. Already before the "takeover of power" it had been the creation of the most modern, hugely successful, political "marketing" strategy of its time, masterminded by Goebbels. And once the monopoly of state control of propaganda fell into Nazi hands in 1933, there was no obstacle in the mass media to the rapid spread of Hitler's "charismatic" appeal.

But even the slick* and sophisticated techniques behind the creation of the Führer Myth would have been ineffective, had not fertile terrain been prepared long before Hitler became Reich Chancellor. Expectations of national salvation were by 1933 widespread, not just among Nazi supporters, and had already become vested* in the person of Hitler. By the time that he took power, over 13 million voters had at least partially swallowed the Führer cult, which was more fully embraced by the huge (if fluctuating) mass membership of the Party and its myriad* subordinate

adulation overenthusiastic praise

slick smart, clever

vested fully and unconditionally guaranted as a legal right, benefit, or privilege

myriad innumerable

The British historian Ian Kershaw

affiliations. The organizational basis was therefore laid for the wider transmission of the Führer cult.

Given the failure of Weimar democracy and the crisis conditions in which the Hitler government came to power, it was clear that if the new Reich Chancellor could swiftly attain some successes, he would substantially increase his popularity. The scope for the rapid widening of the adulation of Hitler, the winning of "the majority of the majority" who had not voted for him in March 1933 had been laid. The speed with which the Hitler cult now spread has to be seen from this background, as well as from the masterly deployment of propaganda imagery.

There were a number of crucial areas where Hitler could win great support by acting in what seemed to be the national, not partisan party-political, interest, and through converting his image from that of Party to national leader. Even his opponents recognized the growth of his popularity. The exiled Social Democratic organization, the Sopade, based in Prague, acknowledged in April 1938 the widely-held view it had repeatedly echoed, "that Hitler could count on the agreement of the majority of the people on two essential points: 1) he had created jobs and 2) he had made Germany strong."

acclaim praise

Readily Accepted the Acclaim*

In the early years of the Third Reich, most people sensed that after the dismal years of hopelessness there was new direction, energy, and dynamism. There was a widespread feeling that finally a government was doing something to get Germany back on her feet. Of course, Hitler, whose knowledge of economics was primitive, had not personally guided the economic recovery in the early years of the Third Reich. The reasons for the rapid revival were complex and varied. If any single individual could be said to have masterminded the recovery, then it was Hjalmar Schacht, President of the Reichsbank and Reich Minister of Economics. Hitler's contribution was above all to alter the climate, to build an air of confidence that Germany was being revitalized. But propaganda portrayed the economic upturn as Hitler's own achievement. He readily accepted the acclaim, and most people thought it was warranted*.

warranted berechtigt

It was the first major step towards winning over those who had not supported him in 1933. It seemed undeniable: while other European countries (and America) still suffered drastically from mass unemployment, Hitler had removed the scourge* from Germany and ushered in* a kind of "economic miracle". [...]

scourge [skɜrdʒ] plague, torment, affliction
to usher sth. in etw. einleiten, etw. in Gang bringen

Left a Lasting Mark

By 1936, there was full employment. [...]

That Hitler had rid Germany of mass unemployment and rescued the country from the depths of the depression was seen by many Germans long after the war as a major achievement, whatever disasters had later followed. Good living conditions and full employment were among the positive attributes of Hitler recorded in opinion surveys in the American occupied zone in the late 1940s, while a sample of young Germans in north Germany around a decade later thought Hitler had done much good in abolishing unemployment. As late as the 1970s, Ruhr workers still had positive memories of the peacetime years of the Third Reich, which they associated with full employment and the pleasures of excursions with the Nazi leisure organization, "Kraft durch Freude," or Strength Through Joy.

The second point singled out by the Sopade as the basis of Hitler's support was without doubt a key factor. Hitler never ceased to hammer home the humiliation

Germany had suffered in defeat in 1918 – allegedly the work of the "November criminals" – and in the Treaty of Versailles signed the following year. The detestation* of the Treaty and its perceived unfairness crossed the political spectrum in Germany. The reduction of the army to a mere 100,000 men was the lasting manifestation of national weakness. The bold moves in foreign policy that Hitler undertook to overthrow the shackles* of Versailles and reassert Germany's national strength and prestige were, therefore, guaranteed massive popular support as long as they could be accomplished without bloodshed.

detestation loathing, hatred

shackles *Fesseln*

Vast Approval for Hitler's Iron Fist

The withdrawal from the League of Nations in 1933, the Saar plebiscite in 1935, the re-introduction of compulsory military service and announcement of a big new Wehrmacht the same year, the re-militarization of the Rhineland in 1936 and the "Anschluss" or annexation of Austria two years later were all seen as huge national triumphs, openly demonstrating the weakness of the western powers which had lorded it over* Germany since the war, and a feat – unimaginable only a few years earlier – solely possible through Hitler's "genius" as a statesman. [...]

In addition to his presumed achievements in bolstering Germany's external standing, Hitler unquestionably won much support through what was taken to be the restoration of "order" at home. Nazi propaganda had been influential in the last, crisis-ridden years of the Weimar Republic, in instilling* in much of the population an exaggerated image of criminality, decadence, social disorder and violence (much of which the Nazis themselves had instigated*). Once in power, Hitler had much to gain through seeming to represent "people's justice," and the "wholesome national sensibility." His public image was that of the upholder of public morality who would clamp down, wherever he encountered it, on those posing a threat to law and order. [...]

to lord it over sth. to dominate, to be overbearing, to be imperious

to instil to implant

to instigate to influence, to provoke, to bring about

The view that Hitler had brought order to Germany was one that persisted well into the post-war era. That, despite "mistakes" (presumably those which had brought his country's ruination through war, and death and destruction to millions) he had "cleaned up" Germany, putting an end to disorder, stamping out criminality, making the streets safe to walk again at night, and improving moral standards, belonged – together with the credit for eradicating mass unemployment and building the motorways – to the lasting elements of the Führer Myth. Alongside economic recovery, rebuilding military strength and restoring "order", Hitler gained support by personifying the "positive" values invested in national unity and the "Volksgemeinschaft" or national community. Propaganda incessantly depicted him as the stern but understanding paterfamilias*, prepared to sacrifice normal human contentments* and to work day and night for no other end than the good of his people. Whatever the frequent criticism of his underlings* and the negative image of the "little Hitlers" – the Party functionaries whom people daily encountered and often found wanting – Hitler himself was widely perceived as standing aloof from sectional interests and material concerns, his selflessness contrasting with the greed and corruption of the Party big-wigs. [...]

paterfamilias patriarch, man of the house
contentment comfort, happiness
underling subordinate

The 'Dynamic Hatred' against Minorities

How many fully swallowed the nauseating* personality cult can, of course, never be established. Not a few obviously did. [...] There was a rise in the early years of the Third Reich in the numbers of parents naming their new-born babies Adolf,

nauseating [ˈnɔziˌeɪtɪŋ] disgusting, abhorrent

even though a decree of 1933 had instructed local registry offices to discourage the practice to protect the Führer's name. [...]
The national community gained its very definition from those who were excluded from it. Racial discrimination was inevitably, therefore, an inbuilt part of the Nazi interpretation of the concept. Since measures directed at creating "racial purity," such as the persecution later of homosexuals, Roma and "a-socials," exploited existing prejudice and were allegedly aimed at strengthening a homogeneous ethnic nation, they buttressed* Hitler's image as the embodiment of the national community. Even more so, the relentless denunciation of the nation's alleged powerful enemies – Bolshevism, western "plutocracy"*, and most prominently the Jews (linked in propaganda with both) – reinforced Hitler's appeal as the defender of the nation and bulwark against the threats to its survival, whether external or from within.
Though Hitler's anti-Semitic paranoia was not shared by the vast bulk of the population, it plainly did not weigh heavily enough in the scales on the negative side to outweigh the positive attributes that the majority saw in him. The widely prevalent latent dislike of Jews, even before monopolistic Nazi propaganda got to work to drum in the messages of hatred, could offer no barrier to the "dynamic" hatred present in a sizeable minority – though after 1933 a minority holding power. [...]

Ian Kershaw: "How Hitler Won Over the German People", in: DER SPIEGEL, 30.1.2008, www.spiegel.de/international/germany/the-fuehrer-myth-how-hitler-won-over-the-german-people-a-531909.html [27.04.15]

to buttress to strengthen

plutocracy society or system ruled by a small minority of the wealthiest people

S 26 Brautvorführung

This cartoon was published in the Swiss satirical magazine *Nebelspalter* in February 1933. It was drawn by Gregor Rabinovitch.

Pre-task
1. Have a look at the symbolic elements and the people labelled in the cartoon. Before analysing it, identify their meaning.

Tasks
2. Analyse the source.
3. Explain in detail the elements of the cartoon.
4. Take a critical stand on the message conveyed by the cartoon.

Post-tasks
5. "January 30, 1933: the "seizure of power", the "takeover of power", the "handing-over of power" or "sneaking into power"?" Write an article for an online encyclopaedia.
6. In S 69 (chapter 1), you came across the idea of a "German special path" *(Deutscher Sonderweg)*. You did some research about this theory and became familiar with its most famous supporters. From what you have learned about Weimar democracy and Hitler becoming chancellor, add further arguments to support or refute this theory.

National Socialism 425

① Hindenburg =

② dagger hanging from canopy =

③ H. in pyjamas/in bed =

④ v. Papen pushing Germania =

⑤ omnipresent swastikas =

⑥ DNVP leader & press tycoon Hugenberg =

⑦ Germania reluctant/ surprised =

⑧ v. Papen's clothes =

G. Rabinovitch

National Socialist Rule Over Germany and Europe

S 27 Walter Tießler

Nicht Phrasen sondern Klarheit (Excerpts)

Walter Tießler was an early Nazi who held a variety of positions in the propaganda apparatus before and after the Nazis took power. When this pamphlet was published by the party's publishing house in 1942, he was head of the *Reichring für nationalsozialistische Propaganda und Volksaufklärung*, a subsection of the party's propaganda department charged with coordinating propaganda at the local level throughout the country.

Randall Bytwerk, German Propaganda Archive, www.calvin.edu/academic/cas/gap/tiessler3.htm [16.03.2015]

Pre-task
1. Copy the visualization provided below. Then choose one of the concepts as a starting point and, with the help of the information given in the overview section, make an educated guess as to how one concept leads to another or is connected to the others. Compare your findings with a partner.

Tasks
2. After having read the source, make additions or omissions where necessary.
3. Explain the "circle of fundamental National Socialist concepts" (l. 4) by elaborating on the twelve concepts put forward by Tießler.

Circle diagram showing the following concepts connected in a cycle: eternal Germany → honour → courage → racial character → labour → achievement → public health → blood and soil → people's community → Socialism in action → loyalty → family → eternal Germany

wellspring the source of a large or continuous supply

The family is the eternal wellspring* of the people. From it the people is constantly renewed. It is thus one of the most essential requirements for an eternal Germany.

This completes the circle of fundamental National Socialist concepts. An **(1) eternal Germany** can exist only if the German people preserve its **[2] honor**. Only he has honor who is ready to display **[3] courage** even to the ultimate. The battle for Germany can be guided only by deepest conviction by someone who knows that Germany is not a geographical concept, but rather the community of people of German blood who reveal their **[4] German racial character**. One of the fundamentals of this German racial character — in contrast to the views of other people — is **[5] labour**, seen not as a burden, but rather as a requirement if one is to find inner satisfaction. National Socialism, therefore, has concluded that achievement is the measure of the worth of the individual and the community. The **[6] principle of achievement** has thus become the National Socialist leadership principle. Since labour and achievement have a higher meaning for us Germans who serve the community, so also the health of the individual is not his private concern, but rather is a matter of the community, one of **[7] public health**. The more naturally the German sees things and lives his life, the easier it will be to maintain the health of the German people. For this reason, the connection to nature finds its most beautiful expression in the concept of **[8] blood and soil**, a prerequisite* for the eternity of the German people. This does not mean that city and country people have a different value, for both must fulfil their duty to Germany, but rather only a compelling necessity. In National Socialist Germany, each German is of equal value and has equal obligations. Above all the varying tasks stands what we share, the **[9] people's community**. We are not only ready to fulfil our duty toward it, but also to provide ever new support through our sacrifices. **[10] Socialism in action** brings together all of these various sacrifices. It is not to deal with a particular need, but rather it is a demand of Germans at all times. Sacrifice is the final result of **[11] loyalty**, which binds together leadership and followers so firmly that nothing and no one can separate them. It is not only that which holds together the great community of the German people, but also every community of life. The most important individual community within the people's community, for all healthy people at all times, is the **[12] family**. For us National Socialists it means not only the firm foundation of a state, but also the community from which children are born, which are to us the living expression of **[1] eternal Germany**. We experience National Socialism as a totality. Only in that way can we truly understand it, seeing it not from the standpoint of the part, but of the whole. Everything, whether in politics, the economy, culture, or the private life of the individual must be examined, seen, and fulfilled according to the fundamental concepts of National Socialism.

Walter Tießler: Not Empty Phrases, but Rather Clarity, transl. by Randall L. Bytwerk, (Orig.: Nicht Phrasen sondern Klarheit, Berlin 1942), www.calvin.edu/academic/cas/gpa/tiessler3.htm [16.11.14]

prerequisite [priːˈrekwəzɪt]
Grundvoraussetzung

S 28 Joseph Goebbels

Reden über die Aufgaben des Reichsministeriums für Volksaufklärung und Propaganda

Joseph Goebbels was in charge of propaganda, heading the *Reichsministerium für Volksaufklärung und Propaganda* since its establishment on 13 March 1933. In the speech at hand delivered on 15 March 1933, Goebbels elaborates on his aim of establishing a "national revolution".

National Socialism

Pre-task

1. Refresh your knowledge about the definition of a revolution. Have a look at chapter 1, S 22 again.

Tasks

2. Analyse the source.
3. Explain the "revolutionary" aspect involved in establishing the *Reichsministerium für Volksaufklärung und Propaganda* and the role of the government.
4. Goebbels says that propaganda is a means to an end. Explain what this end is, according to Goebbels.

Ich sehe in der Einrichtung des neuen Ministeriums für Volksaufklärung und Propaganda insofern eine revolutionäre Regierungstat, als die neue Regierung nicht mehr die Absicht hat, das Volk sich selbst zu überlassen*. Diese Regierung ist im wahrsten Sinne des Wortes eine Volksregierung. Sie ist aus dem Volke hervorgegangen und wird immer die Vollstreckerin* des Volkswillens sein. Ich verwahre* mich auf das leidenschaftlichste dagegen, dass diese Regierung der Ausdruck irgendeines reaktionären Wollens sei, dass wir Reaktionäre wären. [...] Wir wollen vielmehr dem Volke geben, was dem Volke gebührt, allerdings in einer anderen Form, als es im demokratischen Parlamentarismus geschah.

In dem neueingerichteten Ministerium für Volksaufklärung und Propaganda sehe ich die Verbindung zwischen Regierung und Volk, den lebendigen Kontakt zwischen der nationalen Regierung als der Ausdrucksform* des Volkswillens und dem Volke selbst. Wie wir in den vergangenen Wochen erlebt haben, dass sich in steigendem Maße eine politische Gleichschaltung zwischen der Reichspolitik und der Länderpolitik vollzogen hat, so sehe ich die erste Aufgabe des neuen Ministeriums darin, nunmehr eine Gleichschaltung zwischen der Regierung und dem ganzen Volke herzustellen. Ich glaube nicht, dass wir unser Ziel mit einer 52prozentigen parlamentarischen Mehrheit erreicht haben würden. Eine Regierung, die so große, einschneidende* Maßnahmen treffen muss wie die unsrige, könnte auf die Dauer im Volke nicht die Rückendeckung finden, deren sie für diese einschneidenden Maßnahmen bedarf, wenn sie sich damit zufriedengeben wollte. Sie muss vielmehr alle propagandistischen Vorbereitungen treffen, um das ganze Volk auf ihre Seite zu ziehen. Wenn diese Regierung entschlossen ist, niemals zu weichen, niemals, nimmer und unter keinen Umständen, dann braucht sie sich nicht der toten Macht der Bajonette zu bedienen, dann wird sie auf die Dauer nicht damit zufrieden sein können, 52 Prozent hinter sich zu wissen, um damit die übrigbleibenden 48 Prozent zu terrorisieren, sondern sie wird ihre nächste Aufgabe darin sehen, die übrigbleibenden 48 Prozent für sich zu gewinnen. [...]

Es genügt nicht, die Menschen mit unserem Regiment mehr oder weniger auszusöhnen*, sie zu bewegen, uns neutral gegenüberzustehen, sondern wir wollen die Menschen so lange bearbeiten, bis sie uns verfallen* sind, bis sie auch ideenmäßig einsehen, dass das, was sich heute in Deutschland abspielt, nicht nur hingenommen werden muss, sondern auch hingenommen werden kann. [...]

Denn Propaganda ist nicht Selbstzweck*, sondern Mittel zum Zweck. Wenn nun mit diesem Mittel der Zweck erreicht worden ist, dann ist das Mittel gut; ob es in jedem Falle nun scharfen ästhetischen Forderungen entspricht oder nicht, ist dabei gleichgültig. Wenn dieser Zweck aber nicht erreicht worden ist, dann ist dieses Mittel eben schlecht gewesen. Der Zweck unserer Bewegung war, Menschen zu mobilisieren, Menschen zu organisieren und für die nationalrevolutionäre Idee

---

sich selbst überlassen here: to leave to its own devices
Vollstreckerin executor
sich gegen etw. verwahren to strongly object to sth.

Ausdrucksform form of expression

einschneidend radical, far-reaching

aussöhnen to reconcile
jdm. verfallen sein to be under someone's spell
Selbstzweck an end in itself

zu gewinnen. Dieser Zweck – das kann niemand, auch der Böswilligste nicht bestreiten – ist erreicht worden, und damit ist das Urteil über unsere propagandistischen Methoden ausgesprochen worden. Das neue Ministerium hat keinen anderen Zweck, als die Nation geschlossen hinter die Idee der nationalen Revolution zu stellen. Wird der Zweck erreicht, dann mag man über meine Methoden den Stab brechen*; das wäre vollkommen gleichgültig, denn das Ministerium hat dann mit seinen Arbeiten den Zweck erreicht. Wird aber der Zweck nicht erreicht, dann könnte ich zwar beweisen, dass meine Propagandamethoden allen ästhetischen Gesetzen genügen, aber dann hätte ich lieber Theaterregisseur oder Direktor einer Kunst-Akademie werden sollen, aber nicht Minister eines Ministeriums für Volksaufklärung und Propaganda. [...]

Die wichtigsten Aufgaben dieses Ministeriums müssen folgende sein: Zunächst müssen alle propagandistischen Unternehmungen und alle volksaufklärenden Institutionen des Reiches und der Länder zentral in einer Hand vereinigt werden. Es muss ferner unsere Aufgabe sein, diesen propagandistischen Einrichtungen einen modernen Impuls einzuhauchen und sie mit der Jetztzeit in Übereinstimmung zu bringen. Es darf der Technik nicht überlassen bleiben, dem Reich voranzulaufen, sondern das Reich muss mit der Technik gehen. Das Modernste ist gerade gut genug. Wir leben nun einmal in dem Zeitalter, wo Massen hinter einer Politik stehen müssen. [...] Die modernen Volksführer müssen moderne Volkskönige sein, sie müssen die Masse verstehen, brauchen der Masse aber nicht nach dem Munde zu reden. Sie haben die Pflicht, der Masse zu sagen, was sie wollen, und der Masse das so klarzumachen, dass diese es auch versteht. [...]

den Stab über etw. brechen to judge sth.

Rede vor der Presse über die Errichtung des Reichspropagandaministeriums (15. März 1933), in Joseph Goebbels: Revolution der Deutschen: 14 Jahre Nationalsozialismus. Oldenburg, 1933, pp. 135–50

S 29 Adolf Hitler
Aufruf an das deutsche Volk

On 1 February 1933, Hitler gave this address on the radio. On that same day, Reichspräsident Hindenburg also gave his permission for the Reichstag to be dissolved and called for the scheduling of new elections. This is why the speech below was also the starting point of a new election campaign.

Pre-task 1. What do you expect Hitler to say in his first address to the German people concerning Germany's current status? Use the words and expressions provided in the box and make an educated guess.

> Tage des Verrates • tiefste Bekümmernis • Gewirr politisch-egoistischer Meinungen • herzzerbrechende Zerrissenheit • innerer Verfall • Verelendung

Tasks 2. Analyse the source and pay special attention to rhetoric and line of argument.
3. What does Hitler say about 9 November 1918 and the "November parties"? Explain.
4. Detect and explain aspects of Nazi ideology in Hitler's speech. Refer to S 27 for help.

Über 14 Jahre sind vergangen seit dem unseligen* Tage, da, von inneren und äußeren Versprechungen verblendet, das deutsche Volk der höchsten Güter unserer Vergangenheit, des Reiches, seiner Ehre und seiner Freiheit vergaß und dabei alles verlor. Seit diesen Tagen des Verrates hat der Allmächtige unserem Volk seinen Segen entzogen*. Zwietracht* und Hass hielten ihren Einzug. In tiefster Bekümmernis sehen Millionen bester deutscher Männer und Frauen aus allen Lebensständen die Einheit der Nation dahinsinken und sich auflösen in ein Gewirr politisch-egoistischer Meinungen, wirtschaftlicher Interessen und weltanschaulicher Gegensätze.

Wie so oft in unserer Geschichte, bietet Deutschland seit diesem Tage der Revolution das Bild einer herzzerbrechenden Zerrissenheit. Die versprochene Gleichheit und Brüderlichkeit erhielten wir nicht, aber die Freiheit haben wir verloren. Dem Verfall der geistigen und willensmäßigen Einheit unseres Volkes im Innern folgte der Verfall seiner politischen Stellung in der Welt.

Heiß durchdrungen* von der Überzeugung, dass das deutsche Volk im Jahre 1914 in den großen Kampf zog ohne jeden Gedanken an eine eigene Schuld und nur erfüllt von der Last der Sorge, das angegriffene Reich, die Freiheit und die Existenz des deutschen Menschen verteidigen zu müssen, sehen wir in dem erschütternden Schicksal, das uns seit dem November 1918 verfolgt, nur das Ergebnis unseres inneren Verfalls. Allein auch die übrige Welt wird seitdem nicht minder von großen Krisen durchrüttelt. Das geschichtlich ausgewogene Gleichgewicht der Kräfte, das einst nicht wenig beitrug zum Verständnis für die Notwendigkeit einer inneren Solidarität der Nationen, mit all den daraus resultierenden glücklichen wirtschaftlichen Folgen, ist beseitigt.

Die Wahnidee vom Sieger und Besiegten zerstört das Vertrauen von Nation zu Nation und damit auch die Wirtschaft der Welt. Das Elend unseres Volkes aber ist entsetzlich! Dem arbeitslos gewordenen, hungernden Millionen-Proletariat der Industrie folgt die Verelendung* des gesamten Mittel- und Handwerksstandes. Wenn sich dieser Verfall auch im deutschen Bauern endgültig vollendet, stehen wir in einer Katastrophe von unübersehbarem Ausmaß. Denn nicht nur ein Reich zerfällt dann, sondern eine zweitausendjährige Erbmasse* an hohen und höchsten Gütern menschlicher Kultur und Zivilisation.

Drohend künden die Erscheinungen um uns den Vollzug dieses Verfalls. In einem unerhörten Willens- und Gewaltansturm versucht die kommunistische Methode des Wahnsinns das in seinem Innersten erschütterte und entwurzelte* Volk endgültig zu vergiften und zu zersetzen*, um es einer Zeit entgegenzutreiben, die sich zu den Versprechungen der kommunistischen Wortführer von heute noch schlimmer verhalten würde als die Zeit hinter uns zu den Versprechungen derselben Apostel im November 1918.

Angefangen bei der Familie, über alle Begriffe von Ehre und Treue, Volk und Vaterland, Kultur und Wirtschaft hinweg bis zum ewigen Fundament unserer Moral und unseres Glaubens, bleibt nichts verschont von dieser nur verneinenden, alles zerstörenden Idee. 14 Jahre Marxismus haben Deutschland ruiniert. Ein Jahr Bolschewismus würde Deutschland vernichten. Die heute reichsten und schönsten Kulturgebiete der Welt würden in ein Chaos und Trümmerfeld verwandelt. Selbst das Leid der letzten anderthalb Jahrzehnte könnte nicht verglichen werden mit dem Jammer eines Europas, in dessen Herzen die rote Fahne der Vernichtung aufgezogen* würde. Die Tausende von Verletzten, die unzähligen Toten, die dieser innere Krieg schon heute Deutschland kostet, mögen ein Wetterleuchten* sein der Warnung vor dem Sturme. In diesen Stunden der übermächtig hereinbrechenden Sorgen um das Dasein und die Zukunft der deutschen Nation rief uns Männer nationaler Parteien und Verbände der greise Führer des Weltkrieges auf, noch einmal wie einst an den Fronten, nunmehr in der Heimat in Einigkeit und Treue für des Reiches Rettung unter ihm zu kämpfen. Indem der ehrwürdige Herr Reichspräsident uns in diesem großherzigen Sinne die Hände zum gemeinsamen Bunde schloss, wollen wir als nationale Führer Gott, unserem Gewissen und unserem Volke geloben*, die uns damit übertragene Mission als nationale Regierung entschlossen und beharrlich* zu erfüllen.

Das Erbe, das wir übernehmen, ist ein furchtbares. [...]

So wird es die nationale Regierung als ihre oberste und erste Aufgabe ansehen, die geistige und willensmäßige Einheit unseres Volkes wieder herzustellen. Sie wird die Fundamente wahren und verteidigen, auf denen die Kraft unserer Nation beruht. Sie wird das Christentum als Basis unserer gesamten Moral, die Familie als Keimzelle* unseres Volks- und Staatskörpers in ihren festen Schutz nehmen. Sie wird über Stände und Klassen hinweg unser Volk wieder zum Bewusstsein seiner volklichen und politischen Einheit und der daraus entspringenden Pflichten bringen. Sie will die Ehrfurcht vor unserer großen Vergangenheit, den Stolz auf unsere alten Traditionen zur Grundlage machen für die Erziehung der deutschen Jugend. Sie wird damit der geistigen, politischen und kulturellen Nihilisierung* einen unbarmherzigen Krieg ansagen. Deutschland darf und wird nicht im anarchistischen Kommunismus versinken. [...]

Mit dieser gigantischen Aufgabe der Sanierung unserer Wirtschaft wird die nationale Regierung verbinden die Aufgabe und Durchführung einer Sanierung* des Reiches, der Länder und der Kommunen in verwaltungsmäßiger und steuertechnischer Hinsicht*. [...]

Zu den Grundpfeilern dieses Programms gehört der Gedanke der Arbeitsdienstpflicht und der Siedlungspolitik.

Die Sorge für das tägliche Brot wird aber ebenso die Sorge sein für die Erfüllung der sozialen Pflichten bei Krankheit und Alter.

In der Sparsamkeit ihrer Verwaltung, der Förderung der Arbeit, der Erhaltung unseres Bauerntums sowie der Nutzbarmachung der Initiative des einzelnen liegt zugleich die beste Gewähr* für das Vermeiden jedes Experimentes der Gefährdung unserer Währung. Außenpolitisch wird die nationale Regierung ihre höchste Mission in der Wahrung der Lebensrechte und damit der Wiedererringung der Freiheit unseres Volkes sehen. Indem sie entschlossen ist, den chaotischen Zuständen in Deutschland ein Ende zu bereiten, wird sie mithelfen, in die Gemeinschaft der übrigen Nationen einen Staat gleichen Wertes und damit allerdings auch gleicher Rechte einzufügen. Sie ist dabei erfüllt von der Größe der Pflicht, mit diesem freien, gleichberechtigten Volke für die Erhaltung und Festigung des Friedens einzutreten, dessen die Welt heute mehr bedarf als je zuvor.

Möge auch das Verständnis all der anderen mithelfen, dass dieser unser aufrichtigster Wunsch zum Wohle Europas, ja, der Welt, sich erfüllt.

So groß unsere Liebe zu unserem Heere als Träger unserer Waffen und Symbol unserer großen Vergangenheit ist, so wären wir doch beglückt, wenn die Welt durch eine Beschränkung ihrer Rüstungen eine Vermehrung unserer eigenen Waffen niemals mehr erforderlich machen würde.

Soll aber Deutschland diesen politischen und wirtschaftlichen Wiederaufstieg erleben und seine Verpflichtungen den anderen Nationen gegenüber gewissenhaft

---

geloben to vow
beharrlich unwaveringly, perseveringly

Keimzelle nucleus

Nihilisierung nihilation

Sanierung reorganization

in verwaltungsmäßiger und steuertechnischer Hinsicht in terms of administration and taxes

Gewähr guarantee

erfüllen, dann setzt dies eine entscheidende Tat voraus: die Überwindung der kommunistischen Zersetzung Deutschlands.

Wir Männer dieser Regierung fühlen uns vor der deutschen Geschichte verantwortlich für die Wiederherstellung eines geordneten Volkskörpers und damit für die endgültige Überwindung des Klassenwahnsinns und Klassenkampfes. Nicht einen Stand sehen wir, sondern das deutsche Volk, die Millionen seiner Bauern, Bürger und Arbeiter, die entweder gemeinsam die Sorgen dieser Zeit überwinden werden oder ihnen sonst gemeinsam erliegen*. Entschlossen und getreu unserem Eide wollen wir damit angesichts der Unfähigkeit des derzeitigen Reichstages, diese Arbeit zu unterstützen, dem deutschen Volke selbst die Aufgabe stellen, die wir vertreten. [...]

Nun, deutsches Volk, gib uns die Zeit von vier Jahren, und dann urteile und richte uns! Getreu dem Befehl des Generalfeldmarschalls* wollen wir beginnen. Möge der allmächtige Gott unsere Arbeit in seine Gnade nehmen, unseren Willen recht gestalten, unsere Einsicht segnen und uns mit dem Vertrauen unseres Volkes beglücken*. Denn wir wollen nicht kämpfen für uns, sondern für Deutschland!

etw. erliegen to succumb to sth., to be consumed by sth.

Generalfeldmarschall here: Hindenburg

beglücken to make happy

„Aufruf der Reichsregierung vom 31. Januar 1933", in: Hans-Adolf Jacobsen/Werner Jochmann [Eds.]: Ausgewählte Dokumente zur Geschichte des Nationalsozialismus, 1933–1945. Vol. 2, Bielefeld, 1961, (Dokument 31. 1. 1933)

S 30 Verordnung des Reichspräsidenten zum Schutz von Volk und Staat („Reichstagsbrandverordnung")

On 27 February 1933, the Reichstag building went up in flames and Hitler took advantage of this by making Hindenburg enact this Decree for the Protection of People and State, also known as the "Reichstag Fire Decree".

Pre-task
1. Refresh your knowledge about the basic rights of the Weimar constitution and have a look at S 5a again. Which basic rights are granted in the constitution?

Tasks
2. Sum up the most important measures to be taken.
3. Explain the function of the *Reichstagsbrandverordnung* for Hitler (i. e. what did he want to achieve by this means) and its importance for "Phase 1 – control at the centre".
4. On what grounds are the government's new powers justified? Explain.
5. Take a critical stand on the statement that this act served as a "Basic Law of the Third Reich", as historian Helmut Krausnick puts it.

Abwehr defence

Auf Grund des Artikels 48 Abs. 2 der Reichsverfassung wird zur Abwehr* kommunistischer staatsgefährdender Gewaltakte folgendes verordnet:

§ 1

Die Artikel 114, 115, 117, 118, 123, 124 und 153 der Verfassung des Deutschen Reichs werden bis auf weiteres außer Kraft gesetzt*. Es sind daher Beschränkungen der persönlichen Freiheit, des Rechts der freien Meinungsäußerung, einschließlich der Pressefreiheit, des Vereins- und Versammlungsrechts, Eingriffe in das Brief-, Post-, Telegraphen- und Fernsprechgeheimnis, Anordnungen von Haussuchungen* und von Beschlagnahmen* sowie Beschränkungen des Eigentums auch außerhalb der sonst hierfür bestimmten gesetzlichen Grenzen zulässig.

außer Kraft setzen to suspend

Haussuchung house search
Beschlagnahme confiscation

Collage by John Heartfield

§ 2
Werden in einem Lande die zur Wiederherstellung der öffentlichen Sicherheit und Ordnung nötigen Maßnahmen nicht getroffen, so kann die Reichsregierung insoweit die Befugnisse der obersten Landesbehörde* vorübergehend wahrnehmen.
[...]
§ 4
Wer den von den obersten Landesbehörden oder den ihnen nachgeordneten Behörden zur Durchführung dieser Verordnung erlassenen Anordnungen oder den von der Reichsregierung gemäß § 2 erlassenen Anordnungen zuwiderhandelt* [...] wird, [...], mit Gefängnis nicht unter einem Monat oder mit Geldstrafe von 150 bis zu 15 000 Reichsmark bestraft. [...]
§ 5
[...]
Mit dem Tode oder, soweit nicht bisher eine schwerere Strafe angedroht ist, mit lebenslangem Zuchthaus oder mit Zuchthaus bis zu 15 Jahren wird bestraft:
1. Wer es unternimmt, den Reichspräsidenten oder ein Mitglied oder einen Kommissar der Reichsregierung oder einer Landesregierung zu töten oder wer zu einer solchen Tötung auffordert, sich erbietet*, ein solches Erbieten annimmt oder eine solche Tötung mit einem anderen verabredet;
2. wer in den Fällen des § 115 Abs. 2 des Strafgesetzbuchs (schwerer Aufruhr*) oder des § 125 Abs. 2 des Strafgesetzbuchs (schwerer Landfriedensbruch*) die Tat mit Waffen oder in bewusstem und gewolltem Zusammenwirken mit einem Bewaffneten begeht;
3. wer eine Freiheitsberaubung (§ 239) des Strafgesetzbuchs in der Absicht begeht, sich des der Freiheit Beraubten als Geisel im politischen Kampfe zu bedienen.
§ 6
Diese Verordnung tritt mit dem Tage der Verkündung in Kraft.
Berlin, den 28. Februar 1933.
Der Reichspräsident von Hindenburg
Der Reichskanzler Adolf Hitler
Der Reichsminister des Innern Frick
Der Reichsminister der Justiz Dr. Gürtner

Verordnung des Reichspräsidenten zum Schutz von Volk und Staat vom 28. Februar 1933, Reichsgesetzblatt 1933, I, Nr. 17, S. 83.; www.westfaelische-geschichte.de/que845 [27.03.15]

oberste Landesbehörde highest state authority

zuwiderhandeln to act in opposition to sth.

sich erbieten to offer services, to volunteer

schwerer Aufruhr serious rioting
Landfriedensbruch serious disturbance of the peace

S 31 Gesetz zur Behebung der Not von Volk und Reich (Ermächtigungsgesetz)

On 23 March 1933, this Act was debated on during the Reichstag session in Berlin's Kroll Opera House. One day later it was passed.

Pre-task 1. Have a look at the table provided and describe it. Then make an educated guess as to why only one party, namely the SPD, voted against the Enabling Act.

Party	Seats	Share (%)	Consent	Refusal
NSDAP	288	45	288	0
DNVP	52	8	52	0
Centre Party	73	11	72*	0
BVP	19	3	19	0
DStP (former DDP)	5	1	5	0
CSVD (Christlich-Sozialer Volksdienst)	4	1	4	0
DVP	2	0,3	1**	0
DBP (Deutsche Bauernpartei)	2	0,3	2	0
Landbund	1	0,2	1	0
SPD	120	19	0	94
KPD	81	13	0	0
Total	**647**	**100**	**444 (69 %)**	**94 (15 %)**

*One deputy was absent with a valid excuse.   **One deputy was ill.

n.N.: „Ermächtigungsgesetz", in: Wikipedia, Version v. 17. April 2015, http://de.wikipedia.org/w/index.php?title=Erm%C3%A4chtigungsgesetz&oldid=140936790 [27.04.15]

Task 2. Explain to what extent the Enabling Act undermined the Weimar constitution, in spirit and in fact.

Der Reichstag hat das folgende Gesetz beschlossen, das mit Zustimmung des Reichsrats hiermit verkündet wird, nachdem festgestellt ist, dass die Erfordernisse verfassungsändernder Gesetzgebung erfüllt sind:

Artikel 1. Reichsgesetze können außer in dem in der Reichsverfassung vorgesehenen Verfahren auch durch die Reichsregierung beschlossen werden. Dies gilt auch für die in den Artikeln 85 Abs. 2 und 87 der Reichsverfassung bezeichneten Gesetze.

Artikel 2. Die von der Reichsregierung beschlossenen Reichsgesetze können von der Reichsverfassung abweichen, soweit sie nicht die Einrichtung des Reichstags und des Reichsrats als solche zum Gegenstand haben. Die Rechte des Reichspräsidenten bleiben unberührt.

Artikel 3. Die von der Reichsregierung beschlossenen Reichsgesetze werden vom Reichskanzler ausgefertigt und im Reichsgesetzblatt verkündet. Sie treten, soweit sie nichts anderes bestimmen, mit dem auf die Verkündung folgenden Tage in Kraft. Die Artikel 68 bis 77 der Reichsverfassung finden auf die von der Reichsregierung beschlossenen Gesetze keine Anwendung.

Artikel 4. Verträge des Reichs mit fremden Staaten, die sich auf Gegenstände der Reichsgesetzgebung beziehen, bedürfen nicht der Zustimmung der an der Gesetzgebung beteiligten Körperschaften. Die Reichsregierung erlässt die zur Durchführung dieser Verträge erforderlichen Vorschriften.

20 Artikel 5. Dieses Gesetz tritt mit dem Tage seiner Verkündung in Kraft. Es tritt mit dem 1. April 1937 außer Kraft; es tritt ferner außer Kraft, wenn die gegenwärtige Reichsregierung durch eine andere abgelöst wird.
Berlin, den 24. März 1933.
Der Reichspräsident von Hindenburg
25 Der Reichskanzler Adolf Hitler
Der Reichsminister des Innern Frick
Der Reichsminister des Auswärtigen Freiherr von Neurath
Der Reichsminister der Finanzen Graf Schwerin von Krosigk

Gesetz zur Behebung der Not von Volk und Reich (Ermächtigungsgesetz) (23. März 1933), Reichsgesetzblatt, 1933, Teil I, Nr. 25, S. 141; in: Rolf-Peter Magen: Staatsrecht: Eine Einführung, Springer Verlag 2013, pp. 119 f.

S 32 Otto Wels

Speech against the Enabling Act

Otto Wels (see also biography, on p. 411) gave this speech on 23 March 1933 during the debate on the Enabling Act.

Pre-task 1. Make an educated guess as to Wels's criticism concerning the Enabling Act. Refer to the given expressions below taken from the speech.

> Kontrolle der öffentlichen Angelegenheiten [...] ausgeschaltet • Allmacht der Regierung • Reichstag ausschalten

Tasks 2. Compare your findings with your results from the pre-task.
3. Which achievements does Wels ascribe to the SPD in the course of German history and what does he accuse the NSDAP of destroying with their policy? Explain.

[...] Nach den Verfolgungen, die die Sozialdemokratische Partei in der letzten Zeit erfahren hat, wird billigerweise* niemand von ihr verlangen oder erwarten können, dass sie für das hier eingebrachte Ermächtigungsgesetz stimmt. Die Wahlen vom 5. März haben den Regierungsparteien die Mehrheit gebracht und damit die
5 Möglichkeit gegeben, streng nach Wortlaut und Sinn der Verfassung zu regieren. Wo diese Möglichkeit besteht, besteht auch die Pflicht. Kritik ist heilsam* und notwendig. Noch niemals, seit es einen Deutschen Reichstag gibt, ist die Kontrolle der öffentlichen Angelegenheiten durch die gewählten Vertreter des Volkes in solchem Maße ausgeschaltet worden, wie es jetzt geschieht, und wie es durch das
10 neue Ermächtigungsgesetz noch mehr geschehen soll. Eine solche Allmacht* der Regierung muss sich umso schwerer auswirken, als auch die Presse jeder Bewegungsfreiheit entbehrt*. [...]
Die Herren von der Nationalsozialistischen Partei nennen die von ihnen entfesselte* Bewegung eine nationale Revolution, nicht eine nationalsozialistische. Das
15 Verhältnis ihrer Revolution zum Sozialismus beschränkt sich bisher auf den Versuch, die sozialdemokratische Bewegung zu vernichten, die seit mehr als zwei Menschenaltern die Trägerin sozialistischen Gedankengutes gewesen ist und auch bleiben wird. Wollten die Herren von der Nationalsozialistischen Partei sozi-

billigerweise reasonably

heilsam salutary

Allmacht omnipotence

etw. entbehren to lack sth.

etw. entfesseln to unleash sth.

alistische Taten verrichten, sie brauchten kein Ermächtigungsgesetz. Eine erdrückende Mehrheit wäre Ihnen in diesem Hause gewiss. Jeder von Ihnen im Interesse der Arbeiter, der Bauern, der Angestellten, der Beamten oder des Mittelstandes gestellte Antrag könnte auf Annahme rechnen, wenn nicht einstimmig, so doch mit gewaltiger Majorität.

Aber dennoch wollen Sie vorerst den Reichstag ausschalten, um Ihre Revolution fortzusetzen. Zerstörung von Bestehendem ist aber noch keine Revolution. Das Volk erwartet positive Leistungen. Es wartet auf durchgreifende* Maßnahmen gegen das furchtbare Wirtschaftselend, das nicht nur in Deutschland, sondern in aller Welt herrscht. Wir Sozialdemokraten haben in schwerster Zeit Mitverantwortung getragen und sind dafür mit Steinen beworfen worden. Unsere Leistungen für den Wiederaufbau von Staat und Wirtschaft, für die Befreiung der besetzten Gebiete werden vor der Geschichte bestehen. Wir haben gleiches Recht für alle und ein soziales Arbeitsrecht geschaffen. Wir haben geholfen, ein Deutschland zu schaffen, in dem nicht nur Fürsten und Baronen, sondern auch Männern aus der Arbeiterklasse der Weg zur Führung des Staates offensteht. Davon können Sie nicht zurück, ohne Ihren eigenen Führer preiszugeben. Vergeblich wird der Versuch bleiben, das Rad der Geschichte zurückzudrehen. Wir Sozialdemokraten wissen, dass man machtpolitische Tatsachen durch bloße Rechtsverwahrungen* nicht beseitigen kann. Wir sehen die machtpolitische Tatsache Ihrer augenblicklichen Herrschaft. Aber auch das Rechtsbewusstsein des Volkes ist eine politische Macht, und wir werden nicht aufhören, an dieses Rechtsbewusstsein zu appellieren*.

Die Verfassung von Weimar ist keine sozialistische Verfassung. Aber wir stehen zu den Grundsätzen des Rechtsstaates, der Gleichberechtigung, des sozialen Rechtes, die in ihr festgelegt sind. Wir deutschen Sozialdemokraten bekennen uns in dieser geschichtlichen Stunde feierlich zu den Grundsätzen der Menschlichkeit und der Gerechtigkeit, der Freiheit und des Sozialismus. Kein Ermächtigungsgesetz gibt Ihnen die Macht, Ideen, die ewig und unzerstörbar sind, zu vernichten. Sie selbst haben sich ja zum Sozialismus bekannt. Das Sozialistengesetz hat die Sozialdemokratie nicht vernichtet. Auch aus neuen Verfolgungen kann die deutsche Sozialdemokratie neue Kraft schöpfen.

Wir grüßen die Verfolgten und Bedrängten. Wir grüßen unsere Freunde im Reich. Ihre Standhaftigkeit und Treue verdienen Bewunderung. Ihr Bekennermut, ihre ungebrochene Zuversicht verbürgen eine hellere Zukunft.

Rede des Sozialdemokratischen Reichstagsabgeordneten Otto Wels gegen den Erlass des Ermächtigungsgesetzes (23. März 1933), in: Paul Meier-Benneckenstein [Eds.]: Dokumente der deutschen Politik, Vol. 1: Die Nationalsozialistische Revolution 1933, Juncker & Dünnhaupt 1935, pp. 36–38

durchgreifend here: effective

Rechtsverwahrung legal protest

an etw. appellieren to appeal to sth.

S 33 Adolf Hitler

Memorandum on the Four-Year Plan

Hitler's Four-year plan aimed at making Germany's military ready for war in four years. However, the problem was that the private industry also had to make its contribution, meaning that those responsible in the industrial field had to be put under pressure by Hermann Göring, then in charge of the realization of the Four-year plan. In this secret memorandum drawn up in August 1936, Hitler elaborates on the most important aims of the plan.

National Socialism

Pre-task

1. With the help of the visualization, describe how the Nazis wanted to solve Germany's economic problems.

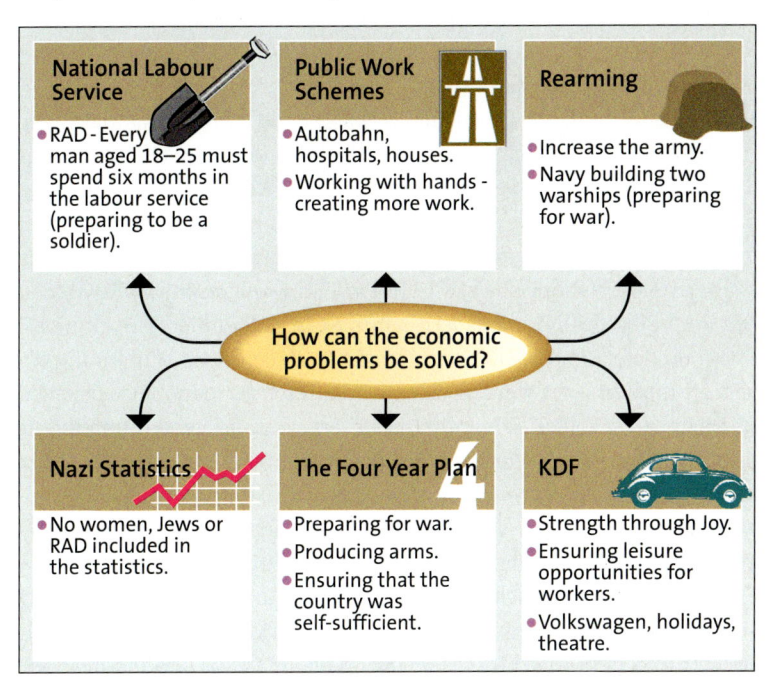

How can the economic problems be solved?

- **National Labour Service**
  - RAD - Every man aged 18–25 must spend six months in the labour service (preparing to be a soldier).

- **Public Work Schemes**
  - Autobahn, hospitals, houses.
  - Working with hands - creating more work.

- **Rearming**
  - Increase the army.
  - Navy building two warships (preparing for war).

- **Nazi Statistics**
  - No women, Jews or RAD included in the statistics.

- **The Four Year Plan**
  - Preparing for war.
  - Producing arms.
  - Ensuring that the country was self-sufficient.

- **KDF**
  - Strength through Joy.
  - Ensuring leisure opportunities for workers.
  - Volkswagen, holidays, theatre.

Tasks

2. Analyse the source.
3. Explain which task Hitler ascribes to the economy as a whole.
4. Which ideological assumption constitutes the basis of Hitler's Four-year plan? Explain.
5. Turn the statistics into a line graph for better visualization. Then assess in how far Hitler's economic policy proved to be successful or not.

Unemployment in Germany from 1933 to 1939	Total
January 1933	6 million
January 1934	3.3 million
January 1935	2.9 million
January 1936	2.5 million
January 1937	1.8 million
January 1938	1.0 million
January 1939	302,000

So wie die politische Bewegung in unserem Volk nur ein Ziel kennt, die Lebensbehauptung* unseres Volkes und Reiches zu ermöglichen, d. h. alle geistigen und sonstigen Voraussetzungen für die Selbstbehauptung unseres Volkes sicherzustellen, so hat auch die Wirtschaft nur diesen einen Zweck. Das Volk lebt nicht für
5 die Wirtschaft oder für die Wirtschaftsführer, Wirtschafts- oder Finanz-Theorien, sondern die Finanzen und die Wirtschaft, die Wirtschaftsführer und alle Theorien haben ausschließlich diesem Selbstbehauptungskampf zu dienen.
Die wirtschaftliche Lage Deutschlands ist aber, in kürzesten Umrissen gekennzeichnet, folgende:

Lebensbehauptung assertion of life

1) Wir sind überbevölkert und können uns auf der eigenen Grundlage nicht ernähren. [...]

6) Die endgültige Lösung liegt in einer Erweiterung des Lebensraumes bez. der Rohstoff- und Ernährungsbasis unseres Volkes. Es ist die Aufgabe der politischen Führung, diese Frage dareinst* zu lösen. [...]

Die Abwehrfähigkeit* Deutschlands basiert auf einigen Faktoren. An die Spitze möchte ich stellen zunächst den inneren Wert des deutschen Volkes an sich. Das deutsche Volk, politisch einwandfrei* geführt, weltanschaulich gefestigt* und militärisch durchorganisiert, stellt sicherlich den hochwertigsten* Widerstandsfaktor dar, den die Welt heute überhaupt besitzt. Die politische Führung ist sichergestellt durch die Nationalsozialistische Partei, die weltanschauliche Geschlossenheit* seit dem Sieg des Nationalsozialismus ist in einem bisher noch nicht erreichten Maße eingeleitet*. Sie muss auf der Grundlage dieser Auffassung immer mehr vertieft und erhärtet werden. Dies ist das Ziel der nationalsozialistischen Erziehung unseres Volkes. Die militärische Auswertung* soll durch die neue Armee erfolgen. *Das Ausmaß und das Tempo der militärischen Auswertung unserer Kräfte können nicht groß und nicht schnell genug gewählt werden!* Es ist ein Kapitalirrtum*, zu glauben, dass über diese Punkte irgendein Verhandeln oder ein Abwägen* stattfinden könnte mit anderen Lebensnotwendigkeiten.

I. Ähnlich der militärischen und politischen Aufrüstung bzw. Mobilmachung unseres Volkes hat auch eine wirtschaftliche zu erfolgen und zwar im selben Tempo, mit der gleichen Entschlossenheit* und wenn nötig auch mit der gleichen Rücksichtslosigkeit*. [...]

II. Zu diesem Zwecke sind auf all den Gebieten, auf denen eine eigene Befriedigung durch deutsche Produktionen zu erreichen ist, Devisen* einzusparen, um sie jenen Erfordernissen* zuzulenken, die unter allen Umständen ihre Deckung nur durch den Import erfahren können.

III. In diesem Sinne ist die deutsche Brennstofferzeugung* nunmehr im schnellsten Tempo vorwärtszutreiben und binnen* 18 Monaten zum restlosen Abschluss

Adolf Hitler speaking on the subject of the Enabling Act in the Kroll Opera House

zu bringen. Diese Aufgabe ist mit derselben Entschlossenheit wie die Führung
eines Krieges anzufassen und durchzuführen; denn von ihrer Lösung hängt die
kommende Kriegsführung* ab und nicht von einer Bevorratung* des Benzins*.
IV. Es ist ebenso augenscheinlich* die Massenfabrikation* von synthetischem
Gummi* zu organisieren und sicherzustellen. [...] Entweder wir besitzen heute
eine Privatwirtschaft, dann ist es deren Aufgabe, sich den Kopf über die Produktionsmethoden zu zerbrechen, oder wir glauben, dass die Klärung der Produktionsmethoden Aufgabe des Staates sei, dann benötigen wir keine Privatwirtschaft mehr.
V. Die Frage des Kostenpreises dieser Rohstoffe ist ebenfalls gänzlich belanglos.
Ich stelle somit folgende Aufgabe:
I. Die deutsche Armee muss in 4 Jahren einsatzfähig sein.
II. Die deutsche Wirtschaft muss in 4 Jahren kriegsfähig sein.

Wilhelm Treue (Eds.): Denkschrift Hitlers über die Aufgabe eines Vierjahresplans. Vierteljahrshefte für Zeitgeschichte 3. (DVA), Stuttgart 1955. p. 204 ff.

Kriegsführung warfare
Bevorratung supply
Benzin petrol, gasoline
augenscheinlich obvious
Massenfabrikation mass production
Gummi rubber

S 34 Adolf Hitler

Ansprache vor der NS-Frauenschaft

On 8 September 1934, Hitler delivered this speech on the role of women to the National Socialist Women's League.

Pre-task 1. Work with a partner. Each of you either focuses on the male or the female persons depicted in the poster. Describe the persons in detail. Concentrate especially on facial expressions and posture.

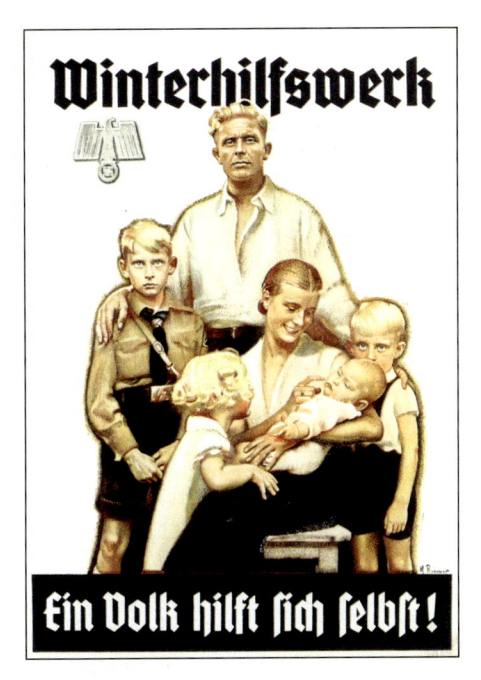

Embedded text:
Winterhilfswerk
Ein Volk hilft sich selbst!

Poster of the *Winterhilfswerk* (Winter Relief), a Nazi welfare organization which helped to finance charitable work, around 1933

Tasks 2. Find expressions in the source which underline your results from the pre-task and explain them.
3. Hypothesize why Hitler envisages a patriarchal social structure for Germany.

[...] Das Wort von der Frauen-Emanzipation ist nur ein vom jüdischen Intellekt erfundenes Wort, und der Inhalt ist von demselben Geist geprägt. Die deutsche Frau braucht sich in den wirklich guten Zeiten des deutschen Lebens nie zu emanzipieren. Sie hat genau das besessen, was die Natur ihr zwangsläufig als Gut zur Verwaltung und Bewahrung gegeben hat, genauso, wie der Mann in seiner guten Zeit sich nie zu fürchten brauchte, dass er aus seiner Stellung gegenüber der Frau verdrängt werde.

Gerade von der Frau wurde ihm sein Platz am wenigsten streitig* gemacht. Nur wenn er selbst nicht sicher war in der Erkenntnis seiner Aufgabe, begann der ewige Instinkt der Selbst- und Volkserhaltung* in der Frau zu revoltieren. Dann begann nach dieser Revolte eine Umstellung, die nicht der Natur gemäß war, und sie dauerte so lange, bis wieder beide Geschlechter zurückkehrten zu dem, was eine ewige weise Vorsehung ihnen zugewiesen hat.

Wenn man sagt, die Welt des Mannes ist der Staat, die Welt des Mannes ist sein Ringen*, die Einsatzbereitschaft für die Gemeinschaft*, so könnte man vielleicht sagen, dass die Welt der Frau eine kleinere sei. Denn ihre Welt ist ihr Mann, ihre Familie, ihre Kinder und ihr Haus. Wo wäre aber die größere Welt, wenn niemand die kleine Welt betreuen wollte? Wie könnte die größere Welt bestehen, wenn niemand wäre, der die Sorgen um die kleinere Welt zu seinem Lebensinhalt machen* würde? Nein, die große Welt baut sich auf dieser kleinen Welt auf! Diese große Welt kann nicht bestehen, wenn die kleine Welt nicht fest ist. Die Vorsehung hat der Frau die Sorgen um diese ihre eigenste Welt zugewiesen, aus der sich dann erst die Welt des Mannes bilden und aufbauen kann.

Diese beiden Welten stehen sich daher nie entgegen. Sie ergänzen sich gegenseitig, sie gehören zusammen, wie Mann und Weib zusammengehören.

Wir empfinden es nicht als richtig, wenn das Weib in die Welt des Mannes, in sein Hauptgebiet eindringt, sondern wir empfinden es als natürlich, wenn diese beiden Welten geschieden* bleiben. In die eine gehört die Kraft des Gemütes*, die Kraft der Seele! Zur anderen gehört die Kraft des Sehens, die Kraft der Härte, der Entschlüsse und die Einsatzwilligkeit*! In einem Falle erfordert diese Kraft die Willigkeit des Einsatzes des Lebens der Frau, um diese wichtige Zelle zu erhalten und zu vermehren, und im anderen Falle erfordert sie die Bereitwilligkeit, das Leben zu sichern, vom Manne.

Was der Mann an Opfern bringt im Ringen seines Volkes, bringt die Frau an Opfern im Ringen um die Erhaltung dieses Volkes in den einzelnen Fällen. Was der Mann einsetzt an Heldenmut* auf dem Schlachtfeld, setzt die Frau ein in ewig geduldiger Hingabe*, in ewig geduldigem Leid und Ertragen*. Jedes Kind, das sie zur Welt bringt, ist eine Schlacht, die sie besteht für das Sein oder Nichtsein ihres Volkes. Und beide müssen sich deshalb auch gegenseitig schätzen und achten, wenn sie sehen, dass jeder Teil die Aufgabe vollbringt, die ihm Natur und Vorsehung zugewiesen hat. So wird sich aus dieser Stellung der beiden Aufgaben zwangsläufig die gegenseitige Achtung ergeben.

Nicht das, was jüdischer Intellekt behauptet, ist wahr, dass die Achtung bedingt sei durch das Übergreifen* der Wirkungsgebiete* der Geschlechter, sondern diese Achtung bedingt, dass kein Geschlecht sich bemüht, das zu tun, was dem anderen zukommt. Sie liegt letzten Endes darin, dass jeder Teil weiß, dass der andere aber alles tut, was notwendig ist, um das Gesamte zu erhalten! [...]

So ist unsere Frauenbewegung für uns nicht etwas, das als Programm den Kampf gegen den Mann auf seine Fahne schreibt, sondern etwas, das auf sein Programm den gemeinsamen Kampf mit dem Mann setzt. Denn gerade dadurch haben wir die neue nationalsozialistische Volksgemeinschaft gefestigt, dass wir in Millionen von Frauen treueste fanatische Mitkämpferinnen erhielten. Kämpferinnen für das gemeinsame Leben im Dienste der gemeinsamen Lebenserhaltung. Kämpferinnen, die dabei den Blick nicht auf die Rechte richten, die ein jüdischer Intellektualismus vorspiegelt, sondern auf Pflichten richten, die die Natur uns gemeinsam aufbürdet*.

Wenn früher die liberalen intellektualistischen* Frauenbewegungen in ihren Programmen viele, viele Punkte enthielten, die ihren Ausgang vom sogenannten Geiste nahmen, dann enthält das Programm unserer nationalsozialistischen Frauenbewegung eigentlich nur einen einzigen Punkt, und dieser Punkt heißt: das Kind, dieses kleine Wesen, das werden muss und gedeihen soll, für das der ganze Lebenskampf ja überhaupt allein einen Sinn hat. [...]

from: Max Domarus: Hitler. Reden und Proklamationen 1932–1945. Bd. I: Triumph, Erster Halbband, 1932–1934, Wiesbaden: R. Löwit, 1973, pp. 450–52

jdm. etw. aufbürden to impose sth. on sb.
intellektualistisch intellectualist

S 35 Inge Scholl

Die Attraktivität der Hitlerjugend

Inge Scholl was the sister of the famous siblings Sophie and Hans Scholl, who, with their group *Die Weiße Rose*, resisted National Socialism. In this account, she talks about the impact National Socialism had on her brother Hans.

Pre-task
1. Brainstorm on reasons why young people join youth organizations. What are possible benefits and what makes them attractive? Exchange your ideas with a partner.

Tasks
2. State which aspects of being part of the Hitler youth were attractive for Inge and her siblings.
3. Explain why Hans Scholl suddenly felt unease after having attended the Nuremberg Rally. Consider the photograph as well.

The *Totenehrung* at the Nuremberg Rally in 1934

Vocabulary	
Auftrieb boost	
jdn./etw. würdigen to appreciate sb./sth.	
sich an etw. beteiligt fühlen to feel oneself a part of sth.	
anöden to annoy	
schal flat, insipid	
sich geben to pass by, to ease off, to let up	
unvermittelt abruptly, suddenly	
die will mir nicht hinunter here: I cannot stomach/tolerate that	
um einer Sache willen for the sake of	
Elternhaus parental home, family	
über etw. hinwegtäuschen to belie sth., to deceive sb. about sth.	
Klampfe guitar	
störend disturbing	
ins Leben treten to enter sb.'s life	
Vorhaltung expostulation	
sich taub stellen to turn a deaf ear	
ersinnen to devise, contrive, conceive	
etw. einsehen to accept sth.	
jdn. bedrücken to depress sb.	
Unbekümmertheit carefreeness, airiness	
Standort base	
Eigenart peculiarity [pɪˌkjuːliˈærɪti]	
Schablone pattern	

Wir hörten, dass wir für eine große Sache leben sollten. Wir wurden ernst genommen, in einer merkwürdigen Weise ernst genommen, und das gab uns einen besonderen Auftrieb*. Wir glaubten, Mitglieder einer großen, wohlgegliederten Organisation zu sein, die alle umfasste und jeden würdigte*, vom Zehnjährigen bis zum Erwachsenen. Wir fühlten uns beteiligt* an einem Prozess, an einer Bewegung, die aus der Masse Volk schuf. Manches, was uns anödete* oder einen schalen* Geschmack verursachte, würde sich schon geben* – so glaubten wir. Einmal sagte eine fünfzehnjährige Kameradin im Zelt, als wir uns nach einer langen Radtour unter einem weiten Sternenhimmel zur Ruhe gelegt hatten, ziemlich unvermittelt*: „Alles wäre so schön – nur die Sache mit den Juden, die will mir nicht hinunter*." Die Führerin sagte, dass Hitler schon wisse, was er tue, und man müsste um der großen Sache willen* manches Schwere und Unbegreifliche akzeptieren. Das Mädchen jedoch war mit dieser Antwort nicht ganz zufrieden, andere stimmten ihr bei, und man hörte plötzlich die Elternhäuser* aus ihnen reden. Es war eine unruhige Zeltnacht – aber schließlich waren wir doch zu müde. Und der nächste Tag war herrlich und voller Erlebnisse. Das Gespräch der Nacht war vorläufig vergessen.

In unseren Gruppen entstand ein Zusammenhalt, der uns über die Schwierigkeiten und die Einsamkeit jener Entwicklungsjahre hinwegtrug, vielleicht auch hinwegtäuschte*.

Hans hatte sich einen Liederschatz gesammelt und seine Jungen hörten es gerne, wenn er zur Klampfe* sang. Es waren nicht nur die Lieder der Hitlerjugend, sondern auch Volkslieder aus allerlei Ländern und Völkern. [...]

Aber nach einiger Zeit ging eine merkwürdige Veränderung in Hans vor, er war nicht mehr der alte. Etwas Störendes* war in sein Leben getreten*. Nicht die Vorhaltungen* des Vaters waren es, nein, denen gegenüber konnte er sich taub stellen*. Es war etwas anderes. Die Lieder sind verboten, hatten ihm die Führer gesagt. Und als er darüber lachte, hatten sie ihm mit Strafen gedroht. Warum sollte er diese Lieder, die so schön waren, nicht singen dürfen? Nur weil sie von anderen Völkern ersonnen* waren. Er konnte es nicht einsehen*; es bedrückte* ihn, und seine Unbekümmertheit* begann zu schwinden.

Zu dieser Zeit wurde er mit einem ganz besonderen Auftrag ausgezeichnet. Er sollte die Fahne seines Standorts* zum Parteitag nach Nürnberg tragen. Seine Freude war groß. Aber als er zurückkam, trauten wir unseren Augen kaum. Er sah müde aus, und in seinem Gesicht lag eine große Enttäuschung. Irgendeine Erklärung durften wir nicht erwarten. Allmählich erfuhren wir aber doch, dass die Jugend, die ihm dort als Ideal vorgesetzt wurde, völlig verschieden war von dem Bild, das er sich von ihr gemacht hatte. Dort Drill und Uniformierung bis ins persönliche Leben hinein – aber er hätte sich gewünscht, dass jeder Junge das Besondere aus sich machte, das in ihm steckte. Jeder einzelne Kerl hätte durch seine Phantasie, seine Einfälle und seine Eigenart* die Gruppe bereichern helfen sollen. Dort aber, in Nürnberg, hatte man alles nach einer Schablone* ausgerichtet.

Inge Scholl: Die Weiße Rose. Fischer Taschenbuch: Frankfurt/M. 1989 (erw. Neuausg.), pp. 16 f.

S 36 Richtlinien für den Geschichtsunterricht

These guidelines for teaching history were published in 1938.

Pre-task

1. The extract provided below is taken from the new *Kernlehrplan für die Sekundarstufe II* for History as a school subject and describes its tasks and aims. Together with a partner, make up your mind about which of these tasks would go totally against ideas on school education under the Nazi regime.

[...] [D]ie Fächer des gesellschaftswissenschaftlichen Aufgabenfeldes [tragen] [...] zur kritischen Reflexion geschlechter- und kulturstereotyper Zuordnungen*, zur Werteerziehung*, zur Empathie und Solidarität, zum Aufbau sozialer Verantwortung, zur Gestaltung einer demokratischen Gesellschaft, zur Sicherung der natür-
5 lichen Lebensgrundlagen, auch für kommende Generationen im Sinne einer nachhaltigen Entwicklung*, und zur kulturellen Mitgestaltung* bei. Darüber hinaus leisten sie einen Beitrag zur interkulturellen Verständigung [...] sowie zur Vorbereitung auf Ausbildung, Studium, Arbeit und Beruf.

Kernlehrplan für die Sekundarstufe II Gymnasium/Gesamtschule in Nordrhein-Westfalen, Geschichte, Ministerium für Schule und Weiterbildung des Landes Nordrhein-Westfalen, Heftnummer 4714, Düsseldorf 2014, pp. 11, www.schulministerium.nrw.de [22.04.15]

Zuordnung classification
Werteerziehung values education

nachhaltige Entwicklung sustainable development
Mitgestaltung participation

Tasks

2. Now explain the tasks and aims of history classes as presented in the source below.
3. Identify means of indoctrination (= to teach (someone) to fully accept the ideas, opinions, and beliefs of a particular group and to not consider other ideas, opinions, and beliefs[1]) in the source and state in how far the Nazis tried to indoctrinate youth instead of educating them.

---
[1] „Indoctrination". Merriam-Webster.com, Merriam-Wester, 2015 [22.04.15]

Das deutsche Volk in seiner Wesensart und Größe, in seinem schicksalhaften* Ringen um innere und äußere Selbstbehauptung ist Gegenstand des Geschichtsunterrichts. Er baut auf der naturgegebenen Verbundenheit des Kindes mit seinem Volke auf und ist, indem er die Geschichte als den schicksalhaften Daseins-
5 kampf der Völker verstehen lässt, in besonderen Maße berufen, die Jugend zu erziehen zur Ehrfurcht* vor der großen deutschen Vergangenheit, zum Glauben an die Sendung* und Zukunft des eigenen Volkes und zur Achtung vor dem Lebensrecht anderer Völker. Der Geschichtsunterricht soll die Vergangenheit so zum jungen Deutschen sprechen lassen, dass sie ihm das Verständnis für die
10 Gegenwart erschließt*, ihn die Verpflichtung jedes einzelnen gegenüber dem Volksganzen fühlen lässt und ihm einen Ansporn* gibt für sein eigenes politisches Tun. Damit weckt er im jungen Geschlecht jenes Verantwortungsgefühl gegenüber den Ahnen und Enkeln, das es fähig macht, sein Leben aufgehen* zu lassen im ewigen Deutschland. [...]
15 Aus dem Glauben der nationalsozialistischen Bewegung an die Zukunft des deutschen Volkes ist ein neues Verständnis der deutschen Vergangenheit erstanden. Der Geschichtsunterricht muss aus diesem legendigen Glauben hervorgehen, er muss die Jugend mit dem Bewusstsein erfüllen, einem Volke anzugehören, das von allen europäischen Nationen den längsten und schwersten Weg bis zu seiner

schicksalhaft fateful

Ehrfurcht respect
Sendung mission

erschließen to open up
Ansporn encouragement

in etw. aufgehen to be subsumed

Zuversicht confidence

Stetigkeit der Erbanlagen continuity of the hereditary characteristics
bedingt limited

Einigung zurückzulegen hatte, das aber heute, am Beginn eines neuen Zeitalters, voller Zuversicht* auf das Kommende blicken darf. [...]

Die Gewissheit eines großen nationalen Seins [...] gründet sich [...] für uns zugleich auf die klare Erkenntnis von den immer wirksamen und unzerstörbar fortdauernden rassischen Grundkräften des deutschen Volkes. Die Einsicht in die Stetigkeit der Erbanlagen* und der nur bedingten* Bedeutung der Umwelt ermöglicht ein neues und tiefes Verständnis von geschichtlichen Persönlichkeiten und Zusammenhängen. [...]

Die Geschichte soll in ihrem Ablauf unserer Jugend nicht als eine Chronik erscheinen, die unterschiedslos alle Ereignisse aneinanderreiht, sondern wie in einem Drama soll nur das Bedeutende und in seiner Wirkung Lebensmächtige im Geschichtsunterricht dargestellt werden. Bedeutend und lebensmächtig sind nicht nur die erfolgreichen, sondern auch die tragischen Gestalten und Zeitabschnitte, nicht allein die Siege, auch die Niederlagen. Immer aber muss er das Große zeigen, da in ihm, auch wo es abschreckend wirkt, das ewige Gesetz sichtbar wird. Nur wo große Taten empfunden und verstanden werden, ist die Voraussetzung für das Auffassen geschichtlicher Zusammenhänge gegeben, das Ohnmächtige und Kleine hat keine Geschichte.

Reichsministerium für Wissenschaft, Erziehung und Volksbildung, Erziehung und Unterricht in der Höheren Schule. Amtliche Ausgabe des Reichs- und Preußischen Ministeriums für Wissenschaft, Erziehung und Volksbildung. Weidmann: Berlin 1938, pp. 69–70

CONNECT

Resisting the Nazi Regime – "Fighting for Human Rights"?

Task Presenting and evaluating different forms of resistance in the form of a jigsaw puzzle.
According to the German judge and prosecutor Fritz Bauer (1903–1968), resistance against the NS regime was nothing less than a "fight for human rights".
In order to prove this statement right or wrong, split up into groups, each group dealing with one person/group (expert groups). Copy and fill in your parts of the table. Then form new groups in which all aspects of comparison are represented (jigsaw groups). Exchange your information and fill in the other parts of the table. Afterwards, get together in your expert groups again. Together, discuss in how far Bauer's claim is true for the different examples of resistance you have dealt with. Include S 37a in your discussion as well.

Person/group	Motivation	Aims	"Fighting for Human Rights?"
Hans und Sophie Scholl (Die Weiße Rose)			
Carl Friedrich Goerdeler			
Kreisauer Kreis			
Claus Schenk Graf von Stauffenberg			

S 37a) Detlev Peukert

Stufen abweichenden Verhaltens im Dritten Reich

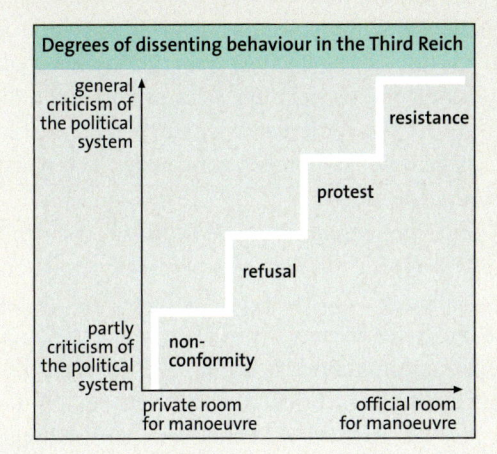

Degrees of dissenting behaviour in the Third Reich

(Diagram: a staircase rising from "partly criticism of the political system / private room for manoeuvre" to "general criticism of the political system / official room for manoeuvre", with steps labelled from bottom to top: non-conformity, refusal, protest, resistance)

Language support

Stufe degree • **abweichendes Verhalten** dissenting behaviour • **Handlungsspielraum** room for manoeuvre • **Nonkonformität** non-conformity • **Verweigerung** refusal • **Widerstand** resistance

The German historian Detlev Peukert (1950–1990) invented a categorization of dissenting behaviour in the Third Reich.

S 37b) Die Weiße Rose

Fünftes Flugblatt

The siblings Hans (1918–1943) and Sophie Scholl (1921–1943) are the most famous members of the Munich-based student group *Die Weiße Rose*. During the years 1942 and 1943, the students distributed leaflets in which they called for resistance against the Nazi dictatorship and an end to the war. While distributing the sixth leaflet, Sophie Scholl was spotted by the caretaker of the Ludwig Maximilian University in Munich and reported to the authorities. On 22 February 1943, Sophie Scholl, her brother Hans and their friend Alexander Schmorell were all sentenced to death and beheaded.
This leaflet dates back to January 1943.

Hans Scholl, Sophie Scholl and Christoph Probst, 1942

Aufruf an alle Deutsche!
Der Krieg geht seinem sicheren Ende entgegen. Wie im Jahre 1918 versucht die deutsche Regierung alle Aufmerksamkeit auf die wachsende U-Boot-Gefahr zu lenken, während im Osten die Armeen unaufhörlich zurückströ-
5 men, im Westen die Invasion erwartet wird. Die Rüstung Amerikas hat ih-

ren Höhepunkt noch nicht erreicht, aber heute schon übertrifft sie alles in der Geschichte seither Dagewesene. Mit mathematischer Sicherheit führt Hitler das deutsche Volk in den Abgrund*. Hitler kann den Krieg nicht gewinnen, nur noch verlängern! Seine und seiner Helfer Schuld hat jedes Maß unendlich überschritten. Die gerechte Strafe rückt näher und näher! Was aber tut das deutsche Volk? Es sieht nicht und es hört nicht. Blindlings folgt es seinen Verführern* ins Verderben. Sieg um jeden Preis! haben sie auf ihre Fahne geschrieben. Ich kämpfe bis zum letzten Mann, sagt Hitler – indes ist der Krieg bereits verloren.

Deutsche! Wollt Ihr und Eure Kinder dasselbe Schicksal erleiden, das den Juden widerfahren ist? Wollt Ihr mit dem gleichen Maß gemessen werden wie Eure Verführer? Sollen wir auf ewig das von aller Welt gehasste und ausgestoßene Volk sein? Nein! Darum trennt Euch von dem nationalsozialistischen Untermenschentum! Beweist durch die Tat, dass Ihr anders denkt! Ein neuer Befreiungskrieg bricht an. Der bessere Teil des Volkes kämpft auf unserer Seite. Zerreißt den Mantel der Gleichgültigkeit*, den Ihr um Euer Herz gelegt! Entscheidet Euch, ehe es zu spät ist!

Glaubt nicht der nationalsozialistischen Propaganda, die Euch den Bolschewistenschreck in die Glieder gejagt hat! Glaubt nicht, dass Deutschlands Heil mit dem Sieg des Nationalsozialismus auf Gedeih und Verderben* verbunden sei! Ein Verbrechertum kann keinen deutschen Sieg erringen. Trennt Euch rechtzeitig von allem, was mit dem Nationalsozialismus zusammenhängt! Nachher wird ein schreckliches, aber gerechtes Gericht kommen über die, so sich feig und unentschlossen verborgen hielten.

Was lehrt uns der Ausgang dieses Krieges, der nie ein nationaler war? Der imperialistische Machtgedanke muss, von welcher Seite er auch kommen möge, für alle Zeit unschädlich gemacht werden. Ein einseitiger preußischer Militarismus darf nie mehr zur Macht gelangen. Nur in großzügiger Zusammenarbeit der europäischen Völker kann der Boden geschaffen werden, auf welchem ein neuer Aufbau möglich sein wird. Jede zentralistische Gewalt, wie sie der preußische Staat in Deutschland und Europa auszuüben versucht hat, muss im Keime erstickt werden. Das kommende Deutschland kann nur föderalistisch sein. Nur eine gesunde föderalistische Staatenordnung vermag heute noch das geschwächte Europa mit neuem Leben zu erfüllen. Die Arbeiterschaft muss durch einen vernünftigen Sozialismus aus ihrem Zustand niedrigster Sklaverei befreit werden. Das Truggebilde der autarken* Wirtschaft muss in Europa verschwinden. Jedes Volk, jeder einzelne hat ein Recht auf die Güter der Welt!

Freiheit der Rede, Freiheit des Bekenntnisses, Schutz des einzelnen Bürgers vor der Willkür verbrecherischer Gewaltstaaten, das sind die Grundlagen des neuen Europa.

Unterstützt die Widerstandsbewegung, verbreitet die Flugblätter!

Fünftes Flugblatt der Weißen Rose, Jan. 1943, in: Inge Scholl: Die Weiße Rose. Frankfurt/M., Hamburg: Fischer Bücherei, 1955, pp. 147–50

Abgrund abyss

Verführer seducer

Gleichgültigkeit indifference

auf Gedeih und Verderb for good or for evil

autark self-sufficient

S 37c Carl Friedrich Goerdeler

Denkschrift an die Generalität

Carl Friedrich Goerdeler (1884–1945) was a German politician (DNVP) and opponent of the Nazi regime. Shortly after the beginning of WWII, civil resistance formed in conservative circles of the German population. The so-called Goerdeler Circle had close connections to the military resistance centred round Ludwig Beck. In the event that the 20 July plot had turned out to be successful, Goerdeler would have become chancellor in the new German government.
This memorandum dates back to 26 March 1943.

Stamp commemorating Carl Friedrich Goerdeler, 1964

[...] Heute stehen wir unter einer Führung, die sich nicht nur als unfähig erwiesen hat, sondern vermessen* und wahnwitzig ist und jedes sittlichen Gehalts entbehrt, weil sie sich des Verbrechens bedient, Verbrechen anordnet und Verbrechen sowie Korruption duldet.
5 Das deutsche Volk hat in allen seinen Schichten, insbesondere in der Arbeiterschaft, dies erkannt. Stalingrad, die Zerstörungen durch Luftangriffe und die Schließungen von Geschäften haben diese Erkenntnis wesentlich gefördert. Das Volk hat, von Teilen der Intellektuellen abgesehen, das Vertrauen zu Hitler verloren, soweit dies je wahrhaftig vorhanden und nicht
10 durch Demagogie erschlichen* war. [...] Ein Mann kann führen, entweder durch die Stärke seiner sittlichen Kraft oder durch Erfolge. Fehlt, wie hier, jene vollkommen und hören diese auf, so ist er erledigt. Das Volk ist nicht nur reif, sondern es wartet, dass eine rettende Tat geschieht. [...]
Wie ist es möglich, dass das so anständige deutsche Volk so lange ein so
15 unhaltbares System trägt? Die Erklärung ist einfach: nur weil sich alle Verstöße gegen Recht und Anstand im Schutze der Geheimhaltung und unter dem Druck des Terrors vollziehen. Dies ändert sich mit einem Schlage, wenn das Licht der Wahrheit in aller Öffentlichkeit auf die unhaltbaren Zustände gerichtet wird. Man stelle dem deutschen Volk in klaren Worten,
20 aber öffentlich, dar, was es im geheimen schon weiß und bespricht: nämlich die Folgen unfähiger militärischer Führung, das Übermaß* von Korruption, die zahllosen Verbrechen, die mit unserer Ehre nicht vereinbar* sind, und richte dann öffentlich an alle die Frage, wer bereit ist, diesen Zustand gutzuheißen*, und wer es für richtig hält, dass er bestehen bleibt. Ich
25 übernehme die Bürgschaft dafür, dass niemand dann vortritt; denn es gibt in der ganzen Welt niemand, selbst keinen geborenen Verbrecher, der sich öffentlich zu einem System der Verbrecher bekennt.
Es ist ein großer Irrtum anzunehmen, dass die seelische Kraft des deutschen Volkes erschöpft* sei; sie ist nur geradezu planmäßig verschüttet*.
30 Es ist also die Aufgabe einer rettenden Tat, die Deckmasse, d. h. das Ge-

vermessen foolhardy

sich etw. erschleichen to obtain sth. surreptitiously

Übermaß excess
mit etw. nicht vereinbar sein to be incompatible with sth.
gutheißen to approve of

erschöpft exhausted
verschüttet buried

Anstand decency

heimnis und den Terror, hinwegzuräumen, Recht und Anstand* wiederherzustellen und damit einen ungeheuren seelischen Kraftzuwachs frei zu machen. [...]

Gerhard Ritter: Carl Goerdeler und die deutsche Widerstandsbewegung. Deutsche Verlagsanstalt, Stuttgart 1954, pp. 577 ff.

S 37d Kreisauer Kreis

Grundsätze

The Kreisau Circle consisted mostly of people from the middle class and was formed in 1940. After its leading personality Helmuth James Graf von Moltke was arrested at the beginning of 1944, the resistance group broke up. However, some of its members then joined the group around Claus Schenk Graf von Stauffenberg. Von Moltke was sentenced to death for high treason and was executed on 23 January 1945.
The basic declaration at hand from May 1942 can be considered one of the key documents of opposition against Hitler.

Helmuth James Graf von Moltke before the People's Court in Berlin, 10 January 1945

sittlich ethical

Die Regierung des Deutschen Reiches sieht im Christentum die Grundlage für die sittliche* und religiöse Erneuerung unseres Volkes, für die Überwindung von Hass und Lüge, für den Neuaufbau der europäischen Völkergemeinschaft.
[...] Die Reichsregierung ist daher entschlossen, folgende nach innen und 5 außen unverzichtbare Forderungen mit allen ihr zur Verfügung stehenden Mitteln zu verwirklichen:

zertreten downtrodden, suppressed

1. Das zertretene* Recht muss wieder aufgerichtet und zur Herrschaft über alle Ordnungen des menschlichen Lebens gebracht werden. Unter dem Schutz gewissenhafter, unabhängiger und von Menschenfurcht freier Rich- 10 ter ist es Grundlage für alle zukünftige Friedensgestaltung.

2. Die Glaubens- und Gewissensfreiheit wird gewährleistet. [...]
3. Brechung des totalitären Gewissenszwangs und Anerkennung der unverletzlichen Würde der menschlichen Person als Grundlage der zu erstrebenden Rechts- und Friedensordnung. Jedermann wirkt in voller Verantwortung an den verschiedenen sozialen, politischen und internationalen Lebensbereichen mit. Das Recht auf Arbeit und Eigentum steht ohne Ansehen der Rassen-, Volks- und Glaubenszugehörigkeit unter öffentlichem Schutz.
4. Die Grundeinheit* friedlichen Zusammenlebens ist die Familie. Sie steht unter öffentlichem Schutz, der neben der Erziehung auch die äußeren Lebensgüter: Nahrung, Kleidung, Wohnung, Garten und Gesundheit sichern soll. [...]
6. Die persönliche politische Verantwortung eines jeden erfordert seine mitbestimmende Beteiligung an der neu zu belebenden Selbstverwaltung der kleinen und überschaubaren Gemeinschaften. In ihnen verwurzelt und bewährt, muss seine Mitbestimmung im Staat und in der Völkergemeinschaft durch selbstgewählte Vertreter gesichert und ihm so die lebendige Überzeugung der Mitverantwortung für das politische Gesamtgeschehen vermittelt werden.
7. Die besondere Verantwortung und Treue, die jeder einzelne seinem nationalen Ursprung, seiner Sprache, der geistigen und geschichtlichen Überlieferung seines Volkes schuldet, muss geachtet und geschützt werden.

Grundeinheit basic unit

Kreisauer Kreis: Grundsätze 1943, in: Walter Hofer (Eds.): Der Nationalsozialismus. Dokumente 1933–1945, Fischer TB, Frankfurt/M. 1983, pp. 333 f.

S 37e) Claus Schenk Graf von Stauffenberg

Geplanter Aufruf an das deutsche Volk

This source from 1944 is Claus Schenk Graf von Stauffenberg's planned appeal to the German people.

Hitlers Gewaltherrschaft ist gebrochen. Ungeheuerliches hat sich in den letzten Jahren vor unseren Augen abgespielt. Nicht vom deutschen Volke gerufen, sondern durch Intrigen schlimmster Art an die Spitze der Regierung gekommen, hat Hitler durch dämonische Künste und Lügen, durch ungeheuerliche Verschwendung*, die allen Vorteile zu bringen schien, in Wahrheit uns aber in Schulden und Mangel* stürzte, in unserem Volke Geister und Seelen verwirrt, ja selbst außerhalb Deutschlands verhängnisvolle* Täuschung erzeugt. Um sich an der Macht zu halten, hat er eine Schreckensherrschaft errichtet. Unser Volk durfte einst stolz auf seine Redlichkeit* und Rechtlichkeit sein. Hitler aber hat die göttlichen Gebote

Claus Schenk Graf von Stauffenberg, 1934

Verschwendung waste

Mangel lack

verhängnisvoll fatal

Redlichkeit honesty

verfemen to ostracize	verhöhnt, das Recht zerstört, den Anstand verfemt*, das Glück von Millionen vernichtet. Er hat Ehre und Würde, Freiheit und Leben anderer für nichts erachtet. Zahllose Deutsche, aber auch Angehörige anderer Völker,
schmachten to languish	schmachten* seit Jahren in Konzentrationslagern, den größten Qualen ausgesetzt und häufig schrecklichen Foltern unterworfen. [...] 20
Selbstüberheblichkeit arrogance	In diesem Kriege haben Machtrausch, Selbstüberheblichkeit* und Eroberungswahn ihren letzten Ausdruck gefunden. Tapferkeit und Hingabe unserer Soldaten sind schmählich* missbraucht. Ungeheure Opfer des ganzen Volkes sinnlos vergeudet. Wider den Rat der Sachverständigen* hat
schmählich ignominious	
Sachverständige/r expert	
Machtdünkel power conceit [kən'sit], power pretensions	Hitler ganze Armeen seiner Ruhmsucht, seinem Machtdünkel*, seiner 25 gotteslästerlichen Wahnidee geopfert, berufenes und begnadetes Werkzeug der Vorsehung zu sein.
	So durfte es nicht weitergehen! Unserer Väter wären wir nicht würdig, von unseren Kindern müssten wir verachtet werden, wenn wir den Mut nicht hätten, alles, aber auch alles zu tun, um die furchtbare Gefahr von uns ab- 30
Gefahr abwenden to avert danger	zuwenden* und wieder Achtung vor uns selbst zu erringen. [...]
	Unser Ziel ist die wahre, auf Achtung, Hilfsbereitschaft und soziale Gerechtigkeit gegründete Gemeinschaft des Volkes. Wir wollen Gottesfurcht an Stelle von Selbstvergottung, Recht und Freiheit an Stelle von Gewalt und
Eigennutz selfishness	Terror, Wahrheit und Sauberkeit an Stelle von Lüge und Eigennutz*. Wir 35 wollen unsere Ehre und damit unser Ansehen in der Gemeinschaft der Völker wiederherstellen. Wir wollen mit besten Kräften dazu beitragen, die
Wunden schlagen to cut wounds	Wunden zu heilen, die dieser Krieg allen Völkern geschlagen* hat, und das Vertrauen zwischen ihnen wieder neu beleben.
	Die Schuldigen, die den guten Ruf unseres Volkes geschändet und so viel 40 Unglück über uns und andere Völker gebracht haben, werden bestraft werden. [...]

Auszug aus dem geplanten Aufruf der Gruppe Stauffenberg an das deutsche Volk. Aus den Kaltenbrunner-Berichten an Bormann und Hitler, Anlage 3, 4. August 1994, qtd. in: Wolfgang Michalka (Eds.): Das Dritte Reich, München 1985, pp. 367 ff.

S 38 Adolf Hitler

Ausführungen gegenüber Befehlshabern des Heeres und der Marine

On 3 February 1933, Hitler talked about the aims of German policy as a whole.

Pre-task
1. Go back to S 29 and scan the text for Hitler's plans concerning German foreign policy.

Tasks
2. Read the source below and compare its contents with those of S 29. Hypothesize about the differences.
3. Identify aspects of Nazi ideology in the source (for help cf. S 27).
4. Relate the contents of S 29 and this source to the cartoon provided on page 451.

Ziel der Gesamtpolitik allein: Wiedergewinnung der pol. Macht. Hierauf muss gesamte Staatsführung eingestellt* werden (alle Ressorts!).

1. Im Innern. Völlige Umkehrung der gegenwärt. innenpol. Zustände in D. Keine Duldung der Betätigung irgendeiner Gesinnung, die dem Ziel entgegen steht (Pazifismus!) Wer sich nicht bekehren* lässt, muss gebeugt* werden. Ausrottung des Marxismus mit Stumpf und Stiel*. Einstellung der Jugend u. des ganzen Volkes auf den Gedanken, dass nur d. Kampf uns retten kann u. diesem Gedanken gegenüber alles zurückzutreten hat. (Verwirklicht in d. Millionen d. Nazi-Beweg. Sie wird wachsen.) Ertüchtigung* der Jugend u. Stärkung des Wehrwillens mit allen Mitteln. Todesstrafe für Landes- u. Volksverrat. Straffste autoritäre Staatsführung. Beseitigung des Krebsschadens* der Demokratie!

2. Nach außen. Kampf gegen Versailles. Gleichberechtigung in Genf; aber zwecklos, wenn Volk nicht auf Wehrwillen eingestellt. Sorge für Bundesgenossen.

3. Wirtschaft! Der Bauer muss gerettet werden! Siedlungspolitik! Künft. Steigerung d. Ausfuhr zwecklos. Aufnahmefähigkeit d. Welt ist begrenzt u. Produktion ist überall übersteigert. Im Siedeln liegt die einzige Mögl., Arbeitslosenheer z. T. wieder einzuspannen. Aber braucht Zeit u. radikale Änderung nicht zu erwarten, da Lebensraum für d[eutsches] Volk zu klein.

4. Aufbau der Wehrmacht wichtigste Voraussetzung für Erreichung des Ziels: Wiedererringung der pol. Macht. Allg. Wehrpflicht muss wieder kommen. Zuvor aber muss Staatsführung dafür sorgen, dass die Wehrpflichtigen vor Eintritt nicht schon durch Pazif., Marxismus, Bolschewismus vergiftet werden oder nach Dienstzeit diesem Gifte verfallen.

Wie soll pol. Macht, wenn sie gewonnen ist, gebraucht werden? Jetzt noch nicht zu sagen. Vielleicht Erkämpfung neuer Export-Mögl., vielleicht – und wohl besser – Eroberung neuen Lebensraums im Osten u. dessen rücksichtslose* Germanisierung. Sicher, dass erst mit pol. Macht u. Kampf jetzige wirtsch. Zustände geändert werden können. Alles, was jetzt geschehen kann – Siedlung – Aushilfsmittel*. Wehrmacht wichtigste u. sozialistischste Einrichtung d. Staates. Sie soll unpol. u. überparteilich bleiben. Der Kampf im Innern nicht ihre Sache, sondern der Naziorganisationen. Anders wie in Italien keine Verquickung v. Heer und SA beabsichtigt. – Gefährlichste Zeit ist die des Aufbaus der Wehrmacht. Da wird sich zeigen, ob F[rankreich] Staatsmänner hat; wenn ja, wird es uns Zeit nicht lassen, sondern über uns herfallen […].

Contemporary US cartoon, published in *The Nation*, spring 1933

jdm. auf etw. einstellen to gear sb. to sth.

bekehren to convert
beugen to break
Stumpf und Stiel root and branch

Ertüchtigung training

Krebsschaden cancer

rücksichtslos ruthless

Aushilfsmittel stop-gap measures

Language support

Friedenstaube peace dove •
Kanonenrohr muzzle • **Olivenzweig** olive branch

Handschriftliche Aufzeichnungen des General Leutnant Liebmann. München, in: Thilo Vogelsang: „Neue Dokumente zur Geschichte der Reichswehr 1930–1933", Vierteljahreshefte für Zeitgeschichte 2 (1954), Heft 4, pp. 434–35

| S 39 | David Low

Stepping Stones to Glory

This cartoon was published on 8 July 1936 in the British daily newspaper *Evening Standard*.

Pre-task 1. Have a look at the map provided and describe it (for help cf. Skills page Talking about Maps, p. 591).

Nazi Germany on the March, 1936–1939

Legend:
- Germany, 1933
- Rhineland remilitarized, 1936
- Areas annexed, 1938
- Areas annexed, 1939
- Slovakia (becomes German „protectorate", March 1939)

Tasks
2. Analyse the cartoon.
3. Take a critical stand on the cartoon's message.

Embedded text: Boss of the Universe/ Spineless "Leaders" of Democracy? !!!/!!/??/?/ Danzig/Rhineland Fortification/Re-armament

Listed personalities (left to right): Hitler, Adolf Baldwin, Stanley (British Prime Minister) Eden, Anthony (British Foreign Secretary)

STEPPING STONES TO GLORY.

S 40 Frank McDonough

Neville Chamberlain, Appeasement and the Road to Munich, 1937–38

In this extract from the book *The Origins of the First and Second World Wars*, the author Frank McDonough elaborates on possible alternatives to the British policy of appeasement.

Pre-task
1. Together with a partner, think of alternatives to a policy of appeasement. Consider possible effects as well. Then, join another pair and exchange your ideas.

Tasks
2. Draw a mind map which includes the aspects which influenced Britain's decision to opt for a policy of appeasement, according to McDonaugh.
3. Explain which alternatives British foreign policy had, according to the author.

Appeasement and the alternatives

It was pretty clear by 1937 that international relations were in a state of turmoil. Germany and Italy were threatening peace in Europe, Japan was at war with China, and a bitter civil war was under way in Spain. It was against this background that Neville Chamberlain, aged 68, became the British prime minister. He was a
5   dull* figure, with the appearance of a bank manager. In his case, however, appearances were misleading. Chamberlain was a man with a mission, who wanted to bring order and lasting peace to international relations through a policy known as 'appeasement'. The task of explaining why appeasement became the policy adopted by the British government to meet the deepening crisis of the 1930s is complex.
10 Any consideration of the reasons for appeasement must mention several factors.
1. There was a widespread horror at the idea of a second world war.
2. Too much faith had been placed in the League of Nations, which proved ineffective when faced with military aggression.
3. There was a widespread feeling that Germany had been punished too harshly by
15   the Treaty of Versailles.
4. British public opinion constantly opposed the rearmament of Britain.
Furthermore, the position of France, Britain's only firm ally, had sharply deteriorated in the face of the growing fascist threat. The Locarno Treaty, designed to protect France from attack, had been ignored by Germany, the Franco-Italian
20 agreement had broken down, and Belgium had opted for neutrality. The German army was moving into a position of superiority, while the Spanish Civil War had raised the prospect* of another hostile power over the French border. In such circumstances, the French government had no desire to go to war, and was increasingly looking to Britain to provide a new direction in Franco-British relations with
25 Nazi Germany and Italy. Finally, the poor state of Britain's armed forces also influenced the policy of appeasement and often justified it. Britain was in no position to offer any help to France, either to defend its cities from air attack, or to defend its possessions in the Far East from Japan.
The policy of appeasement grew out of an intermingling* of all these factors. This
30 is not to suggest that it was inevitable, but in the difficult circumstances of international affairs in the late 1930s it seemed rational and logical to Chamberlain. It

dull boring

prospect outlook for the future

to intermingle to mix

was not, however, the only policy available. There were two alternative directions which British foreign policy could have taken in the late 1930s. The first was to support peace by collective security through the League of Nations, but this policy had never been implemented, even when the league was strong, and stood less chance of success in 1937, when the league was weak and discredited*. A second alternative was to create a 'grand alliance' of the anti-fascist powers, a policy championed* by Winston Churchill, who suggested that the dictators would only respond to military force. Yet this policy amounted to a return to the pre-1914 alliance system, and very few leaders like to adopt a past policy which has already proved unsuccessful, even though in this case it might have prevented war.

The only other option was to satisfy the grievances* created by the Paris Peace Settlement, and Chamberlain, along with the majority of the 'National Government', favoured this stance. A bold* policy of appeasement came to be seen by Chamberlain as the only choice if war was to be avoided. He believed that unless he could negotiate a revision of the Treaty of Versailles with Hitler, then a second world war would probably break out.

The sudden desire of Chamberlain to champion appeasement as an active policy with which to solve the grievances of Nazi Germany was not appreciated by Hitler. In May 1937, for example, Chamberlain invited von Neurath, the German foreign minister, to the coronation of George VI, but Hitler refuses to let him go, on account of the negative coverage* of Nazi Germany in some British newspapers. In November 1937, Chamberlain sent Lord Halifax, a kindred* spirit, to meet leading Nazi figures, much to the annoyance of Sir Anthony Eden, the foreign secretary, who felt that Chamberlain's attempt to court* the dictator might end in failure. At his meeting with Hitler, Halifax said that Britain would support any legitimate German claims in Europe, provided they were negotiated peacefully.

Frank McDonough: The Origins of the First and Second World Wars, Cambridge 1997, pp. 74 ff.

to discredit to damage the reputation of sb.
to champion to favour, to advocate
grievance feeling of having been treated unfairly
bold daring
coverage reporting
kindred similar
to court to give a lot of attention and praise to (someone) in order to get approval, support, etc.

Neville Chamberlain (1869–1940)

Arthur Neville Chamberlain was a British conservative politician born in Edgbaston on 18 March 1869 as the son of a politician. From 1890 until 1897 he lived as a farmer on an island in the Bahamas. After having returned to England, Chamberlain became Lord Mayor of Birmingham in 1915. In 1918, he was elected to the House of Commons, from 1923–1931 he was Minister of Health and from 1931–1937 he served as Chancellor of the Exchequer before becoming Prime Minister on 28 May 1937. Chamberlain became particularly well-known for his policy of appeasement. After several meetings with Adolf Hitler, Chamberlain was of the opinion that he could avoid another war by giving in to Germany's territorial demands. On 30 September 1938, the Munich Agreement was signed between Great Britain (Chamberlain), Germany (Adolf Hitler), France (Edouard Daladier) and Italy (Benito Mussolini). However, when German troops invaded Prague on 15 March 1939, Chamberlain announced an end to appeasement in a speech at Birmingham (S 42). In the period that followed, he made guarantee agreements with Poland, Greece, Romania and Turkey for the event of a German attack. On 3 September 1939, Britain declared war on Germany in response to Germany's attack on Poland two days previously. Having lost the support of his Conservative Party and due to his irresolute leadership, Chamberlain resigned on 10 May 1940 as Prime Minister. His successor in office was Winston Churchill. Chamberlain died shortly after the war on 9 November 1949 in Heckfield near Reading.

S 41 Winston Churchill

The Defence of Freedom and Peace

This speech was a radio broadcast to the United States and to London transmitted on 16 October 1938.

Pre-task
1. In his speech, Churchill makes use of the historical example of Alexander the Great. Alexander allegedly claimed the people of Asia were slaves because they had not learned how to pronounce the word "no". How does that example fit the situation the world finds itself in in 1938?

Tasks
2. Compare your hypothesis from the pre-task with what Churchill actually says.
3. Explain why, for Churchill, a call to arms is not enough to combat Nazism.
4. In the end, Churchill asks himself if this is a call to war. How does he answer his own question? Explain.

I avail* myself with relief of the opportunity of speaking to the people of the United States. I do not know how long such liberties will be allowed. The stations of uncensored expression are closing down; the lights are going out; but there is still time for those to whom freedom and parliamentary government mean something, to
5 consult together. Let me, then, speak in truth and earnestness while time remains. The American people have, it seems to me, formed a true judgment upon the disaster which has befallen Europe. They realise, perhaps more clearly than the French and British publics have yet done, the far-reaching consequences of the abandonment and ruin of the Czechoslovak Republic. I hold to the conviction I
10 expressed some months ago, that if in April, May or June, Great Britain, France, and Russia had jointly declared that they would act together upon Nazi Germany if Herr Hitler committed an act of unprovoked aggression against this small State, and if they had told Poland, Yugoslavia, and Rumania what they meant to do in good time, and invited them to join the combination of peace-defending Powers, I
15 hold that the German Dictator would have been confronted with such a formidable array* that he would have been deterred from his purpose. This would also have been an opportunity for all the peace-loving and moderate forces in Germany, together with the chiefs of the German Army, to make a great effort to re-establish something like sane and civilised conditions in their own country. If the risks of
20 war which were run by France and Britain at the last moment had been boldly faced in good time, and plain declarations made, and meant, how different would our prospects be today! [...]
All the world wishes for peace and security. Have we gained it by the sacrifice of the Czechoslovak Republic. Here was the model democratic State of Central Eu-
25 rope, a country where minorities were treated better than anywhere else. It has been deserted, destroyed and devoured*. It is now being digested*. The question which is of interest to a lot of ordinary people, common people, is whether this destruction of the Czechoslovak Republic will bring upon the world a blessing or a curse. [...]
30 There is another question which arises out of this. Can peace, goodwill, and confidence be built upon submission to wrong-doing backed by force?

to avail oneself of sth. to use

array line-up

to devour [dɪˈvaʊər] to swallow, to consume
to digest verdauen

One may put this question in the largest form. Has any benefit or progress ever been achieved by the human race by submission to organized and calculated violence? As we look back over the long story of the nations we must see that, on the contrary, their glory has been founded upon the spirit of resistance to tyranny and injustice, especially when these evils seemed to be backed by heavier force. Since the dawn of the Christian era a certain way of life has slowly been shaping itself among the Western peoples, and certain standards of conduct* and government have come to be esteemed*. After many miseries and prolonged confusion, there arose into the broad light of day the conception* of the right of the individual; his right to be consulted in the government of his country; his right to invoke the law even against the State itself. [...]

We are confronted with another theme. It is not a new theme; it leaps out upon us from the Dark Ages – racial persecution, religious intolerance, deprivation of free speech, the conception of the citizen as a mere soulless fraction of the State. To this has been added the cult of war. Children are to be taught in their earliest schooling the delights and profits of conquest and aggression. A whole mighty community has been drawn painfully, by severe privations*, into a warlike frame. [...]

No one must, however, underrate the power and efficiency of a totalitarian state. Where the whole population of a great country, amiable*, good-hearted, peace-loving people are gripped by the neck and by the hair by a Communist or a Nazi tyranny – for they are the same things spelt in different ways – the rulers for the time being can exercise a power for the purposes of war and external domination before which the ordinary free parliamentary societies are at a grievous practical disadvantage. We have to recognise this. [...]

This combination of medieval passion, a party caucus*, the weapons of modern science, and the blackmailing power of air-bombing, is the most monstrous menace to peace, order and fertile progress that has appeared in the world since the Mongol invasions of the thirteenth century.

The culminating question to which I have been leading is whether the world as we have known it – the great and hopeful world of before the war, the world of increasing hope and enjoyment for the common man, the world of honoured tradition and expanding science – should meet this menace by submission or by resistance. Let us see, then, whether the means of resistance remain to us today. We have sustained an immense disaster; the renown* of France is dimmed. In spite of her brave, efficient army, her influence is profoundly diminished. No one has a right to say that Britain, for all her blundering, has broken her word – indeed, when it was too late, she was better than her word. Nevertheless, Europe lies at this moment abashed* and distracted before the triumphant assertions* of dictatorial power. [...]

Far away, happily protected by the Atlantic and Pacific Oceans, you, the people of the United States, to whom I now have the chance to speak, are the spectators, and I may add the increasingly involved spectators of these tragedies and crimes. We are left in no doubt where American conviction and sympathies lie; but will you wait until British freedom and independence have succumbed*, and then take up the cause when it is three-quarters ruined, yourselves alone? I hear that they are saying in the United States that because England and France have failed to do their duty therefore the American people can wash their hands of the whole business. This may be the passing mood of many people, but there is no sense in it. If things have got much worse, all the more must we try to cope with them.

---

conduct behaviour
to esteem to appreciate
conception understanding, idea

privation hardship, poverty

amiable friendly

caucus any group or meeting organized to further a special interest or cause

renown glory, honour

abashed ill at ease, disconcerted, humiliated
assertion declaration

to succumb to die, to perish, to collapse, to surrender

For, after all, survey the remaining forces of civilisation; they are overwhelming. If only they were united in a common conception of right and duty, there would be no war. On the contrary, the German people, industrious, faithful, valiant*, but alas*! lacking in the proper spirit of civic independence, liberated from their present nightmare, would take their honoured place in the vanguard* of human society. Alexander the Great remarked that the people of Asia were slaves because they had not learned to pronounce the word "No." Let that not be the epitaph* of the English-speaking people or of Parliamentary democracy, or of France, or of the many surviving liberal States of Europe.

There, in one single word, is the resolve which the forces of freedom and progress, of tolerance and good will, should take. It is not in the power of one nation, however formidably armed, still less is it in the power of a small group of men, violent, ruthless men, who have always to cast their eyes back over their shoulders, to cramp* and fetter* the forward march of human destiny. The preponderant* world forces are upon our side; they have but to be combined to be obeyed. We must arm. Britain must arm. America must arm. If, through an earnest desire for peace, we have placed ourselves at a disadvantage, we must make up for it by redoubled exertions, and, if necessary, by fortitude in suffering.

We shall, no doubt, arm. Britain, casting away the habits of centuries, will decree national service upon her citizens. The British people will stand erect, and will face whatever may be coming.

But arms – instrumentalities, as President Wilson called them – are not sufficient by themselves. We must add to them the power of ideas. People say we ought not to allow ourselves to be drawn into a theoretical antagonism between Nazidom and democracy; but the antagonism is here now. It is this very conflict of spiritual and moral ideas which gives the free countries a great part of their strength. You see these dictators on their pedestals, surrounded by the bayonets of their soldiers and the truncheons* of their police. On all sides they are guarded by masses of armed men, cannons, aeroplanes, fortifications, and the like – they boast and vaunt themselves* before the world, yet in their hearts there is unspoken fear. They are afraid of words and thoughts; words spoken abroad, thoughts stirring at home – all the more powerful because forbidden – terrify them. A little mouse of thought appears in the room, and even the mightiest potentates are thrown into panic. [...]

Is this a call to war? Does anyone pretend that preparation for resistance to aggression is unleashing war? I declare it to be the sole guarantee of peace. We need the swift gathering of forces to confront not only military but moral aggression; the resolute and sober acceptance of their duty by the English-speaking peoples and by all the nations, great and small, who wish to walk with them. Their faithful and zealous* comradeship would almost between night and morning clear the path of progress and banish from all our lives the fear which already darkens the sunlight to hundreds of millions of men.

Winston Churchill: The Defence of Freedom and Peace, 16 Octobre 1938, Broadcast to the United States, London. In: Never Give In!: Winston Churchill's Speeches. A & C Black: London 2013

valiant brave, fearless
alas unfortunately, sadly
vanguard forefront

epitaph inscription on a gravestone

to cramp to hinder
to fetter to chain, to hinder, to restrict
preponderant predominant

truncheon stick

to vaunt oneself to speak vaingloriously of; boast of

zealous enthusiastic

Winston Churchill (1874–1965)

Winston Leonard Spencer Churchill was born on 30 November 1874 as the son of the conservative politician Lord Randolph Spencer Churchill and the American Jennie Jerome near Woodstock (Oxford). He attended the Royal Military Academy of Sandhurst from 1893–1895 and participated in military campaigns in South Africa, India and Sudan. In 1900, he was elected a Conservative member of the House of Commons, however, in 1904, he joined the Liberal Party and due to their election victory of 1904, Churchill became Under-Secretary of State for the Colonies in 1905, President of the Board of Trade in 1908 and Home Secretary in 1910. From 1911 to 1915, Churchill was responsible for the British naval armament since there had not been an agreement with the German Reich. Churchill resigned from the government due to the failure of a military campaign on the Dardanelles in the First World War, for which he, as one of the political and military engineers, had been responsible. When the Liberal Party started to disintegrate in 1924, Churchill again joined the Conservative Party.

Churchill held no political position during the years 1929–1939. Nevertheless, his writings on the subject of British Prime Minister Neville Chamberlain's appeasement policy and his warnings against the German Nazi regime became increasingly known among the British public. When Nazi Germany started its Battle of France [*Westfeldzug*] in 1940, Churchill gave in to public pressure and became Prime Minister and Minister of Defence. During WWII, Churchill turned out to be the motor of British opposition against Hitler and a symbol of the perseverance of his nation. Furthermore, he was the main initiator of the Grand Alliance between Great Britain, the USSR and the USA. From 17 July–2 August 1945. Churchill attended the Potsdam Conference, however, he had to resign as Prime Minister due to the election defeat of his Conservative Party. On 5 March 1946, he gave his famous speech in Fulton, Missouri, coining the term "Iron Curtain" (S 6a), chapter 4) to describe the policy of the USSR. From 1951–1955, he again was Prime Minister of Britain and during his term of office he promoted a policy of détente in the Cold War. In 1956, the city of Aachen awarded him the *Internationaler Karlspreis der Stadt Aachen (Charlemagne Prize)* for his achievements in furthering a united Europe. Sir Winston Churchill died in London on 24 January 1965.

S 42) Neville Chamberlain

Speech at Birmingham

Britain's Prime Minister Neville Chamberlain delivered this speech on 17 March 1939, two days after Germany had invaded Czechoslovakia. Here, he justifies his policy of appeasement.

Pre-task 1. With the help of the expressions provided in the box, try to anticipate Chamberlain's line of argument as to why he saw himself compelled to pursue a policy of appeasement.

> averting a European war • the terms of settlement […] were disapproved • no new problem • surgical operation was necessary • the most immediate object of my visit was achieved • never could we have reconstructed Czecho-Slovakia • exercise of mutual goodwill and understanding • this was the last of his territorial ambitions in Europe

Tasks 2. Reconstruct Chamberlain's argumentation and check your ideas from the pre-task.
3. Point out the reasons Chamberlain gives for pursuing a policy of appeasement.
4. Explain in detail the aspects underlined below.

When I decided to go to Germany I never expected that I was going to escape criticism. Indeed, I did not go there to get popularity. I went there first and foremost because, in what appeared to be an almost desperate situation, that seemed to me to offer the only chance of averting* a European war. And I might remind you that, when it was first announced that I was going, not a voice was raised in criticism. Everyone applauded that effort. It was only later, when it appeared that the results of the final settlement fell short of the expectations of some who did not fully appreciate the facts – it was only then that the attack began, and even then it was not the visit, it was the terms of settlement that were disapproved.

to avert to prevent from happening

Well, I have never denied that the terms which I was able to secure at Munich were not those that I myself would have desired. But, as I explained then, I had to deal with no new problem. This was something that had existed ever since the Treaty of Versailles – a problem that ought to have been solved long ago if only the statesmen of the last twenty years had taken broader and more enlightened views of their duty. It had become like a disease which had been long neglected, and a surgical operation was necessary to save the life of the patient.

After all, the first and the most immediate object of my visit was achieved. The peace of Europe was saved; and, if it had not been for those visits, hundreds of thousands of families would today have been in mourning for the flower of Europe's best manhood. I would like once again to express my grateful thanks to all those correspondents who have written me from all over the world to express their gratitude and their appreciation of what I did then and of what I have been trying to do since.

Really I have no need to defend my visits to Germany last autumn, for what was the alternative? Nothing that we could have done, nothing that France could have done, or Russia could have done could possibly have saved Czecho-Slovakia from invasion and destruction. Even if we had subsequently gone to war to punish Germany for her actions, and if after the frightful losses which would have been inflicted upon all partakers* in the war we had been victorious in the end, never could we have reconstructed Czecho-Slovakia as she was framed by the Treaty of Versailles.

partaker sb. who takes part in sth.

But I had another purpose, too, in going to Munich. That was to further the policy which I have been pursuing ever since I have been in my present position – a policy which is sometimes called European appeasement, although I do not think myself that that is a very happy term or one which accurately describes its purpose. If that policy were to succeed, it was essential that no Power should seek to obtain a general domination of Europe; but that each one should be contented to obtain reasonable facilities for developing its own resources, securing its own share of international trade, and improving the conditions of its own people. I felt that, although that might well mean a clash of interests between different States, nevertheless, by the exercise of mutual goodwill and understanding of what were the limits of the desires of others, it should be possible to resolve all differences by discussion and without armed conflict. I hoped in going to Munich to find out by personal contact what was in Herr Hitler's mind, and whether it was likely that he would be willing to co-operate in a programme of that kind. Well, the atmosphere in which our discussions were conducted was not a very favourable one, because we were in the middle of an acute crisis; but, nevertheless, in the intervals between more official conversations I had some opportunities of talking with him and of hearing his views, and I thought that results were not altogether unsatisfactory.

egy. But the Prime Minister had little doubt as to where the trouble might next flare up. 'He thought that Poland was very likely the key to the situation ... The time had now come for those who were threatened by German aggression (whether immediately or ultimately) to get together. We should enquire how far Poland was prepared to go along these lines.' The British Guarantee to Poland and the genesis of the summer crisis which, this time, would end in war were foreshadowed in Chamberlain's remarks.

Similar reactions were registered in Paris. Daladier let Chamberlain know that the French would speed up rearmament and resist any further aggression. The Americans were told that Daladier was determined to go to war should the Germans act against Danzig or Poland. Even strong advocates of appeasement were now saying enough was enough; there would not be another Munich.

Ian Kershaw (2000): Hitler: 1936–1945 Nemesis. New York: Norton 2000, pp .173–175

S 44 David Low

Rendezvous

This cartoon by David Low was published in the *Evening Standard* on 20 September 1939.

Pre-task
1. Revise your knowledge about the Hitler-Stalin Pact. What was it about?

Tasks
2. Analyse the source.
3. Put the source into its historical context and explain the pictorial elements.
4. Take a critical stand on the cartoonist's message.

Embedded text:
Hitler: "The scum of the earth, I believe?"
Stalin: "The bloody assassin of the workers, I presume?"

S 45 Winston Churchill
"Blood, Toil, Tears and Sweat"

Winston Churchill delivered this speech in the House of Commons on 13 May 1940 and, apart from his "Iron Curtain" speech of 1946, it is his most famous one.

Pre-task
1. Hypothesize about the content and the purpose of the speech. Consider its title and the historical context (cf. biography on p. 458).

Tasks
2. Sum up the content of the speech.
3. How does Churchill try to convince both the House of Commons and the British public that fighting against Nazi Germany is necessary? Focus on his choice of words here and explain.

On Friday evening last I received from His Majesty the mission to form a new administration. It was the evident will of Parliament and the nation that this should be conceived on the broadest possible basis and that it should include all parties. I have already completed the most important part of this task. A war cabinet has
5 been formed of five members, representing, with the Labour, Opposition, and Liberals, the unity of the nation. It was necessary that this should be done in one single day on account of the extreme urgency and rigor* of events. [...] I now invite the House by a resolution to record its approval of the steps taken and declare its confidence in the new government. The resolution:
10 "That this House welcomes the formation of a government representing the united and inflexible resolve* of the nation to prosecute* the war with Germany to a victorious conclusion."
To form an administration of this scale and complexity is a serious undertaking in itself. But we are in the preliminary phase of one of the greatest battles in history.
15 We are in action at many other points – in Norway and in Holland – and we have to be prepared in the Mediterranean. The air battle is continuing, and many preparations have to be made here at home. In this crisis I think I may be pardoned if I do not address the House at any length today, and I hope that any of my friends and colleagues or former colleagues who are affected by the political reconstruc-
20 tion will make all allowances for any lack of ceremony with which it has been necessary to act. I say to the House as I said to ministers who have joined this government, I have nothing to offer but blood, toil*, tears, and sweat. We have before us an ordeal* of the most grievous* kind. We have before us many, many months of struggle and suffering. You ask, what is our policy? I say it is to wage
25 war by land, sea, and air. War with all our might and with all the strength God has given us, and to wage war against a monstrous tyranny never surpassed in the dark and lamentable* catalogue of human crime. That is our policy. You ask, what is our aim? I can answer in one word. It is victory. Victory at all costs – Victory in spite of all terrors – Victory, however long and hard the road may be, for without victory
30 there is no survival. Let that be realized. No survival for the British Empire, no survival for all that the British Empire has stood for, no survival for the urge*, the impulse of the ages, that mankind shall move forward toward his goal. I take up my task in buoyancy* and hope. I feel sure that our cause will not be suffered to fail among men. I feel entitled at this juncture*, at this time, to claim the aid of all
35 and to say, "Come then, let us go forward together with our united strength."

Winston Churchill: "Blood, Sweat and Tears", May 13, 1940, The Churchill Centre, www.winstonchurchill.org/learn/speeches/speeches-of-winston-churchill/92-blood-toil-tears-and-sweat [07.12.2014]

rigor harshness

resolve determination, firmness, resoluteness
to prosecute here: to follow through, to pursue

toil hard work
ordeal test, trial, trouble, suffering
grievous severe, serious, painful

lamentable miserable, sad, deplorable

urge very strong desire
buoyancy ['bɔɪənsi] the ability of sb. or sth. to continue to be happy, strong, etc., through difficult times
juncture crossroad, point

S 46 Franklin D. Roosevelt
"The Four Freedoms"

US President Franklin D. Roosevelt delivered his famous State of the Union Address on 6 January 1941. At that time, the USA did not participate in WWII (they declared war on Japan on 8 December 1941). However, in the face of the ongoing world war on the European continent, Roosevelt left behind US isolationist policy and embarked on a new strategy, namely that of helping allies in need.

Pre-task

1. With this speech, US president Roosevelt opened up a new chapter in US foreign policy. Go back to S 28 in chapter 2 and revise your knowledge about the Monroe Doctrine.

Tasks

2. State why Roosevelt thinks that the USA is no longer safe and explain how he wants to protect the USA in the future.
3. Roosevelt names four freedoms: freedom of speech and expression, freedom of worship, freedom from want and freedom from fear. Copy the grid and complete the second column by referring to violations of these rights at that time.

	Why necessary?
1) freedom of speech and expression	
2) freedom of worship	
3) freedom from want	
4) freedom from fear	

Mr. President, Mr. Speaker, members of the 77th Congress:
I address you, the members of this new Congress, at a moment unprecedented in the history of the union. I use the word "unprecedented" because at no previous time has American security been as seriously threatened from without as it is today. [...]
I suppose that every realist knows that the democratic way of life is at this moment being directly assailed* in every part of the world – assailed either by arms or by secret spreading of poisonous propaganda by those who seek to destroy unity and promote discord in nations that are still at peace. During 16 long months this assault* has blotted out* the whole pattern of democratic life in an appalling number of independent nations, great and small. And the assailants are still on the march, threatening other nations, great and small. [...]
There is much loose talk of our immunity from immediate and direct invasion from across the seas. Obviously, as long as the British Navy retains its power, no such danger exists. Even if there were no British Navy, it is not probable that any enemy would be stupid enough to attack us by landing troops in the United States from across thousands of miles of ocean, until it had acquired strategic bases from which to operate.
But we learn much from the lessons of the past years in Europe – particularly the lesson of Norway, whose essential seaports were captured by treachery and surprise built up over a series of years. The first phase of the invasion of this hemisphere would not be the landing of regular troops. The necessary strategic points

to assail to attack

assault attack
to blot out to crush, to wipe out

would be occupied by secret agents and by their dupes* – and great numbers of them are already here and in Latin America. As long as the aggressor nations
25 maintain the offensive they, not we, will choose the time and the place and the method of their attack. [...]

In the future days, which we seek to make secure, we look forward to a world founded upon four essential human freedoms.

The first is freedom of speech and expression – everywhere in the world.

30 The second is freedom of every person to worship God in his own way – everywhere in the world.

The third is freedom from want, which, translated into world terms, means economic understandings which will secure to every nation a healthy peacetime life for its inhabitants – everywhere in the world.

35 The fourth is freedom from fear, which, translated into world terms, means a world-wide reduction of armaments to such a point and in such a thorough fashion that no nation will be in a position to commit an act of physical aggression against any neighbor – anywhere in the world. [...]

Since the beginning of our American history we have been engaged in change, in
40 a perpetual*, peaceful revolution, a revolution which goes on steadily, quietly, adjusting itself to changing conditions without the concentration camp or the quicklime* in the ditch*. The world order which we seek is the cooperation of free countries, working together in a friendly, civilized society.

This nation has placed its destiny in the hands and heads and hearts of its millions
45 of free men and women, and its faith in freedom under the guidance of God. Freedom means the supremacy of human rights everywhere. Our support goes to those who struggle to gain those rights and keep them. Our strength is our unity of purpose.

To that high concept there can be no end save victory.

Franklin D. Roosevelt's "Four freedoms speech" Annual Message to Congress on the State of the Union, June 1st 1941, Franklin D. Roosevelt Presidential Library and Museum, www.fdrlibrary.marist.edu [23.04.15]

dupe sb. who is tricked into believing or doing sth. stupid or illegal

perpetual continuing all the time

quicklime Ätzkalk
ditch trench

S 47 Franklin D. Roosevelt
"A Call for Sacrifice"

While US President Franklin D. Roosevelt delivered this speech on 28 April 1942, the Japanese were still advancing across the Pacific. Roosevelt asks the American population to make sacrifices for the war effort since the US has to face a "total war".

Pre-task 1. Describe the poster. What kind of sacrifice did the woman make and what is the American population expected to do?

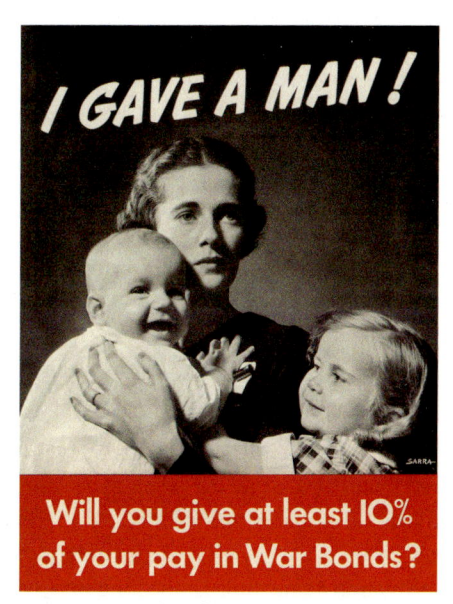

American war bonds poster, 1942

Tasks

2. State what, according to Roosevelt, must be the contribution of the Americans on the home front in order to win the war.
3. Explain how the president describes those people who are not willing to make these sacrifices.
4. Take a critical stand on Roosevelt's appeal by considering the circumstances under which you would be willing to accept it today.

to dislocate to disrupt, to disturb
to dispatch to send

My Fellow Americans, it is nearly five months since we were attacked at Pearl Harbor. For the two years prior to that attack this country had been gearing itself up to a high level of production of munitions. And yet our war efforts had done little to dislocate* the normal lives of most of us. Since then we have dispatched* strong forces of our Army and Navy, several hundred thousands of them, to bases and battlefronts thousands of miles from home. We have stepped up our war production on a scale that is testing our industrial power, our engineering genius, and our economic structure to the utmost. We have had no illusions about the fact that this is a tough job – and a long one. American warships are now in combat in the North and South Atlantic, in the Arctic, in the Mediterranean, in the Indian Ocean, and in the North and South Pacific. American troops have taken stations in South America, Greenland, Iceland, the British Isles, the Near East, the Middle East and the Far East, the continent of Australia, and many islands of the Pacific. American war planes, manned by Americans, are flying in actual combat over all the continents and all the oceans. On the European front the most important development of the past year has been without question the crushing counteroffensive on the part of the great armies of Russia against the powerful German army. [...] Although the treacherous attack on Pearl Harbor was the immediate cause of our entry into the war, that event found the American people spiritually prepared for war on a worldwide scale. We went into this war fighting. We know what we are fighting for, We realize that the war has become what Hitler originally proclaimed it to be – a total war. Not all of us can have the privilege of fighting our enemies in distant parts of the world. Not all of us can have the privilege of working in a munitions factory or a shipyard, or on the farms or in oil fields or mines, producing the weapons or the raw materials that are needed by our armed forces. But there is one front and one battle where everyone in the United States – every man, woman, and child – is in action, and will be privileged to remain in action throughout this war. That front is right here at home, in our daily lives, in our daily tasks. Here at home everyone will have the privilege of making whatever self-denial is necessary, not only to supply our fighting men, but to keep the economic structure of our country fortified and secure during the war and after the war. This will require, of course, the abandonment not only of luxuries but of many other creature comforts*. Every loyal American is aware of his individual responsibility. Whenever I hear anyone saying, "The American people are complacent* – they need to be aroused," I feel like asking him to come to Washington to read the mail that floods into the White House and into all departments of this government. The one question that recurs through all these thousands of letters and messages is, "What more can I do to help my country in winning this war?" To build the factories, to buy the materials, to pay the labor, to provide the transportation, to equip and feed and house the soldiers and sailors and marines, and to do all the thousands of things necessary in a war – all cost a lot of money, more money than has ever been spent by any nation at any time in the long history of the world. We are now spending, solely for war purposes, the sum of about $100 million every day in the week. But, before

creature comfort any small item or detail that makes a person feel comfortable and at home
complacent self-satisfied, contented, smug

this year is over, that almost unbelievable rate of expenditure will be doubled. All of this money has to be spent – and spent quickly – if we are to produce within the time now available the enormous quantities of weapons of war which we need. [...]

All of us are used to spending money for things that we want, things, however, which are not absolutely essential. We will all have to forgo* that kind of spending. Because we must put every dime and every dollar we can possibly spare out of our earnings into war bonds and stamps. Because the demands of the war effort require the rationing of goods of which there is not enough to go around. [...] As I told the Congress yesterday, "sacrifice" is not exactly the proper word with which to describe this program of self-denial. When, at the end of this great struggle, we shall have saved our free way of life, we shall have made no "sacrifice". The price for civilization must be paid in hard work and sorrow and blood. The price is not too high. If you doubt it, ask those millions who live today under the tyranny of Hitlerism. Ask the workers of France and Norway and the Netherlands, whipped to labor by the lash, whether the stabilization of wages is too great a "sacrifice." Ask the farmers of Poland and Denmark and Czechoslovakia and France, looted of their livestock, starving while their own crops are stolen from their land [...]. Ask the businessmen of Europe, whose enterprises have been stolen from their owners, whether the limitation of profits and personal incomes is too great a "sacrifice." Ask the women and children whom Hitler is starving whether the rationing of tires and gasoline and sugar is too great a "sacrifice." We do not have to ask them. They have already given us their agonized answers. This great war effort must be carried through to its victorious conclusion by the indomitable* will and determination of the people as one great whole. [...]

I shall use all of the executive power that I have to carry out the policy laid down. [...] Never in the memory of man has there been a war in which the courage, the endurance, and the loyalty of civilians played so vital a part. Many thousands of civilians all over the world have been and are being killed or maimed* by enemy action. Indeed, it is the fortitude of the common people of Britain under fire which enabled that island to stand and prevented Hitler from winning the war in 1940. The ruins of London and Coventry and other cities are today the proudest monuments to British heroism. [...]

As we here at home contemplate* our own duties, our own responsibilities, let us think and think hard of the example which is being set for us by our fighting men. Our soldiers and sailors are members of well-disciplined units. But they're still and forever individuals, free individuals. They are farmers and workers, businessmen, professional men, artists, clerks. They are the United States of America. That is why they fight. We too are the United States of America. That is why we must work and sacrifice. It is for them. It is for us. It is for victory.

Franklin D. Roosevelt: 'A Call for Sacrifice', 28 April, 1942, in: The Public Papers and Addresses of Franklin D. Roosevelt, 1942 vol., ed. Samuel I. Roseman, New York: Macmillan 1941, pp. 227 f.

to forgo sth. to give up, to do without

indomitable unyielding, steadfast

to maim to cripple, to disable

to contemplate to consider thoroughly; think fully or deeply about

S 48 Joseph Goebbels

Sportpalastrede

German Propaganda Minister Joseph Goebbels gave this speech on 18 February 1943 in the Sportpalast in Berlin, two days after the 6th Army had lost the Battle of Stalingrad. It became especially famous since Goebbels appealed for a "total war" and got the absolute approval of his audience.

Leaflet dropped on Germany by the US Air Force in WWII

„Wollt ihr den totalen Krieg?"

Am 18. Februar 1943, wenige Wochen nach der Katastrophe von Stalingrad, richtete Dr. Goebbels an eine Massenversammlung im Berliner Sportpalast die Frage:

Ein begeistertes „Ja" war die Antwort der Nazi-Versammlung. Heute weiss Deutschland, was „totaler Krieg" bedeutet, besser als es Dr. Goebbels und seine Ja-Schreier im Sportpalast voraussahen. Der totale Krieg, den die Nazis wollten, wird mit immer stärkerer Wucht und Wirkung fortgeführt werden, bis Deutschland bedingungslos kapituliert.

DAS DEUTSCHE VOLK MUSS SELBST WÄHLEN:
ENTWEDER Fortsetzung des totalen Nazi-Kriegs bis zur völligen Vernichtung der deutschen Arbeitskraft und Industrie — ODER:

Pre-task

1. Consider the sub-chapter "The First 'Modern' and 'Total' War" of chapter 2 again. What made WWI "total"?

Tasks

2. How does Goebbels try to convince his audience to agree to a "total war"? Consider the structure of the speech.
3. Compare this speech with Churchill's (S 45). To what extent do both speeches differ from each other?

[...] Ich möchte aber zur Steuer der Wahrheit an euch, meine deutschen Volksgenossen und Volksgenossinnen eine Reihe von Fragen richten, die ihr mir nach bestem Wissen und Gewissen* beantworten müsst. Als mir meine Zuhörer auf meine Forderungen am 30. Januar spontan ihre Zustimmung bekundeten, behauptete die englische Presse am anderen Tag, das sei ein Propagandatheater gewesen und entspreche* in keiner Weise der wahren Stimmung des deutschen Volkes.

Ich habe heute zu dieser Versammlung nun einen Ausschnitt des deutschen Volkes im besten Sinne des Wortes eingeladen. Vor mir sitzen reihenweise deutsche Verwundete von der Ostfront, Bein- und Armamputierte*, mit zerschossenen Gliedern, Kriegsblinde, die mit ihren Rote-Kreuz-Schwestern gekommen sind, Männer in der Blüte ihrer Jahre, die vor sich ihre Krücken* stehen haben. Dazwischen zähle ich an die fünfzig Träger des Eichenlaubes* und des Ritterkreuzes*, eine glänzende Abordnung* unserer kämpfenden Front. Hinter ihnen erhebt sich ein Block von Rüstungsarbeitern und -arbeiterinnen aus den Berliner Panzerwerken. Wieder hinter ihnen sitzen Männer aus der Parteiorganisation, Soldaten aus der kämpfenden Wehrmacht, Ärzte, Wissenschaftler, Künstler, Ingenieure und Architekten, Lehrer, Beamte und Angestellte aus den Ämtern und Büros, eine stolze Vertreterschaft unseres geistigen Lebens in all seinen Schichtungen*, dem das Reich gerade jetzt im Kriege Wunder der Erfindung und des menschlichen Genies verdankt. Über das ganze Rund des Sportpalastes verteilt sehe ich Tausende von deutschen Frauen. Die Jugend ist hier vertreten und das Greisenalter. Kein Stand, kein Beruf und kein Lebensjahr blieb bei der Einladung unberücksichtigt*. Ich kann also mit Fug und Recht* sagen: Was hier vor mir sitzt, ist ein Ausschnitt aus dem ganzen deutschen Volk an der Front und in der Heimat. Stimmt das? Ja oder nein!

---

nach bestem Wissen und Gewissen in all conscience

etw. entsprechen to correspond to sth.

Amputierte/-r amputee

Krücken crutches

Ritterkreuz des Eisernen Kreuzes mit Eichenlaub Knight's Cross with Oak Leaves (highest military award made by Nazi Germany)

Abordnung delegation

Schichtung layer

unberücksichtigt disregarded

mit Fug und Recht justifiably so

Ihr also, meine Zuhörer, repräsentiert in diesem Augenblick die Nation. Und an euch möchte ich zehn Fragen richten, die ihr mir mit dem deutschen Volke vor der ganzen Welt, insbesondere aber vor unseren Feinden, die uns auch an ihrem Rundfunk zuhören, beantworten sollt:

30 Die Engländer behaupten, das deutsche Volk habe den Glauben an den Sieg verloren. Ich frage euch: Glaubt ihr mit dem Führer und mit uns an den endgültigen Sieg des deutschen Volkes? Ich frage euch: Seid ihr entschlossen, mit dem Führer in der Erkämpfung des Sieges durch dick und dünn* und unter Aufnahme auch schwerster persönlicher Belastungen zu folgen?

durch dick und dünn through thick and thin

35 Zweitens: Die Engländer behaupten, das deutsche Volk ist des Kampfes müde. Ich frage euch: Seid ihr bereit, mit dem Führer als Phalanx* der Heimat hinter der kämpfenden Wehrmacht stehend, diesen Kampf mit wilder Entschlossenheit und unbeirrt durch alle Schicksalsfügungen fortzusetzen, bis der Sieg in unseren Händen ist?

Phalanx phalanx

40 Drittens: Die Engländer behaupten, das deutsche Volk hat keine Lust mehr, sich der überhandnehmenden* Kriegsarbeit, die die Regierung von ihm fordert, zu unterziehen. Ich frage euch: Seid ihr und ist das deutsche Volk entschlossen, wenn der Führer es befiehlt, zehn, zwölf und – wenn nötig – vierzehn und sechzehn Stunden täglich zu arbeiten und das Letzte herzugeben für den Sieg?

überhandnehmen to increase alarmingly

45 Viertens: Die Engländer behaupten, das deutsche Volk wehrt sich gegen die totalen Kriegsmaßnahmen der Regierung. Es will nicht den totalen Krieg, sondern die Kapitulation. Ich frage euch: Wollt ihr den totalen Krieg? Wollt ihr ihn, wenn nötig, totaler und radikaler, als wir ihn uns heute überhaupt noch vorstellen können?

Fünftens: Die Engländer behaupten, das deutsche Volk hat sein Vertrauen zum
50 Führer verloren. Ich frage euch: Ist euer Vertrauen zum Führer heute größer, gläubiger und unerschütterlicher* denn je? Ist eure Bereitschaft, ihm auf allen seinen Wegen zu folgen und alles zu tun, was nötig ist, um den Krieg zum siegreichen Ende zu führen, eine absolute und uneingeschränkte?

unerschütterlich steadfast

Ich frage euch als sechstens: Seid ihr bereit, von nun ab eure ganze Kraft einzuset-
55 zen und der Ostfront die Menschen und Waffen zur Verfügung zu stellen, die sie braucht, um dem Bolschewismus den tödlichen Schlag* zu versetzen?

tödlicher Schlag mortal blow
etw. geloben to vow sth.
heiliger Eid holy oath

Ich frage euch siebtens: Gelobt* ihr mit heiligem Eid* der Front, dass die Heimat mit starker Moral hinter ihr steht und ihr alles geben wird, was sie nötig hat, um den Sieg zu erkämpfen?

60 Ich frage euch achtens: Wollt ihr, insbesondere ihr Frauen selbst, dass die Regierung dafür sorgt, dass auch die deutsche Frau ihre ganze Kraft der Kriegsführung zur Verfügung stellt*, und überall da, wo es nur möglich ist, einspringt*, um Männer für die Front frei zu machen und damit ihren Männern an der Front zu helfen?

zur Verfügung stellen to provide
einspringen to help out
etw. billigen to approve of sth.
Drückeberger shirker, quitter
Schieber profiteer
eigensüchtig selfish
sich vergehen an to harm the cause of, to sin against

Ich frage euch neuntens: Billigt* ihr, wenn nötig, die radikalsten Maßnahmen
65 gegen einen kleinen Kreis von Drückebergern* und Schiebern*, die mitten im Kriege Frieden spielen und die Not des Volkes zu eigensüchtigen* Zwecken ausnutzen wollen? Seid ihr damit einverstanden, dass, wer sich am Krieg vergeht*, den Kopf verliert?

Ich frage euch zehntens und zuletzt: Wollt ihr, dass, wie das nationalsozialistische
70 Programm es gebietet*, gerade im Krieg gleiche Rechte und gleiche Pflichten vorherrschen, dass die Heimat die schwersten Belastungen des Krieges solidarisch auf ihre Schultern nimmt und dass sie für hoch und niedrig und arm und reich in gleicher Weise verteilt werden?

gebieten to demand

Ich habe euch gefragt; ihr habt mir eure Antworten gegeben. Ihr seid ein Stück

Volk, durch euren Mund hat sich damit die Stellungnahme des deutschen Volkes manifestiert. Ihr habt unseren Feinden das zugerufen, was sie wissen müssen, damit sie sich keinen Illusionen und falschen Vorstellungen hingeben. [...]

Rede im Berliner Sportpalast, 18. Febr. 1943 v. Joseph Goebbels, in: Helmut Heiber (Eds.): Goebbels Reden 1932–1945. Bindlach: Gondrom Verlag, 1991, pp. 203 ff.

S 49 Gottfried Fabian

A Letter from the Trenches *(Feldpostbrief)*

This letter from 1 April 1945 tells about the experiences of Gottfried Fabian, a soldier at the east front. He writes to his sister and his children.

Pre-task
1. You have already come across a letter from the trenches in chapter 2 (S 55). Recall what you have learned from this letter and anticipate what the following letter might contain.

Tasks
2. Sum up what the soldier experienced at the eastern front.
3. Describe the overall mood of this letter by focusing on the soldier's choice of words.

Gottfried Fabian

sich mit etw. abfinden to resign oneself to sth.

Iwan here: Russian soldiers

wehsinnig crazy, insane

Huscherchen a very shy person

Liebste Hanni und Kinder!
Also muss ich mich wohl damit abfinden*, dass ich alles verloren habe, was ein Mensch nur verlieren kann. Ich danke Dir herzlichst für Deine lieben Zeilen, nur Du bist jetzt die Einzige, an die wir drei Brüder, mit unsern angelegten Sorgen denken können, wenn das Toben der Materialschlachten zur Hölle wird. Du musst mir glauben, liebe Schwester, dass ich von dem Zeitpunkt an, wo es mir zur Gewissheit wird, dass ich Eltern und Familie verloren habe, mein eignes Leben mir soviel wert ist, wie der Dreck an meinen Klamotten.
Am 11.1. fuhr ich morgens um 5 Uhr von Daheim fort, und habe seitdem nichts mehr erfahren.
Am 15.1. war ich bei Neidenburg eingesetzt, dann in Westpreußen, Pommern, Niederschlesien und Niederlausitz bei Guben.
Nach diesen Kämpfen kam ich zum Führer-Begleit-Bataillon, wo ich bis jetzt die Ehre habe, trotz meiner letzten Verwundung, als Elite Soldat zu kämpfen. Heute soll wohl Ostersonntag sein, deshalb will uns der Iwan* nicht in Ruhe lassen; trotzdem es regnet, hat er am Vormittag zweimal angegriffen. Jedesmal blieb er liegen und hat uns dann aus Wut die ganze schöne Stellung zertrommelt, an der wir uns die ganze Nacht geplagt haben. Es wird Dich nicht interessieren, liebe Hanni, warum ich Dir solche Kleinigkeiten schreibe, aber schau, ich muss mich dauernd mit dem in Gedanken beschäftigen, was ich greifen und anfassen kann; denn wenn ich anfange nachzudenken, werde ich ganz gewiß wehsinnig*. Es brennt mir in den Fingern, Dir davon zu schreiben, liebe Schwester, wie es wohl meinem kleinen Huscherchen* ergangen ist, oder was wohl unsere Mutter macht, die ihr ganzes Leben nichts weiter als Arbeit und Sorge gekannt hat und jetzt vielleicht als Dank dafür irgendwo unter entsetzlichsten Umständen gestorben ist. Oder wie wird Vater sich umgeguckt haben, der den Krieg in dieser Form sich nicht einmal in seinen Träumen zur Darstellung billigen konnte, und der immer meinte, wir übertreiben. Hoffentlich ist es Ihm nicht schwer gefallen, als Ihn der russische Panzer überrollte. Ja, liebe Hanni, solche Bilder stürmen auf mich ein

30 und ich muss dann ganz schnell etwas tun, sonst springe ich aus dem Deckungsloch und fange etwas sehr Unüberlegtes an. Die Zentral-Auskunftsstelle für Rückgesuchte aus dem Osten denkt wohl gar nicht daran, mir sowohl wie Gustav etwas über Ostpreußen zu berichten.
Leider musste auch Jutta mit den Kleinen bis auf die letzte Minute dableiben.
35 Mein einziger Trost bist Du noch, liebe Hanni, weil ich Dir schreiben kann und somit doch mich ab und zu auf Post zu hoffen habe, was in den letzten 3 Monaten nicht der Fall war. Liebe Schwester, Deine Adresse ist jetzt bei meiner Einheit eingetragen und somit erhälst Du die Nachricht, wenn es soweit ist, dass mir nichts mehr weh tut. Ich glaube, es wird mir nicht schwer fallen. Verzeih bitte,
40 dass ich so schlecht geschrieben habe, aber ich besitze leider keinen Schreibtisch. Jetzt bleibt alle recht gesund. Denkt mal an mich und lasst Euch recht herzlich grüßen von
Eurem Fritz

Gottfried Fabian an seine Schwester und Kinder am 1.4.1945; Museumsstiftung Post und Telekommunikation 3.2002.0299

S 50 Landing in Europe

This source is an interview with Clay Christensen, a soldier in the U.S. army, who landed on the beaches of France shortly after D-Day. He talks about the crossing of the Atlantic and landing in France and how he experienced the landing in Europe.

Pre-task 1. Make yourself familiar with the geographical location of Operation Overlord by looking at the map provided below. Take turns with a partner and describe what you can see on the map.

Map of Operation Overlord, 6 June 1944

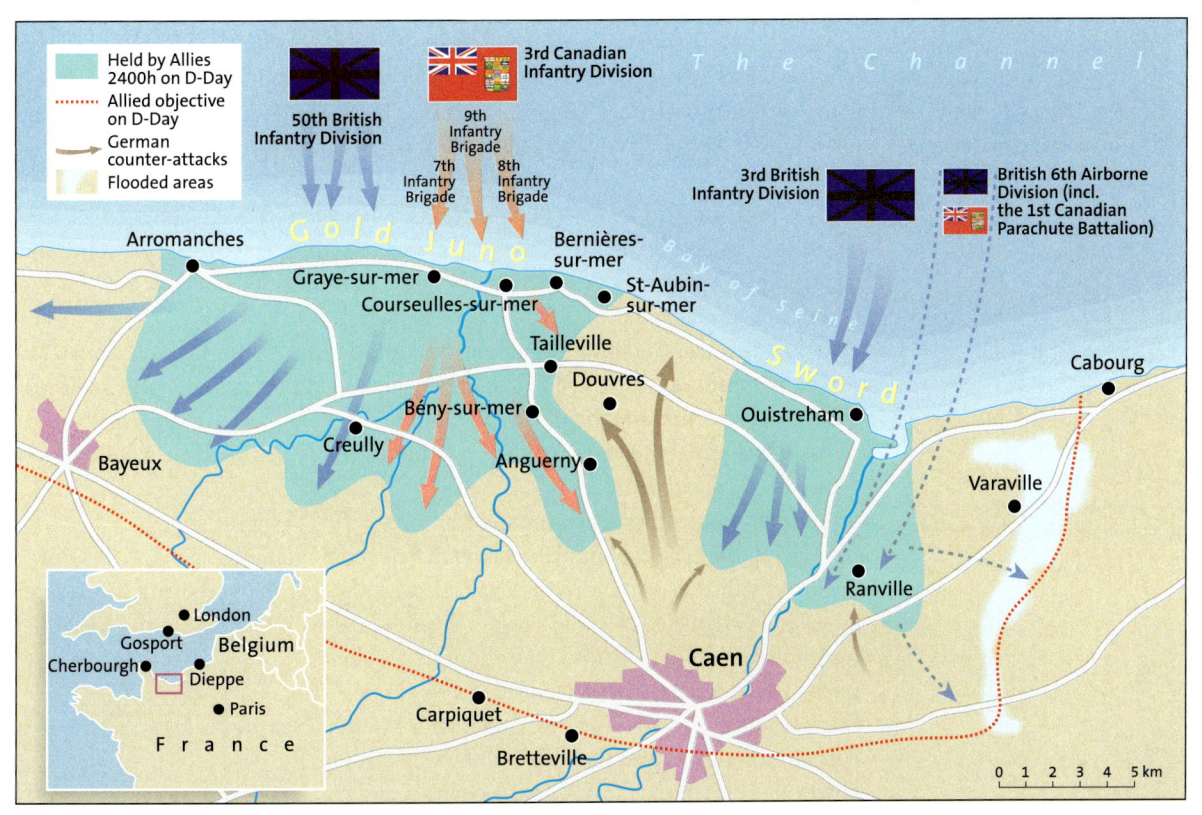

Tasks

2. Describe what Christensen saw when he landed on the beach in Normandy.
3. Explain what Christensen means when he says that his division was "greeted" by the Germans when arriving at the front line.
4. Taking both S 49 and S 50 into consideration, assess the importance of the of both source types, i. e. letters from the trenches and eyewitness accounts/oral history.

I[nterviewer]: Do you remember the crossing? (From the U.S. To Europe)
Chr[istensen]: I do, I remember in the Gulf Stream two to three days out from the United States, it was hot after the Gulf Stream, we stripped down to just skivvies* for whatever you were doing. Not any work cause they had permanent people on the ship for the mess hall and I didn't get seasick myself, so I had the luxury and with a little bit of rank, I managed to stay up on the deck or hanging in the doorway most of the way over.
I: How long did crossing take?
Chr: Took about 10 days and over near France we were supposed to land in Cherbourg, France, but we got word that the harbor was so full of landing craft that had been sunk, had to go backtrack and drop anchor under the White Cliffs of Dover and you can see those cliffs for many miles away. So we dropped anchor there until about 4:00 in the afternoon and then we pulled up anchor and went into the port of Southhampton in England and then we were there for several weeks, about 50 miles north of Southhampton in several quonset huts.
I: This was after D-Day at this time?
Chr: That was after D-Day and then after two weeks of running around loose in England, we boarded ships, various ships and I crossed with my company commander. A small craft, I guess is land craft infantry, a small ship about 30–40 feet long would hold two vehicles and 15–20 men and it had a drop front on it and going across the channel at night. Oh I had been in the hospital, caught double pneumonia* because we went on a forced march one morning.
I: In England?
Chr: In England and about 9:00, the sun came out and then it clouded over and began to rain and on the way back in, it was snowing. It was sort of weird, but typical English weather.
I: You caught a bad cold?
Chr: Caught a bad cold that turned into pneumonia and I went to the hospital. My company commander came down to the hospital a couple days later and told me it was payday and he brought all my gear and told me they were getting ready to go across the channel the next day and I told him, don't leave me. If he'd help me get dressed, I'd go with him.
I: Who was your company commander?
Chr: His name was Captain A.J. Harverstick, a most intelligent person, just down to earth, with tons of common sense. During the war, he saved my life several times and I managed to save his several times. He knew everything the Germans were going to do to us before they attempted to do it.
I: Had you served with him stateside or you just …
Chr: He was our company commander after I went back to Texas to radio school in Fort Monmouth, stayed with him all the way through the war.
I: Now this craft took you across the channel and you ended up where?

skivvies underwear

pneumonia [njuːˈməʊniə] *Lungenentzündung*

Chr: It did and it seems that we, our little craft and several others landed at either Utah Beach or Cold Beach, it was sort of deserted at the time. Going across, it was a moonlit night with scattered clouds and it made the light from the moon shimmer on the waters and then it would cloud over and then it would come out again and I'm looking off to my left and I see, boy that sure is bright water out there shimmering, it turned out it was a torpedo, German submarine had already zeroed in on us or something that was behind us and I screamed at the Navy man who was running the ship. I told him to turn hard left and let's head into that oncoming torpedo and by that time, I could tell that there were two torpedoes and one was probably 20' behind and 6–8' off to the left and the first torpedo missed us no more than that. Pretty scary.

I: Did you see it go by?

Chr: I watched both of them go by.

I: At night in the dark?

Chr: At night in that moonlit night. So we went on over to France.

I: When you say this craft that you were in, which is like a landing craft.

Chr: A small landing craft.

I: About 30 men.

Chr: Well I don't believe we had more than a dozen men with us but it held two vehicles and a jeep and a weapons carrier and I was driving the weapons carrier.

I: Where any other men going over at the same time in other crafts?

Chr: Yeah, our whole company was on various crafts and all of us went over as a small group and that group was a part of 30 or 40 or 50 vehicles out there. You could see different crafts and ships scattered all over the ocean that night.

I: And you landed at the beaches of Normandy?

Chr: Dropped anchor on the beach and my captain says, "Sergeant, don't you lose my damn vehicle in the water here" so when I hit the water, I headed in low range in second gear and wide open.

I: A jeep?

Chr: I had the weapons carrier.

I: Who rode in it, who was supposed to ride in it?

Chr: I was in it by myself. All the men who were in the boat with us, they all waded through the waters.

I: This was at night, in the dead of the night?

Chr: Well we crossed the channel, took us all night long to cross. We were actually landing at daybreak.

I: Were you able to see any signs of the D-Day invasion?

Chr: Not really because the beaches you know were swept clean with the tides. Then as soon as I hit the beach, my captain motioned for me to follow him and we immediately started moving on out of there and I saw the physical evidence of the battles being fought as we went north. We went on up to a little town called Albell, Belgium.

I: You traveled all the way from the French coast to Belgium in one day after you landed?

Chr: We stopped somewhere in bivouac the first night, but I don't remember where it was. It was close to this little place called Albell, Belgium.

I: No sign of the enemy at this time?

Chr: No, they were further off shore. Albell, Belgium was probably 15 miles from the German border or from the German Siegfried line. Albell was maybe 10 miles from the German border.

I: What happened after you got there?
Chr: Well we went into combat mode and we just dug in there. The Germans greeted us.
I: This was at the front lines then?
Chr: This was at the front lines.
I: Did you relieve any other unit or did you just arrive...
Chr: We did, but I don't really know who we relieved, but the Germans had big loudspeakers up there and they welcomed the 99th division. We were sort of a sleeping incognito outfit to the Germans supposedly, but they knew all about us. On the loudspeakers, they gave us our complete history from the day that the unit was activated until we got to the German lines and they quit speaking to us over the loudspeakers and for the next few weeks, if they would fire a rifle shot or an artillery shell, we would answer in kind and if we fired one artillery piece or weapon, they would answer back in kind.

Excerpts from Clayton A. Christensen Oral History, June 26, 2000. http://randall3.uncw.edu/ascod/index.php?p=digitallibrary/digitalcontent&id=738&q=Clayton+A.+Christensen. Oral History Collection, William Madison Randall Library, the University of North Carolina Wilmington, Wilmington, North Carolina

S 51 Victor Klemperer

Tagebucheintrag

This diary entry by Victor Klemperer (1881–1960) dates back to 31 March 1933. Klemperer, a writer and philologist, was born into a Jewish family but converted to Protestantism in 1912 and was married to an "Aryan" woman, which saved him from being persecuted. However, he lost his job as professor at the Technical University of Dresden when the *Gesetz zur Wiederherstellung des Berufsbeamtentums* (Law for the Restoration of the Professional Civil Service) was passed in 1933.

SA members hang up boycott posters on the windows of Jewish shops on 1 April 1933.

Pre-task

1. The photograph on page 474 was taken one day after Klemperer wrote his diary entry. Describe what you see and anticipate the mood of Klemperer's diary entry.

Tasks

2. Compare your ideas from the pre-task concerning the mood evoked in the source with what you have now read.
3. Describe what Klemperer observed on 31 March.

31. März, Freitagabend
Immer trostloser*. Morgen beginnt der Boykott. Gelbe Plakate, Wachen. Zwang, christlichen Angestellten zwei Monatsgehälter zu zahlen, jüdische zu entlassen. Auf den erschütternden Brief der Juden an den Reichspräsidenten und die Regie-
5 rung keine Antwort. [...] Niemand wagt sich vor. Die Dresdener Studentenschaft hat heute Erklärung: geschlossen hinter ... und es ist gegen die Ehre deutscher Studenten, mit Juden in Berührung zu kommen. Der Zutritt zum Studentenhaus ist ihnen verboten. Mit wieviel jüdischem Geld wurde vor wenigen Jahren dies Studentenhaus gebaut!
10 In München sind jüdische Dozenten* bereits am Betreten der Universität verhindert worden.
Der Aufruf und Befehl des Boykottkomitees ordnet an: „Religion ist gleichgültig", es kommt nur auf die Rasse an. Wenn bei Geschäftsinhabern der Mann Jude, die Frau Christin ist oder umgekehrt: so gilt das Geschäft als jüdisch. –
15 Gestern Abend bei Gusti Wieghardt. Gedrückteste Stimmung*. In der Nacht gegen drei – Eva schlaflos – riet mir Eva, heute die Wohnung zu kündigen, um eventuell einen Teil davon wieder zu mieten. Ich habe heute gekündigt. Die Zukunft ist ganz ungewiss. [...]
Am Dienstag im neuen „Universum"-Kino in der Prager Straße. Neben mir ein
20 Reichswehrsoldat, ein Knabe noch, und sein wenig sympathisches Mädchen. Es war am Abend vor der Boykottankündigung. Gespräch, als eine Alsbergreklame lief. Er: „Eigentlich sollte man nicht beim Juden kaufen." Sie: „Es ist aber so furchtbar billig." Er: „Dann ist es schlecht und hält nicht." Sie, überlegend, ganz sachlich, ohne alles Pathos: „Nein, wirklich, es ist ganz genauso gut und haltbar,
25 wirklich ganz genauso wie in christlichen Geschäften – und so viel billiger." Er: schweigt. – Als Hitler, Hindenburg etc. erschienen, klatschte er begeistert. Nachher bei dem gänzlich amerikanisch jazzbandischen, stellenweise deutlich jüdelnden Film klatschte er noch begeisterter.
Es wurden die Ereignisse des 21. März vorgeführt, Stücke aus Reden gesprochen.
30 Hindenburgs Proklamation mühselig*, mit Atemnot, die Stimme eines uralten Mannes, der physisch fast zu Ende ist. Hitler pastoral deklamierend*. Goebbels sieht ungemein jüdisch aus [...]. Man sah Fackelzug und allerlei marschierendes, erwachendes Deutschland. Auch Danzig mit Hakenkreuzflagge. [...]

Victor Klemperer: Ich will Zeugnis ablegen bis zum letzen. Tagebücher 1933–1941. Berlin: Aufbau-Verlag, 1995, pp. 16–17

trostlos desolate

Dozent lecturer

gedrückte Stimmung gloom

mühselig laborious
deklamieren to declaim

S 52a Reichsbürgergesetz

The following two sources are pieces of legislation known as the so-called Nuremberg Laws (*Nürnberger Gesetze*) from 15 September 1935.

Pre-task
1. Scan S 5a again for the basic civil rights granted in the Weimar Constitution.

Tasks
2. State which rights are taken away from the German Jews and what effect this will have on the Jewish fellow citizens.
3. Take S 52b into account as well and examine the inevitable consequences of this legislation for the coexistence of the Jewish and the non-Jewish population.

[...]

§ 1

(1) Staatsangehöriger ist, wer dem Schutzverband* des Deutschen Reiches angehört und ihm dafür besonders verpflichtet* ist.
(2) Die Staatsangehörigkeit wird nach den Vorschriften des Reichs- und Staatsangehörigkeitsgesetzes erworben.

§ 2

(1) Reichsbürger ist nur der Staatsangehörige deutschen oder artverwandten Blutes*, der durch sein Verhalten beweist, dass er gewillt und geeignet ist, in Treue dem deutschen Volk und Reich zu dienen.
(2) Das Reichsbürgerrecht wird durch Verleihung des Reichsbürgerbriefes* erworben.
(3) Der Reichsbürger ist der alleinige Träger der vollen politischen Rechte nach Maßgabe der Gesetze*.

[...]

Nürnberg, den 15. September 1935,
am Reichsparteitag der Freiheit.
Der Führer und Reichskanzler
Adolf Hitler
Der Reichsminister des Innern
Frick

Reichsgesetzblatt, 1935, Nr. 100, S. 1146

Schutzverband protective union
jdm. verpflichtet sein to be beholden to, to be committed to

artverwandtes Blut kindred blood
Reichsbürgerbrief Reich citizenship papers
nach Maßgabe der Gesetze in accordance with the provisions of the law

S 52b Gesetz zum Schutze des deutschen Blutes und der deutschen Ehre

Durchdrungen von der Erkenntnis, dass die Reinheit des deutschen Blutes die Voraussetzung für den Fortbestand* des deutschen Volkes ist, und beseelt* von dem unbeugsamen* Willen, die deutsche Nation für alle Zukunft zu sichern, hat der Reichstag einstimmig das folgende Gesetz beschlossen, das hiermit verkündet wird.

§ 1

(1) Eheschließungen zwischen Juden und Staatsangehörigen deutschen oder artverwandten Blutes sind verboten. Trotzdem geschlossene Ehen sind nichtig*, auch wenn sie zur Umgehung dieses Gesetzes im Auslande geschlossen sind. [...]

Fortbestand survival
beseelt inspired
unbeugsam unyielding, unrelenting, unfaltering

nichtig null and void

§ 2
Außerehelicher Verkehr* zwischen Juden und Staatsangehörigen deutschen oder artverwandten Blutes ist verboten.

§ 3
Juden dürfen weibliche Staatsangehörige deutschen oder artverwandten Blutes unter 45 Jahren nicht in ihrem Haushalt beschäftigen.

§ 4
(1) Juden ist das Hissen* der Reichs- und Nationalflagge und das Zeigen der Reichsfarben verboten.
(2) Dagegen ist ihnen das Zeigen der jüdischen Farben gestattet. [...]

§ 5
(1) Wer dem Verbot des § 1 zuwiderhandelt, wird mit Zuchthaus bestraft.
(2) Der Mann, der dem Verbot des § 2 zuwiderhandelt, wird mit Gefängnis oder mit Zuchthaus bestraft.
(3) Wer den Bestimmungen der § 3 oder § 4 zuwiderhandelt, wird mit Gefängnis bis zu einem Jahr und mit Geldstrafe oder mit einer dieser Strafen bestraft. [...]

§ 7
Das Gesetz tritt am Tage nach der Verkündung, § 3 jedoch erst am 1. Januar 1936 in Kraft.
Nürnberg, den 15. September 1935,
am Reichsparteitag der Freiheit.
Der Führer und Reichskanzler
Adolf Hitler
Der Reichsminister des Inneren
Frick
Der Reichsminister der Justiz
Dr. Gürtner
Der Stellvertreter des Führers
R. Heß
Reichsminister ohne Geschäftsbereich

Reichsgesetzblatt, 1935, Nr. 100, S. 1146 f.

außerehelicher Verkehr adultery

hissen to raise a flag, to hoist a flag

S 53 Samuel Honaker

Letter to Hugh R. Wilson, American Embassy, Berlin

On 12 November 1938, three days after the November Pogrom, the American Consul Samuel Honaker reports the events of the *Reichskristallnacht* to the American ambassador to Berlin, Hugh R. Wilson.

Pre-task 1. Describe the photographs provided to get an impression of what happened on 9/10 November 1938.

The looted and wrecked Jewish Community House in Kassel, 10 November 1938

Badly damaged synagogue in Munich, 10 November 1938

Shattered shop windows in Berlin, 10 November 1938

Jews in Regensburg are led to the train station, 10 November 1938

Tasks

2. State how Honaker describes the situation of the Jews.
3. What does Honaker's description of the burning of the synagogues and devastation of Jewish shops tell you about who was responsible for the deeds? Discuss.

American Consulate
Stuttgart, Germany, November 12, 1938
No. 307
Subject: Anti-Semitic Persecution in the Stuttgart Consular District
The Honorable Hugh R. Wilson, American Ambassador, Berlin

[...] Sir:
I have the honor to report that the Jews of Southwest Germany have suffered vicissitudes* during the last three days which would seem unreal to one living in an enlightened country during the twentieth century if one had not actually been a witness of their dreadful experiences, or if one had not had them corroborated* by more than one person of undoubted integrity. To the anguish of mind* to which the Jews of this consular district have been subjected for some time, and which suddenly became accentuated on the morning and afternoon of the tenth of November, were added the horror of midnight arrests, of hurried departures in a half-dressed state from their homes in the company of police officers, of the wailing* of wives and children suddenly left behind, of imprisonment in crowded cells, and the panic of fellow prisoners.
These wholesale arrests were the culmination of a day of suffering on the part of the Jews. The desecration* and burning of synagogues started before daylight and should have proved a warning signal of what was to come during the course of the next few hours. At 10:30 A.M. about twenty-five leaders of the Jewish community were arrested by a joint squad of policemen and plain clothes men. The arrested persons ranged from thirty-five to sixty-five years of age and were taken from their community officer (*Israelitischer Oberrat*) to the police station in two motor vehicles. As the victims passed from the building to the motor cars bystanders cursed and shouted at them.
Other arrests took place in various parts of Stuttgart. While this city was the scene of many anti-Semitic demonstrations during the course of the day, similar events were taking place all over Württemberg and Baden. Jews were attacked here and there. So great had become the panic of the Jewish people in the meantime that, when the consulate opened after Armistice Day, Jews from all sections of Germany thronged* into the office until it was overflowing with humanity, begging for an immediate visa or some kind of letter in regard to immigration which might influence the police not to arrest or molest* them. Women over sixty years of age pleaded on behalf of husbands imprisoned in some unknown place. American mothers of German sons invoked the sympathy of the Consulate. Jewish fathers and mothers with children in their arms were afraid to return to their homes without some document denoting their intention to immigrate at an early date. Men in whose homes old, rusty revolvers had been found during the last few days cried aloud that they did not dare ever again to return to their places of residence or business. In fact, it was a mass of seething*, panic-stricken humanity.
Burning of Synagogues.
Early on the morning of November 10th practically every synagogue – at least twelve in number – in Württemberg, Baden and Hohenzollern was set on fire by well-disciplined and apparently well-equipped young men in civilian clothes. The procedure was practically the same in all cities of this district, namely, Stuttgart, Karlsruhe, Freiburg, Heidelberg, Heilbronn, et cetera. The doors of the synagogues were forced open. Certain sections of the building and furnishings were

vicissitudes changing conditions of fortune

to corroborate to confirm

anguish of mind mental suffering, distress

to wail to cry loudly, to sob, to weep

desecration violation, abuse

to throng to push

to molest to abuse, maltreat

to seethe to be very angry

to confine to limit, to restrict

heap pile

to ransack to turn inside out, to loot, to plunder

drenched with petrol and set on fire. Bibles, prayer books, and other sacred things were thrown into the flames. Then the local fire brigades were notified. In Stuttgart, the city officials ordered the fire brigade to save the archives and other written material having a bearing on vital statistics. Otherwise, the fire brigades confined* their activities to preventing the flames from spreading. In a few hours the synagogues were, in general, heaps* of smoking ruins.

Devastation of Jewish Shops.

Practically all the Jewish shops in the Stuttgart consular district are reported to have been attacked, ransacked*, and devastated. These actions were carried out by young men and half-grown boys. It was easy to recognize under the civilian clothes of the former trained and disciplined S.A. or S.S. men, while in the case of the latter the Hitler Youth uniform was evident in some instances. The young men set about their task in most cases quietly and efficiently. They first smashed windows, destroyed furnishings, and then began to throw merchandise into the street. Throughout these actions the police looked on, either smilingly or unconcernedly. Most of the Jewish shops in Stuttgart are situated in the main business section of the city. On the Königsstrasse, the principal business street, no looting was observed, but in the side streets looting was noticed in a number of cases. In front of one shop people were seen trying on shoes which had been thrown into the street. Before the Café Heimann was demolished, people helped themselves to cake and so forth. [...]

American Consul Samuel Honaker's description of Anti-Semitic persecution and *Kristallnacht* and its aftereffects in the Stuttgart region (November 12 and November 15, 1938), State Central Decimal File (CDF) 862.4015/2002, Records of the Department of State in the National Archives, Record Group 59, General Records of the Department of State; in: John Mendelsohn (ed.), The Holocaust, Vol. 3, New York: Garland, 1982, pp. 176–89

S 54 Wannsee Protokoll

On 20 January 1942, leading representatives of the SS, the NSDAP and the government met in Berlin Wannsee in order to decide on the "Final Solution to the Jewish Question".

Pre-task **1.** The Wannsee Minutes constitute a very prominent example of the use of euphemisms. According to the Macmillan Dictionary, a euphemism is "a word or expression that people use when they want to talk about something unpleasant or embarrassing without mentioning the thing itself"[1]. Consider the following expressions from the source and make an educated guess what their actual meaning might be. Copy the table and complete it. Compare your results with a partner.

expression used by the Nazis	actual meaning
Zurückdrängung	
Beschleunigung der Auswanderung	
Evakuierung	
Endlösung der Judenfrage	
entsprechende Leitung	

in geeigneter Weise zum Arbeitseinsatz kommen	
durch natürliche Verminderung ausfallen	
Restbestand wird [...] entsprechend behandelt werden müssen	

---

[1] "Euphemism." Macmillan Dictionary. Macmillon Publishers 2015, www.macmillandictionary.com/dictionary/british/euphemism

Tasks

2. After having read the source, make corrections in your table if necessary.
3. Explain the functions of the euphemisms.
4. Against the backdrop of the Wannsee Minutes, discuss when the "final solution" was actually decided on.

[...]
II. Chef der Sicherheitspolizei und des SD, SS-Obergruppenführer *Heydrich*, teilte eingangs seine Bestellung* zum Beauftragten für die Vorbereitung der Endlösung der europäischen Judenfrage durch den Reichsmarschall mit und wies darauf hin, dass zu dieser Besprechung geladen wurde, um Klarheit in grundsätzlichen Fragen zu schaffen. [...]
Der Chef der Sicherheitspolizei und des SD gab sodann einen kurzen Rückblick über den bisher geführten Kampf gegen diesen Gegner. Die wesentlichsten Momente bilden
a) die Zurückdrängung* der Juden aus den einzelnen Lebensgebieten des deutschen Volkes,
b) die Zurückdrängung der Juden aus dem Lebensraum des deutschen Volkes.
Im Vollzug dieser Bestrebungen wurde als einzige vorläufige Lösungsmöglichkeit die Beschleunigung der Auswanderung der Juden aus dem Reichsgebiet verstärkt und planmäßig in Angriff genommen. [...]
III. Anstelle der Auswanderung ist nunmehr als weitere Lösungsmöglichkeit nach entsprechender vorheriger Genehmigung durch den Führer die Evakuierung der Juden nach dem Osten getreten.
Diese Aktionen sind jedoch lediglich als Ausweichmöglichkeiten* anzusprechen, doch werden hier bereits jene praktischen Erfahrungen gesammelt, die im Hinblick auf die kommende Endlösung der Judenfrage von wichtiger Bedeutung sind. Im Zuge dieser Endlösung der europäischen Judenfrage kommen rund 11 Millionen Juden in Betracht* [...]
Unter entsprechender Leitung sollen im Zuge der Endlösung die Juden in geeigneter Weise im Osten zum Arbeitseinsatz kommen*. In großen Arbeitskolonnen, unter Trennung der Geschlechter, werden die arbeitsfähigen Juden straßenbauend in diese Gebiete geführt, wobei zweifellos ein Großteil durch natürliche Verminderung* ausfallen wird.
Der [...] verbleibende Restbestand* wird, da es sich bei diesem zweifellos um den widerstandsfähigsten* Teil handelt, entsprechend behandelt werden müssen, da dieser, eine natürliche Auslese* darstellend, bei Freilassung als Keimzelle* eines neuen jüdischen Aufbaus* anzusprechen ist. [...]

„Das Wannsee-Protokoll", 20.1.1942, Politisches Archiv des Auswärtigen Amtes, Inland IIg 177 (T120/1512/372024-28), in: Léon Poliakov/Joseph Wulf: Das Dritte Reich und die Juden, Frankfurt/M., Berlin: Ullstein 1983, pp. 116–126

Bestellung appointment

Zurückdrängung repression, expulsion

Ausweichmöglichkeit alternative possibility, fallback procedure, provisional action

in Betracht kommen to come into consideration

zum Arbeitseinsatz kommen to be allocated for labour

durch natürliche Verminderung by natural causes

Restbestand remnant, remainder

widerstandsfähig tough, resilient

natürliche Auslese natural selection

Keimzelle nucleus, germ cell

jüdischer Aufbau Jewish reconstruction

tional elites and within the wider reaches of the population*, anti-Jewish attitudes were more in the realm of tacit acquiescence* or varying degrees of compliance*. Despite most of the German population's full awareness, well before the war, of the increasingly harsh measures taken against the Jews, there were but minor areas of dissent (and these were almost entirely for economic and specifically religious-ideological reasons). It seems, however, that the majority of Germans, although undoubtedly influenced by various forms of traditional anti-Semitism and easily accepting the segregation of the Jews, shied away from widespread violence against them, urging neither their expulsion from the Reich nor their physical annihilation. After the attack on the Soviet Union, when total extermination had been decided upon, the hundreds of thousands of "ordinary Germans" (as distinct from the highly motivated SS units, among others) who actively participated in the killings acted no differently from the equally numerous and "ordinary" Austrians, Rumanians, Ukrainians, Balts, and other Europeans who became the most willing operatives* of the murder machinery functioning in their midst.

Nonetheless, whether they were conscious of it or not, the German and Austrian killers had been indoctrinated by the regime's relentless anti-Jewish propaganda, which penetrated every crevice of society and whose slogans they at least partially internalized, mainly in the context of the war in the East.

By underscoring that Hitler and his ideology had a decisive impact on the course of the regime, I do not mean in any way to imply that Auschwitz was a preordained* result of Hitler's accession to power. The anti-Jewish policies of the thirties must be understood in their context, and even Hitler's murderous rage and his scanning of the political horizon for the most extreme options do not suggest the existence of any plans for total extermination in the years prior to* the German invasion of the Soviet Union. But at the same time, no historian can forget the end of the road. [...] The crimes committed by the Nazi regime were neither a mere outcome of some haphazard*, involuntary, imperceptible*, and chaotic onrush of unrelated events nor a predetermined enactment of a demonic script; [...]. General ideological objectives and tactical policy decisions enhanced one another and always remained open to more radical moves as circumstances changed.

Saul Friedländer: Nazi Germany and the Jews. Volume I: The Years of Persecution 1933–1939, London 1997, pp. 3–5

---

wider reaches of the population *weitere Kreise der Bevölkerung*
tacit acquiescence *stillschweigende Einwilligung*
compliance consent

operative *Mitarbeiter, Handlanger*

preordained predetermined

prior to sth. before sth.

haphazard without plan or order
imperceptible that cannot be noticed or felt

| Overview | Sources | Paper practice | Vocabulary | National Socialism | 487 |

Paper Practice: Analysing a Cartoon

S 57 David Low

"Europe Can Look Forward to a Christmas of Peace"

This cartoon by the British cartoonist David Low was published on 10 October 1938.

Model solution
→ p. 605

Tasks
1. Analyse the source.
2. Incorporate the source into the historical context of Nazi foreign policy and explain in detail the elements of the cartoon.
3. Take a critical stand on the cartoonist's assessment of the situation in 1938 and of the cartoon as now seen from a present-day perspective.

"EUROPE CAN LOOK FORWARD TO A CHRISTMAS OF PEACE" – (HITLER)

Embedded text:
Deutschland über alles
Ex French-British Family
Austria – Czechoslovakia – Poland – Hungary – Jugoslavia – Rumania – Bulgaria – Greece – Turkey

Language support

Bettgestell bed-head

to abandon sb.; abandonment (n.) here: to stop supporting sb.
anti-Semitic (adj.); anti-Semitism (n.) [ˌænti'seməˌtɪz(ə)m] *antisemitisch (Adj.); Antisemitismus (N.)* (hatred directed against Jews)
to appease sb.; appeasement (n.) *jdn. beschwichtigen; Beschwichtigung (N.)*
(re)armament *hier: (Wieder-)Aufrüstung*
arson; arsonist *Brandstiftung; Brandstifter/in*
to ban sth.; ban (on sth.) (n.) to say officially that people must not do, sell, or use sth.
to besiege [bɪ'siːdʒ] **(syn.: to lay siege to); siege (n.)** [siːdʒ] *belagern; Belagerung*
to bring sb. to justice to bring sb. before a court in order to find out whether they are guilty of a crime or not
burden *Bürde/Last*
to close in on sth./sb. *etw./jdn. einkesseln*
(to form/make) coalitions *Koalitionen bilden*
(to make) concessions *Zugeständnisse (machen)*
to collaborate; collaborationist (adj.); collaborator (n.); collaboration (n.) here: to work secretly to help an enemy or opponent
to collapse; collapse (n.) here: to fail or stop existing
coming to terms with the past *Vergangenheitsbewältigung*
concept of the enemy *Feindbild*
to consolidate; consolidation (n.) to make the power, position, or achievements you already have stronger or more effective so that they are likely to continue
to conspire against sth./sb.; conspiracy (n.) [kən'spɪrəsi] *sich gegen etw./jdn. verschwören; Verschwörung*
currency *Währung*
debt [det] an amount of money that you owe
to deceive sb. [dɪ'siːv]; **deceit (n.)** to trick sb. by behaving in a dishonest way
to decry to say publicly that you do not approve of sb./sth.
to deport sb.; deportation (n.) to send sb. out of a country
to deprive sb. of sth.; deprivation (n.) to take sth. away from sb./to deny sb. sth.
détente ['deɪtɒnt] **(syn.: rapprochement)** a relaxation of tensions between countries
to devalue; devaluation (n.) to officially reduce the value of a country's money; to treat sb. as if they were not important
to deviate from sth. ['diːvieɪt]; **deviation (n.)** to do sth. in a different way from what is expected or agreed

dictatorship *Diktatur*
to discriminate against sb.; discrimination (n.) *jdn. diskriminieren; Diskriminierung*
eligible (to vote); eligibility (n.) *wahlberechtigt; Wahlberechtigung*
electorate *Wählerschaft*
to execute sb.; executioner (n.); execution (n.) *jdn. hinrichten; Henker/Scharfrichter; Hinrichtung*
to expel; expulsion (n.) here: to force sb. to leave a place or country
to exterminate; extermination (n.) here: to kill a person or a group of people
five-percent threshold *Fünf-Prozent-Hürde*
to fortify; fortification (n.) to protect a place; to make sth. stronger
genocide ['dʒenəsaɪd] **(of/against)** *Völkermord/Genozid*
grassroots democracy *Basisdemokratie*
to humiliate sb.; humiliating (adj.); humiliation (n.) *jdn. demütigen; demütigend; Demütigung*
ideological warfare *ideologische Kriegsführung*
ignominious [ˌɪgnə'mɪniəs] **(adj.)** *schändlich/schmachvoll*
to impose sth. on sb.; imposition (n.) to introduce sth. such as a new law or new system, and force people to accept it
to indoctrinate; indoctrination (n.) to teach sb. a set of beliefs so thoroughly that they do not accept any other ideas
international law *Völkerrecht*
to intimidate; intimidation (n.) to deliberately make sb. feel frightened, especially so that they will do what you want
law of the jungle *Recht des Stärkeren*
to loot to pillage/to plunder
majority vote (syn.: first-past-the-post system) *Mehrheitswahlrecht*
to mutiny; mutiny (n.) *meutern; Meuterei/Aufstand*
to naturalize sb.; naturalization (n.) to allow sb. who was not born in a particular country to become an official citizen of that country
to obliterate; obliteration (n.) to destroy sth. completely
to occupy; occupant (n.); occupation (n.) *besetzen; Besetzer/in; Besetzung*
one-party state *Einparteienstaat*
plebiscite ['plebɪsaɪt] **(syn.: referendum, pl.: referenda)** *Volksabstimmung/Plebiszit*
(handing over of/seizure of/sneaking into/taking over of) power *Macht (-übertragung/-ergreifung/-erschleichung/-übernahme)*

to preserve sth.; preservation (n.) to keep sth. up, to maintain sth.
prisoner of war (POW) *Kriegsgefangener*
proportional representation *Verhältniswahlrecht*
putsch [pʊtʃ] an attempt to get rid of a government by using force, organized and carried out by military leaders or politicians
racist (adj., n.); racism (n.) *rassistisch, Rassist/in; Rassismus*
to reconcile with sb. ['rekənsaɪl] **sth.; reconciliation (n.)** ['rekənsɪ'eɪʃ(ə)n] *sich mit jdm./etw. versöhnen; Versöhnung*
to resist; resistance (n.) *Widerstand leisten; Widerstand*
to resort to sth. to do sth. extreme or unpleasant to solve a problem
to retaliate; retaliation (n.) (syn.: retribution, revenge) to do sth. harmful to sb. because they have done sth. harmful to you
to revise sth.; revision (n.) here: to change sth.
scapegoat *Sündenbock*
scope of action, room for manoeuvre *Handlungsspielraum*
self-determination *Selbstbestimmung*
separation of powers (into judicial, executive and legislative branches) *Gewaltenteilung (in Judikative, Exekutive und Legislative)*

slump a sudden large reduction in amount
special path *Sonderweg*
to suspend sth.; suspension (n.) here: to officially stop sth. for a short time (such as reparation payments)
turmoil ['tɜː(r)mɔɪl] a state of excitement or uncontrolled activity
unconditional surrender; to surrender unconditionally *bedingungslose Kapitulation; sich bedingungslos ergeben/kapitulieren*
to violate sth.; violation (n.) to do sth. that is in opposition to a law, agreement, principle etc., to contravene, to infringe
war of aggression *Angriffskrieg*
war of annihilation [ə,naɪə'leɪʃ(ə)n] *Vernichtungskrieg*
war captivity *Kriegsgefangenschaft*
war criminal/crime *Kriegsverbrecher/-verbrechen*
to withdraw from; withdrawal (n.) to stop taking part; to leave a place
to wreak (– wrought – wrought) havoc ['hævək]**/destruction** to cause great harm or damage
to wreak revenge/vengeance ['vendʒ(ə)ns] to punish sb. for sth. bad they have done to you

The Post-war World –

- Conflicts and Peace After the Second World War
- The Cold War: Cooperation and Conflicts
- The Reunification of Germany After the Peaceful Revolution of 1989

8 May 1945	Aug 1945	1946	1947	1948	1949	1955
Germany's unconditional surrender ("Zero Hour")	nuclear bombs dropped on Hiroshima and Nagasaki; Potsdam Agreement	Churchill's "iron curtain"-speech	Truman Doctrine, ERP (Marshall Plan), Bizonia	Berlin Blockade and Airlift	foundation of the two German states: FRG and GDR; NATO	FRG joins NATO; Warsaw Pact

On the Verge of the Apocalypse?

People sitting and standing on the Berlin Wall near the Brandenburg Gate, 1989

> **Task** — First, come up with a suitable definition of the word "apocalypse" in the context of the Cold War. Then, making use of the timeline provided and taking into consideration further examples of cooperation and conflicts between the Western world and the Soviet Union you remember from previous history classes, discuss in class at which points in the period from 1945 to 1990 you think the world was closest to this apocalypse.

1956	1961	1962	1968	1972	9 Nov 1989	3 Oct 1990
Hungarian and Poznań Uprisings	Berlin Wall	Cuban Missile Crisis	Prague Spring	Basic Treaty, CSCE	Fall of the Berlin Wall	Reunification of Germany

The Post-War World

Topics & Key Questions	Key Terms	Translations
Conflicts and Peace After the Second World War		
The Division of Germany and Europe, 1945–1949 • Was there a "Zero Hour" in Germany in 1945? • 8 May 1945: day of liberation and/or defeat? • In how far is the situation in Germany after WWII comparable to the situation in 1918? What was worse/better? • What was the effect of the Potsdam Conference on post-45 Germany? • Which effect did the changing leadership of the "Big Three" have on the results at Potsdam? • Which of the "Big Three" got most of what they wanted? • Why did a Cold War develop in Europe between 1945 and 1949? • Who was responsible for the start of the Cold War? • What impact did the Berlin Airlift Crisis have on the Cold War? • Was the ERP an American altruistic action only? • How did the USSR establish control over Eastern Europe from 1945 to 1949? • In how far did differences in the aims and measures of occupation policy contribute to the division of Germany?	• Tehran Conference • Yalta Conference • Potsdam Conference ("5 Ds": Denazification, Democratization, Demilitarization, Decentralization Decartelization; "3 Rs": Reeducation, Reparations, Resettlement) • Morgenthau Plan • occupation zones • Allied Control Council • displaced persons (DPs) • Zero Hour • forced labourer • Nuremberg Trials • Iron Curtain • satellite states • puppet government • bizone/bizonia; trizone • Truman Doctrine/containment policy • European Recovery Program (ERP)/Marshall Plan • COMECON (Council for Mutual Economic Aid) • London Conference • currency reform • Berlin Blockade; Berlin Airlift	• Teheran-Konferenz • Konferenz von Jalta • Potsdamer Konferenz (5 Ds: Entnazifizierung, Demokratisierung, Demilitarisierung, Dezentralisierung, Dekartellisierung; 3 Rs: Umerziehung, Reparationen, Umsiedlung) • Morgenthau-Plan • Besatzungszonen • Alliierter Kontrollrat • Heimatlose • Stunde Null • Zwangsarbeiter/in • Nürnberger Kriegsverbrecherprozesse • Eiserner Vorhang • Satellitenstaaten • Marionettenregierung • Bizone; Trizone • Truman-Doktrin/Eindämmungspolitik • Europäisches Wiederaufbauprogramm/Marshallplan • RGW (Rat für gegenseitige Wirtschaftshilfe) • Londoner Sechsmächtekonferenz • Währungsreform • Berlin-Blockade; Berliner Luftbrücke
Basic Law and Foundation of the FRG and the GDR • What were the lessons learned from Weimar with regard to the creation of the Basic Law? • Did the FRG's integration into the Western bloc prevent an early German reunification? • Was Adenauer a "Chancellor of the Allies"?	• London Documents • Parliamentary Council • Basic Law • Federal Republic of Germany (FRG)/German Democratic Republic (GDR) • Occupation Statute	• Frankfurter Dokumente • Parlamentarischer Rat • Grundgesetz • Bundesrepublik Deutschland (BRD)/Deutsche Demokratische Republik (DDR) • Besatzungsstatut
The Cold War: Cooperation and Conflicts		

The Cold War Outside of Europe • Did NATO and the Warsaw Pact make Europe more secure or less secure? • When did the Cold War come closest to turning into a "hot" war?	• NATO (North Atlantic Treaty Organization) • Warsaw Pact • proxy war • MAD (mutually assured destruction) • nuclear arms race ≠ détente • Cuban Missile Crisis • Prague Spring • Brezhnev Doctrine	• NATO (Organisation des Nordatlantikvertrags) • Warschauer Pakt • Stellvertreterkrieg • Gleichgewicht des Schreckens • nukleares Wettrüsten ≠ Entspannung • Kuba-Krise • Prager Frühling • Breschnew-Doktrin
Germany as a "Focal Point" • Why was German rearmament a major issue in the early 1950s? • Why was Germany a "focal point" in the Cold War? • How did the "German question" affect the creation of détente between East and West after 1962? • Brandt's Eastern treaties: solution or sell-out?	• Schuman Declaration • ECSC (European Coal and Steel Community) • Stalin Notes (March Notes) • Treaty of Rome/European Economic Community (EEC) • Berlin Wall • Hallstein Doctrine • Basic Treaty • Ostpolitik/"change through rapprochement" • CSCE (Conference on Security and Cooperation in Europe); Helsinki Accords	• Schuman-Erklärung • EGKS (Europäische Gemeinschaft für Kohle und Stahl) • Stalin-Noten (März-Noten) • Römische Verträge/Europäische Wirtschaftsgemeinschaft (EWG) • Berliner Mauer • Hallstein-Doktrin • Grundlagenvertrag • Ostpolitik/„Wandel durch Annäherung" • KSZE (Konferenz für Sicherheit und Zusammenarbeit in Europa); Schlussakte von Helsinki

The Reunification of Germany After the Peaceful Revolution of 1989

The Collapse of the Soviet Union and the Revolutions in Eastern Europe • In how far was it difficult for the USSR to maintain control of Eastern Europe between 1949 and 1989? • Why did the Cold War come to an end and who won it? • Was the collapse of the USSR inevitable?	• "peace through strength" (Reagan Doctrine) • glasnost (openness)/perestroika (restructuring) • Commonwealth of Independent States • Reykjavik Summit • START 1 (Strategic Arms Reduction Treaty) • Solidarnosz (Solidarity Movement)	• „Friede durch Stärke" (Reagan-Doktrin) • glasnost (Offenheit)/perestroika (Umstrukturierung) • Gemeinschaft Unabhängiger Staaten (GUS) • Islandgipfel • START 1 (Vertrag zur Verringerung strategischer Waffen) • Solidarnosc (Solidarität)
The Reunification of Germany 1989/90 • What were the Anglo-French attitudes towards a reunification of Germany? • Why was Germany eventually reunified? • 1989 – an epochal year? • *Ende/Wende/Revolution*? Revolution after all?	• oppositional groups • Monday demonstrations • fall of the Berlin Wall • Ten Point Plan • "We are the people" → "We are one people" • Treaty on the Final Settlement with Respect to Germany ("Two-plus-Four Treaty") • Unification Treaty	• Oppositionsgruppen • Montagsdemonstrationen • Mauerfall • Zehn-Punkte-Plan • „Wir sind das Volk" → „Wir sind ein Volk" • Vertrag über die abschließende Regelung in Bezug auf Deutschland („Zwei-plus-Vier-Vertrag") • Einigungsvertrag

Conflicts and Peace After the Second World War

The Division of Germany and Europe, 1945–1949

⇨ S 1–12

When examining how Germany was dealt with after its unconditional surrender* on 8 May 1945, it has to be considered that two ideologies and policies collided that envisaged a different future for Europe as a whole. However, the three major powers (USA, the USSR and Great Britain) managed to set up the framework for a new order at three conferences: at the **Tehran Conference*** (November/December 1943), the **Yalta Conference*** (February 1945) and the **Potsdam Conference***. These conferences were accompanied by lively public discussions and many ideas were brought forward as to how Germany should be treated. One controversial idea was that of the US Secretary of the Treasury, Henry Morgenthau, who proposed that Germany should be deprived of all its industrial plants in order to turn it into a mere agricultural country (**Morgenthau Plan***). Already in 1943, the European Advisory Commission (EAC, consisting of representatives of the "Big Three") had developed suggestions for a common policy on Germany and these suggestions were put into practice at the Yalta Conference. It quickly became clear that Germany was to be fragmented*, but not in terms of dismantling it into constituent states*. It was rather to be maintained as a whole after some cessions of territory*. The different German parts were to become **occupation zones*** administered by American, British and Soviet troops and one central commission consisting of the three supreme commanders was to coordinate the administration from Berlin (**Allied Control Council***). The Polish eastern border was to be moved westwards and compensated for through German eastern territories. However, France did not agree to these measures since it had been excluded from previous negotiations, and it only became a fourth occupation power when it was clear that the French zone was to be made up of territory taken from the American and the British zones.

The WWII Allies assumed supreme power over Germany with the Berlin Declaration of 5 June 1945. The so-called **5 Ds*** agreed on at the Potsdam Conference (17 July – 2 August 1945) played an important role in the treatment of Germany:
- **Denazification*** meant the destruction of the NSDAP with all its associated institutions;
- **Democratization*** meant local self-government according to democratic principles;
- **Demilitarization*** meant complete disarmament;
- **Decentralization*** was geared towards the administration and the economy and
- **Decartelization*** meant the destruction of state-run businesses and monopolies.

These agreements were accompanied by the so-called **3 Rs***:
- **Re-education*** was closely linked to democratization and denazification;
- **Reparations*** were to be paid by Germany as a compensation for the damage and losses caused and
- **Resettlement*** affected the German population of the disconnected eastern territories as well as the minorities in Czechoslovakia and other eastern European states since they had to be expelled to central and west Germany.

Resettlement in particular caused unrest among the German population (and this is still the case even today). Although expulsions were not intended to be the rule and removal was to be carried out under humanitarian circumstances, the reality turned out to be different since the distress caused by Nazi Germany during WWII now backfired on the German population. These measures have to be seen as a reaction to the unprecedented* systematic policy of aggression and annihilation carried out by the SS, the German troops and the administrations in Eastern Europe. The approximately 11 million so-called **displaced persons (DPs)*** still living on German soil were a different issue altogether. These former **forced labourers*** had been displaced* by the Nazis during the war for racial, religious or political reasons. With the end of the war, Germany faced a **Zero Hour***. The consequences of war had, as a rule, the greatest effect on people who survived in the debris* of the cities. For the western occupation zones it was estimated that 18 per cent of the flats in the cities were completely destroyed and 28 per cent were at least damaged. People's health suffered owing to the fact that the energy and water supplies had broken down, resulting in the lack of heating and cooking possibilities and of sanitary installations. These factors not only had a negative effect on babies and elderly people, but also on the adult population as well. Added to this came the problem of nutrition, which could not be solved by simply rationing food strictly. Hunger marches and demonstrations were the results and some people even claimed that conditions under the Nazis had been better than under the Allies.

A common goal of the Allies at Potsdam was that of bringing former Nazis to justice. Taking the main war criminals to the international military court in Nuremberg (**Nuremberg Trials***) and promoting denazification was intended to provide the preconditions for democratic behaviour in Germany. In autumn 1945, 24 political and military representatives of the Third Reich as well as NSDAP and state organizations were put on trial accused of crimes against humanity* and peace and war crimes. In fact, the majority of the German population accepted the necessity of punishing the war criminals. All in all, the importance of these trials lies in the fact that they helped make previously unknown crimes known to the broad public

unprecedented not done or experienced before

displaced persons (DPs) *Heimatlose*

forced labourer *Zwangsarbeiter/in*

to displace to force (people or animals) to leave the area where they live

Zero Hour *Stunde Null*

debris [ˌdeˈbriː] the pieces that are left after something has been destroyed

Nuremberg Trials *Nürnberger Kriegsverbrecherprozesse*

crime against humanity *Verbrechen gegen die Menschlichkeit*

Some of the accused in the Nuremberg Trials, front row from left to right: Hermann Göring, Rudolf Heß, Joachim von Ribbentrop (cf. S3). The verdicts* were announced in autumn 1946: twelve main war criminals were sentenced to death, and other accused persons had to face life sentences* or prison for many years. Furthermore, the individual occupation zones put physicians, lawyers, industrialists, members of the Department of Foreign Affairs* and the supreme command of the Wehrmacht on military trial. In total, 668 death sentences were pronounced in the western zones only.

On 10 February 1947, the Allies signed peace treaties with the former allies of Germany (Italy, Hungary, Bulgaria, Romania and Finland). However, finding a solution for Germany itself proved a lot more difficult. Already in 1946, the British Prime Minister Winston Churchill had coined the term **"Iron Curtain*"**, meaning that the Soviet policy has led to an "iron curtain" going down on Europe (cf. S6a). Churchill felt confirmed in his observations by developments in Eastern Europe. Poland's government in exile had been massively hindered in the political participation involved in building a new democratic form of government. The Communist Party of Czechoslovakia had suppressed democratic groups and their work and, in Greece, a civil war had broken out between the western-oriented government and communist associations. Political groups in Hungary, Romania and Bulgaria wishing to follow the example of western democracies had no chance of succeeding due to Soviet leader Stalin's tight grip. Within only a few years, the Soviet Union had been successful in establishing **satellite states*** with **puppet governments*** in almost all the countries of Eastern Europe, sometimes even under conditions akin to civil war.

The Allies' common interests were characterized by the need for security, plans for punishment, and compensation demands, and, as a result, the Potsdam Agreement did not formulate concrete provisions for governing the occupation zones. Thus, Germany's future was relatively open when it came to a restructuring of the economic, social and political structures. This openness, however, also bore the danger of alienation between the major powers since the USA and the USSR differed in their basic ideology and ideas for society.

Taking a closer look at the USA, it becomes clear that three political streams of thought developed after Roosevelt's death in 1945. The first one was a traditional isolationist approach, the second promoted a "one world" policy and continued cooperation with the USSR, and the third reflected the views of the "realists" who pursued a balance of power in Europe which was to be achieved with the help of the backing of the USA. The American diplomat John F. Kennan first sketched the latter policy in his "Long Telegram" (cf. S7). The USA wanted a dynamic and progressive development for Europe according to their liberal understanding since the alternative would have been long-lasting, expensive support. Furthermore, the USA wanted to have Europe as a partner whom they could trade with and cooperate with politically.

When negotiations between the foreign secretaries failed at the Paris Peace Conference in spring 1946, it became more and more obvious how difficult it would be to find a common solution for the future of the Ruhr area, the realization of reparations, and the treatment of Germany as one single unit. At the second conference in July, the US Secretary of State proposed a combination of the US zone with every other zone and the treating of this enlarged zone as a common economic unit. Although the French and the Soviets rejected this offer, it turned out to be a welcome opportunity for the British. The newly founded **bizone** (also called **bizonia**)* (the foundation of the **trizone***, including the French zone, followed in March 1948)

---

verdict decision made by a jury in a trial
life sentence *lebenslange Haft*

Department of Foreign Affairs *Auswärtiges Amt*

Iron Curtain *Eiserner Vorhang*

satellite states *Satellitenstaaten*
puppet government *Marionettenregierung*

bizone/bizonia; trizone *Bizone; Trizone*

soon developed its own political dynamics and in May 1947 already, a parliamentary board with the authority for legislation was introduced. However, in order to avoid the impression that this constituted a newly founded German state, administration work was distributed among different locations in Stuttgart, Bielefeld, Minden, Bad Homburg and Frankfurt am Main.

Several demands of the Soviets were seen by the USA as evidence for an expansionist policy, i.e. the question of possible control over all of Germany, the demand to participate in the allied occupation of Italy, the demand for military bases* in the Dardanelles and the refusal to end the occupation of northern Persia. This assessment revived old ideological contrasts and the only solution seemed to be to set the course for a possible division of Europe. This came about in connection with the **Truman Doctrine*** of 12 March 1947 (cf. S11). It provided for American support for every country which saw itself threatened by communism or the USSR. The underlying assumption of this doctrine was that communism itself, as the root of bondage*, threatened the free, non-communist world in an aggressive way. Another aspect of American **containment policy*** was the offer of a **European Recovery Program (ERP)*** also called the **Marshall Plan*** after its initiator US Secretary of State George Marshall, which was introduced only three months after the Truman Doctrine (cf. S9, S10). The plan promised the European countries aid in terms of goods and money for recovery purposes. The USA demanded that the beneficiaries* should cooperate with each other on an international level; furthermore, the aid was linked to consultations with the donor country*, i.e. the USA. Thus, the aid incorporated the beneficiary countries into the western system of currency and economy and since every European country was in need of economic and financial support, this programme acted as an instrument in the division of East and West.

Not surprisingly, the Soviet Union rejected the programme on 2 July 1947 and the other Eastern European countries followed this lead soon after. A relatively short time after the introduction of the Marshall Plan, the Soviet Union presented their own programme in which US policy was portrayed as imperialist and aggressive, whereas communism offered real democracy and peace. Furthermore, the Soviet Union stated that American policy endangered the security of the USSR, referring to the experience gained in both world wars, when the West had been the aggressor. Thus, the Soviet Union introduced their own economic institution, the **COMECON (Council for Mutual Economic Aid)***, on 25 January 1949.

The process of alienation* between East and West was not only due to different power-political or economic interests, it also came about because both sides pursued the strategy of eliminating the other or at least of undermining its status wherever possible. It would have been possible for both sides to divide the world amongst themselves but that did not happen because the contradicting interests were inextricably connected with antagonistic ideological motives, i.e. a federal structure, a rather weak central government, a multi-party system, an extensive market economy, stress on individual rights and a sense of mission in terms of democracy and capitalism on the side of the USA. The Soviet Union, in its turn, saw itself as the USA's antagonist and the problem was that both sides considered their system to be the only appropriate one.

After the introduction of the Truman Doctrine and the Marshall Plan, the affected countries had to take sides. At the **London Conference*** (February to June 1948), the western European states (Great Britain, France, the Benelux states) and the USA made important decisions on the new order of Western Europe including the Ger-

base headquarters

Truman Doctrine/containment policy *Truman-Doktrin/ Eindämmungspolitik*

bondage state of being unfree

European Recovery Program/ Marshall Plan *Europäisches Wiederaufbau Programm/ Marshall-Plan*

beneficiary person who gains, benefits

donor country country which gives

COMECON (Council for Mutual Economic Aid) *RGW (Rat für gegenseitige Wirtschaftshilfe*

alienation separation, estrangement, division

London Conference *Londoner Sechsmächtekonferenz*

man occupation zones. The Soviet Union had not been invited to the negotiations. Already during the talks, measures promoting the economic integration of West Germany were taken by incorporating the western zones of Germany into the ERP. The Soviet Union reacted to this conference by having its representative leave the Allied Control Council on 20 March 1948. Now the time was ripe for a **currency reform*** in the western zones, a step which had become particularly necessary because these zones were now becoming increasingly incorporated into the field of international economic policy.

On 20 June 1948, the Deutsche Mark (DM) replaced the Reichsmark in the western zones. Every German got 40 DM and four weeks later another 20. The immediate reaction of the Soviet Union was twofold: first, they introduced their own currency only three days later and second, they started a blockade of West Berlin (**Berlin Blockade***) on the very same day. The western Allies responded to this blockade by supplying West Berlin with everything it needed by plane (**Berlin Airlift***, cf. S12). This blockade clearly marked the final breach* within the former alliance of victors and any idea of economic unity for the whole of Germany now had to be revoked.

This blockade had been the most radical reaction of the Soviet Union so far and it was therefore no surprise that the Cold War was about to turn into a hot one. The Soviet military administration blocked freight traffic and passenger traffic* to Berlin, which seriously challenged the USA. For the USA, it was impossible to give up West Berlin since that would have meant a loss of political prestige and influence. Lucius D. Clay, the American military governor, had first thought about a military breakthrough from the western zones to Berlin, but this idea was soon dismissed. It was also Clay who came up with the idea of an airlift. As it turned out, this airlift was able to provide the population of West Berlin with all the goods it needed for nearly one year. During this time, the population of West Berlin constantly resisted the Soviet pressure. From September 1948 on, the deputies of Berlin met in the western part of the city and new legislative and executive institutions were installed in East Berlin. In the summer of 1948 already, the western military governors had imposed a blockade of goods on East Berlin and the Soviet occupation zone. It took a long period of negotiations, but, finally, on 12 May 1949, both blockades were ended. Despite the fact that the airlift had been a very costly enterprise for the West, it inflicted losses on the Soviet Union. This case shows that no ordinary weapons were used in the Cold War, the weapons were those of propaganda and psychology. Stalin's actions had confirmed the prejudice against him since he had taken a whole city hostage* and soon he was compared to Hitler.

The consequences of the Berlin Blockade for Germany were clear: the country's political and economic integration into the West was strengthened sustainably, while, at the same time, the position of the Western Powers was reinforced.

---

currency reform *Währungsreform*

Berlin Blockade *Berlin-Blockade*
Berlin Airlift *Berliner Luftbrücke*
breach split, rupture

freight traffic and passenger traffic transport of goods and people

to take sb. hostage *jdn. als Geisel nehmen*

Basic Law and the Foundation of the FRG and the GDR

⇨ S 13–17

Der Parlamentarische Rat hat das vorstehende Grundgesetz für die Bundesrepublik Deutschland in öffentlicher Sitzung am 8. Mai des Jahres Eintausendneunhundertneunundvierzig mit dreiundfünfzig gegen zwölf Stimmen beschlossen. Zu Urkunde dessen haben sämtliche Mitglieder des Parlamentarischen Rates die vorliegende Urschrift des Grundgesetzes eigenhändig unterzeichnet.

BONN AM RHEIN, den 23. Mai des Jahres Eintausendneunhundertneunundvierzig.

PRÄSIDENT DES PARLAMENTARISCHEN RATES

I. VIZEPRÄSIDENT DES PARLAMENTARISCHEN RATES

II. VIZEPRÄSIDENT DES PARLAMENTARISCHEN RATES

The original document signed by Konrad Adenauer (president of the Parliamentary Council), Adolph Schönfelder (vice president) and Hermann Schäfer (second vice president)

The **London Documents*** (cf. S 14a/b) of 1 July 1948, which were handed to the German Minister Presidents and two governing mayors by France, Great Britain and the USA, served as a guideline for the development of a future constitution for West Germany. Drawing this up was the task of the **Parliamentary Council*** and it was not an easy one, since the Allies had to agree to this **Basic Law***. No political group had a majority and the political parties also differed considerably when it came to the question as to which character the new Basic Law should have. The SPD, for instance, opted for a kind of organization statute with a rather provisional character because they wanted to leave the door open for a reunification with the East, whereas the CDU wanted the Basic Law to have a model character for a later-envisaged Germany as a whole. Further questions that arose were whether Germany should have a strong central government or strong single governments in the federal states and how strongly the individual institutions should be involved in matters of legislation. Furthermore, it was not definitely settled which economic system the newly founded state was to have, i.e. a market economy or a planned economy (although property was put under state security). Once these issues were solved (sometimes after dramatic arguments), the western Allies had to agree as well. The French and Americans mainly criticized the fact that the Basic Law was too centralist and weakened the federal states too much. However, the western Allies eventually agreed to the Basic Law on 8 April 1949. On 8 May 1949, the Basic Law was put to the vote in the Parliamentary Council and accepted by a vote of 53 to 12 (six CDU members, two KPD members, two Centre Party members and two DP members voted against it). On 12 May, ratification by the Landtage followed. An interesting fact is that all the Landtage agreed with the exception of the Bavarian Landtag since they believed that there was not enough independence for the Länder,

London Documents *Frankfurter Dokumente*

Parliamentary Council *Parlamentarischer Rat*
Basic Law *Grundgesetz*

but nevertheless they did accept the law as being legally binding*. Thus, on 23 May 1949, the law was enacted* and the **Federal Republic of Germany (FRG)*** came into being.

Not long after this, a second foundation of a state came about: that of the **German Democratic Republic (GDR)***. On 4 October 1949, the party executive committee* of the SED (*Sozialistische Einheitspartei Deutschlands*, the leading party in the Soviet occupation zone) started consultations with other parties and "mass organizations" about the formation of a provisional government and just three days later, on 7 October, the German People's Council (*Deutscher Volksrat*) enacted an already accepted constitution and declared Otto Grotewohl (SED) the first Minister President of the GDR. This act defined the foundation of two German states and soon both began to work on consolidating their existence. In a government declaration of 21 October, Germany's first chancellor Konrad Adenauer (CDU) claimed that the FRG was the "only legitimate governmental organization of the German people" because the governmental organization of the Soviet zone had been established with the participation of only "a minority of loyal Germans".

What scope of action did the two German states have? The GDR stood under the complete direct political and military control of the USSR, while the government of the FRG was restricted by the **Occupation Statute*** (cf. S 14b), which made a completely independent economic and foreign policy impossible. Furthermore, economic policy was also restricted by the International Authority for the Ruhr*, which enabled the Allies to control the coal and steel industry of the Ruhr area. In addition, all the non-communist parties of the FRG agreed that they would not entertain plans and initiatives which would make it possible for the Soviet Union to participate in future developments in Germany as a whole and to influence the situation of the whole of Germany. This, in turn, meant either making West Germany economically so attractive that it would have an effect on East Germany or securing the exclusive mandate* of the FRG through integrating it into the West. The latter strategy was the one pursued by Adenauer. SPD party leader Kurt Schumacher, for his part, detested any "cosying up"* to the ideas of the Western Allies. Eventually, Adenauer considered his strategy to be successful when, on 22 November 1949, he signed the Petersberg Agreement, which foresaw that the FRG would become a member of the OECD (Organization for Economic Co-operation and Development). Furthermore, the FRG was allowed to commence diplomatic relations, an end of dismantlement was planned, and it was agreed that the rights of legislation in regard to economic matters were to be transferred to the FRG, whereby, however, the importance of the already settled restrictions was once again stressed very clearly.

---

legally binding *rechtsverbindlich*
to enact a law *ein Gesetz erlassen*
Federal Republic of Germany (FRG) *Bundesrepublik Deutschland*
German Democratic Republic (GDR) *Deutsche Demokratische Republik*
party executive committee *Parteivorstand*

Occupation Statute *Besatzungsstatut*
International Authority for the Ruhr *Ruhrstatut*

exclusive mandate *Alleinvertretungsanspruch*
to cosy up to sb. *sich bei jdm. einschmeicheln, anbiedern*

The Cold War: Cooperation and Conflicts

The Cold War Outside of Europe

⇨ S 18–24

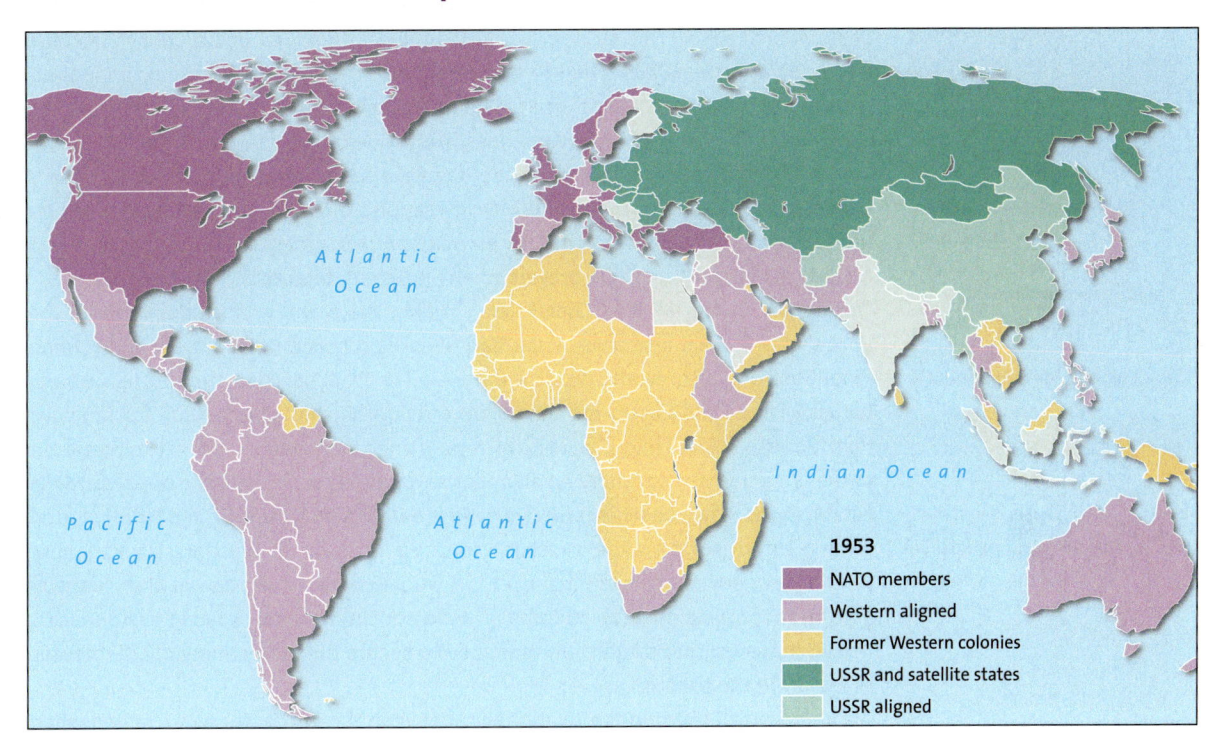

1953
- NATO members
- Western aligned
- Former Western colonies
- USSR and satellite states
- USSR aligned

The division of the world became especially apparent with the foundation of two institutions, each representing the interests of one of the parties involved in the Cold War. On 4 April 1949, **NATO (North Atlantic Treaty Organization)**★ was founded in Washington D.C. This military alliance is defined as a defensive alliance between its member states and its aims have not changed since 1949. During the Cold War, the main task of NATO was to secure its member states' security through deterrence and armament. Its underlying idea of mutual defence is still valid, namely that if one member state is attacked by a non-NATO state, the others will help to defend it. Germany joined NATO on 9 May 1955. The counterpart of NATO was the **Warsaw Pact**★, founded on 14 May 1955. It can also be seen as the military complement to COMECON.

The Cold War carries its name because the two opposing blocs never fought against each other directly, instead they fought so-called **proxy wars**★. The Korean War, for example, lasted from 25 June 1950 until 27 July 1953. Korea had been occupied by Japan since 1910. Japan was defeated by the Allies of WWII and both American and Soviet troops occupied Korean territory. The 38th **degree of latitude**★ became the separating line between these troops and soon negotiations for a joint Korean government failed due to ideological differences. Mediation on the part of the United Nations also proved to be unsuccessful and so Korea was divided into two states: the democratic Republic of Korea in the south and the communist Democratic People's Republic in the north. This division is still in effect today.

Coming back to the strategy of deterrence, it must be pointed out that in the case of the Soviet Union and the USA, both superpowers potentially strived for a form of

NATO (North Atlantic Treaty Organization) *Organisation des Nordatlantikvertrags*

Warsaw Pact *Warschauer Pakt*

proxy war *Stellvertreterkrieg*

degree of latitude *Breitengrad*

world domination and both had a strong sense of mission*. Another important factor is that both states did not share a common border, in which case neighbouring states would have had a reason for cooperation. In the event of a possible war, the stock* of atomic weapons available would have allowed both parties to completely destroy each other. This strategy of **MAD (mutually assured destruction)*** became well-known in the 1950s. The key thing here was the fact that if one opponent attacked the other with a first strike, it had to expect a counterstrike and thus the chance of finally prevailing became less likely. Given this enormous risk for the attacker, atomic weapons increased the degree of deterrence in a way that made a stable peace quite likely. Thus, WMDs (weapons of mass destruction)* were no longer seen as "real" weapons but as political instruments. The outcome was a **nuclear arms race*** and this prevented any policy of **détente***.

During the **Cuban Missile Crisis*** (cf. S 20), the world was on the verge of the apocalypse for the first time. Cuba had become a communist state in 1959 when Fidel Castro overthrew the dictator Battista. The USA stopped supporting Cuba financially and thus Castro more and more relied on the Soviet Union for financial help. For the Soviet Union, in its turn, supporting Cuba meant a chance to break out of the encirclement of American alliances and military bases and the opportunity to establish their own basis far away from their own territory. In 1962, the USSR started to ship intermediate-range missiles* to Cuba. As a direct reaction, US President John F. Kennedy announced that the USA would destroy every Soviet ship suspected of transporting missiles to Cuba. The Soviet Union finally gave in to Kennedy's threat, however, they unofficially managed to secure the dismantling of US missiles in Turkey in the process.

Another critical point in the relationship between the two blocs was reached when Soviet troops invaded Czechoslovakia on 21 August 1968. The background to this was that the Czechoslovakian Communist Party had started a reform movement, called the **Prague Spring***, by means of which it wanted to make socialism more democratic. The USSR, however, saw a counter-revolutionary movement in this attempt and sent in troops to crush it. This approach was in accordance with the later said **Brezhnev Doctrine***, named after the Soviet party leader Leonid Brezhnev. It basically postulated that the Soviet satellite states were limited in their sovereignty and that the Soviet Union always had the right to interfere in the affairs of other Warsaw Pact states if the cohesiveness* of the Eastern bloc was endangered.

Germany as a "Focal Point"

The Korean War and the communist threat were two reasons why Germany's military future was also a subject of discussion among the Americans. One important question was, for instance, whether Germany should have an army at all and if so to what extent Germany should be responsible for itself in respect of its military defence. In the course of this discussion, the first German chancellor Konrad Adenauer demanded on the one hand a "rampart* against the threat from the East" and on the other hand he wanted armed forces, whether in the form of a strong federal police or in the form of a German contingent in an international army. For Adenauer, having a military force was an inherent characteristic of a sovereign and equal state. At a conference of the foreign ministers in September 1950, the FRG was granted several concessions such as, but not limited to, the annulment* of the state of war, the revision of the occupation statute (cf. S 14b), its exclusive mandate, and the setting up of a Foreign Service*. Despite this, Adenauer could not gain the approval of all Western Europeans for German rearmament and France in particular had massive reservations. However, in May 1950, the French foreign minister Robert Schuman had already proposed combining the complete French and German steel and coal production in one institution in order to help prevent another war between France and Germany. This **Schuman Declaration*** turned out to be realistic since the participants could rely on the experience gathered with the International Authority for the Ruhr. And so, on 18 April 1951, the **ECSC (European Coal and Steel Community)*** was founded. The six acceding countries* (Italy, Luxemburg, FRG, Belgium, the Netherlands and France) appointed nine representatives to a High Authority* which was responsible for securing the well-regulated supply of a common market transcending national borders. Furthermore, the High Authority could interfere in matters of national rights, such as customs.

On 8 February 1952, the Bundestag formulated several conditions under which it would agree to rearmament. Among these was the revocation of the occupation statute and full sovereignty in respect of domestic and foreign affairs. Any future peace treaty for Germany as a whole was not to interfere with the treaties regulating the integration of the FRG into the West. Furthermore, Berlin was to count as a part of the FRG and any future reunited Germany was to be oriented towards the FRG in terms of society and politics. Finally, no restrictions were to remain from the period of occupation concerning legislation, industrial production, research etc. However, since the FRG had as yet no sovereignty in terms of its foreign policy, it could not establish an army on its own. The fact that the Western Allies now approved of the formation of a German army showed that one very important aim of the occupation statute, namely security and control, had become obsolete in the face of a tense international situation. To complicate matters, the Soviet Union also tried to take the initiative by sending the so-called **Stalin Notes*** (or **March Notes***) to the West German government on 10 March 1952. In the first note, Stalin offered the Western Allies negotiations about a peace treaty with Germany (as a whole). The provisions for such a peace treaty were that Germany would be restored as a sovereign state (but without its eastern territories), the occupation armies would be withdrawn and democratic parties and organizations would be permitted. However, according to Stalin, a reunited Germany would not be allowed to form any coalitions or military alliances aimed against any former state which had previously fought against Germany. Three further notes followed in which several questions were discussed, but in the end the exchange of notes stopped when the Western Allies remained steadfast in their demand for discussing the organization of free elections, a point to which the Soviet Union failed to answer.

With the signing of the **Treaty of Rome*** on 25 March 1957, the FRG's integration into the west came to a preliminary completion. The treaty established the

Foreign Service *Auswärtiger Dienst*

Schuman Declaration *Schuman-Erklärung*
ECSC (European Coal and Steel Community) *Europäische Gemeinschaft für Kohle und Stahl*
acceding country *Beitrittsland*
High Authority *Hohe Behörde*

Stalin Notes (March Notes) *Stalin-Noten (März-Noten)*

Treaty of Rome/European Economic Community (EEC) *Römische Verträge/Europäische Wirtschaftsgemeinschaft (EWG)*

European Economic Community (EEC)★ and the European Atomic Energy Community (EURATOM). Considering the decisions taken by politicians in West Germany in this period, one can say that their scope of action as well as the sovereignty of the FRG itself were somewhat limited both politically, by allying with Western Europe and identifying with American policy, and legally, through the treaties concluded with the West and the prevailing authority of the Four Powers over Germany.

Germany became a focal point of the Cold War again in 1961, when work commenced on the **Berlin Wall★** on 13 August. For the GDR, security policy meant, in the first place, securing the existence of the GDR as a state. The USSR was the only state which guaranteed the GDR's existence as a state, first as an occupying power, later as an alliance partner. The following aspects are only a few of the factors which prevented the GDR from being accepted as a state: first, the **Hallstein Doctrine★**, which stated that assuming diplomatic relations with the GDR was an "unfriendly act" towards the FRG; second, the territorial location of Berlin; and third, the political and social profile of the GDR itself. The latter was also a reason, apart from a rather low living standard, why many inhabitants of the GDR wished to leave their home. The GDR wanted to solve the problem of Berlin by declaring it a "free city" through releasing it from the responsibility of the Four Powers. However, this attempt failed and the building of the wall started in 1961, also with a view to reducing the mass exodus of skilled workers. When the border of the FRG also became more difficult to penetrate, the stream of fugitives★ decreased and finally came to an almost complete stop. Relations between the two German states were then finally settled in the **Basic Treaty★** of 21 December 1972.

The Basic Treaty was the result of a new policy pursued by the FRG under Chancellor Willy Brandt (SPD). Egon Bahr, Under-Secretary of State in the Federal Chancellery, (1969–1972), can be called the creator of Brandt's **Ostpolitik★** since he opted for **"change through rapprochement"★**. Until 1969, Western German policy had looked upon the collapse of the regime in the East as a means of achieving the reunification of the two German states. Furthermore, the Hallstein Doctrine burdened the relationship with otherwise neutral states. The new strategy was now geared not only towards Western Europe but also towards Eastern Europe. One very famous event, connected with Chancellor Brandt, is his genuflection★ when visiting a memorial ceremony commemorating the Warsaw Ghetto Uprising of 1943. This gesture was so sensational because Brandt, who himself had left Germany in 1933 already and had been expatriated★ by the Nazis in 1938, nevertheless took over responsibility for Germany's past. Soon Ostpolitik celebrated its first successes, the first being the Moscow Treaty and the Treaty of Warsaw in 1970 in which the inviolability of current borders was confirmed, territorial integrity respected, and further territorial claims as well as the use of violence disclaimed. As a result, the relationship with the GDR was intensified in the following year, and then the Basic Treaty was signed and both German states joined the United Nations as official member states. Eventually, both German states also took part in the **CSCE (Conference on Security and Cooperation in Europe)★**, which, in its final document, the **Helsinki Accords★** of 1 August 1975, made declarations on principles relating for example to the renunciation of violence, and cooperation and social communication in Europe.

Berlin Wall *Berliner Mauer*

Hallstein Doctrine *Hallstein-Doktrin*

fugitive person escaping from law or other pursuer
Basic Treaty *Grundlagenvertrag*

Ostpolitik/"change through rapprochement" *Ostpolitik/ „Wandel durch Annäherung"*

genuflection *Kniefall*

to expatriate sb. to throw sb. out of a country

CSCE (Conference on Security and Cooperation in Europe); Helsinki Accords *KSZE (Konferenz für Sicherheit und Zusammenarbeit in Europa); Schlussakte von Helsinki*

The Reunification of Germany After the Peaceful Revolution of 1989

The Collapse of the Soviet Union and the Revolutions in Eastern Europe

⇨ S 25–29

The collapse of the Soviet Union and the revolutions in Eastern Europe are inextricably intertwined. When the economic problems in the USSR increased in intensity in the mid-1970s, the effects became noticeable for the satellite states as well. One aspect contributing to the prevailing financial difficulties was the war in Afghanistan, which was started by the USSR in 1979. This proxy war had almost the same impact on the Soviet Union as the Vietnam War had had on American society.

In terms of foreign policy, the Helsinki Accords of 1975 and the phase of the Second Cold War (1977–1985) also had a marked effect on the devastation of the socialist system. The Helsinki Accords contained ten points (also called the Decalogue), one being respect for human rights and fundamental freedoms. Although the communist regimes had tried to suppress political opposition by all means, they had not been able to erase critical thinking and internal opposition completely. Opposition groups had every reason to feel heartened by the Helsinki Accords. Then, in 1981, Ronald Reagan was elected president in the USA and with him the policy of détente ended. Reagan coined the phrase **"peace through strength"**★ which also became known as the **Reagan Doctrine**★.

"peace through strength" (Reagan Doctrine) „Friede durch Stärke" (Reagan-Doktrin)

In order to solve its economic problems, the USSR started a reform programme under its new general secretary Mikhail Gorbachev, who was elected in 1985. His assumption was that the communist state could only tackle its economic problems by means of extensive domestic reforms. Thus, he introduced two concepts, **glasnost (openness)**★ and **perestroika (restructuring)**★. Whereas the former was not only geared towards making economic decisions more transparent and calculable, but also towards opening processes in the state and society for the citizens, the latter aimed at a debureaucratisation and decentralisation of the planned economy in order to make it more efficient. However, it was not Gorbachev's aim to abolish the socialist system, instead he wanted to modernize and stabilize it. Soon, the victims of the Stalin era were rehabilitated, freedom of speech, religion and the press were guaranteed and private companies were allowed. Furthermore, a market economy was introduced, a new constitution paved the way for a presidential system, and the single republics of the Soviet Union gained a broad degree of autonomy. The new policy soon developed its own dynamics and thus many people started to question the ideological and territorial foundations of the system. When the three Baltic states, Estonia, Latvia and Lithuania, proclaimed their independence in spring 1990, the Soviet Union once again resorted to military means in order to stop these plans. However, the military intervention failed and all three states were recognized by the EU in the summer of 1991. The heads of state of the three remaining Soviet republics (Russia, the Ukraine, and Belarus) agreed on the dissolution of the Soviet Union on 8 December 1991 and founded the **Commonwealth of Independent States**★ (CIS, also called the Russian Commonwealth).

glasnost (openness)/perestroika (restructuring) Glasnost (Offenheit)/Perestroika (Umstrukturierung)

Commonwealth of Independent States Gemeinschaft Unabhängiger Staaten (GUS)

Gorbatchev's reform policy also had a decisive impact on the peaceful end of the conflict between East and West because this defensive strategy led to the USA changing their collision course. US President Reagan and Soviet leader Gorbachev

Reykjavik Summit *Islandgipfel*

both attended the **Reykjavik Summit*** in October 1986 and achieved progress on the matter of nuclear disarmament, which later resulted in the signing of the Intermediate-Range Nuclear Forces Treaty (INF Treaty) in December 1987. In 1982, US President Reagan had already initiated the Strategic Arms Reduction Talks, but it was only in 1991 that **START 1 (Strategic Arms Reduction Treaty)*** was signed by Reagan's successor George Bush and Gorbachev. In the same year, 1991, the Warsaw Pact was dissolved and with it one of the two military blocs which had dominated world policy for decades.

START 1 (Strategic Arms Reduction Treaty) *Vertrag zur Verringerung strategischer Waffen*

Coming back to Gorbachev's reform programme, the policy of glasnost and perestroika was vital for the further development of the Warsaw Pact states, since it, together with the Helsinki Accords, provided opposition groups with the necessary arguments for their enterprise. The change had its beginning with the foundation of the Polish trade union **Solidarnosz (Solidarity movement)***, led by Lech Walesa. Faced with rising prices, workers of the Gdansk* shipyard* went on strike in August 1980. One month later, the trade union was founded and was very much supported by the Polish Pope John Paul II. The workers demanded free speech, the release of political prisoners, and access to mass media and independent courts. The Polish communist regime first recognized the movement and commenced negotiations but these were ended when the government did not achieve any success. Under General Jaruzelski, martial law* came into effect in December 1981 and, in its course, opponents of the state were arrested and Solidarnosz abolished. The movement was forced to go underground. Nevertheless, Walesa was awarded the Nobel Peace Prize in 1983. The policy of glasnost and perestroika was also responsible for the Polish government being forced to start talks with representatives of the trade union in spring 1989. These so-called round table talks broke the monopoly of power of the communist party and the first free elections in the Eastern Bloc were then held in summer 1989. The new Polish government started to restructure the political system, introduced a market economy and oriented Poland more towards the West. Finally, Poland joined NATO in 1999 and the European Union (EU) in 2004.

Solidarnosz (Solidarity movement) *Solidarnosc (Solidarität)*
Gdansk *Danzig*
shipyard place where ships are built or repaired

martial law *Kriegsrecht*

The front page of an Australian newspaper, 26 August 1991

Further revolutions followed, for example in Hungary, Czechoslovakia, Romania, Bulgaria and Albania, all of which share some common features: first, they took advantage of the economic weakness of the communist regimes; second, the governments faced political pressure from foreign countries; and third, opposition members displayed great personal bravery. One further effect of the former Soviet states breaking free from their suppressor was a renaissance of nationalism, which, in some cases, such as for example the former Yugoslavia, was also accompanied by displays of aggression.

The Reunification of Germany 1989/90

Global politics also had an impact on the German communist regime in the GDR. The SED regime became more and more isolated since it totally rejected any reforms connected with glasnost and perestroika. However, there had always been **oppositional groups*** in the GDR. In particular the large number of people who had left the GDR in 1953 and before the building of the wall in 1961 and again in 1989 made it clear that the population was politically and economically dissatisfied. Another form of opposition took place within the Christian churches and a third form was made up of oppositional political groups. Most of the time, the two latter groups opted for a "third way", something between socialism and capitalism or a form of democratic socialism. Another opposition group formed inside the SED itself. They were mostly dissatisfied with the ideal of socialism and its realization in the GDR.

The trigger for the **Monday demonstrations*** can be seen in the local elections of May 1989. The **inconsistency*** lay in the fact that over 99 per cent of the people had, according to the official state figures, voted for the National Front (an alliance of political parties and mass organizations) although many had voted "no" or had **nullified*** the ballot paper, encouraged by the reforms in the USSR. Thus, church **congregations*** and oppositional citizens filed a complaint against the responsible authorities. As a result, the opposition gained more and more in confidence and on 19 September 1989, the New Forum *(Neues Forum)* was granted its **accreditation*** as an independent political organization. The GDR government rejected the demands made but could not prevent the oppositional movement from growing immensely popular. The situation became even more bizarre when Gorbachev visited East Berlin to celebrate the 40th anniversary of the GDR on 7 October 1989. Here, he openly called upon the SED government to introduce political reforms, which, in turn, effectively backed up the demonstrators' demands. Two days later, on 9 October, the last day of the GDR dawned with over half a million people peacefully demonstrating for freedom, the rule of law, and free elections in East Berlin. On 17 Oc-

oppositional groups
Oppositionsgruppen

Monday demonstrations
Montagsdemonstrationen
inconsistency puzzle

to nullify to make sth. legally null
congregation people who regularly attend religious services
accreditation official authorization to or approval of

Monday demonstrations in the GDR

tober, Erich Honecker was forced to resign as general secretary of the Central Committee of the SED.

Parallel to the events in Berlin, a massive wave of refugees from the GDR hit the Permanent Missions of the Federal Republic of Germany* in Budapest, Warsaw and Prague. After long negotiations with the UN, German foreign minister Hans-Dietrich Genscher was able to announce that the refugees had been granted exit permits*. When Hungary opened its borders to Austria in the night of 10 to 11 September, a mass exodus on the part of GDR citizens was the result and the movement became unstoppable. The GDR government's reaction was a press conference on 9 November, in which the draft text of new cross-border travel regulations was announced by Günther Schabowski, the Politburo's Secretary (cf. S 25), who also confirmed that he believed them to come into effect immediately. And that very night, the **fall of the Berlin Wall*** was initiated by tens of thousands of people who gathered at the wall in the centre of the city.

Soon events came thick and fast* in the GDR and on 28 November the German chancellor Helmut Kohl (CDU) presented a **Ten Point Plan*** in the German Bundestag. It included immediate measures in favour of the GDR in terms of humanitarian aid and extensive financial help and demanded a fundamental change in the political system. The long-term aim was to achieve German reunification. During this time, demonstrations had not stopped and the people's slogans changed from **"We are the people"*** to **"We are one people"***, not only emphasizing the demand for civil rights but also calling for German unity as well.

Some foreign countries reacted in a rather affronted fashion since Kohl had not informed them about his plan. Altogether, foreign countries displayed different reactions to the events in Germany. French President François Mitterrand was worried that the events in Germany and in Europe might become uncontrollable and that Germany could emerge as an independent power. The British Prime Minister Margaret Thatcher feared a collapse of European stability and wanted to maintain the

Permament Mission of the Federal Republic of Germany *Ständige Vertretung der Bundesrepublik Deutschland*
exit permit the permission to leave a country

fall of the Berlin Wall *Fall der Berliner Mauer*
to come thick and fast *sich überschlagen (Ereignisse)*
Ten Point Plan *Zehn-Punkte-Plan*

"We are the people" → "We are one people" *„Wir sind das Volk" → „Wir sind ein Volk"*

The signing of the "Two-Plus-Four Treaty". Front row from left to right: James Baker (USA), Douglas Hurd (Great Britain), Eduard Shevardnadze (USSR), Roland Dumas (France), Lothar de Maiziere (GDR), Hans-Dietrich Genscher (FRG)

(economic) balance of power in Europe. The USA, however, viewed events in a more positive light because it was felt that they constituted a strong blow against communism. US president Bush supported Kohl's diplomatic negotiations, and Kohl, in turn, promised that a future reunited Germany would be oriented towards the West (cf. S27). However, the USA also emphasized that NATO as well as the EU had to be involved in the process of reunification.

In the GDR, a "round table" had formed, which included representatives of the old elite as well as representatives of the opposition. This institution operated as a kind of substitute government under minister president Hans Modrow and worked towards the political independence of the GDR, whereas the population more and more wished for a quick unification with the FRG. This could not, however, be achieved by Germany alone since the four victorious powers of WWII demanded a say as well. Thus, the so-called "Two + Four process" was initiated on 13 February 1990 in Ottawa, Canada, and on 17 July, Polish representatives joined the negotiations over the German eastern border, the Oder-Neisse line. The **Treaty on the Final Settlement with Respect to Germany (Two-Plus-Four Treaty)*** was signed on 12 September in Moscow by the foreign ministers of the USA, Britain, the USSR, France, the GDR and the FRG (cf. S28). It paved the way for the **Unification Treaty*** between the FRG and the GDR, which was approved of by both German parliaments, the Bundestag and the Volkskammer, on 20 September 1990. On 3 October, the five new federal states joined the FRG and the allied powers abstained from exercising their hitherto existing rights in Germany. Two more treaties followed, one regulating the withdrawal of Soviet troops from German territory (12 October) and the German-Polish Border Treaty (14 November 1990).

Treaty on the Final Settlement with Respect to Germany (Two-Plus-Four Treaty) Vertrag über die abschließende Regelung in Bezug auf Deutschland („Zwei-plus-Vier-Vertrag")
Unification Treaty Einigungsvertrag

Conflicts and Peace After the Second World War

S1 How to Deal with German Civilians

The source at hand features excerpts from an official briefing for British soldiers in Germany, telling them how to behave appropriately in the defeated country. Thus it dates back to 1945.

Pre-tasks

1. Have a look at the photograph provided which shows an Allied soldier with a photograph of Hitler. Can you imagine what he might be thinking? Write a thought bubble in your exercise book and make sure your thought bubble matches up with the emotion expressed through his facial expression.
2. Now put yourself into the shoes of the officials who are to brief the British soldiers about how to deal with German civilians they meet. In your exercise book, write their speech bubbles and include:
   - how the British soldiers are supposed to behave, and why,
   - what they should prepare themselves for hearing from the German civilians they meet and
   - how they should deal with that.

Tasks

3. Point out the positive and the negative characteristics the British officials ascribe to "the" Germans.
4. Explain the references to the National Socialist rule over Germany, starting with the "seizure of power" in 1933.
5. Examine the reasons given for why Hitler could come to power in Germany, against the backdrop of the theory of a German "special path".
6. Take a critical stand on the view of guilt and responsibility expressed.

Post-task

7. Revise what you have learned about nationalism and the (difficult) idea of a nation-state, for example Herder's concept of a "national spirit" (*Volksgeist*) that defines the characteristics of a people. Keeping all this in mind, discuss the way "the Germans" are presented in this briefing.

Allied soldier with a photograph of Hitler

To Begin With –
You are going into Germany.
You are going there as part of the Forces of the United Nations which have already dealt shattering blows on many fronts to the German war-machine, the most ruthless the world has ever known. But most of the people you will see when you get to Germany will not be airmen or soldiers or U-boat crews, but ordinary civilians – men, women and children. Many of them will have suffered from overwork, underfeeding and the effects of air raids, and you may be tempted to feel sorry for them.

[…] **There will be no brutality about a British occupation, but neither will there be softness or sentimentality.**

You may see many pitiful sights. Hard luck stories may somehow reach you. Some of them may be true, at least in part, but most will be hypocritical attempts to win sympathy. For, taken as a whole, the German is brutal when he is winning, and is sorry for himself and whines for sympathy when he is beaten.

So be on your guard against "propaganda" in the form of hard-luck stories. Be fair and just, but don't be soft.

There is no need for you to bother about German attempts to justify themselves. All that matters at present is that you are about to meet a strange people in a strange, enemy country.

What The Germans Are Like
When you meet the Germans you will probably think they are very much like us. They look like us, except that there are fewer of the wiry type and more big, fleshy, fair-haired men and women, especially in the north.

But they are not really so much like us as they look. The Germans have, of course, many good qualities. They are very hard-working and thorough; they are obedient and have a great love of tidiness and order. They are keen on education of a formal sort, and are proud of their "culture" and their appreciation of music, art and literature.

But for centuries they have been trained to submit to authority – not because they thought their rulers wise and right, but because obedience was imposed on them by force.

The old Prussian army – and the Nazi army too – set out intentionally to break the spirit of recruits. They were made to do stupid and humiliating things, in order to destroy their self-respect and turn them into unquestioning fighting machines. This method produced a formidable military force, but it did not produce good human beings. It made the Germans cringe* before authority.

That is one reason why they accepted Hitler. He ordered them about, and most of them liked it. It saved them the trouble of thinking. All they had to do was obey and leave the thinking to him.

It also saved them, they thought, from responsibility. The vile cruelties of the Gestapo and the S.S. were nothing to do with them. They did not order them; they did not even want to know about them. The rape of Norway, Holland and Belgium was not their business. It was the business of Hitler and the General Staff.

That is the tale that will be told over and over again by the Germans. They will protest with deep sincerity that they are as innocent as a babe in arms.

But the German people cannot slide out of their responsibility quite so easily. You must remember that Hitler became Chancellor in a strictly legal way. Nearly half

to cringe to move back slightly from sth. that is unpleasant or frightening

the German electors voted for him in the last (comparatively) free election of 1933. With the votes of his National Socialist allies he had a clear majority. The Germans knew what he stood for – it was in his book – and they approved it. Hitler was immensely popular with the majority of the Germans: they regarded him as the restorer of German greatness. They welcomed the abolition of unemployment although they knew that it arose from conscription and rearmament. **After the fall of France most Germans supported his military conquests with enthusiasm. It was only when they felt the cold wind of defeat that they discovered their consciences.**

[...] It is possible that some civilians will welcome your arrival, and may even look on you as their liberators from Hitler's tyranny. These will be among the Germans who consistently opposed Hitler during his years of success. Not that they made speeches against him or committed sabotage: any who did that are unlikely to be alive to welcome you. But there are many who kept their own counsel and passively opposed Hitler all along.

As a rule they are loyal members of the political parties suppressed by Hitler, mostly workers, but often honest people of the middle classes. Or they are Catholics or Protestants, who have opposed Hitler because of his persecution of Christianity.

But many Germans will pretend they have been anti-Nazis simply because they want to be on the winning side. Among them will be many doubtful characters. Even those who seem to have the best intentions cannot be regarded as trustworthy; [...].

While you are serving in Germany you are representatives of Britain. Your behaviour will decide their opinion of us.

It is not that we value their opinion for its own sake. It is good for the Germans, however, to see that soldiers of the British democracy are self-controlled and self-respecting, that in dealing with a conquered nation they can be firm, fair and decent. The Germans will have to become fair and decent themselves, if we are to live with them in peace later on.

Leitfaden für britische Soldaten in Deutschland 1944: Zweisprachige Ausgabe (Englisch/Deutsch)/The Bodleian Library. Übers. v. Klaus Modick. Köln: Kiepenheuer & Witsch 2014

S 2) Richard von Weizsäcker

Speech to the German Bundestag

Richard von Weizsäcker (1920–2015) was a German CDU politician. He was Governing Mayor (*Regierender Bürgermeister*) of Berlin from 1981 to 1984 and served as the sixth Federal President of the Federal Republic of Germany from 1984 to 1994.

Pre-task 1. On the next page, there is a "word cloud" containing words from Weizsäcker's speech. With a partner, decide on one antithesis [ænˈtɪθəsɪs] that you think characterizes 8 May 1945 (the date of Germany's unconditional surrender) best. Write down the two terms making up this antithesis in two different colours and be prepared to explain your choice against the backdrop of the historical context.

Language support

Gedenken commemoration •
Gefangenschaft captivity •
Kapitulation surrender •
Befreiung liberation •
Stunde Null Zero Hour •
Ungewissheit uncertainty •
Unrecht injustice

Tasks

2. Focus on lines 1 to 35: In this part of the speech, von Weizsäcker mostly speaks about the perception of 8 May in 1945. Point out remarks referring to the past (= before 1945), the present (= 8 May 1945) and the future (= the time after 8 May 1945).
3. Focus on lines 36 to 63: In this part of the speech, von Weizsäcker mostly speaks about the perception of 8 May in 1985. Point out remarks referring to the past (= before 1945), the present (= 8 May 1945) and the future (= the time from 1945 to 1985).
4. Copy and fill in the table below with your results from tasks 1 and 2. Use key words only and add the respective line numbers.

	Past	Present	Future
View in 1945	?	?	?
View in 1985	?	?	?

5. Use the visualization to explain how, according to von Weizsäcker, the year 1985 can finally give answers to questions raised in 1945.
6. Examine von Weizsäcker's view that 8 May 1945 was a "Day of Liberation" and that there was no "Zero Hour" after all. In doing so, explain his references to the historical context, meaning the period of National Socialism and thereafter.

Post-tasks

7. Richard von Weizsäcker died on 31 January 2015. This prompted many leading politicians to make public statements about the former Federal President. Vice-Chancellor Sigmar Gabriel, for example, said: "Seine [von Weizsäckers] Einordnung [classification] dieses Tages als Tag der Befreiung hat das Geschichtsverständnis [view of history] der Deutschen nachhaltig [in a lasting way] beeinflusst. Diese Rede wird für immer als Zäsur [caesura, break] in den Geschichtsbüchern seinen Platz haben." (www.tagesschau.de/inland/weizsaecker-tod-reaktionen-101.html [31.3.15])
Discuss to what extent and why Gabriel calls the speech a "break" in the Germans' view of history. In order to do that, you should know that the speech was not unanimously approved of when it was delivered in 1985, and that some of the politicians present refused their applause. Consider possible reasons for that in 1985, against the backdrop of the question whether 8 May 1945 was a day of liberation or a day of defeat.

8. 8 May 1945 is commonly celebrated as "VE-Day" – Victory over Europe Day. What would probably have been von Weizsäcker's stance towards this label? Give an evaluation.

---

gedenken to commemorate

Befreiung liberation
Unrecht injustice
Fremdherrschaft foreign rule
Machtverschiebung shift of power

Schonung protection

Beschönigung extenuation [ɛksˌtɛnjʊˈeɪʃən]
Einseitigkeit one-sidedness
Gang course

Folgen consequences

bewusst conscious(ly)

Gefangenschaft captivity

verbittert embittered, filled with bitterness
geschenkt given, here: the gift of
Ungewissheit uncertainty
bedingungslos unconditional
entgelten to pay

gute Sache good cause
sich herausstellen to turn out
vergeblich in vain

Viele Völker gedenken* heute des Tages, an dem der Zweite Weltkrieg in Europa zu Ende ging. Seinem Schicksal gemäß hat jedes Volk dabei seine eigenen Gefühle. Sieg oder Niederlage, Befreiung* von Unrecht* und Fremdherrschaft* oder Übergang zu neuer Abhängigkeit, Teilung, neue Bündnisse, gewaltige Machtverschiebungen* – der 8. Mai 1945 ist ein Datum von entscheidender historischer Bedeutung in Europa.

Wir Deutsche begehen den Tag unter uns, und das ist notwendig. Wir müssen die Maßstäbe allein finden. Schonung* unserer Gefühle durch uns selbst oder durch andere hilft nicht weiter. Wir brauchen und wir haben die Kraft, der Wahrheit so gut wir es können ins Auge zu sehen, ohne Beschönigung* und ohne Einseitigkeit*.

Der 8. Mai ist für uns vor allem ein Tag der Erinnerung an das, was Menschen erleiden mußten. Er ist zugleich ein Tag des Nachdenkens über den Gang* unserer Geschichte. Je ehrlicher wir ihn begehen, desto freier sind wir, uns seinen Folgen* verantwortlich zu stellen.

Der 8. Mai ist für uns Deutsche kein Tag zum Feiern. Die Menschen, die ihn bewußt* erlebt haben, denken an ganz persönliche und damit ganz unterschiedliche Erfahrungen zurück. Der eine kehrte heim, der andere wurde heimatlos. Dieser wurde befreit, für jenen begann die Gefangenschaft*. Viele waren einfach nur dafür dankbar, daß Bombennächte und Angst vorüber und sie mit dem Leben davongekommen waren. Andere empfanden Schmerz über die vollständige Niederlage des eigenen Vaterlandes. Verbittert* standen Deutsche vor zerrissenen Illusionen, dankbar andere Deutsche vor dem geschenkten* neuen Anfang.

Es war schwer, sich alsbald klar zu orientieren. Ungewißheit* erfüllte das Land. Die militärische Kapitulation war bedingungslos*. Unser Schicksal lag in der Hand der Feinde. Die Vergangenheit war furchtbar gewesen, zumal auch für viele dieser Feinde. Würden sie uns nun nicht vielfach entgelten* lassen, was wir ihnen angetan hatten?

Die meisten Deutschen hatten geglaubt, für die gute Sache* des eigenen Landes zu kämpfen und zu leiden. Und nun sollte sich herausstellen*: Das alles war nicht nur vergeblich* und sinnlos, sondern es hatte den unmenschlichen Zielen einer

verbrecherischen Führung gedient. Erschöpfung*, Ratlosigkeit* und neue Sorgen kennzeichneten die Gefühle der meisten. Würde man noch eigene Angehörige finden? Hatte ein Neuaufbau in diesen Ruinen überhaupt Sinn?
Der Blick ging zurück in einen dunklen Abgrund* der Vergangenheit und nach
35 vorn in eine ungewisse dunkle Zukunft.
Und dennoch wurde von Tag zu Tag klarer, was es heute für uns alle gemeinsam zu sagen gilt: Der 8. Mai war ein Tag der Befreiung. Er hat uns alle befreit von dem menschenverachtenden* System der nationalsozialistischen Gewaltherrschaft*. Niemand wird um dieser Befreiung willen vergessen, welche schweren Leiden für
40 viele Menschen mit dem 8. Mai erst begannen und danach folgten. Aber wir dürfen nicht im Ende des Krieges die Ursache für Flucht, Vertreibung und Unfreiheit* sehen. Sie liegt vielmehr in seinem Anfang und im Beginn jener Gewaltherrschaft, die zum Krieg führte.
Wir dürfen den 8. Mai 1945 nicht vom 30. Januar 1933 trennen.
45 Wir haben wahrlich keinen Grund, uns am heutigen Tag an Siegesfesten zu beteiligen. Aber wir haben allen Grund, den 8. Mai 1945 als das Ende eines Irrweges* deutscher Geschichte zu erkennen, das den Keim der Hoffnung* auf eine bessere Zukunft barg*. [...]
Es gab keine „Stunde Null", aber wir hatten die Chance zu einem Neubeginn. Wir
50 haben sie genutzt so gut wir konnten. An die Stelle der Unfreiheit haben wir die demokratische Freiheit gesetzt.
Vier Jahre nach Kriegsende, 1949, am 8. Mai, beschloß der Parlamentarische Rat unser Grundgesetz. Über Parteigrenzen hinweg gaben seine Demokraten die Antwort auf Krieg und Gewaltherrschaft im Artikel 1 unserer Verfassung:
55 „Das Deutsche Volk bekennt sich darum zu unverletzlichen und unveräußerlichen Menschenrechten als Grundlage jeder menschlichen Gemeinschaft, des Friedens und der Gerechtigkeit in der Welt."*
Auch an diese Bedeutung* des 8. Mai gilt es heute zu erinnern. [...]
Ehren wir die Freiheit.
60 Arbeiten wir für den Frieden.
Halten wir uns an das Recht.
Dienen wir unseren inneren Maßstäben der Gerechtigkeit.
Schauen wir am heutigen 8. Mai, so gut wir es können, der Wahrheit ins Auge*.

Richard von Weizsäcker: Rede, Gedenkveranstaltung im Plenarsaal des Deutschen Bundestages zum 40. Jahrestag des Endes des Zweiten Weltkrieges in Europa, Bonn, 8. Mai 1985, Bundespräsidialamt, www.bundespraesident.de/SharedDocs/Reden/DE/Richard-von-Weizsaecker/Reden/1985/05/19850508_Rede.html [27.04.15]

Erschöpfung exhaustion
Ratlosigkeit helplessness

Abgrund abyss [əˈbɪs]

menschenverachtend inhuman
Gewaltherrschaft despotism, tyranny

Flucht, Vertreibung und Unfreiheit escape, expulsion and bondage

Irrweg wrong path
Keim der Hoffnung seed of hope
bergen to hold

Das ... Welt. The German people therefore acknowledge inviolable and inalienable human rights as the basis of every community, of peace and of justice in the world.
Bedeutung sense, meaning
der Wahrheit ins Auge schauen to face the truth

S 3 „Diese Schandtaten: Eure Schuld!"

This is one of the posters the Americans put up in public places in Germany with the intention of spreading the message that the atrocities the allied soldiers were confronted with when liberating the concentration camps were, in effect, not committed by just a few, but by many Germans. This "shock therapy" was meant to appeal to the conscience of the German people and to warn them that they would not be able to escape their share of the blame.

Tasks You can work on these tasks in English or in German, whatever makes you feel more comfortable.

1. Take turns and describe the photographs to each other. Read the captions of the photographs. Ho do they make you feel?
2. Together, think about how the German population might have felt in the cities in which these kinds of posters were displayed in public places.
3. Assess the possible success of such a campaign and explain your opinion. In your assessment, also consider the intention of the campaign as explained in the introduction to the source.[1]

---

[1] Nach einer Idee von Ralph Last: „‚Diese Schandtaten: Eure Schuld!' Reaktionen der deutschen Bevölkerung auf die amerikanische Plakatkampagne"; in: Geschichte lernen 163 (2015), S. 38–47

„Diese Schandtaten: Eure Schuld!" American poster from 1945

Embedded text:
In zwölf Jahren haben die Nazi Verbrecher Millionen Europäer gefoltert, verschleppt und ermordet. Männer, Frauen und Kinder wurden von Hitlers vertierten Henkersknechten gehetzt und zu Tode gequält, nur weil sie Juden, Tschechen, Russen, Polen oder Franzosen waren.
Ihr habt ruhig zugesehen und es stillschweigend geduldet.
Im Kampf erhärtete Soldaten der Alliierten haben ihren Ekel und ihre Empörung angesichts der vergasten, verkohlten und ausgemergelten Leichen der Opfer in den K. Z. Buchenwald nicht verbergen können.
In Buchenwald wurden nach deutschen Lagerberichten 50 000 Menschen verbrannt, erschossen, aufgehängt.

In Dachau fanden amerikanische Soldaten allein 50 Güterwagen mit verwesenden Leichen. Seit Beginn dieses Jahres erlagen dort 10 000 Menschen ihren Foltern.
In Belsen fanden britische Truppen Folterkammern, Verbrennungsöfen, Galgen und Auspeitschungspfähle. 30 000 Menschen sind dort umgekommen.
In Gardelegen, Nordhausen, Ohrdruf, Erla, Mauthausen, Vaihingen fielen unzählige Zwangsverschleppte und politische Gefangene einem Inferno, wie es die Weltgeschichte noch nie gesehen hat, zum Opfer!
Ihr habt untätig zugesehen. Warum habt ihr mit keinem Wort des Protestes, mit keinem Schrei der Empörung das deutsche Gewissen wachgerüttelt?
Das ist Eure große Schuld – Ihr seid mitverantwortlich für diese grausamen Verbrechen!

Captions underneath the pictures:
1) Güterwagen vollgeladen mit Leichen wurden in Dachau von den amerikanischen Soldaten entdeckt.
2) Wie Brennholz aufeinandergeschichtete Leichen wurden im Dachauer Konzentrationslager von den amerikanischen Truppen gefunden. Das Blut floss über den Boden, als die Soldaten ankamen.
3) Dieser Insasse des Dachauer Schandlagers wurde hohläugig und abgemagert vor Hunger von den amerikanischen Soldaten aufgefunden.
4) Ein Teil der in einer Grube gefundenen 1000 Leichen, die von britischen und amerikanischen Soldaten bei der Befreiung eines Lagers vorgefunden wurden.
5) Amerikanische Soldaten besichtigen ein Greuellager, wo die verbrannten Leichen der Nazi-Opfer aufgestapelt liegen.
6) Verkohlte Leichname der politischen Gefangenen, die von SS-Truppen im Dachauer Lager in den Tod gehetzt wurden.
7) Ein Insasse des Dachauer Lagers betrachtet die Leichen seiner Kameraden, die Opfer vertierter SS-Truppen wurden. Die Nazis gossen Benzin über die Leichen und verbrannten sie.

S 4 Max Radler

„SCHWARZ WIRD WEISS oder MECHANISCHE ENT-NAZIFIZIERUNG"

This cartoon by Max Radler was published in the German satirical magazine *Simplicissimus* in 1946 and takes an ironical stand on the process of denazification.

Pre-task 1. Focus on the title of the cartoon and the accompanying poem only. Pinpoint the message that is included in both by relating the textual elements to each other.

Tasks 2. Describe the cartoon in detail, including striking aspects of composition.

3. With reference to the accompanying cartoon, explain the cartoonist's message and how religious references in word and picture help to convey it.

Post-task 4. "Denazification" was one of the "5 Ds" agreed on at Potsdam, "Reeducation" one of the "3 Rs". Do further research and come up with definitions for both that clearly set them apart.

SCHWARZ WIRD WEISS oder MECHANISCHE ENTNAZIFIZIERUNG

M. Radler

Embedded text on banner:
Über einen reuigen Sünder ist mehr Freude als über zehn Gerechte!
Entnazifikator. Patent H. Schmitt

Springt immer rein! Was kann euch schon passieren,
Ihr schwarzen Böcke aus dem braunen Haus!
Man wird euch schmerzlos rehabilitieren.
Als weiße Lämmer kommt ihr unten raus.

Wir wissen schon: Ihr seid es nie gewesen!
(Die andern sind ja immer schuld daran – –)
Wie schnell zum Guten wandeln sich die Bösen,
Man schwarz auf weiß im Bild hier sehen kann.

J. Menter

Language support

- **mechanisch** automatic
- **Entnazifikator** denazifier
- **Fließband** assembly line
- **Kanzel** pulpit ['pʊlpɪt]
- **Lamm** lamb[3]

Embedded text:
Über einen reuigen Sünder ist mehr Freude als über zehn Gerechte![1]
Entnazifikator. Patent H. Schmitt[2]

Jump right in! What can happen to you,
You black sheep from the brown house!
You'll be painlessly rehabilitated.
You'll come out as snow-white lambs.
We know: you were never involved!

(The others are always the guilty ones – –
How quickly the bad turn into good,
Here you see it in black and white.

---

[1] "There will be more joy over one sinner who repents than over ten righteous persons," an ironic reference to Luke 15:7 (the parable of the lost sheep).

[2] Heinrich Schmitt was a Bavarian special minister who was responsible for carrying out the denazification programme.

[3] "I will bring them down like lambs to the slaughter," an allusion to Jeremiah 51:40 (Babylon's punishment).

CONNECT

One Nation, One People, One Theory? The Goldhagen Debate

Task Getting to know and taking sides in the "Goldhagen Debate" of 1996:
The so-called "Goldhagen Debate" once more stimulated discussions about guilt and responsibility for the Holocaust, not only in Germany. One of the main objectives of history classes is to enable you to participate in such public debates and to take a critical stand, defending your point of view with the help of valid arguments (judgement of facts) and, especially as far as this topic is concerned, with reference to norms and values, such as human rights (value judgement). With the help of the short biographical account of Goldhagen as well as with an excerpt from a book review of Goldhagen's hotly debated 1996 bestseller (cf. S5), write an argumentation in which you evaluate Goldhagen's approach.

Daniel Jonah Goldhagen (*1959)

Born in Boston in 1959 to a father who had survived the Holocaust, Goldhagen earned his doctor's degree in history, specializing in National Socialism and the Holocaust. His 1996 work "Hitler's Willing Executioners: Ordinary Germans and the Holocaust" triggered a public debate in the reunified Germany about the origins of the Holocaust. Goldhagen's controversial thesis was that German anti-Semitism was a unique and specific phenomenon since it included an eliminatory component and also carried it out – Goldhagen called this "eliminationist anti-Semitism".
Goldhagen argued that this German anti-Semitism had become deeply embedded in the German mentality in the course of the 19th and the early 20th century, which meant in consequence that German Wehrmacht soldiers did not develop any mens rea* in the face of their mass executions. From this, Goldhagen concluded that the anti-Semitism of the "ordinary" German made the National Socialist genocide of the Jews possible.
This thesis once again made the idea of a "collective guilt" on the part of the Germans the focus of attention, a view which was, however, adamantly* rejected by the German public.

---

mens rea ['mɛnz 'riːə] *Unrechtsbewusstsein* • **adamantly** resolutely, strictly, decisively

S5   Fritz Stern

The Goldhagen Controversy: One Nation, One People, One Theory?

Fritz Stern (*1926) is an American historian of German descent. The text at hand is an excerpt from Stern's book review of Goldhagen's "Hitler's Willing Executioners", published in the November/December issue of *Foreign Affairs* in 1996. Note: in view of the brevity of this excerpt a link to the website has been provided to enable the reading of the entire review and the attainment of a more comprehensive understanding of Stern's criticism.

[...] The book is a deliberate provocation – I consider this a neutral judgment. Provocations can shock people out of their settled, comfortable views; they can also be self-promoting attacks on earlier work and professional standards. Goldhagen's title is provocative and delivers his thesis: the executioners of Jews were willing murderers, who willingly chose to torment and kill their victims; they were ordinary Germans, not Nazi monsters, not specially trained or indoctrinated by party membership or ideology, but simply acting out of what Goldhagen calls the common German "eliminationist mind-set." And being "ordinary" Germans responding to a common "cognitive model" about Jews, their places could have been taken by millions of other ordinary Germans. [...] Goldhagen draws on the rich literature about German antisemitism [sic] even as he dismisses it, distills what is useful for his thesis while ignoring whatever might contradict or complicate it, and then celebrates the originality of his own version. The result is a potpourri of half-truths and assertions, all meant to support his claim that German antisemitism was unique in its abiding* wish to eliminate Jews, its "eliminationist mind-set." He suggests that one needs to look at Germans as anthropologists look at preliterate societies*; they are not like "us," meaning Americans or Western Europeans. [...]

Fritz Stern: "The Goldhagen Controversy: One Nation, One People, One Theory?" Foreign Affairs. April 28, 2015, www.foreignaffairs.com/articles/52630/fritz-stern/the-goldhagen-controversy-one-nation-one-people-one-theory [28.04.15]

abiding lasting, enduring, continuing, unlikely or impossible to change
preliterate society one that does not have a written language

S 6a) Winston Churchill

Sinews of Peace

In 1946, the British Prime Minister Winston Churchill (cf. chapter 3 for a biographical account) gave his "Sinews of Peace" speech (sinews, pl. = fig.: strength, power) in Westminster College in Fulton, Missouri, on 5 March 1946. However, since he coined a metaphor in this speech which was then commonly used to illustrate the division of East and West in the bipolar, post-45 world, it has come to be known as the "iron curtain" speech.

Pre-task
1. Have a look at the introductory pages to this chapter. Describe the "iron curtain" as depicted in the two photographs and speculate on the meaning of this metaphor in the context of the beginning of the Cold War.

Tasks
2. Describe the situation the "Continent" (l. 9) currently finds itself in, according to Churchill.
3. Explain the "iron curtain" metaphor (l. 8).
4. Characterize the Russian people, as claimed by Churchill, and examine which further course of events Churchill has in mind.

Post-task **5.** Which arguments do you believe Stalin might advance to justify the expansion of the Soviet sphere of influence? Make an educated guess.

[...] I have a strong admiration and regard for the valiant* Russian people and for my wartime comrade, Marshal Stalin. There is deep sympathy and goodwill in Britain – and I doubt not here also – towards the people of all the Russians and a resolve to persevere* through many differences and rebuffs in establishing lasting
5 friendships [...]. It is my duty, however, for I am sure you would wish me to state the facts as I see them to you, to place before you certain facts about the present position in Europe.
From Stettin in the Baltic to Trieste in the Adriatic, an iron curtain has descended across the Continent. Behind that line lie all the capitals of the ancient states of
10 Central and Eastern Europe. Warsaw, Berlin, Prague, Vienna, Budapest, Belgrade, Bucharest and Sofia, all these famous cities and the populations around them lie in what I must call the Soviet sphere, and all are subject, in one form or another, not only to the influence but to a very high and, in many cases, increasing measure of control from Moscow. [...] The Communist parties, which were very small in all
15 these Eastern States of Europe, have been raised to pre-eminence and power far beyond their numbers and are seeking everywhere to obtain totalitarian control. Police governments are prevailing in nearly every case, and so far, except in Czechoslovakia, there is no true democracy. [...] Whatever conclusions may be drawn from these facts – and facts they are – this is certainly not the Liberated Europe we
20 fought to build up. Nor is it one which contains the essentials of permanent peace. [...] I do not believe that Soviet Russia desires war. What they desire is the fruits of war and the indefinite expansion of their power and doctrines. But what we have to consider here today, while time remains, is the permanent prevention of war and the establishment of conditions of freedom and democracy as rapidly as pos-
25 sible in all countries. Our difficulties and dangers will not be removed by closing our eyes to them. They will not be removed by mere waiting to see what happens; nor will they be removed by a policy of appeasement. What is needed is a settlement, and the longer this is delayed, the more difficult it will be and the greater our dangers will become.
30 From what I have seen of our Russian friends and Allies during the war, I am convinced there is nothing they admire so much as strength, and there is nothing for which they have less respect than for weakness, especially military weakness. For that reason the old doctrine of a balance of power is unsound*. We cannot afford, if we can help it, to work on narrow margins, offering temptations* to a trial of
35 strength. If the Western Democracies stand together in strict adherence to the principles of the United Nations Charter, their influence for furthering those principles will be immense and no one is likely to molest* them. If however they become divided or falter in their duty and if these all-important years are allowed to slip away, then indeed catastrophe may overwhelm us all [...].

Winston Churchill: Sinews of Peace, March 5, 1946, reprinted in: Jussi Hanhimäki (ed.): The Cold War. A History in Documents and Eyewitness Accounts. Oxford (OUP) 2004, pp. 47 f.

valiant very brave and determined, esp. in a difficult situation

to persevere [ˌpɜː(r)sɪˈvɪə(r)] to continue trying to achieve sth. difficult

unsound not based on sensible ideas
temptation Versuchung

to molest to abuse, to interfere with, to behave in a violent or threatening way towards sb.

Josef Stalin (1879–1953)

Born in Georgia in 1879, Stalin (born Josef Wissarionowitsch Dschugaschwili) only learned Russian at the age of eleven. Upon his entry into a seminary* in 1894, he was first confronted with Marxist writings. He became a member of the Russian Social Democratic Labour Party in 1898 and was excluded from the seminary one year later because of his involvement in revolutionary activities.

When the Labour Party was divided in 1903, Stalin joined the Bolsheviks, led by Lenin (cf. chapter 2) and was shortly afterwards banned to Siberia. He fled Siberia and was frequently arrested and sentenced in the period that followed, but never spent much time in prison.

In 1912, Lenin appointed him a member of the Bolsheviks' central committee. From this time onwards, he called himself Stalin ("the one of steel").

Upon the end of tsarist rule in 1917, Stalin became People's Commissar for Questions of Nationality and used the Red Army to violently reintegrate those Caucasus peoples who had seceded* from Russia. He became more and more influential in the Bolshevik Party, and the newly-created office of General-Secretary which he assumed in 1922 was used to combat adversaries and to consolidate his position of strength. Even though Lenin had warned of Stalin's ambitions, Stalin retained his offices upon Lenin's death and suppressed any oppositional aspirations, eliminating his opponents during the years 1925 to 1929.

Under the maxim "Socialism in One Country"* Stalin then used his unrestricted power to enforce the collectivization of agriculture and a rigorous programme of industrialization with the help of five-year-plans. From 1934 to 1939, the "Great Purge"* eliminated Stalin's potential or alleged opponents. Show trials were used to judge over and eventually execute the remaining Bolshevik leadership dating back to the time of Lenin.

When Nazi Germany began its attack on the Soviet Union ("Operation Barbarossa", cf. chapter 3) despite the Hitler-Stalin Pact of 1939, Stalin took over the military leadership of the country. At the conferences of Yalta and Potsdam in 1945, he asserted the kind of expansionist striving for power which was to determine the post-war world until 1990. An example of this was the Korean War, which clearly showed Stalin's determination to expand the Soviet sphere of influence.

Stalin died on 5 March 1953. In the wake of the so-called process of "destalinization" from 1956 onwards, the principle of sole rule was restricted and replaced by the collective leadership of the party. In addition, crimes committed by Stalin and his henchmen* were identified and condemned.

---

*seminary *Priesterseminar* • **to secede** *sich abspalten* • **"Socialism in One Country"** „*Sozialismus in einem Land*" • **the "Great Purge"** *die „große Säuberung"* • **henchmen** *Schergen*

S 6b Josef Stalin

Reply to Churchill

In a 1946 interview with *Pravda*, the Russian daily newspaper associated with the Communist Party, Stalin responded to Churchill's speech.

Pre-task
1. In his response, Stalin compares Churchill to Hitler. Can you think of reasons? Discuss.

Tasks
2. Describe the similarities between Churchill and his "friends" (l. 2) and "Hitler and his friends" (l. 4), as seen by Stalin, and state his justifications for the expansion of the Soviet sphere of influence.
3. Explain Stalin's justifications in their historical context.

Post-tasks
4. Write an argument between Churchill and Stalin in which they justify their positions.
5. Read the box containing information about the Sovietization of the satellite states (on page 524). Against this backdrop, take a critical stand on Stalin's view of Communism as contained in the last part of his interview.

[...] In substance, Mr. Churchill now stands in the position of a firebrand of war. And Mr. Churchill is not alone here. He has friends not only in England but also in the United States of America.
In this respect, one is reminded remarkably of Hitler and his friends. Hitler began
5 to set war loose by announcing his racial theory, declaring that only people speaking the German language represent a fully valuable nation. Mr. Churchill begins to set war loose, also by a racial theory, maintaining that only nations speaking the English language are fully valuable nations, called upon to decide the destinies of the entire world.
10 The German racial theory brought Hitler and his friends to the conclusion that the Germans, as the only fully valuable nation, must rule over other nations. The English racial theory brings Mr. Churchill and his friends to the conclusion that nations speaking the English language, being the only fully valuable nations, should rule over the remaining nations of the world. [...]
15 As a result of the German invasion, the Soviet Union has irrevocably* lost in battles with the Germans, and also during the German occupation and through the expulsion of Soviet citizens to German slave labor camps, about 7,000,000 people. In other words, the Soviet Union has lost in men several times more than Britain and the United States together.
20 It may be that some quarters are trying to push into oblivion* these sacrifices of the Soviet people which insured the liberation of Europe from the Hitlerite yoke*. But the Soviet Union cannot forget them. One can ask therefore, what can be surprising in the fact that the Soviet Union, in a desire to ensure its security for the future, tries to achieve that these countries should have governments whose rela-
25 tions to the Soviet Union are loyal? How can one, without having lost one's reason, qualify these peaceful aspirations of the Soviet Union as 'expansionist tendencies' of our Government?
[...] Mr. Churchill wanders around the truth when he speaks of the growth of the influence of the Communist parties in Eastern Europe [...]. The growth of the in-
30 fluence of Communism cannot be considered accidental. It is a normal function. The influence of the Communists grew because during the hard years of the mastery of fascism in Europe, Communists showed themselves to be reliable, daring and self-sacrificing fighters against fascist regimes for the liberty of peoples.
from "Stalin's Reply to Churchill", March 14, 1946 (interview with *Pravda*), *The New York Times*, p. 4

irrevocably here: permanently, once and for all, conclusively

oblivion obscurity, a situation in which sth./sb. has been completely forgotten
the Hitlerite yoke *das Hitler'sche Joch*

The Sovietization of the Satellite States: "Salami Tactics"

The term "salami tactics" was allegedly first used by the Hungarian Communist Mátyás Rákosi in the late 1940s to describe how the Communist Party silences opposition and takes over from its opponents by "cutting them off like slices of a salami". Generally speaking, "salami tactics" implies taking over control of a country by steps so that the country only realizes it has been taken over when it is too late. As regards the Sovietization of the satellite states, the "salami tactics" employed by the Soviet Union could be divided into six steps:

In a first step, the Red Army supported communist minorities in the country who set up resistance groups.

In a second step, provisional governments were established, with key positions given to exiled Communists.

In a third step, allegedly free elections were held after which key ministries were given to Communists. After this, nationalization and collectivization began.

In a fourth step, terror was used to form new coalition governments with similar-minded parties ("bloc politics") and leaders of the opposition were eliminated.

In a fifth step, Communist governments were established by controlled elections using single lists*.

In a sixth and last step, the country conformed to the Soviet example by concluding treaties of friendship and mutual assistance, etc.

---

* **single list** *Einheitsliste*

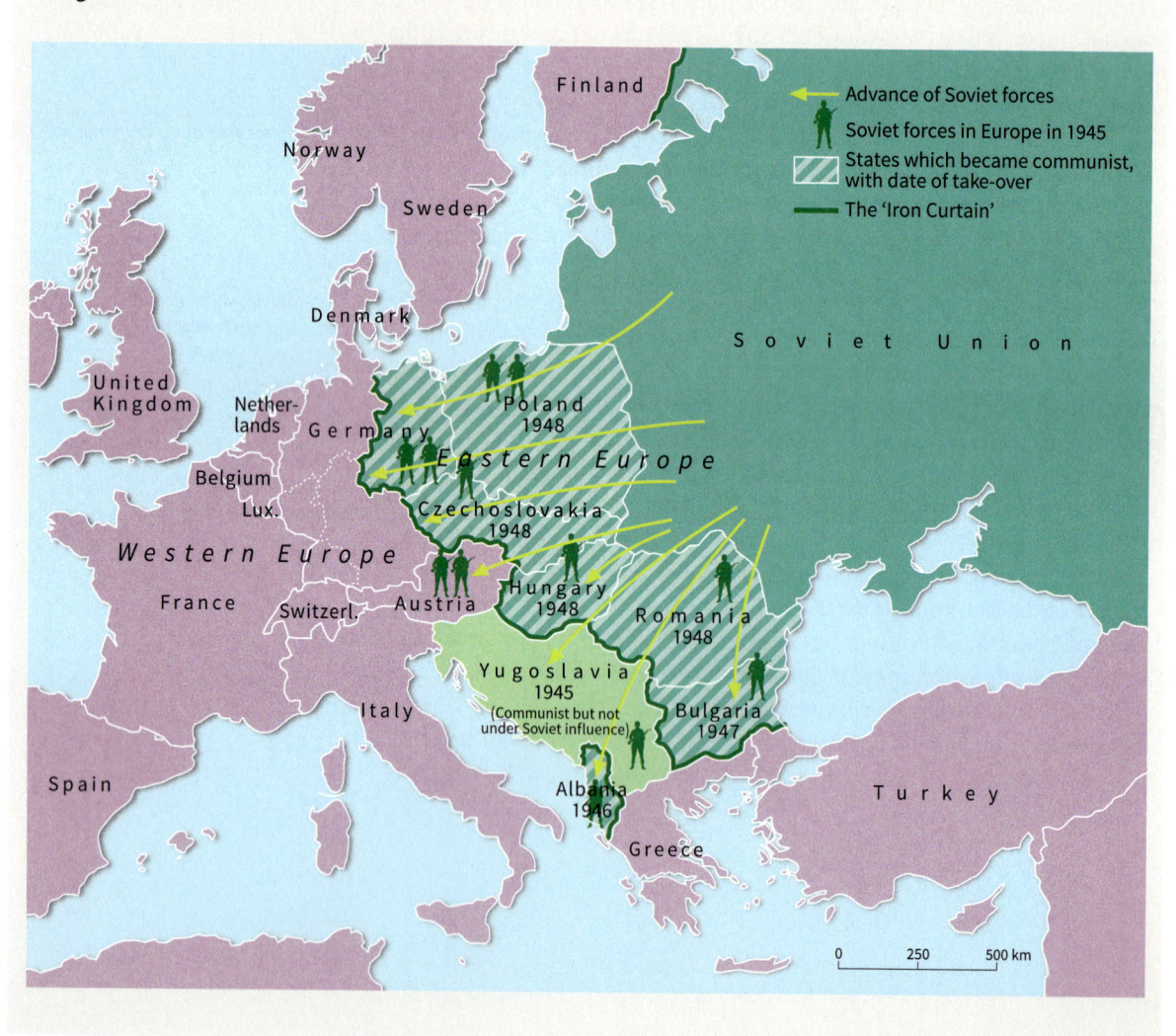

S 7 George F. Kennan

Long Telegram

You have already come across the American diplomat George F. Kennan, who coined the phrase "seminal catastrophe" to characterize the First World War (cf. chapter 2). Living in Moscow since 1933, US Embassy official Kennan analysed the Soviet policy at the request of the American State Department. His findings are contained in the so-called 'Long Telegram' of February 1946.

Pre-task

1. Kennan states that "[w]orld communism is like [a] malignant parasite which feeds only on diseased tissue." (ll. 39 f.) Paraphrase this sentence in your own words and discuss what it reveals about:
   a. Kennan's view on Communism and the reasons for this view and
   b. Kennan's possible suggestions to the American State Department on how to combat Communism effectively.

Tasks

2. Summarize the background context necessary to understand Kennan's statement from lines 39 following (cf. task 1).
3. Examine the persuasive techniques Kennan makes use of in order to convince the American State Department that a policy of strength is necessary.
4. Discuss to what extent the "Long Telegram" contributed to a deterioration in US-Soviet relations, taking into consideration the reliability of Kennan's assessments and the consequences which would result from adhering to his suggestions.

The Chargé* in the Soviet Union to the Secretary of State★
SECRET
Moscow, February 22, 1946 (0.00 p.m.)

USSR still lives in antagonistic "capitalistic encirclement" with which in the long
5 run there can be no permanent peaceful coexistence. [...]
Wherever it is considered timely and promising, efforts will be made to advance official limits of Soviet power. For the moment, these efforts are restricted to certain neighboring points conceived of here* as being of immediate strategic necessity, such as Northern Iran, Turkey, possibly Bornholm*. However, other points
10 may at any time come into question, if and as concealed Soviet political power is extended to new areas. [...]
In summary, we have here a political force committed fanatically to the belief that with US there can be no permanent *modus vivendi,*★ that it is desirable and necessary that the internal harmony of our society be disrupted, our traditional way of
15 life be destroyed, the international authority of our state be broken, if Soviet power is to be secure. [...] I cannot attempt to suggest all answers here. But I would like to record my conviction that problem is within our power to solve – and that without recourse to any general military conflict. And in support of this conviction there are certain observations of a more encouraging nature I should like to make:
20 (1) Soviet power, unlike that of Hitlerite Germany, is neither schematic nor adventuristic. It does not work by fixed plans. It does not take unnecessary risks. Impervious* to logic of reason, and it is highly sensitive to logic of force. For this reason it can easily withdraw – and usually does – when strong resistance is encountered

chargé senior diplomat (so Kennan himself)
Secretary of State James F. Byrnes, cf. S 8

of here in the Soviet government
Bornholm island in the Baltic Sea, belonging to Denmark

modus vivendi (Lat.) an arrangement that helps people who have very different opinions to live or work together

impervious not affected by sth.

at any point. Thus, if the adversary has sufficient force and makes clear his readiness to use it, he rarely has to do so. If situations are properly handled there need be no prestige-engaging showdowns.

(2) Gauged against Western World as a whole, Soviets are still by far the weaker force. Thus, their success will really depend on degree of cohesion, firmness and vigor* which Western World can muster. And this is factor which it is within our power to influence.

vigo(u)r mental energy, enthusiasm, and determination

(3) Success of Soviet system, as form of internal power, is not yet finally proven. It has yet to be demonstrated that it can survive supreme test of successive transfer of power from one individual or group to another. Lenin's death was first such transfer, and its effects wracked Soviet state for 15 years. After Stalin's death or retirement will be second. [...]

For those reasons I think we may approach calmly and with good heart problem of how to deal with Russia. As to how this approach should be made, I only wish to advance, by way of conclusion, following comments: [...]

Much depends on health and vigor of our own society. World communism is like malignant parasite which feeds only on diseased tissue. This is point at which domestic and foreign policies meets *[sic]*. Every courageous and incisive* measure to solve internal problems of our own society, to improve self-confidence, discipline, morale and community spirit of our own people, is a diplomatic victory over Moscow worth a thousand diplomatic notes and joint communiqués*. If we cannot abandon fatalism* and indifference in face of deficiencies of our own society, Moscow will profit – Moscow cannot help profiting by them in its foreign policies. We must formulate and put forward for other nations a much more positive and constructive picture of sort of world we would like to see than we have put forward in past. It is not enough to urge people to develop political processes similar to our own. Many foreign peoples, in Europe at least, are tired and frightened by experiences of past, and are less interested in abstract freedom than in security. They are seeking guidance rather than responsibilities. We should be better able than Russians to give them this. And unless we do, Russians certainly will.

incisive expressed in a clear and direct manner

communiqué an official statement
fatalism the belief that one cannot prevent things from happening, esp. bad things

Finally we must have courage and self-confidence to cling to our own methods and conceptions of human society. After all, the greatest danger that can befall* us in coping with this problem of Soviet communism, is that we shall allow ourselves to become like those with whom we are coping.

to befall to happen to

KENNAN

Telegram, February 22, 1946, History and Public Policy Program Digital Archive, National Archives and Records Administration, Department of State Records (Record Group 59), Central Decimal File, 1945–1949, 861.00/2-2246; reprinted in US Department of State, ed., Foreign Relations of the United States, 1946, Volume VI, Eastern Europe; The Soviet Union (Washington, DC: United States)

Portrait of George Kennan by Ned Siedler (1947), showing him behind a chessboard on which an American and a Russian chess piece stand

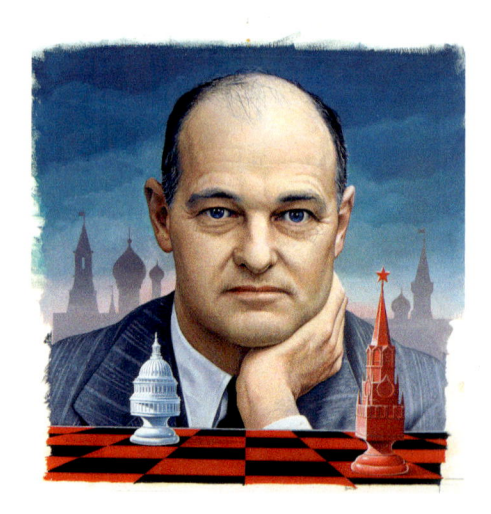

S 8 James F. Byrnes
Stuttgart Speech

This speech was delivered in Stuttgart on 6 September 1946, almost exactly a year to the day after Japan surrendered to the U.S., thus ending the Second World War. United States Secretary of State James F. Byrnes (succeeded in office by George Marshall in 1947) spoke to U.S. military personnel, journalists and leading German officials. Officially entitled "Stuttgart Speech", it has come to be known as the "Speech of Hope" – at least in Germany.

Pre-task

1. Anticipate what Byrnes could state that would make this a "speech of hope" for Germany. Consider Germany's unconditional surrender in May 1945, the carrying out of the Potsdam Agreement and the development of the relations between the occupying powers from 1945 to September 1946.

Tasks

2. Point out Byrnes's criticism of the Allied Control Council as regards the economic unity of Germany and outline the USA's view of how Germany should develop in the future.
3. With the help of the overview section, put the source into the historical context of the division of Germany until 1949 and explain Byrnes's intentions.
4. Byrnes states that no one is interested in turning Germany into "a pawn in a military struggle for power between the East and the West" (ll.2f.). Against the backdrop of the speech and considering the historical context of the division of Germany and Europe from 1945 to 1949, discuss whether Germany was a cause of conflict or caught between the fronts.
5. Evaluate whether Byrnes's speech was a "speech of hope" for Germany, or a "speech of challenge" to the Soviet Union.

Post-task

6. Put yourself into the shoes of the journalists listening to Byrnes's speech. Split up into four groups, representing journalists from Germany (western zones), Britain, France and the Soviet Union. Write their coverage of the speech to be broadcast by their respective radio stations.

[...] It is not in the interest of the German people or in the interest of world peace that Germany should become a pawn* in a military struggle for power between the East and the West. [...] The carrying out of the Potsdam Agreement has, however, been obstructed by the failure of the Allied Control Council to take the neces-
5 sary steps to enable the German economy to function as an economic unit. Essential central German administrative departments have not been established, although they are expressly required by the Potsdam Agreement. The equitable* distribution of essential commodities between the several zones so as to produce a balanced economy throughout Germany and reduce the needs for imports has
10 not been arranged, although that, too, is expressly required by the Potsdam Agreement. The working out of a balanced economy throughout Germany to provide the necessary means to pay for approved imports has not been accomplished, although that too is expressly required by the Potsdam Agreement.
The United States is firmly of the belief that Germany should be administered as

pawn a person who is being used by sb. who is more powerful than them to achieve an aim

equitable fair and reasonable because everyone is treated in the same way

to obliterate to destroy completely

an economic unit and that zonal barriers should be completely obliterated* so far as the economic life and activity in Germany are concerned. The conditions which now exist in Germany make it impossible for industrial production to reach the levels which the occupying powers agreed were essential for a minimum German peacetime economy. Obviously, if the agreed levels of industry are to be reached, we cannot continue to restrict the free exchange of commodities, persons, and ideas throughout Germany. The barriers between the four zones of Germany are far more difficult to surmount than those between normal independent states.

The time has come when the zonal boundaries should be regarded as defining only the areas to be occupied for security purposes by the armed forces of the occupying powers and not as self-contained economic or political units. That was the course of development envisaged by the Potsdam Agreement, and that is the course of development which the American Government intends to follow to the full limit of its authority. It has formally announced that it is its intention to unify the economy of its own zone with any or all of the other zones willing to participate in the unification. So far only the British Government has agreed to let its zone participate. We deeply appreciate their cooperation. Of course, this policy of unification is not extended to exclude the governments not now willing to join. The unification will be open to them at any time they wish to join. We favor the economic unification of Germany. If complete unification cannot be secured, we shall do everything in our power to secure the maximum possible unification. [...]

It is the view of the American Government that the German people throughout Germany, under proper safeguards, should now be given the primary responsibility for the running of their own affairs. [...] It is our view that the German people should now be permitted and helped to make the necessary preparations for setting up a democratic German government [...]. While we shall insist that Germany observe the principles of peace, good-neighborliness, and humanity, we do not want Germany to become the satellite of any power or powers or to live under a dictatorship, foreign or domestic. The American people hope to see peaceful, democratic Germans become and remain free and independent. [...]

The American people want to return the government of Germany to the German people. The American people want to help the German people to win their way back to an honorable place among the free and peace-loving nations of the world.

Stuttgart Speech ("Speech of Hope") by J. F. Byrnes, United States Secretary of State: Restatement of Policy on Germany (September 6, 1946), US Policy; http://usa.usembassy.de/etexts/ga4-460906.htm [28.04.15]

American poster advertising the ERP (European Recovery Program AKA Marshall Plan)

S 9 ▸ The "Marshall Plan" – Selling Democracy?

The United States of America launched the European Recovery Program in 1947, unofficially called the "Marshall Plan" after the US Secretary of State George C. Marshall who first presented his ideas on reconstructing Europe in a speech to students on 5 June 1947. Up until 1952, the USA delivered goods worth about 15 billion dollars to Europe. Marshall Aid was also offered to the eastern European states but Stalin had prevented this, fearing subjugation to capitalism in return for the help.

Pre-task 1. The "Marshall Plan" – Selling Democracy? Discuss possible answers to this question, seen from the perspectives of the USA, the western European countries and the eastern European countries. TIP: Have a look at Kennan's "Long Telegram" again (cf. S 7 ▸).

Tasks

2. Describe both cartoons in detail, including the arrangement of pictorial elements.
3. Explain the view of the Marshall Plan by examining the pictorial elements. Also consider the background of the artist(s) and how this helps to explain the standpoint taken.
4. Discuss to what extent the Marshall Plan aimed at "selling democracy" after all.

Neighbours. Come on Sam! It's up to us again!"
Cartoon by E. H. Shepard, published in the British magazine *Punch* on 1 October 1947

Embedded text:
AMERICAN AID
SELF HELP

Russian cartoon, 1949

Embedded text:
On the skeleton: crisis
On the horse: Marshall Plan
On the flag: to Western Europe

Language support

Zweiteilung here: division into two parts • **Schaufel** shovel

Language support

Pferdegeschirr, Zaumzeug harness • **Sporen** spurs • **ausgemergelt** emaciated

CONNECT

The Berlin Airlift – "Island" of Democracy and Freedom?

Task Designing pre-, while- and post-listening tasks for a podcast about the Berlin Airlift for younger students:
On the website of the German radio station *Bayern 2*, there is a podcast about the Berlin Airlift (approximately 19 minutes) entitled "Die Berliner Luftbrücke: Flieger mit Kohlen und Kartoffeln".
→ www.br.de/radio/bayern2/wissen/radiowissen/geschichte/berliner-luftbruecke-dossier-100.html

Your teacher wants to make use of your bilingual expertise and has asked you to design pre-, while- and post-listening tasks for his Year 9 class that is also dealing with this topic at the moment.

This is what you want your fellow students to learn (learning objectives):
- the preliminary events leading to the Berlin Blockade and to the Airlift,
- how the Airlift was carried out and how it impacted the lives of the Berlin citizens,
- why the Allies did not give up on Berlin,
- how the Airlift impacted the relationship between the German/Berlin population and the Allies,
- how the Airlift contributed to the division of Germany (and Europe) from 1945 to 1949.

In S 12, you find some information about the function and variations of pre-, while- and post-listening tasks.
First, listen to the whole podcast and decide which vocabulary you have to explain in English, since the podcast is in German.
Second, work in groups and design pre-, while- and post-tasks that ensure the attainment of your learning objectives (see above). Try them out in Year 9 if possible!

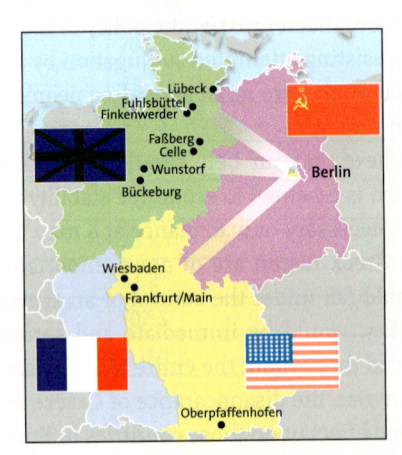

S 12 Pre-, While-, Post-listening Tasks

pre-listening	What help do the students need in advance to prepare or make possible their understanding of the podcast and to help enable them to talk about it? • e.g. collecting words in context, hypotheses, activating already existing knowledge …
while-listening	Which tasks help students to understand the podcast, content-wise and language-wise? • e.g. true/false exercises, gap-filling, matching exercises, odd one out, multiple choice, putting events into the correct chronological order …
post-listening	Which tasks help to consolidate the newly won knowledge and to prepare the students for a balanced assessment, taking into consideration the pros & cons of the issue in question? • e.g. defining central terms, playing taboo, designing a quiz, visualizations (Mind Map, fishbone diagram) …

S 13 Fritz Meinhard

So muss er ja gedeihen!

The German cartoon "This'll make it thrive" by Fritz Meinhard was published in the *Stuttgarter Zeitung* on 19 October 1949, shortly after the foundation of the GDR on 7 October 1949.

Pre-task
1. Revise what you have learned about the antagonism between East and West and communism and capitalism so far and how this antagonism impacted development in the respective German occupation zones.

Tasks
2. Work with a partner. Partner A describes the left side of the cartoon, partner B the right side. Afterwards, agree on commonalities and differences in your descriptions.
3. Now swap sides. Partner A explains the elements on the right-hand side of the cartoon, partner B the elements on the left-hand side. Afterwards, agree on commonalities and differences in your explanations.
4. Considering your findings from tasks 1 to 3 and taking the title of the cartoon into consideration, explain the cartoonist's message.
5. Take a critical stand on this message, both from a contemporary perspective and from a present-day perspective.

Language support

gedeihen to thrive • **Wappenadler** heraldic eagle • **füttern** to feed • **Zylinder** top hat • **Handschuhe** gloves • **Hammer und Sichel** hammer and sickle • **Gefieder** feathers • **struppig** scrubby • **Wappen** coat of arms, crest

S 14a London Documents

The London Documents (*Frankfurter Dokumente*) from 1 July 1948 were the result of the London Conference and authorized the summoning of a Constituent Assembly to work out a draft constitution for the FRG.

Pre-task
1. The London Documents included some guidelines for the draft constitution. What would the Allies demand from the Constituent Assembly? Speculate.

Tasks
2. Point out the guidelines for the Constitution, as demanded by the Allies.
3. Explain the importance of these constitutional provisions for a new governmental organization in Germany.

4. Evaluate to what extent the London Documents seem to be the logical result of the policies employed by the western Allies in their respective occupation zones.

Beschlüsse resolutions

Verfassungsgebende Versammlung Constituent [kən'stɪtjʊənt] Assembly
einberufen to summon
zusammentreten to convene
geeignet suited
zerrissen torn
wiederherstellen to restore
angemessene Zentralinstanz appropriate central authority

Vorlage submittal

In Übereinstimmung mit den Beschlüssen* ihrer Regierung autorisieren die Militärgouverneure der amerikanischen, britischen und französischen Besatzungszone in Deutschland die Ministerpräsidenten der Länder ihrer Zonen, eine Verfassungsgebende Versammlung* einzuberufen*, die spätestens am 1.9.1948 zusammentreten* sollte.
[...] Die Verfassungsgebende Versammlung wird eine demokratische Verfassung ausarbeiten, die für die beteiligten Länder eine Regierungsform des föderalistischen Typs schafft, die am Besten geeignet* ist, die gegenwärtig zerrissene* deutsche Einheit schließlich wiederherzustellen*, und die Rechte der beteiligten Länder schützt, eine angemessene Zentralinstanz* schafft und Garantien der individuellen Rechte und Freiheiten enthält.
Wenn die Verfassung in der von der Verfassungsgebenden Versammlung ausgearbeiteten Form mit diesen allgemeinen Grundsätzen nicht im Widerspruch steht, werden die Militärgouverneure ihre Vorlage* zur Ratifizierung genehmigen. Die Verfassungsgebende Versammlung wird daraufhin aufgelöst.

Frankfurter Dokumente, 1. Juli 1948, Büro der Ministerpräsidenten des amerikanischen, britischen u. französischen Besatzungsgebietes (Ed.), Dokumente betreffen die Begründung einer neuen staatlichen Ordnung in den amerikanischen, britischen und französischen Besatzungszonen, Wiesbaden 1948, pp. 15–17

S 14b London Documents: Occupation Statute

The London Documents did not only contain the call to draft a constitution, but also restricted the sovereignty of a future West German state in the so-called "occupation statute" (*Besatzungsstatut*).

Pre-task 1. In which aspects of sovereignty would the Allies probably restrict the future West German state so that they would be able to interfere quickly if needed? Make an educated guess.

Tasks 2. Describe which restrictions of sovereignty a future West German state would be subject to.
3. Explain why the Allies decided to restrict these aspects of sovereignty in particular.
4. Against the backdrop of the question whether Germany was a cause of conflict or caught between the fronts in the initial stages of the Cold War, give an evaluation of the London Documents.

Post-task 5. Do further research to find out when and why the Occupation Statute ended.

verfassungsmäßig constitutional

Befugnis authority

Die Schaffung einer verfassungsmäßigen* deutschen Regierung macht eine sorgfältige Definition der Beziehungen zwischen dieser Regierung und den Alliierten Behörden notwendig. Nach Ansicht der Militärgouverneure sollen diese Beziehungen auf den folgenden Grundsätzen beruhen:
A: Die Militärgouverneure werden den deutschen Regierungen Befugnisse* der Gesetzgebung, der Verwaltung und der Rechtsprechung gewähren und sich sol-

che Zuständigkeiten* vorbehalten*, die nötig sind, um [...] die Militärgouverneure in die Lage zu setzen:

a) Deutschlands auswärtige Beziehungen vorläufig wahrzunehmen und zu leiten.
b) Das Mindestmaß* der notwendigen Kontrollen über den deutschen Außenhandel [...] auszuüben.
c) Vereinbarte oder noch zu vereinbarende Kontrollen [...] auszuüben.
d) Das Ansehen der Besatzungsstreitkräfte zu schützen und [...] ihre Sicherheit [und] ihre Bedürfnisse [...] zu gewährleisten.
e) Die Beachtung der von ihnen gebilligten* Verfassungen zu sichern.

B. Die Militärgouverneure werden die Ausübung ihrer vollen Machtbefugnisse wieder aufnehmen, falls ein Notstand die Sicherheit bedroht, und um nötigenfalls die Beachtung der Verfassungen und des Besatzungsstatutes zu sichern.

C. Die Militärgouverneure werden die oben erwähnten Kontrollen nach folgendem Verfahren* ausüben:

a) Jede Verfassungsänderung ist den Militärgouverneuren zur Genehmigung vorzulegen. [...]
c) Die Beobachtung, Beratung und Unterstützung der föderativen Regierung und der Länderregierungen bezüglich der Demokratisierung des politischen Lebens, der sozialen Beziehungen und der Erziehung werden eine besondere Verantwortlichkeit der Militärgouverneure sein. [...]

Der Parlamentarische Rat 1948–1949. Akten und Protokolle, Bd. 1 Vorgeschichte. Boppard 1975, pp. 33 ff.

Zuständigkeit competence
vorbehalten to reserve

Mindestmaß minimum

billigen to approve

Verfahren proceedings

Conference of the West German Minister Presidents in Koblenz on 8 July 1948. The Minister Presidents attending expressed serious concerns about the London Documents, fearing they would finalize the division of Germany.

S 15 ADN *(Allgemeiner Deutscher Nachrichtendienst)*

The Founding of the GDR

When it became more and more obvious that the Western powers were planning for the foundation of a West German state, the SED (*Sozialistische Einheitspartei Deutschlands*) began to summon People's Congresses that were approved by single lists and that worked out a constitution for an East German state. On 7 October 1949, the German Democratic Republic was eventually proclaimed, as announced in press releases such as the one below, issued by the news agency ADN (*Allgemeiner Deutscher Nachrichtendienst*, founded in 1946, the only officially approved news agency of the GDR).

Pre-task

1. Put yourself into the shoes of the news presenter who is reading out the press release for the public. Use the words and phrases provided in the box and write your announcement about the founding of the GDR along these lines, keeping the same order.

> 7. Oktober 1949 • neuer, unabhängiger, freier gesamtdeutscher Staat • Wille des Volkes • Abwehr der vom Westen drohenden Gefahr der Spaltung • schwere nationale Notlage • frei von Bevormundung • drückende Fesseln des Besatzungsstatuts • Friede, Aufbau, nationale Einheit • Ausgangspunkt einer Entwicklung

Tasks

2. Scan the press release for the words and phrases in the box and check how close your announcement came to the original.
3. Characterize the GDR, as presented in this press release, especially in contrast to the FRG.

---

gesamtdeutsch all-German
Deutscher Volksrat German People's Council

Wiederherstellung restoration
vollstrecken to execute
Notlage state of emergency
John McCloy was High Commissar and the highest-ranking representative of the Allies
Tagung meeting
Volkskammer People's Parliament
beauftragen to commission
Bevormundung paternalism
einstimmig unanimous(ly) [juːˈnænɪməs]
weltanschaulich ideological

die Bahn frei machen für to pave the way for
Aufbau reconstruction

Am 7. Oktober 1949 wurde in der deutschen Hauptstadt Berlin die Grundlage eines neuen, unabhängigen und freien gesamtdeutschen* Staates geschaffen. Eine neue Ära deutscher Geschichte hat damit begonnen. Der Deutsche Volksrat*, in dem alle Parteien und Massenorganisationen vertreten sind, hat das Schicksal Deutschlands in seine Hand genommen und ist darangegangen, den Willen des deutschen Volkes zur Wiederherstellung* der Einheit und zur Abwehr der vom Westen drohenden Gefahr der Spaltung zu vollstrecken*. Angesichts der schweren nationalen Notlage*, wie sie durch die Gründung der amerikanischen McCloy*-Republik in Bonn entstand, hat sich der Deutsche Volksrat auf seiner 9. Tagung* als Provisorische Deutsche Volkskammer* konstituiert. Er hat gleichzeitig die vom Dritten Volkskongress beschlossene Verfassung der Deutschen Demokratischen Republik in Kraft gesetzt und Otto Grotewohl mit der Bildung einer demokratischen deutschen Regierung beauftragt*, die frei ist von der Bevormundung* irgendwelcher Hohen Kommissare, frei von den drückenden Fesseln eines Besatzungsstatuts.

Der Volksrat nahm vor Beendigung seiner Tätigkeit einstimmig* ein Manifest der Nationalen Front des demokratischen Deutschland an, das sich an alle Deutschen ohne Rücksicht auf ihre politische, soziale und weltanschauliche* Stellung wendet und sie auffordert, durch Unterstützung der Nationalen Front die Bahn frei zu machen* für Frieden, Aufbau* und nationale Freiheit.

Der 7. Oktober 1949 ist der Geburtstag eines neuen, demokratischen und freien Deutschlands, der Ausgangspunkt einer Entwicklung, die, folgerichtig zu Ende gegangen, das deutsche Volk neuem Wohlstand und einem dauerhaften Frieden entgegenführen wird.

Erklärung des AND anlässlich der Gründung der Deutschen Demokratischen Republik, Berlin, 7. Okt. 1949, www.zum.de/psm/n45/adn_45_2.php [28.4.15]

Konrad Adenauer (1876 – 1967)

Konrad Adenauer was born in Cologne on 5 January 1876. After studies at the universities of Munich and Bonn, he became a lawyer and found his way into politics via the Catholic Centre Party (cf. chapter 1) becoming mayor of Cologne in 1917. In 1921, Adenauer was elected President of the Prussian State Council and, in 1929, he was re-elected mayor of Cologne. His resolute opposition to the Nazis led to his deposition as mayor soon after Hitler's "seizure of power" in 1933. Adenauer was forbidden to live in Cologne and was put under house arrest in his house in Rhöndorf near Bonn.

In 1948, the Western occupational powers appointed Adenauer President of the Parliamentary Council that was to function as the Constituent Assembly and as such to work out a constitution for West Germany. After having taken over the chairmanship of the CDU (a party he himself had helped to create), Adenauer was elected as the first Chancellor of the FRG on 15 September 1949. Until 1955, he was simultaneously the FRG's foreign minister.

Under the motto "Keine Experimente!", Adenauer stood for the western integration of the FRG and a unified Europe which he considered the only sensible solution in the bipolar world characterized by the Cold War. The trust he had gained among the population made it possible to include the FRG in the process of European unification. In addition, the FRG gained the right to rearm after joining NATO in 1955. One other concern of Adenauer was reconciliation* with France, culminating in the Franco-German Treaty of Friendship of 1963.

On 10 October 1963, Adenauer resigned from office and he gave up the chairmanship of the CDU in 1966. He died in his house in Rhöndorf in 1967, aged 91.

---

reconciliation [ˌrekənsɪliθeɪʃ(ə)n] *Wiederversöhnung, Aussöhnung*

S 16 Konrad Adenauer

Ansprache nach der Schlussabstimmung über das Grundgesetz

As its President, Adenauer gave a speech to the Parliamentary Council after it had voted on the Basic Law on 8 May 1949.

Pre-task
1. Adenauer himself calls the draft constitution a "compromise", implying that the Basic Law did not meet with unconditional support. What would speak against drafting a constitution for a West German state in general? Hypothesize.

Tasks
2. Skim through the speech for reservations about the Basic Law which Adenauer talks about "between the lines".
3. Describe Adenauer's wishes for Germany's future.
4. Discuss to that extent it would be justified to call Adenauer a "Chancellor of the Allies", taking into consideration the autobiographical account and S 16 .

Post-task
5. Who was responsible for the division of Germany and Europe between 1945 and 1949: the Western Allies or the Soviet Union? Revise this chapter and give an evaluation.

bestreiten to deny	[...] Meine Damen und Herren! Es ist wohl in Wahrheit – und ich glaube, auch keiner von denen, die ihre Nein-Stimme begründet haben, wird das bestreiten* – für uns Deutsche der erste frohe Tag seit dem Jahre 1933. Wir wollen von da an rechnen und nicht erst von dem Zusammenbruch an, so schwer die Jahre des Zusammenbruchs auch waren. Die Jahre von 1933 bis 1945, die uns in einer fürchterlichen Knechtschaft* sahen, dürfen nicht aus unserem Gedächtnis gewischt werden. Die Zeit, die hinter uns liegt, war schwer, und wir beginnen erst langsam einen Blick und einen Schritt in eine bessere Zukunft zu tun. [...]
Knechtschaft bondage	
Mängel shortcomings	Wir haben ein Kompromiss geschlossen. Über das Kompromiss ist manches gesagt worden. Jedes Kompromiss hat Fehler und Mängel*. Aber ein Kompromiss hat auch einen großen Vorteil. Es lehrt die Parteien, die so gezwungen waren, miteinander zu arbeiten, auch im politischen Gegner den überzeugten, den ehrlichen Gegner zu schätzen. [...]
menschenwürdig humane	Wir wünschen die Einheit Deutschlands, wir wünschen sie von ganzem Herzen und von ganzer Seele. Wir wünschen ein freies Deutschland, in dem der deutsche Mensch ein menschenwürdiges* Dasein führen kann wie jeder andere europäische Mensch. Wir in der Westzone sind auf dem Wege zur politischen Freiheit.
Zustände conditions	Wie die Zustände* in der Ostzone sind, haben Sie eben gehört. Das, was bei uns, und das, was in der Ostzone geschieht, ist ebenso wenig zu vergleichen, wie Feuer und Wasser zu vergleichen sind. Feuer und Wasser kann man nicht miteinander mischen. Deswegen möchte ich in dieser bedeutungsvollen Stunde den alliierten Mächten zurufen: Wir wollen nicht, dass durch die Verhandlungen in Paris* etwa eine Annäherung der Zustände in den Westzonen an die in der Ostzone erreicht wird.
die Verhandlungen in Paris the last conference of the Council of Foreign Ministers from 23 May to 20 June, confirming the end of the Berlin Blockade	
Bodenreform land reform	(Abg. Renner: Keine Bodenreform*!) Wir wollen keine solche Vermischung, sondern wir möchten, dass die Ostzone zu den gleichen Zuständen gelangt, in denen wir leben, (Lebhafte Zustimmung.) damit wir dann die Einheit und die Freiheit Deutschlands als gesichert ansehen können. [...]
Kriegsgefangene prisoners of war (POWs)	Wir haben noch weitere Wünsche; wir wünschen auch, es möge auf dieser Pariser Konferenz endgültig dafür gesorgt werden, dass unsere Kriegsgefangenen* zurückkehren. (Bravo!)
Verschleppte displaced persons (DPs) Ausgetriebene the expelled göttlich divine	Wir wünschen auch die Rückkehr der Verschleppten*, die Rückkehr der Ausgetriebenen*, und wir wünschen schließlich auch, dass man dort über die Grenzziehung im Osten spricht und über die Oder-Neiße-Linie, so wie wir es nach göttlichem* und menschlichem Recht verlangen können. (Bravorufe und Händeklatschen rechts und bei der SPD.)
Missklang discord Verpflichtung obligation	Wir haben den größten Teil der Arbeit an den Aufgaben, die dem Parlamentarischen Rat gestellt worden waren, vollendet, auch wenn hier und da ein Missklang* dazwischentönte, doch getragen von dem Gefühl der Liebe und der Verpflichtung* gegenüber dem deutschen Volke. Meine Damen und Herren! Wir wünschen, dass Gott dieses Volk und dieses Werk segnen möge, zum Segen Europas und zum Segen des Friedens in der Welt! (Erneute lebhafte Bravorufe und Händeklatschen.) Ich schließe die Sitzung.

Parlamentarischer Rat. Stenographischer Bericht. 10. Sitzung. 8. Mai 1949, S. 241–243; www.konrad-adenauer.de/dokumente/reden/ansprache-parlamentarischer-rat [28.4.15]

CONNECT

„Bonn ist nicht Weimar."

Task Explaining the lessons learned from Weimar in the form of a jigsaw puzzle:
"Bonn ist nicht Weimar" is the title of a 1956 book by the journalist Fritz René Allemann, putting the emphasis on differences between the Weimar Constitution of 1919 and the Basic Law of 1949. However, instead of focussing on the differences only, it is your task to explain the lessons learned from Weimar.
In order to do so, split up into groups, each group dealing with one aspect of comparison (expert groups). Copy and fill in your parts of the table. Then form new groups in which all aspects of comparison are represented (jigsaw groups). Exchange your information and fill in the other parts of the table. Afterwards, get together in your expert groups again. Together, discuss which lessons from Weimar the creators of the Basic Law have learned, and why they were deemed necessary.

For the fast ones: Go back to chapter 1 and discuss to what extent the Basic Law is a continuation and realization of the demands and ideas of 1848/49.

Link to the Basic Law in English translation: www.btg-bestellservice.de/pdf/80201000.pdf
Weimar Constitution: cf. chapter 3.

S 17 Aspects of Comparison

ASPECT ↓	1919	1949	Lesson learned?
President			
Chancellor			
Basic Rights			
Voting System			
Political Parties			
Bundestag and Bundesrat			
Status of Judges			
Referenda			

The Cold War: Cooperation and Conflicts

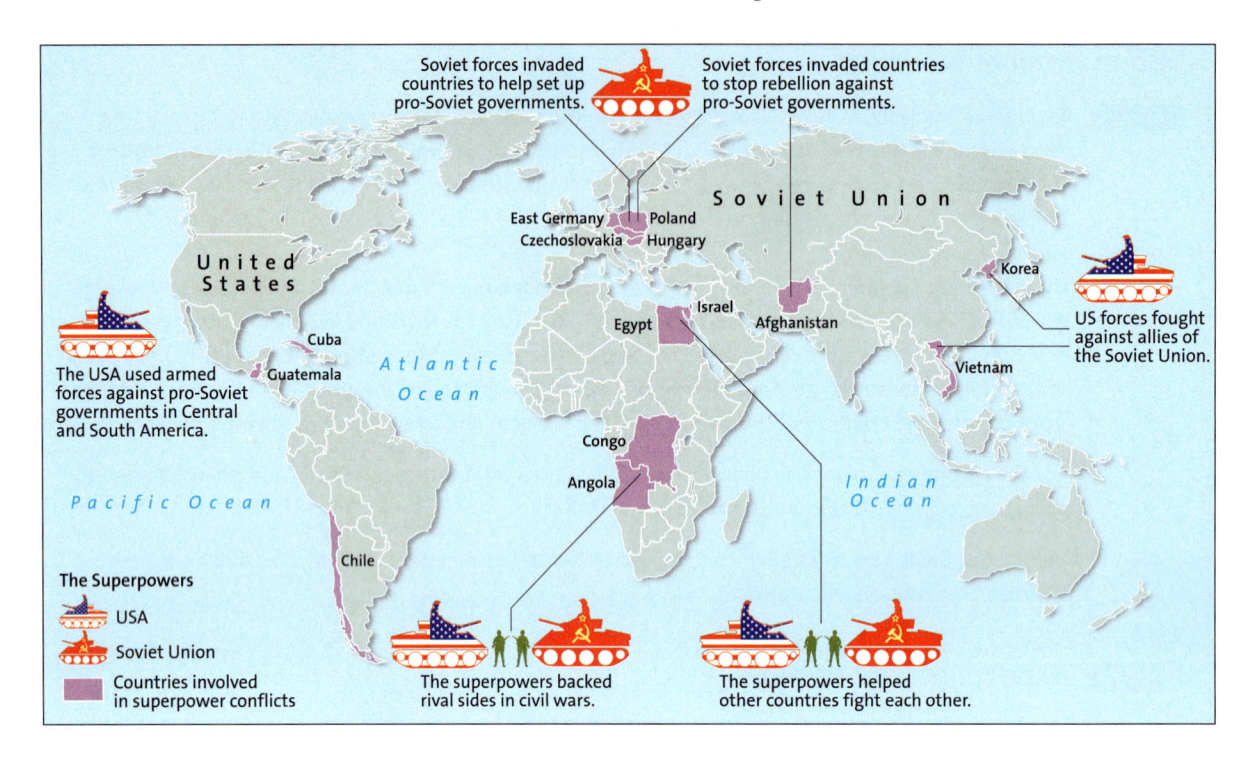

Map labels:
- Soviet forces invaded countries to help set up pro-Soviet governments.
- Soviet forces invaded countries to stop rebellion against pro-Soviet governments.
- The USA used armed forces against pro-Soviet governments in Central and South America.
- US forces fought against allies of the Soviet Union.
- The superpowers backed rival sides in civil wars.
- The superpowers helped other countries fight each other.

Countries labelled: United States, Soviet Union, East Germany, Poland, Czechoslovakia, Hungary, Korea, Cuba, Guatemala, Israel, Egypt, Afghanistan, Vietnam, Congo, Angola, Chile

The Superpowers
- USA
- Soviet Union
- Countries involved in superpower conflicts

S 18 Cooperation and Conflicts: On the Verge of the Apocalypse?

The Cold War period is characterized by a series of conflicts, but also by cooperation, for example the process of the European unification.

Task Distribute the given examples of cooperation and conflicts that occurred during the period of the Cold War and prepare two-minute-presentations on each to be given in class when fitting. All the examples should be covered – feel free to add more if you like. After the presentations, copy the chart provided below and draw the "Cold War Fever Curve" by classifying each aspect, stating how much it contributed to either apocalypse or détente.

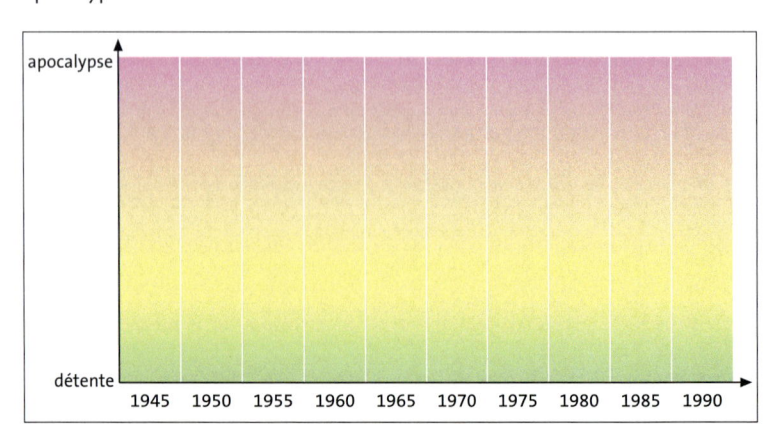

Chart: y-axis from "détente" (bottom) to "apocalypse" (top); x-axis years 1945, 1950, 1955, 1960, 1965, 1970, 1975, 1980, 1985, 1990.

Schuman Declaration, 1951; ECSC	Stalin (March) Notes, 1952	NATO, 1949 and Warsaw Pact, 1955	Korean War, 1950 ff.
17 June 1953	Vietnam War, 1955 ff.	Hungarian Uprising, 1956	Poznań Uprising 1956
Treaty of Rome, 1957; EEC	U2 Incident, 1960	Élysée Treaty, 1963	"space race", 1955 ff.
Prague Spring, 1968; Breshnev Doctrine	Quadripartite Agreement on Berlin, 1972	CSCE, 1973 and Helsinki Accords	SALT I, 1969 ff. and SALT II, 1972 ff.
War in Afghanistan, 1979 ff.	Able Archer 83	?	?

S 19 Eric J. Hobsbawm

The Golden Years

Eric Hobsbawm (1917–2012) was a British historian and Professor of World and Western History. In this excerpt from his work "The Age of Extremes", he gives three reasons why the Cold War changed the whole world.

Pre-task
1. What are the three reasons Hobsbawm might put forward to explain why the Cold War changed the whole world? Identify the odd one out and give reasons for your choice.
   a. It largely eclipsed pre-WWII-conflicts.
   b. It revived colonialism and imperialism.
   c. It made a provisional state of affairs permanent for a long time.
   d. It led to the establishment of immense reservoirs of armaments.

Tasks
2. Scan the text and find the odd one out.
3. Explain the title of Hobsbawm's book (cf. introductory remarks) with the help of the text.
4. Against the backdrop of the text excerpt, discuss Hobsbawm's stance towards the idea that the world was on the verge of the apocalypse.

The Cold War had transformed the international scene in three respects. First, it had eliminated, or overshadowed, all but one of the rivalries and conflicts that shaped world politics before the Second World War. Some disappeared because the empires of the imperial era vanished, and with them the rivalries of the colo-
5 nial powers over dependent territories under their rule. [...] France and (West) Germany buried the old hatchet* after 1947 not because the Franco-Germany conflict had become unthinkable – the French government thought about it all the time – but because their common membership of the U.S. camp and the hegemony of Washington over Western Europe would not allow Germany to get out of
10 hand. [...]
Second, the Cold War had frozen the international situation, and in doing so had stabilized what was an essentially unfixed and provisional state of affairs. Germany was the most obvious example. For forty-six years it remained divided [...] into

to bury the hatchet *das Kriegsbeil begraben*

four sectors: the West, which became the Federal Republic in 1949; the middle, which became the German Democratic Republic in 1954; and the East, beyond the Oder-Neisse line, which expelled most of its Germans and became part of Poland and the U.S.S.R. The end of the Cold War and the disintegration of the U.S.S.R. reunited the two western sectors and left the Soviet-annexed parts of East Prussia detached and isolated, separated from the rest of Russia by the now independent state of Lithuania. It left the Poles with German promises to accept the 1945 frontiers, which did not reassure them. Stabilization did not mean peace. [...]

Third, the Cold War had filled the world with arms to a degree that beggars belief [sic]. This was the natural result of forty years when major industrial states had constantly competed to arm themselves against a war that might break out at any moment; forty years of superpowers competing to win friends and influence people by distributing arms all over the globe, not to mention forty years of constant "low intensity" warfare with occasional outbreaks of major conflict. [...]

In 1947 the U.S.A. had recognized the need for an immediate and gigantic project to restore the West European economies, because the supposed danger to these economies – communism and the U.S.S.R. – was easily defined. The economic and political consequences of the collapse of the Soviet Union and Eastern Europe were even more dramatic than the troubles of Western Europe, and would prove even more far-reaching.

Eric J. Hobsbawm: The Age of Extremes. A History of the World, 1914–1991. New York 1996, pp. 252–255

John Fitzgerald Kennedy (JFK) (1917–1963)

JFK was born in Brookline, Massachusetts on 29 May 1917. In 1940, he graduated from Harvard in International Studies. A member of the Democratic Party, JFK became the United States' youngest President (the 35th) when he was elected in 1961, aged 43. Up until the present day, he is also the only Catholic ever to become US President.

In the short time of his term in office, JFK had to master the Cuban Missile Crisis (cf. S 20) and afterwards pursued a policy of détente towards the Soviet Union, for example establishing the so-called "red telephone", a direct telephone line from the Oval Office to the Kremlin to facilitate communication between the USA and the SU and to prevent a nuclear war from breaking out.

On 22 November 1963, JFK and his wife Jackie visited Dallas, Texas, and here he was assassinated, shot while driving through the city in a convertible. The circumstances of the assassination remain unclear up to this day.

Nikita Khrushchev (1894–1971)

Nikita Khrushchev was born in the Ukraine on 17 April 1894, the son of a miner. He worked as a machinist in the mines and became a member of the Communist Party in the wake of the Russian Revolution. In the Russian Civil War, he fought on the side of the Red Army.

In the 1920s Khrushchev worked as party secretary, for example in Kiev, and then moved to Moscow in 1929 where he became chairman of the Communist Party in 1935.

After the end of the Second World War, Khrushchev became the head of state of Ukraine in 1947, but again moved to Moscow only two years later to work in the Central Committee of the Party. After Stalin's death, Khrushchev was elected First Secretary of the Party's Central Committee in 1953 and embarked on the process of "destalinization".

Despite attempts to establish a peaceful coexistence between East and West and several state visits, no solution was found for the "German Question". The situation between East and West then deteriorated, for example with Khrushchev's decision to support the building of the Berlin Wall in 1961, or with his diplomatic defeat in the Cuban Missile Crisis in which he was eventually forced to back down (cf. S 20).

After growing criticism of his rule from within the Party, Khrushchev was overthrown by the Central Committee in October 1964 and was succeeded in office by Leonid Breshnev. Banned from public life as a "non-person", Khrushchev spent his last years in seclusion and died in Moscow in 1971.

CONNECT

The Cuban Missile Crisis – Evaluating "Histotainment"

Task Evaluating the historical accuracy of Ken Follett's description of the beginning of the Cuban Missile Crisis in "Edge of Eternity" in a letter to his publishing house:

The Cuban Missile Crisis of 1962 has frequently been covered in semi-fictional works, such as the film "Thirteen Days" by Roger Donaldson (2000), but also in the third part of Ken Follett's trilogy entitled "Edge of Eternity" (2014). Even though works of fiction usually do not lay claim to historical accuracy, they do of course influence the readership. Thus it makes sense to focus on one example, in this case Follett's novel, and, by means of comparison with a historical source, to evaluate its accuracy since we are frequently confronted with "histotainment" (a blend of 'history' and 'entertainment') and should be able to deal with this critically.

You are to compare the two descriptions of a meeting of Kennedy and his advisors on 16 October 1962 during which the existence of Soviet nukes on Cuba becomes clear and further proceedings and their implications are discussed.

This is what you should do:

STEP 1: Get an overview of the Cuban Missile Crisis. Use the given map and do further research.

STEP 2: Read the transcript of the "off-the-record" meeting on 16 October provided by the US Department of State (http://microsites.jfklibrary.org/cmc/oct16/doc3.html). Then copy and fill in the respective column of the table provided.
STEP 3: Read the extract from Follett's "Edge of Eternity" which is about exactly this meeting. Fill in the other column of the table.
STEP 4: With the help of your table, evaluate the historical accuracy of Follett's text.
STEP 5: Write a (formal!) letter to Follett's publishing house in which you include your evaluation and in which you comment on "histotainment" as such. What are the advantages/disadvantages? What do you recommend when it comes to dealing with and publishing "histotainment"?

Aspects to consider: ↓	Transcript	Follett
Length (actual/felt):		
Participants:		
Information revealed:		
Topics discussed:		
Atmosphere (+ reasons for your impression):		

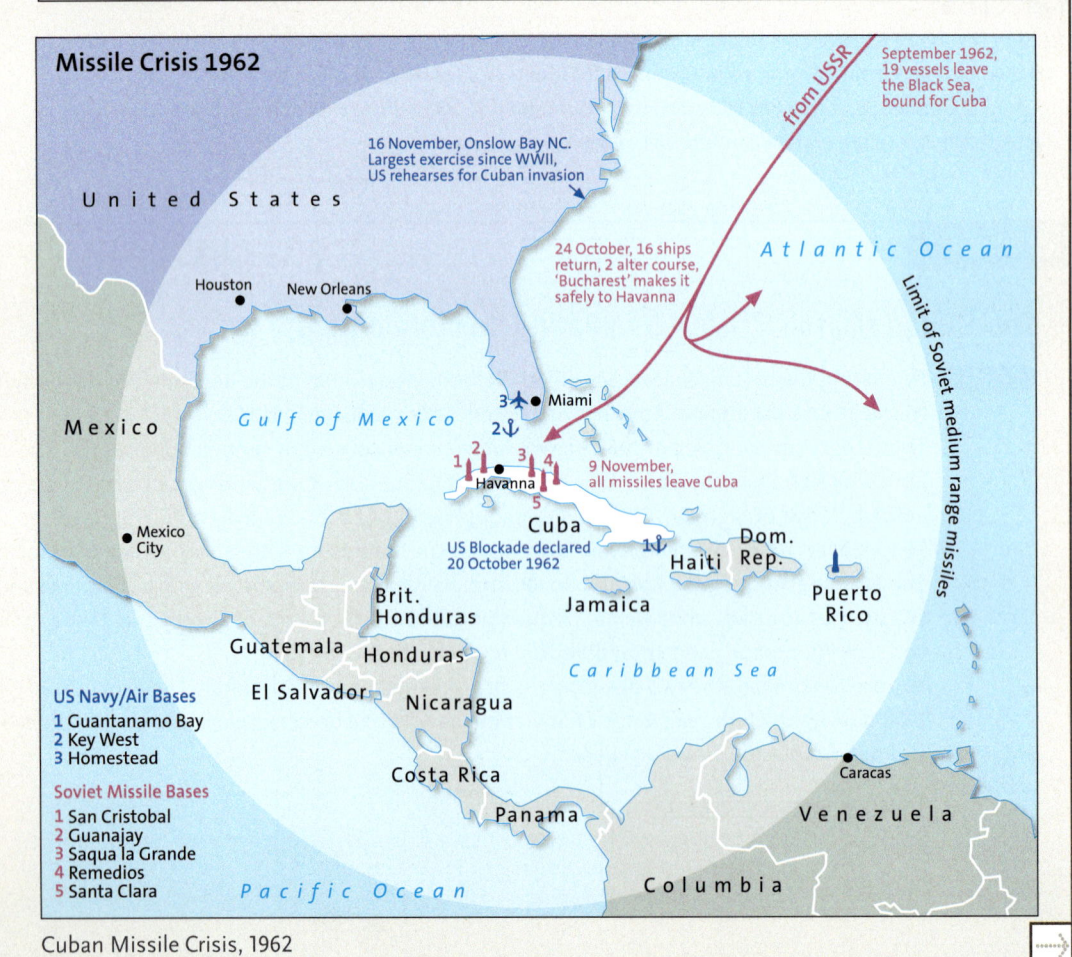

Cuban Missile Crisis, 1962

S 20 Ken Follett

Edge of Eternity

George Jakes, a character created by Follett, is called on to join an emergency meeting in the White House. Jakes is a lawyer and works for Robert F. Kennedy (cf. annotations).

George Jakes did not know what the emergency meeting was. Bobby Kennedy* summoned him and Dennis Wilson* to a crisis meeting in the White House on the morning of Tuesday, 16 October. [...]
'The CIA has some news for us,' the President said. 'Let's begin.'
5 At one end of the room, in front of the fireplace, stood an easel* displaying a large monochrome photograph. The man standing next to it introduced himself as an expert photo interpreter. George had not known that such a profession existed. 'The pictures you are about to see were taken on Sunday by a high-altitude U-2 aircraft of the CIA flying over Cuba.'
10 Everyone knew about the CIA's spy planes. The Soviets had shot one down over Siberia two years ago, and had put the pilot on trial for espionage.
Everyone peered at the photo on the easel. It seemed blurred and grainy, and showed nothing that George could recognize except maybe trees. They needed an interpreter to tell them what they were looking at.
15 'This is a valley in Cuba about twenty miles inland from the port of Mariel,' the CIA man said. He pointed with a little baton*. 'A good-quality new road leads to a large open field. These small shapes scattered around are construction vehicles: bulldozers, backhoes*, and dump trucks. And here –' he tapped the photo for emphasis – 'here, in the middle, you see a group of
20 shapes like planks of wood in a row. They are, in fact, crates eighty feet long by nine feet across. That is exactly the right size and shape to contain a Soviet R-12 intermediate-range ballistic missile, designed to carry a nuclear warhead.'
George just stopped himself from saying *Holy shit*, but others were not so
25 restrained, and for a moment the room was full of astonished curses.
Someone said: 'Are you sure?'
The photo interpreter replied: 'Sir, I have been studying air reconnaissance* photographs for many years, and I can assure you of two things: one, this is exactly what nuclear missiles look like, and two, nothing else looks like this.'
30 God save us, George thought fearfully; the goddamn Cubans have nukes*.
Someone said: 'How the hell did they get there?'
The photo interpreter said: 'Clearly, the Soviets transported them to Cuba in conditions of utter secrecy.'
'Snuck them in under our fucking noses,' said the questioner.
35 Someone else asked: 'What is the range of those missiles?'
'More than a thousand miles.'
'So they could hit ... '
'This building, sir.'

Bobby Kennedy Robert F. Kennedy, the President's brother (in 1962, he was Attorney General)
Dennis Wilson character created by Follett, aide to Robert Kennedy (sb. whose job is to help another person in their work)
easel a frame used for supporting the paper or board that you are painting or drawing on

baton a stick

backhoe *Tiefbagger*

reconnaissance [rɪˈkɒnɪs(ə)ns] the use of soldiers or aircraft to go into an area and get information about an enemy
nuke a nuclear weapon

George had to repress an impulse to get up and leave right away.

'And how long would it take?'

'To get here from Cuba? Thirteen minutes, we calculate.'

Involuntarily, George glanced at the windows, as if he might see a missile coming across the Rose Garden.

The President said: 'That son of a bitch Khrushchev lied to me. He told me he would not deploy nuclear missiles in Cuba.'

Bobby added: 'And the CIA told us to believe him.'

Someone else said: 'This is bound to dominate the rest of the election campaign – three more weeks.' [...]

We have to do something about the missiles, George thought.

He had no idea what.

Fortunately, Jack* Kennedy did.

'First, we need to step up U-2 surveillance of Cuba,' the President said. 'We have to know how many missiles they have and where they are. And then, by God, we're going to take them out.'

George perked up. Suddenly the problem did not seem so great. The US had hundreds of aircraft and thousands of bombs. And President Kennedy taking decisive, violent action to protect America would do no harm to the Democrats in the midterms.

Everyone looked at General Maxwell Taylor, chairmen of the Joint Chiefs of Staff and America's most senior military commander after the President. His wavy hair, slick with brilliantine* and parted high on his head, made George think he might be vain. He was trusted by both Jack and Bobby, through George was not sure why. 'An air strike would need to be followed by a full-scale invasion of Cuba,' Taylor said.

'And we have a contingency plan* for that.'

'We can land a hundred and fifty thousand men there within a week of the bombing.'

Kennedy was still thinking about taking out the Soviet missiles. 'Could we guarantee to destroy every launch site in Cuba?' he asked.

Taylor replied: 'It will never be one hundred per cent, Mr President.'

George had not thought of that snag. Cuba was 777 miles long. The air force might not be able to find every site, let alone destroy them all.

President Kennedy said: 'And I guess any missiles remaining after our air strike would be fired at the US immediately.'

'We would have to assume that, sir,' said Taylor.

The President looked bleak, and George had a sudden vivid sense of the dreadful weight of responsibility he bore. 'Tell me this,' said Kennedy. 'If one missile landed on a medium-sized American city, how bad would that be?' [...]

General Taylor conferred with his aides for a few moments, then turned back to the table. 'Mr President,' he said, 'our calculation is that six hundred thousand people would die.'

Ken Follett: Edge of Eternity. London (Macmillan) 2014, pp. 203–207

Jack John

brilliantine a hair-grooming product (pomade)

contingency plan Notfallplan, Alternativplan

English headlines on Cuban Missile Crisis; October 23, 1962: These were the headlines of England's daily newspapers after President Kennedy's announced the blockade of Cuba.

S 21 John F. Kennedy

„Ich bin ein Berliner"

The speech provided is one of the most famous in history. It was given by the American President John F. Kennedy on the occasion of his visit to Berlin on 26 June 1963, in order to commemorate the 15th anniversary of the Berlin Airlift.

Pre-task
1. „Ich bin ein Berliner." – What does Kennedy express with the help of this sentence? Discuss.

Tasks
2. Point out Kennedy's statements on Communism and present his view of freedom.
3. Examine the persuasive techniques Kennedy makes use of, including his Rome – Berlin equation.
4. Explain why Kennedy singles out the city of Berlin by putting his remarks into their historical context.

Post-task
5. Do further research on JFK and hypothesize on how much he could possibly have contributed to détente had he not been assassinated in 1963.

I am proud to come to this city as the guest of your distinguished Mayor, who has symbolized throughout the world the fighting spirit of West Berlin. [...]
Two thousand years ago the proudest boast was "civis Romanus sum.*" Today, in the world of freedom, the proudest boast is „Ich bin ein Berliner."
5 I appreciate my interpreter translating my German!
There are many people in the world who really don't understand, or say they don't, what is the great issue between the free world and the Communist world. Let them come to Berlin. There are some who say that communism is the wave of the future. Let them come to Berlin. And there are some who say in Europe and else-
10 where we can work with the Communists. Let them come to Berlin. And there are even a few who say that it is true that communism is an evil system, but it permits

civis Romanus sum (Lat.) literally "I am a Roman citizen"; with this sentence Romans would invoke their Roman citizenship that granted them certain privileges (the phrase is often cited in Cicero's speeches against Verres)

us to make economic progress. Lass' sie nach Berlin kommen. Let them come to Berlin.

Freedom has many difficulties and democracy is not perfect, but we have never had to put a wall up to keep our people in, to prevent them from leaving us. I want to say, on behalf of my countrymen, who live many miles away on the other side of the Atlantic, who are far distant from you, that they take the greatest pride that they have been able to share with you, even from a distance, the story of the last 18 years. I know of no town, no city, that has been besieged for 18 years that still lives with the vitality and the force, and the hope and the determination of the city of West Berlin. While the wall is the most obvious and vivid demonstration of the failures of the Communist system, for all the world to see, we take no satisfaction in it, for it is, as your Mayor has said, an offense not only against history but an offense against humanity, separating families, dividing husbands and wives and brothers and sisters, and dividing a people who wish to be joined together.

What is true of this city is true of Germany – real, lasting peace in Europe can never be assured as long as one German out of four is denied the elementary right of free men, and that is to make a free choice. In 18 years of peace and good faith, this generation of Germans has earned the right to be free, including the right to unite their families and their nation in lasting peace, with good will to all people.

You live in a defended island of freedom, but your life is part of the main. So let me ask you, as I close, to lift your eyes beyond the dangers of today, to the hopes of tomorrow, beyond the freedom merely of this city of Berlin, or your country of Germany, to the advance of freedom everywhere, beyond the wall to the day of peace with justice, beyond yourselves and ourselves to all mankind.

Freedom is indivisible, and when one man is enslaved, all are not free. When all are free, then we can look forward to that day when this city will be joined as one and this country and this great Continent of Europe in a peaceful and hopeful globe. When that day finally comes, as it will, the people of West Berlin can take sober satisfaction in the fact that they were in the front lines for almost two decades.

All free men, wherever they may live, are citizens of Berlin, and, therefore, as a free man, I take pride in the words „Ich bin ein Berliner!"

John F. Kennedy; „Ich bin eine Berliner", Speech, June 26, 1968, http://millercenter.org/president/speeches/speech-3376 [28.4.15]

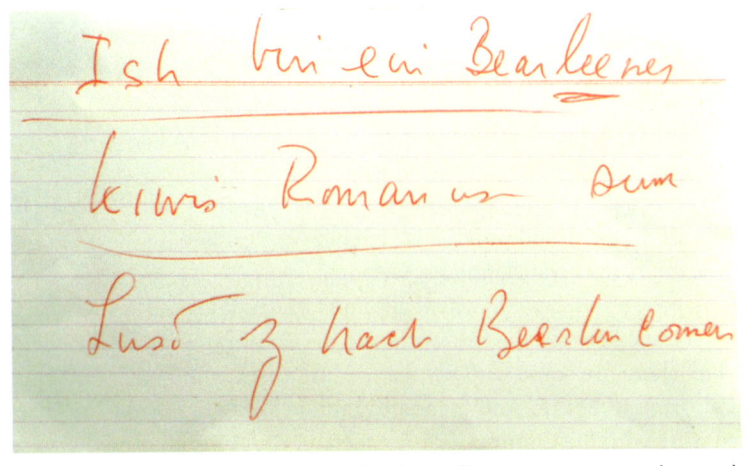

Kennedy's handwritten note, reminding him of how to pronounce the words correctly

Willy Brandt (1913–1992)

Willy Brandt was born as Herbert Ernst Karl Frahm in Lübeck on 18 December 1913. He was affiliated* with the SPD from the beginning, due to his grandfather's influence, but changed to the Socialist Workers' Party (SAP) in 1931. After Hitler's "seizure of power", the SAP commissioned Brandt to build up a party outpost in Oslo. For this, he gave himself the alias "Willy Brandt". Nazi Germany expatriated* him in 1938, and when Norway was occupied by the Wehrmacht in 1940, he became a prisoner of war but was released soon since he was not recognized. After the war, he reported on the Nuremberg Trials for the Scandinavian press and became press attaché* for the Norwegian military commission in Berlin, where he officially called himself Willy Brandt after he had been given back his German citizenship.

From 1949, he was an SPD member of the German Bundestag and became mayor of Berlin in 1957. In 1964, Brandt was elected chairman of the SPD – a post which he was to keep for 23 years. From 1966 to 1969, he was Vice-Chancellor and Foreign Minister, and in 1969 he was elected German Chancellor.

The main characteristic of his time in office was his Eastern Policy that was aimed at "change through rapprochement"*. One example of this was the Warsaw Genuflection (cf. S 22). On the one hand, this policy led some people to call him a traitor and to accuse him of a "sell-out", of standing in the way of Germany's reunification. On the other hand, Brandt was awarded the Nobel Peace Prize for his contribution to the reconciliation of Germany and Poland in 1971.

When one of his closest staff members, Günter Guillaume, was unmasked as an agent of the Stasi, the GDR's Ministry for State Security, Brandt had no choice but to resign on 6 May 1974.

When the Berlin Wall came down on 9 November 1989, Brandt commented on this event proverbially using the words "Jetzt wächst zusammen, was zusammengehört". After the reunification of Germany, the decision to transfer the seat of government from Bonn to Berlin was decided on Brandt's initiative.

Brandt died of cancer on 8 October 1992.

---

affiliated officially connected with a larger organization or group • **to expatriate sb.** to take away sb.'s citizenship • **attaché** [əˈtæʃeɪ] an official who is in charge of a particular subject or activity at an embassy

S 22 The Warsaw Genuflection

On 7 December 1970, Willy Brandt was in Warsaw to sign the Warsaw Treaty as part of his Eastern Policy. Before the signing of the treaty, Brandt visited a memorial commemorating the Warsaw Ghetto Uprising of 1943, when he – surprisingly – sank down to his knees after laying down a wreath in a gesture of humility and penance. This has come to be known as the Warsaw Genuflection *(Kniefall von Warschau)*.

Pre-task
1. In a survey by the German magazine DER SPIEGEL in 1970, 41% of the interviewed found the gesture appropriate, 48% found it exaggerated (cf.: www.spiegel.de/spiegel/print/d-43822427.html [14.02.15]). Can you think of reasons for both attitudes? Discuss.

Tasks
2. Describe the four photographs showing the Warsaw Genuflection.
3. Explain to what extent one's attitude towards the Warsaw Genuflection might be influenced depending on which perspective one is presented with. Based on your results from tasks 2 and 3 and with

the help of the skills pages, discuss the statement "the camera never lies".
4. Do further research on Brandt's Eastern Policy and his motto "change through rapprochement". Include the idea behind it as well as the Warsaw Treaty, the Moscow Treaty and the Basic Treaty. Then put the Warsaw Genuflection into its historical context.
5. With reference to the survey results presented in task 1, discuss whether Brandt's Eastern Policy was a "solution" or a "sell-out" in connection with the German Question after the year 1945.

Ronald Reagan (1911–2004)

Ronald Wilson Reagan was born in Tampico, Illinois, on 6 February 1911. In 1932, he graduated from Eureka College (Tampico) in Economics and Sociology and started working as a sports reporter at a radio station in Iowa. In 1937, Reagan got his first major role in the film 'Love is in the Air'. Further productions followed, for example starring next to Errol Flynn in the 1940 success 'Santa Fé Trail' *(Land der Gottlosen)*.

In 1962, Reagan joined the Republican Party and four years later he became Governor of California. In 1980, he won the Presidential Elections and, in 1981, became the USA's 40th President. In 1984 he was re-elected for a second term in office.

Even though Reagan was regarded as a "Cold Warrior" who had called the Soviet Union an "evil empire" and who had advocated a policy of "peace through strength", he introduced a second phase of détente between the USA and the SU when he met the Soviet leader Gorbachev in Reykjavik and negotiated the limitation of nuclear arms.

Reagan was succeeded by George Bush in 1989. He made his last public appearance in 1996 when he celebrated his 85th birthday. A little later it became known that he suffered from Alzheimer's Disease. Reagan died in Bel Air, Los Angeles, on 5 June 2004, aged 93.

S 23 Ronald Reagan

Speech at the Brandenburg Gate

US President Ronald Reagan visited Berlin on the occasion of the 750th anniversary of the city. His speech at the Brandenburg Gate was delivered on 12 June 1987.

Pre-tasks
1. The most memorable and well-known sentence from this speech is certainly "Mr. Gorbachev, tear down this wall!" (ll. 44 f.). Regarding the tone of this sentence, was this a challenge, a command or a request? Discuss.
2. Have a look at the photograph showing Reagan giving the speech in front of the Brandenburg Gate in the immediate vicinity of the Berlin Wall. Does this deliberately chosen location change your mind in respect of task 1? Discuss the matter again.

Tasks

3. Point out Reagan's statements on communism and present his view of freedom.
4. Examine how the US President singles out the Berlin Wall as the most visible symbol of the bipolar world.
5. Explain Reagan's references to changes taking place in the Soviet Union.
6. Compare his views on communism, freedom and the city of Berlin with Kennedy's (cf. S 21).
7. Based on your findings, discuss once again whether "Mr. Gorbachev, tear down this wall!" was a challenge, a command or a request.

[…] Ladies and gentlemen,
Twenty-four years ago, President John F. Kennedy visited Berlin, speaking to the people of this city and the world at the City Hall. Well, since then two other presidents have come, each in his turn, to Berlin. And today, I, myself, make my second visit to your city.
We come to Berlin, we American presidents, because it's our duty to speak, in this place, of freedom. […]
Behind me stands a wall that encircles the free sectors of this city, part of a vast system of barriers that divides the entire continent of Europe. From the Baltic, south, those barriers cut across Germany in a gash* of barbed wire, concrete, dog runs, and guardtowers. Farther south, there may be no visible, no obvious wall. But there remain armed guards and checkpoints all the same – still a restriction on the right to travel, still an instrument to impose upon ordinary men and women the will of a totalitarian state. Yet it is here in Berlin where the wall emerges most clearly; here, cutting across your city, where the news photo and the television screen have imprinted this brutal division of a continent upon the mind of the world. Standing before the Brandenburg Gate, every man is a German, separated from his fellow men. Every man is a Berliner, forced to look upon a scar.
[…] As long as this gate is closed, as long as this scar of a wall is permitted to stand, it is not the German question alone that remains open, but the question of freedom for all mankind. Yet I do not come here to lament. For I find in Berlin a message of hope, even in the shadow of this wall, a message of triumph. […]
In the West today, we see a free world that has achieved a level of prosperity and well-being unprecedented* in all human history. In the Communist world, we see failure, technological backwardness, declining standards of health, even want of the most basic kind – too little food. Even today, the Soviet Union cannot feed itself. After these four decades, then, there stands before the entire world one great and inescapable conclusion: Freedom leads to prosperity. Freedom replaces the ancient hatreds among the nations with comity* and peace. Freedom is the victor.
And now the Soviets themselves may, in a limited way, be coming to understand the importance of freedom. We hear much from Moscow about a new policy of reform and openness. Some political prisoners have been released. Certain foreign news broadcasts are no longer being jammed*. Some economic enterprises have been permitted to operate with greater freedom from state control.
Are these the beginnings of profound changes in the Soviet state? Or are they token* gestures, intended to raise false hopes in the West, or to strengthen the Soviet system without changing it? We welcome change and openness; for we believe that freedom and security go together, that the advance of human liberty can only

---

gash a long deep cut

unprecedented [ʌnˈpresɪˌdentɪd] never having happened or existed before

comity friendliness, politeness

to jam here: to block electrical signals (and thus prevent broadcasts from being sent)

token false, fake, pretence

strengthen the cause of world peace. There is one sign the Soviets can make that
would be unmistakable, that would advance dramatically the cause of freedom and
peace.

General Secretary Gorbachev, if you seek peace, if you seek prosperity for the Soviet Union and Eastern Europe, if you seek liberalization: Come here to this gate! Mr. Gorbachev, open this gate! Mr. Gorbachev, tear down this wall! [...]

As I looked out a moment ago from the Reichstag, that embodiment of German unity, I noticed words crudely spray-painted across the wall, perhaps by a young Berliner: "This wall will fall. Beliefs become reality." Yes, across Europe, this wall will fall. For it cannot withstand faith; it cannot withstand truth. The wall cannot withstand freedom.

President Ronald Reagan, Speech at the Brandenburg Gate, West Berlin, Germany, June 12, 1987, www.au.af.mil/au/awc/awcgate/speeches/reagan_berlin.htm [02.06.2015]

Mikhail Gorbachev (* 1931)

Mikhail Gorbachev was born in Stavropol on 2 March 1931. After having studied law, he became a member of the Communist Party in 1952 and a member of the Central Committee in Moscow in 1971. Being part of the Politburo* from 1980 onwards, his political achievements were rewarded with the post of the Party's General-Secretary to which he was appointed in 1985.

Upon becoming General-Secretary, Gorbachev initiated his programme of *perestroika* (restructuring) in order to enable the Russian economy to keep up with that of the West. At first believing that the basis of the Russian economy was good and that only minor changes were needed, Gorbachev soon came to realize that major changes were necessary, and that a semi-free market economy would have to replace the centrally planned Russian economy. The second pillar of his reform programme was *glasnost* (openness), essentially bringing Russian society a step towards democracy by allowing for greater freedom of the press and of speech in general.

In 1989, Gorbachev was elected as the first President of the USSR. In that same year, he paid a state visit to the GDR on the occasion of its 40th anniversary where he was greeted by the population, who saw him as a reformer. On this occasion, he allegedly uttered the proverbial statement „Wer zu spät kommt, den bestraft das Leben" to illustrate to GDR head of state Erich Honecker that it was no use anymore trying to keep the GDR alive by force. After the fall of the Wall on 9 to 10 November 1989, Gorbachev agreed to Germany's reunification on 10 February 1990. In that same year, freedom of the press and of religion was introduced in the USSR, as well as a free-market economy. The signing and ratification of the CSCE Charter in Paris on 19 December 1990 marked the official end of the Cold War. In December 1990, Gorbachev was awarded the Nobel Peace Prize for working towards reform and peace.

Even though a Communist coup d'état against him failed in August 1991, it still led to a massive loss of power on his part, which eventually led to him resigning from his post as the Communist Party's General-Secretary on 24 August 1991. On 25 December 1991, he also resigned as President – the post was taken over by his successor Boris Yeltzin. Thenceforth* Gorbachev was to retreat into private life, even though he still takes part in his country's public life and has only recently written an autobiography (cf. S 24).

Politburo *Politbüro* (i.e. the executive committee for a number of political parties that are usually Communist; the first Politburo was created by the Bolsheviks in 1917) • **thenceforth** from then on, from that time on

S 24 Mikhail Gorbachev

Alles zu seiner Zeit

In 2013, Gorbachev published his autobiography „Alles zu seiner Zeit". In the 13th chapter, he elaborates on the motives for perestroika.

Pre-tasks
1. Before reading, come up with concise definitions for "perestroika" and "glasnost". Use the overview section as well as the biographical account of Gorbachev, and add examples of both.
2. In his 2007 work "The Cold War", the American historian John Lewis Gaddis calls the end of the Cold War a "triumph of hope", mainly "because Mikhail Gorbachev chose not to act, but rather to be acted upon." (p. 239) However, in his autobiography, Gorbachev says: „Bis heute wird mir vorgeworfen, ich hätte diese Länder ‚abgegeben'. Nein, ich habe sie nicht abgegeben, sondern nur dem Volk dieser Länder überlassen." (ll. 33 ff) In how far do these two statements match up? Discuss.

Tasks
3. Describe why Gorbachev saw the time as being ripe for perestroika in the Soviet Union.
4. Put Gorbachev's statements into the context of the "peaceful revolutions" of 1989.
5. Compare Gorbachev's view of freedom with Reagan's (cf. S 23).

Post-task
6. Keeping in mind your definitions of "revolution" (cf. chapter 1), take a critical stand on the term "peaceful revolution" against the backdrop of the events of 1989.

Weltsicht world view
unsterblich immortal

aufreibendes Wettrüsten nerve-wracking arms-race

aufschieben to postpone

atomare Bedrohung nuclear threat
unvorhersagbar unpredictable

in einer Sackgasse stecken to be caught in a dead end
höllisch infernal
bremsen to decelerate [diːˈseləreɪt]

Eine neue Weltsicht*: Die Menschheit hat aufgehört, unsterblich* zu sein

Von Anfang an war mir klar: Ohne eine Verbesserung unserer internationalen Beziehungen war an radikale Reformen in unserem Land nicht zu denken. Der Druck, der mit unserer Beteiligung am aufreibenden Wettrüsten* und unserer Involvierung in Konflikte an verschiedenen Punkten des Erdballs zusammenhing, musste herabgesetzt werden. Wenn man eine neue Welt haben wollte, musst Schluss mit dem Kalten Krieg gemacht werden. Versuche, die internationalen Beziehungen zu verbessern, konnten nicht aufgeschoben* werden, sondern mussten Bestandteil unseres politischen Kurses sein.

Wenn man mich nach den Motiven für die Perestrojka fragt, betone ich immer die innenpolitischen Gründe. Aber die außenpolitischen Gründe waren nicht minder wichtig, insbesondere die atomare Bedrohung* mit ihren unvorhersagbaren* Folgen für unser Land und die ganze Welt. Einstein hat als Erster von der Notwendigkeit eines neuen Denkens im Zeitalter der Atomwaffen gesprochen. Die Menschheit hat aufgehört, unsterblich zu sein. Wir müssen den Erhalt des Lebens auf der Erde in den Vordergrund rücken.

Mitte der achtziger Jahre war die Gefahr eines Atomkriegs gestiegen. Die internationale Gemeinschaft steckte in einer Sackgasse*. Das höllische* Wettrüsten hatte eine solche Geschwindigkeit erreicht, dass schwer vorstellbar war, wie man es anhalten oder zumindest bremsen* könne. Es bestand auch die Gefahr, dass es zu einem Atomkrieg hätte kommen können, ohne dass ihn jemand wollte. Man musste etwas tun.

Das neue Denken erlaubte es, die recht verstandenen Interessen unseres Landes mit den Interessen der Menschheit zu verbinden. Auf diese Weise eröffnete sich die Möglichkeit einer fruchtbaren Zusammenarbeit mit anderen Staaten.

Als wir die Perestrojka begannen, deren Sinn ja darin bestand, unserem Volk die Freiheit zu geben, musste die sowjetische Führung dieses Recht auch den anderen Ländern zugestehen*. Das führte zur prinzipiellen Ablehnung jeder Einmischung in die Angelegenheiten der „Bruderländer" des Warschauer Paktes. Damit war einer der wichtigsten Schritte zur Befreiung* vom stalinistischen Erbe* vollzogen.

Die sowjetische Führung hat recht daran getan, sich nicht in die Veränderungen Mittel- und Osteuropas einzumischen. Bis heute wird mir vorgeworfen, ich hätte diese Länder „abgegeben*". Nein, ich habe sie nicht abgegeben, sondern nur dem Volk dieser Länder überlassen*.

Die neuen Prinzipien der Perestrojka haben auch eine große Rolle bei der Wiedervereinigung Deutschlands gespielt. Hauptakteur* der Wiedervereinigung war das Volk dieser Länder. Das ist die sicherste Grundlage für Verständnis und Zusammenarbeit.

etw. zugestehen to grant

Befreiung liberation
Erbe inheritance

abgeben to hand over
überlassen to leave

Hauptakteur main actor

Michail Gorbatschow: Alles zu seiner Zeit. Mein Leben. Übers. von Birgit Veit. Hamburg (Hoffmann und Campe) 2013, pp. 399f.

S 25 Press Conference with Günther Schabowski

On 9 November 1989, an international press conference with representatives of the GDR's Central Committee was scheduled for 6 p.m. Günther Schabowski had just taken over the post of the Politburo's Secretary responsible for the media the day before. Between 5 and 5.30 p.m. Schabowski met Egon Krenz, the last Communist head of the state of the GDR, to inform himself about the session of the Central Committee which had resulted in a draft of a travel law to be presented to the Council of Ministers (who would eventually decide on it). Krenz gave this draft to Schabowski, who did not seem to be aware of the exact content of this "time bomb" ticking among his papers. The text at hand is an excerpt from the transcript of the press conference. Schabowski was accompanied by SED Central Committee members Helga Labs, Gerhard Beil and Manfred Banaschak.

Pre-task 1. Have a look at these photographs of Schabowski, taken at the press conference. Describe his facial expressions and his gestures. Then discuss the likelihood of Schabowski being unaware of the exact wording of the travel law draft and only realizing its impact while actually reading it out to the journalists present.

Tasks 2. Outline the course of the press conference.

3. Examine the way Schabowski presents the travel law draft to the press. Include your findings from task 1.
4. Put the transcript into the historical context of the reunification of Germany and, against the backdrop of the given transcript, explain in detail why the Wall fell on 9 November 1989.
5. Did the Wall thus fall "by accident"? Discuss.
6. Evaluate to what extent the press conference and the decision to draft a travel law provides proof that the GDR was about to collapse in the not too distant future.

Post-task 7. Watch the *Tagesschau* of 9 November 1989 (e.g. www.youtube.com/watch?v=AhKfHKTyZpU) on *YouTube* and discuss to what extent Schabowski's body language and intonation support your findings. Make any necessary additions and/or changes.

[...]

Schabowski: [...] Also, wir wollen durch eine Reihe von Umständen, dazu gehört auch das Reisegesetz*, die Chance also der souveränen Entscheidung des Bürgers zu reisen, wohin er will. (Äh) Wir sind natürlich (äh) besorgt, dass also die Möglichkeit dieses Reisegesetzes, – es ist ja immer noch nicht in Kraft, es ist ja ein Entwurf*.

Allerdings ist heute, soviel ich weiß (*blickt bei diesen Worten zustimmungsheischend in Richtung Labs und Banaschak*), eine Entscheidung getroffen worden. Es ist eine Empfehlung des Politbüros aufgegriffen worden, dass man aus dem Entwurf des Reisegesetzes den Passus* herausnimmt und in Kraft treten lässt, der stän... – wie man so schön sagt oder so unschön sagt – die ständige Ausreise* regelt, also das Verlassen der Republik. Weil wir es (äh) für einen unmöglichen Zustand halten, dass sich diese Bewegung vollzieht (äh) über einen befreundeten Staat (äh), was ja auch für diesen Staat nicht ganz einfach ist. Und deshalb (äh) haben wir uns dazu entschlossen, heute (äh) eine Regelung zu treffen, die es jedem Bürger der DDR möglich macht (äh), über Grenzübergangspunkte* der DDR (äh) auszureisen.

Frage: (*Stimmengewirr*) Das gilt ...?
Riccardo Ehrmann, Journalist, ANSA: Ohne Pass? Ohne Pass? – (Nein, nein!)
Krzysztof Janowski, Journalist, Voice of America: Ab wann tritt das ...? (... *Stimmengewirr*) Ab wann tritt das in Kraft?
Schabowski: Bitte?
Peter Brinkmann, Journalist, Bild Zeitung: Ab sofort? Ab ...?
Schabowski: (*kratzt sich am Kopf*) Also, Genossen*, mir ist das hier also mitgeteilt worden (*setzt sich, während er weiterspricht, seine Brille auf*), dass eine solche Mitteilung heute schon (äh) verbreitet worden ist. Sie müsste eigentlich in Ihrem Besitz sein. Also (*liest sehr schnell vom Blatt*): „Privatreisen nach dem Ausland können ohne Vorliegen von Voraussetzungen – Reiseanlässe und Verwandtschaftsverhältnisse – beantragt werden. Die Genehmigungen* werden kurzfristig* erteilt. Die zuständigen Abteilungen Pass- und Meldewesen* der VP – der Volkspolizeikreisämter – in der DDR sind angewiesen, Visa zur ständigen Ausreise unverzüglich* zu erteilen, ohne dass dafür noch geltende Voraussetzungen für eine ständige Ausreise vorliegen müssen."
Riccardo Ehrmann, Journalist, ANSA: Mit Pass?
Schabowski: (Äh) (*liest*) „Ständige Ausreisen können über alle Grenzübergangsstellen der DDR zur BRD erfolgen. Damit entfällt die vorübergehend ermöglichte

---

Reisegesetz travel law
Entwurf draft
Passus passage
ständige Ausreise permanent departure/leave
Grenzübergangspunkt border crossing
Genosse comrade
Genehmigung permission
kurzfristig at short notice
Pass- und Meldewesen passport and registration
unverzüglich immediately, without delay

Erteilung von entsprechenden Genehmigungen in Auslandsvertretungen der DDR bzw. die ständige Ausreise mit dem Personalausweis der DDR über Drittstaaten*." (*blickt auf*) (Äh) Die Passfrage kann ich jetzt nicht beantworten (*blickt fragend in Richtung Labs und Banaschak*). Das ist auch eine technische Frage. Ich weiß ja nicht, die Pässe müssen ja, ... also damit jeder im Besitz eines Passes ist, überhaupt erst mal ausgegeben werden. Wir wollten aber ...

Drittstaaten third countries

Manfred Banaschak: Entscheidend ist ja die inhaltliche Aussage ...
Schabowski: ... ist die ...
Ralph T. Niemeyer, Journalist, DAPA: Wann tritt das in Kraft?
Schabowski: (*blättert in seinen Papieren*) Das tritt nach meiner Kenntnis ist das sofort, unverzüglich (*blättert weiter in seinen Unterlagen*) ...
Helga Labs: (*leise*) ... unverzüglich.
Gerhard Beil: (*leise*) Das muss der Ministerrat* beschließen.
[...]

Ministerrat Council of Ministers (i. e. the chief executive body of the GDR)

Internationale Pressekonferenz von Günter Schabowski, 9. Nov. 1989, in: Hans-Hermann Hertle: Die Berliner Mauer. Biografie eines Bauwerkes. Berlin (Ch. Links Verlag) 2., aktualisierte Auflage, 2015, pp. 194–195

CONNECT

The Reunification of Germany – Cartoon Workshop

Task Revise and apply your cartoon analysis skills to investigate how the reunification of Germany was perceived in Germany and abroad.

The reunification of Germany gave rise to serious qualms, especially on the part of Britain and France. These qualms were often expressed in the cartoons of 1990 – six examples from different countries are depicted here.

Split up into six groups, each group focusing on one of the cartoons. If possible, bring an enlarged copy of your cartoon to class. Then revise your cartoon analysis skills with the help of the skills pages and apply them to the task at hand, i.e.:

STEP 1: Analyse the formal features of the cartoon.
STEP 2: Describe the cartoon in detail, including its elements and its composition.
STEP 3: Put the cartoon into the historical context of the reunification of Germany.
STEP 4: Explain in detail the elements of the cartoon. Circle and label the elements on your enlarged copy for the presentation of your results.
STEP 5: Take a critical stand on the message expressed, both from a contemporary and from a present-day perspective.
STEP 6: Present your findings in a gallery walk. Copy and fill in the route card provided below while listening to the presentations of the other groups.

ROUTE CARD	QUALMS	CARTOON ELEMENTS EXPLAINED
1) Canada		
2) New Zealand		
3) Britain		
4) Bulgaria		
5) France		
6) Germany		

Cartoon Workshop

S 26

"From these ashes ... Free at last?"
Cartoon by Josh Beutel, published in the Canadian *Telegraph Journal*, February 1990
Persons depicted, from left to right:
Karl Marx, Adolf Hitler

Language support

from these ashes allusion to the phoenix, a bird that rises out of the ashes of its predecessor and is associated with the sun • **free at last** quotation from a Negro spiritual, also quoted by Martin Luther King Jr in his "I have a dream"-speech • **Wappenadler** heraldic eagle

"Dropping the pilots"*
Cartoon by Laurence Clark, published in the *New Zealand Herald* on 4 October 1990
Persons depicted, from top to bottom:
Helmut Kohl, Charles de Gaulle, Josef Stalin, Franklin D. Roosevelt, Winston Churchill

* This cartoon is a deliberate play on the famous one by John Tenniel, showing Bismarck leaving the "ship of state" (cf. chapter 1, S 67).

Language support

pilot Lotse • **Leiter** ladder • **Geländer** handrail • **Bullauge** bull's eye, porthole • **die Arme verschränken** to fold one's arms

"March of the Fourth Reich"
Cartoon by Bill Caldwell, published in the British *Daily Star* in February 1990

Language support

sich in etw. verwandeln to morph into sth.

Cartoon by Milen Radev, published in the Bulgarian satirical magazine *Starschel* in November 1990.
Depicted person: Helmut Kohl

Language support

Krönchen coronet • **Zipfelmütze** jelly bag cap • **Froschkönig** Frog King

"Tonton met les points sur les » I «" (Uncle speaks in plain language/Der Onkel spricht Klartext)
Cartoon by the French cartoonist Ferdinand Guiraud from 22 November 1989
Persons depicted, from left to right:
(unidentified), François Mitterrand, Helmut Kohl, Margaret Thatcher
Embedded text:
L'économie de l'ouest avant celle de l'est. (First the economy of the West, then that of the East.)
Ja, ja nach Paris d'abord. (Yes, yes to Paris first.)

Language support

Kronleuchter lustre • **Pickelhaube** spiked helmet

Cartoon by the German cartoonist Walter Hanel from 15 February 1990
Depicted people/embedded text from top to bottom:
Helmut Kohl (Einheit), Mikhail Gorbachev (UDSSR), François Mitterrand (Paris), Mikhail Gorbachev (UDSSR), Margaret Thatcher (London), Pope John Paul II (Polen), NATO, François Mitterand (Paris), George Bush, ISRAEL

Language support

Skipiste slope • **Hindernis** obstacle • **Slalomstange** slalom ['slaːləm] pole

S 27 Helmut Kohl & George Bush
Telephone Conversation

On 13 February 1990, the German Chancellor Helmut Kohl called up the US President George Bush to discuss the developments in the GDR and to agree on further proceedings.

Pre-task
1. What does the fact that Kohl and Bush frequently conversed via telephone reveal about their aims as regards the reunification of Germany? Make an educated guess.

Tasks
2. Describe the situation of the GDR, as portrayed by Kohl, and point out in which respects Bush promises Kohl support.

3. Characterize the relationship between West Germany and the USA as it becomes apparent in the given telephone conversation, and explain to what extent the nature of the source as such contributes to this perception.
4. Explain the role the FRG and the USA see for themselves when it comes to Germany's reunification. In doing so, also explain Kohl's references to recent events in the GDR.

Post-task 5. Revise what you have learned about other countries' qualms as regards German reunification (overview section, cartoon workshop S 26). Then draw a cartoon that illustrates the US view of Germany's reunification, as presented in S 27 .

Chancellor Kohl: ... [East German] Prime Minister [Hans] Modrow is here today. The situation continues to be dramatic. Between the 1st of January and today, 80,000 have come from the GDR [East Germany] to the Federal Republic [West Germany]. That is why I suggested a monetary union* and an economic community ...

Your support is invaluable.

Let me say a few words about my talks in Moscow. Gorbachev was very relaxed ... But the problems he faces are enormous – nationalities, the food supply situation – and I do not see a light at the end of the tunnel yet.

You know the text we published jointly on the German Question. It was highly satisfactory. We will go in that direction now, and in a parallel way on security policy. We also discussed the same points Jim Baker* had been discussing, that the two German states should be working together with the Four Powers – the U.S., the UK, France, and the USSR ... At Camp David*, this is one thing we will have to discuss thoroughly: the future of NATO and the Warsaw Pact. I feel we will find a solution, but it will be hard work. I told Gorbachev again that the neutralization of Germany is out of the question for me.

The President: Did he acquiesce* or just listen? How did he react?

Chancellor Kohl: My impression is that this is a subject about which they want to negotiate, but that we can win that point in negotiations. The modalities will be important, but I do believe we can find a solution.

The President: We must find a solution. The Camp David meeting will be very important, and I am delighted you are able to come. When I heard your comments from Moscow and heard that Mr. Gorbachev had removed a longstanding obstacle to unification, I was thinking of you as a friend. It must have been an emotional moment for you. The German people certainly want to be together.

Chancellor Kohl: That is quite true. This is a great moment for us ...

The President: ... We have been supporting your stated position that NATO membership would be appropriate. We won't move away from that, but we do need to talk and see where we need to be more flexible and where we need to be more firm.
...

Helmut Kohl and George H. W. Bush, "Telephone Call from Chancellor Helmut Kohl of the Federal Republic of Germany to President George H. W. Bush." Making the History of 1989, # 530

---

monetary union Währungsunion

Jim Baker James (Jim) Baker, US Secretary of State, 1989–1992
Camp David country retreat of the US President, also used for (in)formal meetings

to acquiesce ['ækwɪˌes] to agree to sth. or to accept sth.

Demonstrations in the GDR

S 28 — Treaty on the Final Settlement with Respect to Germany

The "Treaty on the Final Settlement with Respect to Germany" – also called the Two-Plus-Four Treaty – was negotiated between the foreign ministers of the Soviet Union, the USA, France, Britain, the FRG and the GDR. The treaty was signed on 12 September 1990 and gave Germany back full sovereignty. Three weeks later, the GDR officially acceded to the FRG. However, the treaty only came into force when it was also ratified by the Russian Federation in March 1991.

Pre-task
1. Why is the treaty also called the Two-Plus-Four Treaty? Explain.

Tasks
2. Find categories for the articles and classify them accordingly.
3. Explain how the treaty gave back full sovereignty while simultaneously ensuring a peaceful, reunited Germany.

Post-task
4. On 25 May 2011, the UNESCO (The United Nations Educational, Scientific and Cultural Organization) included the Two-Plus-Four Treaty in their "Memory of the World Register". This register consists of just 250 documents which, according to the UNESCO, are exceptional (another example is, for instance, the 42-line Gutenberg Bible). Taking into account the qualms some countries had about Germany's reunification back in 1989/90 as well as the further development of the reunified Germany, evaluate whether the Two-Plus-Four Treaty deserves to be on that list.

[…] ARTICLE 1
(1) The united Germany shall comprise the territory of the Federal Republic of Germany, the German Democratic Republic and the whole of Berlin. Its external borders shall be the borders of the Federal Republic of Germany and the German

Democratic Republic and shall be definitive from the date on which the present Treaty comes into force. The confirmation of the definitive nature of the borders of the united Germany is an essential element of the peaceful order in Europe.

(2) The united Germany and the Republic of Poland shall confirm the existing border between them in a treaty that is binding under international law.

(3) The united Germany has no territorial claims whatsoever against other states and shall not assert any in the future. [...]

ARTICLE 2

The Governments of the Federal Republic of Germany and the German Democratic Republic reaffirm their declarations that only peace will emanate* from German soil. [...]

ARTICLE 3

(1) The Governments of the Federal Republic of Germany and the German Democratic Republic reaffirm their renunciation of* the manufacture and possession of and control over nuclear, biological and chemical weapons. They declare that the united Germany, too, will abide by* these commitments. [...]

(2) [...]

The Government of the Federal Republic of Germany undertakes to reduce the personnel strength of the armed forces of the united Germany to 370,000 (ground, air and naval forces) within three to four years. [...]

ARTICLE 4

(1) The Governments of the Federal Republic of Germany, the German Democratic Republic and the Union of Soviet Socialist Republics state that the united Germany and the Union of Soviet Socialist Republics will settle by treaty the conditions for and the duration of the presence of Soviet armed forces on the territory of the present German Democratic Republic and of Berlin, as well as the conduct of the withdrawal of these armed forces which will be completed by the end of 1994. [...]

ARTICLE 6

The right of the united Germany to belong to alliances, with all the rights and responsibilities arising therefrom, shall not be affected by the present Treaty.

ARTICLE 7

(1) The French Republic, the Union of Soviet Socialist Republics, the United Kingdom of Great Britain and Northern Ireland and the United States of America hereby terminate their rights and responsibilities relating to Berlin and to Germany as a whole. As a result, the corresponding, related quadripartite agreements, decisions and practices are terminated and all related Four Power institutions are dissolved.

(2) The united Germany shall have accordingly full sovereignty over its internal and external affairs.

ARTICLE 8

(1) The present Treaty is subject to ratification or acceptance as soon as possible. On the German side it will be ratified by the united Germany. The Treaty will therefore apply to the united Germany. [...]

American Foreign Policy Current Documents 1990. Department of State, Washington, 1991, http://usa.usembassy.de/etexts/2plusfour8994e.htm [22.4.15]

---

to emanate to come from

renunciation of Verzicht auf

to abide by to follow, to stick to a rule, decision, or instruction

Paper Practice: Analysing a Written Primary Source

S 29 Charles David Powell

Letter to Stephen Wall

Model solution
→ p. 607

The given excerpts were taken from a secret letter reporting about a meeting between the British Prime Minister Margaret Thatcher and the French President François Mitterrand in Paris. The writer Charles David Powell, Baron Powell of Bayswater and life peer in the House of Lords, was one of Thatcher's key foreign policy advisors during the 1980s. His addressee, Sir Stephen Wall, served as the Principal Private Secretary to the Foreign Secretary at the time the letter was written.

Tasks
1. Analyse the source.
2. Put the source into the historical context of the reunification of Germany and explain Mitterrand's and Thatcher's qualms as reported by Powell.
3. Evaluate the qualms expressed by Mitterrand and Thatcher in the context of January 1990 and from a present-day perspective.

10 DOWNING STREET*, 20 January 1990
Secret and Personal

Dear Stephen,
The Prime Minister* had lunch with President Mitterrand at the Élysée Palace in
5 Paris today. [...] Virtually the whole discussion was about German reunification and European security, with a broad measure of agreement, in particular on how the talks should be followed up. It was agreed that neither side would say anything to the press about the substance of the discussion. [...]
President Mitterrand agreed that German reunification was a central theme for
10 both Britain and France. The sudden prospect of reunification had delivered a sort of mental shock to the Germans. Its effects had been to turn them once again into the 'bad' Germans they used to be. They were behaving with a certain brutality and concentrating on reunification to the exclusion of everything else. It was difficult to maintain good relations with them in this sort of mood. Of course the Germans
15 had the right to self-determination. But they did not have the right to upset the political realities of Europe. He did not think Europe was yet ready for German reunification: and he certainly could not accept that it had to take priority over everything else. [...]
The President continued that we had to accept there was a logic to reunification.
20 But everything depended on the how and when, and on the reactions of the Soviet Union. Britain and France were arguing for caution. The trouble was that the West Germans did not want to hear this. They treated any talk of caution as criticism of themselves. Unless you were wholeheartedly for reunification, you were an enemy of Germany. Because the Prime Minister was such a close friend and they had a
25 tradition of working together, he would tell her in strict confidence some things which he had said to Chancellor Kohl and to Herr Genscher*. He had been very blunt with them. He had said to them that no doubt Germany could if it wished achieve reunification, bring Austria into the European Community and even regain other territories which it had lost as a result of the war. They might make even

10 Downing Street headquarters of the British government in London

the Prime Minister i.e. Margaret Thatcher

Hans-Dietrich Genscher (*1927), Germany's Foreign Minister and Vice-Chancellor from 1974 to 1992

envoy an official who represents his/her country in another country, with a rank below an ambassador

more ground than had Hitler. But they would have to bear in mind the implications. He would take a bet that in such circumstances the Soviet Union would send an envoy* to London to propose a Re-insurance Treaty and the United Kingdom would agree. The envoy would go on to Paris with the same proposal and France would agree. And then we would all be back in 1913. He was not asking the Germans to give up the idea of reunification. But they must understand that the consequences of reunification would not just stop at the borders of Germany. [...]

The President said that he drew the conclusion that it would be stupid to say no to reunification. In reality there was no force in Europe which could stop it happening. None of us were going to declare war on Germany. Nor judging by his statements was Mr. Gorbachev. [...]

The Prime Minister said she did not necessarily agree there was nothing to be done. If other countries all made their views felt together, then we could influence Germany. [...] We should say to the Germans that reunification would come one day, but we were not ready for it yet. We should insist that agreements must be observed and that East Germany must take its place in the queue for membership of the Community. If we all spoke up, then the Germans would have to take some notice. German policy was to test how far they could go with the rest of us, and at the moment they were getting away with too much. She accepted that in the end reunification would come about. But we must find some way to slow it down. [...]

This letter contains extremely sensitive information and I should be grateful if it could be given a very limited distribution only. But Sir Ewen Fergusson* in Paris should receive a copy since the Prime Minister mentioned it orally to him.

I am copying this letter, on a strictly personal basis to Simon Webb (Ministry of Defence).

Yours sincerely,
C.D. Powell

Sir Ewen Fergusson British ambassador to France from 1987 to 1992

Letter from Mr. Powell to Mr Wall, 10 Downing Street, 20 January 1990, in: P. Salmon, K. Hamilton, S. R. Twigge (ed.): German Unification 1989–90: Documents on British Policy Overseas, Series III, Vol. 7, Routledge, 2009, pp. 215 ff.

Road sign frequently found at roads that had been blocked because of the division of Germany. Date and time vary depending on the exact date and time the road was opened in the wake of Germany's reunification.

Hier waren Deutschland und Europa bis zum 10. Dezember 1989 um 10:15 Uhr geteilt.

to abide by sth. to follow a rule, decision, or instruction
to acquiesce [ˌækwiˈes]; **acquiescence (n.)** to agree to sth. or to accept sth., although one does not want to
to acquit sb.; acquittal (n.) to state officially that sb. is not guilty of the crime they were accused of
to aid; aid (n.) to help/support
all-German *gesamtdeutsch*
altruistic [ˌæltruˈɪstɪk] **(adj.); altruist (n.); altruism (n.)** *altruistisch/selbstlos; Altruist (N.); Altruismus (N.)*
apocalypse [əˈpɒkəˌlɪps] a time when the whole world will be destroyed
atomic (nuclear) bomb *Atombombe*
to back down to give in
backward (adj.); backwardness (n.) not developing quickly, normally, and successfully
bipolar world *bipolare/zweigeteilte Welt*
border *Grenze*
centrally planned economy *Planwirtschaft*
collective guilt (v. individual guilt) *Kollektivschuld (vs. individuelle Schuld)*
to commemorate; commemoration (n.) (syn.: remembrance) *gedenken*
to condone sth. *etw. dulden*
constructive vote of non-confidence *konstruktives Misstrauensvotum*
to contain sth.; containment (n.) *etw. eindämmen/in Grenzen halten; Eindämmung*
debris [ˈdebriː] **(syn.: rubble)** *Trümmer, Schutt*
to detain sb.; detention (n.) to keep sb. in prison
to deter sb. [dɪˈtɜː(r)]; **deterrent (n.); deterrence (n.)** *jdn. abschrecken; Abschreckungsmittel; Abschreckung*
disgust (syn.: indignation) *Entrüstung/Empörung*
displaced person (DP) *Heimatloser/Zwangsvertriebener*
to eliminate sth./sb.; elimination (n.) to get rid of sth./sb.
to endanger sth. to put sth. in danger
fall of the Wall *Mauerfall*
federal state *Bundesstaat*
to flee to escape
to file a motion *einen Antrag stellen*
follower *Mitläufer/in*
to found (– founded – founded) *gründen*
incompatible (adj.); incompatibility (n.) not able to work or exist together because of basic differences
to liberate; liberation (n.); liberty (n.) *befreien; Befreiung; Freiheit*
mens rea [ˈmɛnz ˈriːə] *Unrechtsbewusstsein*
to merge (syn.: to fuse) to combine to form a bigger part

missile [ˈmɪsaɪl] a weapon that travels under its own power for long distances and explodes when it hits its target
non-aligned a country that is non-aligned does not receive support from a more powerful country
nuclear arms race *nukleares Wettrüsten*
to nuke to attack with nuclear weapons
occupation zone *Besatzungszone*
peaceful coexistence a situation in which people live together peacefully, or things exist together peacefully, at the same time or in the same place
to proliferate sth.; proliferation (n.) to quickly increase in number or amount
to promulgate; promulgation (n.) to make an idea or belief known to as many people as possible; to make an official announcement introducing a law or rule
to prosecute; prosecution (n.) to officially accuse sb. of a crime and ask a court of law to judge them
prosperity wealth
proxy war *Stellvertreterkrieg*
puppet government *Schatten-/Marionettenregierung*
qualms (pl.) [kwɑːmz/] *Bedenken/Vorbehalte*
reconnaissance [rɪˈkɒnɪs(ə)ns] the use of soldiers or aircraft to go into an area and get information about an enemy
to recuperate; recuperation (n.) to recover; recovery (n.)
refugee (n.); (to seek) refuge *Flüchtling; Zuflucht (suchen)*
to rehabilitate sb.; rehabilitation (n.) *jdn. rehabilitieren; Rehabilitation*
to repent; repentance (n.) *etw. bereuen/Buße tun*
reservations *Vorbehalte*
to reunify; reunification (n.) *wiedervereinigen; Wiedervereinigung*
satellite state *Satellitenstaat*
to sentence sb.; (life) sentence (n.) when a judge sentences sb., they officially state what sb.'s punishment will be; *(lebenslängliche) Freiheitsstrafe*
single (unity) list *Einheitsliste*
social market economy *soziale Marktwirtschaft*
standard of living the type of life that a person or society has according to the amount of money that they have
to subjugate sb.; subjugation to defeat a place or a group of people and force them to obey you
supremacy [sʊˈpreməsi] *Vormachtstellung*
to vanish to disappear
women clearing away the rubble *Trümmerfrauen*
world view *Weltsicht*
Zero Hour *Stunde Null*

CONNECT

Peace – Merely the Absence of War?

What exactly is "peace"? There are various answers to this question. The Dutch philosopher Baruch Spinoza (1623 – 1677) defined peace as follows: *Frieden ist nicht Abwesenheit von Krieg. Friede ist eine Tugend, eine Geisteshaltung, eine Neigung zur Güte, Vertrauen und Gerechtigkeit.* (www.philolex.de/spinoza.htm; [22.03.15])

Peace research furthermore differentiates between the concepts of "positive peace" and "negative peace". Whereas the former is not only restricted to the absence of war and international force, but is also characterized by a lack of personal and structural force (thus an absence of structural aggression) in all areas of society, the latter merely describes a status quo that is characterized by the absence of war or international force. Thus the word "negative" here simply refers to the absence of something (in this case: war). This differentiation reflects the effort a society is prepared to make to maintain peace.

The peace researcher Dieter Senghaas has developed a further model with which to maintain peace. This model is called the "civilization hexagon", and it underscores the notion that peace as such is not a "natural state" but that it has to be created.

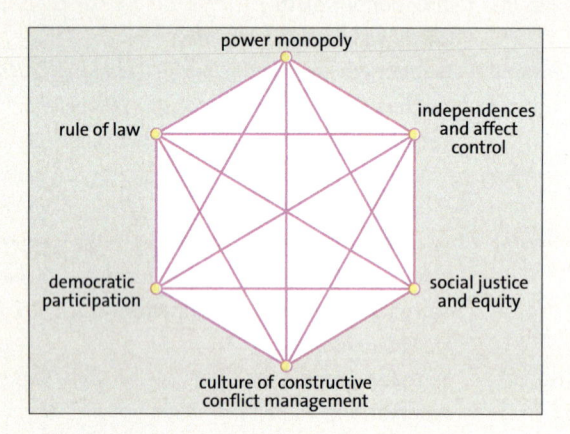

1) <u>Power monopoly:</u> The state has a legitimate monopoly of aggression, if required, not the citizens.
2) <u>Interdependences and affect control:</u> This is achieved through the interaction of the monopoly on aggression and the control exerted by the constitutional state; here, the actual "process of civilization" takes place that might lead to the evolution of national identities.
3) <u>Social justice and equity:</u> Without social justice, there can be no sustainable inner peace.
4) <u>Culture of constructive conflict management:</u> Disagreements can be solved in a constructive way and compromises found.
5) <u>Democratic participation:</u> Emotional involvement and national identities are the precondition for active participation in decision-making processes.
6) <u>Rule of law:</u> A constitutional form of state and the control this provides is necessary to prevent the state monopoly on aggression from turning into despotism.

Overview 〉 Sources 〉 Paper practice 〉 Vocabulary Connect: Revision **569**

Task **Looking back to look ahead.**
In part I of this CONNECT section, you will revise peace agreements from Vienna to Potsdam and assess their (in)effectiveness in creating lasting peace.
In part II of this CONNECT section, you will do research on the process of European unification in order to assess its importance for peace in Europe and Europe's international relations. Finally, you will give a balanced assessment of the question as to under what conditions peace can be secured today and in the future, or respectively of the notion of peace as a "utopia".

PART I: Peace Agreements from Vienna to Potsdam

Task Revise what you have learned about the Congress of Vienna, the Treaty of Versailles and the Potsdam Agreement and copy and fill in the table provided here. Some help/hints are given, but should be elaborated on. Afterwards, compare the peace agreements and evaluate how (in)effective they were in creating lasting peace, and why.

	Congress of Vienna, 1814/15 (Chapter 1)	Treaty of Versailles, 1919 (Chapters 2, 3)	Potsdam Agreement, 1945 (Chapter 4)
Preliminary events that made peace talks necessary	• Napoleonic conquest of Europe • … • … • …		
Major participants			• Harry S. Truman (USA) • Winston Churchill/ Clement Attlee (GB) • Joseph Stalin (SU)
Objectives	• reorganization of Europe after Napoleon's defeat • … • …		
Question of guilt			• Germany = guilty
Outcome	• Holy Alliance, Concert of Europe • … • …	• League of Nations • … • … • …	
Effectiveness in securing lasting peace and reasons			
Overall evaluation, with reference to the civilization hexagon			

Part II: Europe – the Future of History?

Already in 1924, the German artist and sculptor Ernst Ludwig Kircher wrote in his diary: *"Ein einiges Europa wäre das Ende der Kriege und es wird kommen, aber wann?"* (www.kunsthaus.ch/de/ausstellungen/vorschau/europa [25.5.15])

Europe, or the European Union, as a means of securing peace, became increasingly important during and after the Second World War. Originally intended as a bulwark of western European states against the Soviet Union, the idea of European unification has undergone profound changes up to today.

Task — Commenting on Churchill's concept of Europe with the advantage of hindsight and assessing the importance of the process of European unification for peace in Europe and Europe's international relations.

First, put the given speech into its historical context and characterize Churchill's concept of Europe in this context.

Second, do further research on the steps in the process of European unification provided. (Note: Use the following website to complete the picture: http://europa.eu/index_en.htm)

Third, with the advantage of hindsight, comment on Churchill's concept of Europe: to what extent has his vision of a "United States of Europe" come true?

Last, refer back to the civilization hexagon in order to assess the importance (and opportunities/difficulties) of the process of European unification for peace in Europe and Europe's international relations.

Winston Churchill

"Let Europe Arise"

Extracts from a speech at the University of Zurich in 1946.

Mr. President, Ladies and Gentlemen, [...]
I wish to speak to you today about the tragedy of Europe. This noble continent, comprising on the whole the fairest and the most cultivated regions of the earth, enjoying a temperate* and equable* climate, is the home of all the great parent races of the western world. It is the fountain of Christian faith and Christian ethics. It is the origin of most of the culture, the arts, philosophy and science both of ancient and modern time. If Europe were once united in the sharing of its common inheritance, there would be no limit to the happiness, the prosperity and the glory which its three or four million people would enjoy. Yet it is from Europe that have sprung that series of frightful nationalistic quarrels, originated by the Teutonic nations in their rise to power, which we have seen in this twentieth century and even in our own lifetime, wreck* the peace and mar* the prospects of all mankind. [...]

Yet all the while there is a remedy* which, if it were generally and spontaneously adopted by the great majority of people in many lands, would as if by miracle transform the whole scene, and would in a few years make all Europe, or the greater part of it, as free and happy as Switzerland is today. What

---

temperate a temperate climate or region is never extremely hot or extremely cold
equable [ˈekwəb(ə)l] equable weather is not extreme and does not change very much

to wreck to severely damage or destroy
to mar to spoil sth.
remedy help, solution

is this sovereign remedy? It is to re-create the European Family, or as much of it as we can, and to provide it with a structure under which it can dwell in peace, in safety and in freedom. We must build a kind of United States of Europe. [...]

There is also that immense body of doctrine and procedure, which was brought into being amid high hopes after the First World War, I mean the League of Nations. The League of Nations did not fail because of its principles or conceptions. It failed because these principles were deserted by those States who had brought it into being. It failed because the governments of those days feared to face the facts, and act while time remained. This disaster must not be repeated. There is therefore much knowledge and material with which to build; and also bitter dear bought experience to stir* the builders. [...]

I am now going to say something that will astonish you. The first step in the re-creation of the European Family must be a partnership between France and Germany. In this way only can France recover the moral and cultural leadership of Europe. There can be no revival of Europe without a spiritually great France and a spiritually great Germany. The structure of the United States of Europe, if well and truly built, will be such as to make the material strength of a single state less important. [...]

In all this urgent work, France and Germany must take the lead together. Great Britain, the British Commonwealth of Nations, mighty America and I trust Soviet Russia – for then indeed all would be well – must be the friends and sponsors of the new Europe and must champion its right to live and shine.

Therefore I say to you: Let Europe arise!

Winston Churchill's speech to the academic Youth, Zurich, 19 September 1946, www.churchill-society-london.org.uk/astonish.html [28.4.15]

to stir to move, to influence, to arouse

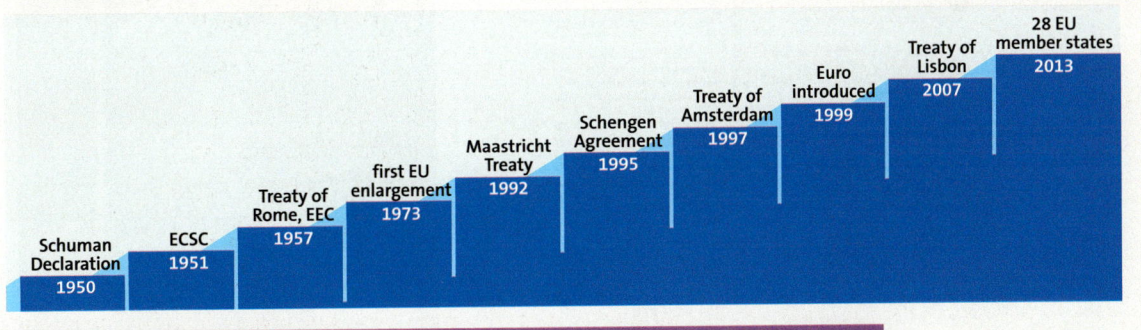

- Schuman Declaration 1950
- ECSC 1951
- Treaty of Rome, EEC 1957
- first EU enlargement 1973
- Maastricht Treaty 1992
- Schengen Agreement 1995
- Treaty of Amsterdam 1997
- Euro introduced 1999
- Treaty of Lisbon 2007
- 28 EU member states 2013

PART III: Peace Today – Merely a "Utopia"?

Taking into account your results from this CONNECT section, give a balanced assessment of the question under which conditions peace can be secured today and in the future. Or is peace as such merely a utopia? Refer to the given definition and provide evidence from history to prove your point.

"utopia [juːˈtəʊpɪə]: An imagined place or state of things in which everything is perfect. [...] The opposite of dystopia." "utopia", Oxford Dictionary, 2015, www.oxforddictionaries.com/definition/english/utopia [28.4.15]

CONNECT

People and Nation – What Is the German's Fatherland?

The very first chapter of this schoolbook is subsumed under the question "What is the German's Fatherland?" and characterizes the question of German national identity as a difficult matter. And, indeed, the question of "people and nation" (*Volk und Nation*) has remained a difficult one up to the present day. What is your personal view on the issue in question?

Task

Answering the question "What is (the German's) Fatherland TODAY?"
In order to answer this question, it is necessary to first of all revise how this question was answered in various periods in German history because the present is based on and derives from history, and answers to present-day questions will in turn influence the way the future is shaped. Take the given visuals as a starting point and focus on:
1.) "People and nation" from the time of the Napoleonic occupation until the end of 1849 (S1).
2.) "People and nation" in the Second Empire until the outbreak of the First World War (S2).
3.) "People and nation" in National Socialist Germany (S3).
4.) "People and nation" in the period of the two German states (S4).
5.) "People and nation" at the time of Germany's reunification 1989/90 (S5).
Consider to what extent the phenomenon of nationalism underwent profound changes from the early 19th century ("internal nationalism") to the time of new imperialism ("external nationalism"), and also take into consideration to what extent National Socialist nationalism impacted the division of Germany after 1945 and also contributed to qualms about Germany's reunification.

S1 A leaflet containing the lyrics of Arndt's song of 1813, published in 1814

S2 Pan-German League postcard, 1914

| Overview | Sources | Paper practice | Vocabulary | Connect: Revision | 573 |

S 3

S 4

Postcard from Nazi Germany, 1938

CDU election poster, 1949

S 5

Cartoon by the British cartoonist Bill Caldwell
Daily Star, 3 October 1990

* Please note that the borders of Germany as depicted here are those of 1937.

Your View?

Task Instructions for Bilingual History Courses

The following grid refers to a structured task instruction, which is the case for nearly all history exam papers. However, you should be aware of the fact that in an exam you might also be expected to work on an unstructured task instruction. In this case, the task instruction would only be "Analyse the source". You are then expected to follow all the steps listed below.

Task 1: Formal Analysis and Reproduction (Anforderungsbereich I)

Task Instruction	Explanation
Primary sources: Analyse the source. Analyse the source and specify on … **Secondary sources:** Analyse the text.	A **reproductive analysis** of a source, regardless of whether it is a primary or a secondary source, requires that you first of all analyse the formal features of the source (cf. "formal analysis of sources") and then give a **structured** (!) outline of the content. "Structured" means that you must include both the main aspects of content and analyse the way the source is structured. In the case of a <u>written source</u>, you should look for a certain train of thought pursued by the author and how the author stresses his/her point(s) or puts forward his/her message(s). You must also quote in task 1 (directly and indirectly). In the case of a <u>visual source</u>, for example, a cartoon, you should not only describe the main elements depicted in the source, but you should also take into account its **composition**. There might be a bisection (*Zweiteilung*) which is worth mentioning, or there might be prominent elements in the foreground and so on.

Task 2: Reorganization and Transfer (AFB II)

Task Instruction	Explanation
Primary sources: Put the contents of this source into its respective context. Incorporate the source into its respective context. Examine … Explain … Give an account of … Give an outline of … **Secondary sources:** Explain (in detail) … Examine the author's intention … Describe … and point out … According to the text, what …/ how …? Give an outline of … Give an account of …	In task 2, you must show that you can link the source at hand to topics you have dealt with in class. If it is a primary source, you will usually be asked to incorporate it into the historical context. However, the task might also be more specific, telling you exactly the time frame you are supposed to cover. If it is a secondary source, you will usually be asked to describe or outline the respective time frame that the source deals with. In general, it is of high importance that you do not just arbitrarily list events in chronological order, but that you link them and explain how they follow on from each other. Additionally, you should refer back to the given source when appropriate, that is, when talking about events or aspects that are also covered in the source.

Task 3: Reflexion and Problem-Solving (AFB III)

Task Instruction	Explanation
Primary sources: Evaluate … How do you judge the author's view concerning …? Discuss whether … Comment on the author's statement … Take a critical stand on … Do you agree with …? Why …? Compare … and give a balanced assessment of … **Secondary sources:** Give an evaluation of … Evaluate … Take a critical stand on …	Task 3 requires you to critically reflect on historically relevant key questions or problems. In general, you should adhere to the following structure: • Introduce the topic by stating what you are about to discuss/evaluate and put forward an initial thesis. • Similar to a comment task in an English exam paper, you should weigh the pros and cons of the issue in question, based on historical arguments. This means you should also definitely avoid "I guess …", "I think …", "I assume …" and focus instead on what you actually know. Make sure that your argumentation or evaluation is balanced, meaning that you have cast a light on all important issues that are connected with the question or problem you are supposed to evaluate. • Finally, come to a conclusion, referring back to your initial thesis. This conclusion should not consist of just a simple repetition of your thesis, but must be based on your argumentation beforehand.

Formal Analysis of Sources

In history papers, the first task is always an analysis. Regardless of whether it is a primary or a secondary source, a written or a visual source, you must always analyse its formal features first. The formal analysis usually gains you around 10 credits, so it is worth learning how to formulate these aspects by heart, so that you do not miss out on any credits here. Your first step would be to determine whether the given text is a primary or a secondary source, since primary sources require a short description of their immediate historical context, in other words, a few statements about the time that they describe. Secondary sources do not need a description of this time since they were produced after the events that they deal with.

Step 1: Primary or Secondary Source?

primary sources

texts or other materials produced during the time in history you are studying

for example: objects, manuscripts, journals, letters, certificates, newspaper articles, cartoons, artefacts

secondary sources

materials produced by people in a later period which use primary sources as evidence and examples and which often express an opinion or argument about a past event or time period

for example: textbooks articles and books on historical topics, biographies

Step 2: Formal Analysis

Formal Features	Explanation/Examples
author/artist	Who wrote the source/drew the cartoon, etc.? If useful additional information is given, make use of it, for example: "the German cartoonist Walter Hanel".
addressees	Who is the source addressed to? In the case of a secondary source, it is usually "students/people interested in history/in that period of time/fellow professors/historians". In the case of a primary source, you should check the text type and source of information to determine who the addressees might be. For example, if it is a speech delivered by President Obama at Cairo University, then you can say quite specifically that the addressees were his audience in Cairo, but also the world public.
topic	What does the source deal with? The "topic" can be quite general, for example, "Streseman's achievements in terms of foreign policy".
intention	Intention is not to be understood as something general, which means that saying that "he/she wants to provide information about the topic of XY" would not be sufficient. Instead, you should look for the underlying aim pursued by the author or artist, for example, "the cartoonist attempts to criticize the economic impact of the Treaty of Versailles on Germany" or "the historian wants to convince his readership that the Cold War charged the world in a profound way".
source type	Is it a primary or a secondary source? (see step 1)
text type and title	Is it a speech, a historical abstract, a pamphlet, a poster, a cartoon? How is it titled?
source of information	Where was the source published? For example: "The cartoon was published in the British satirical magazine *Punch*".
date/year of publication	When was the source published? This is especially relevant in the case of a primary source.
historical context and motivation	As explained above, this only applies to primary sources. In a formal analysis, describing the historical context means giving a short outline of the immediate historical context. In other words, just one or two brief statements about the relevant period of time, for example: "The letter was written when the how and when of Germany's reunification was still debated." In addition, the author or artist's motivation for writing or creating the source is also relevant, since the source usually displays the author's/artist's standpoint on the issue or cause involved.

How to Analyse a Written Primary Source

There are various examples of written primary sources, such as (but not limited to) letters, leaflets, memoirs, newspapers (for further examples, see Formal Analysis of Sources, p. 577).

When confronted with a written primary source in a history paper, there are certain aspects that require consideration.

Task 1: Formal Analysis and Reproduction

Step 1: Formal analysis
Analyse the formal features of the source.

Step 2: Reproduction
Reproduce the source in your own words showing that you have understood the text. Here you have three different options concerning how to structure your text:
1. Divide the source into sense units that allow you to depict the main statements in chronological order and then go through the text step by step, concentrating on the main points presented by the author. You can also find suitable headings for each paragraph.
2. Look for central aspects and reorganize and summarize them.
3. Focus on the author's line of argument (e.g. viewpoint, thesis, arguments) but only mention the crucial aspects.

In contrast to an English exam paper, you **must quote** in task 1, varying between direct and indirect quotations. Make sure your quotations support what you are saying without dominating your writing.

Task 2: Reorganization and Transfer

Step 3:
In task 2, you must incorporate the source into its historical context.
- Give an outline of crucial events leading up to the events that are depicted in the source in a more detailed way.
- Keep in mind, however, that this should not be presented in a random way or have the appearance of a list of largely unrelated facts. Instead, you should link the events and state how they follow on from each other, leading up to the respective moment depicted in the source.
- In this step, it is also of immense importance to refer back to the given source, thereby explaining historical references made by the author.

Task 3: Reflexion and Problem-Solving

Step 4:
Here you are asked to give your own opinion about a certain aspect that is dealt with in the source or about the source as a whole.
- In providing your views, it is essential that you support your interpretation with concrete references to the source, and that all your explanations are linked back to the source
- For this task, it is also of importance that you judge the content of the source against the backdrop of your own historical knowledge within a broader historical context. When asked to take a critical stand on a particular viewpoint, you are expected to develop your own opinion based on your own (moral) concepts and standards.
- The final crucial aspect in this task is to come to a balanced and sophisticated overall assessment with reference to the original question that was asked.

How to Analyse Visual Sources

The term "visual source" subsumes cartoons, photographs, portraits of rulers, and political posters, among many others. When asked to analyse one of these visual sources, you have to keep in mind that each of these forms of visual representation has specific features which need to be dealt with in a particular way.

a) Cartoon

In most cases, you can expect cartoons to be primary sources, since cartoons are usually not created to be passed on to future generations, but instead are more typically intended to ridicule or criticise current, that is, contemporary situations. When confronted with a cartoon in a history paper, the following are some aspects that require consideration.

Task 1: Formal Analysis and Reproduction

Step 1: Formal analysis
First of all, analyse the formal features of the cartoon.

Step 2: Reproduction
Give a detailed description of the elements of the cartoon, also taking into account its composition, for example, whether there are prominent elements in the background/foreground, whether a bisection of the cartoon can be detected and so on. A description never includes interpretation, and requires you to instead stay on the "surface" level only. For instance, even if it is absolutely obvious that the depicted person is Bismarck, you should avoid saying so and should instead just describe him objectively, for example: "The cartoon shows a tall man with a moustache, wearing a spiked helmet and a uniform".

Task 2: Reorganization and Transfer

Step 3:
In task 2, you must incorporate the cartoon into its historical context.
- Give an outline of crucial events leading up to the events that are depicted in a more detailed way in the cartoon. Keep in mind, however, that this should not be presented in a random way or have the appearance of a list of largely unrelated facts. Instead, you should link the events and state how they follow on from each other, leading up to the respective moment shown in the cartoon.
- After or while outlining these events, you should explain how the different elements of the cartoon are related to the historical context. For example, this would be the point at which you would state that the character that you only described on the surface level in task 1 is, in fact, supposed to be Bismarck and then you would give an explanation as to why the cartoonist chose to depict him. Here, you should also explain any symbols the cartoonist has made use of and analyse any special techniques applied, for instance, exaggeration.

Task 3: Reflexion and Problem-Solving

Step 4:
Evaluate the message the artist is trying to convey.
- First of all, state what the message is.
- Then – against the backdrop of your knowledge about the time period covered – state whether, or in which selected points, history has proven the artist right or wrong. Consider also the way in which the message is communicated. Is the presentation of the cartoon elements exaggerated and one-sided, and as such, more polemic or is there room left for the readers to arrive at their own interpretion? In a final step, you should give your overall opinion of the cartoon, based on your argumentation beforehand. You might also be asked to take a critical stand on the cartoonist's message both from a contemporary and a current perspective. If this is the case, try to avoid being "wise after the fact" and to keep in mind that contemporaries did not have access to information about the further course of history.

b) Photograph

People usually believe what they see on photographs since they are supposed to represent reality. However, this is not always the case, particularly in the light of more recent methods enabling the manipulation of photographs with computer programmes. Even without such programmes, however, the photographer can also manipulate reality simply by, for example, choosing a certain motif or shooting from a particular angle, which can distort the proportion of reality.

Task 1: Formal Analysis and Reproduction

Step 1: Formal analysis
- Who took the photograph and what do you know about him/her?
- Which event/person/object is depicted? What is the title of the photograph?
- Is there any information given concerning where and when it was taken?
- Who is/are the addressee/s?
- What was the photographer's intention? What was the purpose of the photograph?

Step 2: Description and composition (cf. portrait)

Task 2: Reorganization and Transfer

Step 3: Examining the photograph against the backdrop of its historical context (cf. portrait)
Keep in mind that photographs can be either highly staged or just be simply snapshots, and as such, are likely to serve different purposes!

Task 3: Reflexion and Problem-Solving

Step 4: Evaluating the photograph
- From today's point of view, give your overall assessment of the depiction of the respective event/historical figure.

c) Portrait

In the case of a portrait, you can be reasonably sure that it is a secondary source, since portraits were usually specially commissioned to "freeze" a decisive moment in time so that it would be remembered by generations to come or to provide a lasting visual reminder of a particular historical figure.

Task 1: Formal Analysis and Reproduction

Step 1: Formal analysis
- Who painted the portrait and what do you know about him/her?
- Which moment in time/historical figure is depicted? What is the title of the portrait?
- Who commissioned the painting and what do you know about him/her?
- Is there any information given concerning where and when it was painted?
- Who is/are the addressee/s?
- What was the artist's intention? Which message did he/she intend to convey?

Step 2: Description and composition
- Which elements of the portrait can you identify (people, places, objects, etc.) and how are they portrayed?
- Which elements of composition are dominant? In this respect, you could consider proportions, perspective, the colours used, spatial distances and so on.
- Were any alterations or manipulations added later on? If so, which ones? Please remember that "reproduction" requires you to stay on the "surface level" only, so you should not analyse at this stage!

Task 2: Reorganization and Transfer

Step 3: Examining the portrait against the backdrop of its historical context
- What is the historical context of the portrait? Elaborate on the context in detail before relating it to the specific elements of the portrait.
- What do the elements of the portrait and the means of portrayal convey?
- Did the portrait have a certain function?
- If possible, compare the portrait with other sources from the respective time period.

Task 3: Reflexion and Problem-Solving

Step 4: Evaluating the portrait
- Does the portrait correspond to what is known about the historical context? Is it accurate? Which criteria can you apply to prove or disprove this?
- From today's point of view, give your overall assessment of the depiction of the respective event/historical figure.

d) Political Poster

As a means of conveying information, posters can be used in various ways, the most prominent amongst these being billboard advertisements or political posters. Advertising posters in particular are almost always designed to appeal to the wishes or dreams of their addressees and make use of various forms of composition (text only, part text and part picture, images only, etc.) to convince their addressees that these wishes and dreams can be fulfilled. Since the beginning of the 20th century, political posters have served as a means of propaganda, and were especially prominent during the time of the First and Second World War.

Task 1: Formal Analysis and Reproduction

Step 1: Formal analysis
- Who is the designer/artist?
- What is depicted? What is its title?
- Who commissioned the poster and what do you know about him/her?
- Is there any information given concerning where and when it was produced?
- Who is/are the addressee/s?
- Which means does the artist make use of? Does the poster present stereotypes and preconceived notions about the enemy?
- Where was the poster displayed and how widely was it spread?
- What was the intention of the artist and/or the person who commissioned the poster? Which message did he/she intend to convey?

Step 2: Reproduction (cf. cartoon)

Task 2: Reorganization and Transfer

Step 3:
In task 2, you must incorporate the poster into its historical context. (cf. cartoon)

Task 3: Reflexion and Problem-Solving

Step 4:
Evaluate the message the artist is/was trying to convey. (cf. cartoon)
Be sure to also take into consideration which attitudes, (secret) desires, beliefs and/or prejudices the poster was designed to appeal to!

How to Analyse Statistics

When dealing with statistics in history, it is important not only to differentiate between the different forms of graphic representation, but also to keep in mind when and how these statistics were produced. In the Middle Ages, for example, few statistics, if any, were recorded by the people living at that time. Nevertheless, it is possible to find materials depicting conditions during this particular time in the forms of statistics. What has to be kept in mind in such cases is that these statistics were produced at a later time by historians, who converted information contained in written sources into the form of statistics. Statistics as a particular scientific branch was not really developed until the 18th century, and it was only from then on that more official and more reliable data collection took place.

Although statistics are more likely to be regarded as an unbiased and objective source, it is important to never lose sight of the fact that any particular issue can be represented from at least two different points of view, depending on which one should be stressed. In this respect, statistics merely provide simplified extracts from more complex interrelations and therefore need to be considered within a broader context.

Task 1: Formal Analysis and Reproduction

Step 1: Formal analysis
- Analyse the formal features of the given statistic(s). Pay special attention to every piece of information provided.

Step 2: Reproduction
- Describe in detail which topic the source deals with. In order to do this, you have to mention which factors are being related to each other.
- Describe the content of the statistic(s): which period is shown, and which geographical area is it related to?

Task 2: Reorganization and Transfer

Step 3:
Similar to the procedure for analysing a historical map, in analysing statistics, you need not place them into their historical context unless you are explicitly asked to do so. This could, for example, be necessary if the statistics involved represent an obviously-biased source, and as such, are designed to convey a certain message. In all other cases, you should instead relate the given statistics to other sources that deal with the same topic/period of time. By explaining what the situation was like at a certain time in this way, you also explain the historical context at the same time.

Task 3: Reflexion and Problem-Solving

Step 4:
If a statistic is in itself a source, as for example, in the case of an unemployment statistic published by a government body (in contrast to one published by a trade union), you should evaluate the statistic against the backdrop of the historical context.
- State the message conveyed by the statistic.
- Elaborate on the historical context that the statistic is embedded in.
- Evaluate whether the message is appropriate or inappropriate by referring to points in which history has proven the message right/wrong or evaluate the purpose of the statistic.
- Arrive at a balanced assessment, based on your argumentation beforehand.

How to Analyse a Historical Map

Most typically, maps are associated with geography lessons. However, maps are also an important source of information for history classes, because they show important political, military, economic or social aspects at a particular point in time.

Task 1: Formal Analysis and Reproduction

Step 1: Formal analysis
- Analyse the formal features of the map. Pay special attention to the map key, as usually all the important information is provided there.

Step 2: Reproduction
- Describe in detail what the map depicts. Here you should also mention which colours have been used in order to emphasise certain aspects or which symbols have been included and which aspects they are designed to represent.
- Describe the overall content of the map: the area shown, the time represented, etc. Sometimes, you may be asked to compare one map with another in order to recognise a certain development over a longer period of time. If you are asked to make a comparison of this type, you should analyse each map separately before comparing them, at which point you can then mention similarities or differences.

Task 2: Reorganization and Transfer

Step 3:
In analysing maps, one major difference compared to most other historical sources is that you generally need not place a map into its historical context unless you are explicitly asked to do so. This could, for example, be necessary if the map itself represents an obviously-biased source, and as such, is designed to convey a certain message. In most other cases, however, you should instead simply relate the map to other sources that deal with the same topic/period of time. By explaining what the situation was like at a certain time in this way, you also explain the historical context at the same time.

Task 3: Reflexion and Problem-Solving

Step 4:
If the map itself is a source, you should evaluate the map against the backdrop of its historical context.
- State the message conveyed by the map.
- Elaborate on the historical context that map is embedded in.
- Evaluate whether the message is appropriate or inappropriate by referring to points in which history has proven the message right/wrong <u>or</u> evaluate the purpose of the map.
- Arrive at a balanced assessment, based on your argumentation beforehand.

How to Analyse a Written Secondary Source

Unlike written primary sources, secondary sources are texts written by historians who give an account of their research results based on careful consideration of primary sources and other specialist literature. In this way, existing interpretations or analyses of historical events are expanded by a further perspective: that of the historian in question.

Secondary sources of this type can be divided into two main groups: scientific and non-scientific literature. Whereas the first group mainly consists of scientific papers dealing with historical issues and questions, the second group includes, for example, historical essays in magazines, journalistic texts dealing with historical topics, but also educational texts in school books and articles published or reproduced on the worldwide web.

Task 1: Formal Analysis and Reproduction

Step 1: Formal analysis
Analyse the formal features of the source without elaborating on the historical context.

Step 2: Reproduction
(cf. How to analyse a written primary source)

Task 2: Reorganization and Transfer

Step 3:
In task 2, you must link the given statements to the historical context, i.e. explain and elaborate on what the author expresses. (cf. How to analyse a written primary source)

Task 3: Reflexion and Problem-Solving

Step 4:
(cf. How to analyse a written primary source)

Making Historical Judgements

There are two types of historical judgements: a judgement of facts and a value judgement. Even though judgements of facts and value judgements might be hard to differentiate from time to time, or might even overlap, it is important that you know the difference between these two kinds of judgements, and that you know the criteria for a good, valid and convincing historical judgement.

Judgement of Facts (*Sachurteil*)	Value Judgement (*Werturteil*)
The North Rhine-Westphalian history syllabus defines a **judgement of facts** as follows: "*Sachurteile gelten der Auswahl, Verknüpfung und Deutung historischer Ereignisse und Zusammenhänge.*" (KLP SII NRW, p. 16) This implies that a judgement of facts is based on and derives from the analysis and interpretation of (primary and secondary) sources. Examples of judgements of facts: • "The reparations Germany had to pay after the end of the First World War cannot be directly linked to the economic slump of 1929." ➔ explanation of a causal relationship • "Bismarck's change of mind as far as Germany's imperial policy is concerned can be traced back to his wish to conserve the power-political structures of the Empire." ➔ evaluation of motives responsible for a change of course	**Value judgements** are defined as follows: „*Bei Werturteilen werden darüber hinaus normative Kategorien auf historische Sachverhalte angewendet und offen gelegt; eigene Wertmaßstäbe werden reflektiert, Zeitbedingtheit bzw. Dauerhaftigkeit von Wertmaßstäben berücksichtigt.*" (KLP SII NRW, p. 16) Thus a thorough judgement of facts must be the basis for a value judgement. Example of a value judgement: • "The death of millions of Russian POWs in captivity cannot be ascribed to the SS alone, the army – the Supreme Army Command – was always involved, too. Death was frequently linked to neglect and not to a lack of food. This can be linked to the fact that Russians were seen as "subhuman", taking away German "living space"." ➔ humanitarian criteria (human dignity, equality) are applied to also accuse the German army of treating Russian POWs in an inhumane way

Quality Criteria for Historical Judgements

General criteria:
- coherence of argumentation and presentation
- logical line of argument
- confirmability of argumentation
- awareness of one's own perspective
- modification and revision of judgement must be possible

Validity:
- analysis of relevant information/materials
- analysis of main information from sources without falsification
- consideration of other judgements
- weighing up of different judgements

Appropriateness:
- display of underlying values and norms
- openness for different judgements
- orientation towards human rights, human dignity, freedom, democracy
- consideration of different value systems both then and now

abridged, altered and translated from: Hoffmann, Frank: „Überlegungen zur Planung von Geschichtsunterricht mit dem Ziel der Förderung historischer Urteilskompetenz"; www.schulentwicklung.nrw.de/materialdatenbank/nutzersicht/materialeintrag.php?matId=3210 [14.02.2015]

Talking about Visual Sources

Talking about Composition

in the top left-hand corner	in the top right-hand corner
top left	top right
	in the background
at the (very) edge of ...	
	away from the centre
far left	far right
	in the centre of ...
on the left	on the right
	in the foreground
front left	front right
in the bottom left-hand corner	in the bottom right-hand corner

Note: Use the present progressive when describing what people <u>are doing</u> in the picture.

English	German
• In the picture, one can see ...	• Auf dem Bild sieht man ...
• The picture shows/illustrates/depicts ...	• Das Bild zeigt ...
• The picture introduces us/the viewer to ...	• Das Bild führt uns/den Betrachter ein in ...
• The picture consists of ...	• Das Bild besteht aus ...
• The picture is subdivided into/composed of ... pictorial elements.	• Das Bild ist unterteilt in/zusammengesetzt aus ... Bildelementen.
• to catch the eye of the viewer	• dem Betrachter ins Auge stechen
• What strikes the eye is ...	• Was ins Auge sticht ist ...
• focus of attention	• Zentrum der Aufmerksamkeit
• The picture/scene is dominated by ...	• Das Bild/die Szene wird dominiert von ...
• There is a difference between ... and	• Es gibt einen Unterschied zwischen ... und ... .
• facial expression	• Gesichtsausdruck
• gesture	• Geste
• posture	• Körperhaltung
• to be shown in profile	• im Profil gezeigt werden
• caption	• Bildunterschrift
• speech/thought bubble	• Sprech-/Gedankenblase
• bisection	• Zweiteilung

• The general impression that is conveyed to the viewer is … • The picture conveys the impression that … • The artist/cartoonist/photographer creates an atmosphere of … • The characters represent/stand for/symbolise … • The caption is ironic/humorous/sarcastic because … • The caption corresponds to the depicted scene to the extent that … • The scene that is captured in the photograph/cartoon/portrait/poster refers to/is related to … . • The artist/cartoonist/photographer compares … to … . • The character/person/body part/animal is drawn/presented in a realistic/unrealistic way. • The size of … is exaggerated in order to suggest/show the viewer that … • The character/person is portrayed favourably/unfavourably as being … • The cartoon/painting relies heavily on the use of traditional symbols. • to allude to (n.: allusion) • to refer to (n.: reference) • on the (visual) surface • on the figurative/symbolic level	• Der allgemeine Eindruck, der dem Betrachter vermittelt wird, ist … • Das Bild vermittelt den Eindruck, dass … • Der Künstler/Karikaturist/Fotograf erschafft eine Atmosphäre von … • Die Charaktere/Figuren repräsentieren/stehen für/symbolisieren … • Die Bildunterschrift ist ironisch/humorvoll/sarkastisch, weil … • Die Bildunterschrift korrespondiert insofern mit der gezeigten Szene als … • Die Szene, die in der Fotografie/der Karikatur/dem Portrait/dem Poster festgehalten ist, bezieht sich auf/ist mit … in Verbindung gesetzt. • Der Künstler/Karikaturist/Fotograf vergleicht … mit … . • Der Charakter/die Figur/die Person/der Körperteil/das Tier ist realistisch/unrealistisch gezeichnet/präsentiert. • Die Größe von … ist übertrieben, um dem Betrachter zu suggerieren/zeigen, dass … • Der Charakter/die Figur/die Person ist vorteilhaft/unvorteilhaft dargestellt als … • Die Karikatur/das Gemälde stützt sich sehr auf den Gebrauch traditioneller Symbole. • auf etw. anspielen • sich auf etw. beziehen • auf der (visuellen) Oberfläche • auf der bildlichen/symbolischen Ebene
• The message the artist/cartoonist/photographer is trying to communicate is that … • The artist/cartoonist/photographer implies that … • to criticise, critique/criticism (of), critic, critical (towards) • to disapprove of sth. (n.: disapproval) • to make fun of/to poke fun at sth./sb. • to ridicule/to mock • to satirise sth.	• Die Botschaft, die der Künstler/Karikaturist/Fotograf zu kommunizieren/vermitteln versucht ist, dass … • Der Künstler/Karikaturist/Fotograf impliziert/unterstellt, dass … • kritisieren, Kritik (an), Kritiker, kritisch (gegenüber) • etw. missbilligen (N.: Missbilligung) • sich über etw./jdn. lustig machen • lächerlich machen/verspotten • etw. satirisch darstellen

Talking about Maps

English	German
• The map covers the time period from ... to ... • In the map key, ... is symbolised by ... • The map depicts the development of ... • The similarities/commonalities/differences between the maps are ... • There is no/little information about ... • The map reveals that ... • The map helps to explain why/how ...	• Die Karte deckt den zeitlichen Rahmen von ... bis ... ab. • ... wird in der Kartenlegende durch ... symbolisiert. • Die Karte zeigt die Entwicklung von ... • Die Ähnlichkeiten/Gemeinsamkeiten/Unterschiede zwischen den Karten sind ... • Es gibt keine/wenige Informationen über ... • Die Karte enthüllt/gibt preis, dass ... • Die Karte ist hilfreich, um zu erklären, warum/wie ...
• to illustrate/to show/to depict • cardinal direction • altitude [ˈæltɪˌtjuːd] • latitude • longitude • sea level • estuary [ˈestjuəri] • to border on • boundary/border • territory • territorial dispute • loss of territory • dependent/independent territory • area • province • empire (emperor, empress) • kingdom (king, queen) • duchy [ˈdʌtʃi] (duke, duchess) • principality (prince, princess) • to be located • to divide between • to become part of sth. • to gain, to regain • to conquer [ˈkɒŋkə(r)] (n.: conquest) • to return to • to occupy (n.: occupation) • to annex (n.: annexation) • to invade (n.: invasion) • to become independent • to come into existence • access to the coastline • mainland • peninsula • archipelago [ˌɑː(r)kɪˈpeləɡəʊ] • straits • isthmus [ˈɪsməs]	• zeigen • Himmelsrichtung • Höhenlage • Breitengrad • Höhengrad • Meeresspiegel • Flussmündung, Meeresarm • grenzen an • Grenze • Territorium, Gebiet • territoriale Auseinandersetzung • Gebietsverlust • (un)abhängiges Gebiet • Bereich, Gebiet, Fläche • Provinz • Kaiserreich (Kaiser, Kaiserin) • Königreich (König, Königin) • Herzogtum (Herzog, Herzogin) • Fürstentum (Fürst, Fürstin) • gelegen sein • aufteilen zwischen • Teil von etw. werden • dazugewinnen, zurückgewinnen • erobern • zurückgehen an • besetzen • annektieren, anschließen • einfallen, eindringen • unabhängig werden • entstehen • Zugang zur Küste • Festland • Halbinsel • Archipel, Inselgruppe • Meerenge • Landenge

Talking about Charts

The three most common charts in history classes:

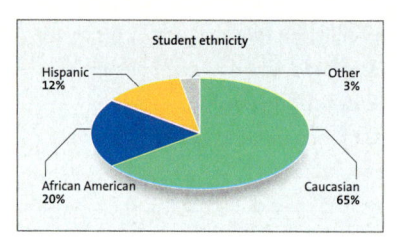

pie chart (*Kuchendiagramm*)

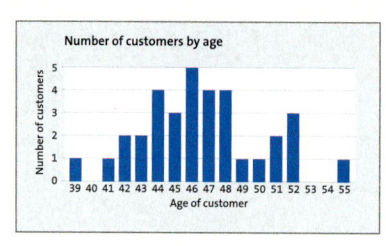

bar chart (*Säulendiagramm*)

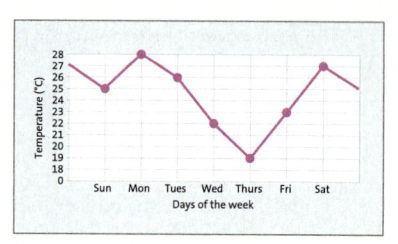

line chart (*Liniendiagramm*)

Prepositions of time	
• in (month/year/afternoon, etc.) • at (7 o'clock, 10 AM etc.) • from (a point in time) to (another point in time) • between (a point in time) and (another point in time) • during (a period of time)	• before (a point in or a period of time) • after (a point in or a period of time) • by (a point of time arrived at) • until (a point of time reached) • since (from a point in the past until now)

English	German
• to fluctuate/alternate between	• fluktuieren/schwanken zwischen
• to rise/increase (slightly/steadily/sharply/dramatically/rapidly) to/by	• auf/um … (leicht/stetig/scharf/dramatisch/schnell) ansteigen
• a rise/increase of	• Anstieg/Steigerung um
• to go up and down	• rauf und runter gehen
• to remain stable at	• bei … stabil/gleich bleiben
• a steady downward trend	• eine stetige Tendenz nach unten
• to go down gradually	• graduell/fortschreitend runtergehen
• a marked upward trend	• eine deutliche Tendenz nach oben
• to go up noticeably	• merklich hochgehen
• to fall/decrease (slightly/steadily/sharply/dramatically/rapidly) to/by	• auf/um … (leicht/stetig/scharf/dramatisch/schnell) fallen
• a fall/decrease of	• Abnahme/Rückgang um
• stay at (a level)	• (auf einem Niveau) bleiben
• to plunge to/by	• plötzlich fallen auf/um
• a drop of 5 %	• Rückgang um 5 %
• figures shoot up from 10 % to 15 %	• Zahlen schießen von 10 % auf 15 %
• to reach a peak	• einen Höchststand erreichen
• to arrive at the highest point	• am höchsten Punkt ankommen
• to (not) change	• sich (nicht) ändern
• to double	• sich verdoppeln
• to halve	• sich halbieren
• around/nearly/slightly more than/approximately/just over (under)	• ungefähr/beinahe/etwas mehr als/etwa/leicht über (unter)

Talking about Democracy

English	German
• to elect/election/electorate	• wählen/Wahl/Wählerschaft
• to vote for/against sth./voter/to cast/to receive a vote	• für/gegen etw. stimmen/eine(n) Wähler(in)/eine Stimme abgeben/bekommen
• to be eligible to vote/eligibility [ˌelɪdʒəˈbɪləti]	• wahlberechtigt sein/(Wahl-)Berechtigung
• franchise (n.)	• Wahlrecht
• to disenfranchise sb. (n.: disenfranchisement)	• jdm. das Wahlrecht aberkennen
• (universal manhood) suffrage	• (allgemeines) Wahlrecht
• to go to the polls	• wählen gehen
• majority/minority	• Mehrheit/Minderheit
• constitutional/unconstitutional (adj.)	• verfassungsgemäß/verfassungswidrig
• federalism	• Föderalismus
• separation of powers	• Gewaltenteilung
• legislative/executive [ɪgˈzekjʊtɪv]/judicial branch	• Legislative/Exekutive/Jurisdiktion
• proportional representation/majority vote	• Verhältniswahlrecht/Mehrheitswahlrecht
• parliamentary seat/mandate	• Sitz im Parlament/Mandat
• to be entrusted with sth.	• mit etw. betraut werden
• to appoint sb.	• jdn. ernennen
• to dismiss sb.	• jdn. entlassen
• to dissolve [dɪˈzɒlv]/dissolution (n.)	• auflösen/Auflösung
• to summon	• einberufen (z. B. das Parlament)
• to resign/resignation (n.)	• ein Amt niederlegen/Amtsniederlegung
• to abdicate/abdication (n.)	• abdanken/Abdankung
• commander-in-chief (of the armed forces)	• oberster Heeresführer
• head of state	• Staatsoberhaupt
• referendum (pl.: referenda)/plebiscite [ˈplebɪsaɪt]	• Volksabstimmung/Plebiszit
• to have the confidence of	• jemandes Vertrauen haben
• vote of no confidence	• Misstrauensvotum
• to propose/pass/veto/approve/disapprove laws	• Gesetze vorschlagen/verabschieden/sein Veto einlegen/billigen/missbilligen
• to petition/petition (n.)	• eine Eingabe machen/beantragen/Bittschrift
• constituency [kənˈstɪtjʊənsi]	• Wahlkreis
• deputy	• Gesandte(r)
• representative	• Repräsentant(in)/Abgeordnete(r)
• to be accountable/responsible/answerable to	• rechenschaftspflichtig sein

Taking Part in a Discussion

Asking for opinions	• Could you tell us where/what/when/who/how/why …? • What led you to this view/opinion/conclusion … ? • What's your opinion on …?

Clarifying	• Are you saying that … ? • Could you explain what you meant by …? • If I understood you correctly, you said that …
Expressing opinions	• As far as I'm concerned, … • Let me just say this to prove my point: … • I have the impression that … • If I'm not mistaken … • The way I see it , … • If it were up to me, … • It is fairly certain that … • I honestly feel that … • Without a doubt, … • Allowing for the fact that …,
Defending your opinions	• What I am trying to say is … • Let me explain what I mean in another way. • As I was saying, …
Agreeing with another opinion	• That's a good point. • What XY says about … is true. • I couldn't agree more. • That makes sense to me. • So/Neither do I. • I support what you've just said.
Disagreeing with another opinion	• That might be true, but … • I'm afraid I have to disagree. • In my view, it's a mistake to … • Contrary to XY, I believe that … • Shouldn't we consider …? • The truth of the matter is … • Frankly, I doubt whether … • Let's face it, … • No way./I don't buy that. • Let's agree to disagree. • You can't make that comparison. • I think you're jumping to conclusions. • That's off the point.
Partly agreeing with another opinion	• Yes, up to a point, but … • I can see where you are coming from, but … • You might be right if we were to consider only this aspect, but … • Obviously, this is true, but isn't it even more important to consider the fact that …
Useful verbs	• to counter [*kontern*] • to rebut/refute [*widerlegen*] – rebuttal (n.) • to argue for/in favour of sth./against sth. • to address [*ansprechen*] • to make a point • to convince sb.

Giving a Presentation

Introduction	• Let me introduce myself/my group members. • What I/we would like to present today is … • Today, I/we will be speaking about … • The topic of my/our presentation is … • Today's topic is of particular interest because … • My/our talk is relevant because … • By the end of this presentation, you will be familiar with … • The purpose/aim/objective of this presentation is … • My/our goal is to … • I/we have divided the presentation into … parts. • In my/our presentation I/we will focus on … major issues, namely … • First, I/we will be looking at …, second … and third … • I/we will begin/start off by/with … Then I/we will move on to … • Then/Next/After that … • I/we will end with … • My/our presentation will take about … minutes. • It will take about … minutes to cover these issues. • Please take a handout and pass them on. • Don't worry about taking notes. There will be/is a handout. • There will be time for questions after the talk. • If you have any questions, feel free to interrupt me/the presenter at any time.
Main part	• In this part of the presentation, I/we would like to talk about/will address the topic … • This brings me to the end of my … point. • Before I move on, I would like to sum up the main issues. • This leads directly to my next point. • This brings us to the next point/part. • … will now continue with the next part. • As I said/mentioned earlier, … • Let me come back to what I said before. • As I pointed out in the … part of the talk, … • What conclusion can we draw from this? • Why do I say that? Because …
Conclusion	• I/we am/are now approaching the end of the presentation. • This brings me/us to the end of the talk. • As a final point/finally, … • Just to summarize the main points of the presentation, … • To conclude/in conclusion/to sum up/in summary/to put it in a nutshell, … • Are there any question? • Now I/we will be happy to answer your questions. • Thank you for your attention.

Task Instructions *(Operatoren)*

Anforderungsbereich	Language support
I: Formal analysis of primary and secondary sources	• The source at hand is …/The given source is … • It is (an extract/excerpt from …) (a book/an essay/a speech/a historical text …) • It was written/drawn by … and was published in [source of information] in [year of publication]. • It dates back to …/stems from the time of …/must be read/seen/viewed against the backdrop/background of [historical context]. • It can be classified as a primary/secondary source. • It is addressed to …/Its addressees are … • The source deals with/is about/describes/is concerned with/considers … • The cartoon depicts/shows/portrays … • The (main) topic of the source is … • The author's/writer's/speaker's/artist's intention was to … • The author/writer/speaker/artist wants to express that/intends to show that …
I: Reproduction Structured outline of content	• The text/source can be divided into … parts/paragraphs/sections/sense units … (which support the author's train of thought/line of argument). • The author/writer/speaker/historian starts off/begins with an explanation of …/by explaining … • The author/writer/speaker/historian introduces the reader/listener to the topic by presenting … • The author/writer/speaker/historian puts forward a thesis which is … • He/she then goes on to say/state that …/continues by … • In order to stress his/her point/to back up his/her arguments, he/she lists examples of … • When mentioning …, he/she is referring to (= historical context). • In line(s) …, it is stated that … which is a reference to (= historical context). • He/she draws the conclusion that/concludes that/sums up his/her main findings …
II: Reorganization and transfer	• The given source depicts/is about/is concerned with/describes the time of … • When examining …, one should start with …/one could take … as a starting point (due to the fact that …/because …) … • A (further) crucial aspect to be considered is … • This is directly linked to … • As a consequence,/Resulting from that, … • The impact of … can further be illustrated by … • There is a causal relationship between … and … because … • This had a major impact on … • The author also refers to this in line(s) … when stating that … • By this, he/she means … • This is also what the author hints at in line(s) … .

III: Reflexion and problem-solving	<ul><li>When asked whether/if …</li><li>At first glance, …</li><li>Taking into account that …, I am of the opinion that …</li><li>On the one hand, … , on the other hand, …</li><li>Whereas …, I am convinced that …</li><li>To further stress/prove this point, one must/could (also) consider that …</li><li>What makes this thesis seem unlikely is …/a counter-argument worth mentioning is …</li><li>Weighing the pros and cons, I come to the conclusion that (my initial thesis is proven correct as/due to the fact that …) …</li><li>To put it in a nutshell,/All in all,/To conclude,/In conclusion,/Summarizing …</li></ul>

Checklist: Am I appropriately prepared for the exam?

I am appropriately prepared when …	☺	😐	☹	tips and tricks
I am familiar with the central questions and am able to incorporate the issues dealt with in class into a broader context.				For each sub-topic, think again about which aspect of the topic has been dealt with and create a mind map which represents that aspect.
I know the basic terms related to the topic and am able to briefly explain their meaning.				You should be able to explain the key terms listed in the topic overview of the chapter: If not, check the key terms again (e.g. in a dictionary or in your glossary).
I know the basic dates related to the topic and am able to explain the significance of the events (key events).				If necessary, read the overview pages again and draw a timeline. You could also create a quiz.
I know the key personalities of this era and am able to classify them politically.				If you are not sure, scan this chapter for the short biographies of the key personalities.
I can analyse visual sources (cartoons, maps, paintings, portraits, posters).				Have a look at the skills pages again. Try using these guidelines for another visual source to practise.
I can analyse the formal features of a source.				Have a look at the skills pages again. Create an aide-memoire with the initials of the required aspects and learn it by heart.
I can explain the gist of a text (as in a reproduction task in an exam paper).				Here you have to link the gist of a text with your background knowledge. To do this, check: • Which statements from the text need to be explained? • Where is the link between your given information and the text? (Remember evidence from the text and quotations!) The main criterion is the relevance of the content for the exam text and the task! Write a mock exam on another source and make use of the skills pages.
I can link the content of a source to the historical context and am able to explain references made in the source.				Have a look at the skills pages and the language support for task instructions.
I can give my own opinion on a text in a reasonable way/express my own reasonable judgement about a certain issue.				Take a very close look at the task: What exactly is to be judged? Most of the time you are asked to give a balanced opinion, i.e. to consider both sides of the coin. The most important thing is the justification for your views, i.e. the conclusiveness of your arguments and your ability to see historical cohesion (cf. skills pages).

Paper Practice: Analysing a Written Secondary Source

What is the German's Fatherland?

Michael Gorman

The Unification of Germany: Introduction

Tasks
1. Analyse the text.
2. Give an outline of the larger context of the unification of Germany and explain the references made by the author.
3. Take a critical stand on historians' assessments of the role played by Bismarck in the process of Germany's unification, as presented in the text.

Task	Model Solution
Analyse the text.	
formal analysis	The source at hand is a historical abstract and the introduction to the book "The Unification of Germany", published in 1994 and written by the then Head of Humanities at Westfield Community School Michael Gorman. Thus it can be classified as a secondary source. Gorman addresses historians as well as students interested in the respective period of time in history. In this extract, he mainly deals with the driving factors that brought about German unification in 1871, intending to characterize it as outstanding and as the most important political event of the 19th century.
structured outline of content	Gorman introduces his text by putting forward the thesis that German unification in 1871 constituted "the most important political event in the history of 19th-century Europe", (l. 2) followed by the Napoleonic Wars. In the following lines (cf. ll. 4–11), he proceeds to elaborate on arguments to prove this thesis, starting off with a shift of power from Paris to Berlin. Here, Gorman already singles out Bismarck as he evolves to become "the leading statesman in European affairs." (l. 7) Furthermore, the profound effects of defeat on Austria, later Austria-Hungary, and France are referred to, the latter developing a lasting hostility towards Germany. Gorman characterizes these effects as "portend[ing] ill for the future." (l. 11) The following paragraphs are concerned with the driving factors of German unification that the author identifies, but which are also important for the history of 19th century Europe in general. From lines 13 to 20, he identifies industrialisation as a phenomenon that speeded up unification from 1850 onwards, leading for example to better and more varied goods, enhanced means of transportation and warfare and, in general, to "vast amounts of wealth." (l. 17 f.) Lines 21 to 29 are dedicated to the increasing attractiveness of the phenomena of liberalism and nationalism. According to Gorman, the middle class in particular profited from Germany's economic union thanks to industrialisation and wanted this to be "translated into political unification" (l. 25) in order to make Germany prosper even more business-wise. In this nation-state, they consequently also wanted to have "a greater say in the running of the country." (l. 24) In the very last paragraph (cf. ll. 27–30), the author refers to fellow historians and singles out the "political genius of Otto von Bismarck" (l. 27) as the most important driving factor for the unification of Germany, characterizing his role as "essential" (l. 28) and "crucial." (l. 29)

Give an outline of the larger context of the unification of Germany and explain the references made by the author.

Since the task requires you to give an outline of the <u>larger</u> context of the unification of Germany, it would be appropriate to include at least a short overview of German nationalism in the first half of the 19th century, even though your focus should certainly be on the Wars of Unification. This is what you should elaborate on:

- the rise of nationalism in the wake of the Napoleonic conquests in Europe (cf. ll. 2 f.)
- nationalist hopes for the creation of a German nation-state are shattered when the Congress of Vienna decides on the German Confederation instead
- nationalist movements in the pre-March period (e.g. Hambach Festival) (cf. ll. 19 f.)
- failure of the 1848/49 Revolutions (as far as the coming into being of a German nation-state is concerned)
- **German-Danish War (1864):** War against Denmark over Schleswig (German-Danish population) and Holstein (mainly Germans, part of the German Confederation); Treaty of Gastein includes joint administration of the territories (Prussia: Schleswig; Austria: Holstein)
- **Austro-Prussian War (1866):** Prussia declares the end of the German Confederation; the Austrians are defeated in the Battle of Königgrätz, but are treated leniently by Prussia in order to prevent an alliance between Austria and potential enemies of Prussia (e. g. France); end of Austro-Prussian dualism (cf. ll. 8 f., 9 f.)
- **North-German Confederation, 1867:** Symbol of Prussian dominance and important step towards unification
- **Customs Union Parliament, 1867:** Forced upon the four southern states, but elected delegates are against political unification; nevertheless, step towards unification via the economy
- **Hohenzollern Candidature and Ems Telegram, 1870:** France is against a "Prussian puppet" on the Spanish throne and demands from the Prussian King that he must reject the offer for all times; Bismarck's edited version of the Ems Telegram provokes France so much that she declares war (cf. ll. 27 ff.)
- **Franco-Prussian War, 1870/71:** The southern German states join the North-German Confederation in the fight against France; in January 1871, the German victory is decided with the fall of Paris (cf. ll. 8 ff.)
- **18 January 1871:** The German Empire is proclaimed in the Hall of Mirrors in Versailles, the Prussian King becomes Emperor William I; the peace treaty forces France to pay reparations, German troops are stationed in France and Germany annexes the coal-rich area of Alsace-Lorraine (cf. ll. 1 ff., 10 f.)

Do not forget to **refer to the text** when explaining the references made by the author, by quoting directly and indirectly, for example:

- The author emphasizes the role Bismarck played in the process of German unification. (cf. ll. 5 ff., 27 ff.)
- Gorman does not mention the terms of the humiliating treaty explicitly, but states that in the years that followed, "France harboured an enduring enmity towards Germany." (ll. 10 f.)

Take a critical stand on historians' assessments of the role played by Bismarck in the process of Germany's unification, as presented in the text.

Historians' assessments, as presented in the text:
According to Gorman, historians have singled out Bismarck as the most important driving factor of German unification, which they attribute to his alleged "political genius" (l. 30) and his ability to "manipulat[e] internal and external forces." (ll. 28 f.) The way the author presents this assessment creates at first glance a positive impression of the statesman Bismarck even though the word "manipulate" also carries negative connotations.

Arguments to support a positive assessment of Bismarck, for example:
- diplomatic mastermind: careful planning, always having the ultimate goal of German unification in mind (under Prussian hegemony), e. g. creation of the North German Confederation, 1867
- lenient treatment of Austria after the Austro-Prussian War in order to avoid the latter making alliances with potential enemies of Prussia/Germany
- political unification via economic unification (Customs Union Parliament, 1867)
- making use of the southern German states' fear of a French attack in order to further political unification

Mitigation/constraint, for example:
- unification by "blood and iron": negative view on the 1848/49 revolutions/parliamentary democracy (cf. "blood-and-iron" speech of 1862, solving the constitutional crisis in Prussia)
- in general: working towards and ensuring Prussian hegemony in Germany
- provoking the Austro-Prussian War by suggesting unacceptable changes to the constitution to the Federal Diet, making Austria declare war
- editing of the Ems Telegram in order to provoke France to declare war
- proclamation of the German Empire in Versailles as the foundation of the "hereditary enmity" between Germany and France
- unification "from above", without the involvement of the people

To put it in a nutshell: Give a brief summary of your opinion based on your argumentation beforehand!
Do not forget **to refer to the text** (ex-/implicitly) in task 3, too. You should make use of arguments given in the text and elaborate on them, but also add further ideas.

Paper Practice: Analysing a Cartoon

The First World War – The "Seminal Catastrophe"?

David Low

Unlimited Indemnity

Tasks
1. Analyse the source (formal analysis and detailed description, including composition).
2. Put the cartoon into the context of the Treaty of Versailles and explain the elements of the cartoon.
3. Compare the message conveyed in the cartoon with Keynes's assessment of the Treaty of Versailles.

Task	Model Solution
Analyse the source.	
formal analysis	The source at hand is a cartoon entitled 'Unlimited Indemnity', drawn by the caricaturist David Low and published in the British evening paper *The Star* on 24 January 1921. It is a primary source which deals with the economic impact of the Treaty of Versailles on Germany. Low addresses the readers of *The Star*, thus the British public, but also the world public. His intention is to criticize the amount of indemnity Germany has to pay as unrealistic, implying that this burden prevents Germany from recovering financially. The cartoon was published about one-and-a-half years after the Treaty of Versailles was signed on 28 June 1919, officially ending the First World War and blaming Germany for its outbreak (Article 231), thus making her liable to pay for the losses and damages caused.
composition and description	**Composition:** • picture + caption ("Perhaps it would gee-up better if we let it touch the earth.") **Description:** • **in the foreground, centre** – harnessed horse tied to a cart and lifted up into the air by the sheer weight of the cart's freight; head bent down, wearing blinkers; on the neck, the word "GERMANY" is inscribed; beads of sweat are dripping from the horse's head • **on the left:** cart packed full with a very large load, resembling a mountain in shape; the load is labelled "UNLIMITED INDEMNITY"; cart seems to be stuck; a shovel stuck into the ground is shown in front of the cart • **in the foreground, to the right:** two men are depicted; the left of the two is holding the reins of the horse in his right hand and has a whip in his left hand which he is holding up as if he was about to use it; the man has untidy hair and his face features a moustache; he is dressed in black trousers, wearing a black waistcoat over a white shirt; the man in the very right of the picture is holding a shovel in his left hand and is looking at the horse hanging in the air; he is smaller than the other man and dressed in bright colours, wearing a cap on his head and an apron; the sleeves of his shirt are rolled up, his right hand is resting on his chin as if he was thinking about something.

Put the cartoon into the context of the Treaty of Versailles ...

End of the war:
- Allies on the Western front are reinforced by US troops that did not have to endure the war of attrition; German troops cannot withstand a joint allied counter-attack in August 1918; the Supreme Army Command advises suing for an armistice
- 9 November 1918: republic proclaimed, forced abdication of the Emperor
- 11 November 1918: Germany signs the armistice

Background of the Treaty of Versailles:
- German population was hoping to be treated in accordance with US President Wilson's "14 Points"
- deliberations of the "Big Three" (Four: Clemenceau, Lloyd George, Wilson, Orlando) difficult because of partly incompatible aims (e.g. France's wish for "revenge" v. self-determination as included in the "14 Points")
- German delegation not allowed to participate in the talks; merely confronted with the treaty draft and forced to sign as the loser of the war

Most important treaty terms:
- demilitarization (an army of no more than 100,000 men (*100 000 Mannheer*), ban on tanks and submarines, conscription forbidden)
- Germany's sole guilt ("War Guilt Clause", Article 231) as a legal precondition for
- reparation payments
- demilitarization of the Rhineland
- loss of territories (e.g. Alsace-Lorraine, Danzig, establishment of the so-called "Polish Corridor") and loss of all colonies

... and explain the elements of the cartoon.

For example:
- the title "Unlimited Indemnity" → allusion to the high reparation payments imposed on Germany in the Treaty of Versailles as a logical consequence of Germany's (alleged) sole guilt
- caption → criticism of the futility of the task Germany is confronted with ("let it touch the earth" = unrealistic demands that cannot be fulfilled); use of pun "gee-up" to stress that the "unlimited indemnity" prevents Germany from any possible recovery
- presentation of Germany as a horse → to show how Germany is to be "domesticized" by the victors of the war and to utter criticism of the hard labour she has to endure
- blinkers → Germany should solely focus on working off her debts
- beads of sweat → represent Germany trying hard but standing no chance in the face of the sheer amount she has to pay
- cart and harness → stand for the burden the payments means for Germany, one that she cannot get rid of
- shovels → show that the victors keep loading the "cart" with indemnities despite the fact that the horse Germany is not able to "gee-up" anymore
- Briand with a whip holding the reins in his hand → criticism of France's desire for revenge and the harsh treaty terms she was negotiating for
- Lloyd George uttering the sentence contained in the caption → allusion to Great Britain ultimately finding the Treaty of Versailles too harsh and thus favouring a moderation of its terms

Compare the message conveyed in the cartoon with Keynes's assessment of the Treaty of Versailles.

The task instruction "compare" requires you to focus on similarities and commonalities as well as differences. Please note that in this case, you are not asked to give an evaluation of the two views on the Treaty of Versailles since this would require extensive knowledge about the impact the Treaty of Versailles had on the Weimar Republic and about the extent to which it provided a breeding ground for extremist groups such as the National Socialists (→ Chapter 3). A comparison of these two sources makes sense since they both address the same issue and stem from the same time (1920, respectively 1921).

First, introduce your comparison, for example:
"At first glance, Keynes's and Low's assessments of the Treaty of Versailles seem to be quite similar due to the fact the both of them focus on the economic impact the Treaty of Versailles has or might possible have on Germany. However, this thesis requires further elaboration by focussing on the details of their respective assessments."

Similarities/Commonalities	Differences
• both focus on the economic impact of the Treaty of Versailles • the French desire for revenge is addressed in both (cartoon: Briand with a whip; text: Clemenceau's wish to crush the enemy economically) • both do not present the British as vengeful • in both sources, the treaty is presented as short-sighted, neglecting the role Germany plays in Europe (cartoon: "gee-up"; text: delicate system of supplies that is destroyed by Germany's economic obliteration)	• Keynes expressly focuses on the intricate economic system that feeds Europe which has been destroyed by the Treaty of Versailles and thus he foreshadows the war to come as a consequence of famine and starvation • Low expressly focuses on the improbability that Germany will be able to meet its obligations and the futility involved • the role played by Great Britain (cartoon: makes suggestions for a more realistic approach; text: happy to present a compromise that was to be accepted at least for a short time)
Useful words/phrases: • Likewise … Similarly … A major similarity/commonality is … The sources have in common that … In comparison …	Useful words/phrases: • Whereas … In contrast to … Contrary to … A major difference is … In comparison …

Your comparison in a nutshell: are there more commonalities or differences? What is most important? Refer back to your introductory sentence here.

Appendix 605

Paper Practice: Analysing a Cartoon

National Socialism – Germans' Nemesis Up to Today?

David Low

"Europe Can Look Forward to a Christmas of Peace"

Tasks
1. Analyse the source.
2. Incorporate the source into the historical context of Nazi foreign policy and explain in detail the elements of the cartoon.
3. Take a critical stand on the cartoonist's assessment of the situation in 1938 and of the cartoon as now seen from a present-day perspective.

Task	Model Solution
Analyse the source.	
formal analysis	"The source at hand is a cartoon entitled "Europe Can Look Forward to a Christmas of Peace", drawn by the caricaturist David Low and published on 10 October 1938. It is a primary source which deals with possible consequences, as envisaged by the artist, of the Munich Agreement, which was signed on 30 September in the same year. Since it can be assumed that the cartoon was published in a British newspaper (although no publication place is given), the cartoonist addresses readers of the respective newspaper, thus the British public, but also the world public. He intends to criticize the Munich Agreement, implying that Hitler will not stop taking the countries of Europe."
composition and description	**Composition:** • picture and caption ("Europe Can Look Forward to a Christmas of Peace" – Hitler) **Description:** • ***in the foreground, left*** – man with a moustache and a smug satisfaction on his face, dressed like Father Christmas, dropping babies in a sack labelled "DEUTSCHLAND ÜBER ALLES" ("GERMAN RULING ALL"); two babies are already in the sack, one upside down, the other one lurking out of the sack • ***in the foreground, middle/right:*** five babies on a large bed, all with frightened facial expressions; the bed-head reads "EX-FRENCH-BRITISH FAMILY", below it reads "AUSTRIA – CZECHOSLOVAKIA – POLAND – HUNGARY – JUGOSLAVIA – RUMANIA – BULGARIA – GREECE – TURKEY"
Put the source into the historical context of Nazi foreign policy ...	
	Outline of foreign policy: double-tracked after Hitler being appointed chancellor → pretending to have peaceful intentions in order to calm down the other European powers: • speeches by Hitler; • German-Polish Non-Aggression Pact 1934; • Anglo-German Naval Agreement 1935; • Olympic Games in Berlin 1936. → preparation for war/aggressive policy: • rearmament (March 1935 announcement of a German navy meant a breach of the Versailles Treaty); • Rhineland Fortification in March 1936 (France and Great Britain protest but without military opposition); • participation in the Spanish civil war in order to test German troops and weapons;

- Hossbach Memorandum 1937 describes Hitler's plans for annexing Austria and destroying Czechoslovakia;
- in 1937/38 the pressure on the eastern governments is increased and Hitler fuels uprisings in German-speaking territories (Austria, Czechoslovakia);
- March 1938 annexation of Austria *(Anschluss)* → breach of the Versailles Treaty (but no opposition from the allies;
- 1938 crisis over the Sudetenland, Hitler has territorial claims and negotiations with British PM Chamberlain start which end in the Munich Agreement on 30 September;
- August 1939 Hitler-Stalin Pact includes an additional secret protocol in which the division of Poland and the Baltic states between Germany and the Soviet Union is settled;
- 1 September 1939: German attack on Poland → beginning of WWII

... and explain in detail the elements of the cartoon.

E.g.:
- caption "Europe Can Look Forward to a Christmas of Peace" → contradicts what is happening in the cartoon, thus ironic
- presentation of Hitler as "bad" Father Christmas who steals children → Hitler is evil and up to take over the world
- presentation of other countries as babies waiting in line → they are weak and vulnerable and will be stolen as well
- bag labelled "DEUTSCHLAND ÜBER ALLES" → allusion to Nazi ideology of German supremacy
- empty pillow under „Austria" → annexation of Austria has already taken place
- bed-head labelled "EX-FRENCH-BRITISH FAMILY" → since Britain did not interfere in the *Anschluss* of Austria, they are betraying their allies and the other countries fall prey to Hitler

Take a critical stand on the cartoonist's assessment of the situation in 1938 and of the cartoon as now seen from a present-day perspective.

Start off with a **short introductory sentence** in which you present the cartoonist's assessment in a condensed way, for example:
"The cartoonist criticizes the Munich Agreement as being useless since he thinks that Hitler will not be satisfied with the concessions made for him."

October 1938 (confirmation of the artist's assessment):
- Hitler's policy violated the terms of the Versailles Treaty over and over again
- Hitler's plans for Germany were public at a very early time ("Mein Kampf")
- Germany's armament and the aggressive character of its regime were very obvious at that time and must have been perceived as a threat
- until 1937, British appeasement policy towards Germany had been largely uncontroversial and alternatives had not been proven

Today (mitigation/constraint):
- policy of appeasement attempted to prevent a war in case of political conflicts by diplomatic means
- fear of a new war after the experiences of WWI
- lack of support by the British public for a war
- British armament was not developed enough back then; the Munich Agreement provided a gain in time for British armament
- Britain could not have been certain in how far they would have been supported by their partners/ allies or the League of Nations: France was domestically weak, the communist system of the Soviet Union was feared and the USA pursued an isolationist policy

To put it in a nutshell? Your opinion based on your argumentation beforehand! Do not forget to include the political events after the Munich Agreement into your assessment.

Paper Practice: Analysing a Written Primary Source

The Post-War World – On the Verge of the Apocalypse?

Charles David Powell
Letter to Stephen Wall

Tasks
1. Analyse the source.
2. Put the source into the historical context of the reunification of Germany and explain Mitterrand's and Thatcher's qualms as reported about by Powell.
3. Evaluate the qualms expressed by Mitterrand and Thatcher in the context of January 1990 and from a present-day perspective.

Task	Model Solution
Analyse the source.	
formal analysis	"The source at hand is a private, thus non-public letter written by then British Prime Minister Margaret Thatcher's key foreign policy advisor Charles David Powell, addressed to Stephen Wall, the Principal Private Secretary to the British Foreign Secretary. Copies of the letter were also forwarded to the British ambassador to France, Sir Ewen Fergusson, and to Simon Webb in the Ministry of Defence. It can be classified as a primary source and deals with a meeting between the British Prime Minister and the French President in Paris during which they discussed their worries about the impending reunification of Germany and its possible impact on European security. Powell intends to inform the Foreign Secretary (and the Ministry of Defence) of the French and British views on the issue in question and to forward Thatcher's standpoint that reunification should be slowed down. It is important to mention that by the time the letter was written, the Berlin Wall had already fallen two months before. In the month to follow, talks about the "Two-Plus-Four Treaty" would begin, leading to the treaty's ratification in September which in turn paved the way for the Unification Treaty. On 3 October 1990, Germany would then officially be reunified."
structured outline of content	"Powers starts off by presenting the situation and the main topic of the conversation between Thatcher and Mitterrand to his addressee. Here, he already emphasizes that the letter contains strictly confidential information. (cf. ll. 1–8) In the next section, extending from lines eleven to 18, the writer focuses on qualms expressed by the French President who uttered concern that the "mental shock" (l. 11) of the possibility of German reunification might turn the Germans "once again into the 'bad' Germans they used to be." (ll. 12 f.) Mitterrand found it unacceptable to prioritize the topic of reunification, believing that "Europe was [not] yet ready," (l. 16), says Powell. The British foreign policy advisor commences with the President's elaborations on his fears. (cf. ll. 19–36) Even though Mitterrand conceded that "there was a logic to reunification," (ll. 19 f.) he advised to be cautious, also because the Soviet Union's reaction could not be predicted. According to Powell, Mitterrand told Thatcher he had openly expressed his worries to the Germans, asking them to "understand that the consequences of reunification would not just stop at the borders of Germany" (ll. 36 f.) by confronting them with his fear that Germany might expand its territories again, like in Nazi Germany, and that this might catapult Europe back into the situation before the outbreak of the First World War.

However, Powell reports Mitterrand to conclude that "no force in Europe [could] stop [reunification] happening," (ll. 38 f.) and that there is actually no way war would break out.

In the following section, (cf. ll. 41–49) the writer proceeds with presenting the British Prime Minister Thatcher's reactions to the President's remarks, which initially was disagreement with the latter's assessment that "there was nothing to be done." (ll. 41 f.) On the contrary, Powell describes Thatcher's view that Germany could indeed be influenced in case all countries stand together against, having her emphasize "that agreements must be observed" (ll. 44 f.) and having her express criticism of Germany "test[ing] how far they could go [...]." (l. 47) Powell says the British Prime Minister was willing to accept that reunification would happen, but also insisted on "find[ing] some way to slow it down." (l. 49)

In the very end, the writer reiterates the strict confidentiality of his information (cf. l. 50) and explains who else is to receive a copy of the letter only, expressing his gratefulness for the letter's "very limited distribution only." (l. 51)"

Put the source into the historical context of the reunification of Germany …

Even though the task is restricted to the reunification of Germany, it makes sense to make short reference to changes in the USSR and the "peaceful revolutions" of 1989/90 because otherwise the context of Germany's reunification cannot be explained properly.

- **Helsinki Accords**, 1975: Decalogue containing human rights and fundamental freedoms
- **Solidarity** in Poland (1980 ff.)
- 1985 ff.: Gorbachev's policies of **'perestroika'** and **'glasnost'**
- **Reykjavik summit** (Gorbachev and Reagan), 1986: progress regarding nuclear disarmament
- **Monday demonstrations** in the GDR after the elections of May 1989, **Neues Forum**
- **40th anniversary of the GDR** (7 October 1989): Gorbachev calls in SED to introduce political reforms
- **Hungary opens border to Austria** (10/11 September 1989): mass exodus of GDR citizens via first breach in the 'Iron Curtain'
- **Fall of the Wall** (9 November 1989): pressed on by thousands gathering at the wall after press conference with Schabowski and the presentation of the new travel law
- **Ten Point Plan** (November 1989) by FRG's Chancellor Kohl
- **"Two-Plus-Four Treaty"** (September 1989)
- **Unification Treaty** (September 1989)
- **Reunification of Germany:** 3 October 1990

… and explain Mitterrand's and Thatcher's qualms as reported about by Powell.

Qualms, e.g.:
- Mitterrand: The Germans might resort to extremism again once reunified (cf. ll. 11 ff., 29 f.)
- Mitterrand: German unwillingness to compromise or accept criticism of reunification foreshadows future diplomatic difficulties (cf. ll. 21 ff.)
- Mitterrand: A reunified Germany might once more expand its territory to the east by regaining territories lost after the war (cf. ll. 26 ff.); thus Germans are not aware that their reunifications also affects the borders within Europe (cf. ll. 35 f.)
- Mitterrand: if the Germans indeed expanded to the east, this would very probably lead to a chain reaction that would bring Europe back to the pre-WWI state of affairs (cf. ll. 30 ff.)
- Mitterrand: expression of fear and helplessness that nothing can be done to stand up against Germany (cf. ll. 38 f., 41 f.)
- Thatcher: fear that speed of reunification prevents the observation of agreements made (cf. ll. 43 f.)
- Thatcher: doubts about westward orientation of reunified Germany (cf. ll. 44 f.)
- Thatcher: in favour of slowing down the process of reunification (cf. ll. 49 f.), fear of a lack of economic stability in Europe

Do not forget to **refer to the text** where appropriate and necessary, by quoting directly and indirectly, for example:
- Powell reports that Mitterrand expressed his fear that the Germans might try to regain territories lost after the war and in doing so "might make even more ground than had Hitler." (ll. 29 f.)
- According to Powell, Thatcher did not deny that reunification was about to happen, but was in favour of decelerating the process. (cf. ll. 48 ff.)

Evaluate the qualms expressed by Mitterrand and Thatcher in the context of January 1990 and from a present-day perspective.

Start off with a **short introductory sentence** in which you present the qualms in a condensed way, for example:
In the letter, Powell reports about Mitterrand's and Thatcher's qualms about German reunification which mainly centre around worries that a reunified Germany would endanger the political and economic equilibrium in Europe.

January 1990:
- experience of two world wars for which Germany was responsible
- fear of a politically and economically strong reunified Germany which might disturb the European balance of power
- experience from the past: Germany's alleged "special path"
- situation of the GDR was uncertain and with it the one of the Soviet Union

Today:
- reunited Germany is a reliable member of the international community (EU, NATO, UN) and stands for peace
- communist system collapsed completely and turned out to be unable to tackle the problems it was confronted with

To put it in a nutshell? Your opinion based on your argumentation beforehand!
Do not forget to refer to the text (ex-/implicitly) in task 3, too. You should make use of aspects given in the text and elaborate on them, but also add further ideas.

Glossary

14 Points (*14 Punkte*) Programme presented to Congress on 8 January 1918 by US President Woodrow Wilson, its strongest idea being the **self-determination** of the people. During the negotiations for the Treaty of Versailles, the USA relied on these points when formulating their position.

20 July plot (*Attentat vom 20. Juli 1944*) Failed assassination attempt on Adolf Hitler, carried out by Claus Schenk Graf von Stauffenberg. He wanted to kill Hitler by placing a bomb in the military headquarters.

25-Points Programme (*25-Punkte-Programm*) Programme of the Nazi Party published on 24 February 1920 in which the party's principles and aims are written down.

Allied Control Council (*Alliierter Kontrollrat*) A committee founded after WWII comprised of the supreme commanders of the four victorious powers with the task of establishing a provisional administration in the occupied Germany. Its main task was to demilitarize and demobilize Germany. Formally, the Allied Control Council was dissolved only in 1990 when the **"Two plus Four Treaty"** settled Germany's full sovereignty after its reunification.

Anschluss (*Anschluss*) After WWI, Germany was forbidden to include the German part of Austria into its territory, thus the **Anschluss** (= connection) was forbidden.

anti-Semitism (*Antisemitismus*) Hostility against Jews, having its roots in the Middle Ages. Part of Nazi ideology.

Anti-Socialist Laws (*Sozialistengesetze*) Laws introduced by Bismarck in 1878 which banned Socialist and Social Democratic organizations and their actions.

appeasement policy (*Beschwichtigungspolitik*) A policy pursued by the British government during the 1930s which aimed at making concessions to the Nazis in order to prevent a war.

April Theses (*Aprilthesen*) Theses set up by Lenin in 1917 in the course of the **Russian Revolution** which basically were a political programme as to how to proceed in the revolution.

Aryanization (*Arisierung*) A Nazi term which describes the act of depriving Jews of their property and giving it to Germans.

"Aryan master race" (*"arische Herrenrasse"*) According to Hitler, it was the state's duty to breed a supreme German race which should rule the world.

Atlantic Charter (*Atlantik-Charta*) US and British goals for a post-war world after the German attack on the Soviet Union in 1941.

Austro-Prussian dualism (*österreichisch-preußischer Dualismus*) The question of whether either Austria or Prussia was to rule in a German **nation-state**. The question arose in the course of the national assembly's decision for a **Smaller German Solution (Little Germany)**.

Austro-Prussian War (*Deutscher Krieg*) The second of the three **Wars of Unification**, starting in 1866 over the question of how to govern Schleswig and Holstein after the **German-Danish War**. It was ended by the **Battle of Königgrätz** in which Austria was decisively defeated by Prussia.

autocracy (*Autokratie*) A system of government in which one person has unlimited power.

balance of power (*Gleichgewicht der Mächte*) The idea that no single state has more power than another one in order to prevent war or military conflict.

Balkan Wars (*Balkan-Kriege*) Wars in 1912/13, which were also triggered by the **Bosnian Crisis**, between Turkey and, among others, Serbia and Bulgaria.

Basic Law (*Grundgesetz*) Name for the German constitution.

Basic Rights (*Grundrechte*) A set of rights which had already been passed by the **Paulskirche Parliament** in 1848 but were later rejected by the bigger German states. In the **Weimar Constitution**, however, these rights gained a much more important status and settled in how far the state was allowed to interfere in the citizens' private affairs. In today's **Basic Law**, some of the **Basic Rights** cannot be changed at all, and some need a two-thirds majority in the Reichstag.

Basic Treaty (*Grundlagenvertrag*) Treaty from 21 December 1972 which settled the relations between the **FRG** and the **GDR** and was a result of Chancellor Brandt's **Ostpolitik**.

Battle of Britain (*Luftschlacht um England*) The attack of Nazi Germany on Great Britain between August 1940 and spring 1941.

Battle of Königgrätz (*Schlacht bei Königgrätz*) cf. **Austro-Prussian War**

Battle of Nations (*Völkerschlacht (bei Leipzig)*) Decisive battle near Leipzig in 1813 which ended the **Wars of Liberation** against Napoleon Bonaparte.

Battle of Sedan (*Schlacht bei Sedan*) cf. **Franco-Prussian War**

Battle of Stalingrad (*Schlacht um Stalingrad*) cf. **Operation Barbarossa**

Battle of the Somme (*Schlacht an der Somme*) A battle at the Western Front in 1916 between German and French troops which turned into a **war of attrition**.

Battle of Tannenberg (*Schlacht bei Tannenberg*) A battle fought at the Eastern Front in 1914 between German and Russian troops which was won by Germany under General Hindenburg.

Battle of Verdun (*Schlacht um Verdun*) One of the most decisive battles of WWI fought at the Western Front between Germany and France in 1916.

Berlin Blockade; Berlin Airlift (*Berlin-Blockade; Berliner Luftbrücke*) The Soviets started a blockade of West Berlin on 24 June 1948 as a reaction to the **currency reform** in the three western zones. The western **Allies**, however, responded to this blockade by supplying West Berlin with goods by plane, which is called the **Berlin Airlift**.

Berlin (Congo/West Africa) Conference (*Kongo-Konferenz (Westafrika-Konferenz)*) A conference which was to settle the conflicts which had emerged from the **Scramble for Africa** in 1884/85. As a result, the African continent was partitioned among the European powers.

Berlin Wall (*Berliner Mauer*) A wall built on 13 August 1961 by the **GDR** with the official aim to protect the GDR's citizens from the Western imperialist influence. In fact, it was a reaction of the SED (Socialist Unity Party of Germany) government to the increasing number of people leaving the **GDR**.

Biedermeier (*Biedermeier*) A conservative, restorative and politically resigned form of literature and opposing model to **pre-March**.

big-stick diplomacy (*Big Stick*) A strategy pursued by US President Roosevelt at the end of the 19th century when dealing with South America, namely to make use of military means to intervene on the American continent.

the "Big Three" (*die "Big Three"*) The Allies of WWII: USA, Great Britain and the **Soviet Union**.

bizone/bizonia; trizone (*Bizone; Trizone*) A combination of the US and the British occupation zone (**bizone/bizonia**) in 1947, which became the **trizone** when the French zone joined in in 1948.

"blank cheque" (*"Blankovollmacht"*) During the **July Crisis**, the German affirmation for Austria-Hungary to support them in any case. Behind lay the assumption that Russia should be deterred.

Blitzkrieg (*Blitzkrieg*) Form of warfare in which quick wars of aggression are waged.

Bolsheviks (*Bolschewiken*) A party in the **Russian Revolution** whose members wanted to install socialism in Russia after the overthrow of the tsar in 1917.

Bosnian Crisis (*Bosnien-Krise*) Conflict from 1908 when Austria-Hungary occupied and annexed Bosnia and Herzegovina.

Brezhnev Doctrine (*Breschnew-Doktrin*) Introduced by Soviet party leader Leonid Brezhnev, saying that the **Soviet Union** has the right to interfere (militarily) in case socialism is threatened in any satellite state.

British East India Company (*Britische Ostindien-Kompanie*) Founded in 1600, this British company was granted the right to carry out the trade between the Cape of Good Hope (South Africa) and the Strait of Magellan (South America).

Cabinet of Barons (*Kabinett der Barone*) Ironic name for the cabinet of Chancellor von Papen, due to some of its members being of noble heritage only and some having no ties to any political parties at all.

"Cape-to-Cairo" (*"Kap-bis-Kairo"*) The idea to expand the British sphere of influence from South Africa into northern Africa and similar advances from Egypt into southern Africa.

Carlsbad Decrees (*Karlsbader Beschlüsse*) Repressive measures taken by Metternich against students and universities supporting and/or spreading revolutionary ideas.

Catalogue of Fundamental Rights (*Grundrechtekatalog*) A set of rights agreed on by the **national assembly** which gathered on 18 May 1848, among them the loss of privileges for the nobility, equality before the law, and freedom of assembly, opinion and speech.

central powers (*Mittelmächte*) A military alliance (in the very centre of Europe) of the German Empire and Austria-Hungary during WWI opposed by the **Triple Entente**. Later, the Ottoman Empire and Bulgaria joined the alliance.

Centre Party (*Zentrum*) Political party of the German Empire, representing Catholicism.

child labour (*Kinderarbeit*) As a result of **industrialization** and increasing production, more and more workforce was needed and thus children were used.

Code Napoleon/Code Civil (*Code Napoleon*) A code of law [*Gesetzbuch*] introduced in France by Napoleon already in 1804 which was the first complete and homogenous regulation of civil rights.

COMECON (Council for Mutual Economic Aid) (*RGW (Rat für gegenseitige Wirtschaftshilfe)*) Soviet counterpart of the **European Recovery Program (ERP)** launched by the US.

Commonwealth of Independent States (*Gemeinschaft Unabhängiger Staaten (GUS)*) The successor state of the **Soviet Union**, founded in 1991.

communism (*Kommunismus*) A political system based on the theory of **Marxism-Leninism** in which the means of roduction lie in the hands of the population and nobody owns private property. The core idea was to overcome social classes thus making society more equal and just.

(the) Communist Manifesto (*(das) Kommunistische Manifest*) A document written by Karl Marx and Friedrich Engels and published in 1848 in which the idea of **communism** is presented.

concentration/extermination camps (*Konzentrationslager/Vernichtungslager*) Special labour camps created by the Nazis to which they deported Jews, political opponents, homosexuals, etc. Prisoners in the **concentration camps** had to do **forced labour** and they were exploited also in terms of medical experiments. The **extermination camps**, especially during WWII, were places of mass murder.

Concert of Europe (*Pentarchie (Fünfherrschaft), „Europäisches Konzert der Großmächte"*) A common European policy agreed on at the **Congress of Vienna** in which Austria, Prussia, Russia and the UK embarked on preserving a **balance of power**, putting down revolutionary aspirations and securing peace.

concordat (*Konkordat*) In general, a treaty between a state and a religious group. The **concordat** from 20 July 1933 between the Vatican and Nazi Germany settled the relations between the Catholic Church and Nazi Germany.

Confederation of the Rhine (*Rheinbund*) A confederation of German states formed on the initiative of Napoleon in 1806. As a consequence, the **Holy Roman Empire of the German Nation** ceased to exist.

Congress of Berlin (*Berliner Kongress*) Taking place in 1879, this congress met due to a crisis in the Balkans between Austria-Hungary and Russia. Bismarck presided over the congress and gained the nickname **"honest broker"**.

Congress of Vienna (*Wiener Kongress*) Meeting of the major European rulers from October 1814 until June 1815 with the task of reshaping the political map of Europe after Napoleon's defeat.

Confessing Church (*Bekennende Kirche*) Part of the Protestant Church, led by Dietrich Bonhoeffer. They opposed Nazi policy and the integration of Protestant Christians into the Nazi state.

Continental Blockade (*Kontinentalblockade*) An economic blockade of British goods, ordered by Napoleon in 1806 in order to weaken the British economy.

council democracy (*Rätedemokratie*) A political system in which the political power lies within directly elected councils. The members of these councils are directly responsible to the electors, i.e. their decisions have to be in accordance with their voters.

Council of the People's Deputies (*Rat der Volksbeauftragten*) A parliament-like institution formed at the end of WWI in Germany which served as a revolutionary government.

CSCE (Conference on Security and Cooperation in Europe) (*KSZE (Konferenz für Sicherheit und Zusammenarbeit in Europa)*) A forum founded in 1973 which should promote projects between eastern and western European states, Canada and the USA in the fields of culture, science, economy, environmental protection and disarmament and to make a contribution to securing and enforcing human rights in Europe. The numerous cooperations supported confidence building among the states and eventually contributed to the end of the East/West conflict. The forum ended with the **Helsinki Accords**.

Cuban Missile Crisis (*Kuba-Krise*) A conflict between the USSR and the USA over the issue of stationing Soviet missiles on the Caribbean island of Cuba.

cultural nation (*Kulturnation*) A people which defines itself as a nation without specific reference to an already existing state. Commonalities could be language, art, culture or history.

currency reform (*Währungsreform*) The introduction of a new currency. In Germany, this happened in 1923 under Chancellor Stresemann after the **Ruhr occupation** and the following **hyperinflation** (*Rentenmark*). The Deutsche Mark (DM) was introduced in the three western German occupation zones on 20 June 1948 and thus replaced the Reichsmark. Another currency was introduced in the Eastern zone by the **Soviet Union** four weeks later.

Customs Union (*Zollverein*) A monetary union founded by Prussia in 1818 with the aim of expanding Prussian trade and industry. It experienced an expansion in 1834 with Bavaria and Wurttemberg joining.

Customs Union Parliament (*Zollparlament*) A parliament in session from 1860 until 1870 with the aim of binding the southern German states closer to North German Confederation dominated by Prussia.

Operation Overlord/D-Day (*D-Day/Operation Overlord*) Military operation carried out by the Allies on **D-Day** (4 June 1944).

Daily Telegraph Affair (*Daily-Telegraph-Affäre*) A diplomatic incident from 1908 caused by the publication of a conversation between German Emperor William II and British colonel Edward Montagu-Stuart-Wortley in the British daily newspaper *Daily Telegraph*.

Dawes Plan (*Dawes Plan*) A plan from 1924 which dealt with a resettlement of **reparation** payments for Germany. The result was an increase of annual rates until 1929.

Day of Potsdam (*Tag von Potsdam*) On 21 March 1933, the first Reichstag after the Nazis had taken over power was opened in a ceremonial act in Potsdam.

Decree for the Protection of People and State ("Reichstag Fire Decree") (*Verordnung des Reichspräsidenten zum Schutz von Volk und Staat ("Reichstagsbrandverordnung")*) cf. **Reichstag Fire**

deflationary policy (*Deflationspolitik*) A financial policy which is geared towards a downsizing of the economy by cutting expenditures of the state. Chancellor Brüning relied on this policy during the **Great Depression/slump**.

demilitarisation (*Entmilitarisierung*) Disarmament and a reduction of the army.

deportation (*Deportation*) The act of forcibly moving people from one place to another on the order of the state. During WWII, the Nazis deported thousands of Jews to the **concentration and extermination camps**.

displaced persons (DPs) (*Heimatlose*) People who have lost their home because of war. Most of the **DPs** were forced labourers who had been deported by the Nazis into **concentration camps**.

division of labour (*Arbeitsteilung*) The process of separating labour evening among workers in order to increase the productivity.

dollar imperialism (*Dollar-Imperialismus*) The American strategy to invest capital in less developed parts of the world in order to boost American foreign trade while at the same time asserting foreign-political goals.

Dual Alliance (*Zweibund*) An alliance between Germany and Austria-Hungary signed in 1879. When Italy joined in 1882, it became the **Triple Alliance**.

duma (*Duma*) Name of the Russian parliament.

Ebert-Groener pact (*Ebert-Groener-Pakt*) A collaboration between the "old elite", i.e. leaders of the OHL and the People's Deputies in the beginning of the Weimar Republic which should secure peace and stability in the time of political unrest.

ECSC (European Coal and Steel Community) (*EGKS (Europäische Gemeinschaft für Kohle und Stahl)*) Founded on 18 April 1951, this supranational organization had the aim of creating a common market without customs or subsidies for its member states (Belgium, France, Italy, Luxemburg, the Netherlands and the **FRG**) for coal, iron ore, steel and scrap.

economic liberalism (*Wirtschaftsliberalismus*) An economic theory coined by the British economist Adam Smith ("father" of the free-market economy) stating that the state must not interfere in economic matters.

emergency decree (article 48) (*Notverordnung (Artikel 48)*) An article of the **Weimar Constitution** which allowed the Reichspräsident to disempower the Reichstag in case of an emergency.

Ems Telegram/Dispatch (*Emser Depesche*) Telegram edited by Bismarck in a way that it offended the French and made them start the **Franco-Prussian War**.

Enabling Act (*Ermächtigungsgesetz*) A law introduced by Hitler on 23 March 1933 in which he dissolved the separation of powers by combining the legislative with the executive branch.

enemies of the Reich (*Reichsfeinde*) Mainly the Centre Party (for supporting the dogma of **Papal Infallibility**) and the Social Democrats as identified by Bismarck. The struggle with the former group culminated in the **Struggle for Culture/Culture Struggle**, the latter were faced with the **Anti-Socialist Laws** passed by Bismarck.

Entente Cordiale (*Entente Cordiale*) A friendly agreement between France and England signed after the **Fashoda Incident/Crisis**.

epochal year (*Epochenjahr*) A year in which decisive events happen which also have long-term effects. Examples are 1789 (French Revolution), 1917 (USA entering WWI, **Soviet Union** comes into existence) and 1989 (**fall of the Berlin Wall**).

European Recovery Program (ERP) (*Europäisches Wiederaufbauprogramm*) Part of the US **containment policy**. This plan promised the European countries financial aid and goods for recovery purposes and incorporated the beneficiaries into the Western system of currency and economy.

euthanasia (*Euthanasie*) A euphemistic term for the systematic murder of people the Nazis considered being "unworthy of life" and for the part of the Nazi ideology of "racial hygiene".

fall of the Berlin Wall (*Mauerfall*) cf. **Monday demonstrations**

Fashoda Incident/Crisis (*Faschoda-Krise*) A crisis about a territory in Sudan in 1898, when British and French military forces met at the upper stretch of the River Nile. It can be seen as an example of clashes connected with the **Scramble for Africa**.

February Revolution (*Februarrevolution*) A revolution which broke out in 1848 in Paris and whose trigger was the high prices for bread and an economic slump connected with social injustice. The French king had to abdicate and the revolution also had an effect on the German states.

Federal Republic of Germany (FRG) (*Bundesrepublik Deutschland*) German state (parliamentary democracy) founded on 23 May 1949, comprising the former three western occupation zones (**trizone**). On 3 October 1990, the **GDR** joined the **FRG**, according to the **Unification Treaty**.

Final Recess of the Imperial Deputation (*Reichsdeputationshauptschluss*) Passed in 1803, this law was the last law of the **Holy Roman Empire of the German Nation**. The results were **secularisation** and **mediatisation**.

"Final Solution to the Jewish Question"/Wannsee minutes („*Endlösung der Judenfrage"/Wannseeprotokoll*) The **"Final Solution to the Jewish Question"** was agreed on at the Wannsee Conference taking place on 20 January 1942. Basically, it meant that all Jews should be deported to **extermination camps** where they should be killed.

forced labourers (*Zwangsarbeiter/in*) Mostly foreign people, war prisoners or German prisoners who had to work for the Nazis in **concentration camps**.

formal vs. informal empire (*formelle vs. informelle Herrschaft*) An **informal empire** denotes an indirect system of control, whereas in the **formal empire** of the **new imperialism** direct military occupation and taking over political and administrative power was the case.

Forty-Eighters (*48er*) A group of former delegates of the **national assembly** of 1848 who had fled after the failure of the revolution.

Four-Year Plan (*Vierjahresplan*) Financial plan set up by Hitler in 1936 with the aim of strengthening German economy by reducing imports.

Free Corps (*Freikorps*) Paramilitary groups consisting of former soldiers and volunteers who fought against left-wing extremist groups in the name of the **Council of the People's Deputies** since they had no military means to defend the newly found German democracy.

free-market economy (*freie Marktwirtschaft*) An economic system in which demand determines supply without any interference from the state.

Franco-Prussian War (*Deutsch-Französischer Krieg*) The third of the three **Wars of Unification**, starting on 15 July 1870, triggered by the **Ems Telegram/Dispatch**. Only two months later, the French were decisively defeated in the **Battle of Sedan** and the French king was taken prisoner.

fulfilment policy (*Erfüllungspolitik*) A policy pursued by the early Weimar government, which aimed at strictly adhering to the demands of the victorious powers of WWI with the goal of showing them how improbable it was to fulfil their demands.

genocide (*Genozid*) cf. **Holocaust/Shoa**

German Confederation (*Deutscher Bund*) A loose confederation of 35 German principalities and four free cities founded on 8 June 1815 after the **Congress of Vienna** with the aim of a better mutual protection and defence.

German Conservative Party (*Deutschkonservative Partei*) A right-wing party in the German Empire advocating for a strong monarchy.

German-Danish War (*Deutsch-Dänischer Krieg*) The first of three **Wars of Unification**, starting in 1864 and triggered by the Danish annexation of Schleswig.

German Democratic Republic (GDR) (*Deutsche Demokratische Republik (DDR)*) Socialist German state founded on 7 October 1949 as a **satellite state** of the **Soviet Union** (cf. **Federal Republic of Germany (FRG)**).

German Labour Front (*Deutsche Arbeitsfront (DAF)*) A Nazi organization which, in the course of **Gleichschaltung/Bringing into Line**, replaced all other **trade unions**.

German Progressive Party (*Deutsche Fortschrittspartei*) A party in the German Empire, critical of the government.

Gestapo (*Gestapo (Geheime Staatspolizei)*) Political police in Nazi Germany responsible for fighting political opponents.

glasnost (openness) (*Glasnost (Offenheit)*) Part of Soviet leader Gorbachev's reform programme introduced in the mid-1980s as a reaction to the economic crisis in the Soviet Union. It was geared towards making economic decisions more transparent and opening processes in the state and society for the citizens. It went along with **perestroika (restructuring)**.

Gleichschaltung/Bringing into Line (*Gleichschaltung*) Nazi term for making alike all parts of politics, society and economy.

Golden Twenties (*Goldene Zwanziger*) A period of the Weimar Republic which was characterized by a cultural boom in arts, literature, architecture, etc.

Good Neighbor Policy (*Politik der guten Nachbarschaft*) A policy pursued by the USA after the **Great Depression** in order to improve relations with Central and South America (≠ **big-stick diplomacy**).

Göttingen Seven (*Göttinger Sieben*) A group of German nationalists (the Brothers Grimm and five university professors) who were persecuted and arrested and whose writings were forbidden in the aftermath of the **Carlsbad Decrees**.

Grand Coalition (*Große Koalition*) cf. **Weimar Coalition**

Great Depression/slump (*Große Depression/Abschwung*) A severe economic crisis which started in 1929 and which had an enormous impact on world economy.

Greater German Solution/Greater Germany (*Großdeutsche Lösung/Großdeutschland*) A possible option discussed in the **national assembly** in 1848 as to the territory for the future Germany. It favoured unifying all German-speaking peoples under one state within the borders of the **German Confederation** (≠ **Smaller German Solution (Little Germany)**).

Hague Conventions (*Haager Friedenskonferenzen*) Conferences taking place in 1899 and 1907 by invitation of the Russian Tsar and the Dutch Queen with the aim of developing an international legal order and norms on to how to settle conflicts peacefully.

Hallstein Doctrine (*Hallstein-Doktrin*) A policy in effect between 1955 and 1969, named after Walter Hallstein, State Secretary at the Foreign Office. The **FRG** considered diplomatic relations of third countries with the **GDR** as an "unfriendly act" since an isolation of the GDR with regard to foreign affairs was the aim. However, German Chancellor Brandt abandoned this policy.

Hambach Festival (*Hambacher Fest*) A festival organised by **student unions** in 1832 with a programme similar to that of the **Wartburg Festival** but with a closer focus on European issues.

Helsinki Accords (*Schlussakte von Helsinki*) cf. **CSCE (Conference on Security and Cooperation in Europe)**

Hitler-Stalin Pact/Additional Secret Protocol (*Hitler-Stalin-Pakt/Geheimes Zusatzprotokoll*) A non-aggression pact between Hitler and Soviet dictator Stalin from August 1939 in which Germany was assured Soviet neutrality in case of a war with the Western powers or Poland. The **Additional Secret Protocol** settled the partition of Eastern Europe between both states.

Hitler Youth (*Hitlerjugend*) The youth organisation of the Nazi Party for teenagers from 10 to 18.

Holocaust/Shoa (*Holocaust/Shoa*) Greek for "completely burned", the term denotes the **genocide** of approximately 6 million people of Jewish origin committed by the Nazis. The Hebrew word for it is **Shoa**.

Holy Alliance (*Heilige Allianz*) An alliance between Austria, Prussia and Russia formed after the **Congress of Vienna** with the aim of preserving Christian values and monarchist rule.

Holy Roman Empire of the German Nation (*Heiliges Römisches Reich Deutscher Nation*) In the Middle Ages, the German Empires saw themselves as successors of the Roman emperors, thus their realm was called the Holy Roman Empire and its territory was larger than today's Germany. In the 15th century, it gained the addition "of the German Nation". However, it was dissolved in 1806 in the course of the **Wars of Coalition**.

"honest broker" (*„ehrlicher Makler"*) cf. **Congress of Berlin**

Hossbach Memorandum (*Hoßbach-Niederschrift*) Minutes taken at a meeting between Hitler and his top ministers in 1936 in which he informed his commanders of the need to increase rearmament efforts in order to prepare for war in the 1940s.

hyperinflation (*Hyperinflation*) In 1923, the result of the strike following the **Ruhr occupation**. The German currency rapidly lost its value.

ignominious [ˌɪɡnəˈmɪnɪəs] **peace** (*Schandfrieden*) cf. **Treaty of Versailles**

Imperial Council Convention (*Reichsrätekongress*) The first meeting of the **workers' and soldiers' councils** after the **November Revolution** in Berlin.

indemnity/reparations (*Entschädigung/Reparationen*) In general, financial compensation which has to be paid by the defeated country.

industrialization (*Industrialisierung*) A process which began at the start of the 18th century in Europe and which had such a profound impact on society and economy that it sometimes is also called the "Industrial Revolution".

integration (*Integration*) In the context of emerging nationalism in the early 19th century, the principle of founding a state based on national sovereignty.

Iron Curtain (*Eiserner Vorhang*) Term coined by the British Prime Minister Winston Churchill in a speech delivered in 1946, describing the Soviet policy of isolating itself and its **satellite states** from any western influence.

jingoism/chauvinism (*Hurrapatriotismus/Chauvinismus*) An arrogant patriotism of the masses which is often combined with a strong enthusiasm for war, especially during the time of **new imperialism**.

July Crisis (*Juli-Krise*) Basically, the events in July 1914 on the eve of WWI starting with the assassination of the Austrian heir to the throne, Franz Ferdinand.

July Revolution (*Juli-Revolution*) Breaking out in France in 1830, this revolution had its origins in the fact that the parliament was not recognized by the government. Furthermore, the first effects of **industrialization** contributed to an explosive political atmosphere.

Kapp Putsch (*Kapp-Putsch*) A failed putsch in 1920 directed against the newly formed Weimar government and carried out by right-wing extremists.

Kissingen Dictation (*Kissinger Diktat*) A diplomatic document dictated by Bismarck in 1877 in Bad Kissingen in which he outlined the cornerstones of his diplomacy, i.e. the isolation of France and a stable European system of alliances.

Kreisau Circle (*Kreisauer Kreis*) A middle-class resistance group against the Nazis.

Kruger telegram (*Krüger-Telegramm*) A diplomatic incident from 1896 when German Emperor William II sent a telegram to the Boer president of the Transvaal, congratulating him on successfully fending off an attack by the British.

"latecomer nation"/"belated nation" (*„verspätete Nation"*) Self-image of the German Empire in the 19th and 20th century which had its roots in the idea that the German Empire could not fall back on older colonial possessions and thus had to lay claim to unappropriated places in the world.

"Law against the establishment of political parties" (*"Gesetz gegen die Neubildung von Parteien"*) In the course of **Gleichschaltung/Bringing into Line**, a law from 14 July 1933 which forbade all other political parties, making the NSDAP the only legal party in Germany.

leader principle (*Führerprinzip*) A political concept of National Socialism according to which the "Führer", i.e. Hitler, should have supreme military, political and judicial power.

League of German Girls/National Socialist Women's League (*Bund Deutsche Mädel/nationalsozialistische Frauenschaft*) A Nazi women's organization.

League of Nations (*Völkerbund*) The forerunner institution of today's United Nations, which came into being on US President Wilson's initiative.

legitimacy (*Legitimität*) A principle of the **Congress of Vienna** which justified that the princes governed their territories by divine right.

liberalism (*Liberalismus*) Having its roots in the Age of Enlightenment, **liberalism** is an ideology which centres on individual freedom or liberty of every human being. Together with nationalism, it opposed societal or political paternalism in the beginning of the 19th century.

living space (*Lebensraum*) Key term of Nazi ideology and the idea that the German people need a place to dwell. The precondition for starting a war for territory in the East.

London Conference (*Londoner Sechsmächtekonferenz*) A conference held in 1948 and attended by the USA, Great Britain, France and the Benelux States. Topics were the incorporation of the three western zones of Germany into the European Community of States, as well as the economic reconstruction of western and central Europe after WWII.

London Documents (*Frankfurter Dokumente*) On 1 July 1948, the USA handed the German minister presidents documents by the representatives of the western Allies which served as a guideline for the development of a future constitution for West Germany.

MAD (mutually assured destruction) (*Gleichgewicht des Schreckens*) A military strategy which is geared towards deterrence. The fact that every belligerent party could totally destroy the other should serve as a deterrent.

manifest destiny (*Manifest Destiny*) An American doctrine of the 19th century implying that the USA has the divine mission to expand.

March Demands (*Märzforderungen*) Political and social demands issued by the middle class, the urban lower classes and the rural population in the period of **pre-March**.

March Ministries (*Märzministerien*) In the course of the revolutionary year 1848, the **March Ministries** were installed by rulers in the **German Confederation**. These were governments with the task of fulfilling some of the **March Demands**.

Marshall Plan (*Marshall-Plan*) cf. **European Recovery Program (ERP)**

Marxism-Leninism (*Marxismus-Leninismus*) cf. **communism**

mediatisation (*Mediatisierung*) The act of making free cities dependent on a territorial ruler (agreed on at the **Final Recess of the Imperial Deputation**).

Mediterranean Agreement (*Mittelmeerabkommen*) An agreement encouraged by Bismarck in 1887 between Britain, Austria-Hungary and Italy. It should prevent Russia from challenging Austria-Hungary further in the Balkans.

Ministry of Public Enlightenment and Propaganda (*Reichsministerium für Volksaufklärung und Propaganda*) A ministry installed by the Nazis which should control all parts of public life.

(to) missionize/proselytise (*bekehren*) The act of colonisers bringing "civilization" to the "heathens". This **missionizing/proselytising** was one justification for imperialism since the colonisers considered it their duty to help heathens.

Monday demonstrations (*Montagsdemonstrationen*) Demonstrations held on Mondays at the end of the 1980s, when Soviet leader Gorbachev's reform programme (**glasnost** and **perestroika**) strengthened the pressure on the GDR government culminated in the movement against the political leaders who more and more lost control. The slogans changed from **"We are the people"** to **"We are one people"**. Finally, the **GDR** government resigned on 8 November 1989 and one day later the **Berlin Wall** fell (**fall of the Berlin Wall**).

Monroe Doctrine (*Monroe-Doktrin*) Named after US President James Monroe, this doctrine implies that the USA would no longer be subject to European colonisation, which, in turn, was the beginning of US isolationist policy.

Morgenthau Plan (*Morgenthau-Plan*) The plan to turn Germany into an agricultural state after WWII, formulated by US Secretary of the Treasury Morgenthau in 1944.

(First and Second) Moroccan Crisis (*(Erste und Zweite) Marokko-Krise*) Both crises (the first crisis lasting from 1904-1906, the second in 1911) centred on expanding French influence in Morocco, which collided with German interests. Although Germany was diplomatically defeated by the Entente powers (France and Great Britain) in the first crisis, they started another advance in 1911 with the sending of a gunboat to the port of Agadir. However, this military manoeuvre also failed.

Munich Agreement (*Münchner Abkommen*) An agreement reached on 30 September 1938 between Hitler and British Prime Minister Chamberlain over the question of the Sudetenland. The result was that the land should be handed over to Germany. Part of British **appeasement policy**.

Munich Beer Hall Putsch (*Hitlerputsch*) A failed putsch carried out by Hitler in November 1923.

national assembly (*Nationalversammlung*) Generally, the term for parliamentary assemblies in history. The first German **national assembly** gathered on 18 May 1848 in the Paulskirche in Frankfurt, which is why it is also called the **Paulskirche Parliament**. The representatives were mainly comprised of educated personalities of the middle class (**Parliament of Professors**).

nationalism (*Nationalismus*) The idea that the most important commonality in a society is nationality. Negatively speaking, it defines an ideology which exaggerates the features of one's own ethnic group. Positively speaking, it means an identification of a community with a "nation".

National Liberal Party (*Nationalliberale Partei*) A moderate conservative party in the German Empire supporting the idea of a nation.

national prestige (*Nationalprestige*) An aspect especially important in connection with imperialism. Here, the single European powers strived for more overseas possessions and political and economic influence.

nation-state (*Nationalstaat*) A form of a state in which the politically acting nation is the crucial figure, thus the nation is the sovereign.

NATO (North Atlantic Treaty Organization) (*NATO (Organisation des Nordatlantikvertrags)*) Founded on 4 April 1949, this organization forms a defensive alliance between its member states. Its task is to ensure the security of its member states through deterrence and armament.

naval arms race (*maritimes Flottenwettrüsten*) A competition between Great Britain and the German Empire about who would be the world's leading naval power. It was a long-term cause for WWI.

naval blockade (*Seeblockade*) A blockade imposed by the British on Germany during WWI in order to cut off the central powers from overseas supplies.

Navy League (*Flottenverein*) An interest group at the beginning of the 20th century promoting the importance of a German fleet.

New Course (*Neuer Kurs*) A world policy pursued by German Emperor William II after Bismarck's resignation in 1890. William II wanted **national prestige** for Germany.

new imperialism (*Hochimperialismus*) A new phase of imperialism from the 1880s onwards, tying in with the era of European expansion in the wake of the voyages of discovery from the 15th to the 18th century.

"Night of Broken Glass"/November Pogrom (*„Reichskristallnacht"/November Pogrom*) The night of 9 to 10 November 1938, when many Jewish shops and synagogues were looted and destroyed Germany-wide.

Night of the Long Knives (*Röhm-Putsch*) The killing of **SA** leader Ernst Röhm and the complete top management of the **SA** by the Nazis due to ideological differences between the **SA** and the NSDAP.

"nightmare of coalitions" (*„Albtraum der Koalitionen"*) Bismarck's fear of an alliance between France and Russia, or any other alliance directed against Germany.

North German Confederation (*Norddeutscher Bund*) A confederation formed in 1867 after the **Austro-Prussian War**, including all the German states north of the river Main.

November Revolution (*Novemberrevolution*) The revolution which took place in Germany at the end of WWI and out of which the Weimar Republic, Germany's first democracy, emerged.

nuclear arms race (*nukleares Wettrüsten*) (≠ **détente**) A process during the Cold War in which both great powers, the USA and USSR, embarked on producing ever more nuclear weapons in order to deter the other power, whom they saw as the enemy.

Nuremberg Law of Citizenship and Race (*Nürnberger Rassegesetze*) Introduced in autumn 1935, this law officially legalized the exclusion of Jewish citizens from public life and from German citizenship.

Nuremberg Trials (*Nürnberger Kriegsverbrecherprozesse*) Trials against the major Nazi war criminals held in Nuremberg in autumn 1945.

Occupation Statute (*Besatzungsstatut*) On 21 September 1949, the three western Allies signed this law which granted the federal states and the government the legislative, executive and judicial power with the coming into being of the **Basic Law**. However, at the beginning the Allies reserved their right for extensive sovereign powers in Germany. The Occupation Statute was revised in 1951 and repealed in 1955 at the London and Paris Conferences.

occupation zones (*Besatzungszonen*) Four zones (American, British, Soviet and later French) Germany was divided into after WWII, decided on at the **Potsdam Conference**.

Oder-Neisse line (*Oder-Neiße-Linie*) The Polish-German border after WWI which is formed by the two rivers, the Oder and the Neisse.

open-door policy (*Politik der offenen Tür*) Originally, a policy dating back to the 18th century which grants every great power the same commercial terms in China. Later, this policy was expanded to every territory which was not under colonial control. The USA was the first great power embarking on this policy.

Operation Barbarossa (*Operation Barbarossa*) Nazi German attack on the **Soviet Union**, starting on 22 June 1941 in order to conquer **living space** in the East. This advance ended with the **Battle of Stalingrad** in which the German army had to surrender in February 1943.

oppositional groups (*Oppositionsgruppen*) In general, a group which has organized in order to criticize the government in office (and even act against it).

Ostpolitik/"change through rapprochement" (*Ostpolitik/„Wandel durch Annäherung"*) A policy of détente pursued by West German Chancellor Brandt in the 1970s with the aim of easing the tensions between the two German states. The idea was to achieve a **"change through rapprochement"** (developing friendlier relations between countries or groups of people who have been enemies).

outlet markets (*Absatzmärkte*) An area in which surplus production can be sold. One motive of imperialism was to establish these markets for surplus production in order to expand domestic and foreign markets.

Pan German League (*Alldeutscher Verband*) Established in 1891, this association claimed that Germany should have colonies as well and agitated in this spirit.

Pan-Slavism (*Pan-Slawismus*) An independence movement of the Slav peoples in the Balkans who wanted to create a Greater Slav state.

Papal Infallibility (*päpstliches Unfehlbarkeitsdogma*) A religious dogma proclaimed by Pope Pius IX in 1870 which should secure his authority in matters of faith. It demanded that a Catholic's first loyalty had to be to the Pope and not to the state. It was a reason for the **Struggle for Culture/Culture Struggle**.

Parliament of Professors (*Professorenparlament*) cf. **national assembly**

Parliamentary Council (*Parlamentarischer Rat*) The institution commissioned with the task of drawing up a constitution for West Germany, according to the **London Documents**.

parliamentary democracy (*parlamentarische Rätedemokratie*) The opposite of a **council democracy**. Here, the representatives elected by the people are only responsible to their own conscience.

Paulskirche Parliament (*Paulskirchen-Parlament*) cf. **national assembly**

pauperism (mass poverty) (*Pauperismus (Massenarmut)*) Widespread poverty of the 19th century during **industrialization** which led to miserable living conditions and social unrest among the German population.

Pax Britannica (*Pax Britannica*) A principle of world and colonial rule in the 19th century according to which peace and prosperity is established by British rule.

"peace through strength" (Reagan Doctrine) (*„Friede durch Stärke" (Reagan-Doktrin)*) The core principle of US foreign policy during the 1980s. The governments of pro-Soviet countries should be weakened (and eventually overthrown) by militarily supporting anti-communist groups in those respective countries.

Pearl Harbor (*Pearl Harbor*) Literally, the headquarters of the US Pacific Fleet on the Hawaiian island of Oahu. In general usage, the name stands for the Japanese attack on these headquarters which incurred severe losses on the US navy.

People's Community (*Volksgemeinschaft*) Part of Nazi ideology and the idea of a homogenous unity to which all Germans belong.

perestroika (restructuring) (*Perestroika (Umstrukturierung)*) Like **glasnost (openness)**, a part of Soviet leader Gorbachev's reform programme introduced in the mid-1980s. Its aim was a debureaucratisation and decentralisation of the planned economy in order to make it the economy more efficient.

policy of Germanisation (*Germanisierungspolitik*) A policy pursued by Bismarck in the German Empire which was against an independent Polish state. The main aim of this policy was to suppress the national and cultural identity of the Poles and to limit the rights of the Polish population.

"Polish Corridor" (*„Polnischer Korridor"*) According to the **Treaty of Versailles**, the strip of land which had formerly separated East Prussia from the German main land was now to be given back to Poland.

political assassinations (*politische Morde*) Several political murders of leading German democratic politicians in the years 1920/21 committed by right-wing extremists.

political nation (*politische Nation*) A state in which the people, i.e. citizens, have the power and the government is accountable to them.

policy of détente (*Entspannungspolitik*) In general, a policy which aims at easing tensions between states. German Foreign Minister Stresemann pursued this kind of policy in order to ease the tensions between Germany and the victorious powers of WWI. The **Ostpolitik** of West German Chancellor Brandt in the 1970s also aimed at easing the tensions between the **FRG** and the **GDR** (cf. **Basic Treaty**).

Potsdam Conference (*Potsdamer Konferenz*) The third conference of **the "Big Three"** held in July/August 1945, at which the **5 D's (Denazification, Democratization, Demilitarization, Decentralization and Decartelization)** and the **3 R's (Re-education, Reparations and Resettlement)** were decided on.

"pragmatic colonisation" (*„pragmatische Kolonisierung"*) Bismarck's strategy for colonisation, i.e. to not establish a **formal empire** but to resort to mercantile or trading rule in the colonies only.

Prague Spring (*Prager Frühling*) A reform movement of the Czechoslovakian Communist Party in August 1968 which wanted to make socialism more democratic. This movement was crushed by Soviet troops who acted according to the **Brezhnev Doctrine**.

preliminary parliament (*Vorparlament*) A parliament set up by Southern German democrats and liberals in March 1848 which should set up elections for a German **national assembly**.

pre-March (*Vormärz*) Period between the Congress of Vienna (1815) and 1848/49 and the umbrella term for the oppositional and revolutionary literature of that time which aimed at arousing the political consciousness of the citizens.

Presidential Cabinets (*Präsidialkabinette*) Name for the last three governments of the Weimar Republic which were installed by the Reichspräsident, who ruled in accordance with the **emergency decree (Article 48)**.

propaganda (*Propaganda*) In general, any means which aim at manipulating public opinion in favour of a ruler.

protectorate (*Protektorat, Schutzgebiet*) A state-like territory, which is partly independent and sovereign.

proxy war (*Stellvertreterkrieg*) In general, a war which is not directly fought between two belligerent great powers but between smaller states which are influenced by the great powers.

Pulpit Law (*Kanzelparagraph*) A law introduced by Bismarck during the **Struggle for Culture/Culture Struggle** in order to strengthen the authority of the state by dissolving Catholic religious orders, placing schools under state supervision, forbidding priests to speak about state affairs and reforming the training of priests.

puppet government (*Marionettenregierung*) A government installed by a foreign great power (cf. **satellite states**).

raj [rɑːdʒ] (*Raj*) Name for the British rule over India.

Reichstag Fire (*Reichstagsbrand*) The burning of the Reichstag building on 27 February 1933. This was used as a pretext by the Nazis to introduce the **Reichstag Fire Decree (Decree for**

the Protection of People and State) which basically restricted the Germans' civil rights.

Reich Labour Service (*Reichsarbeitsdienst*) A Nazi organization in which every German citizen had to serve one year. Part of Nazi education.

Reinsurance Treaty (*Rückversicherungsvertrag*) A part of Bismarck's alliance system signed in 1887 which stated that Germany and Russia (secretly) promised neutrality except for the event that Germany would attack France or Austro-Russia.

resistance (*Widerstand*) In general, the refusal to obey an authority or the oppositional act against an authority.

restoration (*Restauration*) A principle of the **Congress of Vienna** implying that the political and social standards of the period before the French Revolution were to be re-established.

Reykjavik Summit (*Islandgipfel*) A meeting between US President Reagan and Soviet leader Gorbachev in October 1986 during which progress was achieved in terms of nuclear disarmament.

risorgimento (re-birth, resurrection) (*Risorgimento (Wiedergeburt, Wiederauferstehung)*) Period in Italian history (1789–1870) and political movement inspired by the ideas of the Enlightenment and the French Revolution.

Rome-Berlin Axis (*Achse Berlin-Rom*) Alliance between fascist Italy and Nazi Germany.

Roosevelt Corollary (*Roosevelt-Zusatz*) An addition to the **Monroe Doctrine** made by US President Roosevelt in 1904 which introduced the USA's role as an "international police power" with the task of interfering in the affairs of South American states to guarantee law and order.

Ruhr occupation (passive resistance) (*Ruhrbesetzung (passiver Widerstand)*) Occupation of the Ruhr area in 1923 by French troops after the German government had fallen behind with its **reparation** payments. As a reaction, the German trade unions and the government started a campaign for a strike.

rump parliament (*Rumpfparlament*) A small number of Southern German delegates who were still in session in Stuttgart in June 1849 after the failure of the **national assembly** in Frankfurt in 1848. However, the group was dissolved by the Württemberg military on 18 June 1849.

rural exodus (*Landflucht*) During **industrialization** a movement of farmers leaving their land and moving to towns and cities boosted by the more frequent use of technical novelties.

Russian Revolutions (*Russische Revolutionen*) Two revolutions of 1917 which turned Russia into the **Soviet Union**, i.e. turning a monarchy into a communist state.

SA (*SA (Sturmabteilung)*) A paramilitary group of the NSDAP already formed in the Weimar Republic.

sabre-rattling (*Säbelrasseln*) In politics, the strategy to demonstrate military strength as a threat.

sailors' mutiny (*Matrosenaufstand*) In the course of the **November Revolution**, sailors mutinied in the German ports and demonstrated against the ongoing war.

satellite states (*Satellitenstaaten*) In general, smaller states which are protected by larger ones, i.e. a great power. The **Soviet Union** established a system of **satellite states** with **puppet governments** in almost all countries of Eastern Europe after WWII.

Schlieffen Plan (*Schlieffen-Plan*) A plan which should prevent Germany from being involved in a two-front war, developed in 1894. Its goal was a quick defeat of France by first marching through and invading neutral Belgium. This should be quickly done before Russia could mobilize her troops completely. The success of the plan depended on Britain not supporting its ally Belgium, which they did.

Schuman Declaration (*Schuman-Erklärung*) Named after the French Foreign Minister Robert Schuman, this declaration from May 1950 proposed the ombination of the French and the German steel and coal production in one institution with the aim making another war between France and Germany ever more unlikely. The result was the **ECSC (European Coal and Steel Community)** founded in 1951.

Scramble for Africa (*Wettlauf um Afrika*) The colonisation of the African continent between 1880 and WWI.

SD (*SD (Sicherheitsdienst)*) Part of the **SS** and secret police which operated Germany-wide.

Second Empire (*Deutsches Kaiserreich*) Name of the German Empire founded in 1871.

secularisation (*Säkularisation*) The act of taking away territory owned by the church and giving it to secular princes (agreed on at the **Final Recess of the Imperial Deputation**).

segregation (*Segregation, Absonderung*) In the context of 19th century **nationalism**, a state in which nationalism leads to the creation of a common enemy and thus a **segregation** from everything which is "different".

self-determination (*Selbstbestimmung*) cf. **14 Points**

Shoa (*Shoa*) cf. **Holocaust**

Smaller German Solution/Little Germany (*Kleindeutsche Lösung/Kleindeutschland*) The solution agreed on by the **national assembly** of 1848 as to the territorial borders of a united Germany. In contrast to the **Greater German Solution (Greater Germany)**, it was easier to realize since German territory in Austria was not considered.

Social Darwinism (*Sozialdarwinismus*) A theory which became very popular in the second half of the 19th entury until WWI. It combined aspects of biology and evolution theory with the attempt to explain and justify the rule of the western "civilized" world over the "uncivilized" indigenous peoples.

Social Democracy (*Sozialdemokratie*) A political movement and ideology which advocates for a socially fair society. These ideas came up in the course of **industrialization**.

Social Democratic Party (*Sozialdemokratische Partei*) The oldest German political party, founded in 1863 as the General German Workers' Association (*Allgemeiner Deutscher Arbeiterverein*) which represented the interests of the workers.

social imperialism (*Sozialimperialismus*) A motive of new imperialist policy in attempting to divert attention away from domestic problems by pointing out the successes of imperialism in order to legitimize political power structures and social hierarchies in the colonies.

(the) Social Question (*(die) Soziale Frage*) An issue which came up during the **industrialization** and which asked how to improve the (working) conditions of the workers in factories in particular.

social security system (*Sozialversicherungssystem*) A system introduced by Bismarck which basically fulfilled Socialist demands, i.e. health care insurance, old-age pensions, and care for the bereaved.

solidarity (*Solidarität*) A principle of the **Congress of Vienna** meaning that the European dynasties mutually assured to protect their interests from revolutionary ideas.

Solidarnosz (Solidarity Movement) (*Solidarnosc (Solidarität)*) A Polish **trade union** founded in 1980 after a strike of workers of the Gdansk shipyard against rising prices. The longer the strike went on, the more rights the workers demanded, among others freedom of speech and the release of political prisoners.

Soviet Union (USSR) (*Sowjetunion (UdSSR)*) The **communist** state (**council democracy**) which was the result of the two **Russian Revolutions** in 1917.

Spartacists (*Spartakus-Gruppe*) A **communist** group led by Rosa Luxemburg and Karl Liebknecht at the beginning of the Weimar Republic.

Spartacist uprising (*Spartakusaufstand*) A general strike and uprisings in January 1919 after which the **November Revolution** ended.

Spirit of 1914 (*Augusterlebnis*) Euphoria felt in August 1914 by the population of the countries involved in WWI about war, which was fuelled by **nationalism**. Furthermore, the people believed that war was inevitable and that they only waged a defensive war.

Springtime of the Peoples (*Völkerfrühling*) The German struggle for national liberty and unity in 1848.

SS (*SS (Schutzstaffel)*) A Nazi military organization under the leadership of Heinrich Himmler and Hitler's personal guard. Later also responsible for controlling and watching over the **concentration camps**.

stab-in-the-back legend/myth (*Dolchstoßlegende*) A legend spread by the German military high command at the end of WWI, saying that the German army had not been defeated in the field but at the home front by the supporters of the November Revolution.

stalemate (*Pattsituation*) A situation the warring parties faced already at the beginning of WWI, when neither the German nor the French forces could gain any more territory in the trench warfare.

Stalin Notes (March Notes) (*Stalin-Noten (März-Noten)*) Several diplomatic notes by Soviet leader Stalin addressed to the **FRG** in March 1952, in which Stalin offered the Western Allies negotiations about a peace treaty with Germany as a whole. The crucial point why the Western Allies rejected Stalin's proposals was that the condition for such a peace treaty would have been that Germany as a whole should not have any coalitions or military alliances against any former state which had previously fought against Germany.

START 1 (Strategic Arms Reduction Treaty) (*START 1 (Vertrag zur Verringerung strategischer Waffen)*) A treaty signed in 1991 between the **Soviet Union** (later Russia) and the USA which settled the gradual reduction of strategic arms. Further treaties followed.

steam engine (*Dampfmaschine*) A steam-powered machine newly invented in the course of **industrialization** which massively facilitated production.

Struggle for Culture/Culture Struggle (*Kulturkampf*) Bismarck's fight against Catholicism in the **Second Empire**.

student unions/fraternities (*Burschenschaften*) Student associations founded in the 19th century which supported national and liberal ideas and a German unification.

sunrise industries (*Zukunftsindustrien*) In the course of **industrialization**, the electrical and the chemical industries were called this since they were of special importance for Germany in overtaking the leading industrial nation of England in terms of export.

Tehran Conference (*Teheran-Konferenz*) First conference of **the "Big Three"** about how to further proceed on the European continent in terms of warfare and how to deal with Germany after WWII, held at Tehran in November 1943.

Ten Point Plan (*Zehn-Punkte-Programm*) Plan developed by German Chancellor Kohl about how to organize German reunification.

terra nullius (no-man's land) (*Terra Nullius (Niemandsland)*) The name for land which does not belong to anybody and thus can be claimed by everybody.

three-class voting system (*Dreiklassenwahlrecht*) A Prussian, pre-democratic voting system in effect from 1850 until 1918 according to which the voters are classified into three groups on the basis of their income.

Three Emperors' Alliance (*Dreikaiser-Bund*) An alliance between Germany, Austria-Hungary and Russia formed in 1881 and part of Bismarck's alliance system. It stated that in the case of war with a fourth power, Germany would stay neutral.

Three Emperors' League (*Dreikaiser-Abkommen*) An alliance formed by Germany, Austria-Hungary and Russia in 1873 and part of Bismarck's alliance system.

Three Emperors' Year (*Dreikaiserjahr*) The year 1888, since three German emperors were in power in succession, namely William I, Frederick III and William II.

total war (*totaler Krieg*) A warfare in which each and every resource is geared towards war, including society.

trade union (*Gewerkschaft*) cf. workers' movement

Treaty of Brest-Litovsk (*Vertrag von Brest-Litowsk*) A peace treaty signed by Germany and the **Soviet Union** in 1918 which ended the war between them. The **Soviet Union** had to make territorial concessions and thus lost a large number of their population and natural resources.

Treaty of Frankfurt (*Frieden zu Frankfurt*) In this peace treaty between France and Germany, which ended the Franco-Prussian War, France had to cede Alsace-Lorraine to Germany.

Treaty of Locarno (*Vertrag von Locarno*) A treaty signed in 1925 in which Germany as well as France and Belgium declared to refrain from violently changing their existing borders. As a consequence, Germany entered the **League of Nations**.

Treaty of Rapallo (*Vertrag von Rapallo*) A treaty of 1922 which settled the resumption of diplomatic relations between Germany and Russia.

Treaty of Rome/European Economic Community (EEC) (*Römische Verträge/Europäische Wirtschaftsgemeinschaft (EWG)*) Signed on 25 March 1957 by the Benelux states, Italy and the **FRG**, the Treaty of Rome established the **European Economic Community (EEC)**, which was the next step towards a European integration. The **EEC** had the aims of establishing a customs union with a common external tariff (*gemeinsamer Außenzoll*), establishing a common market and the reduction of trade restrictions, establishing mobility of goods, people, services and capital and closely cooperating in the peaceful usage of nuclear energy.

Treaty of Versailles (*Versailler Vertrag*) The peace treaty which settled WWI. Due to the **War Guilt Clause** and the high amount of **reparations** Germany had to pay, it was perceived as an **ignominious peace** by a majority of the Germans.

Treaty on the Final Settlement with Respect to Germany ("Two-plus-Four Treaty") (*Vertrag über die abschließende Regelung in Bezug auf Deutschland ("Zwei-plus-Vier-Vertrag")*) Signed on 12 September 1990 by the two German states and the four victorious powers of WWII, this treaty restored the full sovereignty of the united German state.

trench warfare (*(Schützen-)Grabenkrieg*) A special type of warfare in which trenches are dug at the front line and soldiers of both warring parties hide in these trenches and fight each other.

Triple Alliance (*Dreibund*) An extension of the **Dual Alliance** after Italy had joined in 1882.

Triple Entente (*Triple Entente*) An extension of the **Entente Cordiale** after Russia had joined in 1907.

Truman Doctrine/containment policy (*Truman-Doktrin/Eindämmungspolitik*) A doctrine from 1947 stating that every country which saw itself threatened by **communism** or the **Soviet Union** can expect American support. Part of US **containment policy**, which aimed at limiting Soviet influence on European states.

Tsar/czar (*Zar*) Title of the Russian monarch.

unconditional surrender (*bedingungslose Kapitulation*) A military surrender in which the defeated party does not pose any conditions. Germany surrendered unconditionally on 8 May 1945.

Unification Treaty (*Einigungsvertrag*) Signed on 20 September 1990 by both German parliaments, this treaty sealed the reunification of Germany.

unrestricted submarine warfare (*uneingeschränkter U-Boot-Krieg*) A military strategy which German admiralty had embarked on in 1914, meaning that German submarines would attack any vessels without warning.

urbanization (*Urbanisierung/Verstädterung*) A result of the **rural exodus** in which the population of towns and cities increased.

victory peace (*Siegfrieden*) The opposite of a peace based on compromise and understanding. This concept was pursued by a majority of the German executive branch of the government in 1917.

Wall Street Crash/Black Friday (*Börsencrash/Schwarzer Freitag*) The breakdown of the American stock exchange on 24 October 1929 which affected the European stock exchanges the next day (a Friday, **Black Friday**). The trigger for the **Great Depression/slump**.

War Guilt Clause (*Kriegsschuldartikel*) Article 231 of the **Treaty of Versailles** which said that Germany and her allies are solely to blame for the outbreak of WWI.

war of annihilation (*Vernichtungskrieg*) Ideological warfare pursued by the Nazis in WWII with the aim of destroying all "sub-human races".

war of attrition (*Stellungskrieg*) A defensive warfare in which the front line is a static one. Typical examples are the **Battle of Verdun** (February to December 1916) and the **Battle of the Somme**. Such a type of warfare leads to a very high number of casualties.

Wartburg Festival (*Wartburg-Fest*) A festival of 1817 organised by students at which students and university professors delivered speeches on German unity and liberty.

Wars of Coalition (*Koalitionskriege*) Wars fought by Napoleon from 1792 until 1812 against European monarchies in which the idea of a nation spread throughout Europe.

Wars of Liberation (*Befreiungskriege*) The wars waged by the European powers against Napoleon Bonaparte from 1813 to 1815. They ended with the **Battle of Nations**.

Wars of Unification (*(Reichs-)Einigungskriege*) Three wars fought in order to unify Germany (cf. **German-Danish War**, **Austro-Prussian War** and **Franco-Prussian War**).

Warsaw Pact (*Warschauer Pakt*) The counterpart of **NATO (North Atlantic Treaty Organization)**, founded on 14 May 1955 on the initiative of the **Soviet Union**.

"We are the people" → "We are one people" (*„Wir sind das Volk" → „Wir sind ein Volk"*) cf. **Monday demonstrations**

weapons of mass destruction (WMDs) (*Massenvernichtungswaffen*) In general, any kind of weapon which has severe effects on the environment and life itself. Mostly atomic, biological and chemical weapons.

Weimar Coalition (*Weimarer Koalition*) The first political coalition of the Weimar Republic, consisting of the SPD, DDP and **Centre Party**.

Weimar Constitution (*Weimarer Verfassung*) The constitution of the Weimar Republic and the first democratic German constitution in effect.

welfare (*Sozialhilfe, Fürsorge*) In the course of the **industrialization**, also the state saw the necessity of caring for the weak ones of society (cf. **social security system**).

world policy (*Weltpolitik*) cf. **New Course**

workers' and soldiers' councils (*Arbeiter- und Soldatenräte*) During the **November Revolution** of 1918 in Germany, these councils formed with the aim of not only representing the interests of the workers and soldiers, but also of establishing a communist system in Germany.

workers' movement (*Arbeiterbewegung*) A movement which started during the **industrialization** when a new social class emerged, namely the workers. Soon they started to organize themselves in **trade unions**, for example, in order to fight for their rights.

Yalta Conference (*Konferenz von Jalta*) The second conference of **the "Big Three"** held in February 1945 during which a division of Germany after the war was decided on.

Young Italy (*Junges Italien*) A secret organization founded by Giuseppe Mazzini in the course of the risorgimento which wanted to solve the Italian question by creating an independent republic.

Young Plan (*Young Plan*) A plan developed in 1929 according to which Germany's **reparation** payments were delayed until 1987/88.

Zero Hour (*Stunde Null*) Term for the end of WWII at which Germany was almost destroyed.

Zimmermann Telegram (*Zimmermann-Telegramm*) A coded telegram sent by the German Arthur Zimmermann to the German ambassador to Mexico in 1917 in which Germany offered Mexico support against the USA. The British intercepted the telegram and decoded it. The content had a huge impact on US public opinion in favour of an entry into war.

Index

14 Points 187–188, 297, 315–316, 319, 322, 325, 328, 330, 603
20 July plot 341, 357, 360, 447
25-Points Programme 341, 354, 399 f.

Adenauer, Konrad 492, 499, 500 ff., 531, 539 f.
(Tsar) Alexander I of Russia 23, 63 ff., 70
Allied Control Council 492, 494, 498, 527,
Anschluss 361, 404 f., 423, 606
anti-Semitism 11, 41, 142 f., 341, 353 f., 366, 380, 382 f., 398, 485 f., 488, 519
Anti-Socialist Laws 11, 40 f., 137, 139, 214
appeasement policy 342, 361, 363, 453 f., 458 ff., 488, 521, 606
April Theses 162, 184, 302
Arndt, Ernst Moritz 52 f., 101, 572
Aryanization 342, 366
"Aryan master race" 227, 341, 354,
Atlantic Charter 342, 364
Austro-Prussian dualism 11, 34 f., 114, 600
Austro-Prussian War 9, 11, 35 f., 116 f., 139, 149, 600 f.
autocracy 84, 161, 184 f., 299, 325 f.

balance of power 10, 24, 62–66, 73, 114, 127, 156, 178, 183, 296, 496, 509, 521, 609
Balkan Wars 158, 161, 178
Basic Law 33, 101, 345, 356, 419, 432, 492, 499, 515, 539, 541
Basic Rights 32 f., 298, 338, 340, 345, 356, 432, 541
Basic Treaty 491, 493, 504, 552
Battle of Britain 342, 364,
Battle of Königgrätz 11, 22, 35, 311, 600
Battle of the Nations 8, 10, 18 f., 24, 56, 59, 67
Battle of Sedan 11, 36, 139, 311
Battle of Stalingrad 342, 364, 467
Battle of the Somme 159, 161, 183, 292 f., 334
Battle of Tannenberg 159, 161, 183
Battle of Verdun 159, 161, 183
Berlin Blockade; Berlin Airlift 490, 492, 498, 534, 540, 549

Berlin (Congo/West Africa) Conference 175, 252
Berlin Wall 491, 493, 504, 508, 545, 551, 553 f., 607
Biedermeier 10, 25, 80 ff.
big-stick diplomacy 160, 174, 244 ff.

the "Big Three" 162, 188, 317 f., 320, 322, 339, 395 f., 492, 494, 603
Bismarck-Schönhausen, Otto von 9, 11 f., 34 – 36, 38–43, 113–155, 159, 166, 174–178, 214–220, 251 ff., 266–271, 356, 560, 580, 588, 599 ff.
bizone/bizonia; trizone 492, 496
"blank cheque" 161, 179, 277, 280
Blitzkrieg 342, 364
Bolsheviks 89, 162, 184 f., 301 ff., 307, 392, 522, 555
Bonaparte, Napoleon 8, 10, 13, 16–26, 46 f f., 55–70, 97, 139, 569, 572
Bosnian Crisis 158, 161, 178
Brandt, Willy 493, 504, 551 f.
Brezhnev Doctrine 493, 502
British East India Company 160, 170

Cabinet of Barons 340, 351 f.
"Cape-to-Cairo" 160, 171, 237
Carlsbad Decrees 8, 10, 25 f., 29, 52, 67, 77 f., 137
Castlereagh, Robert Stewart 23, 62 f., 71 f.
Catalogue of Fundamental Rights 11, 32, 38, 101
central powers 161, 180, 183–187, 282, 296, 305–308
Centre Party 11, 38 ff., 132 f., 151, 187, 340, 344 f., 347, 350 f., 356 f., 378 f., 384, 404, 409, 411, 434, 499, 539
Chamberlain, Neville 349, 361, 453 f., 458–462, 606
child labour 28, 160, 165, 336
Churchill, Winston 364, 454–458, 463, 468, 490, 496, 520–523, 560, 569 ff.
Code Napoleon/Code Civil 10, 19, 21, 25
COMECON (Council for Mutual Economic Aid) 492, 497, 501
Commonwealth of Independent States 493, 505
communism 162, 185, 211, 214, 217, 354, 362, 497, 509, 523, 525 f., 532–535, 544, 549, 554
(the) Communist Manifesto 160, 165, 211, 299
concentration/extermination camps 342, 356 f., 359, 365 f., 482, 515
Concert of Europe 10, 24, 67, 71, 569
concordat 341, 357, 361
Confederation of the Rhine 8, 10, 17, 19
Congress of Berlin 9, 12, 42, 146
Congress of Vienna 8, 10, 14, 20 f., 23–25, 62–69, 74, 85, 569, 600
Confessing Church 341, 360,
Continental Blockade 10, 18, 47, 58

council democracy 162, 185f., 299, 302, 340, 344f., 368–371
Council of the People's Deputies 340, 344
CSCE (Conference on Security and Cooperation in Europe) 491, 493, 504, 543, 555
Cuban Missile Crisis 491, 493, 502, 544–549
cultural nation 10, 13, 26, 44f.
currency reform 492, 498
Customs Union 10f., 26f., 35f., 86, 165, 186, 204, 600f.
Customs Union Parliament 11, 35f., 600f.

D-Day/Operation Overlord 342, 364, 471
Daily Telegraph Affair 161, 178, 273
Dawes Plan 340, 348f., 413
Day of Potsdam 311, 338, 341
Decree for the Protection of People and State ("Reichstag Fire Decree") 341, 356, 432
deflationary policy 340, 351
demilitarization 162, 188, 492, 494, 603
deportation 342, 365f., 488
displaced persons (DPs) 492, 495, 540
division of labour 160, 165, 195–198, 226, 305, 336
dollar imperialism 160, 173f., 247
Dual Alliance 12, 42, 180,
duma 161, 184, 298–300

Ebert, Friedrich 343–345, 374, 378, 385–388, 394f.
Ebert-Groener pact 340, 345, 385
ECSC (European Coal and Steel Community) 493, 503, 543
economic liberalism 160, 164, 197
emergency decree (article 48) 340, 345, 351
Enabling Act 283, 341, 356, 411, 434f., 438
enemies of the Reich 11, 39, 135–137, 141
Engels, Friedrich 165, 185f., 197, 210f.
Entente Cordiale 160, 171, 178
epochal year 44, 159, 161, 177, 183–186, 304, 308, 493,
European Recovery Program (ERP) 492, 497, 528, 532
euthanasia 341, 355, 360, 365

Fall of the Berlin Wall 491, 493, 508
Fashoda Incident/Crisis 158, 160, 171
February Revolution 11, 30, 91,
Federal Republic of Germany (FRG) 130, 261, 345, 492, 500, 508, 512, 563f.
Fichte, Johann Gottlieb 17, 47–50, 375,
Final Recess of the Imperial Deputation 10, 17
"Final Solution to the Jewish Question"/Wannsee minutes 342, 367, 480

Fischer, Fritz 278–282
forced labourer 181, 492, 495
formal v. informal empire 160, 167, 173f.
Forty-Eighters 11, 32, 91f., 110
Four-Year Plan 341, 358, 436f.
(Emperor) Francis I of Austria 67
free Corps 26, 84, 278, 340, 346, 390f.
free-market economy 160, 164, 197, 336, 555
(King) Frederick William III of Prussia 23, 64, 70, 97, 139
(King) Frederick William IV of Prussia 30, 32, 64, 95, 97ff., 103–105, 110, 139
Franco-Prussian War 9, 11, 36, 42, 118, 121–126, 267, 311, 600
fulfilment policy 340, 346f.

genocide 14, 261ff., 342, 367, 485, 488, 519
German Confederation 10, 16, 23–27, 30, 32, 34f., 46, 52, 67, 74f., 78, 85, 89, 91, 94, 115, 165, 203f., 600
German Conservative Party 11, 38, 133
German-Danish War 9, 11, 34, 139, 600
German Democratic Republic (GDR) 492, 500, 538, 544, 563f.
German Labour Front 341, 357,
German Progressive Party 11, 38,
Gestapo 341, 357, 359, 511
Glasnost (openness)
Gleichschaltung/Bringing into Line 341, 356, 428,
Golden Twenties 340, 348
Goldhagen, Daniel Jonah 519f.
Good Neighbor Policy 160, 174, 247
Gorbachev, Mikhail 505–507, 553–556, 561f., 566, 608
Göttingen Seven 10, 26,
Grand Coalition 340, 350, 404,
Great Depression/slump 174, 340, 350–354, 358, 361f.
Greater German Solution/Greater Germany 11, 32, 101,

Hague Conventions 161, 171f., 255
Haig, Douglas Sir 292, 334
Hallstein Doctrine 493, 504,
Hambach Festival 8, 10, 26, 82f.
Helsinki Accords 493, 504–506, 543, 608
Hindenburg, Paul von 140, 154, 183, 187, 307f., 311–313, 338, 351f., 355, 358, 383, 387f., 399, 420f., 425, 429, 432f., 435, 475
Hitler, Adolf 113, 116, 153f., 280, 311, 338, 341f., 347f., 350–367, 382f., 392f., 398f., 401f., 411f., 418, 420–424, 429–442, 446–462, 466f., 475–480, 485f., 498, 510ff., 516, 519, 522–525, 539, 551, 560, 566, 605f., 609

Hitler-Stalin Pact/Additional Secret Protocol 342, 364, 462, 522, 606
Hitler Youth 341, 359, 441, 480
Holocaust/Shoa 261, 342, 365, 519
Holy Alliance 10, 24, 65, 67
Holy Roman Empire of German Nation 10, 17, 54, 74
"honest broker" 12, 43, 146, 271,
Hossbach Memorandum 342, 361, 606
hyperinflation 340, 346 f., 417,

ignominious peace 188, 322
Imperial Council Convention 340, 344, 368 ff., 388
indemnity/reparations 17, 23, 36, 66, 156, 162, 173, 186 ff., 242, 261, 306, 317–323, 327, 335 f.,
industrialization 159 ff., 163–165, 168, 181, 189 f., 194 f., 200, 203, 206, 208, 217, 222 f., 268, 522
integration 10, 14, 44
Iron Curtain 458, 463, 490, 492, 496, 520 f.

jingoism/chauvinism 160, 169, 248, 333, 336, 392
July Crisis 161, 179, 276–280
July Revolution 10, 25 f., 66

Kapp Putsch 340, 346, 411
Kennedy, John Fitzgerald (JFK) 502, 544–550, 554
Khrushchev, Nikita 545–548
Kissingen Dictation 12, 42, 145
Kohl, Helmut 508 f., 530 f., 560–562, 565, 608
Kreisau Circle 341, 360, 448
Kruger telegram 140, 161, 178

"latecomer nation"/"belated nation" 161, 175
"Law against the establishment of political parties" 341, 357
leader principle 341, 354
League of German Girls/National Socialist Women's League 341, 358, 439
League of Nations 162, 187 f., 297, 322, 325, 328–331
legitimacy 10, 24, 45, 65–67, 91, 233, 344
Lenin 169, 184–187, 226, 298 f., 301–303, 306 f., 522, 526
liberalism 10, 14 f., 25, 39, 45, 62, 64, 67, 97, 106, 116, 155, 160, 164, 197, 225, 398, 599
living space 280, 341, 354, 364, 366, 588
London Conference 492, 497, 535
London Documents 492, 499, 535–537
Luxemburg, Rosa 344, 346, 371–373

MAD (mutually assured destruction) 493, 502
Manifest destiny 160, 172, 243
March Demands 11, 29 f., 93, 101
March Ministries 11, 30
Marshall Plan 490, 492, 497, 528–532
Marx, Karl 38, 165, 185 f., 197, 210 f., 560
Marxism-Leninism 162, 185 f.,
mediatisation 10, 18
Mediterranean Agreement 12, 42, 148
Metternich-Winneburg, Klemens Wenzel Nepomuk Lothar von 23, 25 f., 30, 62, 66 f., 70, 74, 76–78, 91–93, 101, 212, 405
Ministry of Public Enlightenment and Propaganda 341, 354
Monday demonstrations 493, 507, 608
Monroe Doctrine 160, 173 f., 183, 241–246, 325
Morgenthau Plan 492, 494
(First and Second) Moroccan Crisis 158, 178 f., 273
Munich Agreement 342, 361 f., 454, 460, 605 f.
Munich Beer Hall Putsch 340, 347

National Assembly 9, 11, 31–33, 52, 100–102, 105, 115 f., 118, 156, 344–346, 368, 372, 374, 376, 384, 411
nationalism 8, 10, 13–17, 21, 25, 44–49, 60, 67, 73, 76, 85, 143, 155, 169, 176, 180, 248, 268 f., 305, 354, 382, 506, 510, 572, 599 f.
National Liberal Party 11, 38, 404
national prestige 14, 160, 167, 169 f., 176
nation-state 8, 10, 13 f., 19 f., 24, 32, 34 f., 44, 73–75, 83, 132 f., 248, 510, 599 f.
NATO (North Atlantic Treaty Organization) 490, 493, 501, 506, 509, 536, 539, 543, 561 f., 609
naval arms race 140, 161, 177, 181,
naval blockade 161, 183, 308
Navy League 161, 176 f., 269
New Course 140, 160 f., 176, 268
New Imperialism 126, 159–161, 167 f., 177, 224, 239, 267 f.,
(Tsar) Nicholas II 298, 300
"Night of Broken Glass"/November Pogrom 339, 342, 366,
Night of the Long Knives 341, 357
"nightmare of coalitions" 12, 42, 140, 145, 147, 178
North German Confederation 11, 35 f., 38, 118, 120, 130, 139, 600 f.
November Revolution 299, 302 f., 340, 343, 394
nuclear arms race 493, 502, 567
Nuremberg Laws of Citizenship and Race 339, 366, 476

Nuremberg Trials 492, 495, 551

Occupation Statute 492, 500, 502 f., 536
occupation zones 492, 494–497, 535 f.
Oder-Neisse line 162, 188, 509, 544
open-door policy 160, 173 f.
Operation Barbarossa 342, 364, 522
oppositional groups 359, 493, 507
Ostpolitik/"change through rapprochement" 493, 504, 551
Otto-Peters, Louise 108
outlet markets 160, 164, 168

Pan-German League 161, 176, 186, 269, 572
Pan-Slavism 161, 178, 274
Papal Infallibility 11, 39
Parliament of Professors 11, 31, 100
Parliamentary Council 492, 499, 515
Parliamentary democracy 38, 62, 115, 340, 344, 368, 370, 394 f., 457, 601
Paulskirche Parliament 11, 31, 33 f., 131
Pauperism (mass poverty) 11, 28,
Pax Britannica 160, 170, 226
"peace through strength" (Reagan Doctrine) 493, 505, 553
Pearl Harbor 342, 364, 466
People's Community 341, 354, 358, 426 f.
perestroika (restructuring) 493, 505–507, 555 f., 608
policy of Germanization 11, 41
"Polish Corridor" 162, 188, 405, 603
political assassinations 340, 347
political nation 10, 13, 44 f.
policy of détente 340, 349, 458, 502, 505, 544
Potsdam Conference 458, 492, 494
"pragmatic colonisation" 160 f., 174–176, 251 f.
Prague Spring 491, 493, 502, 543
preliminary parliament 11, 31
pre-March 10, 24 f., 78, 80, 89, 101
Presidential Cabinets 340, 350, 352
propaganda 162, 187 f., 254–256, 287, 289, 294 f., 307, 309 f., 323 f., 327, 354–357, 360, 366, 396, 421–424, 426–429, 446, 464–468, 486, 498, 511, 583
(to) proselytise/missionize 160, 168
protectorate 161, 171, 174, 249, 266, 336
proxy war 493, 501, 505, 532, 567
Pulpit Law 11, 40, 135 f.
puppet government 492, 496, 567

raj 160, 170
Reagan, Ronald 493, 505 f., 553–556, 608
Reichstag Fire 341, 356 f., 432
Reich Labour Service 341, 358
Reinsurance Treaty 12, 42, 140, 148, 271
resistance 341, 359 f., 365 f., 444–450, 456 f., 489
restoration 10, 23 f., 65, 89, 157, 187
Reykjavik Summit 493, 506, 608
Rhodes, Cecil 170, 237–239
risorgimento (re-birth, resurrection) 10, 20
Rome-Berlin Axis 342, 362
Roosevelt Corollary 160, 174, 183, 244–246
Roosevelt, Theodore "Teddy" 174, 244
Ruhr occupation (passive resistance) 340, 346, 348, 404
rump parliament 11, 32
rural exodus 160, 163
Russian Revolutions 161, 185, 187, 195

SA 341, 356 f., 359, 366, 385, 451, 474
sabre-rattling 161, 178,
sailors' mutiny 340, 343
satellite states 19, 492, 496, 502, 505, 523
Schlieffen Plan 159, 161, 180, 284, 308
Schuman Declaration 493, 503, 543
Scramble for Africa 158, 160, 171, 175, 265–267,
SD 341, 357, 366 f., 481, 485
Second Empire 8, 11 f., 16, 37 f., 42, 114, 126, 130, 135, 142, 145, 147, 151, 153, 165, 208, 572
secularisation 10, 17
segregation 10, 14, 44, 486
self-determination 45, 162, 187 f., 218, 321, 343, 361, 489, 565, 603
Shoa 342, 365
Smaller German Solution/Little Germany 11, 32, 34, 101
Social Darwinism 160, 169, 235, 268, 333, 341, 354
Social Democracy 40 f., 137, 139, 141, 160, 165, 301
Social Democratic Party (SPD) 11, 38, 133, 137, 214, 217–219, 340, 343–348, 350 f., 356 f., 359 f., 371, 374, 379, 383 f., 404, 410 f., 417, 434 f., 499 f., 504, 530, 540, 551
social imperialism 160, 169, 175,
(the) Social Question 160, 165, 209, 214–222,
social security system 11, 41, 160, 165, 208, 336
solidarity 10, 19, 24, 140
Solidarnosz (Solidarity Movement) 493, 506,
Soviet Union (USSR) 162, 183–186, 303–306, 360, 362–364, 367, 458, 486, 491 f., 493 f., 496–498, 500–505, 507–509, 522–527, 530, 539, 544, 553–556, 562 f., 565 f., 570, 606 f., 608 f.

Spartacists 340, 344, 346, 388 f.
Spartacist uprising 340, 345 f., 354, 371
Spirit of 1914 161, 180, 283
Springtime of the Peoples 8, 11, 30, 82
SS 341, 357, 359, 480–486
stab-in-the-back legend/myth 162, 187
stalemate 161, 182, 284, 287, 308, 336
Stalin, Josef 301 f., 360, 462, 496, 498, 503, 505, 521–523, 526, 528, 531, 545, 560, 569
Stalin Notes (March Notes) 493, 503,
START 1 (Strategic Arms Reduction Treaty) 493, 506
steam engine 160, 164 f., 192 f., 195, 203, 336
Stresemann, Gustav 340, 348 f., 382, 403–408, 413–415
Struggle for Culture/Culture Struggle 11, 39 f., 135 f., 214, 220
student unions/fraternities 10, 24–26
sunrise industries 160, 165, 203, 205

Talleyrand-Périgord, Charles-Maurice de 23, 59, 65 f., 70
Tehran Conference 339, 492, 494
Ten Point Plan 493, 508, 608
terra nullius (no-man's land) 160, 167
three-class voting system 11, 32, 38
Three Emperors' Alliance 12, 42, 148
Three Emperors' League 12, 42, 147
Three Emperors' Year 9, 12, 43, 114, 134, 140
total war 161, 181, 285, 309, 332, 342, 365, 465–467
trade union 40, 133, 160, 165, 215, 337, 346, 357, 359 f., 374, 379, 383, 411, 506, 585
Treaty of Brest-Litovsk 162, 185, 187, 305 - 308
Treaty of Frankfurt 11, 36, 42
Treaty of Locarno 340, 349, 408–413,
Treaty of Rapallo 340, 349, 410
Treaty of Rome/European Economic Community (EEC) 493, 503, 543
Treaty of Versailles 159, 162, 188, 297, 317–327, 335, 346, 361, 395 f., 423, 453 f., 459, 569, 577, 602–604
Treaty on the Final Settlement with Respect to Germany ("Two plus Four Treaty") 493, 509, 563
trench warfare 161, 182, 289, 292, 337
Triple Alliance 12, 42, 140, 148 f., 161, 178, 272
Triple Entente 140, 161, 178, 180,

Truman Doctrine/containment policy 490, 492, 497, 532 f.
unconditional surrender 339, 342, 365, 489, 490, 494, 512, 527
Unification Treaty 493, 509, 607 f.
unrestricted submarine warfare 161, 183, 294, 297, 308
urbanization 160, 163, 200, 208

victory peace 162, 187 f., 309

Wall Street Crash/Black Friday 340, 350,
War-Guilt Clause 162, 188, 603
war of annihilation 342, 365, 489
war of attrition 161, 182, 183, 285, 287, 337, 603
Wartburg Festival 8, 10, 24–26, 76, 82
Wars of Coalition 10, 17, 20
Wars of Liberation 10, 19, 24, 26, 97, 139, 267
Wars of Unification 11, 34, 78, 114, 122, 126, 600
Warsaw Pact 490, 493, 501 f., 506, 543, 562
"We are the people" → "We are one people" 493, 508
weapons of mass destruction (WMDs) 181, 285, 337, 502
Weimar Coalition 340, 345, 350
Weimar Constitution 340, 345, 376–385, 419, 476, 541
welfare 85, 94, 139–142, 153, 160, 166, 172, 245, 337
Wels, Otto 409–411, 435 f.
(Emperor) William I of Germany 36, 139
(Emperor) William II of Germany 18 f., 43, 113 f., 134, 139–141, 150 f., 160, 176–179, 254–258, 268, 270–275, 309, 311
Wilson, Woodrow 187 f., 294, 296 f., 303, 315–330
world policy 161, 167, 174, 176 f., 244, 260, 268
workers' and soldiers' councils 184, 338, 340, 343
workers' movement 160, 165, 185, 190, 359

Yalta Conference 339, 492, 494
Young Italy 10, 21, 72
Young Plan 340, 349, 417

Zero Hour 490, 492, 495, 513, 515, 567
Zimmermann Telegram 161, 183, 294

Bildquellenverzeichnis

S. 8: Napoleonmuseum Thurgau; S. 9: Germanisches Nationalmuseum; S. 14: 40 000 Meisterwerke, AS-Versand, Directmedia Publishing; S. 15: ullstein bild – LEONE; S. 18: picture-alliance © ZB-Fotoreport; S. 19: picture alliance/Westend61; S. 20, 27, 54, 57, 69, 127, 265, 284, 306, 363, 364, 376, 452 (o.), 471, 501, 503, 524, 534, 542, 546: Franz-Josef Domke, Hannover/Verlagsarchiv Schöningh; S. 23: picture-alliance/Judaica-Sammlung Richter; S. 25: Peter Willi – ARTOTHEK; S. 29: Wikimedia Commons (l.); Wikimedia Commons/Pischdi (r.); S. 31: picture-alliance/akg-images; S. 35: bpk/Staatsbibliothek zu Berlin/Ruth Schacht; S. 37: Collection Persmuseum (Amsterdam); S. 39: Lothar Gall/Karl-Heinz Jürgens: Bismarck – Lebensbilder, Bergisch-Gladbach/Lübbe 1990, Nr. 187; S. 41, 52, 76, 80, 96, 97 (u.), 105, 121, 122, 137, 138, 175, 208: bpk; S. 43: picture alliance/blickwinkel/McPHOTO; S. 46: Shifteh Somee – Fotolia; S. 48: akg-images GmbH; S. 50: picture-alliance/akg-images; S. 51: flowofhistory.com/C. Butler; S. 55: picture alliance/Heritage Images; S. 56: nach: Horizonte. Westermann: 2004. p. 118; S. 59: Library of Congress Prints and Photographs Division Washington, D.C. 20540 USA; S. 63: Wikimedia Commons/The Royal Collection; S. 64: picture-alliance/akg-images; S. 65: Wikimedia Commons; S. 66: Wikimedia Commons/Metropolitan Museum of Art; S. 67: akg-images GmbH (o.); Wikimedia Commons/Heeresgeschichtliches Museum (u.); S. 70: ullstein bild – Granger, NYC; S. 72: Wikimedia Commons; S. 77: picture-alliance/dpa dena; S. 81, 82: akg-images GmbH; S. 83: Hambacher Fest 2.0; S. 84: Wikimedia Commons/Hannelore Gärtner: Georg Friedrich Kersting. Seemann, Leipzig 1988; S. 91: Wikimedia Commons/Library of Congress; S. 95: www.strasse-der-demokratie.eu; S. 97: Wikimedia Commons/Lecen (o.); S. 99: bpk/Dietmar Katz; S. 100: nach: Horizonte, Westermann, 2006, S. 172, Grafik 929G; S. 108: Wikimedia Commons/Lumos3; S. 110: Wikimedia Commons/Düsseldorfer Monatshefte, 1848; S. 111: Picture-Alliance GmbH/Foto: Karlheinz Schindler; S. 113: DER SPIEGEL 7/1998; S. 114: Bundesarchiv, Bild 183-R68588/P. Loescher & Petsch/CC-BY-SA 3.0; S. 116: © The Heartfield Community of Heirs/VG Bild-Kunst, Bonn 2015/akg-images; S. 124: Harper's Weekly; S. 125: bpk/Hermann Buresch; S. 133: bpk/Dietmar Katz; S. 139: Wikimedia Commons/Fotograf: Wilhelm Kuntzemüller; S. 170: Wikimedia Commons/ Fotograf: Reichard & Lindner; S. 143: akg-images; S. 146: bpk/Klaus Göken; S. 149: Universal History Archive/Getty Images; S. 150: Lothar Gall/Karl-Heinz Jürgens: Bismarck – Lebensbilder, Bergisch-Gladbach/Lübbe 1990, Nr. 191 (S. 215); S. 154: Deutsches Pressemuseum im Ullsteinhaus e. V.; S. 158: © Harris Morgan – Wikimedia Commons (http://commons.wikimedia.org/wiki/File%3AWWI-Causes.jpg) (licensed under (CC BY-SA 3.0)); S. 159: picture alliance/empics; S. 164: picture-alliance/akg-images; S. 166: akg-images/Archiv für Kunst und Geschichte; S. 168: Picture-Alliance GmbH; S. 169: bpk/adoc-photos; S. 172: Wikimedia Commons/Jeff G.; S. 175: akg-images/arkivi UG; S. 177: picture-alliance/United Archives/TopFoto; S. 179: ullstein bild – TopFoto; S. 181: British Library/Wikimedia Commons (CC0 1.0 Universal (CC0 1.0)); S. 182: nach: Praxis Geschichte 6 (2013): "Der Erste Weltkrieg", p. 14 (Westermann); S. 183: New York Times, March 1, 1917; S. 186: Review of Reviews, Vol. 58, No. 4, October 1918; archived at the Ohio State University Cartoon Research Library; S. 189: Wikimedia Commons/Library of Congress (ID pga 00019); S. 191: © Science Museum of Minnesota www.smm.org; S. 194: Museum of Art, Philadelphia; S. 198: picture alliance/akg-images; S. 199: akg-images GmbH/E. Lessing; S. 200: Wikimedia Commons/Stephen J. Lee: Aspects of British Political History, 1815–1914. Routledge, London/New York 1994; S. 204: © ullstein bild/Archiv Gerstenberg; S. 205: Electrolux Hausgeräte GmbH, Markenvertrieb AEG; S. 210, 211, 215, 220, 275, 278 (o.), 311, 320, 382, 414, 449, 451, 530: akg-images GmbH; S. 213: In: P. Lane: British Social and Economic History from 1760 to the present day. Oxford: Oxford University Press 1979, S. 44/Wikimedia Commons; S. 217: picture alliance/ZB; S. 224: picture-alliance/KPA/TopFoto; S. 227: PAUL D STEWART/SCIENCE PHOTO LIBRARY/akg-images; S. 229: www.bridgemanart.com; S. 230: akg/North Wind Picture Archives; S. 233: picture-alliance/Mary Evans Picture Library; S. 237: picture-alliance/united archives; S. 238: Punch Magazine, 10 December 1892; S. 241: ullstein bild – Granger, NYC; S. 244: Pach Brothers Portrait Photograph Collection/Wikimedia Commons; S. 245: ullstein bild – Granger, NYC (l.); TM, ® & © 2015 Paramount Pictures. All Rights Reserved. (r.); S. 246: © Cagle Cartoons; S. 247: Wikipedia.org [12.02.2015]; S. 250: © Koloniales Bildarchiv, Universitätsbibliothek Frankfurt am Main; S. 251: picture-alliance/akg-images; S. 253: © Zelfit – Fotolia.com (l.); Wikimedia Commons/Bundesarchiv, (Bild 146-2004-0098A/CC-BY-SA) (r.); S. 256: akg-images/Universal Images Group/Universal History Archive; S. 257: www.bridgemanart.com; S. 260: picture-alliance/(c)Robert Hunt Library/Mary Evan; S. 261: Deutscher Kolonialatlas mit Jahrbuch 1918: auf Veranlassung der deutschen Kolonialgesellschaft herausgegeben 1918: Jahrbuch von Karstedt; S. 263: © ullstein bild/ullstein bild; S. 268: © Matthias Haas – Fotolia.com; S. 270: ullstein bild/TopFoto; S. 272: ullstein bild/Granger, NYC; S. 274: John Tenniel, Alice in Wonderland/from: Wikimedia Commons; S. 276: Time Life Pictures/Getty Images (l. o.); ullstein bild/Granger, NYC (l. u.); picture alliance/AP Photo (r. o.); Hulton Archive/Getty Images (r. u.); S. 278: picture-alliance/dpa (u.); S. 283: SZ Photo/Süddeutscher Verlag GmbH (o.); Wikimedia Commons/Magnus Manske (u.); S. 286: © EdwardSamuel – Fotolia.com; S. 288: Lebenszeichen – Feldpostbriefe erzählen : pädagogische Handreichung/von Christof Beitz. Volksbund Deutsche Kriegsgräberfürsorge e. V., Landesverband Bayern. – München : Volksbund Dt. Kriegsgräberfürsorge, 2003; S. 289: action press/Collection Christophel; S. 290: ullstein bild – Granger, NYC; S. 292: Wikimedia Commons/Hohum; S. 293: Andrew Wrenn: The First World War, 1997, © Cambridge University Press 1997, reproduced with permission.; S. 294: MPI/Getty Images; S. 295: Library of Congress, LC-DIG-ds-03216 (o.); Wikimedia Commons/Infrogmation (u.); S. 297: Picture-Alliance GmbH/dpa (o.); Library of Congress, National Photo Company Collection, LC-DIG-npcc-20162/Wikimedia Commons (u.); S. 298: picture alliance/Heritage Images; S. 301: picture-alliance/RIA Nowosti (o.); Russian Picture Service/akg (u.); S. 304: Praxis Geschichte, Ausgabe Januar Heft 1/2007: Epochenjahr 1917, Westermann Verlag; S. 310: IAM/akg-images (l. o.); akg-images/Universal Images Group/Universal History Archive (r. o.); Mansfield Library, Archives & Special Collections (l. u.); ÖNB/Wien/KS 16320460 (r. u.); S. 314: Anschläge/Verlag Langewiesche-Brandt; S. 318: © Donets – Fotolia.com (o.); © Barry Barnes – Fotolia.com (Mitte); akg-images/Universal Images Group/Universal History Archive (u.); S. 319 (v.o.n.u.): © Barry Barnes – Fotolia.com; picture alliance/Heritage Images; © Barry Barnes – Fotolia.com; akg-images; S. 317, 323, 324, 355, 359, 362, 403, 417, 441, 482, 483, 495, 499, 518, 537: bpk; S. 326: Daily Herald, 13th May, 1913; S. 328: Wikimedia Commons/Vectors by Mysid, based on FOTW; S. 329: Punch Magazine 10 December 1919/Wikimedia Commons (o.); Hulton Archive/stringer/Getty images (u.); S. 330: The Ohio State University Billy Ireland Cartoon Library & Museum; S. 331: ullstein bild – CARO/Rupert Oberhäuser; S. 332: © I. Faßbender, 2014; S. 334: DER SPIEGEL 1/2014; S. 335: David Low/Solo Syndication; S. 338: bpk (o.); ullstein bild (u.); S. 339: picture-alliance/dpa; S. 344: IAM/akg-images; S. 347: bpk | Bayerische Staatsbibliothek | Heinrich Hoffmann; S. 349: ullstein bild – Roger-Viollet/Albert Harlingue; S. 352: ullstein bild – ADN-Bildarchiv; S. 354: © Deutsches Historisches Museum, Berlin/ A. Psille;S. 369: Wikimedia Commons/ONAR; S. 371: picture-alliance/akg-images; S. 374: Scherl/Süddeutscher Verlag – Bilderdienst; S. 379: © Deutsches Historisches Museum, Berlin/A. Psille (l.); S. 380: Hessisches Landesmuseum Darmstadt/Foto: Wolfgang Fuhrmannek; S. 381: akg-images (o.); Deutsches Historisches Museum, Berlin/A. Anweiler-Sommer (u.); S. 383: Deutsches Historisches Museum, Berlin; S. 384: Deutsches Historisches Museum, Berlin/S. Ahlers; S. 385: © VG Bild-Kunst, Bonn 2015, bpk/Bildarchiv Preußischer Kulturbesitz; S. 386: Süddeutsche Zeitung Photo (l.); picture alliance/IMAGNO/Austrian Archives (S) (r.); S. 388: INTERFOTO/Sammlung Rauch; S. 390: Bundesarchiv, Bild 002-007-128 Grafiker Impekoven. I./1919/1923 ca.; S. 391: ullstein bild – Süddeutsche Zeitung Photo/Scherl; S. 396: © Punch Limited (o.); ullstein bild – Becker & Brede (u.); S. 397: bpk/Kunstbibliothek, SMB, Phototek Willy Römer/Willy Römer (o.); Bundesarchiv, Bild 102-00104 Foto: Pahl, Georg/1923 (u.l.); Franz-Josef Domke, Hannover/Verlagsarchiv Schöningh; S. 398: picture-alliance/akg-images; S. 404: akg-images/Imagno; S. 408: bpk/Dietmar Katz; S. 411: bpk/Kunstbibliothek, SMB, Phototek Willy Römer/Willy Römer; S. 416: nach: John Hite/Chris Hinton (ed.): Weimar & Nazi Germany. London (Hodder) 2000, p. 103; S. 419: SZ Photo/Scherl; S. 422: picture-alliance/dpa; S. 425: Nebelspalter/Gregor Rabinovitch; S. 433: © The Heartfield Community of Heirs/VG Bild-Kunst, Bonn 2015/Deutsches Historisches Museum Berlin; S. 437: nach: "Changing Life in Germany", www.BBC.co.uk; S. 438: picture alliance/akg-images; S. 439: Deutsches Historisches Museum, Berlin/A. Psille; S. 445: Grafik nach: Detlev Peukert: Die Edelweißpiraten. Protestbewegung jugendlicher Arbeiter im Dritten Reich. 2. Aufl., Köln 1983, S. 236 (o.); akg-images/Wittenstein (u.); S. 447: Entwurf des Sonderpostwertzeichens: Prof. Gerd und Erika Aretz; S. 448: picture-alliance/akg-images; S. 452: ullstein bild – TopFoto (u.); S. 454: bpk/adoc-photos; S. 458: Imperial War Museum Collections; S. 461, 462: ullstein bild – Granger, NYC; S. 465: Poster: Sarra, Valentino, 1903-. I gave a man! : will you give at least 10% of your pay in war bonds?. [Washington, D.C.]. UNT Digital Library. http://digital.library.unt.edu/ark:/67531/metadc462/. Accessed March 26, 2015.; S. 468: Wikimedia Commons/Magnus Manske; S. 470: Museumsstiftung Post und Telekommunikation 3.2002.0299; S. 474: bpk | Bayerische Staatsbibliothek | Heinrich Hoffmann; S. 478: bpk/Carl Eberth (l.o.); bpk | Bayerische Staatsbibliothek | Heinrich Hoffmann (r.o.); bpk/Abraham Pisarek (l.u.); bpk (r.u.); S. 484: ullstein bild – Roger-Viollet; S. 485: ullstein bild – ddp; S. 487: David Low/Solo Syndication; S. 490: INTERFOTO/Friedrich Rauch; S. 491: © ullstein bild – Hesse; S. 506: The News, 26 August 1991, News Limited; S. 507: akg-images/AP; S. 508: ullstein – ADN – Bildarchiv; S. 510: bpk/Maurice Zalewski/adoc-photos; S. 512: ullstein bild – pwe Verlag GmbH; S. 513: I. Faßbender; S. 516: Bundesarchiv, Plak 004-005-005 Grafiker: o. Ang./1945-1949 (ca.); S. 519: picture-alliance/ dpa; S. 520: getty images/Popperfoto; S. 522: Sovfoto/UIG via Getty Images; S. 526: © 2015. Photo Nat. Portrait Gall. Smithsonian/Art Resoruce/Scala, Florence; S. 528: bpk/Kunstbibliothek, SMB/Knud Petersen; S. 529: ullstein bild – TopFoto (l.); picture alliance/Heritage Images (r.); S. 353: Stuttgarter Zeitung, 19.10.1949; S. 539, 545: Keystone Pressedienst; S. 544: AP Photo; S. 549: INTERFOTO/JTB PHOTO; S. 550: picture alliance/ZB; S. 551: picture-alliance/akg-images; S. 552: Bundesregierung, B/45 Bild-00182585 Foto: Reinek, Engelbert/7. Dezember 1970 (l.o.); Fotoagentur SVEN SIMON (r.o.); ullstein bild (l.u.); bpk/Hanns Hubmann (r.u.); S. 553: Picture-Alliance GmbH (o.); ullstein bild – Thierlein (u.); S. 555: Picture-Alliance GmbH; S. 557: ullstein bild – Mehner Klaus Mehner; S. 560: © Provincial Archives of New Brunswick (PANB) (l.o.); © Laurence Clark/Haus der Beschichte, Bonn (r.o.); by Bill Caldwell, published in the British Daily Star in February 1990 (l.u.); Milen Radev /Haus der Geschichte, Bonn (r.u.); S. 561: Le Canard Enchaîné/Kiro (l.); © Walter Hanel, Bergisch Gladbach (r.); S. 563: picture alliance/akg-images; S. 565: picture-alliance/ ZB; S. 566: Wikimedia/Foto: Doris Antony, Berlin (GFDL; CC-BY-SA-3.0); S. 568: © Dieter Senghaas; S. 572: Archiv und Bücherei der Deutschen Burschenschaft, Koblenz (l.); akg-images (r.); S. 573: picture-alliance/akg-images/Florian Profitlich (l.o.); KAS/ACDP 10-001: 14 (r.o.); by Bill Caldwell, in: Daily Star, 3 October 1990 (l.u.); weitere: Verlagsarchiv Schöningh

Sollte trotz aller Bemühungen um korrekte Urheberangaben ein Irrtum unterlaufen sein, bitten wir darum, sich mit dem Verlag in Verbindung zu setzen, damit wir eventuell erforderliche Korrekturen vornehmen können.